THE CHURCH
AND CULTURES

The American Society of Missiology Series, in collaboration with Orbis Books, seeks to publish scholarly works of high merit and wide interest on numerous aspects of missiology—the study of mission. Able presentations on new and creative approaches to the practice and understanding of mission will receive close attention.

Previously published in
The American Society of Missiology Series

No. 1   *Protestant Pioneers in Korea,*
        by Everett Nicholas Hunt, Jr.

No. 2   *Catholic Politics in China and Korea,*
        by Eric O. Hanson

No. 3   *From the Rising of the Sun,*
        by James M. Phillips

No. 4   *Meaning across Cultures,*
        by Eugene A. Nida and William D. Reyburn

No. 5   *The Island Churches of the South Pacific,*
        by Charles W. Forman

No. 6   *Henry Venn,*
        by Wilbert R. Shenk

No. 7   *No Other Name?*
        by Paul F. Knitter

No. 8   *Toward a New Age in Christian Theology,*
        by Richard Henry Drummond

No. 9   *The Expectation of the Poor,*
        by Guillermo Cook

No. 10 *Eastern Orthodox Mission Theology Today,*
        by James J. Stamoolis

No. 11 *Confucius, the Buddha, and Christ,*
        by Ralph H. Covell

No. 12 *The Church and Cultures,*
        by Louis J. Luzbetak

No. 13 *Translating the Message,*
        by Lamin Sanneh

No. 14 *An African Tree of Life,*
        by Thomas G. Christensen

American Society of Missiology Series, No. 12

THE CHURCH AND CULTURES

New Perspectives in Missiological Anthropology

Louis J. Luzbetak, S.V.D.

ORBIS BOOKS

Maryknoll, New York 10545

Fourth Printing, September 1991

The Catholic Foreign Mission Society of America (Maryknoll) recruits and trains people for overseas missionary service. Through Orbis Books Maryknoll aims to foster the international dialogue that is essential to mission. The books published, however, reflect the opinions of their authors and are not meant to represent the official position of the society.

Biblical quotations are from the *New American Bible*

Manuscript editor: Joyce Rappaport

ORBIS/ISBN 0-88344-625-1 (pbk.)

To
Father Wilhelm Schmidt, S.V.D.
(February 16, 1868–February 10, 1954)
In appreciation of his pioneering spirit
In serving Faith through Science

CONTENTS

List of Figures   xi

Preface to the Series   xiii

Foreword   xv

Preface   xvii

1. The Theological Foundations of Missiological Anthropology:
    A Preamble   1
    The Primacy of the Holy Spirit   1
    The Need of Spirituality   2
    A Living Faith   3
    Dedication to the Needs of Others   4
    A Humble Sense of Personal Mission   6
    The Importance of Human Knowledge and Skill   8
    Summary   10

2. Missiological Anthropology   12
    Missiology   12
    Nature and Scope   12
    History of Missiology   15
    Missiological Resources   23
    Anthropology   23
    Nature and Scope of Anthropology   23
    Subdisciplines of Anthropology   27
    Applied Anthropology   34
    Anthropology and Other Disciplines   42
    Missiological Anthropology   43
    Nature and Scope of Missiological Anthropology   43
    Justification, Professional Ethics   44
    History of Mission Anthropology   49
    Missionaries and Professional Anthropologists   53

3. Mission Models   64
    Theoretical Models   64
    Ethnocentric Orientations   64

    Accommodational Orientations   67
    Contextual (Incarnational, Inculturational) Orientation   69
  An Historical Overview of Mission Models   84
    Early Expansion: The First Five Hundred Years   85
    The Christianization of Europe—500–1500 A.D.   89
    The Evangelization of New Peoples in Asia and the Americas—
        1500-1800 A.D.   91
    The Nineteenth Century   97
    Contemporary Mission:1914–1945   103

4. Signs of the Times   **106**
  The Moratorium   107
  New Independent Church Movements   107
  Local Theologies, Commitment to the Poor, Basic Communities,
       the Continuing Strength of Popular Religiosity, and New
       Ministries   108
  Vatican II and Beyond   109
    Vatican II: 1962-1965   109
    Beyond Vatican II   111
    Official Catholic Teaching   122
  Conclusion   132

5. The Nature of Culture   **133**
  Cultural Perspective   133
    Early Anthropological Definitions   134
    The Nature of Knowledge   135
    The Nature of Models   135
    Criteria for a Good Model   136
    The Need for a Missiologically Oriented Model of Culture   137
    An Overview of Cultural Models   139
  A Composite Missiological Perspective of Culture: Culture as a
       Socially Shared Design for Living   156
    Culture as a Plan for Living   156
    Culture as a Societal Possession   166
    Culture as a Learned Design   181

6. Integration of Culture   **223**
  Surface Level of Culture: Cultural Forms   225
  Intermediate Level of Culture: Structural Integration   225
    The Notion of Structural Integration   225
    Method of Inquiry   234
    Summary and Missiological Application   238
  Third Level of Culture: Psychological Integration   249
    The "Mentality" of a People   249

World View   252
Religion, Ideology, Philosophy   263
Themes and Counterthemes   276
Summary and Missiological Application   279

7. Cultural Dynamics   **292**
General Notions   292
The Nature of Cultural Dynamics   292
Anthropology and Culture Change   293
The Locus of Culture Change   293
Kinds of Culture Change   294
Summary and Missiological Application: General Notions
        Regarding Cultural Change   300
The Processes by Which Cultures Change   305
The Primary or Innovative Processes of Culture Change   305
Secondary or Integrative Processes   308
The Terminal Processes of Culture Change   314
Summary and Selected Missiological Applications: Processes
        by Which Cultures Change   321
Conditions Favoring Change/Persistence   329
Conditions Favoring Change in General   330
Conditions Favoring Origination   337
Conditions Favoring Diffusion   341
Summary and Missiological Application: Conditions Favoring
        Change   351

8. Epilogue: Anthropology at the Service of Faith   **374**
The Church as Community   376
The Communal Model: Its Meaning, Strengths, and
        Weaknesses   377
Anthropological Application   380
The Church as Universal Sacrament   381
The Sacramental Model: Its Meaning, Strengths, and Weaknesses   381
Anthropological Application   381
The Church as Herald   385
The Kerygmatic Model: Its Meaning, Strengths, and Weaknesses   385
Anthropological Application   386
The Church as Servant   386
The Diaconal Model: Its Meaning, Strengths, and Weaknesses   386
The Diaconal Tasks of the Church: Who Are the Poor?   387
Anthropological Application   390
Supplementary Readings   393
The Church as Institution   395
The Institutional Model of the Church: Meaning, Strengths,
        and Weaknesses   395

Anthropological Application   *396*
Conclusion   397

NOTES   **399**

REFERENCES   **411**

INDEX   **453**

LIST OF FIGURES

1. Flow Chart of Components and Forces in the Missiological
       Process   15
2. The Holistic Nature of Anthropology   26
3. The Basic Structure of the Science of Anthropology   27
4. Missionaries and Anthropologists: Examples of Possible Synthesis
       of Differing World Views   56
5. Major Differences Between (Traditional) Accommodation and
       Inculturation   82
6. Vatican II Documents: A Missiological Overview   110
7. Conversational Space in North and South America   209
8. Terminal Stages of Adjustment to a New Cultural Environment   218
9. A "Photographic" vs. a "Functional" Description of Culture   230
10. American vs. Soviet Semantics   259
11. Correspondence Between African Gods and Catholic Saints in Brazil,
       Cuba, and Haiti   361

PREFACE TO THE SERIES

The purpose of the ASM Series—now in existence since 1980—is to publish, without regard for disciplinary, national, or denominational boundaries, scholarly works of high quality and wide interest on missiological themes from the entire spectrum of scholarly pursuits, e.g., biblical studies, theology, history, history of religions, cultural anthropology, linguistics, art, education, political science, economics, and development, to name only the major components. Always the focus will be on Christian mission.

By "mission" in this context is meant a passage over the boundary between faith in Jesus Christ and its absence. In this understanding of mission, the basic functions of Christian proclamation, dialogue, witness, service, worship, and nurture are of special concern. How does the transition from one cultural context to another influence the shape and interaction between these dynamic functions? Cultural and religious plurality are recognized as fundamental characteristics of the six-continent missionary context in east and west, north and south.

Missiologists know that they need the other disciplines. And those in other disciplines need missiology, perhaps more than they sometimes realize. Neither the insider's nor the outsider's view is complete in itself. The world Christian mission has through two millenia amassed a rich and well-documented body of experience to share with other disciplines. The complementary relation between missiology and other learned disciplines is a key feature of this Series, and interaction will be its hallmark.

The promotion of scholarly dialogue among missiologists may, at times, involve the publication of views and positions that other missiologists cannot accept, and with which members of the Editorial Committee do not agree. Manuscripts published in this series reflect the opinions of their authors and are not meant to represent the position of the American Society of Missiology or of the Editorial Committee for the ASM Series. The Committee's selection of texts is guided by such criteria as intrinsic worth, readability, relative brevity, freedom from excessive scholarly apparatus, and accessibility to a broad range of interested persons and not merely to experts or specialists.

On behalf of the membership of the American Society of Missiology we express our deep thanks to the staff of Orbis Books, whose steadfast support over a decade for this joint publishing venture has enabled it to mature and bear scholarly fruit.

James A. Scherer, Chair
Sister Mary Motte, FMM
Charles R. Taber
ASM Series Editorial Committee

FOREWORD

The Church and Cultures is an excellent book made even better. The 1963 edition by Louis J. Luzbetak, S.V.D. was enthusiastically received and justly praised for its crucial insights and sound advice about the use of anthropology in missions. The 1988 edition has been greatly expanded and brought up to date. In addition to being completely rewritten, it contains a superb bibliography.

What makes this volume unusual is the triad of themes: theology, ecumenicity, and history. These themes play a dominant role and provide the cohesion so essential in any comprehensive treatment of missiological anthropology. Instead of tacking on the theological implications of missions as a kind of final apologia, Fr. Luzbetak begins with a clear statement about the meaning of Christian faith in diverse cultures, and he ends the book with an insightful treatment of the role of the church in an increasingly non-Christian world.

Though written from a Roman Catholic perspective, this discussion of cultural anthropology in missions is truly ecumenical, not only in spirit, but also in the judicious and balanced manner in which the similarities and differences between Roman Catholic and Protestant mission enterprises are treated. For Protestants this volume is an excellent introduction to present-day Roman Catholicism, and for Roman Catholics this book provides an unusually fair and helpful introduction to various aspects of Protestant movements, especially as they relate to missions.

Without exception, Fr. Luzbetak deals with present issues in the light of their historical backgrounds. It is this time-depth perspective that helps the reader understand not only what happened, but also why such events took place and why so many present-day problems are really not as unique as they often appear to be.

Readers of this volume will be particularly pleased by the manner in which Fr. Luzbetak faces up to crucial issues. He does not hesitate to discuss the critical ethical implications of applied anthropology, and he rejects completely the tendency of some persons to use anthropological insights to manipulate people. Furthermore, he does not avoid some of the theological cross-currents in both Roman Catholic and Protestant circles that directly and indirectly affect the proclamation of faith. Above all else, Fr. Luzbetak argues convincingly for the sanctity of cultural distinctiveness in relation to the universal claims of ecclesiastical institutions.

In addition to full coverage of such large issues as contextualization, referred to in current missiology also as indigenization, inculturation, and incarnation, some of the more acute and personal issues of culture shock, going native, estrangement, and re-entry (the return of a missionary to his or her home culture) are also judiciously discussed.

Not only does Fr. Luzbetak demonstrate an excellent grasp of cultural anthropology but he also displays a sanctified common sense based on wide experience in many parts of the world and on a strong personal commitment to Christ and to people. His valuable insights become all the more meaningful in the light of his genuine scholarly humility.

Eugene A. Nida

PREFACE

The first edition of the author's *The Church and Cultures* appeared in 1963, almost twenty-five years ago. That the book filled an important need at the time was evident from the enthusiastic response from grassroots missionaries and from colleagues preparing church personnel for work overseas. After two printings by Divine Word Publications, the William Carey Library reprinted the book four more times, with the last reprinting in 1984. Very encouraging, too, were the French, Spanish, Italian, Polish, and Indonesian translations and adaptations. It was, therefore, at the urging of missionaries and many colleagues that the author undertook the task of rewriting the book and producing a kind of "Phase II" *Church and Cultures*.

The general goals and approaches, and not a few applications and illustrations, have, at the suggestion of many, been retained. The book, however, involved a thorough rewriting to contain the many new dimensions of missiology as well as anthropology. Recent developments in both fields have been duly taken into account. Consistent with such substantial alterations, the subtitle of the book has been changed from *An Applied Anthropology for the Religious Worker* to *New Perspectives in Missiological Anthropology*.

The present version differs from the original work especially in two ways. (1) The Phase II work is addressed primarily to the local Christian *community*, rather than to the foreign missionary as was the case in the original publication. After all, the main goal of applying anthropology to mission is to enable the *"yeast"* of the Gospel, the Christian community, to penetrate "the whole mass of dough" (Lk 13:21). The task of incarnating the Gospel in the minds and hearts of a people, in allowing Christ to be born here and now, lies principally with the local Christian community—with the people themselves under the guidance of the Holy Spirit in communion with the universal Church—and not with the "outsiders," however helpful, and indeed necessary, they may be. One of the chief differences between the Phase I and Phase II works is, therefore, the shift of emphasis from directing change mainly through "outsiders" to directing change mainly from within the community itself. This shift is more in harmony with current missiological thinking and certainly is more in accord with current anthropological thought. (2) The other major difference is in the fact that the Phase II work is not addressed exclusively, or even primarily, to so-called "newer" churches but to *all* local communities. The concepts and principles discussed are usually as applicable and necessary in the West as they are in the Third World and *wherever* the Church is present. We hasten to add, however, that although the emphasis is now on mission rather than on missions, church growth and cross-cultural evangelization remain basic interests in both the theory presented and in the problems and illustrations chosen.

The book is intended particularly for the English-speaking world; references and supplementary readings are therefore mainly in English. Many topics could not be fully developed owing to their specialized nature and space limitations. To supplement the present text, we have, therefore, provided updated references and annotated lists of what we believe to be readable and reliable sources of supplementary and balancing information corresponding to the special needs of our expected readership.

Like the original book, this Phase II work was written not so much for professional anthropologists as for mission practitioners and decision makers (and for those preparing themselves to become such). It is also aimed at colleagues in other fields who might be interested in applying anthropological thinking to their own work in the service of faith. However, the present work is not intended to be a kind of cookbook in which one might find specific recipes, or a kind of telephone directory in which one might look up the numbers for specific individuals or business concerns needed at the moment. To provide important light from an important modern social science called "cultural anthropology"—not to provide ready-answers or the final word—is the purpose of this book. Nor is it our intention to suggest in any way that anthropology, however important, has all the answers.

The book is written primarily with Roman Catholic readers in mind. However, the warm reception that the original work received from other Christian traditions has made the author particularly conscious of the ecumenical potential of any new version. In fact, the author feels greatly honored to have his study appear in the American Society of Missiology Series, a publication of a professional association known for its commitment to ecumenical cooperation.

It should be noted that *purely illustrative* sections have been set off from the text as such and are at the same time distinguishable from longer citations. Some readers will be interested in examples that illustrate otherwise dry and abstract theory, whereas others may prefer to concentrate on concepts and principles and to read the illustrations selectively.

It has been said many times before that writing a book is like baring one's soul before the whole world. To be understood, the author has to state honestly and clearly, and at times boldly, positions that might otherwise remain personal and hidden from others. In fact, as in the present case, what often motivates writers to write is their commitment to such positions, so that the pouring out of the writer's soul becomes an integral part of the message itself. Especially when writing a book dealing with the Christian call to mission, and therefore when writing about the blending of science and religion, about a marriage between nature and supernature, about a partnership between creature and Creator, authors must, so to speak, lay their cards on the table and unequivocally declare, "This I believe; this I hold." Our opening chapter is such a declaration. The first chapter is, in fact, a preamble and a foundation. It is a preamble in the sense that whatever is said here is presupposed by all that follows, even if no further mention of the particular stand is made. The reader is therefore asked to interpret *whatever* is said in the body of the book in light of such underlying faith values. Any other interpretation would be a distortion of the author's message or at least a misreading of his intent. In fact, it is hoped that anyone desiring to put the present theory into practice would do so in light of the fundamental assumptions in question.

Chapter 1 might in abbreviated form very well have been made a part of the present preface if it did not have another, equally important purpose—namely, the laying of a theological foundation for missiological anthropology. The assumptions of chapter 1 constitute, in fact, the solid rock on which the application of anthropology to mission must be based.

Chapter 2 describes in detail what is meant by "Missiological Anthropology"—namely, a blend of missiology and anthropology: the scope and purpose of the book is missiological whereas the process and analysis is anthropological.

In the hope of learning from the culturological failures and successes of the past, chapter 3 examines mission models first theoretically and then histori-cally. At the same time, the theoretical presentation serves as a preview of the theory that is to come; it also serves to clarify some of the terminology that will be used in the chapters to follow.

Chapter 4, entitled "Signs of the Times," looks at the present and the future of mission to see what challenges await missiological anthropology. It also provides the basic theological parameters within which present-day mission anthropology must be applied.

Chapter 5 examines the recent anthropological developments in regard to the concept of culture. It then reformulates this knowledge into a working mis-siological model. Chapter 6 looks at culture as a system, and chapter 7 examines the dynamic character of culture. It should be noted that traditional accommodation generally passed over such important considerations; on the other hand, inculturation (incarnation, contextualization, "evangelization" of cultures—all synonymous) may not do so. Chapters 5, 6, and 7 are, in fact, the heart of inculturational theory. Corresponding missiological applications are made throughout these chapters so as to illustrate the relevancy of the anthro-pological theory discussed.

Chapter 8 is an epilogue. Here the anthropological theory of the earlier chapters is synthesized in the light of the nature and mission of the Church. Important supplementary readings are proposed for further, more-in-depth study.

The present book reflects much of the thinking that has gone on in the mind of the author over many years, some of which has been expressed in his previous publications. The author wishes to acknowledge his indebtedness to the many colleagues consulted or cited, both in anthropology and in mis-siology. He feels particularly indebted to the colleagues who have been kind

enough to review his manuscript, whether in part or whole, and whose suggestions have, no doubt, contributed greatly to the improvement of the present
work. A very special word of appreciation is due to Dr. Ernest Brandewie of the
University of Indiana at South Bend, Rev. Dr. Lawrence Nemer, S.V.D., and
Rev. Dr. Robert Schreiter, C.PP.S, both of Catholic Theological Union in
Chicago, and Dr. Darrell Whiteman of the E. Stanley Jones School of Evangelism and World Mission at Asbury Theological Seminary in Wilmore, Kentucky. The author is grateful for their careful reading of the manuscript and for
their useful suggestions. However, the author alone is responsible for the views
expressed. In a very special way, the author is indebted to two missionary
societies without whose support and encouragement a Phase II work would,
literally, have been impossible. Thanks is due to the Maryknoll Missionaries
for a grant from their Walsh-Price Fellowship program and for their much
appreciated encouragement and patience. Above all, a sincere word of grati-
tude must go to the Superiors of the Divine Word Missionaries for freeing the
author from other duties so as to enable him to complete what turned out to be
a far more difficult and time-consuming, albeit deeply satisfying, undertaking
than had been anticipated.

Washington, D.C.
August 15, 1987

THE CHURCH
AND CULTURES

Chapter One

THE THEOLOGICAL FOUNDATIONS OF MISSIOLOGICAL ANTHROPOLOGY: A PREAMBLE

Science without religion is lame;
religion without science is blind.
Albert Einstein

Missiological anthropology rests on three solid theological assumptions: (1) it insists on the primacy of the Holy Spirit in mission action; (2) it recognizes the need of genuine spirituality in those engaged in mission; and (3) it is convinced of the important role that human knowledge and skill can and should play in "proclaiming the Kingdom of the Father, sharing the life of the Son, and bearing the witness of the Spirit" (Newbigin). We begin our study of missiological anthropology by examining its theological foundations.

1.1 THE PRIMACY OF THE HOLY SPIRIT

The mission of the Church is essentially a spiritual activity—the work of the Holy Spirit. Effectiveness and true success in mission, we maintain, cannot be measured except in terms of the supernatural. Behind every human effort there must be the Power and Free Gift of God (the Holy Spirit and his Grace). We wish, therefore, to emphasize and declare loudly and clearly, leaving no doubt behind whatsoever, that the scientific planning so strongly emphasized in our approach to mission is in no way meant to be a substitute for the Holy Spirit. Rather, we acknowledge the truth of the Lord's warning that "apart from me you can do nothing" (Jn 15:5). Without the Holy Spirit, the Church would be but a lifeless body, a corpse, and at best a "noisy gong, a clanging cymbal" (1 Cor 13:1) and not the vibrant Church of the Acts of the Apostles. Nor can

1

scientific planning, however cleverly executed, ever force the Holy Spirit to act in any particular manner. (*Lumen gentium,* no. 1–5; *Gaudium et spes,* no. 2). Such a task can be carried out only in and through the Spirit (*Evangelii nuntiandi*, no. 75).

1.2 THE NEED OF SPIRITUALITY

If the role of the Holy Spirit is as important as we say it is, it must follow that the effectiveness of mission and the solutions to its problems must first and foremost be sought not in human cleverness—no, not even in anthropology—but elsewhere. *The most important and most desirable ingredient in a person engaged in mission is genuine and deep spirituality*. In fact, we hold that God sometimes chooses those "whom the world considers absurd to shame the wise . . . the weak of this world to shame the strong" (1 Cor 1:27). To borrow the words of Benedict XV:

for those who enter upon the apostolic life there is one attribute that is indispensable. It is of the critical importance . . . that they have sanctity of life. For the one who urges others to despise sin must despise it himself. . . . Give the missionary, if you will, every imaginable talent of mind and intellect, endow him with the most extensive learning and the most brilliant culture. Unless these qualities are accompanied by moral integrity they will be of little or no value in the apostolate. . . .

especially let him be a devout person dedicated to prayer and constant union with God, one who goes before the Divine Majesty and fervently pleads the cause of souls. For as we bind ourselves more and more closely to God, we shall receive the grace and assistance of God to a greater and greater degree. [*Maximum illud*, 26f; cf. *Evangelii nuntiandi*, no. 76]

The Rite of Ordination puts it well when it admonishes the ordinand: "Believe what you read [in the Scriptures], teach what you believe, practice what you teach." This is what Bishop Edward Walsh, M.M., had in mind when he admonished his men:

The task of a missioner is to go to a place where he is not wanted, to sell a pearl whose value, although of great price, is not recognized, to people who are determined not to accept it even as a gift. . . . To accomplish this he need not be a saint but he must come close to passing for one. And in order to achieve this hoax, he must do so many things that a saint does, that it becomes for him a serious question if the easiest way is not simply to be a saint in the first place and be done with it. [Grutka 1977:11]

Similarly, the constitutions of the missionary Society of the Divine Word remind its members, "People must be able to recognize that we [missioners] have experienced in our own lives the kingdom that we proclaim to others" (Const. 106). The constant message of one's life must be that of St. Paul, "Imitate me as I imitate Christ" (1 Cor 11:1). It has been wisely said that the first and most convincing word preached by any missionary does not come from his or her lips but from the missionary's heart and behavior. Suffice it here to emphasize that one of the most basic assumptions of the present approach to mission is that effectiveness presupposes a spirituality that might be summed up as (1) a deep, living faith, (2) a selfless dedication to the needs of others, and (3) a humble, obedient, and trustful sense of personal mission. However we may wish to describe mission spirituality, these three dimensions will somehow always be a kind of lowest common denominator[1] and will constitute the very foundation of the spirituality we are discussing. There are, of course, some excellent treatises on general spirituality and some specifically focused on mission to which the reader might wish to refer.[2]

1.2.1 A LIVING FAITH

Those engaged in mission must be, above all, individuals of deep, living faith, sincerely believing what they preach, with God as the very heart and center of their lives, the mainspring of their innermost selves. It is a basic theological assumption of the present approach to mission that every Christian, but especially those engaged in a ministry, must strive to be of "the mind of Christ" (1 Cor 2:16) to such an extent, in fact, that he or she can say with Paul, "for me 'life' means 'Christ' " (Phil 1:21) and "the life I live now is not my own; Christ is living in me" (Gal 2:19f). To emphasize such personal theocentric oneness and wholeness is merely to re-echo the words of Jesus to the scribe who inquired about "the first of all Commandments" (Mk 12:28–34). Jesus unhesitatingly takes his answer from Deuteronomy, from a passage very familiar to every Jew, in fact heard from earliest childhood over and over again: "you shall love the Lord your God with all your heart, and with all your soul, and with all your strength" (Deut 6:4–7).

This answer calls to mind the response of the wise guru who was approached by a young man in very much the way that Christ once had been addressed:

> "Master," the young man asked, "when can I say that I truly love God?" Instead of giving a direct answer, the guru signaled to two of his disciples, saying, "Give him the answer I gave you when you asked me that very question. Yes, when can we say that we truly love God the way we should?" Completely bewildered, the inquirer allowed himself to be led by the two disciples to a nearby stream, where he was at once submerged and held under water for a very uncomfortable length of time. When finally released, the inquirer, coughing and sputtering, and wondering what all this meant, was brought back to the guru. "Now," the guru solemnly said, "now you are ready for an answer to your question. Tell me, my son, exactly

what were you thinking about when you were held under water?" Still coughing and gasping for air, the young man half-smiling replied, "What could I have been thinking about, but about air, air, and more air?" The wise guru looked sympathetically at the young man and said, "Now you have answered your own question; you love God truly, the way you should love him, as soon as you seek God, and only God, the way you sought air and only air."

This is the type of theocentricity (that is to say, the oneness with Christ through the Holy Spirit and completeness in the Father) that Paul must have had in mind when he said that for him *life* and *Christ* were synonymous (Phil 1:21; Gal 2:19f) and that all things, compared to Christ, were equivalent to rubbish (Phil 3:8). This, too, is what Jesus meant by "with *all* your heart, *all* your soul, and *all* your strength." Although fully realizable only in the hereafter, such a theocentric orientation must be the goal of every true follower of Christ, especially of those who wish to succeed in a ministry. Without theocentricity, even the best anthropological theory applied to ministry and witness would be but an exercise in futility, a gimmick, and a sham. We have no choice in the matter. The primary and driving force of every Christian, particularly of someone called to church leadership and a ministry, must be nothing less than "*Totus tuus!*"—"Lord, I am yours, yours entirely and without reserve!"—the motto John Paul II chose for himself.

1.2.2 DEDICATION TO THE NEEDS OF OTHERS

The second requirement for a true spirituality for mission is Christ's own "second commandment," which, he said, was inseparable from his first (Mt 22:39). This second commandment demands *selfless dedication to the needs of others* (cf. *Evangelii nuntiandi*, no.79). Love of neighbor is not something accessory to mission and is not primarily a kind of lure for winning converts; it is, in fact, nothing less than a basic constitution of the very Kingdom that the Church wishes to extend through mission. According to this constitution, the community of love that we call "Church" must not only *believe* its faith; it must *do* it. Christianity is by its very nature a faith of love (Mt 22:34–40; Jn 13:14f, 34; 15:9–17), whose adherents are to be recognized by their Godlikeness that is reflected especially in their genuine care and active compassion for others.

The demand for selfless, humble service was a lesson impressed on the apostles and disciples of Jesus on many occasions before his supreme immolation on the cross (Mt 20:27f; Mk 10:45; Lk 10:25–37; 21:15–19), not least of all in the beautiful parable of the Good Shepherd (Jn 10:1–21). At the last supper he said:

You address me as "Teacher" and "Lord," and fittingly enough, for that is what I am. But if I washed your feet—I who am Teacher and Lord—

then you must wash each other's feet. What I just did was to give you an example: as I have done, so you must do. [Jn 13:13–15]

Here one should note how deeply conscious the Lord was of his role as teacher and how at the same time he was aware of the importance of the lesson he was teaching. He repeated the fact and emphasized that his intention was to provide an example that was not merely to be admired but also to be followed. His was the example of humble service of the Good Shepherd, who was ever ready to serve and to lay down his life for his sheep (Jn 10:1–21). Responding to the Master's example, Paul wrote to the Corinthians, "I will gladly *spend* myself . . . for your sakes" (2 Cor 12:15). Spending oneself for others is the second dimension of true mission spirituality. Christ's disciples, in turn, passed the lesson of humble service on to their own disciples: "The way we came to understand love was that he laid down his life for us; we too must lay down our lives for our brothers" (1 Jn 3:16; cf. 1 Cor 11:1). It is therefore appropriate that the successor of Peter and head of a "Servant Church" should refer to himself as the "Servant of the Servants of the Lord."

Throughout church history down to our own times, examples of heroic dedication to the needs of others abound. Owing especially to the inability of missionaries to cope with tropical diseases, their life expectancy only a century ago was often brief indeed. Five of the first seven Holy Ghost Fathers who were sent to the Guinea Coast died within the first five weeks of their arrival. In less than seventy years, the SMAs (the Society of African Missions) lost 500 priests and 239 Brothers. The Benedictines of St. Ottilia made similar sacrifices: 75 percent of their missionaries died before reaching the age of thirty-five, with only three surviving to their forties. Of the fifty-two Divine Word Missionaries who died in the first thirty years of the Society's existence, thirty-one died before finishing their fifth year in the missions (Thauren 1927:42). To embrace a vocation that implied that one would live for perhaps only five additional years was indeed to lay down your life for your brothers (1 Jn 3:16). These are, of course, only examples; similar situations prevailed in other parts of the world as, for instance, in Oceania (Forman 1978:52f).

Examples from our own times would include such heroic individuals as Archbishop Romero of El Salvador, who was murdered by right-wing extremists for identifying himself "too closely" with the poorest of the poor of his country (Erdozain 1984). In neighboring Guatemala, in less than two years some fifteen priests and religious have been kidnapped or killed for the "crime" of loving the poor. Mother Theresa of Calcutta would be the first to recognize that today there are dozens, if not hundreds, of modern apostles of all Christian traditions who deserve to share her Nobel Peace Prize.

Although it is still the exception for one to be called upon actually to lay down his or her life, the *readiness* to answer such a call is a requirement of all Christians, particularly for those engaged in mission. However, the most common, most painful, and most important but generally unrecognized form of self-immolation is the call to small but real and continuous daily sacrifices presupposed by the practical anthropological principles and guidelines to be suggested in the present volume. We refer, for instance, to the enormous sacrifices that will be required of all engaged in cross-cultural ministries in learning and appreciating the ways and values of the community ministered to; there are also the drudgery and the countless humiliations and frustrations associated with any real effort to master an apparently "insignificant" local dialect; there is the violence to self that is required when adapting to local standards of human interaction; and there is the humiliation of having to serve as *junior* partner in the Third World only because one is a foreigner, even if the expatriate has had a far better education and far more experience in the particular ministry than his or her indigenous counterpart. Not the sacrifice of the luxuries of one's home nor the consolations of relatives and friends of long standing but the sacrifice of one's ways and values will be the missionary's greatest sacrifice, a sacrifice that, in fact, may even become a slow martyrdom. The missionary who claims that he or she has never felt the weight of this sacrifice has most likely never made it. (Cf. Luzbetak 1970:15.)

1.2.3 A HUMBLE SENSE OF PERSONAL MISSION

A spirituality for mission presupposes *a deep but humble and obedient sense of personal mission, a conviction tied to an unshakable trust in God.* Speaking of every Christian, and therefore *a fortiori* of one called to a leadership role in mission, John Henry Newman wrote:

God has created me to do Him some definite service; He has committed some work to me which He has not committed to another. . . . Somehow I am necessary for His purposes, as necessary in my place as an Archangel in his—if, indeed, I fail, He can raise another, as He could make the stones children of Abraham. Yet I have a part in this great work.

Newman then goes on to draw the important conclusion:

Therefore I will trust Him. [*Meditations and Devotions*, London, 1875. In Harrold 1945:356f]

Moses at first resists God's call. "Who am I," he asks, "that I should go to Pharaoh and lead the Israelites out of Egypt?" God's answer is simple and in fact the very same that he gives to this day to whomever he calls to a special task—"*I* will be with you" (Ex 3:10ff). Similarly, God calls Gideon to lead the Israelites against the powerful and constantly harassing armies of the Midianites. Like Moses, Gideon remonstrates, "My family is the meanest in Menasseh, and I am the most insignificant in my father's house." God's answer was, "It is *I* who send you. . . . *I* shall be with you" (Jgs 6:14ff). The two great heroines of the Old Testament, Judith and Esther, humbly accept their special and very difficult missions. Relying entirely on him who called, Judith courageously proceeds to cut off the head of Holofernes (Jdt 13:7f), an archenemy of God's Chosen People. Before approaching the King at the risk of her life, Esther humbly begs God, "Help me, who am alone and have no one but you, O Lord." Full of trust in him who called, Esther approaches the king and successfully pleads for her people (Est 4). Prophet Jeremiah's call follows the same pattern. God tells Jeremiah, as he tells everyone he calls to mission, "Before I formed you in the womb I knew you, before you were born I dedicated you, a prophet to the nations I appointed you." Jeremiah comes up with the usual excuse, "I know not how to speak. I am too young." But the Lord too comes with *his* usual argument and assurance, "Have no fear . . . *I* am with you" (Jer 1:4–10, 17–19). Paul, the missionary *par excellence,* was thoroughly convinced of his personal mission; at the same time, he was a man of obedience and full trust in God. In his farewell to the elders of the church of Ephesus (Acts 20:17–25), he speaks of how—although he realized that nothing but "bonds and affliction," nothing but "chains and hardships," awaited him in Jerusalem—he nevertheless in imitation of his Master on *his* final trip to Jerusalem would humbly, obediently, and confidently press on toward the city. He was "compelled by the Spirit," with only one ambition left in life—to finish the mission to which he had been called: "I put no value on my life if only I can finish my race and complete the service to which I witness to God's grace" (Acts 20:24). When everyone seemed to have abandoned him, Paul tells us, "the Lord stood by my side and gave me strength, so that through me the preaching task might be completed and all the nations might hear the gospel" (2 Tm 4:16f). Paul had no doubt whatsoever that he would succeed, for "in him who is the source of my strength I have the strength for everything" (Phil 4:13), and "if God is for us, who can be against us?" (Rom 8:31). Paul wrote to the Philippians, "I firmly trust and anticipate that I shall never be put to shame for my hopes; I have full confidence that now as always Christ will be exalted through me [i.e., I will succeed in my mission], whether I live or die" (Phil 1:20; *see* also Rom 8:28; 2 Cor 12:9; Eph 3:20; 2 Tm 1:12).

One cannot help but be reminded of Jesus' own unparalleled example of absolute trust in his call and ultimate success. After only three years in public ministry, Jesus ended his active life in what seems at first to have been a total disaster. His belief in mission, his obedience, and his trust, however, were absolute. No situation, not even death, could weaken his confidence in the Father and in the ultimate success of his mission.

A humble and firm trust and openness to the will of the Father were virtues characteristic of all great missionaries and founders of missionary orders and societies. This is true of all Christian traditions. Arnold Janssen (1837-1909), the founder of the Divine Word Missionaries, was an outstanding example of a leader who exhibited these missionary virtues. More than once, people shook their heads in wonderment, saying, "Here you have either a great saint or an outright fool," reminding us of what had been said also of Jesus—that he too was "out of his mind" in carrying out his mission (Mk 3:21). Arnold Janssen was trying to do the impossible—founding a Catholic mission society in Germany during the *Kulturkampf*. No wonder Janssen succeeded against such odds (Bornemann 1975). As Arnold Janssen is described in the current constitutions of the Society he founded, he was "a man of prayer, trust in God, openness to God's direction and apostolic commitment" (Const. 406; cf. Const. 122). Some Protestant examples include Hudson Taylor in China (Kane 1984) and William Carey in India (*infra*, 3.2.4.1.1).

1.3 THE IMPORTANCE OF HUMAN KNOWLEDGE AND SKILL

After unequivocally proclaiming that mission presupposes the primacy of the Holy Spirit and deep spirituality on the part of those engaged in mission, our theological preamble professes at the same time *a deep appreciation of the contribution that human knowledge and skill can make toward more effective mission policies and practices*. Our preamble insists that "science without religion is lame; religion without science is blind" (Albert Einstein).

This partnership between the natural and the supernatural rests on solid theological grounds. According to God's own way of doing things, there is a very close connection between nature and supernature, between human effort and Grace. "Do your best and God will do the rest" was a bit of practical theology that the present author learned from the Benedictine Sisters in the first grade of parochial school. He firmly believes this statement to this day. Although faith can move mountains (1 Cor 13:2), it would be anything but sound theology if we were to follow an exclusively supernatural approach. Mission calls for a supernatural-plus-natural strategy in imitation of God himself—the God of the Bible (cf. Stott, Coote 1979:21–131) and the God of History (Luzbetak 1969:118ff). The Koran teaches the Muslim to trust in Allah but at the same time reminds him to *tie* his camel so as to keep it from wandering off. Or in the words of Colossians 3:23, "Whatever you do, work at it with your *whole* being." *Whole being* certainly demands the utilization of human knowledge and skill. We believe that faith can indeed move mountains, but we also know that God wants us to use picks and shovels, and, if we have them, dynamite and bulldozers as well.

A particularly strong argument may be found in the words of St. Paul: "But how shall they call on him in whom they have not believed? And how can they believe unless they have heard of him? And how can they hear unless there is someone to preach?" (Rom 10:14). Our anthropological approach to mission maintains that, according to God's own plan, mission normally presupposes, besides the Holy Spirit, a human partner. There must be a preacher and a hearer; that is, the principles and skill of *human* communication must also be applied. The preacher must be "heard" (Rom 10:13ff); that is, the hearer must be made to understand and must be moved, for to preach in any other way would be tantamount to not preaching at all (and therefore the normal channel of Grace would be absent). Just as it is impossible today to practice theology without taking the secular sciences into account, so it is impossible to practice missiology without taking the secular sciences, particularly anthropology, into account. The secular sciences do not remove God from mission. On the contrary, they support the Christian's supernatural attitude toward his or her work by presenting mission problems in their natural but true and overwhelming immensity, thus forcefully convincing the Christian of his or her inadequacy, and forcing those in the ministry to seek the assistance that really counts—*God's* assistance. Abraham Lincoln said, "I have been driven to my knees many times by the conviction that there was nowhere else to go." Our preamble states that a humble appreciation of science will do the same for those engaged in mission; it will drive them to their knees too. Science will make them say with Peter, "Lord, to *whom* shall we go?" (Jn 6:68). Although almost any human knowledge can prove useful in mission work, it is especially in cultural anthropology that those engaged in mission action learn to know the nature that Grace presupposes and builds upon.

Anthropology is sometimes looked upon as a suspect, if not a heretical, tool. However, we are justified in applying anthropological theory to mission in no less a way than Billy Graham is justified when he employs twentieth-century psychology, oratorical skills, and sophisticated advertising and organizational techniques in his campaigns, or when John Paul II employs his public relations and linguistic adeptness in his many audiences and travels around the globe.

Although St. Paul's dependence on the Holy Spirit was absolute and unwavering, he did not hesitate to use a variety of human skills, however natural and purely-human such skills may have been. We read in the Acts of the Apostles 19:8 how in Ephesus Paul entered the synagogue and over a period of three months "debated fearlessly, with persuasive arguments" about the Kingdom of God. We read that he "urged and insisted" that both Jews and Greeks repent and accept the Lord Jesus Christ (Acts 20:21). Words like *debate*, *persuade*, *urge*, and *insist* certainly connote an effort in communication that is important to mission, even if it is essentially a human effort.

Jesus himself employed in a most masterful manner what were purely human techniques. He did not hesitate to employ such oratorical and pedagogical approaches as were present in his deeply moving parables of the prodigal son (Lk 15:11–32), the Good Samaritan (Lk 10:25–37), and the Good Shepherd (Jn 10:1–18). We note also the beautiful similes of the birds of the air and the lilies of the field (Lk 12:24–30). In fact, Jesus was actually applying anthropology here (i.e., contextualizing, incarnating, and inculturating the Good News; in the truest sense of the word tailoring his message to the culture of his audience without compromising it). That is what this book is all about: the tailoring of the Good News to the context of local churches.

Jesus even believed in such human tools as drama. To proclaim his message about the sacredness of the temple, he overturned tables and drove the money-changers out of the sacred precincts with a whip (Jn 2:13–17), thus *dramatizing* how holy his Father's house really was. At the last supper, Jesus not only instructed his disciples in love for one another but, by washing their feet, he *dramatized* his message of humble service, a ministry aptly called the "ministry of the towel" (R. Foster 1983b). The mysterious signs of grace that we call *sacraments* are all dramatic ritual acts in which God becomes actively present among his People. Just as Jesus and his followers did not have to apologize for employing the various human communication skills of their age, the Church today need not take too seriously the charge that an anthropological approach to mission is an attempt to put the Holy Spirit "out of business." If we are to love God with *all* our heart, *all* our mind, and *all* our strength, and if we are to love our neighbor *as ourselves* (Dt 6:4–7; Mk 12:30f), we who live in the Age of Science have no choice but to love God and our neighbor also with all the *scientific* strength available to us in our times. And let us not forget that the scientific field particularly relevant to mission is anthropology, which literally means "the science of human beings."

The anthropological approach does not seek to replace the Holy Spirit with human cleverness. The intention is rather to be as perfect an instrument in God's hands as possible, using to the fullest every God-given capacity at our disposal. We are merely saying in the words and in the spirit of St. Francis of Assisi, "Lord, make me a *channel* of your peace." Or as Cardinal Newman stated it, "I am born to serve Thee, to be Thine, to be Thy *instrument*" (Harrold 1945:356f [emphasis added].) We are merely recognizing that God in his infinite love and wisdom found it fitting to enter into partnership with his Church and with us personally to carry out his Son's mission of love to the world, despite all our limitations, all our weaknesses, and sinfulness—in fact, despite our objective uselessness (Lk 17:10; 1 Cor 1:27). God's Master-Instrument is the Body of Christ, with the Spirit as the Source of Life and Strength, the Incarnate Word as the Head, and we weak, useless, sinful human beings as the limbs (1 Cor 12:12–31; cf. Rom 12:4–8; 1 Cor 10:17; Eph 1:22f; 2:16; 3:6; 4:12; 5:23; Col 1:18,24; 2:19). Apropos is the story of a greatly admired crucifix that is said to have been found in the rubble of a bombed-out church during World War II. Remarkable was the fact that the whole lifesize body had been well preserved, except for the two hands that had vanished in the fire. There followed much debate about what should be done with the corpus. Some suggested that a sculptor be hired to restore the hands. However, it was finally decided to mount the body of Christ onto a new cross without restoring the hands. The message of a handless Christ would be only too clear, especially to those aspiring to continue his mission on earth: "*You* are my hands; I have no hands but yours!" In a word, we aim *to be as perfect a channel of Grace as possible, to be as worthy an instrument in God's hands as possible, to be as good, wise, and faithful a servant (Mt 24:44–48) as is humanly possible. That, and that alone, is our intention and theological justification for insisting on anthropological knowledge and skill in mission.*

1.4 SUMMARY

When applying anthropology to mission, we can never overemphasize the threefold message of our preamble. In missiological anthropology, the centrality of the Holy Spirit, the need of spirituality, and the importance of human knowledge and skill must be studied and meditated on, and ever kept alive. The threefold message of our preamble must at all times constitute the solid rock on which the application of anthropology to mission action must rest.

Chapter Two

MISSIOLOGICAL ANTHROPOLOGY

> *Anthropology holds up for us a*
> *great mirror and lets us look at*
> *ourselves in our infinite variety.*[1]
> Clyde Kluckhohn

Missiological anthropology might best be regarded as a specialized form of applied anthropology. We call our field *missiological anthropology* because it is a blend of missiology and anthropology: its scope and purpose are missiological, whereas the processes and analyses are anthropological. Missiology suggests the issues, parameters, and goals; anthropology provides the particular (culturological) perspective, approach, and standards for studying the issues. More specifically, our field seeks (1) to bring together in an organized fashion the various concepts, insights, principles, theories, methods, and models of anthropology that are particularly relevant to the mission of the Church, and (2) to show how such an organized body of knowledge might be employed for a better understanding and realization of that mission (Luzbetak 1961). Our aim is to *understand* missiology and to *do* anthropology. We shall therefore have to describe both fields if we are to describe what we mean by *missiological anthropology*.

2.1 MISSIOLOGY

2.1.1 NATURE AND SCOPE

2.1.1.1 The Name "Missiology"

The name *missiology* is derived from the Latin *missio* ("a sending forth with a special message to bring or with a special task to perform") and the Greek *logos* ("a study, word, or discourse"). Etymologically, missiology is a study of the sending forth or expansion of the Church.

The study of Church mission and of the specific missions of the Church has been known by a variety of names. Both Gustav Warneck, the father of

12

modern Protestant missiology, and Joseph Schmidlin, Warneck's Roman Catholic counterpart, used the term *Missionslehre* ("mission theory"), a name that was superseded by *Missionswissenschaft* ("mission science"). In the earlier days of modern missiology, there were suggested such high-sounding but awkward names as *kerystics* ("theory of announcing the Gospel"), *prosthetics* ("theory of adding to the community"), *auxanics* ("the study of growth"), *halieutics* ("theory of fishing"), *agrics* ("theory of the field"), *plethunics, organics, evangelistics,* and so on (Schmidlin 1931:1). Fortunately, these never received acceptance. Donald Anderson McGavran and his associates still prefer "church growth theory."[2] The name *theology of mission(s)* seems to be the preferred British usage, while *science missionaire* has found acceptance mainly among French-speaking missiologists. We have adopted *missiology* because the basic meaning of the term is readily understood and because the term is used most widely.

2.1.1.2 Definition

Some missiologists define their field with their own particular understanding of mission in mind. Such a definition describes *their* variety of missiology, but, we might ask, what about the missiologies that do not fit into the authors' concepts? Do they cease to be missiology? Thus, Johannes Verkuyl defines the science of mission as "the study of the salvation activities of the Father, Son, and Holy Spirit throughout the world geared toward bringing the kingdom of God into existence" (1978:5). This is, no doubt, a good theological understanding of mission, but the understanding seems to be too narrow for defining missiology. The field calls for a definition that would be more compatible with the great variety of understandings of mission throughout the history of the field, especially today, whether or not we are personally in agreement with the particular understanding. The definition must, among other things, not overlook the nontheological interdisciplinary aspects of missiology (*infra*, 2.1.1.4)

2.1.1.3 Missiology as Theology and/or History

Kenneth Scott Latourette (1884–1968), being the outstanding historian that he was (Sterling Professor in Missions and Oriental History at Yale University, president of the American Historical Association, and "Dean of American Church Historians") not surprisingly at all preferred to view missiology from his own particular perspective. He regarded it simply as history (Hogg 1978).

Most mission theorists, however, consider missiology to be basically theological. Thus the two eighteenth-century pioneers of missiology, Protestant Schleiermacher (1768–1834) and Catholic Hirscher (1788–1865), considered all study of mission as a form of pastoral theology. Warneck looked upon his *Missionslehre* as a three-branched theological study—namely of church history, scriptural foundations for mission, and practical missionary theology. Schmidlin's *Missionslehre* similarly consisted of church history, theological and rational foundations for mission, and pastoral theology. To this day, there is no real consensus among missiologists as to how one might best fit missiology into an overall scheme of theology. No matter how missiology might be structured within theology, theology will always occupy the central place and will always play the determining role. The object of missiology (i.e., the mission of the Church and the evaluation of the norms according to which this mission is to be carried out) must repeatedly be examined, tested, and re-tested, not so much in the light of human wisdom (however vital that wisdom may be) but in terms of how *God* understands mission. What counts in missiology above everything else is what *God* regards as genuine salvation activities and what *God* means by "the Kingdom of God." Theology is therefore the real acid test in mission and holds the place of honor among the disciplines involved. All other fields, including anthropology, are essentially supportive in nature and have a cross-fertilizing, expanding, strengthening, and integrating function. In a word, the other fields are essential, but they are supplementary dimensions of a basically theological field.

2.1.1.4 Missiology as an Integrating, Multidisciplinary Field

Although basically theological in nature, missiology, as we understand it today, is unable to deal with its theological concerns without the aid of a variety of other disciplines, both theological and secular. Missiology is multidisciplinary in character and holistic in approach.

Anthropologist Alan P. Tippett (1974a:498–504) developed a model of the missiological process and presented it in the form of an interesting flow chart (Figure 1, see page 15).

Even if some of the details in Tippett's chart are open to question, the model nevertheless well illustrates the dynamics of missiology and the meaning of such terms as *interdisciplinary, integrating, cross-fertilizing,* and *supplementing*. The process begins with actual field situations and ends with *applied* missiology. According to Tippett, the most important flow comes from the ethnosciences, including ethnotheology, ethnohistory, and ethnopsychology. These ethnosciences are solidly based on, flow from, and are enriched by theology, anthropology, history, psychology, sociology, and practical mission experience. The ethnosciences freely interact with one another, while Gospel values serve as the driving force of this cross-fertilization. Further interaction takes place through still other admixtures, such as comparative religion. This total mix is what Tippett calls *missiology*. Flowing from this theoretical missiology are pastoral, educational, administrative, and other practical applications referred to simply as *applied missiology*.

Important to remember is that missiology, like anthropology, is not a *mere conglomeration* of disciplines but a network of disciplines that systematically interact with one another. Missiology is, therefore, more properly regarded as a *field* rather than a discipline. It is a field that studies the expansion and growth of the mission of the Church in all its dimensions—communal, sacramental, kerygmatic, diaconal, and institutional (see chapters 4 and 8).

Figure 1
Flow Chart of Components and Forces
in the Missiological Process

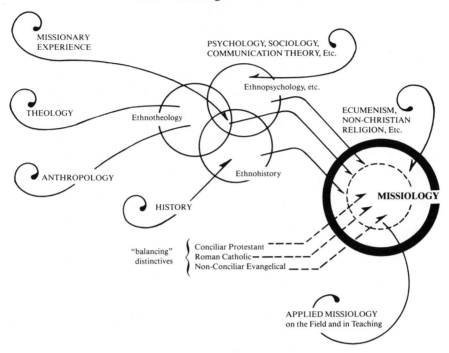

After Arthur F. Glasser, "Missiology—What's It All About?" © *Missiology* 1978, 6:8.

2.1.2 HISTORY OF MISSIOLOGY

2.1.2.1 The Beginnings of Missiology

Patristic literature failed to produce a single systematic treatise dealing professedly with what we might regard as missiological theory, mission history, or the foundations of pagan missions (Schmidlin 1931:66). Nevertheless, patristic writings, especially those of post-Constantinian times, abound with insightful discussions and useful historical information and are therefore of high missiological value (Schmidlin 1931:66–71; Latourette 1937, 1:113–170). One thinks, for instance, of Augustine and John Chrysostom. Two outstanding treatises toward the close of the patristic period were the anonymous tractate *About the Call of All Peoples* and Pope Gregory the Great's *Letters and Instructions,* the latter work dealing with problems affecting practical mission methods, particularly the problem of cultural adaptation (Schmidlin 1931:70; cf. Latourette 1938, 2:62–69). The writings of the Middle Ages include those of St. Boniface and St. Columban, a number of important papal documents, the works of the Scholastics, especially St. Thomas Aquinas' *Summa contra gentiles* and *Opusculum contra Saracenos,* and the writings of Raymond Lull, a Franciscan tertiary, who authored no less than

313 works on mission topics and established training centers for missionaries (Hoffman 1967:901). Lull's Dominican counterpart of this period was Raymond of Penyafort (b. 1175–1180, d. 1275). More, of course, could be said about the Middle Ages and its understanding of the mission of the Church.

In the Age of the Great Discoveries, there was the author of the *Libro de las profecias*, Christopher Columbus himself, in which are combined a zeal for the spread of the Gospel with a passion for discoveries (Hoffman 1967:901). The real mission theorists, however, were José de Acosta, S.J., author of *On the Procuring of Salvation of Indians* (1588); Thomas of Jesus, a Carmelite; and Cardinal Branasti de Laurea, a Franciscan Conventual who authored the first systematic work on evangelism, the *Commentarium in quattuor libros sententiarum Scoti*. The primary concerns of mission theorists of this period, and into the seventeenth century, were problems of a juridical nature both canonical and civil, as well as such concerns as the administration of Sacraments, and the Chinese and Indian rites controversies (Hoffman 1967:901). The chief representative of the Protestant churches was the Dutch Gisbert Voetius (1589–1676), whose mission theory was highly akin to that of the Catholic thinkers of the time.

2.1.2.2 The Pioneers of Modern Missiology

Eighteenth-century Catholicism saw a distinct decline in mission interest. The Protestant attitude was, in turn, indifference and even hostility. It was, in fact, not until the close of the century that Protestants became involved extensively in overseas missions. Responsible for most of this new spirit were the Evangelicals and Pietists; they were supported by the colonial expansion, commerce, and imperialism of the times. It was during this period that missiological studies were first recognized as integral and distinct constitutive parts of the wider system of theology. Important pioneers in this field were Roman Catholic theologian J. B. Hirscher (1788–1865), Orthodox N. I. Ilminsky (1821–1891), and Protestant Friedrich E. D. Schleiermacher (1768–1834), author of the *Kurze Darstellung des theologischen Studiums zum Behuf einleitender Vorlesungen* (1850). Schleiermacher regarded the study of missions as a form of practical theology. Because mission involvement was a new experience for Protestantism, there was a feeling that the biblical justification for such activities had first to be established; past missionary experience had to be evaluated. Among the early significant Protestant attempts to develop an independent science of mission, besides those of Schleiermacher, were the efforts made by the German Lutheran theologian Karl Graul (1814–1864) and Alexander Duff (1806–1878) of the Church of Scotland. Other outstanding Protestant pioneers were Henry Venn (1796–1873) and Rufus Anderson (1796–1880).

Considered as the real founder of *modern* Protestant missiology is the German theologian Gustav Warneck (1834–1910). The first chair of missiology ever to be established, however, was that at the University of Edinburgh. Founded in 1867, it was held by Alexander Duff.

Joseph Schmidlin, the church historian at Münster, began to shift his scholarly interests more and more specifically toward *mission* history and *mission* theory. He was influenced by the growing colonial involvement of the German Empire, encouraged by the example of Protestant mission theorists of Germany, urged on by mission bibliographer Robert Streit and by Arnold Janssen (the founder of the German missionary Society of the Divine Word; his associates were especially Frederick Schwager, Anton Freitag, Theodor Grentrup, Karl Streit, Herman Fischer, and Hubert Hansen). In 1909, Schmidlin offered a course in Catholic missions, stressing the areas then under German colonial control. Particularly important was the encouragement Schmidlin received from Robert Streit, the founder of the now-famous *Bibliotheca Missionum*, a basic bibliographical resource that was greatly appreciated by mission specialists (Henkel 1982:18f). In 1910, a chair of missiology was founded at Münster. The following year, Schmidlin founded the first Catholic missiological journal, the *Zeitschrift für Missionswissenschaft* (later renamed *Zeitschrift für Missionswissenschaft und Religionswissenschaft*) and became the first president of the Internationales Institut für Missionswissenschaftliche Forschungen. Schmidlin published the first modern textbook on Catholic mission theory, the *Katholische Missionslehre im Grundriss* (1919) and the first, richly documented Catholic mission history, the *Katholische Missionsgeschichte* (1925). Robert Streit, because of his great influence on Schmidlin and his monumental bibliographical accomplishments, is rightly regarded, with Schmidlin, as co-founder of modern Catholic missiology.[3]

2.1.2.3 Modern Catholic Missiology

2.1.2.3.1 Pre-Vatican II Missiology

Germany. In the 1920s and early 1930s, the influence of Schmidlin and Streit spread well beyond Münster to such important German universities as Würzburg, Munich, and Bamberg. It also gained acceptance across Europe.

After the devastation of World War II, the leadership in German Catholic missiology passed on to Benedictine Thomas Ohm and Josef Glazik, M.S.C. The Divine Word Missionaries later added their strength to this rapid growth at St. Augustin, near Bonn, through their mission seminary and missiological, sinological, and anthropological institutes.

Belguim. Pierre Charles, S.J. brought missiology to the University of Louvain in 1922. He wrote a "small mission encyclopedia" entitled *Les dossiers de l'activité missionaire,* and a year later inaugurated the missiological workshops known as Semaine des Missions (renamed *Rythmes du Monde*).

Italy. Italy, with Rome as the center of world Catholicism, could not remain passive for very long. In fact, the Pontifical Urban College of the Propagation of the Faith (now generally referred to as the Pontifical Urban University) offered sessions in missiology as early as 1919 and established the Pontifical Institute of Mission Science, officially known as the Pontificium Institutum Missionale Scientificum. Among the best-known mission scholars attached to the institute is André Seumois. The other important center of missiology in

Rome is the Jesuit Gregorian University. A chair of missiology was founded there in 1928, with the addition of a full missiological faculty four years later. Soon thereafter, a missiological journal was founded at the Gregorian University, *Il Pensiero Missionario*. The Pontifical Urban University continued its *Bibliotheca Missionum*, the bibliographical work begun by R. Streit, and introduced a new supplemental publication, the *Bibliografia Missionaria* while it built up and maintained a valuable missiological library of over 100,000 volumes. In 1943, the Gregorian University began to publish its annual *Studia Missionalia*.

France. France owes its interest in mission science to small scholarly circles of enthusiasts. The Catholic Institute of Paris and the missiological conferences held in Paris, Lyons, and Strassburg in the 1920s and early 1930s gave birth to modern French missiology. The *Revue d'Histoire des Missions* first appeared in 1923. Despite the setback that the Church suffered in World War II, and despite the shift of concern from overseas missions to de-Christianized France, such outstanding French theologians as de Lubac, Danielou, Raguin, Rétif, and others remained highly involved in missiological issues.

Spain. Spanish missiologists became active in the early 1930s. The Asociación de Misiología was founded; workshops were held at several Spanish centers; a course in mission science was introduced at the University of Comillas; and publications, both popular and scholarly, began to appear. The primary concern of the Spanish missiologists was history. The main center for study was located at the Seminario des Misiones Extranjeras in Burgos.

Netherlands. The first Roman Catholic chair of missiology in the Netherlands was founded in Nijmegen in 1930. Soon after World War II (1948), an institute of missiology was also established there. The leading scholar was Alphons Mulders.

Switzerland. The first Catholic center of missiology in Switzerland was the Bethlehem Missionary Institute, founded at Schöneck-Beckenried in 1921. Thirteen years later, the University of Fribourg introduced missiological courses into its program, and in 1944 this center of learning founded an institute of missiology. In 1945, the Bethlehem Missionary Institute published the first issue of its *Neue Zeitschrift für Missionswissenschaft* under the editorship of J. Beckmann, the leading Catholic Swiss missiologist in the postwar years. Today the best-known Swiss Catholic missiologist is Capuchin Walbert Bühlmann.

North America. Professional Catholic missiology had a very slow start in North America. Missiology remained on a nonprofessional level, even though popularization of the study of missions began quite early, particularly in missionary training centers and among Catholic youth in general (owing to the efforts of the Catholic Students Mission Crusade that was founded in 1918). In fact, there were practically no professionally trained Catholic missiologists in the United States until well after World War II. The Society of the Propagation of the Faith published its *Worldmission*, which, however, especially in its earlier years, was popular rather than scholarly in nature. The publication of the *Mission Academia* study materials by the Society of the Propagation of the Faith, and the translations of Schmidlin's history and theory (1931 and 1933 respectively) by the Divine Word Missionaries were perhaps the first signs of the slow process of professionalization that was taking place. The annual meetings of the Mission Secretariat of Washington, D.C., in the 1950s and 1960s, and Fordham University's annual workshops for mission specialists that took place around the same time were additional small but significant steps toward more serious Catholic involvement in mission studies. The Catholic University of America began a short-lived missiological program in 1958, some sixteen years after such courses had been offered in Canada at the University of Ottawa. Today, the leading Catholic missiological centers in the United States are the Catholic Theological Union in Chicago and the Washington Theological Union in Washington, D.C. Although there are at present no Catholic schools in the United States granting doctorates in missiology programs, and only one such school exists in Canada, missiological specializations within existing graduate programs are available. For example, a "Religion and Culture" program is offered by the Catholic University of America.

2.1.2.3.2 Vatican II and After

The most significant development in Catholic missiological thought came with the Second Vatican Council, a truly revolutionary development (we shall have opportunity to treat this topic more fully in the next two chapters). Suffice it here to indicate the general direction that Catholic missiology seems to have taken in our times as a result of the Council. Despite the complexity involved in any attempt to assess the vast amount of current publications that must be considered,[4] one cannot but get the impression that (1) much, if not most, of the postconciliar missiological literature tends to be practical rather than theoretical in nature; (2) postconciliar literature is often, if not generally, ecumenical in scope, with applications drawn cross-denominationally; and (3) despite the fact that postconciliar literature is often contradictory and tentative, great advances have indeed been made, as we shall explain more fully especially in chapters 4 and 8. Here we offer only a brief explanation of these characteristics.

That much, if not most, of postconciliar literature is *pastoral* rather than theoretical is evident in the type of problems that seem most frequently to be treated. These include issues of liberation, religious education, liturgy, secularization, dialogue with non-Christians, and the like. Underlying such practical questions are usually the anthropological problems of contextualization and self-determination.

Postconciliar literature, we have said, tends to be *ecumenical*. Missiology today no longer seems to reflect schools of thought, as was the case by contrast several decades ago with the evangelization school of Münster questioning the "church-planting" direction of Louvain. Much less evident today are the interchurch polemics of the pre-Vatican II years. Postconciliar missiology clearly tends to be cross-denominational, corresponding to the theological pluralism that is now found in professional missiological associations and that prevails at missiological symposia and workshops.

Thirdly, as is clear from the concern expressed in Paul VI's exhortation *Evangelii nuntiandi*, Catholic postconciliar mission theology is in many ways *transitional, confused, and contradictory.*[5] That such is the case, however, should not surprise anyone. After all, radical theologizing has affected much, if not most, of recent theology, and there is no reason why missiology should be exempt from this trend. Despite such cross-currents (*infra*, 4.4.2.4), giant steps have been made. Inroads have been made in ecumenical understanding and cooperation, interfaith dialogue, and the appreciation of such concepts as the "Kingdom of God." Unparalleled progress has also been made in local theologies, in the concept of inculturation, and in the understanding of the true nature and mission of the church (*infra*, 4.4.3; 4.4.4; chapter 8).

2.1.2.4 Modern Protestant Missiology

O. G. Myklebust has produced in his two-volume survey, *The Study of Missions in Theological Education* (1955; 1957), the first comprehensive history of mission studies. What follows is intended to be but a very general overview. For more of the development of modern Protestant missiology, one might best consult such authors as Verkuyl (1978:26–86, 261–308), Bassham (1979), and Glasser, McGavran (1983).

Germany. In pre-World War II Germany, the most prominent Protestant missiologist was perhaps Karl Hartenstein (1894–1952), of the Basel mission. His special interest was the purification of missionary motivation through an emphasis on eschatological considerations. In postwar Germany, the outstanding missiologist was Walter Freytag (1899–1959), founder and first professor of the Missionsakademie at the University of Hamburg. Any list of outstanding missiologists of present-day Germany would include such names as Walter Holsten of the University of Mainz, whose emphasis is on the "kerygmatic" dimensions of mission (actually on the Lutheran understanding of justification by faith); Wilhelm Andersen of the Augustana Hochschule of Neuendettelsau, who views mission from the perspective of the Blessed Trinity as the mission of God himself, very much in line with the thinking of Karl Barth; Hans Jochen Margull; Peter Beyerhaus; and Hans Werner Gensichen, the founding president of the International Association for Mission Studies.

Netherlands. The most influential Protestant missiologists in the Netherlands in our times are J. H. Bavinck (d. 1964), Henrik Kraemer (d. 1965), Johannes Hoekendijk (d. 1975), and Johannes Verkuyl.[6]

England. Any list of leading British missiologists of our times would include such figures as Max A. C. Warren (d. 1977), Stephen Charles Neill (d. 1984), Lesslie Newbigin, and John V. Taylor. British missiology has made important progress in mission history and theology—one need but consider the names just mentioned—but the field in that country seems currently to be directed toward strategy-oriented problems.

A special word about a mission strategist who was clearly ahead of his time may be in place here. Roland Allen (1868–1947) of the British Society for the Propagation of the Gospel in Foreign Parts was a missionary to China during the Boxer Rebellion. His views were expressed especially in his *Missionary Methods: St.Paul's or Ours* (1912) and *Spontaneous Expansion of the Church and the Causes Which Hinder It* (1927). In many ways, Allen was a revolutionary. It was his conviction that missionaries ought to imitate Paul by handing over authority and responsibility of missionary churches to indigenous leaders almost immediately—in any case, as soon as possible. He decried paternalism and ecclesiastical colonialism, and emphasized the central role of the Holy Spirit in mission. The task of the missionary was simply to bring non-Christians to Christ rather than to try to remake them according to the missionary's own self-image. He insisted on independence for mission churches, fostered ecumenical cooperation, and opposed the transplantation of Western institutions to newer churches. Allen's ideas had actually to wait until the 1960s to be appreciated. Although clearly ahead of his time, Allen was unrealistic in many ways. For instance, he seemed to imagine that the world of today did not differ from that of St. Paul. He also overlooked the fact that independence of new churches, as desirable as it may be, could at times be brought on prematurely. Allen also downplayed interdependence and overemphasized the autonomy of local churches.[7]

Scandinavia. The influential Scandinavian missiologists today are Olav Guttorm Myklebust (Oslo), Bengt Sundkler (Uppsala), and Johannes Aagaard (Aarhus).

Switzerland. Although the Swiss have given Protestant missiology a number of respected scholars, Karl Barth (d. 1968) stands out not only for his contribution to Protestant systematic theology (his primary achievement), but also for his insights regarding the mission of the church as a continuation of God's own mission and as belonging to the very nature of Christianity itself (Verkuyl 1978:61).

United States. In the United States, the most respected Protestant missiologists of our times are historians Kenneth Scott Latourette (d. 1968), R. Pierce Beaver (d. 1987), and Charles W. Forman. Outstanding work of broad missiological scope is being done today by Gerald H. Anderson, the imaginative editor of the *International Bulletin of Missionary Research*. Like British missiology, but perhaps more so, American missionary science today shows a strong pastoral preference, with emphasis on strategy and practical aspects of mission. Among the better-known mission strategists today are such figures as Eugene A. Nida, Donald Anderson McGavran, and McGavran's colleagues at Fuller Theological Seminary.[8] The leading missiological centers are Yale, Princeton, Asbury Theological Seminary, Fuller Theological Seminary, and, one might add, the Overseas Ministries Study Center.

2.1.2.5 Orthodox Missiology

Although the mission involvement of the Orthodox Church can hardly compare with that of the Catholic and Protestant Churches in intensity,

Orthodox mission history has nevertheless much to offer to Catholic and Protestant mission theory and practice. Orthodox missiology as a science, however, had a very late start. It was only twenty-five years ago that the Orthodox Church experienced a missiological awakening, a missiology based largely on Orthodox past mission experience. Its qualities are seen especially in its deep appreciation of the vernacular language (for both Scripture and liturgy), its insistence on an indigenous clergy, and its emphasis on the rights and responsibilities of the *local* church. (The local church is viewed as a eucharistic community and as the visible expression of God's redemptive action) The chief journal of Orthodox missiology is the *Panta Ta Ethne* (Athens). For a fuller introduction to Orthodox missiology the reader would do well to consult James Stamoolis, *Eastern Orthodox Mission Theology Today* (1986); for more concise surveys, one might consult, for instance, Bria (1986), Meyendorff (1974, 1978), and Stamoolis (1984).

2.1.2.6 Third World Missiology

In the last few decades, Third World missiology, both Catholic and Protestant, has grown enormously. Of particular interest to Third World scholars is the problem of contextualization, regarding liberation in particular. The avalanche of recent missiological publications, much of which is of excellent quality, is impressive indeed. The more outstanding scholars include the Latin American mission thinkers like Gustavo Gutiérrez, Hugo Assman, Leonardo Boff, Enrique Dussel, and Orlando Costas; the Africa specialists like John S. Mbiti, E. Bolaji Idowu, and Aylward Shorter; the Asia experts like Raimundo Panikkar (Hinduism), Heinrich Dumoulin (Buddhism), Kosuke Koyama (Japan), Choan-Seng Song (China), and Stephen Fuchs (aboriginal India).

Perhaps the best survey of Latin American, African, and Asian liberation theology is Dean William Ferm's two-volume *Third World Liberation Theologies* (1986). The first volume is *An Introductory Survey*, a clear, systematic guide to liberation theology written for students at the seminary and college levels. Ferm's other volume is *A Reader*, a representative selection from the writings of outstanding Third World liberation theologians. Other clear and positive introductory overviews of liberation theology that should be studied include Gibellini's *The Liberation Theory Debate* (1988) and L. and C. Boff's *Introducing Liberation Theology* (1987). A beginner in liberation theology would do well to read Gerald Anderson and Thomas Stransky's edited *Mission Trends*, No. 3 and No. 4 (1976, 1979); these works contain carefully selected papers on liberation and Third World theology. The reader should also review the papers from the 1976 Dar es Salaam ecumenical dialogue, edited by Sergio Torres and Virginia Fabella (1978). It is particularly important to be acquainted with the official documents of the Vatican Congregation for Doctrine of the Faith (Ratzinger 1984, 1986) and to keep in mind that the 1984 document was meant to be a *critique* of liberation theology and therefore necessarily negative in tone. However, any doubts about the official attitude of the Roman

Catholic Church and the basic theological soundness of liberation theology have been removed by John Paul II in his address to the bishops of Brazil a year later (*Origins* 1986:681–685) in which the Pope announced that a new document (Ratzinger 1986) would soon be released, emphasizing that "when purified of elements which can adulterate it, i.e., liberation theology, with grave consequences for the faith, this theology of liberation is not only orthodox, but also necessary" (*Origins* 1986:684). *The* classic in liberation theology is Gustavo Gutiérrez's *A Theology of Liberation: History, Politics and Salvation* (1973; revised edition 1988).

The direction that Third World mission theory and practice is making today will be found not so much in the works of mission futurologists like Bühlmann, however useful and enlightening such reading may be, but in the published proceedings of congresses, such as those of the World Council of Churches at Melbourne and the World Evangelicals at Pattaya in 1980, and in proceedings of international workshops, such as that sponsored by the Servizio Documentatione e Studi (SEDOS) of March 1981 (Motte, Lang eds. 1982).

2.1.3 MISSIOLOGICAL RESOURCES

Missiological resources have indeed become plentiful. A detailed survey of both Catholic and Protestant libraries, archives, bibliographies, clearinghouses, general reference works, periodicals, publishers, professional associations, research centers, workshops, and schools is provided in Notes 9 and 10 of this chapter.

2.2 ANTHROPOLOGY

2.2.1 NATURE AND SCOPE OF ANTHROPOLOGY

The word *anthropology* is derived from the Greek *anthrôpos* ("human being") and *logos* ("word, discourse, study"). Anthropology inquires into the basic questions about who human beings are, how they came to be what they are, how they behave, and why they behave as they do. Because the mission of the Church is to human beings, and because anthropology is the systematic study of such beings, a basic knowledge of this science is a *must* for anyone engaged in mission. Anthropology is a coordinating type of science. It is composed, however, not just of bits and pieces of all sorts of sciences, but is rather a science in its own right. It is such, first of all, because it has a very distinct object of study—our humanness. The physical, biological, cultural, social, and psychological understanding of what it means to be human is examined with a view to arriving at as complete and integrated a picture as is possible of what we understand by *anthrôpos*. Anthropology is a science in its own right also because it has an overall method of its own that we might simply call "comparative." What follows is an attempt to concretize two fundamental features of anthropology—holism and the comparative method.

2.2.1.1 Holism

Is it not presumptuous for any science to claim for itself the name of *"the* science of human beings"? After all, other sciences study human beings too—history, psychology, and biology, to mention only a few.

There are a number of reasons for regarding anthropology as the science of humankind *par excellence*. Most importantly, it can be considered as such because it attempts to understand human beings *holistically*. *Holistic* is a word derived from the Greek *holos*, meaning "whole, complete." Whatever issue anthropology examines, it does so in relation to our human wholeness. Unlike other sciences that study human beings, anthropology alone assumes a distinctly holistic role, viewing humanness as a unified system. Consequently, anthropology is best described as a *coordinating science of humanness*. It exists as such without sacrificing the insights and approaches of the particular fields involved. Whereas other sciences may study human beings from a *particular* perspective (for instance, from the physical, biological, psychological, social or historical perspective) anthropology focuses on something more than an understanding limited to any single point of view.

Anthropology helps us avoid the mistake of the four blind men spoken of in the ancient Indian fable. In this tale, each of the blind men insisted that elephants looked the way each of the men visualized the elephant they touched:

> According to a version of this fable, one of the blind men had embraced the elephant's leg and now insisted that the animal was very much like a tree trunk. The second blind man had touched the side of the elephant and was now convinced that the animal was unquestionably very much like a wall. The third blind man had felt the elephant's tail and now insisted that the animal was unquestionably similar to a rope. Another blind man had touched the elephant's tusk and now claimed that the elephant looked like a spear.

The moral is clear: concentration on a specific dimension of humanity is the method of most sciences. Although undoubtedly useful and in fact necessary, the method unfortunately can be misleading. Human beings are more than physical entities that might be described in terms of atoms and chemistry. We do not deny that human beings *are* composed of atoms and chemicals, but at the same time we recognize that they are much more—they are biological, social, cultural, psychological, historical, and spiritual entities. To describe what it really means to be human, we must bring together the various perspectives or models of humanness and superimpose them like transparencies, one on top of the other. They must be interrelated and viewed as a single organized picture. This, in fact, is the goal of anthropology—to produce a composite, coordinated, and fully living picture of the single entity called *anthrôpos*. This complex way of understanding people may explain why anthropologists are sometimes called "licensed lunatics," but theirs is the only true way of understanding humans—or elephants, for that matter.

Physical anthropology, for instance, studies the *biological* processes of the human body, but it does so by relating the various biological processes to other anthropological perspectives, such as the cultural and social. Archaeology, a historical subfield of anthropology, studies various artifacts of *extinct* peoples, but it does so only with other human models in view. Ethnology, a third anthropological subdiscipline, is primarily interested in the ways and values of *living* peoples, but at the same time it asks how these ways and values are affected by the other human dimensions and how they in turn affect and modify other perceptions.

Anthropologists, in fact, behave very much like architects who are in the process of constructing a large, complicated office building. The architect invariably will insist on viewing the object of study (the building) holistically.

The architect will, therefore, need not just one, but a variety of perspectives or *models*. A number of blueprints will be needed, each of which will be highly specialized. However—and this is important—the particular blueprints will always be studied in light of the other blueprints and in light of the whole building. As in architecture, anthropology seeks to integrate into one whole a variety of specialized blueprints of what it really means to be human.

The architect will need, first of all, a basic floorplan which will provide the functions, locations, and dimensions of each room and floor and will indicate such things as the location of the windows, doors, and pillars. This blueprint will have to be supplemented by other blueprints of the building being built, such as those of the structural engineer, which will indicate in detail the type and size of the foundations and footings and the arrangement and dimensions and exact locations of the girders. There will also be blueprints provided by the mechanical engineer and by other highly specialized subcontractors, each providing specific diagrams that will indicate the location and type of pipes and ducts for heating, air conditioning, plumbing, and the like. Carpenters and other craftsmen will draw up plans for cabinets and shelving, all of which must be carefully integrated "holistically" with the other perspectives of the building. Another set of blueprints will be provided by the electrical engineer, reflecting the complexities of the electrical system of a modern office building, such as the location of the lights and outlets, the type and location of conduits that lead to ventilators, elevators, to exit and emergency lights, to a great variety of office appliances like typewriters, computers, word processors, calculators—and one should not forget the doorbells, fire and burglar alarms, and the all-important telephone network. The different blueprints must be constantly cross-referenced, otherwise the plumber's pipes and ducts will be going through girders, the electrician's outlets will be somewhere behind panels, and the structural engineer's pillars will end up in the middle of doorways and elevator shafts.

Figure 2
The Holistic Nature of Anthropology

Anthropology seeks to discover the interrelationships between various scientific models of the human being.

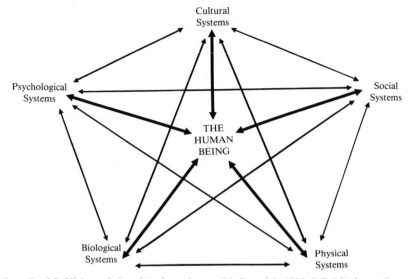

From Paul G. Hiebert, *Cultural Anthropology,* p. 24. Copyright 1976, J. B. Lippincott Co.

A fuller examination of the holism of which we speak would reveal (1) that *each and every* human characteristic is ultimately of concern to anthropology, just as each and every aspect of the building is of concern to the architect; (2) that of concern to anthropologists are *human commonalities as well as human diversities*; (3) that anthropology is holistic also in the sense that its concerns include human beings *of every time and place*; (4) and, finally, that the object of anthropological inquiry, whatever subfield we may have in mind, is the group, not the individual as an individual. Individuals are, after all, members of an organized interacting group.

In a word, only a composite, coordinated, holistically interrelated and integrated picture can fully present what a magnificent "architectural" marvel human beings really are: who they are, where they come from, how they behave, why they behave the way they do, and indeed how similar and yet how different they are—in short, what it truly means to be human. The task of coordinating and integrating the various scientific perspectives of what it means to be a human being is the unique task of the science of anthropology. Anthropology, therefore, rightly regards itself as *the* science of human beings; of all sciences, it alone takes this comprehensive and longitudinal look at the being we call *anthrôpos*. (Cf. Hiebert 1976:75–88.)

2.2.1.2 The Anthropological Method: A Comparative Approach to Knowledge

The second essential and distinctive characteristic of anthropology is its *comparative method*. To be able to present our humanness in a holistic way as just described, the anthropologist must *compare* one group of human beings with another. The anthropologist's laboratory turns out to be the whole world—all natural environments and times, from the very first appearance of humanity. The laboratory method used is that of comparison. The approach followed by anthropologists is therefore rightly called the "comparative approach" to knowledge.

2.2.2 SUBDISCIPLINES OF ANTHROPOLOGY

No anthropologist could possibly master the entire field of anthropology. The science of anthropology is therefore broken into many subdisciplines and ever-finer specializations.There are, for instance, such subfields as psychological anthropology, ecological anthropology, urban anthropology, and economic anthropology. Some anthropologists focus their efforts on art, music, cognitive systems, laws, or religion. Figure 3 presents the *basic* structure of anthropology.

Figure 3
The Basic Structure of the Science of Anthropology

The Study of Human Beings	Orientation	
	Historical or Descriptive	*Scientific*
as a *biological* animal Physical Anthropology	Paleoanthropology	Race
as *rational* animal Cultural Anthropology	Archaeology Linguistics Ethnology	Social Anthropology

Anthropology branches off into two general areas. The first centers its attention on human beings *as biological organisms* (physical anthropology); the second focuses on that which is *distinctive of human beings*—culture (cultural anthropology). Scholars in continental Europe regard these two areas as being so different in object and method that the two cannot and should not be considered under the same general science or name. However, in light of what we have just said about the holistic and coordinating nature and scope of anthropology, most anthropologists, especially those of the Anglo-Saxon world, feel that the union is well justified. It is true that the international meetings of anthropologists are officially referred to as the International Congress of Anthropological *and* Ethnological Sciences as if anthropology and ethnology were distinct fields. The fact is that the conjunction *and* was added only as a compromise after a bitter debate at one of the organization's early formative meetings. It is revealing to note that the same anthropologists who insist on a distinction in names maintain a close relationship with one another and hold their international meetings as a single association of professionals. The structure of the American Anthropological Association, by contrast, clearly reflects the holistic character of the field and the affinity of the various anthropological disciplines. This attitude is reflected in the departmental arrangements of American colleges and universities.

Physical and cultural anthropology are further subdivided according to the particular *orientation* of the discipline in question. Thus a study can be regarded as "historical/descriptive" on the one hand, or "scientific" on the other. If the primary goal of the discipline or subdiscipline is to discover and document the uniqueness of facts, the discipline or subdiscipline is historical or descriptive. If the primary goal focuses on the formulation of generalizations ("laws"), the discipline is regarded as scientific (Hoebel 1958:12). Figure 3 seeks to throw some light on the ensemble of anthropological disciplines and major subdisciplines, and to show how they can be neatly structured by reason of their particular orientation.

2.2.2.1 Physical Anthropology

Physical anthropology studies human beings as biological organisms. The field is therefore sometimes regarded as "biological anthropology" or "human biology." True to its holistic character, physical anthropology seeks out all possible causes (genetic, ecological, social, and so on) that might explain the evolution and variations of the human body. When physical anthropology focuses on the origin and evolution of the human body, the discipline is called human paleontology (Gr. *palaios* "old" + *onta*, "existing things" + *logos*, "word, discourse, study") or paleoanthropology (Gr. *palaios* + *anthrôpos* + *logos*, or in simple English, "the study of fossil man"). When physical anthropology assumes a scientific orientation, with a focus on structure and function of contemporary forms, it is called "the study of race" or somatology (Gr. *sôma*, "body" + *logos*). To achieve its goals, physical anthropology has recourse to highly specialized auxiliary fields, such as anthropometry (Gr.

anthrôpos + *metron*, "measure"), biometrics (Gr. *bios*, "life" + *metron*), and human genetics. Somatology branches off into such subfields as human morphology (Gr. *morphê*, "form" + *logos*) and comparative human physiology (Gr. *physis*, "nature" + *logos*).

By taking very minute and detailed measurements and making comparisons of fossilized and unfossilized bone structures from human and prehuman forms, the paleoanthropologist tries to discover the origins of the human body, its genetic relationships to lower forms, and its evolution through the thousands of years since the first appearance of humankind on earth. In studying prehistoric humans, the anthropologist relies mostly on the analysis of bone structures. However, when *living* races are studied, the whole human animal can be examined. Anthropologists then inspect such anatomical details as the skin, hair, eyes, internal organs, blood, and the various bodily secretions. They especially follow the clues and tools of modern genetics. A good physical anthropologist will be an expert anatomist and physiologist; he or she may have even more knowledge in such areas than physicians generally have. Because anthropology is interested in groups rather than individuals as individuals, the physical anthropologist is concerned with averages and indices rather than with individual measurements as such.

Although at first sight physical anthropology seems to be unrelated to the mission of the Church, it nevertheless *is*, inasmuch as the discipline provides some of the most basic scientific arguments that support the universal brotherhood of all peoples. Physical anthropology offers strong scientific arguments against claims of racial superiority of one group over another. It makes important contributions also to the general health of peoples, a major element of the social mission of the Church. Moreover, physical anthropology provides much useful background information for cultural anthropology, the chief mission-related form of anthropology.

2.2.2.2 Cultural Anthropology

Cultural anthropology analyzes, describes, and compares the distinctly human aspect of peoples. It explores lifeways and mentalities of living societies as well as of those from past ages. Cultural anthropology, unlike physical anthropology, studies human behavior that is *learned* rather than genetically inherited. Depending on its orientation, cultural anthropology may be historical, descriptive, or scientific in the sense described above and used in Figure 3. Anthropology's ultimate concern, it must be emphasized, is not description but a better understanding of *why* people are what they are.

Today, cultural anthropology is subdivided into three major areas: archaeology (prehistory), linguistics, and ethnology. Whereas archaeology focuses on the description and historical interpretation of *extinct* cultures, ethnology is concerned with *living* cultures. Linguistics is the study of one of the most distinctly human characteristics, human speech; the area deals with both living and extinct languages.

2.2.2.2.1 Archaeology

Archaeology (Gr. *archaios*, "ancient" + *logos*) is sometimes called "ethnology of extinct societies." It studies prehistory or prehistoric archaeology. There are two forms of archaeology: classical and anthropological. Classical archaeology deals with early human history that occurred after the art of writing was discovered about five thousand years ago. Anthropological archaeology retrieves, analyzes, compares, and interprets human relics, internments, inscriptions, drawings, and other cultural products. It aims to discover as much as possible about cultures of prehistoric times. Of concern is the *preliterate* history that covers the period between the emergence of human beings and the invention of writing, a period estimated by some anthropologists as covering as much as three million and more years. Today, archaeologists show considerable interest in the study of culture change (processual archaeology). Increasingly, prehistorical inquiries are also being related to the cultures of living peoples.

Investigation into prehistory, like all historical research, is necessarily interested in establishing the time when a phenomenon took place. However—unlike popular writers, journalists, and historians in general—prehistorians are not concerned so much about setting an absolute date for their archaeological finds. Prehistorians often wish to discover a *chronology*, a time-sequence rather than a specific date. The scientific tools used to establish such chronologies are derived from a variety of sciences, including geology, climatology, chemistry, zoology, and botany. More recently, a variety of sophisticated mathematical and computer-related applications have become important parts of the archaeological method.

2.2.2.2.2 Linguistics

Linguistics (Latin *lingua*, "tongue, speech, language") is the study of language across space and time. Because speech is a distinctly human feature (cf. Umiker-Sebeok, Sebeok 1981, 1982) and because the methodology of linguistics is highly specialized, the study of language as an anthropological subfield is well justified. (Just as some anthropologists concentrate on such areas of culture as music, myth, law, economics, or religion, so a linguist, a highly specialized cultural anthropologist, concentrates on linguistic aspects of culture.) Linguistics, as indicated in Figure 3, has a "historical/descriptive" orientation. Historical linguistics focuses on the evolution of languages and seeks to reconstruct ancestral languages. It aims to show the relationship of one language to another and of one group of languages to another. Taxonomic (descriptive or comparative) linguistics seeks to describe the fundamental constituents of languages and the rules by which languages are constructed into actual speech.

Noam Chomsky (b. 1928), regarded by many as the most influential linguist of our times, rejects the view that language is learned passively. He maintains instead that human beings have a built-in capacity to acquire language; that is, people have an inborn competence to abstract the basic grammar rules from the infinitude of speech sounds heard in early childhood. People can generate a new infinitude of novel sentences. Chomsky's approach to language is called *transformational* or *generative* linguistics. Today, however, Chomsky's views are being questioned more and more, especially outside America, as being reductionist.

Some linguists, namely those involved in the subfields known as sociolinguistics and anthropological linguistics, are interested in the relationship of language to thought and human behavior. Anthropological linguistics is concerned with the discovery of evolutionary relationships of languages. The anthropological linguist is interested in human communication and in identifying the various social functions that a language has in a culture. The field of sociolinguistics emerged in the 1940s as a study of language as a cognitive system reflected throughout a given culture. In the 1960s, it took new directions. The Chomsky school focuses on language competency of individuals. Other sociolinguists are concerned more with the usage of language by distinct subgroups rather than by individuals as individuals; for instance, these researchers study the language used by different age groups, by men in contrast to women, or by the different social classes of the same society. Also of interest to sociolinguists are the language differences based on differences in topic and occasion, and such questions as how and when bilinguals switch from one language to another. We shall have much more to say about linguistics when we deal with the subject of communication, an important consideration in mission. Communication is, in fact, the most basic human tool at the disposal of the Church in carrying out its role in the world.

2.2.2.2.3 Ethnology

The term *ethnology* (Gr. *ethnos*, "nation, people" + *logos*) may be somewhat confusing because it is used by anthropologists in three different ways. In a loose sense, *ethnology* refers, first, to historical studies that focus on *living* or *recent* cultures. This usage is made in contradistinction to *archaeology*, a discipline that focuses on extinct lifeways. The second sense of the term is applied in contradistinction to studies that have a *scientific* orientation. The term can thus mean an *historically* oriented anthropological study of living or of recent cultures. In its third sense, the term can refer to a descriptive study of *a particular* living culture. Today, it should be noted, scientifically oriented cultural anthropology predominates, and generalizations about human behavior, rather than about history, have become the more common concern of ethnologists. Missiological anthropology is basically missiological ethnology.

Ethnology, as a descriptive study of a particular living culture, continues to be an important concern to researchers studying living cultures. Such descriptive studies are sometimes referred to as *ethnography* (Gr. *ethnos*, "nation, people" + *graphein* "to write, describe"). Ethnographies are the result of detailed first-hand field research. The particular focus of description and method of ethnographic information-gathering will largely reflect the particular underlying theory or concept of culture held by the particular ethnographer.

Ethnographers live among the people studied. They observe and interview the bearers of culture. On assuming a role in the society being studied, the ethnographer participates as much as possible in the life being observed so as to feel and to understand the environment before attempting to describe it.

Certain culturological disciplines closely related to ethnology in object and method are generally looked upon as ethnological subspecializations. Other related areas, like comparative religion, folklore, and mythology, may be regarded as independent disciplines. The subfields of ethnology include, among others, ethnohistory, economic anthropology, ethnomusicology, ethnolinguistics, and psychological anthropology. Ethnohistory, for example, aims to reconstruct the past of simple, usually preliterate societies, by seeking historical clues and evidence, including unwritten "documents" such as oral tradition, folk history, archaeological finds, and a variety of linguistic clues. Psychological anthropology, another example, studies the relationship between culture and personality.

The early ethnologists restricted their studies to so-called "primitive," that is, preliterate and technologically simple peoples. In recent decades, ethnology has broadened its scope to include technologically complex societies as well. The ethnologist's predilection for the simpler, especially untouched lifeways (hardly existing today) was based on sound methodological grounds. For instance, Ralph Linton felt that an anthropologist was less likely to be prejudiced when he or she investigated and described societies that were simpler than his or her own (1945:11f). Or as the leading anthropologists of the 1940s and 1950s pointed out, the closest approximation to a laboratory for a social scientist was a simple, rather than a complex, social situation. In such a "laboratory," the social scientist could approximate the ideal situation of a natural scientist's laboratory. The simple society is generally homogeneous. It is also generally small, manageable, and not so unwieldy as Western societies are. It is quite isolated and is generally free of outside influences. Because such a society is relatively homogeneous, the whole group has more or less the same level of education and experience. All members share a relatively high degree of isolation. In such a human laboratory, the ethnologist and social anthropologist are able to reduce the number of variables to a minimum and are thereby in a better position to describe cultures more accurately and to compare them more objectively. This makes their generalizations easier to test. (Kluckhohn 1949:11–13; Herskovitz 1950:79–93; Benedict 1950:15–18.)

2.2.2.3 Scientifically Oriented Cultural Anthropology

Social Anthropology. Social anthropology is the comparative study of social systems. Sometimes the branch of knowledge is referred to as *comparative sociology*. Social anthropology examines a society's values, institutions, and activities. It observes their interdependence and aims to establish "laws" of social behavior.

The field of social anthropology first emerged in England in the 1920s as a reaction against the subjectivity of evolutionistic interpretations of the origin of social phenomena. Emile Durkheim (1858-1917), the French student of society and one of the founders of modern social sciences, greatly influenced the direction of social anthropology. It was his conviction that social systems were independent "organisms" sustained through the interdependence of their constituent parts. According to Durkheim, the object of sociology was to study such relationships. This concept was applied to anthropology in England by A. R. Radcliffe-Brown (1881-1965) and Polish-born anthropologist Bronislaw Malinowski (1884-1942). Radcliffe-Brown applied the concept to his study of the Andamanese society (*Andaman Islanders*, 1922). He argued that the purpose of social anthropology was none other than to identify the specific functions of the social parts and to show how these parts are responsible for the continuance of the whole. Malinowski in his *Argonauts of the Western Pacific* (1922) independently of Radcliffe-Brown took the cue from Emile Durkheim, arguing that the purpose of social anthropology was indeed to identify the specific functions of the social parts, but in response to basic human needs.

Social anthropology is frequently referred to simply as "functionalism," inasmuch as the concept of function is the unifying element.

Despite the at times rather severe criticism of functionalism (it is condemned especially for assuming that societies are shackled by a kind of law of equilibrium and for attempting to explain social systems exclusively in terms of themselves), the contribution made to our understanding of cultures by British social anthropologists cannot be overestimated. Some of the finest fieldwork and ethnography must be credited to the functionalists. As we shall see, many of their insights and generalizations are directly applicable to the Church's mission. In any case, the study of the origin and past history of such cultural phenomena as puberty rites and ancestor worship, for instance, is far less relevant to missiological anthropology than is the understanding of how the functions of puberty rites and ancestor worship relate to the present-day persistence of such practices. In response to criticism hailed at functionalism, social anthropologists have reconsidered many of their assumptions and have adjusted their views, especially by admitting to a greater flexibility and dynamism in cultures.

Other Comparative Approaches. The comparative approach seeks to uncover general "laws" regarding society and culture. (1) At times, a comparison of *constituent parts* of a given culture will reveal a consistency and harmony that serves to buttress such cultural parts. For example, permissiveness on the part of educators may be looked upon as correct, proper, and logical, for "that is the way our benevolent ancestors and gods always behave." It may also be impossible and unthinkable for a society to sell land to the local missionary for a needed hospital or school "because the only thing one can sell is what one has actually made—and we certainly have not made this land." (2) Sometimes cross-cultural comparisons are made between *similar lifeways within a relatively limited geographical area.* Here the purpose of the comparative approach might be, for instance, to find an explanation for the presence of slavery in a particular society when the practice is totally unknown in otherwise similar neighboring cultures. (3) Sometimes *large-scale comparisons* of fifty or more cultures, or for that matter on a worldwide basis, are made in the hope of discovering broad laws of human behavior. The best-known and perhaps most comprehensive cross-cultural project is that of the Human Relations Area Files (HRAF) at Yale University. The files consist of excerpts from published ethnographies coded for wide use by anthropological institutions and scholars. The coding is by subject and culture, according to Murdock's *Outline of Cultural Materials*, originally published in 1937 and now in a fifth edition (1982). The employment of statistics and modern computer techniques have expanded the usefulness of such large-scale cross-cultural comparisons and generalizations. The chief weakness of the approach is the almost total dependence of the user of the data on the care and judgment of the coders—on their biases, possible misinterpretations, omissions, and other possible coding errors.

2.2.3 APPLIED ANTHROPOLOGY

2.2.3.1 Nature and Scope of Applied Anthropology

When considering the nature and scope of applied anthropology, we should keep in mind that the commonly made distinction between pure and applied sciences does not make any real theoretical or methodological sense; both types of sciences go hand in hand and both are necessary and mutually enriching.

In simplest terms, applied anthropology can be said to utilize anthropological knowledge and skill for practical human needs. It does this in much the way the science of medicine utilizes for the purpose of health and illness the knowledge and skill of physiologists, biologists, chemists, geneticists, and other scientists. Unlike medicine, however, applied anthropology is a relatively recent field and is a social rather than a natural science. It is not surprising, then, that applied anthropology has not yet matured into a full-fledged profession with an organized body of anthropological concepts, principles, theories, and techniques. It is still a long way from being systematized so as to be able constantly to expand and grow in content and applicability in accord with a set of tested methods of experimentation, control, and prediction. Nevertheless, a veritable treasury of useful, holistic knowledge of human beings, at the theoretical as well as practical level, does indeed exist. Anthropology has always been employed with considerable profit by such action-oriented people as educators, social workers, lawyers, judges, city planners, health specialists, military experts, technicians, government administrators, overseas representatives, and church-workers. These people serve in various capacities as cultural interpreters, program evaluators, consultants, planners, strategists, "bridge-builders," and "trouble-shooters." They serve private organizations, industry, churches, governments, and such international operations as *UNESCO*, the World Food Organization, the World Bank, and the Peace Corps. Anthropological applications are as relevant in highly complex societies as they are in remote and technologically simple situations. The following random listing of projects shows the broad applicability that anthropology has in our times:

urban planning

campaigns against hunger and dietary deficiencies

improvements in agricultural methods and animal husbandry

nursing, hospital work, and other health services

school administration, mass education, literacy campaigns, learning and teaching a foreign language

promotion of sanitation and hygiene

child-care education

maintenance of morale in prisons and retention camps

counsel to legislatures and courts

rapid industrialization and social disorganization resulting therefrom

population control

community development programs

the promotion of community morale, pride, and loyalty

drug abuse and alcoholism

coping with factionalism

problems affecting the elderly

violence and riot control

post-disaster planning

programs to counteract racism

identification of human remains by physical anthropologists for criminal action and forensic purposes

crime control

mass emigrations and refugee programs

broadcasting and media utilization

minority relations

opposition to needed technical change

military purposes such as the maintenance of morale among armed forces and prisoners of war, maintenance of good relations with civilians in combat zones or under military rule, psychological warfare, the formulation of treaties and terms of surrender

the organization and management of cooperatives and credit unions

mental health programs

archaeological guidance affecting park services

mining, oil exploration, and major construction projects coming in conflict with values and needs of native peoples

psychiatric counseling

problems arising from the intrusion of tourists into a community training of corporate executives for overseas assignments church-related administration and activities

Most of these applications are laudable, but there have also been highly questionable involvements on the part of anthropologists. One such application was the now-infamous Project Camelot of the late 1960's that sought to undermine governments in Latin America (Horowitz 1965; Wax 1978). A similar incident took place in Thailand (Jorgensen, Wolf 1970). By contrast, the Vicos Project of Cornell University in the late 1950s was an example of how the social sciences can effect deep, meaningful, multifaceted changes in an undesirable feudal system such as had existed in the Vicos Valley of Peru prior to the project (Holmberg 1965; Dobyns, Doughty, Lasswell 1971).

2.2.3.2 History of Applied Anthropology

Rather than try to summarize the complicated general history of anthropology, we shall limit ourselves to the history of applied anthropology. Missiological anthropology is, after all, a form of *applied* anthropology. For the general history we refer the reader to our overview of anthropological theories (*infra*, 5.1.6) and to such full-length studies as Lowie's classic work (1937) or that of M. Harris (1968). There are also short but excellent surveys, such as those of Voget (1973) and Eggan (1977).

2.2.3.2.1 The Beginnings of Applied Anthropology

The idea that anthropology could and indeed should improve the quality of human life is as old as the field of anthropology itself. However, well into the 1930s, anthropological applications were invariably of an incidental nature, loosely connected and of limited duration. They were not the central and primary concern of the anthropologist. Among the early anthropologists who recognized the applicability of their field to practical human problems were evolutionists like the American Lewis Henry Morgan (1818–1881), as well as the British Sir Edward B. Tylor (1832–1917) and Sir John Lubbock (1834–1913). As evolutionists, they interpreted all cultural development according to the inflexible, preconceived, unilineal set of laws that required the simpler to precede the more complex, the less perfect to precede the more perfect. Their assumptions about progress were held as true whether they considered bodily forms, marriage, religious beliefs, or any other socially shared behavior.

Franz Boas (1858–1942), a German-born anthropologist and immigrant to the United States, exerted great influence on an entire generation of American anthropologists, including such leading figures as Kroeber, Herskovits, Sapir, Lowie, Wissler, Hallowell, Radin, Benedict, Hoebel, and Mead. Boas is, in fact, regarded as the father of American anthropology. He took a firm stand against the apriorism of the evolutionists and in 1911 published his *The Mind of the Primitive Man*, a bold defense against racist views. Boas himself, however, remained a "pure" rather than an "applied" anthropologist.

2.2.3.2.2 The Transitional Years: 1920–1944

It had been the common practice for social scientists to shy away from personally involving themselves in action. Such personal involvement was regarded as unbecoming of serious scholars. But, as Partridge and Eddy point out (1978:20–26), this attitude began to change in the 1920s. The change seems to have been due to three developments: (1) interest in contemporary rather than past cultures, (2) the growth of functionalism, and (3) concern for knowledge about *all* cultures, including those of the anthropologists themselves. New types of studies were made, for instance, by Robert Redfield, Ruth Benedict, W. Lloyd Warner, Ralph Linton, and Margaret Mead. Important, too, was the influence of the British functionalists Malinowski and Radcliffe-Brown, who shifted the interest of many anthropologists of Anglo-Saxon countries away from the origins and distribution of cultural traits to questions regarding the function of elements of culture. Anthropologists began to analyze how a custom served a purpose in the particular society studied; they investigated the factors that encouraged the rise of customs; and they studied features that were responsible for the modification and persistence of customs. In 1928, Margaret Mead published her *Coming of Age in Samoa*, in which she compared adolescent Samoan girls with their counterparts in America. Robert and Helen Lynd studied the life of an American community and produced the classic *Middletown* (1929). The Australian psychiatrist Elton Mayo began to apply anthropological concepts and methods to problems of modern industry. Because of his influence, other anthropologists took the cue and began to write about productivity, workmanship, absenteeism, and other industry-related issues (Warner 1941, 1962; Warner, Low 1947; Warner, Lunt 1941).

From the beginning of the 1930s, there was a marked increase in the number of anthropologists employed by the U.S., Mexican, British, Spanish, Portuguese, Dutch, French, and other governments. However, application of anthropology remained on the periphery of the discipline. Unlike the period that followed, the applications until the forties were more or less limited to isolated problems. Nevertheless, the stage for the blossoming of modern applied anthropology had been set.

2.2.3.2.3 World War II: The Birth of Modern Applied Anthropology

Modern applied anthropology can be said to have been born during, and largely owing to, World War II. The patriotism of anthropologists during the war years was high, and the need for their expertise was quite generally recognized. During World War II, of some 303 anthropologists in the United States, over 295 were involved in the war effort *as anthropologists* (Mead 1977:149). Observing the British war effort and the role played by anthropologists, Kluckhohn noted how

> British anthropologists held important posts in the Foreign Office, the Admiralty, the British Information service, the Wartime Social Survey, and in the field. One man was political adviser for the whole Middle East, another carried the main administrative burden for the vast Anglo-Egyptian Sudan, still another handled liaison problems with native peoples in Kenya and Abyssinia. (1949:172f)

He points out how the Japanese invasion of India would have had an entirely different history if it had not been for the confidence that a woman anthropologist, Ursula Graham Bower, enjoyed with the Zemi, a strategically located tribe on the Assam-Burma frontier.

During the war, American anthropologists operated in their professional capacities in many branches of government, both at home and in the field. They were involved in writing practical handbooks on jungle and desert survival; they trained officers in coping with morale problems; they were engaged in psychological warfare, in predicting reactions of enemies, in penetrating Ecuadorian jungles in search of quinine, and even in helping to write the terms of surrender with Japan (Kluckhohn 1949:168-195).

It was in mid-1941 that anthropologists organized themselves into the Society for Applied Anthropology. They also founded their first professional journal, *Applied Anthropology* (later renamed *Human Organization*). The journal emphasized such concerns as community development, industrial relations, health services and psychiatry, food production, and the administration of peoples. Three years later (1945), another important milestone was reached: Ralph Linton edited an insightful anthology entitled *The Science of Man in the World Crisis*, in which outstanding anthropologists discussed such practical issues as the role of their discipline in dealing with internationalism, war, use of resources, population control, the changing lifeway of American Indians, and territorial administration. The forties and fifties witnessed an ever-greater involvement of anthropologists in studying and writing about contemporary issues affecting plantation laborers, peasant farmers, urban laborers, and the like (Eddy, Partridge 1978:33f). It was also at this time that Clyde Kluckhohn of Harvard published his prize-winning *Mirror for Man*, in which he graphically presented the countless contributions that applied anthropology was making in the contemporary world.

The postwar years were a time of rapid expansion for anthropology, in the United States perhaps more than anywhere else. Enrollments in anthropology courses at American colleges and universities grew by leaps and bounds—from only 24 Ph.D.s in 1947–48 to no less than 445 in 1975–76, not to mention the more than 6,000 B.A. and 1,000 M.A. degrees bestowed that same year (cf. Eddy, Partridge 1978:35). In this period, applied anthropologists began to withdraw from their government positions and to return to their teaching posts. "Pure" anthropology was thus not only revitalized but, as we shall see (*infra*, 5.1.6), it blossomed in a great variety of new directions. With so much momentum in the direction of theory, it was not surpising that application suffered.

Nevertheless, there were a number of very significant developments in *applied* anthropology during a period that must be regarded as a period of decline. One thinks not only of the successful Vicos Project (Holmberg 1965) but also of such works as Goodenough's *Cooperation in Change* (1963), G. M. Foster's *Traditional Societies and Technological Change* (1973), E. Spicer's *Human Problems in Technological Change* (1952), and Arensberg and Niehoff's *Introducing Social Change* (1964). Some excellent work was done also in medical anthropology (*see*, for instance, Paul 1955), and in the areas of education and childrearing (Spindler 1955, 1963). Medical anthropology, in particular, developed so rapidly that in 1967 a professional association known as the Society for Medical Anthropology was founded.

Applied anthropology suffered an additional setback during recent times on account of the growing disagreement between anthropologists and their clients regarding the legitimate expectations of an applied social science. To make matters worse, anthropologists became involved in a number of clearly unethical projects (particularly the so-called "Project Camelot," the purpose of which was to influence Latin American countries politically). An already weakened discipline was thus given a severe blow through notoriety.

2.2.3.2.4 Contemporary Applied Anthropology

The postwar years saw a sudden rush from the applied field to academic positions. As a result, academic positions today are all more or less filled. In fact, because of budget cuts and lower college and university enrollments, the number of available positions has actually been reduced. The future for younger anthropologists consequently seems to be outside academia, in the applied field. First and foremost, opportunities seem to be in development, health (physical as well as mental), and education (Goodenough 1978: 264f). Other possibilities are in urban planning, forensics, museum management, national park service, drug and alcohol rehabilitation, social work, overseas industries, and, of course, church-related activities. For more recent information on the state of the art and future direction of applied anthropology, we refer the reader to such works as Erve Chambers, *Applied Anthropology: A Practical Guide* (1985); the American Anthropological Association's special publications and training manuals, for example, Nader, Maretzki (1973); Goldschmidt, ed. (1979); Partridge (1984); van Willigen, DeWalt (1985); van Willigen (1986), and such recent works as Elizabeth M. Eddy and William L. Partridge, eds., *Applied Anthropology in America* (1978), Peggy Reeves Sanday, ed., *Anthropology and the Public Interest* (1976), Michael V. Angrosino, ed., *Do Applied Anthropologists Apply Anthropology?* (1976), and Alden Redfield, ed., *Anthropology Beyond the University* (1973).

Applied anthropology has thus experienced its ups and downs. Today, as Ward Hunt Goodenough and Peggy Reeves Sanday put it,

Though anthropologists still debate whether there should be an applied anthropology and sometimes even deny that there is any opportunity for anthropologists in nonacademic employment, it is clear that a large and growing cadre of anthropologists is fully engaged in such activity. . . . [There is] evidence that the uses of anthropology are again on the increase. . . . The absolute number of anthropologists engaged in nonacademic professional activities is almost as great as at any time in the past, though proportionately they remain a minority. [Goldschmidt, ed. 1979:263]

2.2.3.3 Applied Anthropology and Value Judgments

Despite claims to the contrary, applied anthropology is by no means a value-free science (cf. Geertz 1984). Our argument is simple enough: Whenever anthropology is applied, it is applied to what one calls "human needs"; but anyone—agnostic, materialist, positivist, or Christian believer—who speaks of human needs is making a value judgment. Scientific materialism is itself a philosophical point of view, not a science.

When anthropology is applied, it is applied for something the anthropologist calls a cause. It is applied for the "betterment" of human conditions, for the educational or technological "advancement" of a social group, or for the "rights" of defenseless or needy individuals. Because social scientists are responsible beings who cannot divide themselves into two beings (the one a scientist and the other a moral being), they cannot wash their hands of the consequences of their actions, even in research. Nor can they stand uninvolved as mere spectators or as mere technicians advising the employer about what must be done to assure the employer's stated goals. Nor can the anthropologist pose as a kind of meteorologist, forecasting what will happen if such and such a policy is followed without at the same time assuming responsibility. Roger Keesing was very much to the point when he rejected the

> widespread assumption that social science can be objective and neutral— that it can be free of ideological and political commitments and can seek truth without involvement. . . . If one does not 'notice' oppression or injustice or exploitation because one is only a scientist and science does not concern itself with political issues, then one is being myopic and self-deluding about objectivity.[1976:537]

In any scientific work it is essential that concepts, principles, theories, and techniques be scrupulously and objectively applied according to *strictly scientific* standards. These features may not be predetermined by ideology, world view, or one's religion. However, and this is important, in scientific work moral decisions and value judgments are involved whenever one deals with human needs. Willy-nilly, value judgments must be made about the goals and the particular means to be used to achieve such goals. A physician, although primarily concerned about the strict application of *medical* science, is nevertheless constantly faced with ethical dilemmas and moral decisions that seem outside the province of medicine. What is medically possible, medically permissible, medically correct, and therefore medically advisable is not by that very fact *ethically* correct and advisable. The issue of *in vitro* pregnancies is a good example of what is meant (Ratzinger 1987; Molnar 1987). Anthropologists must, therefore, be less concerned about the rightness of *making* value judgments than about their value judgments *being right*.

Applied anthropologists have been struggling with the ethical dimension of their activities since at least the founding of such professional associations as the Society of Applied Anthropology in 1941 (Mead, Chapple, Brown 1949;

Mead 1977,1978; Rynkiewich, Spradley 1976; Rossi, O'Higgins 1980; Chambers 1985:216–225; Werner, Schoepfle 1986; Cassell, Jacobs 1987). Some anthropologists (mostly cultural relativists and functionalists of the old school) cling to an otherwise very useful consideration—the fact of cultural relativism—but unfortunately insist on absolutizing relativism by declaring the integrity or wholeness of individual cultures as sacred and untouchable (Luzbetak 1985b; Stipe 1980; Hiebert 1978). If a culture were its own ultimate measure of rightness or wrongness, headhunting, racism, and perhaps most social evils, inasmuch as they are integral parts of that "sacred" and "untouchable" whole, would be right and proper. Other anthropologists feel that the best ethical measuring rod would be a catchword like "self-preservation" or "survival value." They say that the question every applied anthropologist should ask himself or herself is, Does my intervention contribute to the preservation of the particular society? (Goldschmidt 1960). This is a useful litmus test indeed, but it is incomplete. Still others look to "self-determination" (Tax 1958, 1977) as the gauge for "rightness." This, too, is unquestionably an important insight, but unfortunately it is one that is not quite adequate. Such criteria, despite their merits, are all too restrictive, at least in the sense that they are all limited to localized microvalues of a particular social group and have little or no relation to the rest of humanity. Such criteria downplay or overlook the macrovalues and universal relations with and responsibility toward the rest of humanity (cf. Fonseca 1982). Perhaps more to the point would be such broader philosophical concepts as "human dignity" (Holmberg), or St. Thomas Aquinas' "human self-realization" (cf. Crollius 1980:253–275; Gritti 1975).

But when is a human being "self-realized"? Over and above the various anthropological insights that we have mentioned, there is available today a philosophical-theological subdiscipline that examines what it means to be truly human. When do we really achieve our full human potential? The subdiscipline called Christian anthropology seeks to provide a more objective and more complete answer to this question. Christian anthropology studies the redeemed human person with all that human existence implies culturally, socially, personally and spiritually. We believe that as Christians our understanding of our humanness outstrips even the loftiest perceptions offered by materialists and positivists. Outstanding thinkers like Rahner, Ricoeur, and Pannenberg examined, and are examining, such concepts as "human dignity," "self-realization," "self-interpretation" and "self-expression" in light of revelation and the Christian perception of God, Christ, universal brotherhood, and our common God-intended human destiny. Granted, such ideological considerations are theology and philosophy, not anthropology, and therefore, as emphasized earlier, they do not enter into the processes of scientific research and data analysis as such. Yet they can and indeed should be part and parcel of what one understands by "being human" and "human self-realization" if one is to be both an applied anthropologist and a believing Christian. (Rahner 1975:880–893; McBrien 1980:101–177; Pannenberg 1985.)

Applied anthropology presupposes a fourfold commitment and responsibility—a commitment and responsibility to (1) one's solidly based personal values or conscience, (2) strict scientific standards, (3) the rights of the people at the micro as well as at the macro levels, and (4) the goals of the client for whom the anthropologist works. These four responsibilities often give rise to tensions and dilemmas. Professional statements on anthropological ethics are helpful but are far from finalized or adequate. Even if they were, such statements would not absolve the individual anthropologist from personal responsibilities in applying such statements. We shall return to the subject when we speak of the justification for missiological anthropology (*infra,* 2.3.2).

2.2.4 ANTHROPOLOGY AND OTHER DISCIPLINES

What is the difference between anthropology and sociology? Between anthropology and other social sciences? Between anthropology and psychology? Between anthropology and the humanities?

2.2.4.1 Sociology

Sociology is the sister discipline of anthropology. In fact, there is very much overlapping and actual convergence in methodologies and theoretical approaches. There are, however, a number of very important differences. Although both disciplines focus on *group* behavior, sociology as a rule focuses on the study of human *interrelationships*. Anthropology, by contrast, goes beyond social interrelationships and includes *all* shared patterns of human behavior (for instance, artifacts as such). Whereas sociology is primarily concerned with highly complex Western societies, anthropology has shown a certain predilection for simpler non-Western societies. Sociology concentrates on the present; anthropology researches the past as well. Sociology is focused on actual social behavior (i.e., on how societies act out their set of cultural norms); cultural anthropology is usually focused on the norms themselves, on the underlying codes for behavior and human interaction. Sociologists study what a speaker *is saying* or *has actually said*; the anthropologist studies what the speaker *could* say.[11] A final and by no means the least important difference is found in the respective methodologies: sociologists rely heavily on statistical methods; anthropologists prefer the participant-observation approach and cross-cultural comparisons. Anthropologists use statistics generally only as a secondary tool.

2.2.4.2 Other Social Sciences

Other social sciences, such as history, economics, and political science, have much in common with anthropology. However, the concepts and methodologies applied in these fields are much more distinct than in the case of sociology. The basic tool in historical research, for instance, is the *written* record, whereas anthropology utilizes not only written records but also all possible clues of the past, including languages, archaeological remains, folklore, oral tradition, present living cultures, and the like.

2.2.4.3 Psychology

Anthropology, as we shall see (*infra*, 5.2.2), is concerned with the norms for behavior for a *society*, whereas psychology focuses its attention on *individual* behavior. There are important differences in methodology between the two fields: while psychology employs what is primarily laboratory experimentation, anthropology takes a cross-cultural approach. These differences, however, do not imply that the two fields are not mutually useful: anthropological cross-cultural theory provides some insights applicable to psychological research, and psychology reciprocates by providing very important information for anthropological research regarding such questions as cognition, learning theory, factors involved in culture change, and the relation between personality and culture.

2.2.4.4 Humanities

The most important difference between the humanities and anthropology is the fact that anthropologists do not study literature and art forms per se, but aim rather to show how literature and art relate to other aspects of culture (*supra*, 2.2.1.1).

2.3 MISSIOLOGICAL ANTHROPOLOGY

2.3.1 NATURE AND SCOPE OF MISSIOLOGICAL ANTHROPOLOGY

Missiological anthropology might best be regarded as a specialized form of applied anthropology. Its scope and purpose are missiological, while the processes and analyses are anthropological. Missiology proposes the basic issues and goals, and anthropology supplies the perspective, approach, and standards for studying them. More specifically, missiological anthropology seeks (1) to bring together in an organized fashion the various concepts, insights, principles, theories, methods, and models of anthropology that seem to be particularly relevant to the mission of the Church, and (2) to show how such an organized body of knowledge might be employed for a better understanding and realization of that mission.

The specific object of missiological anthropology is the *context* in contextualization. It investigates the context in which the Gospel must be viewed, understood, proclaimed, and lived by. God through his revelation, especially through the Incarnation, set the agenda for the Church. The Church is commissioned to carry out this agenda without compromising "the smallest letter of the law, not the smallest part of a letter" (Mt 5:18). This must be done not in some absolutistic manner but in accord with the given social, cultural, and psychological laws that govern human existence. The Gospel must be preached to human beings *as* human beings and *where* they happen to be at this particular point in time and place (Luzbetak 1969:117–130). The lifeway, mentality, tradition, and social conditions of the local community are the context in which God's agenda must be viewed and interpreted and as much as possible be allowed to unfold. The specific task of missiological anthropology, therefore, is not to *set* an agenda—God has already done that for the Church. Our task as missiological anthropologists is rather to help determine the concrete priorities and the *how* of mission. We must help identify the proper emphases and the most effective manner of expressing a society's faith and obedience to God in terms of its ways, values, and soul.

2.3.2 THE JUSTIFICATION FOR A MISSION-RELATED ANTHROPOLOGY: PROFESSIONAL ETHICS

Consistent with what we said about applied anthropology in general (*supra*, 2.2.3.3), a justification for cultural interventionism is called for in mission as well. To "make disciples of all nations" (Mt 28:19), to be "fishers of men" (Mt 4:19), to work toward the establishment of a worldwide Kingdom that is to continue into eternity (Lk 11:2), to set the world on fire with the values of that Kingdom so that the world might be totally consumed (Lk 12:49), to set oneself up as "the salt of the earth" and "the light of the world" (Mt 5:13f)—all this is "interventionism" to the highest degree. The Christian battle cry of "Jesus Christ . . . yesterday, today, and forever" (Heb 13:8) and "at Jesus' name every knee must bend in the heavens, on the earth, and under the earth, and every tongue proclaim to the glory of God the Father: Jesus Christ is Lord!"(Phil 2:10–11) demand a justification. Mission anthropology looks for its justification where it should—*outside* of anthropology, in mission theology (cf. *Lumen gentium*, no.1–17; *Gaudium et spes*, no.1–3; *Ad gentes*, no.1–9).[12] Anthropologists who would wish to condemn Church mission activity, and therefore also missiological anthropology, as baseless ethnocentrism, will themselves have to look *outside* their field for their arguments and for a justification for their own point of view. This holds true whether they consider themselves to be atheists, agnostics, positivists, materialists, or whatsoever.

Mission anthropologists have the same four basic commitments and responsibilities that all applied anthropologists have: (1) a commitment to their conscience (their values, world view, and religious beliefs); (2) a commitment to strict scientific standards; (3) a commitment to the people served; and (4) a commitment to the goals, values, policies, and programs of the client (in the case of mission anthropologists, to the institutional Church, the particular diocese, church-related society, board, or organization). Tensions arising from these responsibilities are unavoidable and must be faced and solved according to sound ethical norms by the weighing of one commitment against the other.

2.3.2.1 A Commitment to the Mission Anthropologist's Conscience

Of the four commitments just stated, the most important and absolutely inviolable one is the commitment to one's conscience—to one's well-founded and well-formed world view and faith values. A few decades ago, some applied anthropologists employed by governments and industry felt that it was quite ethical to sit back, as it were, and merely watch what was taking place on the cultural stage. They believed that they could in a very unattached and objective manner predict for the client what would most likely happen next. It was also assumed by some that anthropologists could be hired as policy advisers to show the client how most effectively and efficiently to carry out a particular goal, whatever that goal was. Such dissociation from the ethical or unethical nature of the anthropologist's involvement is generally rejected by anthropologists today. *Mission* anthropologists have even less reason for any such laissez faire attitude. There is no washing of hands; in fact, the commitment to conscience has precedence over all other responsibilities.

2.3.2.2. Commitment to Scientific Standards

The second most important commitment is the one to scientific standards. Insofar as mission anthropology is a science, it must adhere to strict scientific standards, and it must be uninhibited by other considerations in its processes and analyses. Just as a biblical archaeologist researches the biblical past, using the same archaeological concepts, principles, theories, methods, and skills that any qualified archaeologist does in nonbiblical situations, so the mission anthropologist must "anthropologize" according to the same rigid scientific rules that any other good anthropologist does.

However, and this is what we are emphasizing, ethical considerations do enter into scientific research. Such considerations flow from the scientist's responsibility to his or her conscience. To illustrate the point, we need but recall the fact that the basic anthropological research method is the participant-observation approach. This approach encourages the anthropologist doing fieldwork to be a genuinely sympathetic, empathetic, and objective observer and to become immersed in the day-to-day activities of the community being studied to the extent that the community approves. However, *active* participation, which is a genuinely scientific procedure, would hardly be ethically appropriate in the case of someone researching human sacrifices, infanticide, witch burning, headhunting, sex orgies, or a ritual that would be tantamount to denying one's faith. In short, the choice of a particular scientific method is not made independently of ethical considerations.

In mission anthropology, we are constantly dealing with ideological (non-scientific) matters. Owing to the nature of the issues and objectives of our field, we shall throughout this book be dealing with *faith* matters, especially (1) to *introduce* faith issues that must be examined anthropologically; (2) to *illustrate*

such issues; (3) to spell out the theological, moral, canonical, liturgical, catechetical, and similar *parameters* within which anthropology must be applied or
the particular problem solved; (4) to *indicate the anthropological implications*
of a biblical text, to point out the anthropological weakness of a church
decision or practice, or, on the contrary, to point out the anthropological
wisdom of a doctrine, tradition, or discipline. The general rule, however,
remains: when applying anthropology to mission problems, scientific standards must be upheld.

2.3.2.3 A Commitment to the People Served

Another extremely important and inviolable responsibility is to respect the
rights of the people served. Mission anthropology must at all times be sensitive
to the rights of the people served, not only to the rights of the informant as is
generally insisted upon by anthropologists today, but also to the rights of the
community. Like all applied anthropology, mission anthropology must defend
the rights of the particular society to self-preservation and, as much as possible, to self-determination. Theoretically speaking, this obligation is now much
easier to observe than in the past, because the prevailing Christian thought on
the matter supports the principles of self-preservation, self-determination,
self-expression, and self-realization. It was more than thirty years ago that Pius
XII, expressing the official stand of the Catholic Church, placed the right to
one's culture and national character on the highest possible level of human
rights—on the level of the right to one's good name and to existence itself. To
disregard a people's right to its culture would indeed be a most flagrant
violation of justice.

> The right to existence, the right to the respect from others, the right to
> one's own good name, the right to one's own culture and national
> character . . . are exigencies of the law of nations dictated by nature
> itself. [Allocution, December 6, 1953]

Although understandable in its historical context, nothing could be more
unchristian and objectively unjustifiable than the Spanish Inquisition and the
so-called "two-swords" policy of forced baptism of the Crusaders, Teutonic
Knights, and the Conquistadores. St. Paul expressed his policy in two simple
sentences: "Domineering over your faith is not my purpose. I prefer to work
with you toward your happiness" (2 Cor 1:24). St. Paul clearly believed in the
policy that Goodenough aptly terms "cooperation in change" (1963). There is
no room in mission for any type of manipulation that deprives the individual of
free choice. Vatican II could not have been more emphatic than it was when it
insisted that

> the human person has a right to religious freedom. Freedom of this kind
> means that all men should be immune from coercion on the part of

individuals, social groups and every human power so that, within due limits, nobody is forced to act against his convictions in religious matters in private or in public, alone or in association with others. The Council further declares that the right to religious freedom is based on the very dignity of the human person through the revealed word of God and by reason itself. [*Dignitatis humanae*, no.2]

In the Pastoral Constitution on the Church in the Modern World, Vatican II again bases its argument for freedom of conscience on human dignity, a favorite argument of many anthropologists today.

God willed that man should 'be left in the hand of his own counsel' (Eccl 15:14) so that he might of his own accord seek his creator and freely attain his full and blessed perfection by cleaving to him. Man's dignity therefore requires him to act out of conscious and free choice. [*Gaudium et spes*, no.17]

Dignitatis humanae pursues the argument further by pointing out Christ's own practice:

God calls men to serve him in spirit and in truth. Consequently they are bound to him in conscience but not coerced. God has regard for the dignity of the human person which he himself created; the human person is to be guided by his own judgment and to enjoy freedom. . . . [Christ] supported and confirmed his preaching by miracles to arouse the faith of his hearers and give them assurance, but not to coerce them. . . . [He] refused to use force to impose [his message] on those who spoke out against it. [no.11]

The Declaration on Religious Liberty then goes on to recall the practice of the New Testament churches.

From the very beginnings of the Church the disciples of Christ strove to convert men to confess Christ as Lord, not however by applying coercion or with the use of techniques unworthy of the Gospel but, above all, by the power of the word of God. [no.11]

The main contextualizers of Christianity, as the present book will attempt to show in detail, is the society concerned. The principles of self-determination and self-realization are a basic rule in mission anthropology. Christianity should be *offered* to the world, never imposed on anyone. Besides, both theological and anthropological theory tell us that the Gospel cannot in fact be incarnated into a society (or "integrated" with the rest of its culture, to use anthropological terminology) except from within. (Cf. National Conference of Catholic Bishops 1986a: no.39.)

However—and this is extremely important—the right of a people to its culture is not to be regarded as absolute, as if cultures were totally independent and therefore as if they were untouchable wholes. Societies are parts of the *world* community. If each cultural whole were, as some extreme cultural relativists still insist, an untouchable system, the most suppressive rightist or leftist governments would have to be regarded as being beyond reproach as long as the particular culture or subculture approved suppression. The fact remains that every society has responsibilities that reach beyond itself. Every society has indeed responsibilities toward itself as an integral entity, but it also has responsibilities toward its individual members as individuals as well as toward other societies—toward the rest of humanity. Moreover, local Christian communities as Christian communities are by no means merely local; by becoming Christian they chose to become *worldwide* entities in a very special sense. They chose to cross all cultural boundaries and traditions like the God they worship and call "Father." By becoming Christian, they chose to transcend their localness and be one Body (1 Cor 12:12-31) and the branches of a single vine (Jn 15:5). In a word, mission anthropology admits that individual cultures are sacred, but by so doing it does not claim any type of absoluteness for cultures. Societies are self-determining indeed but not apart from other, wider and narrower considerations. We therefore espouse not an absolute but relative cultural relativism.

2.3.2.4 A Commitment to the Client

Mission anthropologists have a fourth commitment, namely that to the institutional Church they serve—to the international or local church authorities and to the church-related organization served. Today, institutional loyalty has lost much of its popularity; but, even today, without institutional strengths the Christian would be very weak indeed. Human beings by their very nature need teamwork. Without an esprit de corps and community loyalty, mission effectiveness becomes extremely difficult if not impossible. What we are saying is that the mission anthropologist must look upon himself or herself as a member of a team. Like it or not, the Church *is* an institution, even if the institutional character of the Church may not be its most important dimension.

Cooperation and loyalty become particularly difficult whenever there is a serious disagreement between the theoretically inclined, idealistic members of the "team" on the one hand and the more practical and realistic members on the other—between the administrators, lawmakers, and grassroots church-workers, and such "theorists" and "dreamers" as are perhaps most mission anthropologists. Mission anthropologists should recognize the generally superior practical knowledge that administrators and local pastors may have. They should also not oversell their discipline, however useful the discipline may be. The failure to recognize the practical knowledge and experience of other members of the mission team is too often responsible for the impression social scientists give that they are nothing more than idealists and theoreticians floating somewhere on cloud nine.

Yet there is no denying that administrators, in particular, and all decision makers tend to compartmentalize their interests, specifically their personnel, time, and budget, "according to sound business practices and good steward-ship," while anthropologists on principle disdain compartmentalization, advo-cating the holistic perspective of their discipline instead. Ideally, whoever applies anthropology to mission should be acquainted not only with anthropol-ogy but also with whatever anthropology is being applied to. There must be appreciation for the value of the experience and practical knowledge of others who are on the so-called mission "team." Conversely, the administrator and the grassroots practitioner should have training in at least the basics of anthropol-ogy. To our mind, the best anthropological applications are those that reflect *both* the spirit of good practioners *and* the spirit of good theoreticians. This idea goes back to the Greek philosopher Plato. If for some reason or other the ideal is impossible or inadvisable, the second-best should be sought. This does not mean that mission anthropology is easily satisfied with the second-best. Nor should the mission anthropologist hesitate to champion the ideal or to advocate the revolutionary. One should rather tend toward the theoretically ideal and at the same time—as individuals with the down-to-earth views of administrators and practitioners—appreciate the real. Only a blending of these two ingredients, the ideal and the real, will guarantee the type of missiological anthropology we have in mind.

Respect for the client's goals does not mean that mission anthropologists are never to disagree with their clients. In fact, the very contrary is true. They should never stand silently by, tacitly approving the client's policies or pro-grams when they honestly feel that the particular policies and programs are detrimental to the rights of the community served, are contrary to scientific standards, or are incompatible with their own conscience. The fact is that application of anthropology may actually *demand* disagreement and confron-tation. Mission anthropology, however, does not suggest that social scientists at the service of the Church should take the law into their own hands; rather, they should respectfully challenge the law and the lawgiver and together work toward the desired change as loyal members of one and the same team. We are, therefore, speaking of a "loyal opposition." In an extreme case, of course, a mission anthropologist may willy-nilly have to look for another team.

2.3.3 HISTORY OF MISSION ANTHROPOLOGY

2.3.3.1 The Beginnings of Modern Mission Anthropology

There have always been outstanding mission strategists, scholars, and ex-plorers in the Church who knew how to apply cultural concepts to mission even long before applied anthropology was born. There was the apostle Paul, who strongly opposed the Judaizing tendencies of the early Church; there was Pope Gregory the Great who, in the words of Schmidlin, "treated with the utmost forbearance all national, political, social, cultural, and even religious peculiari-ties, and, when these were unusually deep-rooted, even admitted them in a purged or modified form into Christianity" (1931:230); there was Raymond Lull (d. 1316) who believed in what is called today in anthropology "the participant observation" field technique, Lull having made four field trips to Africa. Even centuries ago, this great missionary emphasized the need of specialized cross-cultural training. There were also such experts in cross-cultural communication as Ricci (d. 1610) and de Nobili (d. 1656); there were such champions of human rights as de las Casas (d. 1566). There were also numerous linguists and ethnographers among missionaries, not all as recognized as were Sahagún (d. 1474), Lafitau (d. 1740), or R. H. Codrington (d. 1922), but all nevertheless appreciated by scholars to this day. Much of the Celtic, Germanic, Slavic, and Greenlandic folklore is derived from early missionary ethnography. Contributors included Monk Regino (d. 967), Bishop Thietmar of Merseburg (d. 1019), Canon Adam of Bremen (d. 1076), Nestor (d. 1100), and Bishop Kodlubek of Krakow (c. 1210). The following three centuries (1200–1500) produced even more missionary ethnography that is appreciated by historians to this day; for example, John de Plano, Carpini, William Ruysbroeck, Prince Hayton, John of Corvino, John of Marignola, and Jordanus Catalani. During the period of the great discoveries it was again missionary ethnographers who excelled in describing the cultures and languages of the inhabitants of the Americas, Africa, and Oceania. Among these were Christoval Molino, José d'Acosta, Dobrizhoffer, de Charlevoix. In fact, the work of the French Jesuit Lafitau (*Moeurs des sauvage américains comparées aux moeurs des premiers temps*, published 1724) is regarded by anthropologists as the very first truly anthropological study ever written.

The real beginnings of modern mission anthropology might best be traced to the mission Society of the Divine Word when anthropology in its strict sense of the word was still in its infancy. These beginnings we shall simply call "The Wilhelm Schmidt Legacy." It is to Father Wilhelm Schmidt, S.V.D., that the present book is dedicated, well justifying the somewhat more detailed account of this legacy to be presented toward the close of this chapter.

2.3.3.2 Recent and Current Mission Anthropology

The first anthropological handbooks and guides written in modern times expressly for cross-cultural mission work were modest in scope. They were essentially small ethnographic and linguistic aids, such as those of Louis Le Hunsec, C.S.Sp., *Directoire générale des missions* (1930) and Henri Dubois, S.J., *Traité de missiologie practique* (1932), and such questionnaires as that of Franz Kirschbaum, S.V.D., and Christoph von Fürer-Haimendorf, *Anleitung zu ethnographischen und linguistischen Forschungen mit besonderer Berücksichtigung der Verhältnisse auf Neuguinea und den umliegenden Inseln* (1934).

A further modest attempt was made in 1945 by Gordon Hedderly Smith when he published his treatise, *The Missionary and Anthropology: An Introduction to the Study of Primitive Man for Missionaries*. A true milestone was reached with the appearance of the clear and lively presentation of basic anthropological concepts by linguist-anthropologist and Bible scholar Eugene A. Nida, in his *Customs and Cultures: Anthropology for Christian Missions* (1954). It was also in 1954 that the German theologian-ethnologist Richard Mohr began to publish his cross-cultural studies on human morality, especially his *Richtlinien für eine Missionsmoral* (1959). In 1958, anthropologist Martin Gusinde, S.V.D., published his mission anthropological compendium *Die völkerkundliche Ausrüstung des Missionars* (1958). Except for Wilhelm Schmidt's inspiration and Eugene Nida's classics, none of these early attempts seem to have had any significant impact on missionary attitudes and practices. Important, too, were the journal *Practical Anthropology* (1953–1972), which brought considerable cultural awareness to Protestant grassroots missionaries,[13] and such earlier culturally sensitive periodicals as the *International Review of Mission* (since 1912) and the *International Bulletin of Missionary Research* (since 1950).

In the 1950s and 1960s, the world—and this includes the Christian world—became particularly sensitive to cultural differences. The chief reasons for this development were (1) the self-awareness, the national pride, and the hunger for independence on the part of the Third World countries, and (2) as we shall see in chapter 4, the impact of Vatican II. Among American Catholics, the leading force championing the cause of cultural sensitivity was the Mission Secretariat. It was also in the early 1960s that a paper was read at the Catholic Anthropological Association Meeting. This paper stressed:

the necessity of developing an *organized* body of anthropological concepts, principles, theories, and methods pertinent to mission work; organized so that one could speak of a subdiscipline of Applied Anthropology specifically tailored to the needs of the religious worker engaged in apostolic activities outside his own cultural milieu; organized so that this body of anthropological knowledge could grow; so that, as it grew, it would clarify more and more the very nature of missionary work and would discover new and more effective methods of experimentation, control, and prediction. In a word, such a body of organized anthropological knowledge would aim to help the missionary choose the most effective and least disorganizing techniques and policies truly representative of the scientific age in which he lives. [Luzbetak 1961:165f]

In working toward this goal, the present author was able a few years later to publish his *Church and Cultures* (1963), one of the first full-length systematic treatments of the subject.[14]

The 1970s and early 1980s were years when mission anthropology, like all missiology, took on a strongly ecumenical and interdisciplinary direction in professional publications, associations, meetings, and training programs. The journal *Missiology*, founded in 1973, assumed and expanded the work of *Practical Anthropology*.

Very characteristic of the 1970s was the rapid development of local theologies in Latin America, Africa, India, and, in fact, throughout the world. All involved a vast amount of local ethnology (*supra*, 2.1.2.6). Particularly important too was the Willowbank consultation of the Lausanne Committee for World Evangelization,[15] the proceedings of which were published under the title of *Gospel and Culture* (1979). Also significant was the establishment of the Pontifical Council for Culture[16] in 1982.

Characteristic of our times is the growing importance of interfaith dialogue with Hinduism, Buddhism, and Islam. To be kept in mind is the fact that meaningful dialogue, like local theology, presupposes the application of the principles of cross-cultural communication and genuine cultural sensitivity.

One cannot but appreciate the timeliness of the further development of Christian communication theory. Marvin K. Mayers' *Christianity Confronts Culture* appeared in 1974; four years later David J. Hesselgrave published his excellent handbook, *Communicating Christ Cross-Culturally: An Introduction to Missionary Communication* (1978), followed by Charles H. Kraft's works, his *Christianity in Culture* (1979) and *Communication Theory for Christian Witness* (1983) in particular. Useful too are James E. Engel's *Contemporary Christian Communications: Its Theory and Practice* (1979) and Lyman E. Reed's *Preparing Missionaries for Intercultural Communication: A Bicultural Approach* (1985), and Franz-Josef Eilers' *Communicating Between Cultures* (1987). Eugene Nida and William D. Reyburn's *Meaning Across Cultures* (1981) updated and simplified the invaluable information that had been previously provided by Nida, the best-known mission linguist today, and others (Nida 1960; Nida, Taber 1969).

There are also many useful studies focused on specific cultures, for example, Marguerite G. Kraft's *Worldview and the Communication of the Gospel: A Nigerian Case Study* (1978), Darrell L. Whiteman's *An Introduction to Melanesian Cultures* (1984), and the publications of mission research centers such as the Melanesian Institute in New Guinea and the Centre d'Etude Etnologique de Bandundu in Zaire.

Welcome also are the recent anthropological works of Paul G. Hiebert, *Anthropological Insights for Missionaries* (1985), Sherwood G. Lingenfelter and Marvin K. Mayers, *Ministering Cross-Culturally: An Incarnational Model for Personal Relationships* (1986), and such general coverage of cultural anthropology as that of Grunlan and Mayers (1979). A work very much in harmony with the central message of the present book is Joseph Fitzpatrick's *One Church Many Cultures* (1987).

Most encouraging is the growing interest today among anthropologists in the study of religion. There is at the same time the growing involvement of experts in religion in the study of anthropology. Not only are these specialists reading each other's literature and listening to each other, but they are now also in ever closer communication with one another. Mary Douglas, Victor Turner, Clifford Geertz, and, a few years ago, Edward Evans-Pritchard, are all examples of the high-caliber anthropologists involved. Further evidence of this encouraging trend is, for instance, found in the special issue of the *American*

Ethnologist (*Frontiers of Christian Evangelism*) (Jane Schneider and Shirley Lindenbaum, eds., 1987), which contains such contributions as "The Virgin of Guadalupe in New Spain: An Inquiry into the Social History of Marian Devotion," or the two issues (no.25, 26) of the *Studies in Third World Societies* (1985) dealing with missionaries and anthropologists. Or again, the January 1985 issue of *Theology Today* focuses on the question "What Does Anthropology Have to Do with Theology?" At the same time, the *Biblical Theology Bulletin* (1979:3-12) carries G. S. Worgul's article "Anthropological Consciousness and Biblical Theology." Sociologist Joseph Gremillion has recently edited an important work, *The Church and Culture Since Vatican II* (1985), and sociologist Hervé Carrier took up a similar topic in *Evangile et Cultures de Léon XIII à Jean-Paul II* (1987). Final examples of this trend that might be mentioned are L. Moore and F. E. Reynolds' edited work *Anthropology and the Study of Religion* (1984), Harvie M. Conn's *Eternal Word and Changing Words: Theology, Anthropology, and Mission in Trialogue* (1984), and the various contributions of theologians like Robert Schreiter (1977, 1981, 1985), and Ary A. Roest Crollius (1980, 1984). The following section casts further light on the topic.

2.3.4 MISSIONARIES AND PROFESSIONAL ANTHROPOLOGISTS[17]

There is also another picture to the story. One cannot help but notice the growing antagonism between professional anthropologists and missionaries. Our question is, What are the prospects (1) for a better understanding, and (2) for closer cooperation between the two groups?[18]

2.3.4.1 Toward a Better Understanding

It is a sad fact that while missionaries are growing increasingly more and more sympathetic toward professional anthropologists and more appreciative of the potential good that cross-cultural mission might derive from the work of anthropologists, professional anthropologists are becoming more and more antagonistic. The losers in this case are not only the two groups immediately concerned but also the people whom both groups wish to serve.

The correctives that might lead to a better understanding include (1) avoiding stereotypes, and (2) recognizing the fact that the disagreement rests not so much on anthropological as on ideological grounds.

2.3.4.1.1 Stereotyping As an Obstacle to a Better Understanding

Anthropologist Roger Keesing describes this stereotyping in the following terms:

> The caricatured missionary is a strait-laced, repressed, and narrowminded Bible thumper trying to get the native women to cover their bosoms decently; the anthropologist is a bearded degenerate given to taking his clothes off and sampling wild rites. [1976:459]

Missionaries are portrayed as "opinionated, insensitive, neurotic [individuals] sent to the heathen because they were misfits at home" (to borrow Don Richardson's wording [1976:482]). And anthropologists, in the eyes of some missionaries, fare no better. There are at least three categories of stereotyping that seem to be involved: negativism, reductionism, and a whole category of lesser unfounded generalizations.

Negativism. A substantial number of anthropologists use the term *missionary* as a catch-all derogatory label for anyone involved in cross-cultural church activities. They apply the term to the half-educated and uneducated fire-eater as well as to highly educated mission personnel who may have had as broad an education as anthropologists and who may be no less sensitive to and appreciative of other cultures than they. A negativist does not see any reason for identifying his or her foe; he or she believes that if you have seen one missionary, you have seen them all. Differences among missionaries, be the differences historical, denominational, national, educational, or personal, are all regarded as irrelevant; *missionary* and *undesirable* are, after all, synonymous. In turn, some missionaries, although less commonly so, are no less negative in their views about anthropologists.[19]

Reductionism. The term *reductionism* refers to the identification of the lowest common denominator or the basic explanation for complex historical processes. Here we refer specifically to the oversimplified explanations sometimes given to missionaries' motivations, strategies, and policies. This process reduces two thousand years of mission history to racism, ethnocentrism, and expressions of the spirit of free enterprise. The fact is that mission theology, as well as its motivation, strategies, and policies, have varied greatly even during the same period of history (*infra*, 3.2). In total disregard of the fact that we live in the twentieth century, contemporary mission activity is being condemned for the attitudes and behavior of the contemporaries of Constantine, Charlemagne, the Crusaders, Inquisitors, Conquistadores, and colonialists. Critics overlook the fact that today Christians have a much broadened and a much more enlightened understanding of the role of the Church in the modern world.

One should look at both sides, as Roger Keesing does when he writes as follows:

> But there is another side. Many Christian missionaries have devoted their lives in ways that have greatly enriched the communities where they work. Many, in immersing themselves in other languages and cultures, have produced important records of ways now vanishing. But more important, in valuing these old ways and seeing Christianization as a challenge to creative synthesis of old and new, the best missionaries have helped to enrich human lives and provide effective bridges to participation in a world community. In a great many colonial regions, missions provided educational systems while colonial governments did not, and consequently, when the stage was set for the emergence of Third World

leaders in decolonization, many who took the stage were able to do so because of their mission education. Missionaries living in local communities where colonial exploitation had tragically disruptive consequences, have often been vocal critics of government policy or practice. No treatment of Christianity in the Third World could wisely overlook this humanitarian side. [1976:462]

History tells us, that missionaries of the nineteenth and twentieth centuries were caught in the colonization process of their times. They have, nevertheless, also been the pioneers in the decolonization process. A closer look at that "other side" of the ledger would show that they have also been the chief educators and humanizers throughout mission history and throughout the mission world. Missionaries have also helped to bridge the past with the new. The Constitution of Papua New Guinea, for instance, explicitly and gratefully acknowledges the role of old tribal traditions and the social teachings of the churches. The preamble of the Constitution begins by proclaiming

United in one nation, we pay homage to the memory of our ancestors— the source of our strength and the origin of our combined heritage; we acknowledge the worthy customs and traditional wisdoms of our people which have come down to us from generation to generation, and we pledge ourselves to guard and pass on to those who come after us our noble traditions and the Christian principles that are ours now. [*Mission Intercom*, November 1984]

To label missionaries, particularly those of today, as ethnocentric oppressors, colonizers, and imperialists would mean to be blind to the obvious: today, as a group, the churches are in the forefront, second to no one, in defending human rights and promoting human betterment.

Other Unwarranted Generalizations. Some anthropologists base their unfavorable views of missionaries on isolated experiences they may have had personally or on anecdotes that they may have heard regarding the naiveté, insensitivity, and outright stupidity of missionaries. These critics forget that missionaries may have their own repertoire of amusing and shocking anecdotes about anthropologists. Such generalizations certainly are not conducive to better understanding.

We might best sum up what we have said about negativism, reductionism, and unwarranted generalizations by following F. Salamone's wise suggestion that we at all times must clearly determine "*which* missionaries are likely to have trouble with *which* anthropologists in *which* situation" (1980:174).

2.3.4.1.2 Differences in World View as Barriers to a Better Understanding

It is said that most anthropologists are atheists and agnostics. Whether that be the case or not, the fact remains that very often there is a clash between the world view of the missionary on the one hand and the world view of not a few

Figure 4
Missionaries and Anthropologists: Examples of Possible Synthesis of Differing World Views

| | POLARIZATION | | SYNTHESIS |
	GENERAL MISSIONARY WORLD VIEW	ABSOLUTE CULTURAL RELATIVISM	RELATIVE CULTURAL RELATIVISM
Logic	"Either/or" Logic	"Either/or" Logic	"Both/and" Logic
General Orientation	Supernatural, theocentric	Natural, anthropocentric	Natural AND supernatural
Supernature	1. God is absolute.	1. God is a cultural creation.	1. The Absolute can make cross-cultural sense through contextualization.
	2. God is the Source of all truth, universally normative.	2. Human knowledge and experience are the sole and ultimate source of truth.	2. Faith is compatible with human experience.
	3. Faith is supernatural vision, one's most valued possession.	3. Faith is ethnocentrism. (Beliefs have value only within a given cultural context.)	3. Faith can make cross-cultural sense through contextualization.
	4. Christianity IS mission.	4. Christian mission is imperialism.	4. Missions are justified if other faiths are respected and freedom of conscience safeguarded.

Nature	1. The individual rather than the society is evil.	1. Social systems rather than individuals are evil.	1. Individuals AND social systems can be evil.
	2. Human commonalities are more numerous and more important than diversities.	2. Human diversity is greater and more important than human similarity.	2. Both human similarities and diversities are great and important.
	3. Human beings are endowed with a free will.	3. Human beings are subject to deterministic biological, ecological, and psychological forces.	3. Biological, ecological, and psychological factors are compatible with the notion of free will.
	4. Human brotherhood is universal in extent.	4. The parameters of human brotherhood are determined by the given culture.	4. Universal brotherhood is compatible with culturally defined structures.
Role Concept	Teach, "make disciples," change cultures!	Observe cultures. Preserve them. Hands-off policy!	Cultural adaptation and human progress call for both change AND preservation.

From Louis J. Luzbetak, "Prospects for a Better Understanding and Closer Cooperation Between Anthropologists and Missionaries," in *Studies in Third World Societies*, no. 25, 1985, pp. 9–10.

anthropologists on the other. Anthropologists, without exception, have a "religion" called "cultural relativism." Some are "fundamentalists" who insist on an *absolute* cultural relativism; the rest are broken up into countless *relative* cultural relativistic "sects." Whether the absolute cultural relativists are willing to admit it or not, they are "missionaries" themselves, who zealously preach their "gospel" and proselytize in season and out of season.

Absolute Cultural Relativism. Absolute cultural relativism claims that one culture is as good as any other, and that every culture should be judged exclusively by its own standards, within its own context and as an organic and untouchable whole. According to such absolutists, no outside society, Christian or otherwise, has the right to disturb this sacred wholeness. The worst offenders in this regard are the Christian churches; they impose their values on unwilling, helpless individuals; they destroy cultures; they deprive societies of their self-respect. The mission enterprise is the most ethnocentric form of exploitation imaginable; it is a form of colonialism and imperialism—indeed, it is often nothing less than a form of genocide. Unfortunately, what is being overlooked is the fact that the absolute cultural relativist is discussing ideology, not anthropology. The absolute cultural relativist respects the simple animistic religions and the great non-Christian world faiths but refuses to recognize that Christians have a culture too, an essential aspect of which is mission. Such anthropologists, it has been wisely pointed out, believe in freedom of speech but not in freedom of "preach" (Burridge 1978:8). Such anthropologists are stumbling over their world views rather than dealing with matters of their area of competency (cf. Jarvie 1984).

Relative Cultural Relativism. Fortunately, most church workers and most anthropologists are not absolutists. For most, the impasse of which we speak does not come into question. Being able to think in terms of "both/and," these anthropologists and missionaries need not be polarized; for them a greater or less perfect synthesis is quite possible (Figure 4).

2.3.4.2 Toward Closer Cooperation

2.3.4.2.1 Missiology as Bridge-Builder
Unfortunately, most anthropologists are not even aware of the existence of missiology. Missiologists are invariably relative cultural relativists like most anthropologists; they appreciate the importance of cultural anthropology for both theoretical and practical purposes; they are sensitive to cultural differences and the extremely important role that cultures play in societies; and they readily admit mistakes made by the Church in the past in dealing with non-Western cultures. Above all, they are open to anthropological theory and would welcome both the criticism and insights of anthropology for present and future mission action. They are, in fact, the advance guard and pacesetters for cross-cultural church action. Anthropologists interested in a better relationship with missionaries cannot afford to ignore these important bridge-builders.

2.3.4.2.2 Church Leadership

A further sign that collaboration between mission personnel and anthropologists is indeed possible is the growing cultural sensitivity found today among Christian leaders. The greatest evidence of this sensitivity is illustrated by the transformation taking place in the Third World churches. The transformation may not be taking place as fast as one would wish, but it *is* taking place. The Third World churches are unquestionably passing from dependence to independence and on to interdependence with the older churches of the West (*see* Carrier 1985, 1987; Gremillion 1985). A momentum has been generated and the drive to independence and interdependence will not be stopped. As we shall see in chapter 4, there is today an openness among Church authorities to respectful, constructive criticism not seen before, leaving little doubt that the expertise of anthropologists would be welcome in mission planning and strategy development.

2.3.4.2.3 Missionary Training and Local Leadership: A Further Sign of Possible Collaboration

A third positive sign of possible collaboration is the growing cultural sensitivity on the part of grassroots church workers, thanks to the spirit of the local churches and missionary training (cf. Luzbetak 1985b). The ethnocentric stereotype described earlier is becoming a thing of the past. Local Christians, rather than expatriates, are more and more in charge of their churches. As never before, it is becoming the practice of churches not to send workers to other cultures unless these workers have studied at least the basics of cultural anthropology and sociology and have received an orientation in the local ways and values. The numbers of Church personnel with graduate training in missiology and anthropology have increased. Workshops and continuing education programs[20] in the field and for mission staff home on leave, with a strong emphasis on culturological issues, are now not at all uncommon. Professional missiological associations[21] and research and planning centers strongly committed to cultural adaptation are now to be found in all parts of the world. Missiological journals[22] with a strong culturological tone have multiplied in our times.

2.3.4.2.4 Actual Collaboration between Missionaries and Professional Anthropologists

We have stated that missionaries are as a rule more inclined to be well-disposed toward anthropologists and to collaborate with them than the other way around. Is this perhaps because anthropologists feel that there is little or nothing that might be gained through such collaboration?

We have already referred to the tremendous contribution that missionaries have made to anthropology in the past. Anthropologist Burridge goes so far as to say that missionaries have actually fathered anthropology. He sees a strain of jealousy, a kind of Oedipus complex, lurking in the recesses of the anthropologist's heart (1978:5). Or as Edwin W. Smith, onetime president of the Royal Anthropological Institute, pointed out fifty years ago:

> Because of the missionary's contribution to anthropology, as well as because of the utility of this science for the missionary in his daily activity, social anthropology might almost be considered a missionary science."
> [1934:xxxvii]

Roger Keesing traces this indebtedness to "an old and enduring tradition of great missionary scholarship" (1976:459).

But what about *contemporary* missionary contributions to anthropology? Work by *professional* anthropologists associated with Christian missions goes on and is generally appreciated by their nonmission-related colleagues, just as are the activities of any other qualified and reliable anthropologist. One thinks, for instance, of the journal *Anthropos* and many of the works in the *Studia* Series of the Anthropos Institute of the Divine Word Missionaries. There are, of course, many other examples that might be mentioned. But, one might ask, has anthropology perhaps become so sophisticated that today missionaries who are not professional anthropologists can no longer be of use to anthropology? The fact is that even today one need not have a doctorate in anthropology to make a worthwhile contribution to the field, however desirable such a degree may be. Any missionary with a good education, especially if he or she has had basic training in the social sciences and if the missionary is guided by a qualified anthropologist in his or her fieldwork, can gather invaluable information regarding a local culture that would benefit not only the work of the missions but could at least in some small way help advance anthropological theory itself. Experts in local theology and philosophy, like John Mbiti and countless others associated with church work, have provided invaluable data for anthropologists. The fact is that some of the best ethnographic work on tribal and world religions has been done by mission personnel, by both professional and nonprofessional anthropologists. Then there is the missionary-linguist. As in the past, so it is today; the contribution of missionaries to linguistics can hardly be exaggerated:

> The earliest grammars of the 16th and 17th centuries were the result of missionary efforts. Throughout the following centuries there has been a continuing flow of missionary grammars from all parts of the world. Some are good and some are bad and many are totally unknown to anthropological linguists. Many exist only in manuscript form and many have been lost. But the number of unwritten languages in the world is so great that, even near the end of the 20th century, more grammars of unwritten languages are being composed by missionaries than by linguists. Many of the best of these are being done by missionary linguists who have been trained in modern linguistic methods. Anthropological linguists cannot hope to do the job alone. [Haas 1977:45]

The most active group of missionaries engaged in linguistic work today is the Summer Institute of Linguistics/Wycliffe Bible Translators.[23]

However, there is no better evidence that close collaboration is possible than is illustrated through the eighty years of partnership between missionaries and professional anthropologists initiated by Wilhelm Schmidt and described in the next section.

2.3.4.2.5 The Wilhelm Schmidt Legacy[24]

On the occasion of the seventy-fifth anniversary of the Divine Word Missionaries, the *Osservatore Romano*[25] pointed out that

> From the Middle Ages to our present day, missionaries have constantly enriched our knowledge of unknown languages and cultures; but never has any missionary group so systematically—both theoretically as well as practically—devoted itself to this particular effort with such dedication as the Society of the Divine Word. [December 30, 1950]

This young mission society felt that the scientific study of peoples was somehow a part of the missionary responsibility. The prime mover behind this new and broadened understanding of mission work was a young talented seminary professor, Father Wilhelm Schmidt, a linguist turned ethnologist.

Wilhelm Schmidt was born in Westfalen, Germany on February 16, 1868. Dreaming of someday becoming a missionary, Wilhelm at the age of fifteen entered Arnold Janssen's first missionary seminary located in Holland, just over the border to avoid the antireligious restrictions of the *Kulturkampf*. After nine years of studies, Schmidt was ordained in 1892. However, his dreams of going to the missions were never realized. Instead, his contribution to the young mission society was in the area of anthropology, in cross-cultural sensitization of those assigned to church work overseas.

With data provided by missionaries, especially by his former students of ethnology and linguistics, Schmidt began to publish articles on the languages of New Guinea, Oceania, and Southeast Asia. He discovered the relationship between the languages of Oceania and Southeast Asia; this won for him wide recognition, including an award from the prestigious French Académie des Inscriptions et Belles Lettres and membership in the Austrian Academy of Sciences, two distinctions that began a long series of honors.

Schmidt's ethnology was culture-historical, and his predilection was the study of "primitive" societies, the simple tribal populations whom ethnologists of Schmidt's cultural persuasion regarded as most closely reflecting the lifeway of earliest representatives of the human race. The study of the origin of religion was of very special interest to him.

Schmidt was not only a recognized scholar, a prolific writer,[26] and critic, but he was also a great stimulator. His enthusiasm was contagious. Fearing that invaluable ethnological observations of missionaries would be lost for lack of a suitable archives, he founded in 1906 the journal *Anthropos*. He helped plan field research for his associates, missionaries, and professional ethnologists. He guided missionaries in their study of local languages and cultures. As the number of associates and professional collaborators increased, Schmidt felt the need for organization and in 1932, in response to this need, he founded the Anthropos Institute in Mödling near Vienna, now located at St. Augustin, a suburb of Bonn.

Schmidt felt that anthropology was a basic missionary concern, and his reasons were threefold. (1) Schmidt regarded the fight against Evolutionism as a missionary task. By "Evolutionism" he meant the theories of the times that claimed that there was an inflexible law according to which everything in the universe, including the origin of religion, was determined by an unavoidable straight-line progression from the lower to the higher, from the more simple to the more complex, from the less perfect to the more perfect, from the "savage" and "primitive" to the "civilized." What excited Schmidt was the thought that ethnology and missionaries were best suited to combat such pseudo-science. (2) The second reason for linking ethnology with mission action was the conviction that missionaries, if properly trained and provided with professional guidance in the field, could through ethnographic research make invaluable contributions to humanity's better understanding of itself. In many ways, according to Schmidt, missionaries were in a more favorable position to gather information about cultures than professional anthropologists were, especially because missionaries generally spoke the local language, enjoyed the confidence of the local community, and remained in the field a longer time. (3) There was also a practical consideration, now taken for granted but in Schmidt's days regarded as nothing less than revolutionary. We refer to the view that ethnological training could be useful for a truly sound mission approach.

Schmidt worked as an ethnologist almost to his dying day, when he succumbed to his chronic bronchitis, diabetic condition, and heart problem. He died in Fribourg, Switzerland, on February 10, 1954, at the age of eighty-six. Although he himself never had been active in the missions, he left behind a rich missionary and anthropological legacy.

His personal accomplishments were many indeed. (1) By showing that the Mon-Khmer language was a bridge between the Asian and Oceanic languages, Schmidt disentangled the complex linguistic relationship in that part of the world. (2) Schmidt refined and further developed the *Kulturkreislehre* (the so-called "culture circle theory") that in its day had a major impact on European ethnological thought (*infra*, 5.1.6.2.2). (3) Schmidt, unequaled by anyone, was able to sift, analyze, and order an enormous amount of relevant ethnographic data regarding the origin of the idea of God, especially in his monumental *Der Ursprung der Gottesidee* (12 vols., 1926–1955). He is thus appreciated by students of religion whether or not they accept his basic thesis. (4) Through his respect for non-Christian cultures, Schmidt paved the way for the acceptance of Catholic missiology as a field worthy of serious scholars. (5) Schmidt's high regard for non-Christian cultures, especially for their myths, rites, and religious beliefs, was greatly responsible also for the further development of the missiological concept of *accommodation* (cf. Thauren 1928). (6) Schmidt founded, or was instrumental in founding, such milestones in anthropological history as the Anthropos Institute, the Vatican Museo Missionario-Ethnologico, and a number of professional journals, especially his *Anthropos*. (7) It is also an important part of Schmidt's legacy that he encouraged close collaboration between missionaries and professional anthropologists, a practice continued to this day as a tradition of his institute and its publications. (8) Well ahead of his time, he encouraged missionaries to undertake seriously and professionally the study of linguistics, ethnology, comparative religion, and other anthropological fields.

Raymond Firth, the outstanding British anthropologist, rightly expressed anthropology's indebtedness to Schmidt when he said that it was difficult to measure Schmidt's impact on anthropology "because of its pervasiveness."

> His [Wilhelm Schmidt's] foundation of the Journal *Anthropos* was one of the milestones in the development of more systematic anthropological records from exotic cultures, and the stimulus that he gave to fieldworkers in cultural anthropology and linguistics is difficult to measure because of its pervasiveness. [Quoted from Henninger 1956:56]

In Robert H. Lowie's classic *History of Ethnology*, we find the following evaluation of Schmidt's work. It is no less laudatory than Firth's:

> Ethnology owes much to Schmidt for the establishment of *Anthropos*, a journal second to none in the field. With unsurpassed energy Schmidt enlisted the services of missionaries scattered over the globe and thereby secured priceless descriptive reports. [1937:192]

Or, finally, as A. P. Elkin, another outstanding anthropologist expressed it:

> The establishment of an international anthropological journal, *Anthropos*, by a missionary order, the Society of the Divine Word, and its maintenance . . . has itself been a remarkable contribution to anthropology, and the foundation more recently (in 1937) of a similar journal, the *Annali Lateranensi*, by the Pontificio Museo is also very welcome. Through these media, the anthropological and linguistic studies of Roman Catholic missionaries are made available to the scientific world. [1953:8]

The fact is that the *Anthropos* as well as the Anthropos Institute have been open to all missionaries and anthropologists regardless of their religious affiliation.

The amount of useful anthropological research and publication for which Schmidt, his colleagues, and collaborators are responsible is too vast for us even to attempt a summary here.

Chapter Three

MISSION MODELS

A page of history is worth a volume of logic.

Oliver Wendell Holmes

In discussing mission models, our intention is not so much to condemn past mistakes as to learn from them. By mission models we mean postulates, inferences, and systems of motivation employed for guidance and imitation in carrying out the worldwide task of the Church. Such models are exteriorized in the priorities, strategies, and approaches of those engaged in mission. Because such models form an important part of the scenario for mission anthropology, they will now be examined somewhat more closely, at first conceptually and then historically.

3.1 THEORETICAL MODELS

The countless mission models of the two-thousand year history of mission action, despite their differences, might be placed into one of three major categories depending on whether the dominant traits of the model reveal (1) an ethnocentric, (2) an accommodational, or (3) a contextual orientation. (Luzbetak 1977:51–72.)

3.1.1 ETHNOCENTRIC ORIENTATIONS

3.1.1.1 The Role of Enculturation

Ants and bees and other social animals *inherit* through instinct their particular set of rules for the game of successful living. Human beings, by contrast, must *learn* their set of rules from their societies. This they do through the process of *enculturation*. To survive, a society must work out for itself a set of norms, standards, and expectations for successful living. It must also develop a system of communication to enable the members to interact, to learn, and to transmit their shared behavior. Such a set of norms for successful living and such a system of communication is called *culture*. The process of learning a culture from one's society is called *enculturation*.

A culture, we are saying, shows the members of a given society how they are to communicate with one another and what they must do to live and interact with one another "correctly" and "successfully." Because a set of cultural norms is absolutely necessary for harmonious social living, for solidarity, and for survival itself, it is not at all surprising that the members of a society learn their culture well—in fact, so well that their set of norms becomes a kind of second nature. Such a set of norms makes prediction and interpretation of behavior possible and automatic. It also enables the society to cope with its physical, social, and ideational world.

3.1.1.2 Nature and Types of Ethnocentrism

Although enculturation is advantageous and necessary for *intra*societal living, it may, by turning into ethnocentrism, become dysfunctional at the *inter*societal level. Ethnocentrism is the tendency (to some degree present in every human being) to regard the ways and values of one's own society as *the* normal, right, proper, and certainly the best way of thinking, feeling, speaking, and doing things, whether it be in regard to eating, sleeping, dressing, disposing of garbage, marrying, burying the dead, or speaking with God. Because the Church's mission is worldwide, and therefore cutting across cultural boundaries of all places and times, the concepts *enculturation* and *ethnocentrism* are of the greatest importance to mission anthropology, especially in any discussion about mission models.

There are different types of ethnocentrism. Ethnocentrism may vary, first of all, in *intensity*—from understandable and forgivable minor excesses in group loyalty and group pride to uncontrolled xenophobia, unpardonable cultural imperialism, and such utterly outrageous "superman" madness as that of the Nazis.

Moreover, ethnocentrism may occur at a variety of *levels*—at the cultural, subcultural, or at even lower levels. Subcultural differences exist, for example, between the Islamic Sunnites and Shi'ites, between Bavarian and Westphalian Germans, and among the countless ethnic, socioeconomic, racial, religious, and territorial groups in the United States. Such being the case, we can readily understand why, for instance, an African or Indian bishop could conceivably be more ethnocentric in dealing with his fellow-Africans or fellow-Indians than an expatriate bishop from Europe or America; the ethnocentrism merely occurs on a different level. Ethnocentrism may occur also in a variety of *forms*, the most common, and perhaps also the most serious, being (1) paternalism, (2) triumphalism, and (3) racism.

Paternalism is a misguided compassion that tends to humiliate the would-be beneficiaries, making them even more dependent on the would-be benefactor than they were before. Whereas the call to mission implies a desire eventually to put oneself out of business through success in mission, paternalism implies the very opposite. The paternalistic sending church insists on playing father or mother to the receiving church more or less indefinitely. Paternalism implies a lack of trust in the two primary agents in mission, the Holy Spirit and the local community. Paternalism suggests that the local people are so helpless that by themselves they cannot take care of even the smallest matters pertaining to their spiritual, and sometimes temporal, needs. The chief failing of the Franciscan padres in California, for instance, was their excessive paternalism (Luzbetak 1985a). Invariably, ethnocentrism regards local leadership and self-determination as premature. A paternalistic church may make great sacrifices for the socioeconomic needs of Third World countries but does relatively little to help change institutionalized abuses or to provide opportunities for *self*-help. To listen to the congregation so as to learn from the people ministered to may be regarded as ridiculous as it might be for a parent to seek advice from a small child; children, after all, should be seen, not heard. One of the reasons for the shortage of clergy in Latin America and the Spanish-speaking communities in the United States is the conviction of the people themselves, engendered over the centuries, that the padre had to come from the "outside," from the "*superior*" outside.

Triumphalism, a second form of ethnocentrism, is the conviction of the sending church that it has been so successful and so blessed that it now has a manifest destiny to share with the receiving church not only its faith but, more importantly, the special, purely cultural qualities of that faith. Thus, throughout colonial times, the Western churches generally felt that before non-Westerners could be Christianized, they had first to be "civilized," that is, Europeanized. Similarly, when the Philippine Islands were "liberated" from the Spaniards, American Christians began to feel that God was assigning their young, vigorous and successful Anglo-Saxon democracy a unique role; America's destiny was to bring "genuine" Christianity to the islands, a Christianity with all the "wonderful and providentially planned" trappings clearly marked "Made in U.S.A."

Racism and class prejudice are too well known for us to spend much time and space on the subject. The color of the skin somehow condemns certain "less fortunate" individuals to second-class citizenship, not only in society at large but sometimes in the Church as well. That Latin American Catholicism still lacks an adequate indigenous clergy, even after centuries of Christian presence, can hardly be explained away by attributing the dearth of vocations to conditions brought about by North American capitalistic exploitation; not to be overlooked is the racist feudalism that entered the continent with the conquistadores. Similarly, as a result of racism, blacks in the United States were until recent times regarded as suitable candidates for baptism but definitely not for ordination.

3.1.2 ACCOMMODATIONAL ORIENTATIONS

The principle of missionary accommodation presupposes the recognition of "neutral" and "naturally good" elements in non-Christian ways of life. It believes that other cultures contain elements that are consistent with the Gospel. Accommodation insists that, inasmuch as such non-Christian elements can and indeed do exist, the universal Church and the sending churches may, and indeed should, allow local churches to incorporate such elements as part and parcel of the local Christian community's behavior. In fact, such "neutral" and "naturally good" elements may be employed as contact points with Christianity. They can form a useful and important bridge between Christianity and "paganism."[1] In fact, they may be employed as the human foundation-blocks upon which the new Christian community might be built. According to the accommodational model, the vocation and task of the missionary is

> to make the beautiful in the so-called "pagan" heart even more beautiful, to seek out the naturally good in order to make it supernaturally perfect, to present Christianity not as an enemy of the existing way of life but as a friend possessing the secret that will enable the non-Christian culture to reach its God-intended perfection. [Luzbetak 1963:352]

As we shall see when we review the history of mission models, missionary accommodation is as old as the Church itself, as

> from the very beginning down to our own day [the Church] has followed this wise policy. When the gospel is accepted by diverse races, it does not crush or repress anything good and honorable and beautiful which they have achieved by their native genius and natural endowments. When the Church summons and guides a race to higher refinement and a more cultured way of life, under the inspiration of Christian religion, she does not act like a woodsman who cuts, fells and dismembers a luxurious forest indiscriminately. Rather she acts like an orchardist who engrafts a cultivated shoot on a wild tree so that later on fruits of a more tasty and richer quality may issue forth and mature. [Pius XII, *Evangelii praecones*, no.89]

No less forceful was John XXIII when he spoke of this policy, pointing out that the Church

> does not identify herself with any particular culture not even with the occidental culture to which her history is so closely bound. Her mission belongs to another order, to the order of the religious salvation of man. Rich in her youthfulness which is constantly renewed by the breath of the

Holy Spirit, the Church is ever ready to recognize, to welcome and indeed to encourage all things that honor the human mind and heart. [*Princeps pastorum*, no.16]

Although accommodation has consistently been preached as the official policy of the Catholic Church, in practice it has only too often been token in nature, looked upon as optional, or ignored rather than taken as a serious policy and obligation. Protestant missiologist Gustav Warneck viewed accommodation exclusively from the point of view of excess and abuse, and therefore considered it to be "whitewashed paganism." Owing to the strong ethnocentrism of the times, accommodation had frequently to face and struggle with serious opposition. Moreover, because accommodation was spoken of in generalizations and platitudes and because it was only recently that the implications of the policy could be spelled out in terms of the social sciences, the principle was really never understood. In practice, accommodation tended to be shallow, affecting only the surface of culture, the so-called "garb of the Church." In practice if not in theory, accommodation tended to be overcautious, paternalistic, distrustful of the local community, with the sending church (not the new or local church) determining the type of accommodation. In a word, despite the beautiful theory, in practice the actual accommodation made has only too often been insensitive to the deeply felt longings of the local churches, and little real effort has been made by the Church at large to listen to local churches. Mission history, even today, is interpreted and written by Westerners rather than by indigenous scholars and thinkers. The greatest weakness of accommodation in the past did not lie in its intent or aim (both of which were laudable). As we shall see in our historical overview of mission models, the chief inadequacy lay rather in the fact that, unlike contextualization, accommodation was too much in the hands of outsiders, making mission consist mainly in *transplanting* rather than in *sowing*. The *chief* agents in the process have only too often been outsiders who in fact did not, or perhaps even could not, understand the cultural "language" into which they wished to translate Christianity. A further weakness of the otherwise beautiful principle of accommodation was the assumption that cultural adaptation was a concession on the part of older churches rather than a right and, in fact, a need of every local church. Accommodation was also looked upon as something peripheral to Christian living and as appropriate only for "infant," "immature," and "not-yet-fully-developed" Christian communities. It was viewed mainly as a way of winning converts. As we shall explain, contextualization is for *all* local churches, including the "older," "fully matured," and, in fact, "vibrant" churches, wherever they may be. Unlike accommodation, contextualization is looked upon not as a concession on the part of the universal Church, or the sending church, but a right of the local community. Nor is contextualization by any means something peripheral or accidental. Evangelization of cultures *is* mission. A truly Christian community will be a deeply contextualized community. Having said all this, we must nevertheless re-emphasize that the theory of accommodation as such, that is, the concept and intent of accommodation, was largely sound and laudable, even if from today's point of view it is inadequate. Without accommodation, the next step, contextualization, would have been considerably more difficult, if not impossible.

3.1.3 CONTEXTUAL (INCARNATIONAL, INCULTURATIONAL) ORIENTATIONS

We understand contextualization as the various processes by which a local church integrates the Gospel message (the "text") with its local culture (the "context"). The text and context must be blended into that one, God-intended reality called "Christian living" (Luzbetak 1981:39). As mentioned earlier, contextualization is also known as "inculturation" and "incarnation." The missiological term *inculturation* (not to be confused with the much older anthropological household words *en*culturation and *ac*culturation) was popularized in the mid-1970s, mostly by Jesuit writers[2]. The concept *incarnation*, on the other hand, was used much earlier. In 1945, Pius XII pointed out that

the Church . . . is placed in the center of history of the whole human race. . . . As Christ was in the midst of men, so too His Church, in which he continues to live, is placed in the midst of the peoples. As Christ assumed a real human nature so too the Church takes to herself the fullness of all that is genuinely human wherever and however she finds it and transforms it into a source of supernatural energy. [Christmas Message, 1945]

Unfortunately, Pius XII did not suggest *how* one was to incarnate the Gospel, how one was to go beyond accommodation, beyond merely recognizing its "neutral" and "naturally good" aspects, which is demanded by incarnation.

It was Vatican II and Paul VI in particular who ventured beyond traditional accommodation. Building on the advanced thinking of Vatican II and the Fourth Synod of Bishops on Evangelism (1974), Paul VI insisted in his *Evangelii nuntiandi* that the only correct attitude toward local ways of life would be nothing less than "a radical and profound understanding" of the local ways and values, an adjustment that would be more than "a thin veneer" or that would be "purely decorative" in nature. On the contrary, the only proper attitude toward the ways and values of a local Christian community would have to touch the particular society "in a vital way," "in depth" and "right to the very roots"—in a word, "in the wide and rich sense of the Pastoral Constitution on the Church in the Modern World" (EN18-20). One could hardly have stated in a more emphatic way what we mean by *inculturation*. John Paul II has taken up the concept and developed it by means of the analogy "evangelization of culture" (Carrier 1987:117–139; Gremillion 1985:187–290). In terms of social science, John Paul II is simply saying that the Gospel message must be *institutionalized* (Fitzpatrick 1987:172).

There are a number of major differences between the new contextual approach to mission and the traditional accommodational approach. We shall explain the following differences at some length: (1) *the primary agents* involved in incarnating the Gospel are the *local* Christian community and the Holy Spirit—not the sending church or the universal Church; (2) as important as church planting and the institutional Church may be, *the direct concern of mission* is to proclaim the Kingdom of God and salvation; (3) *the ultimate goal* of incarnating the Gospel is *mutual* enrichment, one that benefits not only the local Christian community but the universal Church and the sending church as well; (4) *the depth* of cultural penetration and identification with the Gospel is incomparably greater in contextualization than in traditional accommodation; (5) as important as the primary processes (*infra*, 7.2.1) may be, the chief processes in inculturation are those connected with *integration* (*infra*, 6.2; 7.2.2).

Contextualization, we said, involves all, but especially the integrative processes by which a local church integrates the Gospel message with its understanding of its culture. One should note how these elements bring out the fundamental differences between incarnation on the one hand and accommodation on the other.

3.1.3.1 The Local Church: The Primary Agent Involved in Inculturation

In traditional accommodation, the focus was placed primarily on outsiders—on the missionary and the institutional and universal Church. It was the *sending* church that "from the abundance of its heart," so to speak, "accommodated" or "bent over backwards" to adjust to local ways and values, while the receiving church had really only a secondary listening and learning role to play. In a contextual model, however, the two most important and immediate agents involved in mission, as we have emphasized a number of times, are the Holy Spirit and the local People of God. In inculturation the task of the universal Church is chiefly to remove obstacles in the way of the Spirit and to share its own experience, light, and judgment. The task of the universal Church is that of John the Baptizer, "to make ready the way" (Is 40:3; Lk 3:4) and, as an elder member of the same family, to help discover God's presence already active in the non-Christian heart. In the incarnational approach, the universal Church views itself as a catalyst, an enabler, a guide, and consultant. In Roman Catholicism, it should be recalled, "local church" means primarily the diocese, with due regard for the cultural divisions and corresponding needs. Unlike the extremely cautious accommodational approach, the inculturational strategy implies genuine trust in the Holy Spirit and the local Christian community. Inculturation assumes that, in mission lands as well as in older churches, the real transformers of human beings into "other-Christs" (for that is what *Christian* means), are, as both good theology and good anthropology maintain, not so much the universal or sending church as the people being evangelized. Members of the local Christian community are the real leaven of the

Gospel (Mt 13:33); it is their mission to permeate their own community and as instruments of the Holy Spirit to take part in transforming it into a community of other-Christs. They and no one else are the necessary cultural *innovators*, a technical term used by anthropologists when speaking of social change, as we shall explain fully in chapter 7. The really significant contextualizers are the members of the local community, however important the nonindigenous authorities, theologians, social scientists, and missionaries of the sending and universal Church, especially in the earlier stages of church planting, may be. True metanoia can be effected only from *within*. The Church is itself in the process of self-constitution (Lonergan). True evangelization is ultimately *self*-evangelization, and the best pastoral advice that can be offered to anyone is, Get the answers to your pastoral problems and strategy *from* and *with* your people. At times the expatriate pastor, religious educator, and national and international church authorities will have to disagree and challenge the local church, but the chances are that if there be an answer it will be found deep in the soul of the community.

Formerly, when speaking of accommodation, one generally had so-called mission countries in mind; today, when speaking of contextualization as we are, *every* local church throughout the world is meant, including the local churches of the West. The Gospel must be inculturated on all six continents and in every age, whether in Britain or in New Britain, in Ireland or New Ireland, whether in a distant non-Christian land or in one's own Western de-Christianized or deeply Christian home parish. In any case, whether it be a mission church or not, the primary agent in inculturation is the *local* church itself; this, we say, is good theology as well as good anthropology. Inculturation, whether it be in the form of a dynamic equivalent translation of Christianity, liberation, or dialectic contextualization—the three forms of inculturation, which we shall explain—is achieved ultimately and primarily by the local community.

In concluding this section on the local church as the primary agent of contextualization, there are a number of important points for the reader to keep in mind. Although deeply concerned about the individual as an individual, the contextualizer does not get lost in the individual at the expense of the community. As Vincent J. Donovan suggests,

> we should not set out to evangelize everyone, or even the majority of people. We [should be] out to evangelize a minority, but a minority in every section . . . and the goal envisaged [should not] be mission compounds or mission stations in every section, but Christian communities in every section. *Missions* belong to the missionaries. Christian communities belong to the people; indeed, they are the people. [1978:38f]

By the same token, although the local community is the primary beneficiary of contextualization, the contextualizer does not lose sight of the repercussions a particular adaptation to the local community may have on other segments of the Body of Christ and on humanity at large. Finally, the contextualizer keeps in mind that the local community will need not only local tradition and local symbols to preserve and strengthen its local identity but, inasmuch as the local church is also universal, it will need universal tradition and universal symbols to keep alive and bolster its universal character as well. Not total independence but unity in diversity is the mark of a truly Christian community. In fact, unity in faith will always be primary and fundamental. As in apostolic times, so today, the local church, although the primary agent in inculturation responsible for initiative and action, must nevertheless always be in communication with the universal Church and must ultimately submit itself to the judgment of the communion of churches (*infra*, 4.4.3.3).

3.1.3.2 The Goal of Contextualization

3.1.3.2.1 The Direct Objective, the Integration of the Text with the Context

Traditional accommodation is basically ecclesiocentric; inculturation, without downplaying the institutional dimension of the Church, is primarily Gospel-centered. The primary emphasis in inculturation is clearly on the integration of culture with Christ and his basic message (salvation and the coming of the Kingdom). The primary concern is the basic Jesus-Gospel (cf. Comblin 1977; Donovan 1978) and true metanoia, not Western technology, medicine, higher education—no, not even humanization and socioeconomic liberation or church planting as such. True contextualization seeks first and foremost the Kingdom of God (Mt 6:33). The fact is that Christians can lose themselves in so-called pre-evangelization, humanization, and political liberation. They can forget the heart of the Christian message.

3.1.3.2.2 The Ultimate Objective of Inculturation, Mutual Enrichment

Although contextualizers emphasize the role and needs of the local, rather than the universal Church, genuine contextualization never loses sight of the fact that, however important the local church may be in itself, it transcends its local nature. In communion with other local churches, it becomes an integral part of the universal Church, which is something more than the sum of its parts. The local church is, therefore, something more than local, and *the ultimate purpose of inculturation is not only the benefit to be derived by the local church qua local but the enrichment of the whole Body of Christ*. The good of the local church is the good of the whole Body of Christ, and the good of the whole Body of Christ is the good of the local church.

All local churches are in fact called to be sending churches as well as receiving churches. Every local church is to strengthen every other. The one must be the brother's keeper of the other by judging, correcting, and edifying one another. Third World churches of Africa, Asia, Latin America, and the Pacific Islands will always need the Western churches; they will always need missionaries from Europe and America. But, we hasten to add, Europe and America will need the vitality, youthfulness, and insights of African, Asian, Latin American, and

Oceanic churches. Missionaries will have to be sent from the newer churches to the older churches; the newer churches will need the older churches if they wish to share in the experience and other strengths of maturity that go back to the Apostles and that have been developed over the centuries. Despite the Western trappings that have accumulated over the two thousand years of the Church's existence, one cannot close one's eyes to the fact that during those same two thousand years the Holy Spirit has been active and that the universal Church has much—very much—to offer to the younger Christian communities. Newer churches also need one another. What we wish to emphasize here is that receiving churches should be, and are in fact becoming, more and more sending churches and that the ultimate goal of inculturation is *mutual* enrichment—the health, growth, and vitality of the *whole* Body of Christ. (Luzbetak 1977:66f; cf. Keyes 1982; National Conference of Catholic Bishops 1986a:no.33–39.)

3.1.3.3 A Difference in Depth—An Anthropological Understanding of Culture

Whereas accommodation respects the local culture as being largely "neutral" and as containing many "naturally good" elements that might serve as contact points and stepping-stones to Christ's full message and full discipleship, contextualization goes much farther; in the words of Paul VI cited earlier, contextualization goes to "the very roots" of culture. Contextualization views local cultures as already containing the germ of Jesus' message, reminding us of the *logoi spermatikoi* of the early Fathers of the Church, the seed brought into existence through the mercy of the Father, planted by Christ through his death and resurrection, and watered through the refreshing rain and energized through the warm rays of love and grace of the Holy Spirit. The active presence of God began on the day of creation. This active presence continues today over the whole world, within and without the Church. The Church is therefore missioned not so much to *introduce* Christ to non-Christians as if he were a total stranger, but rather to help the non-Christian find him already present and active in the non-Christian heart. As T. Stransky, commenting on the attitude of Vatican II toward non-Christian religions, expressed it:

> The Spirit acts in the depths of every person, and "offers to all the possibility to be made partners, in a way known to God, in the paschal mystery" [i.e., passion, death and resurrection of Jesus Christ], whether they are within or without the visible borders of the church (*Gaudium et spes*, no.22; cf. *Lumen gentium*, no.16; *Ad gentes*, no.15; *Dignitatis humanae*, no.6). All grace is of Christ. Without him there is no salvation (cf. *Gaudium et spes*, no.22). [1985:156]

Long before the evangelizer appears, God, who desires the salvation of every individual, is already active building the foundation upon which the evangelizer must now build. The presence of Christ experienced in this germinal form must as much as possible be allowed to grow and blossom in the congenial climate of the particular culture and tradition. As Stransky continues to point out, non-Christian religions contain " 'seeds of the Word,' (*Ad gentes*, nos. 11,15), 'seeds of contemplation' (*Ad gentes*, no.18), 'elements of truth and grace, present as a secret presence of God' (*Ad gentes*, no.9), 'a ray of that truth which enlightens all' (*Nostra aetate*, no.2)." Eventually Christ must be fully born (incarnated) into the given culture through the Christlike ways and values of the individual members of the community. Christ is incarnated once again, not, however, as a Jew of two thousand years ago, or as a Westerner of the twentieth century, but as someone born here and now for the first time: the Gospel is not so much *transplanted* as it is *sown* for faith to rise out of the native soil. Inculturation therefore poses the important and difficult question: How would Christ behave and what would he teach if he were born, for instance, in Japan in our times, or as someone born as an American black in Harlem? Mission must make it possible for Christ to be reborn again and again in every time and place. *It is especially to cultural anthropology that one must go to understand what culture (the "context" in contextualization) is and how it operates. To remember is the fact that the ones who understand the culture most profoundly, however, are the people who live the culture.*

Culture as used in anthropology is a complex concept (*infra*, chapters 5-7). To define *culture* is as difficult as it is to define *Church*. Rather than speak of definitions, we shall describe the anthropological culture-concept by means of models or perspectives. Depending on the perspective taken by the particular anthropologist, a culture may be described as an adaptive system, as a communication network, as an historical development, or as a psychological, ecological, biological, historical, evolutionary, or sociological phenomenon (*infra*, 5.1.6). For most missiological purposes, we feel that it would be most advantageous to employ a *multiple* or *composite* model of culture, with the *primary* (i.e., the dominant or pivotal) perspective being one that would view culture as a society's blueprint for succeeding in life—as a design for living or as a plan for coping with the various demands of life. At the same time, other current anthropological perspectives (especially those that view culture as a communication system) would be employed as secondary or complementary submodels adding important detail and providing needed correction and balance. In other words, we shall view culture as *a dynamic system of socially acquired and socially shared ideas according to which an interacting group of human beings is to adapt itself to its physical, social, and ideational environment*. It should be noted that the interpersonal, organizational, and communicational aspects of culture, all of which are extremely important considerations in contextualization, fall under the area of the *social environment*. This working definition of culture will be fully explained in the coming chapters. What follows is meant to be but a brief and necessarily incomplete preview.

There are three levels of culture: (1) the surface level of *forms*— the symbols as such apart from their meaning, the "shape" of the cultural norms; (2) the middle level of *functions*—the meanings of symbols, the logic, purposefulness, and other relationships underlying and connecting the forms; (3) the deepest level of culture—namely the *psychology* of a society, the basic assumptions, values, and drives, that is, the starting-points in reasoning, reacting, and motivating.

Important is our emphasis on culture as a *system* (chapter 6), in fact, as a *living*, (that is, an interacting and dynamic) system (chapter 7) constantly adapting itself to the demands of life, accumulating group experience, and transmitting it from one generation to the next.

Culture includes *everything one learns* from one's social group—from the irrational, useless, and trivial to real matters of life and death. It covers aspects from the proper way of tying one's necktie to what and how one is to eat, whom one may marry and whom one may not, whom to fight and with whom to be friendly, how to rule and how to be ruled, what art is and what it is not, how to perform black magic and how to cure illnesses, and what god to worship. We are stressing the *totality* of a lifeway because in our inculturational approach to mission nothing less than the *total* cultural content comes into play—not just sporadic or haphazard concessions. Christ must be incarnated on all three levels of form, function, and underlying psychology, and we wish to emphasize that this new totality must be a living, dynamic, organic whole.

3.1.3.3.1 Cultural Forms As the First Level of Contextualization

For the present, it is sufficient to understand the word *form* to mean the "shape" of the particular cultural patterns—the *who, what, when, where, what kind*, and *how*. Such forms are the outward contour of a cultural pattern. We have left out the *why*, which is answered on the deeper, second and third, levels of culture. When speaking of form, we refer to the outward "shape" of a symbol, not the inner meaning or meanings of the symbol; nor are we saying anything about how one symbol is connected with other symbols in the given cultural system.

When speaking of inculturation we must keep in mind two important facts about forms as forms. First of all, incarnating the Gospel with a culture respects *all* forms; it does not prejudge any form as important or unimportant, relevant or irrelevant. In contextualization, the *total* inventory of culture matters. Secondly, there is a related practical principle involved that says, "If it ain't broke, don't fix it!" This may be bad English, but it certainly is sound missiology and applied anthropology. The form for expressing filial love as found in a "pagan" culture may be far more meaningful than a missionary-imported "Christian" form. The guitar, for instance, has often proved to be far more meaningful for youth-liturgies than the "finest" music on the "finest" pipe organ.

A basic principle in contextualization is that forms as forms apart from any meaning that they might carry are as a rule neutral. It matters little to the Holy Spirit what the Bible we happen to be reading calls Pharaoh's horses, whether it be in the original Hebrew, in Septuagint Greek, or whether it is *horse, equus Pferd, cheval, cavallo*, or whatever, provided that the form we use *means*, as

Webster puts it, "a large solid-hoofed herbivorous mammal used as a beast of burden, or draft animal, or for riding, in work, sport, or war." God, who created humans as cultural beings and who is the Father of All, is as a rule not particularly concerned about form or expression, whether verbal or nonverbal; his concern, as we shall presently see, is the "heart," the meaning, the *whys*— that is, not the first level but the second and third. It is of little concern to God as a rule whether a particular society prefers bowing to genuflecting, standing to kneeling, wearing shoes and no hat to being barefooted with head covered in order to show one's reverence and submission to God. In most Western cultures, washing another's feet is as much out of place as brushing someone else's teeth. At the Last Supper it was not the form (the actual washing of feet) that Jesus wanted to be perpetuated as much as the meaning of this dramatic act (the humble service of others). In liturgy, of course, when and where meaningful, washing of feet as a symbol with special meaning might be retained, as it in fact is in many Holy Thursday rituals.

3.1.3.3.2 The Second Level of Culture and Incarnation

The second level of culture is that of usage, purpose, and meaning. Just as forms are the particular society's answers to the *who, what, when, where, what kind*, and *how*, so functions are the society's answers to the immediate *why*. We arrive at our answer by asking such questions as, What are the reasons, usages, presuppositions, prerequisites, needs, associations, repercussions, logical connections, and the like of the particular form? A function is, in fact, any type of logical or purposeful linkage or relationship between forms. Such questions alone will enable us to appreciate the meaning that is attached to the particular cultural element in the given society. To understand the full meaning and value of, say, clothing in Europe or America, we would have to ask ourselves such a question as, What are the *purposes* and *uses* of clothing? Our answer would be, for instance, To deal with the inclemency of the weather, to take care of our concern for modesty, to let everyone know that I am a man or a woman, to indicate that I am wealthy, to be respected by my peers, to enable people to relate more easily and properly to me who happens to be a clergyman, policeman, soldier, bus driver, bellhop, girl scout, patrol boy, train conductor, nun, altar boy, chorister, usher, bride or bridegroom, first-communicant, baseball umpire or football referee, chambermaid, waitress, chef, nurse, judge, or, for that matter, a circus clown. To arrive at the value (function or meaning) of clothing in Western society, we would have to ask what the *repercussions* would be if one failed to wear clothing or if one wore the wrong clothing. If one wore no clothing at all, most likely one would soon be locked up in jail or in an insane asylum. We might ask also, What does clothing *connote*? As we have seen, clothing connotes prestige and respect, a certain occupation, the level of education, and/or participation in a ritual. Clothing tells everyone who sees me that I am a tramp or, on the other hand, that I have good taste. We might ask, With what is clothing *associated*? The answer would be, for example, With the Amish or Jewish religion, graduation, sports, operas, fancy restaurants, religious orders, beauty contests, athletics, swimming, the Olympics, imprisonment, poverty, and seduction. Put all that together and you have the function (and ultimately the value) that Western cultures generally place on the cultural form called "clothing" and which anthropologists call "referents." (Marshall Sahlins has a thorough symbolic analysis of the American clothing system in his *Culture and Practical Reason* [1976:179-204].)

Such meanings or functional linkages at the two deeper levels of culture must be taken into consideration whenever a Christian community undertakes to direct cultural change. The way I walk, the way I close a door when I leave a room, the way I cross my legs when I sit, the way I dress, and the way and when I smile are all cultural forms or symbols to which my society attaches one or more meanings. Thus I am "speaking" all day long even when I do not utter a sound. A wife who keeps unnecessarily but delicately adjusting her husband's necktie most likely loves him; a wife who keeps jerking her husband's tie unnecessarily most likely does not. Forms of behavior learned from one's society to which function has been added are symbols—symbols that, very much like words, carry meanings.

Very often the particular function is hidden and unknown even to the society in question. The function and corresponding meaning, usage, and purposeful or logical relationships and values, however, are definitely *felt*. Function, meaning, usage, and purposeful or logical relationships (all more or less different sides of the same coin) are often very much like the grammatical rules of one's native language. They are rules that one feels and applies, but of which one is unaware or at least unable to articulate.

The sum total of the immediate *whys* constitutes the full value or full meaning of a particular cultural element or cluster of elements in a particular culture. Important in incarnating the Gospel is to remember that in preaching the Good News we must be aware of the meanings in a culture. We must know the price tags attached to each cultural item. Such price tags vary from culture to culture. In contextualizing the Gospel, we examine all the relationships that a particular form has in the given way of life; we must literally somehow be aware of the whole network of meanings, usages, values, presuppositions, prerequisites, needs, associations, reasons for, repercussions, and purposes—in fact, we must be aware not only of the cultural *semantics* but of the cultural *grammar* and the appropriate *usages* of the language as well.

3.1.3.3.3 Underlying Psychology: The Third Level of Culture and Contextualization

The functions just explained are very intricately intertwined by an underlying logic, by the society's psychology or mentality. Underlying the second level of culture (the network of meanings, usages, values, presuppositions, prequisites, needs, associations, reasons, repercussion, purposes, and the like) is the still-deeper third level—the underlying premises, emotionally charged attitudes, basic goals and drives, starting-points in reasoning, reacting, and motivating. This third level is seldom questioned by the members of the society and largely explains 'why the second-level is what it is. What we wish to emphasize at this point is that if the Gospel is to be truly contextualized, it must be *integrated*—as we shall see in chapter 6— also and especially at the third level.

3.1.3.4 Culture Dynamics

In anthropological terms, when Christ is incarnated into a lifeway, and not merely accommodated, the Gospel message is integrated with the rest of culture. It becomes an *integral part of a system*, bound up and operating with the rest of culture on all three levels; it becomes *institutionalized.*In fact, the Gospel, it is hoped, will become the very heart and nerve center of the culture. The aim is to make the Gospel a *living* part of the *living* and *whole* lifeway. Mission activity must, therefore, take into account the balancing and unbalancing processes and the distinctive dynamics at work in the society (i.e., in the actual behavior) and in culture (i.e., in the design for living). It is for this reason that integration and culture dynamics take up such a large portion of the present book.

Although one may well speak of "accomodation" when it occurs only on the first level of form, one cannot have "inculturation" only at the form level. Inculturation is focused on the second and third levels of culture—on the *integrative* processes and on culture as a *dynamic systematic* whole.

Through the various processes of integration—and this, we feel, is extremely important—the inculturated Gospel message becomes *generative* like culture itself. That is to say, the Gospel is sown in such a way as to be able to grow, expand, and develop. It gives the individual and the Christian community a capacity to express meaningfully faith values in ever-new local and indeed creative ways (cf. Schreiter 1985: 91-93, 119). Christians need not be walking encyclopedias on matters Christian; nor need they be professional theologians. Their faith, however, must reflect a *creative* imagination and inspiration, a constant flowering of a truly contextualized Christianity. Their faith, however simple and imperfect, should nevertheless be creative in the sense that it is constantly made relevant to the time and place without compromising the essentials of the Gospel or the essentials of the universal tradition; such at least is the target. The local church must always seek to be essentially ancient and yet ever new—ever changing, changing itself and the world around it; growing with the demands of life; adapting to the changing physical, social, and ideational environment; at all times being fully of the place, fully of the time, and fully Christian. That is to say, it should be changing constantly without ever ceasing to be what it was in the very beginning, thanks to a tripolar dialectic that contextualization presupposes—a challenge and a counterchallenge between the Gospel, universal Church tradition, and the local culture, a constant and respectful interchange that we shall explain more fully in the coming paragraphs.

3.1.3.5 Approaches to Contextualization

There are three different types of contextualizations: a translational type, a dialectical type, and a liberational type. All three types seek to integrate the Gospel message with the local culture in such a way that the message becomes a part of the cultural system itself. The translational type is represented by Charles Kraft's *dynamic equivalence* model (1979, 1983) and by the present author's original version of *The Church and Cultures* (1963); the *dialectical* type is represented by Robert Schreiter (1985) and the present book, both of which seek to integrate the Gospel message, the universal tradition, and the local culture from within through a tripolar dialectic between the Gospel message, the universal tradition, and the local culture; the liberational type integrates the Gospel message by focusing on the specific liberational needs of the particular society. These three approaches to contextualization, it should be noted, are not necessarily mutually exclusive.

But first some remarks about the translational and dialectical approaches. It is assumed that the reader will be sufficiently acquainted with the third approach, so that little need be said about liberation theology here. Otherwise, we suggest that such introductory works on liberation theology be studied as Ferm (1986), Boff and Boff (1987), Gibellini (1987), Kloppenburg (1974a), and Ratzinger (1984, 1986).

3.1.3.5.1 The Translational Approach

Accommodation is essentially a form of translation. However, at the present moment we are speaking not of an accommodational translation but rather of a truly contextualizing translation, made not so much by an outsider but as much as possible by and with the local cultural community through dialogue, which *integrates* the Gospel message with the local culture into a single cognitive, attitudinal, and motivational symbolic system. The aim is to plant the seed that is Christ in such a way that the new plant would be fully of the place, fully of the time, and fully Christian (that is to say, fully incarnated). The new local church must be *of* the soil—planted, not transplanted, not *merely* translated as in the case of traditional accommodation. It should be noted that a certain amount of translation is important and in fact necessary, especially in the initial or primary stage of Christianization. The chasm separating the Christian from the non-Christian cannot be bridged without it.

> But how shall they call on him in whom they have not believed? And how can they believe unless they have heard of him? And how can they hear unless there is someone to preach? [Rom 10:14]

In the initial stages, there is nothing else that can be done but for the sending church to *translate* Christ, even if its translation of Christ into the other culture will unavoidably be faulty. It will be faulty because much of the initial translation will necessarily be imposed on the local community by a sending church that does not, nor can it, fully understand the local ways and values. The weakness stemming from the very nature of translation, however, can be reduced considerably by contextualizing the translation, namely, (1) by seeking an *emic* approach to culture (that of an insider), and (2) by looking for Christ's presence, however rudimentary, in the non-Christian culture, a topic to which we have already referred and shall refer again and again as we go on. The *dynamic equivalence* approach is such an attempt at a contextualized translation.

The dynamic equivalence approach, despite a number of inherent weaknesses and inadequacies (Luzbetak 1981:43–47), has done much to advance our understanding of the nature of a contextual, rather than a superficial accommodational, translation in mission. The concept *dynamic equivalence* has been borrowed from Bible translation theory developed by such linguists and anthropologists as Nida, Taber, and Reyburn, who rightly point out that in any good Bible translation: (1) the essential message of the text will be rendered in the linguistic forms of the time and place for which the translation is being made; (2) the meaning and impact will be as closely as possible equivalent (hence the name "dynamic equivalence") to the meaning and impact that the original, culturally bound wording had on the biblical community that first received the message. According to Kraft, the church that is planted on any local scene must be "dynamically equivalent to the New Testament Church" both in its meaning and impact; that is, in its informational content, value, and motivational force. The cultural expressions, like the words in a translation, should be local rather than those of the biblical culture, the sending church, or the universal Church. Of primary concern to Kraft is the meaning and impact that the Holy Spirit had in mind. The precise cultural forms in which this meaning is *expressed* in word or behavior really matters little to God.[3] In Kraft's words, a dynamic equivalence church

> would be one that (1) conveys to its members truly Christian meanings, (2) functions within its society in such a way that in the name of Christ it plugs into the felt needs of that society and produces within it an impact for Christ equivalent to that which the first-century Church produced in its society, and (3) is couched in cultural forms that are as nearly indigenous as possible. [Stoot, Coote 1979:304]

Cultural translation should by no means be regarded as unnecessary for older and fully matured churches. Even developed Christian communities will be involved in translating Christ into their own and other cultures, because they will always be involved in cross-cultural communication: (1) much cultural translation and interpretation of biblical cultures will be necessary to understand the Bible message and universal symbols and tradition of the Church; (2) cultural translation will be required of every Christian community, young or old, if it is to enter into a dialogue with the universal Church regarding the true meaning of the Gospel and essential universal tradition; (3) cultural translation will always be necessary to communicate across generations and to pass Christian beliefs and values from generation to generation; (4) cultural translation will be necessary for ecumenical and interfaith dialogue; (5) it will be necessary, finally, for cross-cultural mission.

3.1.3.5.2 Dialectical Approach

The dialectic to which we refer is the tension and constant, deeply respectful back-and-forth challenge and exchange that should be going on between the three poles directly involved in contextualization. The three poles are the Gospel, the universal tradition of the Church, and the local culture. It is especially through such challenges and invitation to counter challenges from these three perspectives that genuine unity in diversity can be achieved and true contextualization realized (Schreiter 1985). In the words of John Paul II,

> the Gospel message cannot be purely and simply isolated from the culture in which it was first inserted (the biblical world or more concretely, the cultural milieu in which Jesus of Nazareth lived), nor, without serious loss, from the cultures in which it has already been expressed down through the centuries; it does not spring spontaneously from any cultural soil; it has always been transmitted by means of an apostolic dialogue which inevitably becomes part of certain dialogue of cultures. [*Catechesi tradendae*, no.53]

The triple dialectic must at all times be an honest, collaborative effort on the part of *all* concerned to solve a *common* problem, the problem of how best to incarnate Christ in the given time and place for the good of the local community and the whole Body of Christ without compromising "a jot or tittle" or a "single stroke of a letter" (cf. Lk 16:17) of the essentials of the Gospel. Important indeed is respectful listening on the part of *all* concerned—on the part of the local church and the universal Church, on the part of the receiving church and the sending church, on the part of the local community and the theologians, social scientists, and other experts whom the local community should by no means ignore. We cannot emphasize strongly enough, however, that the most important key to contextualization will always be the soul of the local community—the local ways, values, needs, and traditions. As already emphasized, the best evangelizers are not the best preachers but the best listeners. The best advice that can be given to any expatriate pastor, religious educator, consultant, administrator, or international church authorities will always be, Get the answers to your pastoral problems from and with your people. And if the pastor, religious educator, consultants, or church authorities happen to share the same culture as the community in question, the advice remains largely the same: *Know* your own culture and seek a solution from *within* and *with* those you are guiding.

Figure 5
Major Differences between (Traditional) Accommodation and Inculturation

	ACCOMMODATION	INCULTURATION
PRIMARY AGENT with chief responsibility for initiative and action.	The proclaimers of the Gospel (missionaries, the sending or universal Church.)	The Christian cultural community.
GOAL	The planting of a local church as an extension of the universal Church.	The penetration of the Gospel message into, and its integration with, the community's culture as a single system of belief, values, and behavior, making the Gospel message generative and creative with the culture. (Called also the "evangelization of culture.")
CHIEF PROCESSES	Diffusion. (Translation by outsiders.)	Integration. (The blending of the Gospel message with the rest of culture by insiders.)
DEPTH	Generally superficial and haphazard. Understanding of culture very limited.	"To the very roots" (*Evang. nunt.*, no. 53). Holistic. Based on a good understanding of the nature, structure, and dynamics of culture.

JUSTIFICATION	Viewed as a concession and privilege granted to a "mission" church by sending or universal Church.	Viewed as a necessity and a right to express one's faith in terms of one's own culture.
BENEFICIARIES	*Still "immature"* local churches.	*Every* cultural community.
EMPHASIS	Unity (with limited toleration of diversity).	Unity in diversity (with both unity and diversity considered sacred).
APPROACH	Practical sense of primary agent.	Tripolar dialogue between the Gospel, the universal Church tradition, and the local culture. (Subject to judgment and correction of the communion of churches.)

3.1.3.6 Contextualization and Communication

Contextualization, although always based on Scriptures, nonetheless utilizes as much as possible *local* symbols, genres, and media, especially such that have the greatest impact in the given society. Local *genres and symbols* refers to such conveyors of ideas as parables, folk tales, proverbs, songs, poetry, mythology, rituals, art, dances, drama, historical events and figures. Among the important media in today's world are of course not only the printed word but the cinema, stage, radio, television, video cassette recorders, Gospel-singing, musicals, and the like.

In the United States, basic human and Gospel values might very usefully be buttressed, for instance, by the well-known myths about George Washington, who is, among other things, supposed never to have told a lie; by traditional proverbs like "An ounce of pluck is worth a ton of luck"; by national holidays, parades, and ceremonies honoring such great heroes as Abraham Lincoln or Martin Luther King, Jr.; and by countless stories which children may not believe but unquestionably love to hear, the moral of which they readily understand and accept—yes, including stories about ugly witches, the Sesame Street "gang," the lovable ET, and the many Walt Disney characters—and let's not forget Santa Claus. Lives of Saints may, or may not, be useful, depending on how relevant they are to the culture in question. Liturgy, and ritual in general, when tailored to the worshipping community, can sometimes convey meaning and emotion as perhaps no other medium might (cf. Chupungco 1982). Folk piety, including day-to-day devotional life and such occasional practices as retreats and pilgrimages, have in recent years rightly become objects of serious study by both anthropologists and missiologists (e.g., Turner, Turner 1978; Juste et al. 1981; Schneider, Lindenbaum 1987).

We are not thereby advocating a kind of secular humanism. Traditional genres and symbols have a singular impact on young and old alike. Narrative theology, we are saying, has an important role to play in inculturation (Song 1984; Turner, Turner 1978:73–78; Loewen 1969:147–192).

3.2 AN HISTORICAL OVERVIEW OF MISSION MODELS

The following overview aims to show how varied indeed mission approaches and driving forces have been throughout mission history. It should be noted how (despite their variability) mission approaches, strategies, and motivations can be placed into three major categories, depending on whether their dominant feature could be described as ethnocentric, accommodational, or contextual. It should be noted also how, even in the same historical period and within the same Christian tradition, contradictory models have coexisted, making historical generalizations difficult, if not totally unfounded. More often than not, if anything, the particular models reflect the times (the cultural, social, and political situation) rather than official ecclesiological theories. Evangelizers have always been children of their age, sharing the idealism as well as the foolishness, the selfless dedication as well as the ethnocentrism and errors, of their day and society. Our aim here, as we have stated, is not so much to blame the past as to learn from it. A very common mistake made is to look back at earlier mission efforts and then to pass judgment on them in light of present-day knowledge, opportunities, and general cultural and social context, forgetting that a generation or two from now it will be our turn to be condemned for what is for us today difficult, if not impossible, to understand, appreciate, or change (Luzbetak 1977:51f). The present overview, it is hoped, will also serve later on as useful reference material to illustrate various anthropological concepts and principles, especially those relating to culture dynamics.

This is intended to be only a brief survey of mission approaches and motivations. For a full description of mission models one should consult such excellent historical analyses as K. S. Latourette, *A History of Expansion of Christianity* (7 vols., 1937–1945); Alphons Mulders, *Missionsgeschichte: Die Aüsbreitung der katholischen Glaubens* (1961); Stephen Neill, *A History of the Christian Missions* (1964); and the somewhat outdated but well-documented and definitely still-useful *Catholic Mission History* by Joseph Schmidlin (1933). For excellent shorter coverages of mission history one might consult Latourette's article in the *Encyclopedia of Social Sciences* (1933) under "Mission," as well as Beaver (1970) and Verkuyl (1978:163–193). It should be mentioned that the only other religions of significance that have been engaged in proselytizing besides Christianity are Buddhism and Islam.

It has been rightly said that the Church has survived many serious crises during her long two-thousand year history. The two most serious of such crises were the transition from Jewish to Hellenic or European Christianity (inaugurated by the Council of Jerusalem in 49 A.D.) and the transition from Western to genuine *world* Christianity (inaugurated by the Second Vatican Council). These two epoch-making transitions constitute two supercategories of mission models, the ethnocentric and accommodational models being typical of the first epoch, the inculturational being the direction of the Church of today and tomorrow.

3.2.1 EARLY EXPANSION: THE FIRST FIVE HUNDRED YEARS

3.2.1.1 The Church of the New Testament

The Church began as a tiny Jewish sect. The original Christian community in Jerusalem was fully and exclusively Jewish. It was attached to the Temple and it scrupulously observed the Jewish laws and customs (cf. Acts 2:43–47; 5:12–16). If a Gentile wished to become a Christian, he or she would first have to embrace Judaism and become a Jew—the only route to becoming a member of God's new People. Only then was one really in a position to accept Jesus as Messiah, the Lord and Savior who had died and rose from the dead and who would soon return to finalize the establishment of his Kingdom. The Gentile convert had first to be circumcised. He had to accept the Law of Moses and to follow the customs of the Jews. In a word, it was unthinkable for the first Christians to associate with heathen, much less to enter into religious communion with them.

It took Peter some time to understand through a vision that salvation was also for non-Jews like Cornelius (Acts 10:9–48). According to Peter,

God shows no partiality. Rather, the man of any nation who fears God and acts uprightly is acceptable to him. This is the message he has sent to the sons of Israel, the good news of peace proclaimed through Jesus Christ who is Lord of all. [Acts 10:34–36]

In Antioch, Paul and Barnabas found that a mixed community of Jews and uncircumcised Gentiles was in existence, a community of whom they approved (Acts 11:26). It was this development that led to serious disputes with the Judaizers and to the convocation of the Council of Jerusalem (Acts 15:1–30; cf. Gal 2:1–14). The Council settled once and for all the question of the necessity of the Law. Circumcision was declared no longer binding for Gentile converts; unclean foods were no longer to be regarded as unclean; fellowship with Gentiles was looked upon as compatible with the Good News; in fact, the Good News was to be preached to the Gentiles and to the Jews alike. The influx of Gentiles into the infant Church was in fact so great that a church in Corinth was founded, consisting of uncircumcised Christians. Before long, the church of the New Testament was mainly Gentile.

The mission approach of the church of the New Testament became strongly accommodational. Customs compatible with the apostolic doctrine and usable as a bridge to or as a contact point with the Gospel were tolerated, while whatever was considered contrary to the Gospel or regarded as a scandal or hindrance to the effective proclamation of the Good News was uncompromisingly rejected. In dealing with the Jews, the apostles used familiar Old Testament concepts, images, cults, and promises; in dealing with the Gentiles, the apostles showed respect for the pagan understanding of sin and for a purely natural belief in God. The Council of Jerusalem was eminently accommodational when it declared: "It is the decision of the Holy Spirit, and ours too, not to lay on you any burden beyond that which is strictly necessary" (Acts 15:28). Paul spoke in temples respectfully of the hopes of pagan ancestors. On the Areopagus he approved the pagan worship of the "Unknown God" (Acts 17:22-31). He recognized the fact that God engraved his law on every human heart, including the heart of the pagan (Rom 2:14ff). God made no distinction between Jew and Gentile (cf. Gal 2:11ff). Accommodations were made to local social structures; thus native Cretans were ordained to head Cretan communities (Tit 1:5). Although the Synoptic Gospels are typically Jewish in tone and character, the Fourth Gospel accommodates the Good News to the Greek mentality, making use of the tradition and philosophy of the Hellenistic world. It should be noted that by the time John's gospel was written, the infant Church had ceased to be Jewish and, as already indicated, had become predominantly Gentile, a situation that made a restatement of the Christian message more in tune with a non-Jewish audience desirable. Thus, for instance, while genealogies had been very meaningful to the Jewish Christians and while such concepts as "Son of David," "Messiah," and "Jerusalem" brought great joy and hope to the Jewish heart, the Gentile Christians found Jewish genealogies largely void of sentiment, King David an obscure, if not unknown, figure, the idea of a messiah lacking the deep, emotional impact and connotations that it had for Jews, and Jerusalem as nothing more than a foreign capital. In John's restatement of the Good News, the universality of the church and the originally Jewish symbols took on a new and deeper meaning: Jesus was presented from the very first chapter as the Light and Savior of the *world*, thus embracing the

Gentiles as well. Central to both the Jewish wisdom tradition as well as to the Hellenistic way of thinking was the *Logos* and the "two-worlds" concept—the shadowy, unreal world in which we live and the real world after which our unreal world is modeled. In harmony with both the Jewish and Hellenic thinking, John presents God as the Principle of Rationality (the "Supreme Idea"), while our task in life is presented as the passage from the shadowy world into the world of reality. John's gospel told the now-predominantly Greek Church in terms intelligible to them how this passage might be realized: Jesus was "the Way, the Truth, and the Life" (Jn 14:6); he was the Light of the world (Jn 1:4,9; 3:19; 8:12; 9:5; 12:46); Jesus was Reality and Wisdom Incarnate! What could be easier for the Greek mind to grasp? In the eloquent words of William Barclay, John's accommodated restatement of the Good News is saying to the Graeco-Roman world:

All your lives you [Greeks] have been fascinated by this great, guiding, controlling mind of God. The mind of God has come to earth in the man Jesus. Look at him and you see what the mind and thought of God are like. [1956:8]

John illustrates an excellent example of accommodation—a way of getting on common ground! Although the Evangelist had an eye to interpreting the Gospel message to a non-Jewish audience and actually did so, he found a resource within his own Jewish tradition that allowed him to make the adaptation and at the same time remain faithful to his tradition.

3.2.1.2 The Post-Apostolic, Pre-Constantinian Period

Toleration of "neutral" and "naturally good" pagan customs (accommodation) was the policy advocated by the early Apologists known as the "Irenics" (the "Peace Makers," the "Reconcilors"), such as Clement of Alexandria and Origen, in contradistinction to the "Polemics," the early Christian hardliners. Tertullian (160?–230), coined the expression *testimonium animae naturaliter christianae* ("the testimony of a naturally Christian soul"). St. Justin Martyr spoke of *logoi spermatikoi,* "the seeds of the Word," that existed in the pagan heart. For Eusebius, pagan philosophies were "preparations" for Christ. He demonstrated a distinctly positive attitude toward non-Christian ways, the very basis for accommodation.

3.2.1.3 The Constantinian Period

When the Church was in its infancy, growth was brought about through conversion of individuals and small family groups. Every Christian felt that to be a Christian implied being an evangelizer, not in an organized way but through word of mouth and by witnessing—by living the faith and dying for it. Martyrdom, even as the pagans had to admit, had become "the seed of

Christians." Despite the Great Commission (Mt 28:18) and the missionary work of the apostles and some of their disciples, however, there was no organized campaign to eradicate paganism as such; it was felt that God would do that at Jesus' second coming. The conversion of the world would be sudden and apocalyptic. When, on the other hand, the tables were turned and the Church passed from a minority status to that of a majority, new mission models appeared. Christianity, which only a few centuries earlier had been but a tiny persecuted sect among many competing religions and philosophies, became by the year 400 A.D. the dominant and official religion of the Mediterranean basin and, in fact, throughout the Roman Empire, extending as far as Arabia, Abyssinia, and even to Central Asia and India. This turn of history was to no small measure associated with the propitious cultural, social, and political situation of the times. Various Germanic and other tribes, notably the Burgundians, Franks, Goths, and Celts, accepted Christianity not only as a result of evangelization but often in response to the example of rulers and in some cases in response to legislation, threats, and other pressures.

The conversion of the Franks was largely brought about by two bishops, St. Remigius of Paris and St. Avitus of Vienne, who succeeded in arranging a marriage between King Clovis (466–511), a tribal religionist, and the Christian princess Clotilda. Some years after his marriage, his victory at Tolbiacum convinced him of the power of the God his wife worshipped. This victory and Clotilda's strong influence led Clovis to Christianity, while his example brought the rest of the population to the Church.

Such "matrimonial" mission models have occurred in other places and times as well. Thus, about a hundred years later King Ethelbert's marriage occasioned a similar conversion among the Anglo-Saxons.

The factors involved in the phenomenal growth of the Church in the first five centuries, unparalleled in the history of religions, were varied and many. There was the support and espousal of Christianity by political powers, not only by Constantine but also by a long succession of Roman emperors that followed. There were the power and prestige of the Roman Empire itself with which Christianity was associated. There were the political and expansionistic benefits that rulers could expect from the prestige that Christianity enjoyed and the benefits that flowed from the goodwill and favor of Rome as a result of conversion. There was the political unity of a widespread Empire (the *pax romana*)—the opening of sea lanes and the freeing of them from pirates, the vast road systems and bridges, and the extraordinary expansion of commerce. There was the wide knowledge of two important cultural languages, Greek and Latin. There was the rise, spread, and influence of monasticism that sought to dispel the syncretism and worldliness of the times through a radical lifestyle and witness; this replaced martyrdom and provided important psychological legitimation for whole tribes and populations to accept Christianity. In a word, from the anthropological point of view a more propitious political, social, and cultural scenario for the spread of an idea could hardly have been possible. Yet one should not overlook or downplay the more traditional missionary approaches and motivations such as Christian idealism, asceticism, and ecclesiastical organization. The spirit of accommodation somehow coexisted with both syncretism and intolerance. St. John Chrysostom (345?–407), patriarch of Constantinople, for example, opposed such customs as horse-racing and pantomimes but did not hesitate to dispatch monks with an imperial decree in hand and accompanied by a band of soldiers to destroy the temples of unbelievers. Nevertheless, like much of the early Church, Chrysostom tolerated whatever appeared to be "naturally good" or "neutral." (Latourette 1970,1:192, 271). St. Patrick (d. 461) likewise was an accommodationist, being very tolerant toward such non-Christian practices as those associated with fire, spring festivals, pagan pillars, oak trees, groves, dress, virgins, and the use of the shamrock to illustrate the Blessed Trinity (Schmidlin 1931:145).

3.2.2 THE CHRISTIANIZATION OF EUROPE—500–1500 A.D.

The next thousand years are called somewhat unjustifiably by Latourette "Years of Uncertainty." The fact is, as someone has observed, we are hardly speaking of years of uncertainty: after all, the evangelization and Christianization of Europe is an exciting story in the annals of mission history; to take a sudden leap from Augustine to Luther, as if nothing had happened in the meantime, would be nothing less than to misread history.

The Christianization of Europe continues to reveal a variety of, and at times opposing, mission models. It was Charlemagne's (768–814) practice first to conquer the population militarily and then to secure the conquest by baptism as a sign of true submission. To refuse baptism was to refuse submission; to refuse submission could mean death. On the other hand, accommodational models were also followed. Local folklore had a great influence on Christian forms of piety, on liturgy, on religious feast days, and on Christian living in general. Pope Gregory the Great (590–604) gave express orders to the missionaries sent to England to be understanding and tolerant toward local non-Christian practices (cf. McCulloch 1978:323–334). The pagan temples, he wrote to Mellitus,

> must not be destroyed. The idols in them must be destroyed; but the temples themselves are to be purified by the sprinkling of holy water, and must have altars and relics placed in them. The people will be more easily drawn to places to which they have become accustomed. And because they are accustomed to kill many oxen in sacrificing to demons, some solemnity must be given them in exchange on this account. . . . For there is no doubt that it is impossible to efface everything at once from their obdurate minds, for the man who strives to ascend to the highest place rises by degrees or steps and not by leaps. [Quoted from Schmidlin 1933:152]

Among the most effective mission models of this period was the so-called "monastic model"—actually embracing a number of distinct submodels. Some Irish monks, for instance, acting independently of church authorities, would set out in groups of twelve on what they called "a pilgrimage for Christ," with no particular destination in mind other than to find an appropriate location for a new monastery. Their motivation was primarily ascetical, and the resulting conversions to Christianity for which they were responsible were really a kind of by-product of the monks' ascetical lifestyle. This missionary approach brought large segments of the European population to the church.

Some (non-Irish) Benedictine monks were sent out directly by the Pope (rather than the monks venturing on their own). Their primary goal was church growth, not personal asceticism. The real concern of Irish monks on the continent was not so much evangelization as the deepening of the faith of nominally Christian people. Although this approach was generally sympathetic to local cultures, the monks, typified by St. Boniface, showed little toleration for whatever they regarded as "superstition"; they defied the local gods, cut down sacred trees, and destroyed pagan shrines. The monks did much, however, to teach the people useful domestic arts, animal husbandry, and agricultural skills.

Another mission model of this period, reflecting the Eastern rather than Western mentality of the time, was that of two scholarly brothers from Constantinople, Greeks by birth, Cyril (Constantine) and Methodius, the ninth-century apostles to the Slavic peoples. Theirs was a triple model, embracing the roles of diplomats, bishops, and educators at the service of the church, the Eastern Empire, and the Slavic peoples. It should be noted that Cyril and Methodius did not *bring* the faith to the Slavs as much as consolidate it. Count Ratislav of Great Moravia had appealed to Emperor Michael III of Constantinople in the following remarkable words:

> Although our people have abandoned paganism and observe Christian law, we have no one to explain the true Christian faith to us in our own language. . . . Send us such a bishop and teacher. [Quoted from Tybor 1984:147]

Note the express request for an accommodational approach to mission. Note also the depth of the response: Cyril and Methodius reduced the Moravian language to writing by means of their so-called Slavonic "glagolitic" or "Cyrillic" alphabet. The Scriptures as well as catechetical and liturgical manuals were translated into the local language; liturgy was celebrated in Slavonic; schools were established and indigenous clergy were trained and assigned to Christian communities. This approach was anything but palatable to Latin missionaries who had been evangelizing the Slavs before the arrival of Cyril and Methodius; they complained bitterly to Pope Nicholas I about the "unorthodox" accommodations made by Cyril and Methodius. The Pope, however, was in no position to give much heed to the complaints: the Latin (i.e., German) missionaries were being expelled from the Slav territory, and the Pope was anxious to seize jurisdiction over the region from the Eastern Patriarchate. He wisely named both Cyril and Methodius bishops. (Cyril, it should be noted died in 869.) By becoming bishop, Methodius' problems, however, were not over; in fact, he was twice imprisoned by the German bishops for several years. Note how contrasting indeed the two mission models were: the German or Latinizing model was successful as far as the nobles were concerned, but the missionaries hailed today as the true "Apostles of the Slavic Peoples" are the Greeks, Cyril and Methodius, outstanding believers in the accommodational approach to mission.[4]

It was during this long and dangerous period of history, when no unifying force other than the church itself existed, that a new, competing religion, Islam, was born. It threatened the very existence of both Church and State. During the eleventh, twelfth, and thirteenth centuries, popes and kings would call Crusades, sometimes with mixed and questionable motives. At times they aimed to spread Christianity; at times they wanted primarily to recover lost territory, notably the Holy Land; at times they wished to liberate Christian captives; at times they tried to keep Christian Europe from being overrun and annihilated by Islam; at times, too, their primary goal was to gain political advantage; or, finally, as in the case of Urban II who called for the First Crusade, the goal was to stop conflict among the nobility by encouraging the establishment of new feudal kingdoms. That both sides, the Muslims as well as the Christians, were guilty of injustice and brutality, including forced conversions, is only too well-known. What is of concern to us at this moment is the fact that, in dealing with the Muslims, missionaries of these times followed a *variety* of mission models. Thus, while Innocent III (Pope, 1198–1216) organized a Crusade against Islam, St. Francis of Assisi (1182–1226) and his followers preached peace and love to the Moslems. In the spirit of St. Francis, Ramon Lull forsook his status in the court of Aragon for that of a Franciscan tertiary to work among Muslims as a "fool of love." On the other hand, only shortly before St. Francis appeared on the scene preaching love toward the Muslims, another renowned saint, St. Bernard of Clairvaux (1091–1153), had been preaching that the killing of a Muslim was not so much "a killing of a human being" as it was "a destruction of an evil"—not a *homicidium* as much as a *malicidium*. Similarly, while some sought the conversion of Jews through debate and persuasion, others, like the Byzantine Emperor Leo III and the Spaniards and Portuguese, generally regarded pressure and segregation as the best way to "convert" Jews. The Crusaders were often not satisfied with anything less than the sword. Similarly, the Teutonic Knights, in their efforts to bring the Prussians into the Church, were firm believers in the use of force as an approach to Church growth. In contrast, the Dominicans of the thirteenth century were known for their efforts at convert-making through respectful discussion, debate, and preaching.

3.2.3 THE EVANGELIZATION OF NEW PEOPLES IN ASIA AND THE AMERICAS—1500–1800 A.D.

3.2.3.1 Catholic Growth and Decline

Latourette has called the period extending approximately from 1500 to the beginning of the eighteenth century as "Three Centuries of Advance." It seems more correct to speak of Catholic and Protestant phases instead, with the beginning of the eighteenth century as a kind of line of demarcation. As far as *Catholic* missions are concerned, one might speak of "advance" only to the beginning of the eighteenth century; thereafter, for at least another century and a half, there was a serious decline in mission involvement. The last half of the seventeenth century was still a part of a glorious era for Catholics, evidenced, for instance, by the establishment of vicariates apostolic and the appearance of the Lazarists on the mission scene. On the other hand, as far as *Protestantism* was concerned, one can hardly speak of any type of "advance," because Protestant missions were for all practical purposes nonexistent until the eighteenth century. The "advance" referred to by Latourette is evidently that of Christendom in general: it was during this time that Christianity, geographically speaking, became a *worldwide* religion.

We wish once again to point out how distinct and contrasting mission models throughout this period of Church history really were. We also wish to emphasize that however important the so-called patronage and Spanish and Portuguese imperialism may indeed have been, and however true it is that Christianity was spread *with* colonialism, colonialism was never the single factor explaining the spread of the Gospel in this period. The mission models, as we shall presently explain, were too varied for such a simple interpretation of history to be accurate.

First of all, one must remember that the Reformation did not affect Spain and Portugal in the way it affected northern Europe. Moreover, Spain and Portugal were seafarers, explorers, and colonizers second to no nation. The extension of the Cross with the Crown seemed quite natural to the Spaniards and Portuguese—in fact, it seemed providential. The pope divided the lands that had been discovered, and those that would be discovered in the future, between these two countries. Portugal assumed responsibility for Africa, Asia, and Brazil; Spain, for Central and South America and the Philippine Islands. It has been well said that India thus became of interest to Portugal not only for its "pepper" but for its "pepper and souls." To achieve this double goal, the Portuguese relied heavily on military might. They were intensely ethnocentric in both church and state matters. The style of their places of worship as well as their settlements in general were distinctly Portuguese. Their methods may have brought new members into the Church but at the same time made outcasts of Indians in their own communities. By contrast, the Italian Jesuit Robert de Nobili vigorously opposed the adoption of Western customs that Hindus normally found repugnant. De Nobili, in fact, became a guru, closely following the Brahmin lifestyle in dress, diet, and mores. He mastered the Sanskrit literature and sought to adapt the Christian message to the philosophy and theology of the Hindus. In China, Matteo Ricci (1552–1610) and his Jesuit fellow-workers were similarly noted for their high regard for Chinese ways and values, especially for their knowledge and respect for Confucianism. Ricci adopted the national lifestyle for himself and taught Christian doctrine in terms of Confucian philosophy. Appreciating the fact that filial piety was a basic theme in the Chinese value system, Ricci found no difficulty in regarding ancestor veneration—which included a family altar, a spirit tablet (believed as the dwelling place of the departed soul), candles, incense, food offerings, and memorial banquets—as being essentially a familial and civic rite and therefore as being in no way in conflict with Christianity. This is, however, not to deny that tensions existed in Ricci's own mind as to the proper limits of accommodation. Later jealousies and misunderstandings as well as fears of possible syncretism eventually brought about the condemnation of Ricci's stand. The Chinese Rites Controversy was re-examined in 1919 by Benedict XV and, twenty years later, fully declared in Ricci's favor by Pius XI (Minamiki 1985).

The Japanese story presents still other contrasting mission models. Although Portuguese warships were docked in Japanese ports, it was not submission to such military power that brought the Japanese to the Church as much as the teaching, preaching, and example of missionaries. Portuguese military might served only to cast suspicion on mission activities.

Other contrasting approaches were those of the Portuguese on the one hand and the Spaniards on the other. It was the custom of the Portuguese to build relatively small settlements with weak direct control over the local population. The extension of the Church was brought about by suppressing tribal religions and by driving away the upper class, the chief native resisters. The Portuguese relied, instead, for their conversions on the lower strata of society and mixed-blood descendants. The Spaniards, on the other hand, believed in strong, direct control of indigenous communities. Exploitation and extermination of Caribbean populations went hand in hand with the expansion of the Spanish crown. It would be totally false to imagine that the missionaries stood passively by or that they consented to such atrocities. A notable case in point was Bartolomé de las Casas, who, after undergoing a personal conversion in the New World, vigorously opposed all forms of exploitation of the native peoples. Writing about the missionaries of this period, R. Pierce Beaver points out how, since de las Casas' bold opposition,

> protection of primitive people against exploitation by whites and by colonial governments has been an important function of missions. After that mighty effort abolished slavery and forced baptism, the missionaries were made both the civilizers and protectors of the Indians. . . . Thus the Indians were preserved, civilized, and Christianized, not killed off or displaced as would later be the case in the United States. [1981:192f]

Missionary approaches varied also according to the particular order to which the missionary belonged. The Spanish Franciscans, Dominicans, and Augustinians established central stations—actually monasteries for themselves—and then invited the neighboring Indians to settle around the mission compound. A small garrison of soldiers would usually protect both the missionaries and the Indian community. Generally speaking, the Franciscans, Dominicans, and Augustinians showed a certain amount of cross-cultural sensitivity, but less so than the Jesuits. The contrast, however, was really between the Mendicants who arrived before 1560, who were very culturally sensitive and who wished to preserve the Indian languages on the one hand, and the Mendicants who arrived later and carried out the policy of the government demanding the use of Spanish rather than the vernacular. As a rule, missionaries were dedicated to the needs of the new Christians, whom they taught especially the arts of grazing and agriculture. Unfortunately, as soon as the area was regarded by the government as "sufficiently civilized," the religious-order priests were frequently replaced by diocesan clergy, who were often of low quality and who possessed little respect for the Indians and their ways. Worse still, the land of the Indians was gradually parceled out among Spanish settlers; this forced the native population to peonage.

The California Missions, under the leadership of Franciscan Father Junipero Serra, illustrate an accommodationist approach to mission with deep concern for the welfare of the Indians and a genuine identification with them. The padres were nevertheless bound to many traditional and often ethnocentric missionary ways of the times, especially to paternalism. The "flock" had to live in mission compounds so as to be preserved from "bad" tribal influences. The Indians were but "adult children," not really to be trusted lest they get into some unchristian "mischief." They were at times punished (whipped, shackled, or put in stockades), the padres having felt a strictly parental responsibility for their charges, the way a good Spanish father would feel in regard to his child. The Indians were not to think for themselves; their task was simply to memorize the *doctrina* by song or rote. In a word, the California Missions model might best be described as genuine identification, but an identification trapped in traditional paternalism (Luzbetak 1985a).

Some Jesuits believed in settlements as did other missionary groups of the times, but theirs were unique in many ways. We refer to the so-called "Reductions" of Paraguay, Brazil, and Argentina. The Reductions excluded non-Indians and were clearly focused on community development and on the protection of the Indians from capture and enslavement by the Spanish. The programs associated with the Reductions reflected a remarkable sensitivity to the Guarani ways and values.

The word *Reductions* is derived from the Spanish *reducción*, from the verb *reducir*, which means "to pull together, to reduce the population to a mission station or community." The system lasted only about 150 years, and never were more than fifty or sixty Jesuit priests involved. Although most of the Jesuits were Spaniards, the Jesuit team associated with the Reductions was international. The thirty cities that comprised the system had a combined population of about 140,000. Although the first to organize a Reduction was the Franciscan Luis de Buaños, it was the Jesuits, especially men like Father Ruíz de Montoya, who made the Reductions the remarkable settlements that they were. These cities formed safe havens against Spanish exploitation, especially against the enslavement of Indians. Although the pope had condemned the enslavement of Indians in 1537, in one year alone no less than 30,000 Indians are said to have been killed or captured.[5] Ruíz de Montoya obtained permission from the Crown to set up a military defense system especially to combat slavery, a serious evil that had made 300,000 freedom-loving Indians into slaves. In 1604 the pope declared Paraguay a Jesuit province. The area extended well beyond what is known today as Paraguay. The first Reduction was founded six years later.

Reductions were well-organized, semiautonomous communities that owed fealty to the Crown and paid taxes. As valuable as the Reductions may have been as systems of defense, their value went far beyond survival. They had collective farms and herds, and they stressed community development and both religious and practical education. Today, the ruins clearly testify to the almost unbelievable transformation that the Reductions brought about. City life had been unknown to these simple agricultural tribes, and unlike the Indians of Mexico and Peru who had a well-developed native art, the Guarani had known very little about ceramics and basket weaving. They were, however, fast learners, who mastered especially Baroque art. But this does not mean that they were mere copiers; rather, they proved themselves to be gifted artists who added original details and a new soul to the art they so admired.

The Reductions lasted into the nineteenth century, well beyond the period under discussion. In 1767, Charles III of Spain expelled the Jesuits from Spain and from all its colonies. The expulsion, however, did not mean the immediate end to the Reductions. The fact is that the Spaniards were obliged to continue the system despite several decisions to give it up and to destroy it; when the so-called communistic features of the Reductions were removed, the situation of the Indians quickly deteriorated, forcing the Spaniards to continue the Reductions. However, now with the Jesuits gone, the Reductions were directed by secular administrators or given to other religious orders; never were they administered by the Indians themselves. One of the principal reasons for the demise of the Reductions was the fact that almost the entire Indian population had been wiped out by diseases. While there were an estimated 100,000 to 300,000 Indians on the Reductions under the Jesuits, only 20,000 were still alive in the early 1800s. The Reductions were gradually destroyed by the Brazilians, and the population with its many skilled laborers and capable craftsmen were dispersed to Buenos Aires and other cities. The final blow was dealt by Carlos Lopez in 1848, when he abolished and destroyed all Guarani property. The ultimate aim of Reductions had been the gradual acculturation of the Guarani people, a most noble effort that in the end failed.

Evaluations of the endeavor will vary. Some find fault with the barrack-like life, which was very un-Guaranian. The system, however, was definitely functional, culturally sensitive, and socially conscious. The Reductions may have been monastic and their living conditions were indeed barrack-like, but their communities formed an excellent self-defense. They were also an example of community development and of a serious attempt at guided acculturation and adjustment to the inescapable effects of colonialism. Reasons for the failure of the Reductions are, however, more complex than meets the eye. Anthropologically speaking, the most serious mistake made might best be described as well-intentioned paternalism. In any case, the Reductions suggest an interesting missionary model from which much can be learned (McNaspy 1982).

In North America, the Jesuits of this period had still another model. Isaac Jogues and his fellow-Jesuits did not urge the Indians to settle in a mission community but rather felt that the missionaries should adopt the nomadic life of the Iroquois and move whenever and wherever the Indians moved. Similarly, the Jesuits of Canada believed that it was they, the missionaries, who should adapt to the lifestyle of the Indians rather than vice versa; accordingly, *they* moved into the Indian villages. The approach of the French Jesuits in Vietnam differed again from that of their fellow-Jesuits and countrymen working as missionaries in the Americas; in Vietnam, the emphasis was on native catechists and indigenous clergy, a route that had amazing results.

For Catholic missions, after a flourishing century and a half, there followed a century and a half of decadence. Morale in mission territories was low, while missionary interest and vocations in the homeland had practically disappeared. The reasons for this sad state of affairs were many. For instance, Protestant colonial powers, after having gained the upper hand over Spain and Portugal, began to hamper Catholic mission efforts. The chief explanation for the decline, however, must be sought in the homeland: Christianity was infected by the irreligious currents of the Enlightenment; just when papal leadership was at a low point, absolutist governments infected Europe with their divisive antipapal movements (known in France as Gallicanism and in Germany as Febronianism or Josephism after Emperor Joseph II); religious orders, the main source of mission personnel and mission inspiration, were overrun with jealousies that eventually led to the Rite Controversies and quarrels over jurisdiction and finally in 1773 to the expulsion of the Jesuits from all mission lands. The greatest catastrophe, however, was the French Revolution with its secularistic, anticlerical repercussions that included suppression of monasteries and seminaries and the persecution of priests.

3.2.3.2 The Birth and Growth of Protestant Missions: 1700–1800 A.D.

While Catholic mission revival waited for the Napoleonic Wars to end, Protestantism, at first apathetic if not antagonistic to missionary activities (cf. Gensichen 1984:3–10), gave birth to a new missionary movement. Protestant England and Holland at first equaled, and then surpassed, Catholic Spain and Portugal as colonial powers. Just as the Catholic Church officially had declared the Catholic missions to be the function of Spain and Portugal's military might, so the Protestant missions were officially declared the function of the Dutch and British trading companies.

The first successful Protestant mission was that of the Danes, founded in 1706 in India by Bartholomäus Ziegenbalg, a German Lutheran associated with Pietism at Halle University. Remarkable were Ziegenbalg's appreciation of Hinduism and his emphasis on medical work as a distinct and indeed an integral part of missionary work. One of his successors, Christian Schwarz (1726–1798), became a respected guru noted for his understanding of and high esteem for Brahminism.

Another important early Protestant movement with roots in the Pietism of Halle University was the Moravian Mission, begun under Count Nicholaus von Zinzendorf (1700–1760). In 1722, Zinzendorf, with refugees from Moravia, founded in East Germany the colony of Herrnhut, a community of lay missionaries who twelve years later were able to send their first missionaries to West Indies and Greenland. By the time Zinzendorf died, the Moravian Mission had sent no less than a hundred missionaries abroad. Among the chief characteristics of the Moravian missionaries were their deep spirituality, their biblical emphasis, their simplicity of presentation of the Christian message, their emphasis on God's love and the Holy Spirit, their modeling of Christian living on the New Testament churches, their insistence on personal rather than mass conversions, and their recognition of the importance of both the local and the worldwide Christian community—a model that has much to teach the modern missionary of all traditions.

The Protestant missions with the greatest impact at this early stage were perhaps those of the Puritans. Their approach consisted especially in preaching hell-fire, personal conversion, and the adoption of a strictly English Puritan lifestyle. As a point of policy, they insisted on isolating new Christians from their pagan surroundings in "uncontaminated" towns. To become a Christian, it was believed, one had to be "civilized" first, and "civilization" was understood in terms of British standards that included a basic education and a good practical training in farming, domestic arts, and literacy.

3.2.4 THE NINETEENTH CENTURY

Latourette has dubbed the nineteenth century somewhat triumphalistically as "The Great Century." It was "great" not so much for the number of new converts (the influx was not comparable to that of the twentieth century) but for the formative impact that the century had on Christians of the West (cf. W. Shenk, 1984). The nineteenth century brought a new missionary consciousness to the Christian world, a revitalization to the mission spirit heretofore unknown, that affected Catholics, Protestants, and Orthodox—the clergy, religious, and laity alike. The peace that was enjoyed during much of the nineteenth century, the wealth, influence, and expansion of Western nations during this period, and the new vitality of the Christian faith accompanying the rapid multiplication of popular voluntary missionary organizations all were important factors contributing to the unparalleled health and growth of the nineteenth-century mission effort.

When speaking of missionary processes of this period, one cannot but emphasize the role played by missionary societies. The nineteenth century is in fact sometimes referred to as "the Century of Missionary Societies," a fitting designation for Catholic and Protestant Christianity alike.

3.2.4.1 Protestant Mission Societies

3.2.4.1.1 William Carey (1761–1834)

William Carey, an enthusiastic promoter of the mission cause, was largely responsible for the new missionary spirit in Protestantism and for the eventual founding of the Baptist Mission Society in 1792 called the Particular Baptist Society for Propagating the Gospel Among the Heathen. Carey was chosen to be the Society's first missionary, and the field selected was India. The immediate concern of the new mission and new missionary was the problem of civilizing the non-Christian world as a precondition for Christianizing it. Carey strongly felt that mission work should result in an independent church, one sustained by a literate laity well-versed in the Scriptures and led by a well-educated indigenous ministry. In the hope of reaching this goal systematically, Carey placed great weight on higher education and on the development of indigenous literature. It was with this goal in mind that he established vast central stations headed by expatriate pastors. Like de Nobili, he too was convinced that India could be Christianized only if the Brahmin caste would be converted first (cf. Drewery 1979).

3.2.4.1.2 Henry Venn and Rufus Anderson

The two names Henry Venn (1796–1873) and Rufus Anderson (1805–1855) somehow go together like Peter and Paul. In any list of Protestant mission strategists of the nineteenth century, one would have to include these two thinkers: Anglican Venn and Congregationalist Anderson.

Henry Venn, the Chief Secretary of the Church Missionary Society of London, was, in Max Warren's words, "the outstanding European missionary leader, thinker and administrator of the 19th century" (1971:636). In the estimation of R. Pierce Beaver, Rufus Anderson, the secretary of the American Board of Commissioners for Foreign Missions, and Venn were "the two greatest mission theoreticians and strategists of the nineteenth century" (1981:200). Venn and Anderson stressed the nature of the church as essentially missionary. Anyone engaged in mission work, they insisted, should be active primarily as an evangelist, moving from place to place and leaving the post of resident pastor to local Christians. The very raison d'être of new Christian communities was to give birth to still other Christian communities. Anderson and Venn were independently responsible for the so-called "three-self" formula as goal of mission, namely the establishment of self-governing, self-supporting, and self-propagating Christian communities. Important for the realization of the three selves, according to Anderson, was *vernacular* education. This formula recalls similar views held by Cyril and Methodius, the Apostles to the Slavs. It was Anderson who broke up William Carey's system of vast central stations in favor of ordaining indigenous pastors for small village communities instead. In such communities it was the vernacular, rather than English, that was the important vehicle of communication and education. Anderson showed insight and independence also in his downplaying of the role of "civilization" as a precondition for Christianization. (Cf. Beaver 1967, 1979, 1981:200f; W. Shenk 1977a, 1977b, 1981:172–176, 1983; Warren 1971; Beyerhaus, Lefever 1964:25–33; Verkuyl 1978:184–187.)

3.2.4.2 Catholic Mission Societies

In the vanguard of the Catholic missionary revival of the nineteenth century were the older religious orders, such as the Jesuits and Franciscans, who in the first quarter of the century experienced a profound revitalization of missionary interest. During the nineteenth century alone, some forty new Catholic male religious congregations specifically missionary in purpose were founded. Among them were the Picpus Society, the Marists, the Oblates of Mary Immaculate, and the Divine Word Missionaries. Unparalleled in history was the missionary enthusiasm and involvement of women religious in mission action, with thirty-nine congregations of women founded during this period expressly for missionary work (Schmidlin 1933:560). The hierarchy and diocesan clergy added their strength to that of men and women religious, while a new flood of missionary concern manifested itself in papal encyclicals and in direct action on the part of such popes as Gregory XVI (pope 1831–1846), former head of the Sacred Congregation of the Propagation of the Faith; Leo XIII (pope 1878–1903), whose missionary interest and involvement merited him the title of "The Great Missionary Pope"; and Benedict XV (pope 1914–1922). It was during this period that a large number of Catholic organizations were founded (estimated at about 250) with the purpose of fostering missionary vocations, educating the laity in their mission responsibilities, and soliciting funds for the missions. The most important of these supporting associations was the international Society for the Propagation of the Faith, begun in Lyons in 1822 as a small association. Today the society is established around the world, providing a major portion of the funds for Catholic mission activities. Informing the laity about the work of the missions and seeking financial support were some 300 Catholic mission periodicals and a constant flow of other promotional literature. It was also during this period that the Sacred Congregation of the Propagation of the Faith (today known as the Congregation for the Evangelization of Peoples) was reorganized, revitalized, and given full authority over the entire Catholic mission effort. Missionary training centers were founded for diocesan clergy in Milan, Lyons, and elsewhere. The leading nation in this period of missionary revitalization was France, which provided 70 percent of all Catholic missionaries. (It should be noted that the Pontifical Urban College, a center intended primarily for advanced training of clergy indigenous to mission countries, was founded in 1627, then was closed and later reopened in 1815.)

Whereas in the beginning of the nineteenth century the number of Catholic missionaries had dropped to an astounding low of only 300 by some estimates (Dirven 1971:415f; Bausch 1977:384), there were as many as 25,000 by 1908 (Schmidlin 1933:564). These facts leave no doubt whatsoever that for Catholic missions this was a truly great century. Only fifty years later the numbers were to reach the 100,000 mark. It is therefore no exaggeration to say that the nineteenth century marked an unusual period for the Catholic missions (Schmidlin 1933:556–582; Latourette 1941,4:53–64).

3.2.4.3 Chief Features of the Nineteenth-Century Mission Models

The mere number of Catholic and Protestant mission societies of this time is astounding; we are speaking of hundreds and thousands. Latourette, referring to Protestant societies alone, estimated that just to list these would take "many hundreds of pages" (1941,4:88). Although sharing many common features, such societies, whether Catholic or Protestant, possessed some very distinctive traits.

3.2.4.3.1 Protestant Mission Strategies

Beaver (1981:200–204) and Latourette (1941,4:94–102) provide us with the following profile of the general approach to mission of the times. (1) It was widely accepted in Protestantism that the Church was missionary by her very nature. (2) The primary emphasis was on *personal* conversion. (3) It was commonly held that the goal of mission was the planting of *indigenous* churches, that is to say, "three-self" churches. (The fact is, however, that in the last quarter of the century the mission churches were once again subjected to a colonialist mentality and were looked upon as part of the "white man's burden," with paternalism as the answer to all mission problems.) (4) There was a new emphasis on the formation of *national* churches. (5) Direct involvement of the laity in mission work took on new importance. (6) It was commonly held that the fundamental missionary concerns were evangelism, education, and medicine. (7) The vital role of women in mission work was universally recognized, with the number of women engaged as missionaries increasing dramatically and with great success. (Such was the case especially in the Orient, where normally women alone could relate effectively with women, particularly in educational and social programs. Generally, too, it was felt that once women were converted, children would follow their mother's example and would thus form the nucleus of a solid Christian community.) (8) A very interesting development was the so-called "comity" arrangement by which various Protestant traditions would recognize one another as valid branches of the one Church of Christ. (9) Comity led to greater interdenominational cooperation, which, in turn, led to broadened international consultation and planning. (Such consultation and planning began with the First World Missionary Conference at Edinburgh in 1910 and has continued to this day.) (10) Protestant missions found new strength in students and universities. Student missionary movements, which began in the United States and spread to other countries, proved to be a great source of mission leadership (Truax 1979). It was especially from the last half of the nineteenth century that an ever-increasing number of missions began to bear the names of such outstanding universities as Oxford, Cambridge, London, and Yale, demonstrating that higher education was now entering into the mission enterprise.

3.2.4.3.2 Catholic Mission Strategies: A Catholic-Protestant Contrast

Although there were many similarities between the approaches of Catholic and Protestant mission societies, there were also many marked differences, not only denominational but also national. There were additionally such differences as those associated with the charism of the founder of the society and the amount of dependence on the missionary's homeland government. During the nineteenth century, we might point out, the dependence on governments, strong at times, was definitely weakening, with the mission societies showing a growing but varied self-reliance.

There was a clear difference between Catholic and Protestant societies regarding (1) ecclesiologies; (2) attitudes toward non-Christian religions and cultures; (3) nationalities involved and the degree of nationalism and ethnocentrism; and (4) mission organization—all clearly evident in the particular missionary approach followed by the particular society (Nemer 1979:16–33; 1981).

Ecclesiology. The primary goal of mission in the view of most Protestant groups was individual conversion. It was hoped that the local church would be formed of solidly, rather than partially or nominally, converted Christian members. In contrast, the primary goal of Catholic missionaries was to plant a hierarchical church. The Protestant missions were basically lay; the Catholic missions were clearly clerical. The emphasis placed on personal conversion in the case of Protestants and on sacramental life in the case of Catholics underlay much of the difference of which we speak. The Protestant missionaries were first and foremost preachers, converters of individuals; the Catholic missionaries were primarily priests and teachers. The missionary priest was assisted by a dedicated corps of lay Brothers and Sisters, who were looked upon as *assistants*. While the Protestants hoped for the blossoming of *national* churches, Catholics sought the birth of new Christian communities that would be integral parts of a *universal* Church.

Attitude Toward Non-Christian Religions and Cultures. Whereas Protestant missions sought indigeneity through their "three-self" formula,[6] the Catholic formula was "the development of an indigenous clergy culturally equal to that of the missionary."

If . . . the indigenous clergy is to achieve the results we hope for, it is absolutely necessary that they be well trained and well prepared. We do not mean a rudimentary and slipshod preparation, the bare minimum for ordination. No, their education should be complete and finished, excellent in all its phases, the same kind of education for the priesthood that a European would receive. For the local clergy is not to be trained merely to perform the humbler duties of the ministry, acting as the assistants of foreign priests. On the contrary, they must take up God's work as equals, so that some day they will be able to enter upon the spiritual leadership of their people. [Benedict XV, *Maximum illud*, no.14f]

Both Catholics and Protestants generally felt that civilization and evangelization somehow belonged together; Catholics, however, were less concerned about the relationship between the two, while the Protestants seemed to be divided, some holding that civilization was a precondition for true Christianity, others holding that civilization was a consequence and benefit of Christianity. *Civilization,* of course, was interpreted by both Catholics and Protestants ethnocentrically. Both generally viewed non-Christian religions and cultures as "not all bad" but nonetheless "worthy of pity" and basically in darkness and superstition, that is, in a deplorable moral state and desperately in need of salvation. Both Catholics and Protestants regarded education and medical work as major roles of missionaries. The attitude of both Catholics and Protestants toward non-Christian religions and cultures is clearly reflected in the metaphors used to describe mission work. Missioners were generally described in military terms, as "soldiers of Christ" who were "fighting" and "dying" on the "battlefield" for the cause of Christ.

Nationality and Nationalism. Both Catholic and Protestant missionaries of the nineteenth century generally felt that they had a "duty and obligation" to work in concert with their governments in caring for the spiritual and social needs of the peoples "providentially" entrusted to their respective countries. Britain, for instance, was regarded by British missionaries as the natural means used by Providence to spread Christian truth and justice, just as God had once used the Roman Empire. In the United States, the "manifest destiny" was unquestioned by American missionaries. Missionaries generally felt that it was only right that their countries share the "blessings" that came with colonialism, while some looked upon mission work as a kind of reparation for the sins of their country's exploitation of subjected peoples.

The Role of Clergy and Laity. The fourth important factor determining mission models was the structure of mission societies. Whereas Protestant mission organizations were voluntary *lay* structures, Catholic mission societies were generally limited to priests and/or religious. The members of Catholic societies lived by a Rule or by Constitutions and were bound by vows or promises. Protestant societies were governed through committees; Catholic missionary societies, although internally independent and governed by their own Superior General or his or her equivalent, were all subject regarding missionary work to a single Roman Congregation, that of the Propagation of the Faith which, in turn, was subject to the Supreme Pontiff. Very often, the particular activities and priorities of the Catholic society were preconditioned by the society's special "charism," for example, specialization in education or health care. Catholics lacked the type of student and university movements that Protestants had, mainly because such activities seemed unnecessary, given the fact that many of the Catholic mission societies were themselves specifically educational in character. Some of these mission societies actually conducted schools of higher learning.

3.2.5 CONTEMPORARY MISSION: 1914–1945

Despite the great defections and other profound losses during the period of the two World Wars Christianity in not a few countries,

> far from disappearing, in 1944 was a more potent force in the total world scene than it had been in 1914. Indeed, the thirty years had been one of the greatest ages of faith. Measured by the criteria of geographic extent, Christianity had not lost but gained. [Latourette 1945,7:410]

Catholic recovery from World War I was characterized by a number of significant developments that later affected mission models. (1) Social action was recognized perhaps more than ever before as a genuinely Christian responsibility. As Pius XI's *Quadragesimo anno* of 1931 emphasized, decent human beings need and demand opportunities, not alms. (2) The ecumenical movement in the Catholic Church was born and began its initial growth, evidenced in the Faith and Order Conference of Lausanne, Switzerland in 1927 and in such theological thinking as that of Yves Congar in his *Divided Christendom* (1939). These were, however, only important first steps; jealousies and competition between Catholic and Protestant mission workers still remained strong. (3) The biblical movement, thanks especially to the efforts of Père Marie-Joseph LaGrange (d. 1938) and the encyclical of Pius XII *Divino afflante spiritu*, advanced biblical scholarship to new heights. (4) The liturgical movement took on new life with an emphasis on the fact that liturgy was a *communal* act and indeed one that had to be *intelligible* to the faithful. (5) The lay apostolate promoted by Pius XI and Pius XII encouraged greater involvement of the laity in Church action and leadership. (6) A theological renewal brought new respect for the theology of St. Thomas Aquinas without being uncritically bound to it as before. (7) The missionary movement was given new life by the appointment of indigenous bishops for new mission territories.

These seven developments, which were highlighted by Richard P. McBrien (1980:646f) as reflecting the period under discussion, were clearly evident also in the missionary models that were to follow especially in post-World War II years (such as J. Hofinger's work in catechetics and liturgy, to mention but one example).

Most regrettably, the period between the two World Wars might be considered the highpoint of colonialism, with missions working hand-in-glove with colonial governments. It was only after World War II that mission countries began to be looked upon more and more as colleagues and partners of the Western church leaders.

It was during Latourette's triumphalistic-sounding "Great Century" that Britain was the undisputed leader in Protestant missionary effort. However, shortly before the outbreak of World War I, the United States had taken the lead, surpassing the British as the main supplier of Protestant mission personnel and funds. American ways, values, and spirit became more and more visible in the approach to Protestant mission work.

The involvement of American *Catholics*, on the other hand, was hardly comparable, although not insignificant (Schmidlin 1933:573–575). The Catholic Church in the United States was still struggling to survive—still building churches, schools, and other institutions for its own heavily immigrant and generally poor population, still seeking to provide personnel for its own needs.[7]

It was during the between-wars period that the dream of a world Christendom began to give way to the awareness that Christians would have to reckon with being a minority in an alien and hostile world. For the first time since Constantine, writes Latourette,

> The trend was away from the idea of *corpus Christianum*, or Christendom, a society ostensibly and collectively Christian embracing a given geographic area in which all were baptized as a matter of convention and supposedly accepted Christian standards, even if they did not fully attain them, and towards the *corpus Christi*, into which individuals moved by their own choice and which was in the world but never fully of it. [1945,7:413]

In Wilbert Shenk's words, "the 'Great Century' in missions was both a powerful last thrust of Christendom and an important instrument in bringing about the dissolution of Christendom" (1984:133). What is meant here is that not until after the First World War did Christians begin to think of themselves as they must have during the first three centuries, and not until the 1960s did Rahner's expression "the little flock" (Lk 12:32) become a favorite topic in mission circles. *Now the Christian challenge is to transform the world not by means of a powerful Christendom—by broad political pressures and cultural structures—but within a humble minority status.* As in pre-Constantinian times, it is once more the *individual* and relatively small *minorities* who must, as a part of God's own plan, work toward the realization of the Kingdom. Church growth will still nevertheless be important. As David Barrett, the editor of the *World Christian Encyclopedia* (1982), envisions it, the new mission era (A.D. 1990–   ) "is likely to emphasize, as its main characteristic, total global access to all peoples of the earth." The important word here is *access*. The Great Commission to make disciples of all nations will mean

> "Give people in every ethnolinguistic group across the world an adequate opportunity to become Christian disciples." Instead of aiming simply to reach the world, or to baptize the world, or overambitiously to convert the world, the aim becomes to disciple the world—to elicit universally a final, definitive response either for him or against him. [Barrett 1982:33]

The main characteristic of the new era will therefore be to make Christ *accessible* to all nations. *Anthropological strategies, we wish to emphasize, cannot afford to overlook this extremely important new situation in which Christians will form but a minority and in which the task of the Church will be the global access of Christ rather than actual conversion of the world. It may also very well be, as Bühlmann has been emphasizing, that the future of the Church rests not with the West but with what he calls "the Third Church."*

Chapter Four

SIGNS OF THE TIMES

No army can stop an idea whose time has come.

Victor Hugo

It is not our intention to analyze and describe in detail the signs of the times themselves but rather to indicate that such signs exist and that they all seem to be pointing in the same direction—in the direction of contextualization, inculturation, and incarnation (whatever term one prefers). These are precisely the areas in which cultural anthropology can play a major role. The signs to which we refer are the moratorium; the rapid rise and growth of independent and pentecostal churches; the rapid development of liberation and other local theologies; the spread of base communities; the rise of new ministries; the continuing strength of popular religiosity in many parts of the world; theological pluralism; ecumenical understanding and collaboration; finally, and above all, the Second Vatican Council. As the *International Bulletin of Missionary Research* in introducing its special issue (October 1985) on "Mission since Vatican II" put it,

> In the history of twentieth century Christianity, Vatican Council II stands out as a landmark that is radically affecting the course of the Christian world mission—for all Christians. It is now twenty years since the close of the council and the promulgation of the "Decree on the Church's Missionary Activity" (*Ad Gentes*, Dec. 7, 1965), and ten years since Paul VI issued his apostolic exhortation on evangelization in the modern world, *Evangelii Nuntiandi* (Dec. 8, 1975). In this period since the council there has been more change in Roman Catholic mission theology and practice than in the hundred years prior to the council, and there will be more ferment in the remaining years of this century. [9:145]

It is for this reason that so much emphasis will be placed on the Council in this chapter. Unfortunately, we shall not be able to analyze the theological trends of

106

Protestant conciliar and independent bodies. This should, however, not be interpreted as a lack of appreciation of similar movements in other Christian traditions. We recognize their impact on missiological thought and practice, as evidenced, for instance, in the spirit of the Melbourne and Pattaya meetings. (*See*, for instance, the official reports of the Commission on World Mission and Evangelism, *Your Kingdom Come* [1980], and of the Pattaya Consultation on World Evangelization, *How Shall They Hear?* [1980]. To complement our observations, one might do well also to consult such authors as Verkuyl [1978], Bassham [1979], Glasser, McGavran [1983], and, perhaps most notably, David J. Bosch's *Witness to the World: The Christian Mission in Theological Perspectives* [1980] to see the signs of the times in other Christian traditions.)

4.1 THE MORATORIUM

The end of World War II brought a worldwide awareness of human equality, a new spirit of liberation, and a hunger for political independence. Traditional colonialism was now dead. As the new spirit gained momentum and spread, the churches of the Third World did not just stand by but joined in the fray, condemning what they felt were injustices and cultural imperialism in their very own ranks (cf. Costas 1982; Bühlmann 1979). Some Third World churches, in fact, went beyond decrying what they considered paternalism and ecclesiastical bondage and demanded nothing less than a moratorium on all foreign church aid, both in personnel and money. What they wished more than anything else was for an opportunity to catch their breath and be free of alien pressure to work out their own plans for their future. Their basic argument was simple: "He who pays the piper calls the tune! So please, please don't pay the piper; *we* want to call the tune!" It was felt that nothing less than a radical, determined, and dramatic approach was called for. Outside assistance, they felt, would in fact be counterproductive; it would lead the receiving church to deeper and deeper dependence on would-be benefactors. The moratorium was bitterly debated in mission circles and was frequently written about in missiological journals. Roman Catholics and Evangelicals, although perhaps sympathetic toward the goals of the moratorium, generally rejected the strategy on theological and practical grounds.[1] What the cry for independence and equality and the moratorium clearly show—and this is our central point—is the existence today of a real hunger in both Western and non-Western churches for the opportunity to express one's faith in terms of one's own culture and real-life situation. This is an unmistakable sign of the times.

4.2 NEW INDEPENDENT CHURCH MOVEMENTS

Demands for equality among Christians antedate the recent protests just described: the Greek-speaking Jews of the infant Church complained that their widows were being neglected and that preferential treatment was being given to the widows who spoke Hebrew (Acts 6:1). There have always been schisms in the Church, for political, theological, and other reasons. There have always and everywhere been such movements as messianism, prophetism, revivalism, and, somewhat later in connection with colonialism, the cargo cults. No movement, however, has been so vibrant as the so-called Christian independence movements, especially in Africa in the post-World War II era. According to David Barrett, the number of independent African churches in 1984 was no less than 6,950, with a total membership of over 30 million, or 10 percent (Barrett 1982:782) to 15 percent (Eliade 1987, 1:82) of the entire Christian community in Africa. These churches have an annual increase of 850,000 (cf.Shank 1985:28). Unfortunate are especially the failure of not a few of the African independent churches to recognize Jesus Christ as *sole* Lord and Savior, the presence of a considerable amount of syncretism, and the alienation from the universal Church. The fact is that, despite the efforts made toward ecumenism and the formation of federations, the churches remain mostly isolated.

The reasons for the independence movements are many (Gilliland 1986), and we shall not now enter into them. Of immediate concern is the fact that independent churches are but another sign of the times. Their existence demonstrates a clear expression of a deep longing in the hearts of adherents of such churches for a Christianity that would more closely reflect *local* needs and aspirations.[2]

By contrast, the growing interdenominational understanding and cooperation, now common around the world, is itself a sign of the times that must be heeded.

4.3 LOCAL THEOLOGIES, COMMITMENT TO THE POOR, BASIC COMMUNITIES, THE CONTINUING STRENGTH OF POPULAR RELIGIOSITY, AND NEW MINISTRIES

Local theologies—and here we refer to *all* forms of local theologizing, including the Marxist variety—reflect a felt-need similar to the two just described. A comparable longing for the contextualization of the Gospel is manifested in the phenomenal growth of basic ecclesial communities, especially in Latin America.[3] There is in the world today a genuine hunger for a Christianity that is truly relevant to cultural, socioeconomic, and political situations. Such a hunger is felt especially by the oppressed peoples of the Third World who regrettably have little or no political standing in their broader societies. Developments such as local theologies (the liberation theologies in particular), new lay ministries, basic communities, and the not-so-new popular religiosity (whether we are sympathetic toward such movements or not) are clear signs of the times. Their existence leaves no doubt that contextualization is an idea whose time has indeed come.

The post-World War II years saw the rapid rise and growth of neocolonialism—old colonialism in a new garb—and, as never before, the appearance of the evils of multinational corporations and the worst aspects of capitalism. However, as historians will record, this was also the time when Christianity as never before cast its lot with the poor (Sobrino, Pico 1985). This new challenge, "the ministry of the towel" of our theological preamble (*supra*, 1.2.2), is but a further sign of the times that must speak to us loudly and clearly when we apply anthropology to mission.[4]

4.4 VATICAN II AND BEYOND

4.4.1 VATICAN II: 1962–1965

John XXIII's vision of Vatican II (a council he announced on January 25, 1959) was, as most Catholics and many non-Catholics believe, distinctly prophetic. In John XXIII's own words, the Council was to "rise like daybreak, a forerunner of most splendid light—and it is now only dawn." The Council recognized the signs of the times and was itself perhaps the greatest of such signs. According to Karl Rahner (1979), Vatican II was the most historically significant Council since the Council of Jerusalem (cf. Stacpoole 1986). Both councils marked a clear break in Church history. The Council of Jerusalem in 49 A.D. marked the passing of the infant Church from being a Jewish Christianity to something that was Gentile and Graeco-Roman. It abandoned its Judaic self-image and such revered Judaic practices as circumcision, the Sabbath, and laws regarding unclean food, practices that were not mere externals but traditions with deep theological consequences. Over the centuries, Christianity eventually became thoroughly Europeanized and, as we have seen in chapter 3, was caught up in the desirable as well as less-desirable aspects of Western history. No less revolutionary than the Council of Jerusalem was Vatican II when it assumed the theological stand that the Church is in the most literal sense of the word a *world* Church, in nature *supra*cultural. In its very essence the Church is as Asian and African as European; it must be at home with every way of life and every mentality. For the first time did a council think, feel, judge, make decisions, and act as a world entity in true collegiality and as a single People of God. Rahner, in fact, regards this new understanding of the Church as "the most general thesis on the fundamental understanding of Vatican II"—in fact, he views this stand as a statement of the Council's "theological uniqueness" (1979). The Church was conceived in the truest sense of the word as a "world" Church, not in theory but in actuality. It remains so, even though it is still imperfect and rudimentary (cf. Bühlmann 1986). From the age of the great discoveries, the Church had worldwide influence, but it was more like a large European "firm" (to use Rahner's comparison) that had a big, export program; it delivered European-packaged Christianity, under strictly Western management, and had a self-image that was definitely European. The new course taken by Vatican II is not some sort of aberration or contradiction, but rather is the result of growth and precedent, of previous insight and hope, of actualization of an existing potential. The Church required a Vatican II to steer Peter's bark in this direction. Today, more

than half of the world's 887 million Catholics live in the Third World. This fact
demonstrates a clear sign of the direction the Catholic Church, and Christianity as a whole, is taking. In this connection, it is also interesting to note that at
the 1985 special Synod in Rome called to reassess Vatican II, 6 out of 10 of the
162 bishops were from developing nations.

Figure 6 presents a missiological perspective of the sixteen Vatican II documents. All of these documents deal with the same basic topic, the mystery of
the Church, a Church that is a *world* Church, and has a *worldwide* mission.
One should note how conscious the documents are of the *local* church's
distinctiveness and how the Council is concerned about cultural relevancy.

The Vatican II documents are *basic* for any application of anthropology to
mission. There are some excellent English translations and commentaries to
consult.[5] We refer especially to such conciliar doctrines as: (1) the Church is
missionary *by her very nature* (*Ad gentes*, no.2); (2) the *whole* People of God is
missionary; *every* member (the hierarchy, clergy, religious, and laity) has a
personal missionary responsibility (*Ad gentes*, no.17,35; *Lumen gentium*,
no.33; *Apostolicam actuositatem*); (3) the Church is at the same time universal
and local (*Lumen gentium*, no.22, 26); (4) local self-determination and cultural pluriformity are a matter of justice and by no means a concession made to
a local church. These features are desirable in themselves and, in fact, they
flow from the very nature of the Church (*Christus Dominus*, no.11); (5)
human betterment and social involvement are an essential and constitutive
dimension of the Church's mission (*Gaudium et spes*); (6) ecumenical and
interfaith understanding, respect, and cooperation are an official policy of the
Catholic Church and a Christian obligation (*Unitatis redintegratio*, *Nostra
aetate*, and *Dignitatis humanae*).

Figure 6
Vatican II Documents: A Missiological Overview

I. The NATURE of the Church
    A. Basic Document—*The Dogmatic Constitution on the Church* (*Lumen
       gentium*, November 21, 1964)
    B. Secondary Documents—The Members of the Church and Their Minis-
       tries
         —*The Decree on the Bishops' Pastoral Office* (*Christus Dominus*,
           October 28, 1965)
         —*The Decree on the Ministry and Life of Priests* (*Presbyterorum
           ordinis*, December 7, 1965)
         —*The Decree on the Training of Priests* (*Optatam totius*, October 28,
           1965)
         —*The Decree on the Renewal of Religious* (*Perfectae caritatis*, Octo-
           ber 28, 1965)
         —*The Decree on the Apostolate of Lay People* (*Apostolicam actuosi-
           tatem*, November 18, 1965)

II. The MISSION of the Church
  A. Basic Document—*The Pastoral Constitution on the Church in the Modern World* (*Gaudium et spes*, December 7, 1965)
    —*Dogmatic Constitution on Divine Revelation* (*Dei verbum*, November 18, 1965)
  B. Secondary Documents—The Inner Functioning of the Church
    1. The Major Functions of the Church
      a. Proclamation and Teaching
      —*Declaration on Christian Education* (*Gravissimum educationis*, October 28, 1965)
      —*Decree on Means of Social Communication* (*Inter mirifica*, December 4, 1963)
      b. Worship—*The Constitution on Sacred Liturgy* (*Sacrosanctum concilium*, December 4, 1963)
    2. The Relationship to Other Churches
      a. Uniate Churches—*The Decree on the Eastern Catholic Churches* (*Orientalium ecclesiarum*, November 21, 1964)
      b. Other Christian Churches—*Decree on Ecumenism*, (*Unitatis redintegratio*, November 21, 1964)
    3. Mission to Non-Christians and/or the World at Large
      —*The Decree on the Church's Missionary Activity* (*Ad gentes*, December 7, 1965)
      —*Declaration on Non-Christian Religions* (*Nostra aetate*, October 28, 1965)
      —*Declaration on Religious Liberty* (*Dignitatis humanae*, November 7, 1965)

4.4.2 BEYOND VATICAN II[6]

4.4.2.1 Synods of Bishops

The Fourth International Synod of Bishops on Evangelization (1974) rejected a draft proposal and concluded with only a short and disappointing "Declaration." Nevertheless, the synod represented many months of serious preparation at both the national and regional levels. It was the stimulus for the writing of Paul VI's apostolic exhortation *Evangelii nuntiandi*, the Roman Catholic Magna Charta on the mission of the Church. Ten years later, and twenty years after Vatican II, an Extraordinary Synod of Bishops was called in 1985 to evaluate the Council's impact and to renew the Church's effort in carrying out the agenda set forth by Vatican II.[7]

4.4.2.2 Evangelii Nuntiandi

The preparatory materials and other documents connected with the 1974 synod, especially Paul VI's synthesis of December 8, 1975, the *Evangelii nuntiandi*, proved to be important vehicles for *reaffirming, clarifying, balancing, concretizing,* and indeed *further developing* the mission thinking of Vatican II. Ideas were developed after a decade of thought and worldwide experience (cf. Luzbetak 1979a).

The statements that were *reaffirmed* and *reinforced* included the various conciliar doctrines calling for the mobilization and engagement of the whole Church for evangelization; recognizing the role of the Church in liberation; calling for humanization as an essential part of the Church's mission; appreciating the right of local churches to their own cultural faith-expressions; and accepting non-Christian faiths as, ultimately, a part of God's own plan of salvation.

The *further clarification* of the official teaching of Vatican II to which we refer is the result of Paul VI's serious concern about the need to bring balance to some of the overemphases and exaggerated conclusions drawn from such conciliar doctrines as, for instance, the right of an individual to follow his or her own conscience, the role of the Church regarding liberation and humanization, and the right of local churches to self-determination in harmony with their own cultures and traditions. In the mind of the pope, these all represent areas of concern that have experienced some overemphasis since the Council and that now possibly call for correction. The exhortation stressed the fact that while the Church recognizes the salvific character of non-Christian religions, one must be careful so as to uphold the uniqueness and normative character of Christ as sole universal Savior. *Evangelii nuntiandi* sought balance also for instance by pointing out that while being deeply concerned about church growth to the farthest corners of the earth, the Christian should not overlook the new missionary challenge, the post-Christian neo-paganism at home.

The synod was responsible for more than merely reaffirming and clarifying conciliar teaching and balancing misguided reinterpretations. The synodal documents, especially the *Evangelii nuntiandi*, served to help *concretize* some of the conciliar ideas. Whereas Vatican II called the attention of Chistians to "the signs of the times," *Evangelii nuntiandi* sought to illustrate how such authentic signs of God's presence might more easily be recognized. It showed, too, how these signs might serve as guides for action. Similarly, the apostolic exhortation not only confirmed the important roles of the laity in the life of the Church but also pointed out more concretely how the laity might be directly involved in evangelizing the world. Thanks to this concretization and ten-year experience, Paul VI was also able to introduce many *new ideas*, including the components of evangelization, the relation of liberation and human development, and the roles for base communities. After *Evangelii nuntiandi*, the most important mission-related document was John Paul II's *Catechesis tradendae* (1979b).

4.4.2.3 Other Postconciliar Developments

Besides documents (for which *see*, for instance, the various issues of the newsletter of the Pontifical Council for Culture, the *Church and Cultures*,

1982–1987; Carrier 1987; Gremillion 1985; Flannery 1975, 1982), there is another set of important indicators of the impact of the Council on Catholic understanding of mission. These indicators are the *actual present-day practices of regional churches*. Latin America provides an excellent illustration. Today, Latin American Catholics view the mission of the Church in an entirely new light, with emphasis on self-determination and liberation. This is the direction that the Latin American Catholics will be taking for the foreseeable future. There is in Latin America a new awareness of the close relationship between faith and real life. There has also been a significant increase in the number of Catholic Bible study groups that regularly reflect on Scripture from the point of view of the actual local situation and the particular cultural heritage (*see* Cardenal 1976–1982). With the birth and subsequent development of liberation theology, the Latin American churches have become conscious as never before of the social dimensions of sin and of Christ as the sole and true liberator. New structures, especially the so-called "basic ecclesial communities" have become important features of Latin American Catholic life. This is a fact that is clearly reflected in the Puebla Documents (Eagleson, Scharper 1979:19, 52, 110, 290, 303–305, 317f, 375–337) and that is indicative of the direction that the Church of tomorrow will be taking. A similar phenomenon is observable in other parts of the Third World: there, too, the Good News is being studied and interpreted in terms of symbols, values, and traditions that are truly indigenous and timely. In the United States, the new postconciliar missiological direction has been voiced perhaps best of all in two documents. The first is the joint statement by the Conference of Major Superiors of Men and the Leadership Conference of Women Religious, entitled *Our Hopes and Concerns for Mission* (1976; cf. S. Smith 1977). They express concerns about timid, limited, and shallow understandings of missionary responsibility, while their main hopes were (1) that the U. S. response to the plea of missionary churches for self-determination would avoid all superficiality and tokenism; (2) that American Catholics would be engaged in missionary work not so much *for* newer churches as *with* them; and (3) that the goal of American involvement in mission work would consist not only in giving but in receiving as well, not only in enriching but also in being enriched. One cannot but applaud the anthropological wisdom and the cross-cultural sensitivity reflected in such a selection of mission goals. The second document to which we refer is the National Council of Catholic Bishops' *To the Ends of the Earth: A Pastoral Statement on World Mission* (1986a), a document that is as much a commitment to mission action as it is an exhortation, as much a statement of the laity, religious, and priests as of the bishops themselves.

4.4.2.4 Theological Crosscurrents

4.4.2.4.1 The General Situation

Postconciliar mission anthropologists will have to adjust to postconciliar theology. This is no small challenge, considering the turbulent theological crosscurrents of our times. Although considerable progress in mission thought has been achieved since Vatican II, contemporary mission theology must nevertheless be described as being in no small measure confused, contradictory, and tentative. Much of this confusion and contradiction is understandable. Like all other major councils of the Church, Vatican II represented the close of one phase of theological thinking and the opening of a whole new phase of questioning. For instance, the call of Vatican II for *every* Christian to participate in mission could not but be blurred by the birth of a new nationalism and the demand for independence from Western churches. Similarly, the call of Vatican II for the evangelization of the world as first priority came into direct conflict with the heart-rending pleas for basic human rights and social justice. Surely it is not easy to speak of God's infinite love and mercy to a father whose family is dying of hunger. There were also the ever-present conflicting priorities of the local church and those of the universal Church. There was the urgent need, for example, for internal reform of a homeland church on the one hand, and the seeming luxury of maintaining church growth overseas on the other. There was the choice between combating paganism at home or fighting paganism abroad. There were also the contradictory views regarding the need for openness to pluralism, on the one hand, and the need for loyalty to the Gospel on the other. There were tensions arising from the need for respect for another's conscience and the need for tolerance toward the undesirable consequences of such respect. There were tensions arising from the need to convert individuals to Christ the Lord of Heaven and Earth, on the one hand, and the rightful concern to help make individuals better Hindus, Moslems, or Buddhists (that is, to make them into better children of the One Father of All). Or again, the emphasis on the institutional nature of the Church has sometimes led to a de-emphasis of, or even a disregard for, the Church as a sign of God's loving and active presence in the world among *all* his creatures. An emphasis on the institutional nature of the Church (as has been traditionally the case of pre-Vatican II ecclesiology since St. Robert Bellarmine) has sometimes unduly excluded independent faith-expressions. Some Christian churches, reacting to the excessive role of the institutional Church, have, however, become excessively absorbed in themselves. Whereas some Roman Catholics tend toward institutionalism, evangelical theology tends toward "an emaciated Gospel," a Gospel not of this world. Protestant conciliar theology aims, toward "a diluted Gospel," a here-and-now salvation (cf. Bosch 1980). True Christian witness, however, should be threefold: simultaneously institutional, not of this world, *and* here-and-now.

4.4.2.4.2 Paradigm Shift

Much of the confusion, contradiction, and tension is due to the liberal theologizing occasioned by a paradigm shift; theologians have gone from a deductive to an inductive approach, which in turn sometimes has led them to conclusions that went beyond the official teaching of the Church, if not against the Scriptures (cf. Burrows 1985; Sheehan 1984).

Neither the deductive nor the inductive approach is really new. The "from-above" deductive christology is exemplified in the Gospel of St. John. There we hear of a pre-existent Word who comes down to earth, taking on human flesh and, as God-Man, setting an example for all, redeeming his brothers and sisters by dying on the cross for them, then rising from the dead, returning to heaven to prepare a lasting home for his followers, once again to appear triumphantly and gloriously as Lord and Judge of the living and the dead. Theology "from above" reflects on what Christ was from the beginning—he was God who became man in the Incarnation. Theology "from below," by contrast, reflects on what Christ did especially at the end—how this human being through his dedication and death proved to be God. During the early christological controversies, the "from-above" approach was followed by the Alexandrian School, for instance by Clement, Athanasius, and Origen. Christology "from below," by contrast, does not begin with a proposition declaring the fact of the Incarnation, of a pre-existent Word, but rather with an account about a particular person, Jesus, who was in every way like ourselves except for sin. Unlike the "from-above" theology of the Gospel of St. John, the theology of the Synoptics represents a theology "from below." Although St. Paul occasionally speaks of Christ's pre-existence (e.g., Rom 8:13; Gal 4:4), the central mystery of his theology seems not to be the Incarnation but Jesus' death and resurrection. Such was also the approach of the Antiochene School in the early christological debates. St. Augustine felt that it was through the Man-Christ that we best can progress to the knowledge of the God-Christ (*Sermo* 261, no.7). We mention these strictly theological matters because as missiological anthropologists we shall inescapably have to deal with what seems to be a paradigmatic shift in theological thinking. Today, the "from-below" thinking seems to be the preferred approach of most theologians. Today, the starting point in theologizing is the consideration of the created cosmos, humanity, the current sociopolitical situations of the time and place, and history.

Our task in missiological anthropology is not to argue theology. We feel, however, that some remarks about the subject are quite relevant. When one begins to apply anthropology to mission one must be wary of *both* approaches. An exaggerated "from-above" stance tends to deprive Christ of his humanity. One could, as the Monophysitists and Docetists did, make Christ only appear *as if* he were human. An exaggerated "from-below" emphasis, on the other hand, as in the case of Nestorianism and Adoptionism, would deprive Christ of his divinity, and would attribute to him only a purely human nature, albeit with a very distinctive and key function in God's Kingdom. What is important to keep in mind when applying anthropology to mission is the fact that one can go overboard on either side of Peter's bark.

Much of the present-day theological tentativeness of which we speak is associated with the radicalization and demythologization of theology. The conclusions drawn are often different from, and even contradictory to, traditionally accepted doctrines. Then too, in an attempt to take seriously the faith

experiences of non-Christians, some contemporary missiologists do not hesitate to relativize the Good News and to strip it of its uniqueness, universality,
normativeness, and finality. The resurrection of Jesus and his miracles, for
instance, are interpreted as religious myth rather than history. The argument
goes as follows: The tendency to mythologize is, after all, a normal God-
intended human process present in all sacred books and is a phenomenon that
occurs in all religions. Why, then, should it not occur in the Bible and in the
Judaeo-Christian tradition as well? For a believer, the argument goes, what
counts is not whether the myth as such represents historical events, but rather
that it represents an actual, meaningful faith-value. Thus Christ's resurrection
is sometimes described by modern liberal theologians as something "other than
a physical" resurrection, while Christ's substantive divinity is reduced to mere
divine functions. These are but some examples of the crosscurrents and treacherous whirlpools missiological anthropologists are caught in today.

We come now to a very important question: If a biblical scholar arrives at a
conclusion contrary to a traditional understanding of Scripture, does it follow
that the scholar necessarily denies such articles of faith? Is a mission anthropologist, who is not a theologian but a firm believer in what his or her faith
teaches, to write off such scholars as atheists and heretics? Dealing with the
subject, Thomas Sheehan sees in radical theologizing a most threatening
"revolution" and a veritable "dismantling" of traditional Roman Catholic
theology (1984). David Tracy, on the other hand, distinguishes between faith
and theology.

> The fact is that one would be hard-pressed to find a Catholic biblical
> scholar who denies [the divinity of Christ or the reality of the Trinity].
> They believe those doctrines even while holding that, on the scriptural
> evidence alone as interpreted through historico-critical methods, the
> historian as historian can hardly be expected to know much about what
> Jesus actually thought. Moreover, given the nature of the scriptures as
> confessional documents, the historian can reach the plausible conclusion
> that in many cases it is more likely that statements attributed to Jesus
> were added by Christian believers who wrote these texts to affirm their
> faith in Jesus Christ rather than made by Jesus himself. [Tracy 1984:427]

Before we stamp the label *heretical* on the works of all liberal theologians, we
must, as Tracy reminds us, be careful to determine which of the four possible
Jesuses the particular theologian is talking about: (1) the so-called historical
Jesus, the Jesus as he appears exclusively on the basis of the New Testament
accounts after the accounts have been thoroughly examined under the micro-
scope of purely scientific historico-critical methods; (2) the real Jesus who
actually walked the earth—taking into account all that he actually thought,
actually did, and actually said, whether these actions are included in the New
Testament accounts or not; (3) the Jesus as he was remembered and understood

by his followers decades after his death; (4) the Jesus of faith as witnessed in the Scriptures, tradition, and present-day Christian experience in word and sacrament (Tracy 1984:428).

Without necessarily espousing liberal theology as such, the mission anthropologist could well appreciate the fact that the liberal theologian is trying to say that *on historico-critical grounds alone* (i.e., on the basis of purely scientific criteria, using the Bible as purely human evidence, and therefore apart from faith), one cannot prove or disprove that such Christian beliefs as the virgin birth, the incarnation, the miracles, the resurrection, revelation, and eternal salvation are historical facts.

Without necessarily supporting liberal theology, one can nevertheless appreciate the fact that the historico-critical arguments can be, and often are, only *one* set among many tools used by theologians. Often they are meant primarily as a kind of corrective rather than a constitutive factor in determining what a Christian should believe and be. The theologian's job may not yet be finished, nor does the theologian necessarily claim that it is. As Tracy puts it, "We believe *in* Jesus Christ *with* the apostles." Text *and* tradition come into play as essential and integral parts of the theological process. Whether liberal or conservative or in-between, tradition mediates faith in word, sacrament, and action, a tradition received from the apostles and transmitted to us through the Church. (Tracy 1984:428; cf. *Dei Verbum*, no.7–10.) Tradition needs a critical examination too. *Ecclesia semper reformanda* ("the Church is ever in need of reform") is a maxim particularly congenial to liberal theologians; it is nevertheless a maxim to some degree at least acceptable across the whole spectrum of theological opinion. Just as the interpretation of the Scriptures is subject to constant study and further clarification and development, so the Church's tradition must undergo constant re-examination, re-evaluation, and reformation. The mission anthropologist, like the theologian, needs a hermeneutic of tradition, which would include conciliar documents, papal and episcopal pronouncements, theological opinions, the sense of the faithful, and much more. Those less sympathetic toward liberal theology must nevertheless recognize that some of the "rebellion" against the official teaching of the Catholic Church are really cases of "loyal opposition." (*See* Tracy 1984:429.) As intimated above, these paragraphs are not intended to serve as a kind of defense of liberal opinion as such; rather, we are saying that, theoretically speaking, applied anthropology can be based on a variety of theologies. In actual practice, however, the mission anthropologist must remain faithful to his or her conscience as well as to the official teaching of the Church served (*supra*, 2.3.2.1, 2.3.2.4). The applications presented and advocated in the present work reflect this particular author's faith convictions. Above all, they reflect his belief in the uniqueness and normativeness of Jesus Christ and the author's personal understanding of the official teaching regarding the nature and mission of the Church. As the Extraordinary Synod of Bishops of 1985 emphasized, the agenda for mission set by Vatican II is still valid after twenty years and will be valid for many decades to come. Mission anthropologists with other theological orientations will have to make the appropriate adjustments.

Owing to the close connection between missiology and anthropology, it is impossible to practice mission anthropology today without some acquaintance with the modern theological crosscurrents of which we speak. What follows is but a quick look at the state of the art within Protestantism and Catholicism, at least as a basic background for applying anthropology to mission. For a more complete survey of current trends, especially in regard to the relativization and radicalization of christology and ecclesiology—the two tracts that touch anthropological application most closely—one might profitably refer to such very readable works as Dulles 1974, 1976, 1985; Lane 1975; O'Collins 1977; Richard 1981; McBrien 1980:369–546. For more in-depth study of recent christological and ecclesiological trends one would, of course, have to go to the classics and be acquainted with the views and writings of such well-known Catholic writers as Rahner, Kasper, Küng, Schillebeeckx, Teilhard de Chardin, and many others, as well as such Protestant counterparts as Cobb, Robinson, Altizer, Cox, Pannenberg, and Moltmann, and the early pace-setters Tillich, Bonhoeffer, and Bultmann. McBrien describes the highly diversified theological spectrum in the following terms:

> At the *far left* one might place the *process theologians* (Hulsbosch, Schoonenberg, and Pittenger—Teilhard himself is too complex for categorization, and so, too, perhaps is Cobb) Küng, Bultmann, Tillich, Altizer, and Van Buren. To their right, but still *clearly left-of-center* on the total spectrum, are Schillebeeckx, Mackey, the *liberation theologians* (Boff and Sobrino), Bonhoeffer, Robinson, and Moltmann. At the *center* is Rahner. Slightly to his right, Kasper, Cullmann, and Meyendorff. Further to the right, Pannenberg. Fully to the right, Barth. [1980:504]

We shall, of course, be able to offer only a few examples of this wide range of views, many of which run counter, or more or less counter, to Vatican II. Our purpose is to illustrate the climate of the times rather than to describe each view and to take a corresponding stand on each. We leave this latter task to theologians. It is interesting to note that while Catholic theology has shifted considerably to the left, Protestant theologians (who, by the way, preceded Catholics in radicalizing theology) seem to have now moved more toward the right.

4.4.2.4.3 Crosscurrents within Protestantism

On the one extreme we find Karl Barth (1886–1968), the Fundamentalists, and the Evangelicals (both Conservative and Ecumenical). All three require nothing less than an explicit knowledge—a personal experience of Christ's saving power—and therefore an explicit acceptance of Christ as a *conditio sine qua non* for salvation. On the other extreme are relativists like Troeltsch and radicals like the "death-of-God" theologians. Protestant theology today might, however, be best described as generally striving to steer a middle course.

Karl Barth (1886–1968), perhaps the best-known exclusivist, was a staunch defender of the absoluteness of Christ. To give any recognition at all to a non-Christian religion ("the slightest deviation, the slightest concession") would in itself be a betrayal of Christ.

By contrast, Ernst Troeltsch (1865–1923) claimed that Christ was but one among many other founders of great religions. He felt that Christianity is true only in the Christian context—true only to the believer. Despite this relativity, it should be noted, Troeltsch nevertheless considered Christianity the most complete of such relative religions.

Rudolf Bultmann (d. 1976) followed a basically humanistic approach, claiming that there was very little that we could know from Scriptures about the actual life and personality of Jesus. Accordingly, our knowledge of Jesus merely reflects what the early Church believed him to be; therefore, to reconstruct an "historical Jesus" would be impossible. Jesus' mission consisted in proclaiming the Kingdom of God, a Kingdom conceived as a power within ourselves and focused on ourselves. This Kingdom enables us to be authentically human and to assume fully the responsibility for our lives. Resurrection is something that happened to the disciples' minds and hearts rather than to Jesus; one cannot therefore speak of Christ as being divine.

Altizer and Van Buren, in their "death-of-God" theology of the 1960s, declared the transcendent God to be "dead." To their thinking, the divine and the supernatural are nothing more than *our* way of looking at the human and natural. This most radical of theologies is a denial of God and a clear distortion of the basic mission of the Church. Even if to believe in Christ is to imitate him in the service of one's neighbor, as "death-of-God" theology would have it, the type of humanism advocated does not recognize the Lordship of Christ. In a word, "death-of-God" theology is plain atheistic Christianity, hardly a basis for Christian mission anthropology.

Shubert M. Ogden (1961) argued that "to believe in Christ" was synonymous with "to understand oneself authentically." Accordingly, such authentic self-understanding has necessarily occurred in *all* religions inasmuch as God is the God of the whole world. He is therefore present and active in the whole world and in all religions—not only in Jesus and in the religion of his followers.

Another crosscurrent is evident in the theory of John Cobb (1975) who advocated a "Logos" theology. Christ is *the* Way only relatively speaking—in the sense that this Way does not exclude other ways. In other words, Christ must be relativized according to the given cultural context. The Logos is in fact incarnate in every human being, while Jesus, inasmuch as his very "selfhood" was incarnated, represents the most perfect and normative incarnation.

John Hick (1973) presented a further example of radical contemporary theology, by denying the uniqueness and normative nature of Christ and the Church on the grounds that God, being the God of the whole world, is therefore active also outside of Christianity. Christianity, like all religions, is a human creation; the Gospel presentation of the incarnation must be understood mythologically, and Christ's uniqueness must be interpreted in a purely subjective and relativistic sense. Hick granted that no one has revealed God and his saving power in the way Christ has; nevertheless, in Jesus, God was acting through a purely human being. Jesus was "Christ" in the sense that "Christ" is to be found in all religions. Hick's reasoning flows from his understanding of God as Agape—to be more exact, as a *process* of Agapeing. Jesus is therefore not God himself but only a mythologized expression of what the attitude of human beings toward God should be. Christ differs from us only in degree and as such can be found in other religions as well.

John A. T. Robinson (1973) combines elements of Teilhard de Chardin and John Hick. Like the latter theologian, Robinson claims that God is in the process of Agapeing. Christ is not Agape in substance but is a Christian mythical expression of what the true relationship of human beings with God should be. Like Teilhard de Chardin, Robinson holds that Christ is in process. Jesus is the "clue" to Christ, while Christ is the "clue" to God (Robinson 1973:229). Robinson uses the term "clue" advisedly, since he is speaking of a process rather than of a realization; that is to say, Jesus is not really Christ, nor is Christ really God. In recent times, this "cosmic Christ" concept was taken up by the World Council of Churches (cf. Hallencreutz 1970:56-62) to explain Christ's universality. Christ is head not only of the Church but of all humanity as well. He is therefore present in all religions and in every aspect of human history. He is the *Lord* of History. The mission of the Church is therefore not so much to introduce Christ to the non-Christian as it is to help the non-Christian find Christ in his or her particular non-Christian faith.[8]

Steering—or at least striving to steer—a middle course between exclusivism on the one extreme and relativism on the other are Wolfhart Pannenberg and Carl E. Braaten, a close follower of Pannenberg. According to Pannenberg (1967, 1968), God is indeed present in non-Christian religions and he is truly experienced by non-Christians; however, and this is vital, God cannot be known in such religions sufficiently for a non-Christian to be saved through Christ. In the last analysis, Pannenberg is an exclusivist. Similarly, according to Braaten (1980:2–8), Christ is unique and universal. Christ is unquestionably not *a* Savior or *a* Lord but *the* Savior and *the* Lord of *all* places and times. This exclusive claim

> is not a footnote to the gospel; it is the gospel itself. . . . The issue of Jesus' uniqueness finally has to do with the resurrection. . . . The true identity of Jesus can be acknowledged only by faith in him as the risen Lord and living Christ. We do not expect that anyone will confess the uniqueness of Jesus in the special sense implied by the sum of Christological titles by means of a historiographical reconstruction of the historical Jesus. That Jesus is dead and buried and will always remain sealed in the tomb to people who do not believe. . . . What is unique about Jesus, however, is precisely his universal meaning. [1980:4]

When Braaten discusses salvation, he does not mean just any form of "salvation" (for instance, this-worldly political, economic or psychological salvation). There are admittedly many such "saviors." Braaten has in mind, rather, an *eschatological* salvation. Apart from Christ, eschatological salvation is impossible. In this sense, non-Christian religions are not salvific; such salvation comes through Christ and through him alone. There seems to be no substantive disagreement between the Pannenberg-Braaten point of view and that of the official teaching of the Catholic Church (especially Vatican II and *Evangelii nuntiandi*). This leaves open the question of *how* a non-Christian religion can be salvific.

4.4.2.4.4 Crosscurrents within Roman Catholicism

No less radical than some of the Protestant views described are many of the opinions of Roman Catholic theologians (cf. Burrows 1985). For instance, in Paul Knitter's view (1978, 1985), there are other saviors besides Christ. Knitter attributes Christianity's claim to exclusivity and uniqueness for Jesus to "the historically conditioned world view and thought-patterns of the time" (1978:154). Because God is the God of all that exists, and because he desires the salvation of all human beings, revelation and salvation must be found also in religions other than Christianity. True religion must therefore be *theocentric* rather than Christocentric.

Raymond Panikkar believes that "Christ" is synonymous with "God the Son, the Word, Logos, the Alpha and Omega," but not with "Jesus of Nazareth." Jesus was indeed Christ, but Christ is not to be identified with the person Jesus. The name that is above every other name (Phil 2:9) is not "Jesus" but "Christ." All religions in some way recognize the same Christ, Logos, and Son of God—the mythic Christ that sanctifies and saves also in religions that are not Christian; this Logos is merely called by other names, such as Isvara, Tathagata or even Jahweh, and Allah. Consistent with his *theo*centric focus, Panikkar advocates an *intra*religious dialogue before entering an interreligious one (1978). His is a "universal christology," fundamental in character, that would "make room not only for different theologies but also for different religions." In his own case, Panikkar describes this internal conversion to his understanding of Christ as "I 'left' as a Christian, I 'found' myself a Hindu and I 'return' a Buddhist without ever having ceased to be a Christian" (1978:2).

Hans Küng, especially in his *On Being a Christian* (1976b), *Christianity and World Religions* (1986), and *The Church* (1976a), regards the Incarnation as functional rather than essential, as *representing* God rather than *being* God. The Man-Jesus *represents* God before humanity and humanity before God. The uniqueness of Christ consists in the superiority of his message, and in this sense he is normative for all even while other religions retain their value. Christ, however, should not be regarded as the "Savior of All"; rather, the non-Christian must seek God *in his or her own religion* until he or she is confronted existentially by Christ. Christian proclamation is necessary so as to make such a confrontation possible. Unlike Rahner, Küng does not regard the Church as the Sacrament that *brings about* the Kingdom—God alone can do that. The Church is merely a herald announcing the reign of God and proclaiming his salvific action in the world. Küng views the Church as being both local and universal, with the universal Church being more than the sum-total of its parts. Together, the local churches become a *new* entity, a single organism. Each local church nevertheless manifests the whole Body of Christ. The papacy is important to Küng, but in itself the papacy does not indicate where the Church is. In general, Küng's ecclesiology can be said to be strongly influenced by the thinking of the Reformation, and by Lutheranism in particular.

In general, the radical theology, or aspects of theology, to which we refer seem to be saying that the task of the Church and mission anthropology is not so much that of preaching Christ as that of preaching *God*. The goal is not so much to make disciples of all nations as to help the Moslems, Hindus, and Buddhists become better Moslems, Hindus, Buddhists, or whatever. The main task of tomorrow's Church, therefore, is not to convert peoples to Christ but rather to help them cling more faithfully to the best of their non-Christian traditions so as to live the full personal and social implications of their own religions more authentically (Baum 1974).

Among the various crosscurrents within Roman Catholicism, we must also include the radical versions of liberation theology (*see* Ratzinger 1986, 1984; Kloppenburg 1974a). Meant here are the liberation theologies that politicize the Gospel as if all that mattered in the New Testament were the reconstructed historical Jesus, the revolutionist who would have lived to a ripe old age and who would have died a natural death if he had not been so intent on bringing about *social* change to his homeland. The substance of the Good News according to such extreme liberation theologies seems to be, "Seek ye first the kingdom of this world and all else will be added unto ye!" We do not deny that liberation theology as such makes good sense (Gibellini 1987; Boff, Boff 1987; Ferm 1986; Ratzinger 1984, 1986) and that it can form a solid basis for missiological anthropology. What we are referring to at the moment is the uncritical Marxist ideology and associated assumptions, especially class-hatred and the uncritical and unrestrained rhetoric that sometimes takes over and reduces salvation (and liberation theology itself) to inevitable class struggle and revolution as the determining factor in all of history and in all aspects of life, including the development of the very idea of religion and God.[9]

4.4.3 OFFICIAL CATHOLIC TEACHING

Before proceeding, the reader might do well to review what had been said earlier about value judgments in applying anthropology to mission, especially what has been said about serving the client (*supra,* 2.2.3.3 and 2.3.2). What are the basic Catholic teachings that are presupposed in Catholic mission anthropology?

There are two opposing missiological currents in the understanding of the official Catholic teaching regarding salvation and mission. Our line of reasoning is that of Ferguson (1982, 1984). Both currents claim to be supportive of, and compatible with, Vatican II. The one is classicist; the other, "modern" or "new." The one is based on traditional concepts; the other, on a new ecclesiology and christology. The one follows a deductive "from-above" methodology; the other, an inductive "from-below" approach. The traditional direction is represented, for instance, by André Seumois (*see* especially *Théologie Missionaire*, 5 vols., 1973–1981); the other, the so-called "new" direction, is advocated by more liberal mission thinkers like futurologist Walbert Bühlmann (1977, 1978, 1979, 1980, 1986) and, to a large measure, by most liberation theologians. Karl Rahner would have to be included in this broad "new" or "modern" group. What follows is an an overview of these two contrasting directions. It should be kept in mind that in the description of "the official Catholic teaching" that follows we are speaking of a broad mainstream, with one group more to the right and the other to the left. As just emphasized, both groups respect the thinking of Vatican II, and they both seek to develop a deeper understanding of salvation and mission that is compatible with the "official teaching." Finally, it should be noted that our usage of the term "traditional" in no way implies "out-of-date"; nor do "new" and "modern," as we understand the terms, necessarily connote "correct" and "better." The two directions, however, do suggest important differences, not only in their methodology but also in their basic concepts and conclusions—concepts and conclusions that are of vital importance for any truly meaningful application of anthropology to the mission of the Church.

4.4.3.1 The Nature of Salvation

The classicist's understanding of *salvation* is eschatological and therefore refers *primarily* to soul-saving, to the hereafter, and to final and eternal salvation rather than to any form of salvation or liberation here on earth. To new missiology, on the other hand, salvation is definitely a matter of *both* the now *and* the hereafter, with a strong emphasis on the concerns of the present life; humanization is associated with salvation as a constitutive and essential dimension of salvation.

Vatican II describes salvation as being *primarily* eschatological rather than this-worldly (*see* the basic document, *The Dogmatic Constitution on the Church*). The clear precedence it gives to the eschatological character of salvation is closer to the views of the traditionalists. However, the Council sees an extremely important, and in fact fundamental and *direct*, relationship between salvation and this world: the Church, like Christ, is sent *to* the world and *for* the world. The Church is a *Servant* Church whose option is clearly for the poor, the weak, and the dispossessed (*Lumen gentium*, no.8; *Gaudium et spes*, no.39). One of the two basic conciliar documents, as its title *The Pastoral Constitution on the Church in the Modern World* indicates, is thoroughly this-worldly, historical, and social in character. The Synod of 1971 supported and confirmed the validity and importance of such concerns by its dictum "the participation in the transformation of the world fully appears . . . as *constitutive* of the preaching of the Gospel [emphasis added]."[10]

4.4.3.2 The Uniqueness and Universality of Christ

If Christ were not unique and universal, normative and final, most of what the present author understands as mission, whether in non-Christian or Christian lands, would make little sense indeed. A unique and universal Christ is what the Gospel is all about, current radical theologizing notwithstanding. On this single basic theological premise alone much that an anthropologist may or may not have to suggest will depend.

The age-old debate about the salvation of unbelievers was reopened in the 1960s, shortly before the Second Vatican Council, especially by Karl Rahner. Despite the maxim *Extra ecclesiam nulla salus* ("There is no salvation outside the Church"), it had been held over the centuries that non-Christians through the mercy of God and the merits of Christ were not excluded from salvation but that *somehow* they could be saved through the merits of Christ. This salvation could occur, for instance, by a kind of sacrament of desire, a *desiderium sacramenti*, a *votum fidei*, or in some other way known perhaps only to God himself. Rahner proposed a new philosophically based rather than scripturally based theory of salvation for those who through no fault of their own did not and could not know Christ, a theory called "Anonymous Christianity."[11]

Anonymous Christianity was Rahner's answer to the apparent dilemma that has troubled theologians from the early centuries of Christianity. Theologians have tried to reconcile the idea of the salvific will of God and the maxim that there is no salvation outside the Church. According to Rahner, non-Christians, even without knowing it, possess a religion that bears within itself true saving grace. In fact, this hidden grace is *Christ's* grace, who is the brother of *all* humankind.

Perhaps most non-Christians would find the term *Anonymous Christian* offensive, but Rahner insists that the term is not meant for dialogue but rather for purely internal use. Moreover, Rahner points out, the term has the advantage of being *positive*. It exposes the positive attitude of the Christian toward non-Christians: "God loves *all* his children!" To anyone who accepts the theory of Anonymous Christianity, non-Christians become something more than just "pagans" and "infidels" groping in the darkness of sin and night of heathenism. This is, however, not to say that their knowledge of the God of Love is not limited and incomplete, and that it will remain such until the Anonymous Christian gets to know Christ, experiences and accepts him as Lord and Savior, as the Word and Image of the Father—so much like the Father that who "has seen me has seen the Father" (Jn 14:9). In fact, Rahner claims that the non-Christian society has an obligation to abandon the old religion for the new as soon as the Gospel is sufficiently experienced.

Knitter, who has little use for Rahner's theory, nevertheless presents Rahner's views very clearly and exactly when he describes Anonymous Christianity in the following well-chosen words.

> First, Christ is the *constitutive cause* of salvation (this term is not Rahner's). Whatever saving grace is present in the world has been constituted and caused by the event of Jesus Christ. Rahner, however, does not consider Christ as *efficient* cause of grace, as if Jesus had to *do* something to bring about God's universal love. Rather, Christ is the *final* cause of God's universal salvific will, what God, from the beginning of time, had in mind in calling and offering grace to all humankind. Jesus of Nazareth, then, is the final goal, the end product of the entire process of universal revelation and grace. For Rahner, that final goal is a necessary cause of salvation. Without that goal, realized in one historical individual, the entire process would not take place: "God desires the salvation of everyone; and this salvation is the salvation won by Christ. . . . *This* relationship of God to man [the supernatural existential] . . . rests on the Incarnation, death, and resurrection of the one Word of God become flesh." . . . Jesus Christ as the final, constitutive case [sic] of salvation, tells humanity what it is, where it is going, what it can hope to achieve. [1985:128f]

It should be noted further that although the Church is not identified with Christ, it is nevertheless, according to Rahner, a continuation of him. Although not all grace is channeled exclusively through the Church, non-Christians are nonetheless unconsciously oriented toward the Church as the continuation of Christ (Knitter 1985:129).

By no means does Rahner's theory nullify the Church's worldwide mission. It nevertheless gives mission action an entirely different orientation, a far more positive direction. The dominant goal of mission action is no longer to save pagans from hell-fire and to provide exclusive membership cards for heaven but rather to make the non-Christians more aware of what they already are— that is to say, true children of God (Knitter 1985:129f).

At first, while many Catholic theologians accepted Rahner's theory, others seriously questioned it or rejected it outright. Today, most Catholic theologians accept some form of the theory. As we have seen, some of Rahner's more liberal admirers, however, have gone well beyond Rahner and beyond what might be regarded as the official teaching of their Church.

Although Vatican II left many questions unanswered regarding the relation between Christianity and non-Christian religions, it nevertheless quite insightfully insisted (after McBrien 1980:667–690) that non-Christian religions, such as Judaism, Islam, Hinduism, and Buddhism, deserve the highest respect (*Ad gentes*, no.10); that such religions provide not only human answers to life's problems but precious religious values as well (*Gaudium et spes*, no.12); that non-Christian religions reflect true human goodness expressed in their rites and symbols and that they contain true treasures of the ascetical and contemplative life (*Ad gentes*, no.15,18); that non-Christian religions are part and parcel of God's providence and design (*Ad gentes*, no. 3); that even doctrinal differences often contain elements of truth and that they therefore demand respect (*Dignitatis humanae*, no.2; *Gaudium et spes*, no.2–4); and that Christians should enter into dialogue with non-Christians in a spirit of love and out of a sincere desire for mutual enrichment (*Gaudium et spes*, no.92; *Ad gentes*, no.11,12,16,18,34; *Dignitatis humanae*, no.2,3,5). But all this is quite different from any relativization that would deprive Christ and his Church of their uniqueness, universality, normativeness, and finality. Nowhere does Vatican II state that non-Christian religions, in themselves and apart from Christ, are ways of salvation (*Gaudium et spes*, no.22; Stransky 1985:156f). Even if, as we have just said, the council leaves many questions unanswered, one thing remains beyond the least shadow of doubt: salvation can come through Jesus Christ and through him alone. Relativization would largely void the need for a *world* Christianity and the anthropological principle of unity in diversity that underlies the present approach to mission.

But first, let us consider *the classicist view* regarding the uniqueness and universality of Christ. The argument is simple enough. The undeniable fact is that many individuals and whole societies do not and cannot know Christ. Considering God's infinite love, mercy, and desire for the salvation of all, and considering the universal significance of the death and resurrection of *the* Savior of the *world* Jesus Christ, it follows that somehow through Christ non-Christian religions must be *potentially* salvific.

New theology goes a step farther and insists that in the given circumstances, such religions are nothing less than the *probable and normal* instruments of salvation. The basic argument for this more liberal view is similar to that of the traditionalists, except that the leap is much greater—from possible to probable, from more or less exceptional to normal. God, from the moment of creation, has desired the salvation of every human being. Without depriving the individual of his or her freedom and responsibility, God, the God of History, must have taken the necessary measures to make the desired salvation *existentially* possible for all. The fact is that today the Gospel has already been preached wherever it is politically, psychologically, and culturally possible; and realistically considered, the future will be no different. The best that many non-Christians could now hope to do is to obey their consciences. Obedience in this case would mean to follow the non-Christian religion as the normal means of salvation in the given circumstances. Followers would thereby adhere to what is tantamount to God's own plan of salvation.

4.4.3.3 The Nature of the Church

Vatican II brought to light a new understanding of the Church to Roman Catholics, thanks to a *multiple* perspective of what the Church really is. The Church was viewed by the Council, for instance, as a people, as a sacrament or sign, as a herald, as a servant, and as an institution. The resulting insights and corresponding practical applications to Christian living were indeed revolutionary in many ways, even if they were not the final word on the subject. Thus there was a new emphasis on the fact that the Church is the *whole* People of God; that is to say, although the Church is hierarchical, the clergy, religious, and laity alike are all truly and fully and equally members of the Church. They therefore in their own right as baptized individuals participate in the mission of Christ. The Council also very logically maintained that the Church consisted not only of Roman Catholics but of *all* Christians; the Church is the *whole* Body of Christ. It did, however, insist that the true fullness of Christ's Church was to be found in the Roman Catholic tradition. Although the Church can be properly understood only in relation to the Kingdom of God, the Church should not be identified with it; rather, as the Council pointed out, the Church should be looked upon as a pilgrim people that through constant reform and heralding is only on its way toward the realization of the Kingdom. The Church is the sacrament that brings about the Kingdom—a true *sacramentum mundi*, a sign of God's active presence within and without the Church. These new insights (or should we perhaps say "forgotten truths") have wide practical anthropological implications (see chapter 8).

However, as far as applied mission anthropology is concerned, no conciliar teaching about the Church could be of greater interest than *the principle of unity in diversity*. The Church is more than a confederation, more than a kind of multinational organization with branch offices spread around the world and managed from one central office.

The fact is that the universality of the Church is realized through the local churches. The universal Church is therefore more than the sum of its parts; it is a communion of local churches—with both words, *communion* and *local*, underscored. To be fully the Church of Christ, the local church must be in union with the Successor of Peter, the Bishop of Rome. At the same time, this communion is pluriform, an understanding toward which both the traditionalists and modern theologians are sympathetic. As Schillebeeckx puts it:

The unity of the Church presupposes and implies a multiplicity of local churches, each with its own special "look," even with its own liturgy, its own ecclesiastical order, and its own theology. This diversity is founded on the Bible, and even demanded in the New Testament. But only in the mutual recognition of each other as legitimate representation of the one Church of Christ is the full meaning of "the Church" guaranteed. If this were not the case, then there should be divisions in the Church. For that reason it is of primary importance for the local church to whose leader is also assigned the office of Peter. This ecclesiological structure makes demands both of the other local churches as well as of the local church whose own distinctive "look" serves as an expression of the legitimate multiplicity of the churches, not of an exclusivism wishing to go its own way. This is a point we must not overlook, for to do so would be an absolute denial of the New Testament concept of church. . . . [1967: 7]

Vatican II was not always consistent when it spoke of the "local church." As in the present work, the intended meaning must be obtained from the context. By "local church," Vatican II sometimes means "diocese" and the bishop as *the* pastor; but it also uses the term in reference to churches of the Eastern rite, to worshipping congregations, and to culturally differentiated groupings. The New Code of Canon Law avoids the use of "local church" and speaks of the diocese as a "particular" church.

What is important to note is that the universal Church is realized in and through the local churches. The universal Church, is, therefore, present in all legitimate local congregations. As Joseph Komonchak of the Catholic University of America describes it in his excellent treatise on the local church presented to the Federation of Asian Bishops (FABC Papers, no.42, 1986), every local church is the full reality, the whole Christ, called "Church."

The Church universal arises out of the mutual reception and communion of local churches: the universal Church results *from* the fact that local churches are in communion. It is, of course, presupposed that the local church is modeled after this communion. The diocese of Rome is itself a local church; it is not the universal Church that local churches join, but rather the local church by becoming local becomes universal. It must, however, acknowledge the "one Lord, one faith, and one baptism" (Eph 4:5) and, as the Apostles' Creed insists, it must be "one, holy, catholic and apostolic."

The Bishop's ministry is that of carrier of universal Christian values and meanings. His is the role of the apostles—to maintain the single body of disciples all united in the Lord. The local church gathers around their bishop to worship. The bishop is not first a member of the college of bishops and then head of a diocese; both the entrance into the college and the assumption of authority and responsibility over a diocese are simultaneous (Komonchak 1986).

The pope is the successor of Peter as Bishop of the local church of Rome. Both the church of Rome and its bishop have unique responsibilities in regard to the universal Church serving as the center of communion, presiding over the communion of churches.

Having explained what we believe to be the official teaching of Vatican II, we can now return to our comparison of traditional views with those of "new" theology. Traditional theology describes the nature of the Church primarily, but not exclusively, from the viewpoint of the Church's being a visible institution, God's instrumental cause of salvation. Accordingly, the emphasis is on the universality, unity, orthodoxy, and institutional character of the Church. New theology, by contrast, prefers to view the Church primarily (but, we hasten to add, not exclusively) as a sign of God's active, saving presence in the world. The emphasis is placed on the local rather than on the universal church, and on diversity rather than on unity. In contrast, Vatican II, although employing a variety of images, seems to have preferred the communal People-of-God model of the Church.

Today, in many fields of knowledge, including theology and anthropology, models are often preferred to definitions. Models seem to be able to generate a wider and deeper, albeit partial, understanding of the reality under consideration. We shall adopt a model-approach to describe the nature of culture (*infra*, chapter 5), at which time we shall explain the meaning of model more fully. Here we wish merely to stress that the Church is a very complex reality that, like culture, might best be described by means of models rather than definitions.

No single perspective—institutional, communal, sacramental, or whatever—will by itself describe the Church satisfactorily. In isolation, any single model would in fact be a distortion. We are saying that any sound ecclesiology will complement its preferred model with aspects from other models, thereby filling in gaps and restoring balance. To borrow an apt comparison from Avery Dulles' classic *Models of the Church*—in ecclesiology we must constantly and simultaneously keep a variety of models before us (the dominant as well as the complementary) much the way jugglers concentrate on and deal not with only one but *all* objects tossed in the air. To ignore any one of them might well spell disaster (1978:14).

St. Paul in his earlier writings spoke of a "church" only in the sense of a *local* Christian community. In fact, at first the term referred only to local Judean congregations that happened to be one of the mother churches of Palestine. In the first four chapters of the Acts of the Apostles, the word does not occur at all; and it rarely occurs in the Gospels. In his later epistles, however, Paul broadens his concept of *ekklêsia* and begins to speak of the Church Universal. He uses a variety of analogies, especially that of the Body of Christ (Brown, Fitzmeyer, Murphy 1968:825f). In this connection, the Letter to the Ephesians (4:1–13) is particularly interesting, because Paul's dominant model here is clearly communal. However, he hastens to expand and balance this model with aspects of other images. He describes the Church primarily as a *community* that humbly and lovingly bears with each of its members and makes "every effort to preserve the unity which has the Spirit as its origin just as there is but one hope given all." What ties this ideal community together is the "one Lord, one faith, one baptism; one God and Father of all, who is over all, and works through all, and is in all," with "Christ the head," through whom "the whole body grows, and with the proper functioning of the members joined firmly together by each supporting ligament, builds itself upon love." However, in this community of love, Paul points out, there are distinct gifts and offices, and in this manner Paul complements his basic communal model with an institutional dimension. In Ephesians 4:11–12 he expressly states that Christ has given structure to his community, namely through "the apostles, prophets, evangelists, pastors and teachers in roles of service for the faithful to build up the body of Christ." In his First Letter to the Corinthians he suggests structures that can be traced to Christ himself (1 Cor 10:14–22; 11:23–25; 14:2–19) and mentions disciplinary rules that are pleasing to God (1 Cor 11:16), all of which clearly implies that the Church has an institutional character as well. In fact, in his Letter to the Ephesians, Paul adds certain aspects of still a third model, describing the Church as a *Pilgrim Church* in the process of building up the body of Christ "till we become one in faith and in the knowledge of God's Son, and form that perfect man who is Christ come to full stature" (Eph 4:13).

Although the number of models may be varied almost at will (Dulles 1978:15), as we shall explain in our epilogue (chapter 8), for simplicity's sake Dulles reduces them to five, namely (1) the institutional model, or the church considered primarily as the God-intended visible organization with identifiable offices, authority, structure, order, discipline, and obedience; (2) the communal model, or the Church as a fellowship in Christ, a People of God, united to God and with one another in Christ through the Spirit; (3) the sacramental model, or the Church as a sign of God's active saving presence—more specifically, as a visible sign of Christ's grace and hope for the fulfillment of his promises, visible especially in the liturgy of the Church; (4) the kerygmatic model, or the Church as herald of God's Kingdom; (5) the diaconal model, or the Church as servant striving to transform the sinful world through the values of the Kingdom of God. In Dulles' view (1976, 1978), any of these five models may well serve as the pivotal or dominant perspective, except for the most subordinate of the five, the *institutional*—however important the institutional character of the Church may be.

In missiological anthropology, we do not have a favorite all-purpose dominant model of the Church. Instead we change our dominant perspective in accordance with the problem at issue and the client served. As Dulles observes, "Church officials have a tendency to prefer the institutional model; ecumenists, the community model; speculative theologians, the sacramental model; preachers and biblical scholars, the kerygmatic model; secular activists, the servant model" (1978:200). This openness of applied anthropology to a variety of dominant models, however, calls for a salutary warning: as we shall see in chapter 8, whatever the model be, it will have certain advantages and disadvantages that must never be ignored.

4.4.3.4 The Mission of the Church

The traditionalist argues that because the Church is God's universal *instrument* of salvation, mission must consist essentially in proclaiming the Good News, in conversion, in discipling all nations, and in worldwide Church planting. What is being planted, traditional theology tells us, is the worldwide Church. Thus, mission is basically ecclesiocentric. The new theological view, by contrast, is clearly theocentric. The emphasis is not on the salvific instrumentality of the Church but on the fact that the Church is a *sign* of the saving, merciful presence of God in the world. The emphasis of a theocentric mission is on orthopraxis (i.e., on *living* according to the constitutions of the Kingdom) rather than on orthodoxy (i.e., on *believing* according to the Church's teaching). New theology stresses that "None of those who cry out 'Lord, Lord,' will enter the Kingdom of God, but only the one who does the will of the Father" (Mt 7:21). Traditional theology, however, stresses that "He who hears you, hears me" (Lk 10:16).

Thus the two supporters of the official teaching of the Catholic Church maintain contrasting views. What did Vatican II have to say on the subject? According to Vatican II, the general mission of the Church is threefold: (1) pastoral—a ministry to the faithful, (2) ecumenical—a ministry to divided Christianity, and (3) missionary—a ministry to areas where the Church has not yet been planted or where it is not yet fully established. Moreover, this ministry is to be exercised by the *whole* Church, not only by the clergy but the laity as well, who participate in Jesus' prophetic, priestly, and kingly mission in their own right as Christians. Participants are prophets inasmuch as the members of the Church speak on behalf of God and the Kingdom; they are priests, especially through their roles in the Eucharist and the Sacrament of Reconciliation; they are kings, by carrying their mission with authority. Members of the Church achieve this mission through (1) the proclamation of the Word (*kerygma*), (2) worship (*leiturgia*), (3) witness (*martyria*), (4) fellowship (*koinonia*), and (5) service (*diakonia*). All five activities are essential to the Church's mission. None may be overlooked in the practical efforts of mission anthropologists. These activities, according to Vatican II, must be carried out individually as well as institutionally, and as much as possible they should be culturally relevant.

One can readily understand why the traditionalists say that the Church will always need the classical missionary: after all, is the Church not first and foremost the universal *instrument* of salvation, and does not such an instrument presuppose Church planting and missionaries? New mission theology, however, holds that because the Church has already been planted wherever existentially possible, the era of traditional missions ("missions" in the plural) has actually come to an end. Today there is only one mission ("mission" in the singular). It is this mission that all Christians are called to. This mission is to the *whole* world, including the Christian West—including all six continents, including non-Christians as well as the de-Christianized, including one's own parish and in fact oneself (Comblin 1977; Bühlmann 1982:248). In a word, the modern theologian holds that missionaries will be needed in the future, but that they will have to be a new breed of missionaries. The emphasis in the future, they say, will no longer be on conversion and church planting as before but on that single general mission that is common to every Christian. Because mission is seen primarily as the disclosure or sign of God's presence and his salvific action, the Church's mission will in the future be directed toward such concerns as the Church's authenticity and renewal, toward peace and justice, and toward service to one's Christian community and the rest of the world. Because the God who is being disclosed is present and active within and without the Church, the Church will be deeply involved in dialogue with all religions and, in fact, with all of good will. Looking at the world as it is and peering more deeply into its future, the modern theologian predicts that individuals and societies who actually do get to know Christ will be but a "little flock" (Lk 12:32)—relatively speaking, a tiny handful. New theology insists that it has by no means abandoned mission; rather, it claims that mission must be reinterpreted "from below," recognizing the signs of the times and acknowledging that God is the God of History. The signs of the times tell us that no matter how great the effort made to evangelize the world—and evangelization must continue—Christians will, according to God's own design, always remain but a "little flock." The parable of the mustard seed, in which Christ compares the Kingdom of God to "the smallest seed of all, yet when full-grown . . . is the largest plant" (Mt 13:32) and the parable of the yeast that eventually makes the whole mass of dough to rise (Mt 13:33), and the many other New and Old Testament references to a *world* mission, must be interpreted in light of actual history and in light of the undeniable world conditions. Anthropological applications, we are saying, will vary according to such ecclesiological differences.

4.5 CONCLUSION

A Christian, especially one who is called to a leadership role in mission, is called upon to be a "builder," a builder of God's temple (Eph 2:21f). The basic building tools are the plumb line and level, both of which must be applied during the construction again and again, and, in fact, simultaneously. Chapter 4 has provided the mission anthropologist with a plumb line, a brief theological overview that must be expanded and built upon. The plumb line will assist the mission anthropologist and those he or she is guiding and working with to construct a building that will be vertically straight. The following chapters enter into anthropology itself—into the context in contextualization. They bring together the basic culturological concepts, principles, and theories regarding the nature, structure, and dynamics of culture relevant to the Church's mission—the all-important second tool that we have dubbed as the builder's "level." The final chapter will serve as an epilogue and will seek to show how the Church applies *both* the level *and* the plumb line in being and doing what the Church is—a community, a sign of God's active presence, a herald, a servant, and an institution.

Chapter Five

THE NATURE OF CULTURE

God is interested in luxurious diversity.

Donald S. McGavran

5.1 CULTURAL PERSPECTIVES

Despite the many uncertainties regarding the nature of culture, most anthropologists would agree with Alfred L. Kroeber, one of America's greatest anthropologists, that "the most significant accomplishment of anthropology in the first half of the twentieth century was the extension and clarification of the concept of culture" (1950:87). This understanding of culture is also anthropology's most significant contribution to missiology. We shall be able to understand the human dimension of mission action to the extent that we are able to understand the meaning of culture. We do not deny that there is much that anthropologists cannot tell us about culture, but at the same time we recognize that there is indeed much that anthropologists do know.

⌈Mission consists in incarnating Christ in the given time and place, allowing him to be reborn in the given lifeway. A true Christian is but another "Christ." The all-important question that faces the Church and all engaged in mission action, be it in a ministry or in witnessing one's faith, is, What would *Jesus* teach and how would *he* behave if he were born today, say in Japan, Brazil, Kenya, or, for that matter, in my home parish in London, Paris, Rome, Bonn, or Washington—not two thousand years ago but today here and now? *Contextualization* is the process by which a local Christian community integrates the Gospel message (the "text") with the real-life context, blending text and context into that single, God-intended reality called "Christian living." By "Christian living" we mean living as *Christ* would live *here and now*—that is, as *he* would behave, what he would teach here and now, and what his values and emotions, his underlying premises, attitudes, and drives would be if he belonged to the particular community we are dealing with.⌋Despite the facts that God cannot compromise his unity and consistency (Rv 3:16) and that the

133

Church may not compromise a single iota of the Gospel (Mt 5:18), God nevertheless delights in what mission strategist Donald S. McGavran calls "luxurious human diversity," a luxuriousness that God created when he created human beings as cultural beings. In fact, whenever God deals with human beings, whether it be in the Bible or in our own times, he deals with them *as* cultural beings. Every Christian community must experience Christ— not as a foreigner who somehow after two thousand years has appeared in the community's midst, but as "one of us," as someone sharing the community's culture and therefore possessing its very soul.

But what is culture? Can we define it in a meaningful and useful way? Or should we perhaps try to describe culture in terms of one or more perspectives?

5.1.1 EARLY ANTHROPOLOGICAL DEFINITIONS

One of the earliest definitions of culture was suggested by E. B. Tylor (1832–1917), the father of modern anthropology. He stated in 1871 that culture or civilization is that complex whole including knowledge, belief, art, morals, law, customs, and any other abilities and habits acquired by people as members of society. In the middle of the present century, Kroeber and Kluckhohn, in their attempt to bring order into the confused usage of the term, uncovered almost three hundred definitions of culture (1952:149). Many of these definitions were but echoes of Tylor, mere variations on a theme—the learned behavior of a society. Thus, Robert H. Lowie defined culture as "the sum total of what an individual acquires from his society—those beliefs, customs, artistic norms, food-habits, and crafts which came to him not by his own creative activity but as a legacy from the past, conveyed by formal or informal education" (1937:3). Kroeber defined culture as "the mass of learned and transmitted motor reactions, habits, techniques, ideas and values—and the behavior they induce" (1948:8). Linton, another stalwart of Kroeber's generation of anthropologists, defined culture simply as "social heredity" (1936:78), once again echoing Tylor's definition. Kluckhohn did not add much either when he defined culture as "the total life-way of a people, the social legacy the individual acquires from the group," "the behavior acquired through learning" (1949:17); or finally, as Felix Keesing understood culture, "the behavior acquired through social learning" (1958:18).

Such definitions were nevertheless helpful and legitimate. They identified, for a time at least, the object of anthropological inquiry, and they presupposed and indeed encouraged further clarification, refinement, and elaboration of the concept. What such definitions stated explicitly was true enough; their weakness lay in what they failed to state. Such early definitions were, we might say, useful *technical* terms; they were descriptive rather than essential in nature.

However, we do not wish to say that all earlier definitions were purely descriptive. Some definitions, like those suggested by functionalists (*infra,* 5.1.6.3) and the Viennese School (*infra,* 5.1.6.2.2), reflected a definite and in fact a quite advanced theory of culture.

Today, anthropological definitions of culture almost invariably presuppose a specific theoretical base and reflect a particular perspective or *model*.

But before we enter into such perspectives, we shall first examine the nature of knowledge and the concept of models as such.

5.1.2 THE NATURE OF KNOWLEDGE

In the beginning of the present century, it was still quite generally held that the real world could be observed, studied, and described objectively—that is, *as* the world *actually* exists outside the mind. In more recent times, however, we have become increasingly aware of the fact that human knowledge is very limited and selective and therefore that it does not quite mirror the real world and the laws governing it; that is to say, we can understand and deal with the real world but never with the world exactly as it is.

There are at least three reasons that underlie the current view (Hiebert 1976:4–11). (1) Our experience of the world is *limited* by the very limitations of our senses and by the scientific tools we use to extend those senses. The "scientific tools" to which we refer are especially our concepts, principles, theories, and methods. Thus the atomic theory, and theories about light and sound waves, energy, and all of science, describe the real world in only an abstract and therefore limited way. Science is concerned with sense data and abstractions; it does not deal directly with the world exactly as it is. (2) Human knowledge, besides being limited, is also highly *selective*. To make knowledge more manageable, we screen out those aspects of the real world that we regard as unimportant, irrelevant, and as a kind of "noise." Consciously or unconsciously, we emphasize certain aspects of reality and de-emphasize others. What philosophers and scientists actually investigate and describe depends largely on what they choose to look for and what specific questions they ask, or, given the state of the art, what questions they are even capable of asking. (3) Societies *order*—that is, categorize—their perceptions in a variety of ways. Thus although all societies see the same rainbow, they divide the spectrum into two, three, four or more colors in *their* own way. Kinship relationships may be ordered, for instance, according to different categories of uncles and aunts. Life itself and all that exists might be ordered quite differently by different cultures, but the world as such remains the same (*infra*, 6.3.2).

5.1.3 THE NATURE OF MODELS

The human habit abstracts, selects, and orders knowledge. It leads us partially to understand the world and partially to distort it. We must, therefore, recognize our inability to understand the world *as* it is. Aware of this partial knowledge, anthropologists frequently resort to *models*. Although the term *model* is used in a variety of ways, it has a common core of meaning; invariably it refers to a particular perspective from which the real world is being examined and described. We ourselves have been using the term in slightly different ways. We have, for instance, spoken of models in reference to the different anthropological disciplines, each as viewing human beings holistically but from a different angle; we have also spoken of missionary approaches as models; and we have shown how the nature of the Church might best be described in terms of models rather than in terms of essential definitions.

Models are particularly useful in day-to-day research, especially when an investigation is dealing with complex phenomena. A model may be said to be something between abstract theory and empirical observation. Models must be taken seriously but not literally. Concretely, a model may be, for instance, a picture, a drawing, a diagram, a map, a three-dimensional miniature or full-size replica, a mathematical or other symbol, a chemical formula, a physical object, or a word or statement. Models are simplified rough drafts, rough but effectively able to call up appropriate mental images. They are analogues around which inquiry can be usefully organized (Pelto, Pelto 1978:256). In a word, they are views of reality from a particular perspective.[1]

Models have a great potential for expanding human knowledge. Their utility lies in the fact that they proceed pedagogically from the known to the unknown, not only summing up but, so to speak, dramatizing the implications of the particular analogy. As we have seen, Paul (Eph 4:1–13; 1 Cor 12) made good use of the human body as a model of the Church. The body is an easily understood image from which countless meaningful ecclesiological implications can be drawn. Paul's analogy suggests new and ever-deeper insights into the organic nature of the Church and the interdependence that exists among its members—and there are dozens of such biblical models of the Church.

But models have their drawbacks. For example, the functionalist school of anthropology, in modeling culture after organisms (very much the way Paul did in regard to the Church), has sometimes gone overboard in drawing parallels between cultures and organic wholes. Reification and reductionism thus become a real and constant danger. It was with such dangers in mind that we sounded a warning when we used models to describe the Church.

5.1.4 CRITERIA FOR A GOOD MODEL

Having made these general observations about models, we are now in a better position to offer some criteria for distinguishing desirable from less desirable models. Good models will always be (1) useful, (2) open, (3) fitting, and (4) stimulating (cf. Hiebert 1983:12f). By *useful* we mean that good models are well suited for organizing a body of knowledge. They explain a large quantity of data and allow only few exceptions. Good models are useful also in the sense that they not only serve informational purposes but also help solve practical problems. By *open* we mean that good models recognize their limitations. Models are presented only as approximations of truth, only as tentative statements of reality, as hypotheses, and as invitations and challenges to further refinement and clarification. By *fitting* we mean that good models are logical, consistent, and "neat." That is, they are simple, clear, aesthetic, and balanced. By *stimulating* we mean that good models have a capacity to arouse the imagination and thus to contribute to further and deeper understanding.

5.1.5 THE NEED FOR A MISSIOLOGICALLY ORIENTED MODEL OF CULTURE

In our case, qua missiologists, a model of culture can hardly be called "good" unless it is at the same time *missiologically* relevant. Our model must be useful, open, fitting, and stimulating—not in some general way only, but in the sense that it can be of particular service to missiology. In a word, it must be able to advance *missiology*. Thus according to our first criterion, usefulness, a missiologically oriented model of culture would have to be theoretically and practically useful *for mission*. It would, first of all, have to help us better to understand mission theology and mission history and to facilitate the construction of theoretical local theologies. It would, however, have to go beyond theory and academics. To be truly useful, our model of culture would have to deal also with the nitty-gritty aspects of mission action, such as how to achieve entry into a non-Christian society; how to cross generational barriers; how to achieve identification and maintain rapport with a community or a part of it, especially if its ways, meanings, and values differ from those of the educator, liturgist, or pastor; how to analyze the socioeconomic situation here and now; how to communicate (that is, how to listen and to respond verbally as well as nonverbally in accord with the given culture or subculture); how most effectively and most painlessly to direct desired social change through the cooperation of those directly affected by the change to be introduced. To be missiologically useful, the model of culture must make mission more understandable to the local as well as to the universal Church, to the indigenous leader as well as to the expatriate. The model should be able to serve as a framework around which a local pastoral strategy and Christian living itself might be built, be it in the West, in the Third World, or anywhere else. In other words, the model must be useful for the development of a sound local theology both theoretical and practical. Or again, if the model is to be regarded as missiologically appropriate, it must, according to our fourth criterion, be stimulating. It must be found stimulating not only by the professional anthropologist but also by the mission historian, administrator, pastor, local lay church leader, liturgist, religious educator, community development coordinator, or anyone else engaged in mission. Not filling our fourth requirement would be, for example, the rather popular structuralism of Lévi-Strauss. As stimulating as Lévi-Strauss' theory may be for some, the approach is too limited in application and too difficult especially for those who will be most involved in applying anthropology to mission. This is not to say that a structuralist model cannot provide, or has not provided, some missiological insights, especially by helping a local Christian community understand its own system of classification of the world and the role of myth and ritual in relation to other aspects of its culture. That our model of culture is indeed missiologically relevant, both theoretically and practically, will be adequately substantiated throughout the present work, especially in the sections entitled "Missiological Application."

Because of the complex nature and function of both culture and mission, we are suggesting five additional requirements for a good *missiologically oriented* model very much in harmony with what Schreiter (1985:42–45) suggests. Over and above the four general criteria, *our* understanding of culture must as much as possible (1) be holistic, (2) be emic, (3) be able to deal with change, (4) represent the community's identity, and (5) be composite. It must be *holistic*, as explained earlier (*supra* 2.2.1.1); our humanness must be understood as much as possible as a single whole. The mission of the Church is concerned with human beings in their totality, in their physical, social, and spiritual oneness (2.2.3.3). We cannot, for instance, assume that the physical aspects of humans are primary and all-important, as do the materialists (*infra*, 5.1.6.1) and at the same time downplay the social and psychological aspects. Nor can the so-called "more noble things of life," such as art, music, and elitist liturgies, be emphasized and folk values and behavior belittled. By *emic* we mean that our model should as much as possible be able to help us better to understand the local culture as an insider does, and at times it should even bring to light some aspects of the local culture that an insider takes for granted and normally does not verbalize and is sometimes not even aware of. Effective Christian witness and any form of ministry must as much as possible be geared to the culture *as understood and felt by the community witnessed and ministered to*. This *emic* understanding of the local culture is but another way of saying, "Get the answers to your pastoral problems *from and with* your people!" and "The best evangelizers are not the best preachers but the best listeners" (Luzbetak 1987:70). Moreover, from our emphasis on culture dynamics (*supra*, 3.1.3.5; *infra*, chapter 7), it should be clear that a good model of culture will have to be able to explain *social change*, whereas from our constant emphasis on the "soul" and "spirit" of a society it should be clear that a good model of culture will have to be able to strengthen the sense of identity of a people. But to be holistic, emic, and able to deal with change and the identity of a people, the ideal missiologically oriented model of culture will have to be *composite*. We are suggesting, therefore, an interlacing of a dominant or pivotal perspective with complementary submodels taken from current anthropological theory. The various perspectives should interpenetrate one another and be like transparent overlays. On top of the pivotal perspective would be placed lesser overlays to provide important supplementary detail and to balance and correct the dominant model where necessary. Like theologian Avery Dulles' jugglers, in missiological anthropology we must concentrate simultaneously on all objects tossed in the air as we did when we were dealing with the nature and mission of the Church (*supra*, 4.4.3.3). Like architects, in mission anthropology we cannot be satisfied with just one blueprint—with the floorplan, for instance, or with only the structural or electrical engineer's perspectives (*supra*, 2.2.1.1). To interpret mission history, to understand the culture-bound biblical sources of mission theology, to help separate basic church tradition from mere cultural trappings, to help the local Christian community maintain and strengthen its own identity, to help the missionary appreciate the seriousness of his or her ethnocentrism, to reinterpret the fundamentals of Christianity in terms of basically non-Christian symbols as is necessary in any initial evangelization, to hold dialogue meaningfully with non-Christians, to enable the Gospel to become truly generative (that is, to enable the Christian to express his or her faith in ever-new and creative ways corresponding to the needs of the time and place and in accord with the soul of the community), *in a word, to apply anthropology to mission, it will be necessary to adopt the architect's multimodel approach and the juggler's "holism" suggested earlier.*

We are suggesting that in mission application one should choose a suitable primary, dominant, or pivotal understanding of culture which then should be corrected, complemented, and balanced off with other perspectives. As a general rule, the author has found the perspective of culture *as a society's design for living* particularly suitable for missiology when complemented by secondary psychological, sociological, ecological, historical, cognitive, semiotic, and other overlays for balance and correction. Not all submodels are, of course, to be regarded as equally important or equally usable, or perhaps usable at all. The most useful complementary perspective for missiology seems to be the symbolic or semiotic view of culture. Accordingly, *we shall describe culture from our dominant perspective (that is to say, taking culture as a design for living) and, where appropriate or necessary, we shall add corresponding correctives and balances and other useful details in terms of secondary models.* But first, we will present an overview of the major anthropological perspectives of culture. For a more thorough coverage of models than we are able to offer, one might study such works as John J. Honigmann (ed.), *Handbook of Social and Cultural Anthropology* (1973), Raoul Narroll and Ronald Cohen (eds.), *A Handbook of Method in Cultural Anthropology* (1970), or Robert A. Manners and David Kaplan (eds.), *Theory in Anthropology: A Sourcebook* (1968).

5.1.6 AN OVERVIEW OF CULTURAL MODELS

5.1.6.1 Materialistic Models of Culture

5.1.6.1.1 Early Cultural Evolutionism

Taking their cues from Darwin, and having no scientific evidence to support their views, British Edward B. Tylor (1832–1917) and American Lewis Henry Morgan (1818–1881) claimed that there was a unilineal law governing not only the biological development of humans but their cultural growth as well. Tylor and Morgan took for granted the existence of a straight line progression from the lower to the higher, from the simpler to the more complex, from the less perfect to the more perfect, from the less moral to the more moral, and from the less civilized to the more civilized. Simpler peoples, therefore, represented to them an earlier stage of cultural evolution through which civilized societies had already passed. Tylor's favorite "proof" was the *doctrine of survivals*, survivals being nonfunctional traces of a more primitive culture. Morgan's favorite model of cultural progression was from savagery through barbarism to civilization. Taken as self-understood was that the human race began at a level of lower savagery: there were no moral guides; marriage did not exist, and promiscuity was the rule. Because the identity of a father was unknown, kinship and property rights were determined, as they only could be, by the mother's line. When regularity replaced promiscuity and paternity was identifiable, property became male oriented. As the human brain developed through evolution, culture also grew. Western civilization was, of course, the acme of human development. A third evolutionist of note, who appeared somewhat later on the scene, was the Scottish anthropologist Sir James Frazer (1854–1941), best known for his work on the development of religion, called *The Golden Bough* (1922). The downfall of cultural evolutionism was brought about especially through the scientifically untenable stance taken and by the opposition of anthropologists of the time, including Franz Boas and Wilhelm Schmidt.

There is still a considerable amount of prejudice against cultural anthropology—and against missiological anthropology in particular—on the part of some fundamentalist Christians. This prejudice is based mainly on the unwarranted identification of classical atheistic evolutionism with all anthropology. After all, is not Edward Tylor regarded as the father of modern anthropology, and are not *evolution* and *anthropology* synonymous? Although there is indeed very little that we might learn from the evolutionists, there is no justification whatsoever for rejecting the entire concept of cultural anthropology.

5.1.6.1.2 Marxism

By *Marxism* we mean anthropological theory based primarily on the thinking of Karl Marx (1818–1883) and Friedrich Engels (1820–1895). Marx's most significant theoretical study was his *Das Kapital*, and his program of action was presented in his *Communist Manifesto*. Marx attributed most problems of his time to a single historical process—the rise and development of industrial capitalism. There are three dimensions to Marxism: Marxism as an ideology, as a body of theory, and as a method.

Anthropologists generally agree that a close dynamic relationship exists between the physical, social, and ideational aspects of culture; that is, between technology, social organization, and ideology. They also generally agree that none of the three aspects of culture can be said to be the decisive determining factor responsible for culture change. There is an undeniable interplay among the three. Marxist theory, however, makes the economic factors the most significant and insists that the importance of any constituent part of culture is to be judged by its relationship to the economic realm, namely to modes of production by which a society acquires its means of subsistence. The economic factor, the Marxists admit, is not always the decisive one, because, as the Marxists see also, the three realms are interrelated. However, the economic variables will assert themselves in culture more than the others and will be primarily responsible for the state of the particular culture. (Honigmann 1959:294–295.)

Marxism is referred to as *dialectical materialism*. Social development is not viewed as being deterministic but rather as dialectical. That is to say, the process is creative and it involves a tension between opposites, a back-and-forth struggle, a process in which Marxist socioeconomic hopes will be fulfilled by the tensions themselves. People are viewed as making their own history; they are capable of transforming human life through study and effort. There is, in fact, a double tension: an actual struggle between economic classes and a historical struggle, the tension between the original liberty and fraternity of the past on the one hand and the struggle with the capitalism of the present on the other. In the end, as the Marxist prediction goes, there will be a happy synthesis, a classless society and full communal ownership.

Unlike other animals, human animals *produce* what they need. Through such cultural devices as division of labor and technology, subsistence potential is increased. In fact, even a surplus is produced, and this factor results in a struggle over power and over the manner of distributing the surplus. The group that gains control over the means of production becomes the ruling class. Other classes develop too, but always in relation to the means of production. Culture is thus primarily and most deeply affected by the physical environment and the technology and other economic variables. Indeed, all histories of peoples might be summarized in terms of socioeconomic stages—the ancient, the feudal, and the capitalist. Cultures thus can be best described in economic terms. In a word, *dialectical materialism*, the name most commonly given to Marxism, refers to the twofold theory (1) that matter has priority over the mind, and (2) that the material basis of all reality is constantly changing in a back-and-forth process that inevitably will end in a materialistic synthesis and eventually in the Marxist utopia. (Cf. Rossi, O'Higgins 1980:68–71.)

This basic Marxist theory has split into a number of varieties: (1) Soviet Marxism, sometimes referred to as Marxism/Leninism or Stalinism; (2) Trotskyism, the repudiation of Stalinism; (3) Social Democracy, the view that power can be acquired peacefully by parliamentary means; (4) Maoism, the quest for the Marxist dream in a peasant-agrarian setting; (5) Neo-Marxism, current Marxism in developed and developing nations; (6) Marxist Structuralism, the attempt to combine Marxism and French structuralism; (7) American Marxism, a dialectical-critical anthropology in the United States and Canada (exemplified in the journal *Dialectical Anthropology*); (8) Christian Marxism, the attempt to combine and reconcile Marxism with the Gospel (exemplified in some Latin American liberation theologies).

That Marxist theory is reductionist and clearly subjective, with a strong ideological bias, cannot be denied. Nevertheless, Marxism has called the attention of both the anthropologist and the missiologist to a number of important facts about society and culture that must not be overlooked or dismissed lightly. (1) *Power* is the ability to manipulate people; it is the ability to compel or prevent behavior. This ability, use, and abuse of power is largely (even if not primarily, as the Marxist would have it) based on the means of production and its distribution. Those who control the vital resources, the goods produced, and the services can create a dependency and a form of serfdom. (2) *Authority* is closely associated with power. Those wielding power are sometimes able to legitimize their power: they convince those they manipulate that their power is actually a "right," and even a kind of "divine right." Mission history, as we have seen in chapter 3, has demonstrated again and again how religion can be used and abused in the achieving of power and authority. As a final observation, it might be well to point out that Marxist insistence, for example, on purely material goals, on the superiority of matter over the spiritual, and on the inevitability of violence and class conflict is definitely irreconcilable with the basic teaching of Christianity (cf. Pius XI, *Divini Redemptoris*; Ratzinger 1984, 1986; Kloppenberg 1974a).

5.1.6.1.3 Neoevolutionism

Universal Evolutionism. By the 1920s, cultural evolutionism was abandoned by anthropologists as unscientific. Leslie White (1900–1975), however, soon began to revive the concept in a new form. He was not interested so much in cultures (in the plural) as in the ways and values of *Homo sapiens*. The level of human progress, he claimed, was determined by the amount of energy any segment of humanity could harness and by the efficiency with which energy could be consumed per capita.

Marshall Sahlins (1958) supported White's theory by focusing on the relationship between technology and social stratification. In his studies of Polynesians, he claimed to have identified three levels of stratification that were determined not by type of technology (which was entirely limited by the environment) but by the type of environment itself. The most stratified societies, he insisted, were to be found on large fertile masses, while the least stratified were island people with the least resources.

Multilinear Evolution. Julian Steward (1902–1972), in his *Theory of Culture Change* (1955), rejected both the old evolutionistic concept that all cultures pass through the same stages as well as Leslie White's newer view of universal evolution. He admitted, however, that cultures went through *similar* stages, as exhibited by Mesopotamia, Egypt, China, Mesoamerica, and Peru, all of which passed through stages of hunting, food gathering, and agriculture. Each of these cultures ended up as a highly complex political organization. What appeared particularly significant to Steward was the similar environment in all these areas: each had a fertile river valley surrounded by an arid hinterland. With the birth of agriculture there was an increase in population. An introduction of irrigation was followed by an ever-expanding agricultural economy. Finally, each culture developed a very complex political system. What Steward described was a multilinear evolutionary adaptation.

5.1.6.1.4 Cultural Ecology

Although *cultural ecology* embodies a distinctly materialistic view of culture (like that of the evolutionists), it nonetheless goes a step well beyond evolutionism. The groundwork for this advance was done especially by evolutionists Steward and Sahlins, joined by such anthropologists as Vayda, Rappaport, Harris, Longacre, Meggers, and Flannery. Cultural ecology is focused on the relationship of culture and environment—on how the one influences the other. As Betty J. Meggers puts it:

> Man is an animal and, like all other animals, must maintain an adaptive relationship with his surroundings in order to survive. Although he achieves adaptation principally through the medium of culture, the process is guided by the same rules of natural selection that govern biological adaptation. [1971:41]

Ecologists, however, do not wish to explain culture by physical adaptation alone; the social and ideational aspects of culture as well as history are taken into consideration. In fact, the interplay between the physical, social, and the ideational realms are recognized, each realm having important, interconnected functions. To ecologists, however, most central to human adaptation, and therefore to culture, remain subsistence and those elements of social organization that are directly bound up with production: these influence technology; technology influences division of labor and distribution of products; and these, finally, influence the form of social groupings and the value system. The primary trigger in culture change is the physical environment to which human beings as a part of that environment (called *ecosystem*) must adapt or perish. A people's world view and religion are thus made dependent more on their adaptation to the rest of the ecosystem than vice versa. In fact, Marvin Harris, the champion of the theory of *cultural materialism*, goes so far as to claim that similar techniques in similar environments will produce similar economic, social, and religious systems.

Ecologists utilize a great variety of scientific fields as a part of their method. Among these fields are demography, biology, and medicine. They consider culture to be all those means, the forms of which have not been biologically inherited but that are socially transmitted and that serve to help the society adjust to the ecological setting. Culture is primarily a form of adaptation to the physical environment and indirectly to the social and ideational environment. In the last analysis, culture change is but a kind of natural selection.

Despite their exaggerated materialistic view of humanness, ecologists can teach us some important lessons. A society must produce behavior patterns that will serve the people in the environment in which they find themselves. There has always been a tendency on the part of some church workers to go in the opposite direction and to downplay "the things of this world." This attitude runs contrary to the *aggiornamento* proposed by Vatican II especially in its "Pastoral Constitution on the Church in the Modern World." Human ecology and its close relation to the rest of our humanness is indeed a very basic concern of Christians. Even when the society is unaware of the processes of the ecosystem, considerable influence is being exerted on culture.

The chief weakness of the ecological perspective of culture is its reductionism. In other words, the ecologists' explanation is at best only partial. Unexplained remain countless nonempirical patterns such as myth and ritual. What has environment to do with circumcision and magic? Also unexplained remain the ecological maladaptive aspects of culture. Finally, ecologists downplay the ideational needs of humans who, as R. Keesing emphasizes, are both "pragmatists and symbol manipulators" (1976:222–223).

5.1.6.2 Historical Anthropology

Wilhelm Schmidt was no doubt exaggerating when he said that ethnology was history or it was nothing at all. In any case, an ahistorical anthropology leaves much to be desired. Various attempts to reconstruct culture history have been made, and are being made, notably as forms of diffusionism and ethnohistory.

5.1.6.2.1 Diffusionism

Diffusionism claims that all cultures originated in one or a few areas of the world. From these places, it is thought, the cultures then spread over the globe. The theories have been largely a reaction to evolutionism.

American Diffusionism. In the United States, the leading diffusionist was Franz Boas (1858–1942), who opposed evolutionism on the grounds that it lacked a scientific basis and that it overlooked the most significant cause of culture change, diffusion of culture traits from one society to another. Rather than building grandiose theories on mere assumptions, as did the evolutionists, Boas maintained that anthropologists should gather data about specific cultures and, by studying the forms and geographic distribution of such forms, they could trace the historical path of one culture to another. No anthropologist has left so deep a mark on American anthropology as has Franz Boas, not so much through his diffusionism, however, as through the training he gave so many of the "pillars" of American anthropology like Mead, Kroeber, and Lowie. He well merits the title of "father of American anthropology." His "school" was known as *historical particularism*.

5.1.6.2.2 European Diffusionism

In Europe, a number of diffusionistic theories were propounded in the early twentieth century, the most extreme of which was that of G. Eliot Smith and William J. Perry, who claimed that Egypt was the birthplace of all civilization.

The most exacting school of diffusionism was that of the German anthropologists, among whom Fritz Graebner (1877–1934) and Wilhelm Schmidt (1868–1954) stand out. Their theory was known as the *Kulturkreislehre*, the "culture circle theory," or the *culture historical method of ethnology.* Whatever objections might be directed at the German diffusionists (a name Schmidt strongly resented), they were meticulous in applying their methodology. As Clyde Kluckhohn of Harvard, a leader among American anthropologists of his time, wrote in his introduction to the English translation of Schmidt's *The Culture Historical Method of Ethnology*,

> I cannot forget that I learned, as a student of Professor Schmidt and Professor Koppers, certain phases of method common to all studies in cultural anthropology better, I honestly believe, than I should have from any other teachers. [W. Schmidt 1939:vii]

In its time, the approach enjoyed considerable respect in anthropological circles, especially in the German-speaking countries. It was Schmidt's conviction that the basic role of ethnology was to reconstruct culture history.

According to the culture circle theory, in the beginning isolated groups of primitives had developed distinctive cultures that then diffused through contact among other bands. Subsequently, such clusterings of culture traits blended with one another. These blends, in turn, mixed with one another and diffused further. The role of ethnology, according to the theory, is to identify such blendings or "circles" by applying certain criteria to cultural patterns and, very much in the manner of detective work, to solve the mystery and reconstruct the whole story. (Brandewie 1983:68–106; W. Schmidt 1939.)

Interest in culture history must go on, whatever approach is followed. The *Kulturkreislehre* is dead and buried like so many other theories that played their role for a time and then were replaced by still other theories (Haekel 1959, 1970; *see* also *Current Anthropology* 1964:407–418). But one fact remains: only further research into culture history will tell us to what extent the poorly understood and sometimes maligned efforts of the *Kulturkreislehre* were right or wrong. Perhaps the most serious criticism that might be made against the theory is toward its piecemeal, lifeless treatment of cultures. The culture historical school of ethnology was also far more certain of being able to reconstruct the past than its method warranted. Laudable, on the other hand, was its total dedication to culture history.

5.1.6.2.3 Ethnohistory

A needed corrective for all models of culture, whatever they be, is offered through ethnohistory. Today, anthropologists are effectively and usefully reconstructing the culture history of both preliterate and recently literate ethnic groups by utilizing not only available written documents but also whatever historical evidence or clues that might be uncovered, whether in the form of written records or in the form of folklore, linguistics, archaeology, oral tradition, place names, and so on.

Ethnohistory, although limited in its sources, enjoys one important advantage: it is a study of culture *over a long period of time*. Some aspects of culture cannot be properly understood except longitudinally, over a longer time span.

Much, for instance, is attributed to Pope John XXIII and to the Vatican Council, when actually many philosophical, theological, and other trends deserve the credit, because they had prepared the way for the revolutionary changes in question (cf. O'Connell 1968). Or, to offer another example, most Latin Americans seem to be blind to the fact that their relatively long histories are as responsible for their woes as the more recent North American dependency and imperialism. Or to offer a final example, the painful lesson of the Iranian hostage crisis would not have taken place if the United States had but known a bit of Iranian cultural history—if the United States, the Shah's main supporter, had not been so oblivious to the fact that the Shah's modernizing reforms were totally alien and very menacing to the ancient religious culture of Iran.

Anthropology without history, we are saying, is very much like faith without works. No culture is really isolated. Revolutions affecting radical change often come like tidal waves from without. There are, first of all, worldwide *ideological* revolutions and their worldwide impact. Macrochanges may trigger quantum leaps. One thinks, for instance, of the birth and spread of Hinduism, Buddhism, Christianity, Islam, and Marxism. Then there are the worldwide *economic* revolutions: the discovery of fire, the development of higher forms of hunting, the discovery of agriculture, the invention of the wheel, writing, printing, steam power, electricity, the "horseless carriage," the airplane, radio, television, the discovery of the contraceptive pill and its worldwide impact. There were the jet age, the space age, and the computer age, each revolution rolling over one shore after another like gigantic tidal waves, with one age encountering another. Cultural analysis must be made in light of such intercivilizational contacts of the past, present, and future.

But there are also lesser histories, lesser but nonetheless important. We refer to short-term changes in contradistinction to changes affecting the system itself. It is here that ethnohistory has a major role to play. Not only is there a more general Christian and Islamic history (in the singular), but there are also Christian and Islamic histories that are more local which must be reconstructed if we are to understand the local Christian or Islamic society and culture. Local catastrophes, outstanding personalities, powerful factions, and other historical accidents are anything but insignificant factors in culture change (*infra*, 7.3.1.8, 7.3.3.3.1).

Good examples of how ethnohistory can be used in the study of mission will be found in Darrell Whiteman's "Missionary Documents and Anthropological Research" (1985) and in his *Melanesians and Missionaries: An Ethnohistorical Study of Social Change in the Southwest Pacific* (1983) as well as in the works of Alan R. Tippett, for example, his *Aspects of Pacific Ethnohistory* (1973a), "Towards a Technique for Extracting Anthropological Data from Oceanic Missionary Records" (1974b), and *Oral Tradition and Ethnohistory: The Transformation of Information and Social Values in Early Christian Fiji—1835–1905* (1980).

5.1.6.3 Functionalism

While American anthropologists continued their interest in culture history, the British abandoned all hope of ever being able to reconstruct the pasts of nonliterate peoples. The latter felt strongly that anthropologists should be engaged in tasks that were possible—in studying *living societies*. The British placed emphasis on social institutions and asked what institutions were for, what they do to or for the society, and how such institutions relate to one another logically, purposefully, or otherwise. Such relationships are called *functions*.

British functionalism owes its origin to two anthropologists, the Polish-born Bronislaw Malinowski (1882–1940) and A. R. Radcliffe-Brown (1881–1955). Malinowski in his *Argonauts of the Western Pacific* (1922) and Radcliffe-Brown in his *The Andaman Islanders* (1922) quite independently arrived at the conclusion that cultures could be properly understood only if their constituent parts were viewed as functionally interrelated.

The two founders of British functionalism differed somewhat in their understanding of function. According to Malinowski, culture provided the answer to human needs. There were, first of all, seven *basic* needs: food, reproduction, comfort, protection and safety, relaxation, movement, and growth. Basic needs were met by such patterns as clothing and shelter and by such basic institutions as marriage and the family (these institutions made reproduction and education possible). However, basic needs themselves created other needs, the so-called *derived* needs, to which the responses were said to be the economic and political institutions. Responding to both the basic and derived needs were, for instance, art, recreation, and religion.

Radcliffe-Brown, rather than Malinowski, was a great admirer of Durkheim. Like Durkheim, he viewed society as an organism: institutions were to a society what organs were to the human body, each carrying out special roles. Like the organs of a body, he claimed that institutions were consistent and harmonious with one another. Preservation of the whole and solidarity were the chief purposes or functions of social institutions. It was impossible to understand any part of the whole without relating the part to all the other parts. Furthermore, a change in one part would bring a change throughout the whole. Radcliffe-Brown emphasized the study of kinship because he regarded kinship as the very heart of nonliterate social organization.

Functionalism is rightly criticized for its reductionist view of culture and society, especially for its exaggeration regarding the consistency, harmony, balance, purposefulness, and wholeness of culture and society. At times the search for functions has led functionalists to see them where they did not exist or to fail to see them when similar functions did not exist in Western cultures. Due to the tendency to explain all functions purposefully and to emphasize the *social* aspect of function (the preservation and the solidification of society), functional explanations of *ideational* behavior have been sometimes overlooked or not sufficiently appreciated. While able to deal satisfactorily with problems of identity, as Schreiter (1985:46) points out, functionalism is weak in dealing with change, a consideration no less important for mission than is identity. Functionalism is also rightly accused of ignoring historical explanations and such facts as dysfunction and human commonality. We hasten to add, however, that it would be unfair and in fact incorrect to say that all functionalism, especially the Radcliffe-Brown variety, is unaware or incapable of dealing with change (Martindale 1965).

Although functionalism has its share of weaknesses (Jarvie 1965:18-34), it has contributed much to anthropology as well as to missiology. Schreiter's criticism of functionalism is anything but blind to its contributions. He points out, for instance, the "holistic concerns, the attention to context, and the concern for rich empirical detail"; the usefulness of functionalism in missionary adaptation; the role of functionalism in cross-cultural communication, important especially for initial and early evangelization; and the practicality of functionalism and its relative ease of application (1985:46-47). Malinowski, Radcliffe-Brown, and other early functionalists were also responsible not only for their invaluable concept of function and for their appreciation of the wholeness of society and culture but also for the development of useful field techniques. In fact, some of the finest ethnography has been executed by functionalists, and today functionalism can boast of such outstanding anthropologists as Meyer Fortes (b. 1906), E. E. Evans-Pritchard (1902-1974), Raymond Firth (b. 1902), Victor Turner (1920-1985), and many others, all of whom have grown with anthropology and gone well beyond classical functionalism.

The influence of functionalism is felt most strongly in Anglo-Saxon countries. This is especially true in Britain, so much so that Firth did not hesitate to say that "all British social anthropology today is functionalist" (1955:247). Especially since World War II, functionalism has greatly broadened its interests, improved its methods, and clarified its concepts and terminology (Firth 1955:237-258). Important contributions to functionalism, it must be remembered, have been made also by sociologists—Talcott Parsons (b. 1902) and Robert Merton (b. 1910) in particular.

5.1.6.4 Psychological Anthropology

5.1.6.4.1 Configurationalism

Configurationalism refers to the anthropological trend of the 1930s that emphasized the unique wholeness of cultures, described this uniqueness in terms of "configuration," and attempted to identify the motivating force behind the particular society and culture. Of all proponents of configurationalism, Ruth Benedict (1887-1948) was no doubt its greatest champion. She maintained that cultures had a distinctive character very much like individuals: cultures, too, could be introvert, extrovert, paranoid, megalomanic. Like individuals, cultures were consistent in their thought and action patterns, showing little deviation. The consistency was attributed to certain drives peculiar to the culture. At first, Benedict exaggerated this consistency and was justifiably attacked by her colleagues who regarded her views as "purely intuitive," "subjective," and nothing less than "a distortion," "guess work," and "an oversimplification." The litany of epithets included "poetry" and "mysticism." (The fact is that Ruth Benedict was indeed a poet.) In the face of such criticism, she admitted in her *Patterns of Culture* (1934) degrees of psychological integration, and her book actually became a classic in anthropological literature.

The terminology used by Benedict was borrowed from psychology. The Navaho society, for example, was described as a typical introvert system: individualistic, self-centered, nonconformist, excessive, aggressive—in a word, typically "Dionysian." The neighboring Pueblo Indians were, on the other hand, typically "Apollonian": group-conscious, conformist, ritualistic, restrained, peace-loving. The terms *Dionysian* and *Apollonian* were borrowed from Nietzsche and represented a single, unified, all-pervading trend in culture.

Partly responsible for the growing interest of anthropologists in psychological issues was the popularity of Freudian psychoanalytical theory. Of special interest were questions of child rearing, descriptions of basic personality types, and the general impact of culture on personality formation. Attempts were also made to discover the influence of culture on deviant personalities.

Even complex societies were being studied in the hope of arriving at the *national character* of, for instance, the United States (Mead 1942; Gorer 1948), Russia (Gorer, Rickman 1949), and Japan (Benedict 1942; Gorer 1943). That much unfounded stereotyping was involved cannot, of course, be denied.

5.1.6.4.2 Recent Psychological Anthropology/Personality and Culture Studies

As we shall see in chapter 6, psychological anthropology, despite its questionable beginnings, was by 1950 well on its way toward the adoption of the discipline and rigor of true science. Today, the field has much to offer mission anthropology, particularly in complementing our pivotal model of culture. Responsible for this progress are such well-known anthropologists as Margaret Mead, Abram Kardiner, A. I. Hallowell, J. J. Honigmann, John W. M. Whiting, and many others (Devos 1980; Bourguignon 1973). Modern psychological anthropology has not only become a truly respectable scientific subfield of anthropology but has also greatly widened its scope to include questions that have direct and important bearing on mission action. It investigates, for instance, the relationship between culture on the one hand and thought and perception on the other. Important, too, are such insights as the fact that social organization plays a more important role in personality formation than do most other aspects of culture, or that mental disorders and stress may be peculiar to a given culture.

5.1.6.5 Ideational Models of Culture

5.1.6.5.1 New Ethnography/Ethnoscience/Ethnosemantics/Cognitive Anthropology

In the 1950s, some anthropologists, chiefly North Americans, decided to try to improve their ethnographic field techniques by means of a *new ethnography*. It was felt that somehow the aim of anthropologists to describe cultures in terms of the members of the society being studied was not being realized. Cultures, they now felt, should be analyzed and described *emicly*, and not merely *eticly*, the way a linguist can describe a language from an insider's point of view. (The term *emic* was introduced in 1954 by Kenneth Pike, a linguist, who borrowed the term from *phonemic*, a word employed by linguists in contradistinction to *phonetic*.) Emicists attempt to describe a culture without the use of any preconceived or absolute cognitive categories, the way linguists attempt to describe a particular language without recourse to preconceived notions about phonological and grammatical structures. The goal of the emicists as such was not really new. New, however, were (1) the proposed *object* of study, including culture as a society's body of knowledge (hence the name *ethnoscience*) and the set of ideas that a member of a society must know to be able to cope with life; (2) the *methodology*, including data-collecting techniques, analytic procedures, and record keeping; (3) certain *emphases*, such as the emic/etic distinction and the importance placed on the analysis of categories of concepts as found in the particular cognitive system, including the classifications of kinship, colors, and other semantic domains peculiar to the particular cognitive system. All this seemed to justify calling the new school of thought by several names: new ethnography, ethnoscience, ethnosemantics, and cognitive anthropology.

The methodology is particularly interesting. Ethnoscientists feel that to be able to understand a culture the way someone who was born into it understands it, the fieldworker will have to study nonlinguistic behavior in a manner analogous to the approaches made in linguistics; after all, language reflects the cognitive system, and verbal and nonverbal communication are very similar. Just as the fieldworker must not assume that any speech sound heard in an utterance of an alien is necessarily there to differentiate or create meaning, so the anthropologist must not assume nonverbal categories on the basis of what occurs in the outsider's cognitive system. For example, "friend" is a cognitive category of our behavior that excludes "enemy" (the two concepts are mutually exclusive); in another cognitive system, however, the category "friend" may include "ritual friends" who may happen to be enemies. We include apples, oranges, peaches, and bananas as "fruit," but we regard tomatoes as "vegetables." New ethnography does not *assume* anything on the basis of some outside category; rather, it seeks to *establish* cognitive categories (cultural units) on the basis of the particular culture itself.

Much more, of course, goes into emic analysis than we are able to summarize here. There are, for example, special ways of interviewing an informant, keeping ethnographic records, making a domain analysis, posing structural questions, making a taxonomic analysis, making a componential analysis, and discovering cultural themes. Without entering too deeply into the methodology, however, we wish to point out the emphasis placed by emicists on the necessity of avoiding the transference of the fieldworker's cognitive system to that of the informant's culture. There is, first of all, the insistence on the use of the native language to safeguard the native's categorization of reality. Secondly, questioning of informants takes place as much as possible indirectly, with the informant himself or herself actually or equivalently posing the question he or she answers.

Opening question to informant by ethnographer. What would be an interesting question to ask about that plot of ground where the women are now working?

First question suggested by informant: What is grown there?
First answer given by informant to his/her own question:
Ana (a native vegetable).

The second question by the informant extends the information about *ana*. Each of the other crops is similarly treated. And the questioning continues in this vein. The technique calls for abundant use of question frames. To avoid transferring further the mental categories of the fieldworker onto the information received from the informant, only those personal observations in a participant observation approach are usable that are confirmed by a reliable informant according to emic standards. There is an insistence on keeping a close record of both the informant's response and the question or stimulus; it is assumed that only the question and answer of and by the informant together reflect a basic unit of the informant's cognitive system. Theoretically speaking, if we were to place all such pairs together, we would have the cognitive structure or the cultural "grammar"; we would know the total body of knowledge, the culture, *as* an insider knows it.

Among the leaders in cognitive anthropology are such scholars as S. A. Tyler (1969), Ward Goodenough (1970, 1971), J. P. Spradley (1979, 1980), and M. Agar (1973). For a detailed description of the emic method of field research, one might best study the two works on the subject by Werner, Schoepfle (1986) and J. P. Spradley (1979, 1980) or the short presentation by Pelto and Pelto (1978:54–64). Some of the more significant earlier works on ethnoscience are those of Pike (1954), Goodenough (1956, 1957), Metzger and Williams (1963), Frake (1962, 1964), and Sturtevant (1964). For more recent developments in ethnoscience, one might read Kokot, Lang, and Hinz's survey (1982:329–350).

That new ethnography suffers from some serious weaknesses cannot be denied. First of all, emic procedures are extremely slow-moving; only a relatively few topics might realistically be covered on a field trip. The fact is that to date new ethnography has very few finished products to substantiate its usefulness and validity. Even Sturtevant, one of the emicist stalwarts, had to admit that the ideal goal of a complete ethnography was still a long way from practical attainment:

> The full ethnoscientific description of a single culture would require many thousands of pages published after many years of intensive field work based on ethnographic methods more complete and more advanced than are now available. [1964:123]

Second, the close modeling of culture on language is sometimes exaggerated. There certainly are many striking similarities between language and culture—language, after all, is an integral part of culture—but the similarities are overdrawn by the emicists to the extent that the whole theory seems to suffer from a considerable amount of reductionism. Third, the emic model for culture is too ideational for practical action. The cognitive system may indeed be the main force for action (as we hold), but it is not the only factor determining social behavior; there are factors outside the mind or cognitive system that influence behavior too. For instance, there are limits placed on behavior by the physical environment, the state of technology, intra- and extratribal politics, and the like (*infra*, 5.2.2.2.4).

Despite such weaknesses, however, cognitive anthropology has something to offer to both theoretical as well as applied anthropology. Its scrupulous handling of field data and the constant focus on an insider's perspective may make this still-not-fully-tested, slow-moving approach worth considering in missionary work at least for special pastoral problems (for example, those affecting marriage law) that call for meticulous ethnography and considerable retesting of data by others. Cognitive anthropology has a definite role to play in any composite missiological model of culture.

5.1.6.5.2 Structuralism

In anthropology, *structuralism* means *French* structuralism, of which Lévi-Strauss (b. 1908) is the outstanding figure. One must, however, not overlook or downplay the contributions of other anthropologists. Among these are the Russian formalists, the Swiss psychologist Piaget, and Jakobson of the Prague school of linguistics.

The structuralist premise is that the patterns of all cultures are the product of one and the same psychological process shared by all humans. The interest is in the abstract *culture,* not in *a* culture. As a basic premise, structuralism holds that cultural patterns, however different in different societies, have a common inner logic, a basic human structure. To understand *the human mind*—that is to say, the common universal design of cultures and not the individual cultures as such—is the objective of French structuralism.

Structuralism assumes that human beings have an inborn ability to order their experiences and to classify the world in which this experience takes place. Lévi-Strauss' emphasis is on the extraordinary capacity that the human animal has to arrange perceptions and to categorize them. All humans have the same kind of brain, which operates in the same manner in all societies. Cultural differences, however great they may be on the surface level, are the same on the deeper level. To get at the deeper-level structures is Lévi-Strauss' chief concern.

An important assumption of French structuralism is that the human capacity to form categories is founded on the ability to create *binary distinctions*—that is, a concept and its negative counterpart, such as life versus death, black versus white, male versus female, or right versus left. Such binary pairs are irreconcilable: what is right cannot be left, what is alive cannot be dead.

Lévi-Strauss is particularly fond of analyzing *myths*. He claims that they carry a deep-level message. Thus the opposition between life and death is resolved in mythology through a middle category, namely through the idea of some form of immortality. A Pueblo myth dealing with hunting, war, and agriculture accordingly solves the contradiction between life and death by the following logic: agriculture symbolizes life; war is death; but this contradiction is solved by means of hunting, a mediating category—hunting requires death in order to preserve human life. (J. Friedl 1981:56.)

French structuralism, although received enthusiastically by some anthropologists for its imagination and stimulation, is regarded perhaps by most as too complicated, too limited, too arbitrary, and too mystic to be really useful. Lévi-Strauss' writings unfortunately allow for a variety of interpretation; they do not possess the rigorous singleness of meaning characteristic of scientific writing. Objectionable, too, is the fact that the approach is too subjective. J. Friedl's observation is very much to the point when he says that

> it is, after all, Lévi-Strauss who selects the myths to be analyzed, who arranges the elements and "uncovers" the structure hidden within the myth. [J. Friedl 1981:56]

Structuralists, like the emicists, also decontextualize culture by placing it exclusively in the heads of people rather than where it should be placed, partly in the heads and partly in social interaction.

And yet, we do not wish to dismiss structuralism without giving credit where credit is due. One must recognize the merits that it has. As Schreiter (1985:48) points out, by discovering the working of the binary opposition in culture, the structuralist approach can cast useful light on the relation between different domains of culture. In particular, it can explain how myth and ritual relate to other aspects of culture; it can also cast light on native metaphors and on the system of classification; it can provide a better understanding of identity structures and cohesiveness of a people. These are all major considerations when one is applying anthropology to mission. Our main objection to the approach as a primary model for missiological purposes, however, remains: the model is too complex and too subjective, and it has too limited an application to mission needs.

As basic reading, we recommended the following works: Octavio Paz's *Claude Lévi-Strauss: An Introduction* (1970); Edmund Leach's two small books *Claude Lévi-Strauss* (1974) and *Culture and Communication: The*

Logic by Which Symbols Are Connected (1976); and Ino Rossi (ed.), *The Unconscious in Culture: The Structuralism of Claude Lévi-Strauss in Perspective* (1974). It would also be necessary, of course, to read one or the other of Lévi-Strauss' classics, especially his *Structural Anthropology* (1963) and *The Savage Mind* (1966).

5.1.6.5.3 Symbolic/Semiotic Anthropology

Gaining ever greater respect among anthropologists today is one of the areas of newest direction, known as *symbolic* or *semiotic anthropology*. These names are derived from the Greek *symbolon* ("token, sign") and *sêmiôtikos* ("observant of signs"). In symbolic anthropology, culture is viewed as a shared communication network that sends messages along vast and elaborate interconnected routes. Culture is therefore an interwebbing of signs (bearers of messages and their meanings). These signs may be verbal or nonverbal (persons, things, or events). The particular circuit that they follow is determined by codes (a set of rules). A sign may in fact carry several meanings, as in the case of a smile, which may be a sign of happiness, satisfaction, cynicism, skepticism, welcome, ridicule, humor, love, revenge, or a signal for action, all depending on the given culture and the nature of its code.

Symbolic anthropology is interdisciplinary, with special predilection for linguistic metaphors. Thus the three poles around which the model gravitates are known as *syntactics* (the grammar of the cultural language), *semantics* (the meanings), and *pragmatics* (the rules governing the practical usage of the signs, the "sociolinguistics" of culture). Semiotics has drawn much also from other anthropological schools of thought, such as functionalism and structuralism, and from other fields like sociology, computer science, psychology, philosophy, and mathematics. Much of the inspiration has been derived from Max Weber and Lévi-Strauss.

There are considerable differences in how the symbolic model of culture is described, not only by the three major language groups of semioticists (the French-, Russian-, and the English-speaking) but also within each of these groups. The Anglo-Americans include, for instance, Clifford Geertz, David Schneider, Victor Turner, Mary Douglas, Edmund Leach, and Raymond Firth, who agree that cultures are best viewed as systems of shared meaning but who disagree in their perception of symbols. Schneider, like the structuralists and emicists, disembodies culture. That is to say, he isolates culture from actual behavior and treats it entirely on its own terms, a feature we shall have to reject in our composite model of culture (*infra*, 5.2.2.2.4). Culture is more than what an informant *says*: as Geertz holds, culture is not disembodied but implies a *use* to which the members of a society will put the symbolic system (Rossi, O'Higgins 1980:66). To Geertz, the shared symbols are, as they must be to the mission anthropologist, a set of plans, recipes, rules, and instructions (Geertz 1965:107), not things purely of the mind that have no application or instructions for real life. Like Geertz, Turner sees culture in terms of symbolic *action*. To Turner, the symbolic system is generally instrumental; that is, it possesses human goals, purposes, interests, and concerns, and serves to excite the emotions and to motivate the bearer of culture (*infra,* 6.2.3.3.1). This is a stand clearly adopted in our missiologically oriented model of culture (*infra,* 5.2).

What are some of the advantages of the symbolic/semiotic model? (1) Symbolic anthropology is distinctly *holistic,* an extremely important criterion for a good missiologically oriented model of culture. That it is such is evident from the fact that its concerns include *all* symbols—verbal and nonverbal, empirical and nonempirical (including thoughts, emotions, and values), the nobler aspects of culture (like art, poetry, music, and religion), as well as the other domains of culture (the social, economic, and political). (2) By getting at the configuration of *both culture and society,* a semiotic analysis enables the community to recognize its own uniqueness and to make this uniqueness more understandable to others. (3) *Culture change* is of particular interest to symbolic anthropology: meant are the mechanisms of balance and imbalance, function and dysfunction. Nothing could be more important to mission than change, be the change in the form of conversion (a metanoia, a constant struggle to take off the old person and to put on the new), be it the preaching of the Kingdom, or the difficult journey of the Pilgrim Church on its way to its true and final destination. (4) The emphasis of symbolic anthropology is properly placed on *meaning,* and meaning happens to be what God himself is most interested in and what mission is most concerned about. (5) Moreover, *communication* is the Church's single most important human tool, (cf. Lonergan 1972:355–368, and it is communication that is of foremost interest to semiotics. (Cf. Schreiter 1985:52–53.)

Does that mean that semiotics has no weaknesses? When we dealt with criteria for a missiologically oriented model of culture (*supra,* 5.1.4, 5.1.5), we stressed how important it was that our model be "fitting" (that is, simple and clear) and "stimulating" (that is, able to arouse the imagination of professional theoreticians as well as administrators and grassroots practitioners). Unfortunately, semiotics as presented is largely abstract and difficult, and is often overloaded with linguistic, computer, and academic jargon unfamiliar to most non-anthropologists and particularly strange to the leaders of local churches (especially of non-Western countries) and others most directly responsible for the inculturation of the Gospel. It serves the academician rather than the practitioner and the expert rather than the nonprofessional anthropologist. It is quite true that deeper, long-range concerns are valid for all involved in mission, and ultimately such concerns will perhaps prove to be more important for mission than the nitty-gritty problems facing practitioners at the moment. But it is nevertheless here that its weakness lies: semiotics neglects the nitty-gritty that mission cannot afford to neglect. The practitioner (the primary contextualizer) needs a less abstract, more usable model, one that is more understandable, even if it is lacking some of the depth and sophistication that the proponents of the semiotic model claim for their perspective. The semiotic model, nevertheless, offers considerable promise as far as mission application is concerned and should therefore be pursued, but the development of the perspective and its application will have to be left to the professional, not to the practitioner. The composite mission-oriented model to be suggested in the next section (*infra*, 5.2) borrows liberally from symbolic anthropology as a complementary submodel, even if it does not use its jargon. Our model will always be open to such borrowing for further refinement, balance, and correction. It should not be forgotten that symbolic anthropology is itself a composite with borrowings from cognitive anthropology, structuralism, and functionalism.

The clearest and most successful application of the semiotic model to mission to date is, no doubt, R. Schreiter's *Constructing Local Theologies* (1985). For anthropological theory on semiotics as such, one might study, for example: Clifford Geertz's *The Interpretation of Culture* (1973); Victor Turner's *Dramas, Fields, and Metaphors: Symbolic Action in Human Society* (1974); Victor and Edith Turner's *Image and Pilgrimage in Christian Culture: Anthropological Perspectives* (1978); and Raymond Firth's *Symbols, Public and Private* (1973).

5.2 A COMPOSITE MISSIOLOGICAL PERSPECTIVE OF CULTURE: CULTURE AS A SOCIALLY SHARED DESIGN FOR LIVING

As we have seen (*supra*, 5.1.4, 5.1.5), ours must be a composite view of culture. By viewing a way of life as a society's design for living, we mean that culture is (1) a *plan* (2) consisting of a set of *norms, standards*, and associated *notions* and *beliefs* (3) for *coping* with the various demands of life, (4) shared by *a social group*, (5) *learned* by the individual from the society, and (6) organized into a *dynamic* (7) *system* of control. In the present and following chapters these characteristics will be explained, and their usefulness for theoretical and practical missiology will be illustrated.

5.2.1 CULTURE AS A PLAN FOR LIVING

Culture is not just an open-ended way of life. Rather, it is a plan, map, or blueprint for living that is always in the process of formation and adjustment. It is a code for action, for survival, and for success in life. As we shall see when we discuss culture dynamics, culture is constantly adjusting according to needs and growth of experience. This is in a few words the substance of the model of culture that we feel will be most productive as far as mission application is concerned.

5.2.1.1 Culture Is a Set of NORMS, STANDARDS, NOTIONS, and BELIEFS

By saying that culture is basically a set of *norms for living* we mean that culture consists of control mechanisms—recipes, rules, instructions and guidelines on *how to* live (Geertz 1973:44). Culture also sets *standards* for behavior by providing meanings and values to the constituents of culture. It also supplies countless supplementary details (*notions* and *beliefs*) associated with the various demands of life.

Culture is indeed very much a kind of map or blueprint for living. It is a plan according to which a society is to adapt itself to its *physical, social*, and *ideational* environment. Societies cope with their physical environment by means of norms, standards, and ideas regarding such matters as food production, housing, travel, and various levels of technological knowledge and skill. They adapt to their social environment by means of political guidelines, kinship relationships, and countless norms guiding the interaction between members of the society in question, foremost of which are the norms for communication. These same norms, we mention in passing, are basic for contextualizing the Gospel and for constructing meaningful local theologies. Societies cope with their ideational environment by means of norms affecting such matters as knowledge, art, magic, science, philosophy, ideology, and religion. In other words, when we say that culture is a set of socially shared ideas for coping with the various demands of life, we are speaking not only of ideas affecting physical and social adaptation but also of those affecting thought patterns and knowledge.

5.2.1.2 Culture Is a THING OF THE MIND Underlying Behavior

When speaking of culture, we are therefore speaking not of things or events as such but of *ideas*. Culture is the ideational code *underlying* behavior. It is a blueprint *for* as well as *of* behavior, in the same way that a blueprint is a model for and of a building. But, like a blueprint, it is not the building itself. Culture is, therefore, not the actual reality and historical event as such. Things and events *reflect* culture—history reflects culture—but culture is not the historical reality itself. Norms, standards, and notions are not things or events; they are *ideas* regarding things and events. Culture is a society's set of rules for the game of life, not the played-out game itself. Culture may express itself in artifacts, concrete social interrelationships and observable interaction, and in ritual and magical practices; but these are only *expressions* of ideas and therefore they are not culture itself. Although some anthropologists may regard such expressions as integral components of culture, and although culture never occurs apart from concrete societies and their actual behavior, we regard culture as being essentially an ideational code underlying cultural expressions. We view culture as a *design* for and of behavior the way a cabinetmaker's drawings are a design for and of the furniture produced, but the drawings are not the furniture. Culture refers to what humans *learn*, not what they do or make (R. Keesing 1976:139). Culture in the last analysis is therefore a set of *symbols* and *meanings*.

5.2.1.3 Culture as a More or Less SUCCESSFUL Plan

By viewing culture as being adaptive, we do not wish to imply that everything in culture is purposeful, harmonious, and successful. We wish, rather, to emphasize that culture is the way the particular society *de facto* designs its life, be some of the elements in the plan rational, irrational, or nonrational;

successful or unsuccessful; true or false. We are merely saying that cultures *aim* to be successful. We do not deny that they are at times rightly described as being more like old cities—basically functional but lacking the neat arrangement of a modern suburb or a newly planned urban settlement. In an old city, what is not functional either crumbles away or is torn down, or the citizens simply adjust to the old buildings, the narrow winding streets, and quaint squares, letting them be a part of the city—or of the culture, if you will.

Cultures only *tend* to "cope" and be functional. Although cultures may at times turn out to be dysfunctional, causing problems rather than solving them, they are generally purposeful, at least in the sense that they are the result of a society's shared experience, sometimes over many centuries, and as such generally bring about a lessening of tensions, instill needed confidence, and provide the organization, balance, security, and satisfaction that human exist-ence requires. But because some patterns may sometimes indeed prove to be dysfunctional, our concept of culture prescinds from the success and objectiv-ity of the particular norms, standards, and notions. Cultures, therefore, only *try* or *tend* to cope with the problems of life; they are, after all, only a *plan* or *design* for succeeding in life. They only *promise* success. The plan is constantly being altered, improved on, and experimented with.

5.2.1.4 Culture Is a UNIQUE Plan

Cultures are *unique*. While emphasizing this uniqueness and human diver-sity, however, we must guard against overlooking or downplaying common human traits. Some extreme configurationalists tended to overemphasize hu-man diversity and uniqueness; today, anthropologists generally take into ac-count both human diversity and human commonality. If cultures were so utterly different from one another (as some extremists would have us believe), satisfactory translations would be impossible; the United Nations could hardly hold general assemblies; the World Court, the World Council of Churches, and the Catholic Church would not exist. If such human commonality were not a fact, cross-cultural communication and harmonious cross-cultural interaction—and mission itself—would be impossible. The Bible would not be the universal book that it is; nor would the Good News be good news for all people and all times. While recognizing the great diversity among human societies, one should not grow blind to the many basic human similarities and common human aspirations and values. (As we shall see in the following chapter, we are speaking of similarities, not of identities or universals that would include the details and complexities of cultural organization as well.) Individual cultures are but different answers to fundamentally panhuman questions.

5.2.1.5 Culture Is a COMPREHENSIVE Plan

By speaking of culture as a plan for adapting to the triple human environ-ment, we emphasized that a culture embraces *all* facets of life, the physical, social, and ideational. Our concept of culture is in the strictest sense of the word holistic. Culture is a "complex whole" (Tylor), "the sum total" (Lowie, Linton), "all designs" (Kluckhohn), and "the totality" (F. Keesing). To the anthropologist, the idea of a prosaic garbage heap is therefore as genuinely a part of his or her culture as are the standards regarding the masterpieces of Beethoven, Dante, and Michelangelo. To the anthropologist, a hungry cannibal (if there be such a being)[2] savagely devouring a piece of leg of man and following his society's local design for living would be no less cultured than a socialite daintily nibbling on a piece of leg of lamb. We are not supporting unrestricted cultural relativism, as if all cultures were equally right or wrong; rather, we are saying that the anthropological term *culture* embraces *whatever* one learns from one's society as part of its plan for coping with life—whether objectively right or wrong, whether aesthetically beautiful or repulsive, whether as true as mathematics or as fictitious as ghosts and fairies, whether functional, nonfunctional, or disruptive.

The totality of which we speak embraces the *overt* as well as the *covert* responses to human needs. It includes the *manifest* as well as the *implicit* aspects of a lifeway; the *universals, alternatives,* and the *specialties.* These are the terms that we shall presently define.

A design for coping with life's problems refers to something more than the *manifest* or easily observable—to something more than the so-called *behavioral patterns.* When anthropologists speak of *manifest culture,* they refer to such matters as ideas about food-getting, housing, clothing, ornamentation, eating habits, mating practices, family organization, kinship systems, status, social class, ownership, inheritance rules, trade, government, war, law, religion, magic, and language.

As already partially described (*supra,* 3.1.3.3.1–3.1.3.3.3), there are three levels to culture, namely the levels of form, integration, and configuration. We shall describe these levels at some length later on, but suffice it here to review briefly what these terms mean. (1) The particular norms that make up a culture are expressed in specific *forms,* also referred to as the *explicit* culture, or the *who, what, how, when, what kind,* and *where.* (2) Forms, however, are not mere odds and ends but rather are integral parts of single wholes or subsystems of behavior composed of elements that are linked to one another functionally. *Functions* are the relationships, logical or purposeful, that exist between the various forms. This network of interrelationships anthropologists call *integration.* (3) At a still-deeper level are the starting points of reasoning, reacting, and motivating—the underlying premises, emotionally charged attitudes, and basic drives—the so-called philosophy or mentality of the people in question. This third and deepest level we call *configuration.* In contradistinction to the *manifest* culture, the two deeper levels are sometimes referred to as the *latent* components of culture; they are the *whys* of social behavior.

Anthropologists also speak of *overt* and *covert* aspects of culture. Overt culture refers to the socially shared norms that become externalized through movement and physical activity. Covert culture refers to the patterns of belief, thought, emotion, and evaluation.

5.2.1.6 Missiological Application

5.2.1.6.1 Summary of Relevant Theory

Before we proceed to show the relevance of the theory just presented, it may be useful to summarize the salient points. *Culture as a design for living* is the society's plan for coping with the given physical, social, and ideational environment. Generally, cultures are highly adaptive in purpose. They are more or less complete (covering *all* aspects of life), more or less successful, and always unique. What, we now ask, is the missiological significance of this view of culture? What, in a word, are some of the theoretical and practical implications for mission that flow from the fact that we view culture as a plan for living?

5.2.1.6.2 Missiological Significance of Culture As an ADAPTIVE System

Empathy. One of the most important qualifications for Church leadership and effectiveness in mission is the Lord's advice, "Learn from me, for I am gentle and humble of heart" (Mt 11:29). Jesus was the true servant of Yahweh who could not get himself so much as to break a bruised reed (Is 42:3; Mt 12:20). Commenting on this passage as found in Matthew, Barclay calls Jesus the "Great Encourager," who came not to treat the weak with contempt but with true understanding (1975,2:34). However simple or however complex, however "primitive" or however "advanced" a society's way of life may appear to the outsider, the culture should be viewed indeed as a plan, as an honest attempt to solve genuine human problems. At times the Church may not be able to agree with or approve what the particular society regards as a solution. At times, like Christ himself, the Christian community will be called upon to carry out a prophetic role and therefore will be countercultural. Christians are to be "the salt of the earth" (Mt 5:13) that must penetrate, preserve, give taste, and, at times, sting. A prophet must have deep compassion for AIDS victims without approving homosexuality or drug abuse. Empathy means that the prophet must be able to weep over a sinful city whose lifestyle must nevertheless be condemned. The prophet must be able to condemn prostitution without necessarily condemning the prostitute (Jn 8:11). Empathy is in fact the beginning of both anthropological and missiological wisdom, and the beginning of empathy is the recognition that cultures, however misguided, are as a rule a society's *honest* attempt to cope with life.

It is often difficult to understand how new Christians can so quickly fall back into their "old pagan ways" (cf. Gal 1:6f). Once the novelty of conversion wears off, relapses may become in fact frequent. Recidivism is, however, not so much the result of a weak Faith as it is the result of a very strong faith, a faith in a tested, fulfilling, and apparently successful non-Christian adaptive system. Such a faith has produced harmony in the life of the convert; it has provided the necessary security and has given meaning to life—not *Christian* meaning of course, but meaning nonetheless. Not ill will but the instinct of self-preservation is sometimes at the very root of such relapses. Conversion is normally a process rather than an instantaneous change, and not seldom it involves a constant struggle with the traditional "tested and trustworthy" ways.

Empathy is not something that is to be limited to so-called newer churches. That would be paternalism, not empathy. Keeping in mind what we have said about cultures as being adaptive systems, we must empathize with de-Christianized societies no less than with those in mission lands. Whatever be the reasons for modern de-Christianization and the disenchantment with Christianity (cf. Newbigin 1986), the fact remains that individuals of one-time Christian countries are following an adaptive system (call it neopaganism if you will) that, in their view, serves as a reliable, effective, and satisfying solution to life's problems. In fact, the individuals, especially the youth of such societies, may have been led to believe that Christianity is largely irrelevant. This attitude toward the Gospel is hardly different from that of non-Christians. So-called neopagans are not necessarily individuals of ill will but persons groping in the dark; while seeking solutions, they reach out for nonsolutions offered by their cultures, such as materialism, humanism, hedonism, scientism, sex, drugs, and new cults. In dealing with neopaganism, the Church can never, of course, approve error, never compromise the Gospel, and as a rule cannot remain silent. Our dominant model of culture (culture viewed as an adaptive system) implicitly calls for a truly empathetic insider's appreciation of neopaganism. For the same reason, there is room for empathy even toward lukewarmness, nominal Christianity, and even atheism. "Empathy ever!" we are saying, even if we hasten to add, "Approval never!"

Christ never turned his back to a sinner; it was the sinner who turned away from him. In the document *The Declaration on Religious Liberty*, Vatican II urges Catholics, while adhering uncompromisingly to the Gospel, "to treat with love, prudence, and patience those who are in error or ignorance with regard to faith" (*Dignitatis humanae*, no.14). In the document *The Church in the Modern World*, Catholics are urged to treat atheism with understanding, "reproving, with sorrow yet with the utmost firmness." In fact, Christians are to "seek out the secret motives which lead the atheistic mind to deny God" (*Gaudium et spes*, no.19–21).

Cultural Relevancy. Whether the Church's message be about God and his loving revelation or about such fundamental human needs as food-production, health care, and social justice, it must be presented with culture *as an adaptive system* in mind—that is, as something that promises success in life. Christian doctrines and practices, and for that matter any innovation that the Church may have to offer, be it of a spiritual nature or social, should not be left dangling but should be tailored to the *local* set of needs. Innovations should whenever possible be presented as something that will complete and perfect the existing cultural design. This principle, we must emphasize, applies to technologically advanced societies no less than to developing nations. The undeniable truth is that the Gospel will not be accepted by any society unless the "wares" offered by the Church be presented as missing in the culture, as the preferable solution actually demanded by the existing lifeway itself.

Felt-Needs. Closely related to the principle of cultural relevancy is the principle of felt-needs. Felt-needs are just that—needs that are real. That is to say, they are local, actual, and therefore felt. As such, they are the key to any sound pastoral program and to any genuine contextualization of the Gospel.

The constant awareness that culture is an adaptive system will make those engaged in a ministry and occupying leadership roles to formulate policies based on felt-needs. Such local and actual needs will constitute the starting points, for instance, in religious educational programs. The choice of a catechism or religious textbook should not be determined so much by its popularity in other parts of the world as by the felt-needs here and now and in the foreseeable future.[3] This constant awareness of and sensitivity to felt-needs is unquestionably one of the greatest strengths of Latin American base communities and of most liberation theologies.

As we have just seen, societies will accept only so much of the Gospel as they feel they *need*. One of the chief reasons for the spread of Marxism in the Third World is the ability of its proponents to present Marxist ideology in terms of felt-needs. If the Church is to be successful in the Third World, it too must focus its message on the needs of the local community. Oscar Lewis in his well-known *Five Families* describes how a Mexican gave as reason for abandoning his Catholic faith and joining the spiritists the fact that, unlike traditional Mexican Catholicism, spiritism could help people in trouble, cure sicknesses, and ward off black magic with white (1959:159). The needs of this Mexican Catholic were not being met by the local pastor who was very impersonal, insensitive to local and actual needs, blind to the necessity of making ritual understandable and relevant, and too moralistic; that is, this pastor endlessly preached what people should not do without showing how profoundly relevant God's law was here and now. Culturally-focused scriptural discussions—may we suggest, for instance, Psalm 119, which extols the beauty, power, wisdom, and *relevance* of God's law—would have been the more proper pastoral approach. In northeast Brazil, known for its extreme poverty, a Christian once complained to an American reporter, "See, God gave me all these children, all twelve of them, but I have to go to Marxists to feed them." The social analysis for mission proposed by Holland and Henriot (1983) is particularly meaningful because felt-needs lie at the root of their approach. Excellent examples of what is meant by the principle of felt-needs will be found in such recent works as Masao Takenaka's *God Is Rice* (1986) and Ernesto Cardenal's *The Gospel in Solentiname* (4 vols. 1976–1982).

The many still-unrecognized but nonetheless objective needs must eventually be felt too, but psychologically and pedagogically such objective and still-unfelt needs must wait their turn before they are accepted and integrated with the existing adaptive system. The normal progression in any form of education is from that which is already an integral part of the adaptive system to that which should be, but in fact is not, from the recognized to the still unrecognized, from the known to the still unknown, from the felt to the still unfelt. The starting point in any pastoral plan should be the *existing* set of premises, values, and goals; from these existing assumptions, emotionally charged attitudes, and driving forces, the instructor must lead his or her charges to new conclusions, to new premises, new attitudes, and new goals, and from there, farther and farther, deeper and deeper, to the hoped-for premises, values, and drives, but always from the already felt to the still unfelt. The base communities in Latin America, Africa, the Philippines, and elsewhere find their unusual strength largely in this very ability to move from what is already in the adaptive system to that which seems still to be lacking. St. Augustine, the great knower of the human heart, expressed this basic anthropological and pedagogical principle centuries ago in his *De doctrina christiana*, when he pointed out that an individual will be moved to action

> if what you promise is what he likes, if the danger of which you speak is real, if your censures are directed against something he hates, if your recommendations are in harmony with what he embraces, if he regrets what you say is regrettable, if he rejoices over what you claim is a reason for joy, if his heart is sympathetic toward those whose misery you describe, if he avoids those who you advise should be avoided . . . not merely imparting knowledge about things that ought to be done but rather moving him to do what he knows must be done. [IV,12]

St. Augustine thus maintains that the most usable stepping stones from "pagan" to Christian values are none other than what modern applied anthropology calls felt-needs, needs found in the existing albeit "pagan," adaptive system. St. Paul seems to have applied this principle when at the Areopagus he boldly cried out:

> Men of Athens, I note that in every respect you are scrupulously religious. As I walked around looking at your shrines, I even discovered an altar inscribed, "To a God unknown." Now, what you are thus worshiping in ignorance I intend to make known to you. [Acts 17:22f]

To a society that feels no sense of guilt, as is often the case today in both the modern Western world (Menninger 1973) as well as in less technologically developed lands, the work of redemption as a starting-point or a point of initial emphasis in religious education may not be as effective as a presentation of the personality of Christ. The popularity of the musicals *Godspel* and *Jesus Christ Superstar* illustrates what we mean. Depending on the felt-needs of the particular community, more rapid progress can be expected if Christian education proceeds from an appreciation of Christ as a selfless, lovable, and completely trustworthy person to the culturally more difficult and less appreciated aspects of christology. We are not advocating a kind of selective Christianity but are stressing, rather, the importance of psychological timing that has been tailored to the given felt-needs.

5.2.1.6.3 Missiological Significance of Cultural COMPREHENSIVENESS

What should be contextualized? What is the object of contextualization? The theoretical answer is simple enough: the object of contextualization is nothing less than the *whole* design for living and all that this totality implies. Granted that priorities must be observed, holism, as suggested earlier, must remain one of the major criteria for a good missiological model of culture. Christ must be incarnated first of all in the *manifest* culture. In the words of Paul, "The fact is that whether you eat or drink—whatever you do—you should do all for the glory of God" (1 Cor 10:31). Moreover, contextualization enters above all into whatever we shall have to say about the *implicit* culture, the organization and dynamics of a lifeway. (This very broad holistic view of the object of contextualization will be concretized as we proceed.)

5.2.1.6.4 Missiological Significance of Cultural UNIQUENESS

Every design for living has, so to speak, a personality or individuality of its own (*infra*, 6.2). The natural tendency in observing foreign ways is to give the behavior the same or similar interpretation that we give to our own ways. Identical usages, identical purposes, meanings, and values are attributed to any behavior that shows the slightest similarity to our own. This tendency occurs also at the subcultural level and underlies the common generational clashes:

> New dances, for instance, have always been "shocking" and "immoral," whether the new dance was the polka, mazurka, waltz, or rock'n'roll. Although the high value that is placed on virginity in some cultures is essentially an economic consideration rather than a moral or religious one, the unwary outsider, observing the high esteem for the physical integrity of a bride, compliments the people for their high moral standards when actually they should be complimented for their good economic and purely materialistic sense: in the particular culture the financial compensation to the family of the bride is always much greater for a virgin than a non-virgin. Similarly, just because the Chinese during the Rites Controversy used tapers and incense as a part of their memorial customs, the opponents of the Jesuits regarded the practice as having a strictly religious meaning and therefore as something that had to be condemned as superstitious ancestor worship. After all, the argument went, are not "altars," candles and incense, bows and invocations by their very nature religious in character?

There are very few anthropological principles that are violated as frequently in carrying out the mission of the Church as the following principle: human similarities are not human identities. Insiders generally sense this uniqueness, but outsiders normally do not. Outsiders tend to interpret and evaluate with their own cultural measuring-rods all behavior patterns that remind them of their own:

There is the story told of the Anglo-American couple who on Memorial Day brought some flowers to the grave of their loved ones. They were surprised to see how some Chicanos laid food on the graves instead. Surprised, if not amused, they approached the Chicanos and asked them, "When do you expect your departed to come and eat your food?" Without even looking up, one of the Chicanos replied very nonchalantly, "O, about the same time your loved ones will come up to smell your flowers."

In the Hispanic cultures, for example, a bullfight is regarded as a reputable sport, a most exciting form of entertainment, a kind of ballet, a victory of art over brute force, a pageant of bravery, a *fiesta brava* in the truest sense of the word. However, to many, if not most Americans just north of the Rio Grande, bullfighting, measured of course with a gringo yardstick, is but an "unjustifiable, unfair, and positively cruel slaughter of a helpless and stupid animal by one having the advantage of human intelligence, the assistance of other men, and the use of weapons far superior to even the sharpest bovine horns." The unfairness of our interpretations is brought home to us as soon as ethnocentric deductions are made about our own way of life. Two Frenchmen watching an American football game for the first time would most likely make the following, or similar, comments: "American football is no sport at all. It's sheer brute force! It is outright savagery, nothing else! And do you call that sportsmanship? Is that supposed to be exciting entertainment, with all those boring interruptions called 'huddles'?" Our two imaginary French spectators would be drawing conclusions about American football on the basis of what their soccer would look like if played in such a "rough" and "boorish" fashion and with all those "boring" pauses. On the other hand, if the two Frenchmen would measure American football with an American measuring-rod, they would have to admit that American football is indeed a great sport.

A previous acquaintance with one culture may be a help in understanding a similar culture. Members of subsocieties that are similar should be more easily able to appreciate one another's culture than societies with greatly divergent ways of life. At the same time, we must keep in mind that an acquaintance with similar behavior may become a source of preconceived ideas. The so-called generation gap is a clear example of what we mean by similar but not identical cultural patterns (Luzbetak 1966–67). The Chinese and Japanese are both Orientals, but Chinese are not Japanese, nor are the Japanese Chinese. Previous acquaintance with an Oriental culture may be helpful to us in under-standing another Oriental culture, but such acquaintance, we must remember, may be misleading if we fail to keep the idea of the uniqueness of cultures in mind.

Colombians, Chileans, Mexicans, and Guatemalans are all Latin Ameri-cans, and despite the underlying similarities in their cultures, each of their lifeways must be regarded as unique. Acquaintance with one Latin American people may be helpful in understanding another Latin American people, but such an acquaintance may also become a source of preconceived ideas and a stumbling block. Just because we may have worked many years in Mexico does not mean that we have become authorities on the ways and values of the Hondurans, Costa Ricans, Panamanians, or Puerto Ricans. To an inquiry made by the author some years ago regarding problems of missionary adjust-ment in Mexico, not a few Mexican bishops expressed the opinion that "as difficult as it may be for a North American to be 'de-Yankeeized,' 'de-Yankeeization' always remains possible. That, however, is not the case with many priests and religious coming from Spain. Yankees at least recognize the fact that their culture is different, something the Spaniards unfortunately often fail to do; to them, similarity is identity." It cannot be emphasized enough that one of the first and most important steps to be taken in developing a pastoral strategy at home or anywhere in the world is to recognize the uniqueness of the community. A good example of an empathetic attempt at recognizing local cultural differences is Carl F. Burke's effort to lead lowest-rung youth to God by means of *their* set of shared norms. Burke's *God Is for Real, Man* (1966) portrays Judas as a "stoolie" in Jesus' "gang." "The Lord is my Shepherd" becomes "The Lord is my Probation Officer"—the probation officer being the only true friend that the youths in question have. The word *father* is hardly suitable at this early stage of evangelization, for in the given context, *father* connotes hardly anything more than "a drunken good-for-nothing."

5.2.2 CULTURE AS A SOCIETAL POSSESSION

5.2.2.1 The Meaning of Society

The term *society* refers to organized, interacting, more or less self-sufficient groupings of human beings who share a continuity across generations. Nor-mally, individuals become members of a society by means of a process known as *socialization* (*infra*, 5.3). Common political boundaries are not essential, whereas the sharing of organized relationships, role assignments, cognitive and communication systems, social control, and other forms of systematized interaction among members are. There are two major directions taken by sociologists in their interpretation of society: there is the view of the *functiona-lists*, Talcott Parsons in particular, who view society as being basically in the state of equilibrium; and there is the view of the *conflict theorists*, the chief among whom are perhaps the Marxists, who regard change as the normal state of society and social stability as only a passing phase resulting from the superior power and control of a segment of society that manages to maintain its privileged position. Societies disappear mainly through malaise, assimilation with other societies, biological extermination, and by dispersal of members. (Cf. Hunter, Whitten 1976:361.)

There are still other characteristics of society that one ought to be aware of. As R. Keesing (1976:143ff) observes, the Hopi, as an example, are (1) members of a *society*; that is to say, they are members of a distinct *population*. A population forms a distinct community, generally speaks a common language or dialect, shares a common tradition, and interacts more closely internally than with members of other communities. (2) The Hopi *have* a culture, but they *are not* a culture. (3) A society can be said to be a special kind of *social system*. A social system refers to a unique structure, organization, or set of patterns of interaction within a group, be the group as small as a family, an orchestra, a gang, a convent or a seminary, or as large as an inner city ghetto, a tribe, or a nation.

5.2.2.2 Culture in Relation to Society and the Individual

Culture tells us how a *society* is to behave, although it is really the individual who acts. Culture consists of *patterns*, or expectations in behavior—the standards or guidelines for a society, rather than for an individual as an individual. Let us look more closely at such terms as *society*, *individual*, and *patterns*.

5.2.2.2.1 Culture as the Individual's Theory of His/Her Society's Behavior

Culture, it must be remembered, exists in the mind of the individual member of society. It is the individual's theory as to what his or her society holds as the proper way of coping with life. Just as normal individuals possess an innate linguistic competence that enables them to analyze the vernacular phonemic system and grammar and to generate literally countless "correct" original utterances, so too do they possess an uncanny competence to analyze their culture and to formulate a kind of theory about what the particular culture is. The individual's theory is in substantial agreement with that of the other members of society, just as his or her analysis of the language is substantially in agreement with the society's verbal communication system called "language." Cultural analysis is made further possible through an individual's innate ability to abstract and generalize and through the constant exposure to a dialectic called *enculturation*, a concept we have already touched upon and that we shall treat more fully below (*infra*, 5.2.3).

5.2.2.2.2 Culture as the Anthropologist's Generalization

Going a step farther, we say that cultures are the generalization of the anthropologist about the theories that individual members of a society have regarding their own society's design for living. Culture is therefore a thing of the mind. However, as applied anthropologists we cannot afford to study culture completely disembodied from reality—we cannot regard culture as *only* a thing of the mind. Rather, we relate the "thing of the mind" to real people in real life.

> Meanings are not "in people's heads"; symbols and meanings are shared by social actors between, not in, them; they are public, not private cultural systems. [R. Keesing 1974:79]

In applied anthropology we wish, through cooperation rather than manipulation of any kind, to influence the society's patterns *of* behavior by studying and influencing the patterns *for* behavior (*supra*, 5.2.1.2).

5.2.2.2.3 Cultural Patterns and Individual Variability

No individual knows his or her culture perfectly, and no two individuals will have perfectly the same theories regarding their society's design for living. Moreover, a culture allows for a *range* of behavior; the design for living is not ironclad. As long as the members of a society stay within the set range of approved behavior, they are able to interpret and predict one another's speech, actions, and reactions and to work harmoniously toward the solution of life's problems. Culture might, in fact, be compared to the rules of a game. Although all players understand and follow the same rules, no two players play the game exactly alike. Nor are two games ever played exactly in the same manner. Different situations call for different applications of the same rules. Culture does not define behavior in some absolutistic way. Although the underlying code for behavior (culture) is the central force in shaping behavior, it does not *determine* it.

5.2.2.2.4 Difference Between Actual Behavior and Culture

As we shall see when discussing culture change, the society is constantly adjusting, sometimes innovating, and, in fact, sometimes actually going against its design for living. Human beings are not automatons or slaves of their culture. Because they have a free will and are subject to considerable political, economic, and other pressures; because they have personal preferences, prejudices and biases, doubts, frustrations, fears, and anxieties; because they have distinct personalities, with their own goals and drives, imperfections, weaknesses, and malice; because they are faced with catastrophes, panic, and other situations for which they were not culturally conditioned, individuals will be moved to act contrary to or outside of the rules of the game. Generally speaking, however, they do not give up their design for succeeding in life altogether; they only do not follow the rules in a given situation. Or, a norm may be observed quite scrupulously in public but disregarded in private. The theoretically ideal may in fact sometimes constitute the exception rather than the rule in real life. Gunner Myrdal's classic *An American Dilemma* (1944) illustrates what we mean.

Culture, we stressed earlier (*supra*, 5.2.1.2), is a society's set of symbols *for* and *of* behavior (Geertz 1973:92). However, actual behavior, while reflecting culture, is not to be identified with it, just as a cabinetmaker's drawings are never identified with the table, chair, or cabinet being built. Although the drawing is indeed a picture *of* the chair and is the plan *for* building a chair, the design and the product are two different things. We hasten to add, however, that it is indeed possible for a chair to serve as a model for other chairs, just as it is possible for things and events in a society to function as symbols in its culture. The two must nevertheless be clearly distinguished.

While recognizing the important difference between culture and a community's actual behavior, and while insisting on a clear distinction between the two, we are not forgetting that we are dealing with very closely associated phenomena. As applied anthropologists, we recognize a very close interaction between the two: the underlying code affects actual behavior, while actual behavior affects the code. Culture is, in fact, the central force shaping actual behavior, while behavior is usually the central force shaping culture.

But why do we not just study actual behavior and forget about the cultural code underlying it? R. Keesing offers us two good reasons:

> Codes are finite, while behavior is creative and potentially infinite in variability. Without a code theory we cannot account for the creativity of behavior, for what may happen next as well as what has already happened.
> Codes have sharp edges and neat rules, while behavior has fuzzy edges and only statistical regularities. Without knowing the code we cannot tell which things, acts, and events a people treat as the same and which they treat as different. The psychological code imposes sharp edges and even creates perceptual patterns that do not exist "out there." [1976:163]

5.2.2.3 Idiosyncrasies, Universals, Specialties, and Alternatives

Idiosyncrasies. For a pattern to be a true part of culture, it must represent a society's, rather than an individual's, concept of proper behavior; otherwise it is an *idiosyncrasy*. The latter term as used in anthropology does not necessarily refer to an oddity, but rather to aspects of behavior that are distinctly those of an individual. Any invention or discovery prior to its broader acceptance is an idiosyncrasy. By the same token, although millions may speak the same language or dialect, no two individuals will have exactly the same pronunciation for every detail. Such individual differences in speaking are therefore idiosyncratic, not cultural. Personal skills, doubts, phobias, and all individual behavioral traits, be they queer or not, are idiosyncrasies and therefore are not a part of culture as such.

Specialties. While idiosyncrasies are not regarded as aspects of culture, specialties are. Patterns that are meant exclusively for a particular group within the society—for instance, for a particular group of craftsmen, a certain age group, one of the sexes, a particular occupational group, or a social class—are known as *specialties*. The ways of life of such groups are sometimes referred to as *minicultures*, as, for example, is illustrated in the expression "gang culture." Thus in most societies—(even though efforts are being made today by the modern feminist movement to put an end to sexism) playing with dolls is regarded as normal behavior only for little girls. Playing with dolls is supposed to be one of their specialties. Similarly, there is much that menfolk in a society know that women do not, and vice versa. The husband may not know all the particulars about cooking and housekeeping, but it is generally the man who climbs on the roof to repair the television antenna and who crawls under the car to do the necessary automobile repairs. Ballet dancing and lion training are specialties in our culture, definitely true parts of our way of life but not meant for everyone. It must be noted that a certain role or activity may be assigned by the society to just one single individual (for example, the chieftain or the poet laureate). Such unique roles are not idiosyncrasies, but specialties, because they are not the patterns of an individual as such but that of the society assigned to an individual.

Alternatives. An individual member of society is sometimes free to choose from among a number of patterns. In America, people may choose to live in bungalows, townhouses, ranch-style homes, or trailers; they may live in apartments or condominiums. When people go to their hairdressers, they have a variety of hair styles to choose from. A supermarket offers countless choices of foods. We may travel by airplane, train, bus, or automobile—though horse and buggy might be reserved as a specialty for the Amish, and for the participants of a parade or a military funeral. There are also numerous forms of recreation offered to us as *alternatives*.

Universals. Some patterns are expected of every normal member of the given society. One example is the ability to speak the vernacular language. In African societies, everyone is expected to know how to dance one's feelings, be they in political protest or as an expression of deep religious sentiment. In the United States, the ability to drive a car has practically become a universal. It should be noted that in anthropological literature the term *universal* is sometimes used in an entirely different sense, namely as a pattern that is "basic to human nature" and "common to all societies." Anthropologists are not in agreement about the question of whether any true universals (perfectly identical and not merely similar patterns) exist in different cultures.

5.2.2.4 Culture as Tradition

Culture, we have said, is a society's code for behavior. It is supraindividual, transcending the individual. A culture will continue even after the present generation passes away. Culture is, therefore, rightly called a *social heredity*, a *tradition*.

We must, however, sound a word of caution. The terms *tradition* and *social heredity* should not mislead us to think that culture is something entirely of the past. On the contrary, as we shall see when treating culture dynamics, culture is the here-and-now, with a past and usually a future. The members of a society, the bearers of culture, are very much alive and active. Even nonliterate food-gatherers are constantly changing their way of life. Culture, after all, as we have been emphasizing, is an adaptation to life. Even relatively unchanging simple societies are actually changing, slowly and imperceptibly perhaps, but they are adapting, adjusting, and changing nonetheless. It has been well said that "the only completely static cultures are the dead ones" (Herskovits 1950:20). The members of a society are the architects of their plan for living, their culture. They are not only following their design for living but are constantly modifying it, improving and adjusting their blueprints to the whims and demands of their physical, social, and ideational environments; adjusting and adapting their design in accord with the society's growth in experience and in accord with numberless historical accidents. Details of the culture that remain unchanged are usually those that pass the acid test of time; these details are the social heredity and the tradition that is handed down from one generation to the next. Tradition is extremely important in mission application, because it reflects very basic aspects of the true, living soul of a people.

5.2.2.5 The Extent of Cultural and Societal Boundaries

Are there, then, as many cultures as there are societies? Do the boundaries of a society coincide with those of culture? May we, therefore, define *society* simply as "a cultural group"? The term *culture* is, in fact, used rather loosely in anthropological literature. Especially when speaking of "deviations" and "deviants," we must determine whether we have cultures, subcultures, or one of the other usages in mind.

Strictly speaking, the term *culture* should be restricted to social groups speaking the same or related language and having more or less similar economic, social, and ideological systems. Moreover, culture is largely a tradition, an embodiment of history. Since no two distinct societies can have identical histories and identical experiences, it follows that their cultures can also never be perfectly the same. In this sense one might say that the boundaries of a culture coincide with the boundaries of the corresponding society.

The term *culture*, however, is sometimes used by anthropologists in an *extended sense*. For instance, the term is often used in reference to a number of cultures that happen to be more closely related. Thus we speak of "the Western culture" and "the Oriental culture." In anthropology, we also speak of *culture areas* actually composed of distinct societies and cultures; however, since they occur in a given geographical region and include patterns that are similar in some significant aspects, anthropologists speak, for instance, of the California Culture (in the singular), the North Plateau Culture, the North Pacific Culture, the Eskimo Culture, and so forth, as if each region were but one way of life.[4]

At times the term *culture* is employed when it would be more proper to speak of *subcultures*. A society may include a number of subgroups, the members of which interact with one another more closely than with the rest of the total society. The subgroup has its own values, mores, kinship norms, folklore, ritual, traditions, and group consciousness over and above those that they share with the broader society to which they also belong. Subsocieties are thus partly dependent on and partly independent of the larger social entity; they partly adhere to their own rules of the game of life and partly follow those of the larger social grouping. The actual boundaries of such subsocieties are sometimes difficult, if not impossible, to define because of the complex overlapping that occurs. In the United States, there are hundreds of such subgroups and *sub*-subgroups, differing from one another geographically, historically, ethnically, and religiously and at the same time sharing a common American spirit, identity, history, and basic culture. To name a few, there are Catholics, Protestants, and Jews; southern blacks, northern city blacks; and Chicanos, Puerto Ricans, Cubans, and a dozen and more other Hispanic groupings. Sometimes it is simpler to speak of the broad society's way of life as "culture" and to refer to the subcultures in terms of specialties and alternatives in the sense explained earlier (*supra*, 3.2.2.2.2). Sometimes the discussion of subcultures is greatly simplified by treating them as if they were indeed cultures unto themselves. This is particularly advisable when there is relatively little interaction between the subsociety and the society at large.

The term is used also in a *purely metaphorical* sense, referring to social groups of whose lifeway the anthropologist wishes to emphasize certain alternatives or specialties. For instance, the term "gang culture" is applied with reference to the patterns of a group of delinquents. Similarly, the distinctive lifeway of a neighborhood or a family may be referred to as a "culture." In fact, some anthropologists speak even of a "personal culture."

Finally, there is the fact that at times sociocultural change may be so extensive that the identification of boundaries becomes utterly impossible.

5.2.2.6 Missiological Application: Culture As a Societal Possession

5.2.2.6.1 Summary of Relevant Theory

(1) Although it is the *individual* who is the bearer of culture, culture is actually a *societal* possession. Culture is the set of ideas a *society* has for coping with its physical, social, and ideational environment. (2) A culture is made up of *patterns*, that is, of regularized guidelines for behavior. These patterns, however, allow for individual variability. Some patterns may be expected of all members of the particular society (the *universals*), some only of certain groups or individuals (*specialties*), and some may be facultative (*alternatives*). Behavior that is peculiar to an individual and is not transmitted by the society (*idiosyncrasies*) is not a part of culture. (3) Culture, inasmuch as it is a tested social heritage, is referred to as *tradition*. These traditions are nevertheless constantly changing, improving, deteriorating, growing, developing—and, as is to be expected of an adaptive system, are constantly adjusting and adapting. (4) Strictly speaking, the *boundaries* of a society can be said to coincide with

those of the respective culture. The term *society*, however, is sometimes used in the wider sense of "related cultures" and sometimes in the narrower sense of "subcultures," or at times in a metaphorical sense. Let us now see what bearing these theoretical concepts may have on mission action.

5.2.2.6.2 A Societal Versus an Individual Approach to Mission

Culture is *supra*individual; it is a continuum, the product of *socially* accumulated experiences. Individual members of the society will sooner or later cease to be, but the society and its culture will live on. The choice facing Christian communities is to engage either in a shortsighted, instantly gratifying mission or in one that may perhaps be less satisfying but more meaningful—more meaningful because it could be more continuing. As John XXIII wisely reminded missionaries in his *Princeps pastorum*, "He who sows is not the one who reaps" (no.17). How true indeed it is that if you give a man bread, you feed him once; if you *teach* him to plant, you feed him unendingly. The societal approach that is being suggested here does not aim so much to feed an individual as to teach a social group and generations that will follow.

The individual approach is focused on the individual as an individual, with little regard for social structure and the individual's role in society and his or her potential for facilitating and accelerating a desired social change. The individual approach overlooks the special capacity of certain members of a society to initiate or to perfect the change and to make it an integral part of the culture itself. Certain individuals in the society can in a very special and particularly effective way serve as the leaven of the Gospel that must penetrate the whole mass of dough (Mt 13:33). What we are saying is that the pastors and religious educators should try to develop a mission strategy that will take into account the roles that members of a society qua members play and the relation that these roles have to social structure, to culture change, and to culture persistence. The Church should not merely leave its doors wide open in welcome to any casual and interested passerby; rather, without deliberately closing the door to anyone or unnecessarily passing over anyone, the Church should make every effort to devise a positive plan and, going into the highways and byways, extend a very special invitation to those members of society who in the given time and place, in the given society and culture, have the greatest potential to influence the society. The ultimate target thus becomes the *whole* society. Effective mission strategy, we are saying, will be formulated and carried out within the framework of the given social structure.

The Church has no choice but wisely and responsibly to discriminate in the use of its limited personnel, means, and time. This is, of course, not to deny that in some more unresponsive areas of the world (as was actually the case several decades ago in Kansu and Tibet and as is the case today in some Moslem and Marxist areas), it may be necessary to reduce mission work to patient witnessing of the faith and respectful dialoguing. The basic rule, however, remains: every bit of talent and energy with which the Church is blessed should as much as possible be wisely and conscientiously used to make Christ available to all in accord with the social organization of the society being evangelized. We cannot help but question the practice of some local churches of concentrating their total effort on willing children and submissive women, a situation particularly true in dechristianized and nominally Christian countries. As important as children and mothers may be (and important they are), and as apathetic to the Gospel as the menfolk may appear (and very apathetic they can be), the effort must nevertheless be made to penetrate the *whole* social organism in the most effective and efficient manner. Willy-nilly the male segment must be sought out. In fact, working within the *total* framework of the given social structure as much as possible and helping to bring about a *people's*, rather than only an individual's, conversion, may, in the long run, be the only wise pastoral approach (cf. Donovan 1978: 38f,85; McGavran 1955). The fact that Christ must be made *available* to all does not mean that the Church may not or should not hasten this availability selectively.

We are particularly averse to the common practice of concentrating on children. We are opposed because children are precisely the ones that have the least to say about social change. The children, it is true, will some day grow up and assume adult roles, but unfortunately these roles will to a large measure be kept unchristian by the senior adults who are being ignored as "no-hopers." The fact is that when the children, the so-called "hope for the future" grow up, they may theoretically be able to Christianize such roles, but what not seldom happens is that when such new leaders begin to assume adult roles, they find their hopes unrealizable because of social pressure and the superior authority of their non-Christian, or merely nominally Christian seniors, who, as is frequently the case, choose successors most like themselves. The very institutions that the young adults were supposed to Christianize often force them back into the traditional unchristian ways. This is not a wise mission approach but a vicious circle! The problems of second- and third-generation recidivism in mission lands and much of so-called nominal Catholicism in older churches are traceable to the failure of the church to evangelize *within the framework of the local community*.

At this juncture, one is strongly tempted to enter into an analysis of the whole field of social structure and communication. It would, however, be more profitable for the reader to study Eugene Nida's chapter on the subject in his *Message and Mission* (1960:94–136) and David Filbeck's *Social Context and Proclamation: A Socio-Cognitive Study in Proclaiming the Gospel Cross-Culturally* (1985); see also Reed (1985:33–58) and Holland, Henriot (1983). These works present the basic theory regarding communication and society and show how this theory is directly relevant to different types of societies— tribal, peasant, and modern.

In discussing the relevance of social structure to mission strategy, we should not overlook the all-important role of lay witness and ministries. It is the laity who most fully embody the social relationships of a society. They are generally the educators, editors, union leaders, student organizers, legislators, community leaders, and, above all, are always the heads of families (*Apostolicam actuositatem*, no.13). It should also be remembered, as the World Council of Churches wisely pointed out twenty-five years ago, that

> in a world in which new social groupings are constantly forming, and in which Christians are moving about in their secular occupations as never before, the possibilities of lay witness constitute the Church's greatest opportunity to penetrate new areas with the Gospel. It is essential that laymen would be helped to recognize this fact and to accept the full implications of their baptism. The churches must develop ways of preparing them for effective participation in the one mission. ["The Missionary Task of the Church: Theological Reflections," *Bulletin*, Division of Studies, 1961, no.2, p. 13]

Although full utilization of "woman-power" has not yet been achieved in the Church, the progress that has been made in recent years has been encouraging (cf. Pastoral Letter, *Origins* 1988:757–88). Nevertheless, the old German saying "Kinder, Küche, Kirche!" ("children, chores, and church") to describe the limits of a woman's activities, concerns, and usefulness regrettably still seems to prevail in many Christian quarters.

5.2.2.6.3 Cultural Boundaries and the Church

The theoretical distinctions that we have made regarding cultures, subcultures, universals, alternatives, and specialties have an important bearing on *communication*, the Church's most basic human tool. It is quite possible to reach a limited subgroup without reaching the rest of society. The elite may be reached while the masses may not; the urbanites may be reached, while the rural communities might be completely bypassed. Each subgroup has its own subset of patterns, premises, attitudes, and goals, and unless the Church's message is sent on the specific wavelength corresponding to the differences in question, it may not reach some of those who should be reached. Particularly important to mission is the concept of subculture in a country like the United States. In this country, there are hundreds of cultural subgroups, each calling for social, liturgical, and catechetical adaptations and organizational adjustments. Catholic dioceses are rightly cautious when they consider for one reason or another the discontinuation of an existing ethnic parish; not only are delicate emotional issues at stake but important subcultural values are challenged as well. Minority ethnic parochial structures are often preferred by Hispanics and blacks, not for racial reasons but because their subcultural needs are generally better understood and appreciated under an ethnic pastor and ethnic lay leadership. They also may feel that they are better able to worship God and live as a Christian community if they can worship and live as Hispanics or blacks. Cultural disagreements in arranging parish liturgies and in organizing social and educational programs tend to be less serious than in a multicultural territorial parish. Such an attitude need not be looked upon as a form of racism or segregation. In the past, ethnic organizational structures have done much to preserve and deepen the faith of American Catholics. Ethnic parishes have, generally speaking, facilitated and sped up the necessary cultural adjustment especially during the great migrations from Europe. It is also mainly for socioeconomic reasons that the so-called basic ecclesial communities of Latin America and the so-called homogeneous unit theory advocated by Donald S. McGavran usually make good pastoral and anthropological sense; people "like to become Christian without leaving their own folk" (McGavran 1970:210; cf. Reed 1985:47–48; Wagner 1979), a fact borne out by the many vibrant Hispanic and black parishes in the United States today and the countless national parishes that existed a few generations ago.

To communicate the Gospel effectively, a *constant* awareness of cultural and subcultural boundaries is therefore essential. The theoretical distinctions we have made between societies and subsocieties, and between alternatives, specialties, and idiosyncrasies, have an important practical bearing on the mission of the Church. They are necessary (1) to reach *all* potential beneficiaries (*infra*, 5.2.3.2.4); (2) to be able to communicate in accord with *felt-needs* of the specific group being evangelized (*supra*, 5.2.1.6.2); and (3) to be able to evaluate and deal properly, and as much as possible positively, with *popular religiosity* and *syncretism*—that is to say, to regard these phenomena as possible mirrors of a people's unique soul and tradition—as potential inculturational accelerators (*infra*, 7.3.4.2.3).

One of the most remarkable and at the same time most welcome developments in more recent times, especially since Vatican II, has been the growing *ecumenical understanding and cooperation* among the different Christian traditions. What we have said about subcultures (*supra*, 5.2.2.5) may provide some very useful light for those engaged in ecumenical dialogue and action.

5.2.2.6.4 Group Contacts and Group Conflicts

There have always been conflicts in the Church, some more serious than others. In the present discussion on conflicts within the Church, the focus is not on broad, international schisms, as was the split between the Eastern and Western Churches, or the even more serious disintegration of Christianity in Europe several centuries later, but on conflicts within such narrower confines as a local diocese, parish, institution, or organization. The conflicts in the latter case may be less serious in their consequences but not necessarily in their intensity. In fact, organizational theory has come up with the concept of *scope*—that is, the more inclusive the scope of shared interests and activities, the greater are the chances of tension and conflict.

Although group conflicts can have a variety of causes, they usually arise from the fact that group contact, while perhaps potentially enriching, can lead to misunderstanding. Each group, thanks to its unique enculturative experience, has its own set of norms for "proper" behavior, its own loyalties, and its own interests. Often such enculturative experience becomes a source of tension and conflict.

A culture, being the social group's set of solutions to life's problems, is perforce highly valued and protected. It lies at the very root of a society's identity, group consciousness, esprit de corps, and survival. Enculturation, the process of learning a culture—a process that we shall look into in some detail (*infra*, 5.2.3)—can become the source of serious ethnocentric tensions. Cultural and subcultural (and even *sub*subcultural) groups tend to overvalue and overdefend their own ways and values and at the same time to underappreciate the ways and values of other groups.

There are four basic principles that come into play in group conflicts. (1) There is a deep tendency in human beings to form in-groups and out-groups. (2) Where there are in-groups and out-groups, there may be tensions and conflicts. (3) The danger of conflict becomes real when one of the groups assumes a dominant position in relation to the others. (4) Conflict becomes possible especially when group-consciousness turns into group-centeredness. (For more on ethnocentrism and group conflict, we refer the reader to such full-length works as Le Vine, Campbell [1972].)

There is a deep human tendency in human beings to form in-groups and out-groups. It has been wisely said that "birds of a feather flock together." Human beings are birds who, having similar ways and values, tend to flock together. Their similarity may be at the cultural, subcultural, or specialties level. The in-groups and out-groups thus formed are more a matter of common sympathy rather than organization; they consist of individuals who happen to think, feel, and behave alike and who empathize and identify with one another. Such individuals who share a common set of values and who identify with one another refer to themselves by the pronoun *we* and constitute the *we-group*, whereas the others are referred to as the *they-group*. Such cohesiveness frequently leads to the formation of harmful disruptive cliques and factions.

As social beings, we instinctively take sides, entering in our minds "this" camp or "that" camp, depending on the ways and values that we consider to be "ours" and therefore "proper." We align ourselves into an endless series of *we*s and *they*s. Jews align themselves against the Gentiles; the Irish against the British; the U.S. Marine Corps against the U.S. Navy, Army, and Air Force; teenagers against their elders—and earlier still, when the gang-instinct was alive, it was "we boys" against "those girls." The tendency to form in-groups and out-groups does not disappear with ordination, the pronouncement of religious vows, or departure for overseas missions. The tendency is very much alive in every normal person, including in individuals who are seriously committed to the spreading of the Kingdom of God. The better one understands and appreciates the presence of this natural tendency not only in others but in oneself, the better are the chances of avoiding group tensions and problems. The first step toward group harmony and cooperation in church action, therefore, is to have all concerned, from the highest Church authorities to the lowest member, admit that such a tendency exists "also in *me*."

Where there are in-groups and out-groups there may be tensions and problems. Where there is contact between groups there may be conflict.

In church work, be it in a parish, a church organization, or in an institution, many such internal groupings are possible. To mention only a few of them, there are the "privileged" clerics and the "underprivileged" Brothers and Sisters; the religious "bosses" of an institution and the "voiceless" lay help; the "hard-working" bush missionaries and the "do-nothing" school staffs; the "naive" Americans and the "not-quite-so-naive" Europeans; the "progressive" West Europeans and the "backward" East Europeans; the "born-geniuses" from abroad and the "not-yet-quite-fully civilized" indigenous staff; the younger, "open-minded" staff and the older, "out-of-touch," if not "fossilized," faculty; the "know-it-all" new missionaries and the "will-never-learn" older missionaries. The list can be extended indefinitely. A former missionary from China teaching at the same seminary as the present author wisely observed that the best proof for him that he was middle-aged was the fact that older teachers would come to him to complain about the younger teachers and the younger teachers would come to him to complain about the older. From the examples just given, one can readily see that in-groups can be quite varied and that it is possible to belong to a dozen or more of such wes and theys without necessarily forming a faction or club. At the root of the possible conflicts is our set of learned patterns of thought, attitudes, motivations, and action. A sense of solidarity develops among those who share a common lifeway and standards. This solidarity may become dysfunctional on an inter-group level.

Tensions and conflicts tend to arise whenever there is contact between groups following different norms. We wish to emphasize again that such norms can occur at various levels: they may occur at the cultural level (e.g., an expatriate agricultural specialist versus his indigenous counterpart); at the subcultural level (e.g., someone from the upper class versus someone from the lower class), or at the level of specialties in the same culture or subculture (e.g., medical missionaries versus the elementary school staffs, or the kitchen help versus the laundry department at the same hospital.)

Some dioceses in the United States have become extremely heterogeneous in composition, involving ethnic groups from all parts of the world, with each group maintaining its own national consciousness and loyalties. As a rule, one is inclined to be more sympathetic toward one's own cultural group than toward an outside group. It should not be surprising at all if one finds in the Philippines an indigenous clerical in-group and an expatriate out-group; or in the Archdiocese of Los Angeles, an in-group of American Irish and an out-group of so-called "FBIs" or "Foreign-Born Irish." Language and dialect differences often are at the heart of group division, as is exemplified today in Belgium, Canada, and Yugoslavia.

The danger of conflict becomes real when one of the groups assumes a dominant position in relation to the others. When sociologists speak of "a majority" or of "a dominant group," they do not necessarily mean a numerical majority. The group that is regarded as dominant or as the majority is the group that is recognized as the more influential. In ecclesiastical situations, as is the case for instance in many U.S. city parishes, it is not unusual to find a dozen or more cultural minorities. Similarly, in mission areas, some religious orders may include members from as many as fifteen different countries, each group holding its own cultural conditioning and corresponding preferences. Justified or not, alignments predispose the groups for tensions and misunderstanding. Trouble may indeed be brewing when groups within a Christian community begin to feel uncomfortable on account of their real or imagined "second-class citizenship." We are reminded of the tensions that arose in the early days of Christianity:

> In those days, as the number of disciples grew, the ones who spoke Greek complained that their widows were being neglected in the daily distribution of food, as compared with the widows of those who spoke Hebrew. [Acts 6:1]

Such tensions were in Apostle Paul's mind when he reminded the Romans that there was "no difference between Jew and Greek" (Rom 10:12); or when he reminded the Galatians that "there does not exist among you Jew or Greek, slave or freeman, male or female" (Gal 3:28); or finally, when Paul wrote to the Colossians that "there is no Greek or Jew here, circumcised or uncircumcised, foreigner, Scythian, slave, or freeman" (Col 3:11).

Intolerance seems to become greater as the boundaries of the in-group become smaller and tighter. Thus siblings generally tolerate pluralism far less among themselves than they do in dealing with their playmates; members of the same religious order normally expect and demand far more conformity among themselves than they do from members of other religious orders; Catholics, as a rule, allow less pluriformity among themselves than among their fellow-Christians who are not Catholic.

The relatively minor roles played by lay volunteers in a parish sometimes give the laity the impression, rightly or wrongly, that they are not really trusted, not considered reliable, and not really wanted. The indigenous clergy (or their expatriate counterparts, as the case may be) may feel much the same. Frequently the proverbial last straw that finally breaks the camel's back and causes a so-called moratorium on all foreign church personnel and financial aid or occasions the formation of an independent church may be nothing more than an unfortunate majority-minority relationship.

Human beings crave affirmation from one another. In fact, they suffer psychologically if such support is consistently denied. Particularly dangerous and painful are slurs, unguarded remarks, nicknames, inconsiderateness, and other indications of a lack of appreciation of the minority group by the majority.

It is also true, however, that a minority tends to be oversensitive and to be predisposed to criticize the dominant group unfairly. Again and again, justly or unjustly, the dominant group is condemned by the minority, who ridicule them and make them the butt of countless jokes. Anyone who goes to Poland these days comes back with a repertoire of jokes about the Communist Party, the current dominant group in Poland. A similar situation is found in black communities in the United States regarding the dominant white group. In such a situation rash judgments and rumors can spread like wildfire. Accusations of police brutality and other forms of racism are made against the dominant group automatically and are seldom questioned.

Owing to genuine abuses and frequent cases of injustice, criticism and condemnation of the dominant group by the minority is often justified. Not seldom, however, complaints are unfounded and can very well verge on mass paranoia. The minority begins with the premise that it is the underdog and the Cinderella of the diocese, hospital, school, or church organization and therefore regards itself as being always in the right, always the oppressed and never the oppressor. Neglect and discrimination are the standard explanation of all tensions. There comes the complaint that everyone is given his or her share of the diocesan budget except "our" group. In extreme cases, respect for and cooperation with the dominant group may become well-nigh impossible.

Conflict becomes possible especially when group-consciousness turns into group-centeredness. By group-centeredness we mean ethnocentrism run rampant, whether it be on the cultural, subcultural, or specialized group-level.

Ethnocentrism, we said, is the tendency to evaluate one's own in-group and its norms as being of primary importance and as definitely superior to those of other groups. Whether verbalized or not, ethnocentric thinking embodies such nonsense as these expressions: "Our cooking is the best in the world; we have the best sense of humor; we are the most cultured, best educated, most religious people in the world."

The fact is that any subgroup of a Christian community can become group-centered, whether that subgroup be the majority or minority.

Group-centeredness in a Christian community becomes particularly damaging when a feeling of superiority begins to urge the group to re-educate the out-group after its own image and likeness. As we have seen in our chapter on missionary models (chapter 3), this urge can become a kind of duty, mission, "destiny," or even obsession. It was believed for centuries that people of mission lands could not be truly Christianized unless they were first Europeanized. At least to some degree, such an urge to educate will be found in all human groups. An awareness of one's own group-centeredness and a positive effort to see the good, proper, and beautiful in the ways and values of other groups will go a long way toward the lessening of the temptation to re-educate others. Hispanics in the United States, for example, will resist any effort to make them into "Anglos."

The mere placement of indigenous Superiors at the head of a Third World diocese, parish, or institution—especially if the person placed in authority has been systematically denativized—is no solution to group problems in a diocese, seminary, convent, hospital, or school. This is an important lesson that seems finally to have been learned by the churches.

Dislike of foreign ways is largely a *natural* aversion. Even the kindest individual will harbor a certain amount of undesirable ethnocentrism and exaggerated group loyalty. Even if all members of a culturally mixed Christian community were Saints, the American Saints would feel it their sacred duty to make their parishioners the best Christians possible and therefore to mold them at least to some degree according to the American self-image. The same, of course, would be true of the hypothetical Saints from other countries. And non-Westerners are not exempt from this human frailty. Although Christian values are supposed to be essentially the same the world over, they are expressed in different ways by different peoples. This general cultural bias would cause tensions among even our hypothetical Saints. Without realizing it, the American Christian tends to transform God into an American—and this is true, in varying degrees, also of others, be they Spaniards, Italians, Germans, Fijians, Indians, and so on. All Christians, for example, believe in charity and friendliness, but Americans prefer to exercise these two virtues in a less formal manner, even when dealing with strangers; the European, on the other hand, may insist on a type of charity and friendliness that is heavily colored by etiquette and formality. To most Americans, the flag is a sacred symbol. It stands above politics and its wiles and abuses, and represents the ideals of the nation. In France, a flag is essentially a political symbol. A flag fluttering in front of a factory suggests to many, if not to most, Frenchmen that the particular building is national property, a socialized plant. In a heterogeneous Christian community, each subgroup of hypothetical Saints will be convinced that *its* ways and values are somehow more proper and more correct. We should not be surprised if there is a clash every now and then—yes, even among zealous, devout Christians—between people who sometimes forget that even their understanding of "the mind of Christ" (1 Cor 2:12-16) is influenced by their culture.

If a solution is to be found for group problems in Christian communities, it must be sought in the Creator himself. That is to say, it will be found in an appreciation of the fact that God indeed delights in human diversity.

The vastness and complexity of the Church's mission calls for many specialized groups, professional and otherwise. The mission of the Church calls for recruits from all social strata and from all nations and cultures. The newer and older churches need each other. The task of extending the Kingdom of God is a task entrusted to all professions and all classes—rich and poor, educated and uneducated, clergy and laity—each group with its own esprit de corps and with ways and values distinctly its own, with the countless differences that greatly delight the One Maker of All.

5.2.3 CULTURE AS A LEARNED DESIGN

Bees and ants carry out their social roles, and in fact their whole mode of life, without any previous training; for them, being born is the same as being socialized. With bees and ants, socialization is instinctive. Their way of coping with the environment and survival is purely biological, a matter of genes. Human beings, however, cannot survive by themselves; they must *learn* to survive. This learning must come from one's society. A Norwegian man acts like a Norwegian because he was taught to act like a Norwegian—not because he has Norwegian blood in his veins, but because he has not *learned* to think, speak, feel, and act in any other manner. What is not *learned* from one's society is by that very fact not cultural. That an American eats and that there is a physical difference between men and women does not constitute a part of the American culture. On the other hand, that Americans make and eat ice cream and apple pie and that they play baseball and that American women use lipstick, while men do not, does constitute a part of their culture.

5.2.3.1 Enculturation

5.2.3.1.1 Definition of Enculturation

We were born cultureless and would have remained cultureless if it had not been for the process of *learning* a way of life. This process is called *enculturation*. We were born without a culture but not without a distinctly human competence to *learn* a culture. The term *enculturation*, although often regarded as synonymous with *socialization,* is sometimes considered by anthropologists to be only closely allied to it, not identified with it. To anthropologists, socialization is the process by which one is incorporated into a society by learning its way of life. Socialization, they say, focuses on those patterns by means of which the individual becomes a member of society, adapts to other members of the social group, and is assigned a status and a role. Although many anthropologists understand the term *enculturation* as being focused on a *child's* learning of a culture, we prefer to regard enculturation as a lifelong process of mastering an adaptive system. The duration and scope of enculturation is therefore as broad as life itself.

The terms *enculturation* and *socialization* are extremely important anthropological, sociological, and psychological concepts. They are worthy of far more study than can be given here. One might, for instance, consult such full-length works on enculturation as T. R. Williams' *Introduction to Socialization* (1972) or such culture-and-personality studies as written by Barnouw (1973), Bourguignon (1973), LeVine (1973), and Devos (1980).

5.2.3.1.2 Cultural Relativity

Although much of what the individual learns from his or her society is objective, true, correct, and valid, much is culturally determined. The following examples, many taken from the author's original *Church and Cultures* (1970: 74–77, 85–95), illustrate the relativity of cultures.

In Western cultures one is taught quite early in life to eat with a spoon and fork; to eat with one's fingers would be "primitive" and "savage." However, Western peoples forget their own principles when they eat olives, popcorn, or peanuts; they eat such food with their fingers. Similarly, there seems to be nothing improper in eating a sandwich or a hamburger with one's hands rather than on a plate with knife and fork—yes, very much like "primitives" and "savages." As Indonesians like to put it: "You Westerners are the primitives and savages: you haven't the foggiest idea who had your fork in his mouth last. We're different; *we* don't have the slightest doubt about whose fingers were in *our* mouths last."

There is sometimes very little logic and consistency in culture. Germans are shocked and nauseated to see Americans eat sweet corn on the cob. Isn't that, after all, what one feeds to chickens, horses, and pigs? Americans, in turn, find it difficult to see how Germans can regard seasoned but absolutely raw ground beef as a delicacy. Isn't that what they feed lions? And how can Germans eat their bacon "raw"? Even our mice won't be tempted by our bait unless the bacon we use on our mouse trap is partly singed.

Most people would be shocked, not to say nauseated, to see how some Melanesians season their pork; the chef, during the process of roasting a pig, will chew ginger and salt and spit his seasoning on the meat. (What is overlooked is the fact that the seasoning is sterilized in the fire.) The acceptable way to knead dough in some isolated areas of Europe until rather recent times was to tread on it; and it is also easier to crush grapes for wine and cabbage for sauerkraut with the feet. That's how they make the tastiest sauerkraut.

The Navaho Indians are nauseated at the very thought of swallowing something as smelly and slimy as a fish, while Marc Connely's *Green Pastures* portrayed heaven as the place where you are assured of a delicious fishfry at least once a week for all eternity. Thus the black heaven becomes the Navaho hell. Some people relish horsemeat; and donkey somehow manages to get into Italian salami, giving it that special flavor and extra "kick." In most Western countries the unscrupulous butcher who passed off ground horsemeat for hamburger meat would in fact be brought to court. In a recent scandal, Australian packers were sued for shipping kangaroo meat to American fast-food chains, sued not by the Society for the Prevention of Cruelty to Animals but by patrons who could not quite stomach kangaroo-burgers. T-bone steaks delight the American palate, but, as unbelievable as it may seem, disgust the Hindu. We would find it psychologically and gastronomically impossible to nibble on a piece of tender roast poodle or to swallow even the tiniest piece of southern-fried dachshund, or to take even a small spoonful of a cat casserole made with Uncle Ben's finest rice and the choicest chunks of Felix, that faithful old feline that has become a part of the family and provided the whole neighborhood with dozens of his kind. The fact is that, depending on the culture, roast tomcat could be as appetizing as roast tomturkey. In Taiwan and in parts of Mexico, dogs are sometimes bred for butchering, and, in some Taiwanese restaurants, you may be able to pick out your dog the way we sometimes can pick out our lobster swimming his last swim in the restaurant aquarium.

Nida (1966:58,62) offers us a few more interesting examples: Tibetans enjoy rancid butter, while some Africans enjoy fermented manioc and eat fried or raw termites; Westerners, on the other hand, refuse to eat rancid butter but eat Liederkranz cheese; they refuse fermented manioc but eat sauerkraut; they refuse termites but eat slimy oysters. Ancient Romans ate peacock tongues not for their taste but for the same reason that Westerners eat caviar, as a symbol of status and prestige.

And there are delicacies to consider. Some Africans may be nauseated at the very thought of eating frozen animal secretions we call "ice cream," but the same people find rats, snakes, and worms quite delicious. Cheese, by the way, is even worse; it is a "spoiled" animal secretion, and even the finest yogurt can be "absolutely nauseating." In the Caucasus Mountains, a guest of honor may be presented with a special delicacy, the cooked eyes of a ram. We would most likely forgo such an *hors d'oeuvre* even at the risk of offending our host. The Eskimo, on the other hand, who is fond of bird's eyes, might have no such inhibitions.

To sum up with a final example—in Hong Kong, it is said, people will eat anything that has four legs, except the table they are eating on, or that has two wings, except the airplane they arrived on—an exaggeration which nevertheless brings out our point: you eat whatever your culture tells you to.

Even muscular habits vary from culture to culture, for they have been conditioned by the people's way of life.

We imagine that the normal way to rest is to sit in a "comfortable" chair. But what is comfortable in one culture may turn out to be very uncomfortable in another; the proper way to rest may be to squat, recline on a hard mat, sit on a rock or the ground itself, or to stand on one foot like a flamingo, first resting one limb and then the other. Children in many mission schools at first find sitting at a desk very uncomfortable, preferring to squat on the floor even when writing. Americans avoid as much back bending as possible; they have to work over a bench or table and hire undocumented aliens to pick their pickles and other vegetables. Egyptian farmers, unlike Americans, prefer short-handled hoes and sickles that force them to remain bent over hours on end jackknived very much like their ancestors that are depicted on Egyptian monuments. The Japanese carpenter *pulls* his saw; his Western counterpart *pushes* it. Some Pacific Islanders find a carpenter's plane very awkward and may turn the blade into an adze, since the chopping movement is far more "natural." New Yorkers have their own culturally defined way of going through revolving doors.

Such relativity permeates all human behavior, including the defining of aesthetic/disgusting behavior, music, art, ethics, and thought habits.

In a training program for self-defense, American women are advised to disgust an approaching rapist by picking their noses. If the Eiffel Tower were located in the heart of Washington, D.C. instead of Paris, it would be a relatively easy matter to convince Frenchmen that the tower was but a "monstrosity." Or as Schopenhauer once observed—if we were to ask an ancient Greek what he thought of the magnificent Gothic cathedrals of Europe, his immediate reply would be, "Barbaric to the extreme!" Most North Americans consider cockfights cruel and inhumane; the Filipinos, Indonesians, and not a few other societies do not. There was a time when most Christians regarded cosmetics and the mixing of sexes in schools and churches as immoral. Today teenagers and many young adults go into a veritable rapture on hearing the thundering beat of rock music, while not a few of the older generation stop their ears as they try in desperation to climb the nearest wall. According to news reports, in March, 1979, Moslem Iranians hurled stones and curses, brandished knives and swords, and fired rifles, as thousands of women in Tehran challenged the Islamic law by marching in protest in defense of their "right" to wear blue jeans and skirts instead of the traditional long black dresses and veils—the clash here being subcultural rather than cultural. Islam regards also alcoholic drinks and pork as abominations; only "infidels" like Christians do such things. Western societies shudder at the very thought of infanticide as the normal way of disposing of one of the twins or as a more general form of population control. At the same time many Western societies regard abortion as the normal exercise of the right of a woman over her own body. In Western countries, polygamy (that is, simultaneous plural marriage) is regarded as wrong; divorce, on the other hand (that is, serial plural marriages) as often being desirable. The caste system has always been a scandal to Western societies—why, for instance, should only the lowest caste have to clean latrines and why, if one's parent was a sweeper-bearer, should one have no choice but to be a sweeper-bearer too? On the other hand, racism does not shock many Westerners, just as slavery did not shock perhaps most people only a century ago.

5.2.3.1.3 The Extent and Thoroughness of Enculturation

The number of "proper" things that an individual must learn is great indeed (see Luzbetak 1970: 74–77, 85–95).

> In early childhood one is taught the fundamentals of the "proper" way to eat (that is, with clean hands, using the proper utensils, sitting at a table rather than, for example, squatting on the floor around a large common bowl and eating with one's fingers or chop-sticks, in small bite-sizes, and as much as possible without slurping and messing up oneself and the environs. As one grows older one learns more and more the rules of etiquette and politeness, especially how one is not to be greedy and how one is to say "please" and "thank you." The child before long learns to avoid baby-talk, to say "fought" instead of "fighted" and eventually such "big words" as "disobeyed" instead of "distobeyed," "accident" instead of "askident," and "spaghetti" instead of "pisketti." The child soon learns the fundamentals of personal cleanliness and how to urinate and defecate in a "dignified" manner. As years go on, the child learns to dress with less and less help from others. It is a red-letter day when the child learns to tie its own shoelace, which, of course, must be done according to a very definite and approved pattern. The necktie comes next, which also must be tied in one specific way, although many ways are theoretically possible. (Some men, of course, seem never to be able to master the art.) The hair, too, must be combed "properly." Later on, of course, when the child becomes a teenage lad, he may insist on going to a hair stylist because only a hair stylist, rather than just an ordinary barber, can "bring out the real you," unaware of the fact that it is not so much the "real you" that is brought out as the style of the day that is based on criteria learned from one's social group.

We are endlessly learning *the* way to do things, *the* way to speak and even to feel and to think. Before long, we master our lesson so well that to think, speak, feel, or act in any other way will require effort and considerable violence to self to go contrary to the "proper" way. Culture thus becomes a kind of second nature to us, affecting our behavior and influencing our personality.

> From early childhoood—in fact from the day we were born—we have been drilled to conform. Companions and elders constantly have offered us advice, guidance, and criticism, involving themselves in our choices, making sure that we would choose the "useful," "polite," "true," "disciplined," "civilized," "good," "beau-

tiful," "correct"—in a word, "the proper." We were praised and ridiculed, rewarded and punished, by our peers, at times quite mercilessly. In fact, enculturation is a life-long process into adulthood. As an adult one is constantly learning, for instance, how to interact with fellow employees, how to be "professional" in what one does, how to be a good patient in a hospital, how to be a good husband or wife, parent, or grandparent and, since enculturation continues at least intermittently until death, how to grow old gracefully and how to die peacefully.

The process of enculturation is so thorough and subtle that even one's emotional reactions and muscular movements reflect one's cultural conditioning.

Westerners sometimes regard Oriental behavior as "sheepish" and "self-defacing" while the Oriental finds the behavior of Americans and Europeans as "haughty" and "disrespectful." "Westerners," they say, "walk around as if they owned the world." Subgroups within larger societies are often recognized not only by how they dress and by their bodily adornments and peculiarities of speech but also by their gait, posture, and culturally determined facial expressions. Even an angry person's facial movements, the breathing and the volume, tempo, and rhythm of speech, and, of course, the particular choice of epithets, will vary from subculture to subculture, depending on what the particular subsociety considers to be the "proper" way of being infuriated. In fact, there is a male and female way of being angry. Women and children may cry when they are frustrated and angry; men normally may not. Although it may be psychologically more healthful to cry than to hold back tears, our culture requires of a man a greater reason for tears than a flat tire he might get somewhere along the expressway. Enculturation is so thorough and subtle that it may have actually conditioned some of our glands, involuntary muscles, and nervous system. We sometimes consider psychopathic, as hysteria or compulsion, patterns that are in another culture perfectly normal and that require considerable effort on the part of the individual to learn. The convulsions and unconsciousness freely brought about by a witchdoctor or a shaman are not forms of insanity but genuine achievements praiseworthy in their cultural context. We laugh, shed tears, and faint or vomit at the "proper" times—"proper" perhaps in Europe or America but not necessarily in Fiji or Japan.

The patterns of behavior that one learns in the process of enculturation may indeed be, as Kluckhohn and Kelly put it, "rational, irrational, and nonrational" (1945:89–90, 97; cf. Benedict, R. 1934), the one condition being, as emphasized earlier, that the pattern be *learned* from one's society.

Enculturation aims to make "proper" behavior as automatic as possible. This goal is achieved through a simplifying and regularizing process. The human mind, for instance, operates largely in categories; human behavior is matrixed; the countless speech sounds are learned when one arranges them into a distinct phonemic system; the complexities of a culture are reduced to general "laws" and classes. In a word, simplification and organization of regularities are human characteristics that make habitual and automatic behavior possible. Learning a culture is more than learning countless isolated forms. As we have seen (*supra*, 3.1.3.3.2, 3.1.3.3.3) and as we shall explain fully in the following chapters, in the process of enculturation one learns the culture *as a system*; one learns not only forms but also how these forms are tied to one another through meanings and an underlying philosophy. In a word, one learns the structure and organization of culture—that is to say, the full and true meaning of a culture—the mastery of which makes the culture into a quasi-automatic operation and a kind of second nature.

To emphasize the extent and depth of cultural conditioning is not to make human beings into automatons. We pointed out earlier that a culture pattern is really a *range* of behavior; cultures offer nothing more than *guidelines* for the solution of human problems. Moreover, the norms taught by the society to the individual only *tend* to be shared. In other words, the individual remains free and may actually depart from the standard and approved ways. The fact that cultures are dynamic and that they are constantly changing is the best evidence that cultures do not make automatons out of individuals. Human beings are largely molded by culture and are constantly pressured by it, but never are they shackled to it.

5.2.3.1.4 How Cultures Are Learned

From what we have thus far said about enculturation, one should not conclude that culture learning is a purely passive conditioning process. What Noam Chomsky (b. 1928) holds regarding language learning we can extend to culture learning across the board. Chomsky maintains that humans have a built-in capacity to learn a language, an inborn competence that nonhumans do not have. As cognitive anthropology points out, humans are preprogrammed to be able somehow to analyze the extremely complex sound system of languages. Humans have the ability to abstract the basic rules of grammar to such an extent, in fact, that they are able to understand and generate an infinite number of novel combinations. Similarly, lodged deep in the unconscious seems to be a wider capacity, the innate human capacity to analyze, learn, understand, and live the culture of one's society. In the last analysis, a newborn infant is not born with a *tabula rasa*, a clear slate, but with a distinctly human capacity to learn a culture.

There are three basic ways in which a design for living is learned (Luzbetak 1970: 78–79). First of all, much is learned through deliberate *observation* and *imitation*. Secondly, culture may be learned through direct and conscious instruction called *education*. (*Schooling* is only a special form of education, given by a socially appointed instructor at a given place and time.) Thirdly, perhaps the most important way that a culture is learned is through *unconscious imitation*, by a kind of absorption. These three processes are crucial to the learning of the communication system of one's society. They teach the "grammar" of one's culture, especially the *why* of culture, the functional linkages between the various cultural elements (the logical or purposeful interconnections in a culture), and the underlying premises, emotionally charged attitudes, and basic drives (the starting points of reasoning, reacting, and motivating). We judge a person's character by the company he or she keeps, because we feel that we unavoidably *absorb* the ways of our associates.

As children we were constantly admonished that one rotten apple could spoil a barrel of good ones. Parents in turn are reminded that "words teach but example draws," implying that the best way to educate children is by example, the *absorption* of the habits of the parents themselves. An Italian is not given special instructions on how to gesticulate; nor does an Italian rehearse his or her profuse and expressive gestures before a mirror. Nevertheless, practically every Italian one meets seems to be as eloquent with his or her hands as with his or her voice. We are not taught expressly how and when to blush or shed tears, when to faint, when to be nauseated, or when our mouth is to water; blushing, weeping, fainting, nausea, and a hankering for certain foods are largely responses to *unconscious* absorption of patterns.

We are not exaggerating the importance of this third way of acquiring a culture. It is indeed important in our lives, and in religious formation in particular.

5.2.3.1.5 Enculturation: A Distinctly Human Process

Is enculturation, one might ask, a distinctly human process? Why did Kroeber some forty years ago define culture simply as "that which the human species has and other social species lack" (1948:253)? Animals do not have a culture, because they cannot *learn* it. They not only lack the innate competence mentioned above (5.2.3.1.4) but are also incapable of the symbolic behavior that cultural learning presupposes.

We do not say that animals cannot learn at all. After all, dogs and cats can be housebroken; dogs can learn tricks; and parrots, like children, sometimes say the cleverest things at the most propitious moment. Nevertheless, there is an essential difference between human and animal learning, and, despite the claims of some modern researchers to the contrary, the difference is not only in degree but in kind.

At first sight it would seem that at least the more humanlike animals, the anthropoids, would be able to learn in the same way as human beings do and that, at least in regard to the anthropoids, the difference in learning would be in degree rather than in kind. Do not the many experiments even of older studies of primate intelligence, such as those of Hooton, Köhler, and the Yerkes (e.g.,

Köhler 1925; Yerkes 1929; Kellogg, Kellogg 1933), show the contrary to be true? Do not anthropoids make and use tools, and therefore is it not true that they can reason and that they actually possess an intellect, however primitive? And do not the more recent studies indicate that anthropoids have an ability to communicate in a humanlike fashion? (See Luzbetak 1970: 79–81)

> Chimpanzees, for example, learn to play with toys with even greater dexterity than above-normal children. A common sight in circuses is the line of vivacious chimps pedaling their bicycles with as much enthusiasm and skill as any children in the neighborhood. Apes have even learned to ride motor scooters. They hurl coconuts, sticks, and stones in self-defense. Is not the use of weapons a use of tools and therefore a sign of true intelligence? When an ape finds a nut that is too hard to crack with its hands or teeth, it may have learned to use a stone very much the way human beings did in the Stone Age. When a banana is beyond the chimpanzee's reach, it may have learned to lengthen its reach by joining two sticks. Or, in order to reach its food, the more clever anthropoid may have learned to make a kind of ladder for himself by piling one box on top of the other—not recommended by insurance companies, but only too human nonetheless. Chimpanzees have learned to sharpen a stick with their teeth for special purposes. Does this mean that they *made* tools? They have been taught to distinguish good money (actually chips that fit a slot machine) from counterfeits (chips that do not) and to store their wealth in a kind of bank for a rainy day, later to be deposited into the slot machine and receive food (raisins) in return. Was this the beginning of the supermarket? In fact, the first American astronaut was Sam, a chimpanzee.

And, we might ask further, why could not a group of apes, after one of their more precocious fellows has acquired a bit of new knowledge either by imitation, accident, or trial-and-error, imitate the inventor and thus develop a truly humanlike culture? If apes can imitate human beings—monkey see, monkey do—why should they not be able to imitate one another and develop a true culture? A classic example would be that of the ape who invented the amusing pastime of teasing chickens. The game consisted in poking a stick at a helpless hen in order to make it hop, cackle, and flap its wings in a frantic attempt to escape the teaser. Soon the inventor's relatives and neighbors joined in the fun—and fun it was, for everybody except the helpless fowl. This game may sound like the transmission of group experience through the kind of learning called for in our concept of culture. However, there is a very essential element missing in the type of learning just described.

All these examples of anthropoid intelligence and ability to learn consist in imitating what was actually seen, heard, or felt, in remembering the sensory image and associating it with a new sensory stimulus similar to the first experience. If all chickens were to emigrate from the realm of the anthropoids, the apes would never be able to describe their amusing chicken-game to their offspring, for the learning of even the most intelligent ape is limited in this case to imitating an actual chicken-teasing. Absent is the ability to make abstractions as humans do and to communicate by means of symbolic cues. Human beings, by contrast, are able to prescind from the sensory here-and-now. They can abstract the "whatness," the quiddity or essence, of things and events.

Human beings can, in fact, do more than form and preserve ideas for themselves. They have the power to *share* their abstract ideas and knowledge with their fellow-humans. They are able to describe a game without actually performing, and listeners can get the gist of the game without necessarily seeing it played. Herein lies the difference between human and purely animal learning and communication.

Essentially, culture is a set of norms, or, phrased alternatively, a set of *ideas*. Transmission of culture presupposes the ability to transmit ideas. Ideas are transmitted by the group to the individual by means of symbols understood by the entire group. Human beings have the unique ability to create symbols. Abstract ideas are attached to colors, sounds, tastes, touches, smells, actions, objects, and other sensory phenomena, including silence, time, and space (cf. E. T. Hall 1959, 1976; Hall, Whyte 1960). The object meant need not be physically present. In its place, human beings are able to use arbitrary symbols, the chief of which are the articulate sounds known as *language*. There is, for instance, nothing hen-like about the English word *hen*. Symbols are physical phenomena (like the word *hen*), to which a meaning has been arbitrarily bestowed by the users. Animals may very well use signals, but they never create or use symbols. They may in a rudimentary way perhaps manipulate some signals, but they can never bestow the *meaning* of "chicken" to a symbol.[5] Symbolic behavior, verbal as well as nonverbal, enables humans to have and to transmit ways, goals, premises, values, and a whole philosophy of life, thus largely replacing human dependence on instinct. Through such symbolic behavior and learning, each generation contributes to the growth of group experience. In turn, group experience is preserved in the form of culture and tradition. Although the human conceptual process begins with the senses too, it transcends them; the difference, therefore, is not only in degree but also in essence.

In the last few decades, great interest and excitement has been generated among many psychologists, linguists, anthropologists, and other researchers in the so-called ape-language studies. Although apes cannot produce spoken words, some researchers claim that these animals do possess semantic and syntactic abilities that differ from human communication only in degree. According to Dr. Francine Patterson of the Gorilla Foundation of California, Koko, a 230-pound gorilla, uses more than 500 signs regularly and knows some 500 others in American Sign Language, or Ameslan—the hand language of the deaf (Vessels 1985:110). Allen and Beatrice Gardner claim to have been able to teach their clever female chimpanzee named Washoe over 200 words in Ameslan, and that Washoe can now use these words grammatically. She is also supposed to be able to make generalizations. Here, however, we seem to be dealing with signals, not symbols. Other researchers, like Umiker-Sebeok and Sebeok (1981, 1982), question the validity of such claims on the grounds that the research is based on faulty methodology. The experimenters, they say, unwittingly emit cues to their clever simian subjects, who in turn respond not to symbolic cues (absolutely necessary for human-type communication), but to subliminal signals that even the experimenters may not be aware of. Herbert S. Terrace and other authorities on the subject question the claims by Patterson and the Gardners, pointing out, as the Sebeoks do, that their clever anthropoids may be merely reacting to the promptings of human trainers and not communicating spontaneously at all.

The most that might be conceded is (1) that nonhuman animals can indeed *communicate*, especially through sounds, smells, and body movements, namely, through the use of their senses and instincts; and (2) that some anthropoids (gorillas and chimpanzees) have been trained to combine different signals to form new messages; that is, to "speak" a kind of *subhuman* "language." Hogs, dogs, and frogs, it has been wisely said, can be *trained*, but only humans can be *educated*; that is, enculturated. Enculturation is a process that presupposes a *mind*. Despite their arguments, ape-language protagonists have a long way to go before they can say with anything approaching scientific certainty that they have proven their thesis (Linden 1986). The difference between human and nonhuman communication is in kind and not merely in degree.

5.2.3.2 Missiological Application: Culture Is Learned

5.2.3.2.1 Summary of Relevant Theory

(1) Culture is *learned* from one's society. The process of learning a culture is called *enculturation*. (2) Although much of what the individual learns from his or her society is objective, true, correct, and valid, much is culturally determined and is therefore *relative*. This relativity touches the society's whole culture, including forms, functions, and underlying mentality (the starting-points of thinking, reacting, and motivating). (3) Enculturation is therefore *detailed, deep, and pervasive*, affecting the rational, irrational, and nonrational. (4) Despite the pervasiveness of culture, human beings are by no means automatons; culture is only *a potential set of rules and guidelines* for living. The individual is able to depart from the standard and approved norms of behavior. (5) Culture is acquired when it is learned *through education and conscious and unconscious imitation*. (6) Enculturation is *distinctly human*. (7) The term *enculturation* must be distinguished from *inculturation* (a synonym for *incarnation* and *contextualization*) and *acculturation* (the whole set of processes involved in culture change resulting from close and constant contact between societies over a longer period).

5.2.3.2.2 Enculturation and Ethnocentrism

Enculturation makes social living possible. Without enculturation, there would be no human societies. Communication between members of a society, cooperation, sharing of experience, the transmission of such experience from generation to generation, harmonious (predictable) interaction, and survival of the individual and the society itself are all possible only because human beings have been enculturated by their society.

Enculturation therefore serves a very basic function in society. At the *intra*societal level it is very functional. At the *inter*societal level, however, it often grows dysfunctional by becoming the very source of *ethnocentrism*.

Ethnocentrism is a universal problem. We discussed it earlier in connection with missionary models (chapter 3) and when we discussed group contacts and group conflicts (*supra*, 5.2.2.6.4).

Ethnocentrism is the universal tendency to regard the ways and values of one's own social group as the norm for everyone. As we have pointed out earlier, ethnocentrism can vary in intensity, ranging from an understandable and forgivable minor excess in group enthusiasm, loyalty, and pride to uncontrolled xenophobia, unpardonable cultural imperialism, and such utterly outrageous madness as Nazism. Jews at the time of Jesus regarded the Gentiles as unclean, while Samaritans were detested even more than pagans (McKenzie 1965:765–766). It was only through a bitter struggle that Paul's doctrine of equality between Jew and Gentile was able to prevail. Today, ethnocentrism occurs in older churches as well as in newer Christian communities. It is by no means a monopoly of the older churches. It may occur at the specialties level (for example, among the male population of a society in the form of sexism, or between two different social classes) as well as at the subcultural level (for example, in the case of an indigenous bishop coming from a different part of the country or speaking a different dialect), or at the cultural level, affecting an entire society or even a larger region or a whole race. We have seen in our discussion of mission models in chapter 3 how ethnocentrism has appeared again and again in various forms throughout Church history. An appreciation of human differences and commonalities will go a long way toward reducing our ethnocentric tendencies. Robert Redfield in his article "The Study of Culture in General Education" was very much to the point when he said the following:

For as one comes to understand people who live by institutions and values different from one's own, at the same time one comes to see that these people are, nevertheless, at bottom quite like one's own people. The alien culture at first appears to us as a mask, enigmatic or repugnant. On closer acquaintance we see it as a garment for the spirit; we understand its harmonies and appreciate them. Finally, as acquaintance goes deeper still, we do not see, or for a time forget, the culture, but look only to the common humanity of men and women beneath. [*Social Education*, 1947:262]

A case of ethnocentrism has been graphically described by Aubrey Menen in his *Dead Man in the Silver Market* (1953), a summary of which follows. This is a particularly interesting account, inasmuch as it shows how *anyone* can be ethnocentric—not only the British or other Westerners but, literally, any human group possessing a culture. Ethnocentrism is indeed a *universal* frailty, affecting not only the Western Church but the Church of the Third World as well.

The story Menen relates is about himself and his grandmother, a proud upper caste Malabar Indian whose traditions she was convinced were "superior in every respect to the great majority of other human beings." India, she insisted, was civilized when the British were still running around naked.

Aubrey's father was Indian; his mother, British. Aubrey himself was thoroughly anglicized, and English was his only language. In fact he was so thoroughly enculturated in English ways that he was indistinguishable from other British lads of his age.

Aubrey Menen recounts how, when he was twelve, his grandmother insisted on his being brought halfway round the globe from London to a town near Calicut to receive personally from her instructions on his "real" identity and on "proper" behavior. Summing up his experience, he tells us: "Grandmother took me in hand, and I never thought the English were perfect again." Aubrey's mother traveled to India with him. Since she was "unclean" and would have "defiled" the grandmother's residence, a special house had been prepared for her in a remote corner of the property, where she could remain in her "continuous state of defilement," bothering no one and especially not requiring the complicated Hindu ritual cleansing that would have otherwise been continuously needed.

Aubrey's grandmother painfully recalled how some fourteen years earlier her son, that is to say Aubrey's father, did the most dreadful thing imaginable—he married a non-Hindu without his mother's blessing or consent. It was, as Aubrey put it, "like an American boy of twenty-two wrote home from foreign parts to say that he had taken to cannibalism."

His grandmother had never met the English but somehow she felt that she knew all about them. For one thing, the English were "incurably dirty in their personal habits." Imagine, the British did not bathe twice a day! Besides, they used "contraptions" called "bathtubs" in which they wallowed like filthy water buffalo instead of bathing like civilized people in flowing water. "A really nice person," Aubrey was reminded, "does not even glance at his own bath water, much less sit in it." The British also ate "anything," including *meat*, the way the out-caste Todas did—outcastes who had no nobler role in society than that of making mats and cleaning latrines. Besides, the British had practically "no religion." The British were also very "boorish." Instead of eating their meals alone in a corner of the room the way grandmother did, they ate directly opposite each other so that they could watch "each other thrust food into their mouths, masticate and swallow it." How disgusting! And another thing—why does "that Englishwoman" (Aubrey's mother) insist on covering her breasts? Only harlots do such a despicable thing! Grandmother, of course, always insisted on meeting people "properly," that is formally and in harmony with her social station, proudly with her breasts completely bare, the way a "decent" wife and mother would. There were, of course, many other things that the grandmother failed to understand, for instance, how the British could call themselves civilized and yet allow widows to remarry. She also could not understand how the British could keep all kinds of "extraneous" things in their homes. Grandmother's furniture, on the other hand, consisted only of things that "should" be in a home, namely beds, a few oil-lamps, and brass-bound boxes. Tables were taboo, while chairs were "vulgar" and served no real purpose other than "ostentation."

The grandmother's "riding passion," of course, was racial pride. In fact, "she belonged to the cleverest family of the cleverest people on earth." She laughed at British backwardness "not unkindly but pityingly." Particularly "sad and scandalous" was the fact that Aubrey had reached puberty and was still unmarried. If the English wished their offspring to grow up "decently and not lewdly", why didn't they marry them off as they "should"—while they were still children?

The grandmother was greatly saddened when the time came for Aubrey to leave and return to England to live once again among the "heathen." As a last precaution she gave Aubrey a small book containing all the duties and privileges of his caste, a book that opened with an appropriate prayer of thanksgiving to God "for creating us—our caste, that is—so much superior in every respect to the great majority of other human beings."

The moral of our story is simple: Yes, grandma, ethnocentrism *is* a common human ailment, and you, like most human beings, have more than just a touch of it.

5.2.3.2.3 Enculturation as Habit-Formation

Enculturation is habit-formation. Enculturation aims at nothing less than the mastery of the particular design for living. Moreover, the society as well as the subsocieties and further subdivisions are all concerned about passing their particular set of norms for success in life on to posterity. Enculturation, therefore, sets a high goal for itself—the mastery and perpetuation of the social group's "secret" to success in life.

Cultural ways become a kind of second nature to the individual as well as to the social group. Such socially transmitted sets of habits may be neutral or they may be in harmony or in conflict with Christian attitudes, beliefs, and behavior. Anyone engaged in a ministry would, therefore, do well to review the basic principles of psychology regarding habit formation. At the same time, one should keep in mind the principles of moral theology regarding the influence of habits on human behavior. Into consideration come such principles as the diminution of culpability of evil habits innocently (i.e., culturally) acquired, and the morality of living in unavoidable conditions that make the overcoming of undesirable habits difficult or humanly impossible. It often happens that in order to change one such habit, the person concerned may have to gain control of other habits first, and these in turn may each presuppose the subjugation of still other deeply ingrained habits. Such is the case especially because cultural patterns are not isolated phenomena but are interwebbed and closely structured (this subject is a major topic that we will treat in the following chapter). There are functional linkages between the various constituents of culture— which in turn flow from certain more or less consistent starting points in reasoning, reacting, and motivating—which were likewise largely acquired in the process of enculturation. The various cultural habits are functionally tied to one another into a closely knit system. The mastery of one undesirable habit presupposes a struggle with many other habits, some of which may have an important and continuous role to play in the life of the individual and his or her social group. As a result, additional tensions arise, owing to social control. These come from peer pressure, group loyalty, and reward and punishment (*infra*, 7.3.4.2). With such facts in mind, it is easy to understand and appreciate the force that enculturation and socialization exert even on well-intentioned individuals. Baptism may bring the new Christian the necessary grace to live a good moral Christian life, but it does not neutralize the influence of culturally acquired habits. The struggle is often not with isolated panhuman temptations but with deep-rooted, mutually-fortified habits—habits of thought, speech, judgment, desire, feeling, reaction, and action, all of which rest on premises, values, and goals learned from one's society. These habits are innocently acquired in the process of enculturation and are insisted upon by the society through its set of social controls. Thus, cultures can indeed become a kind of trap or cage, or as E. T. Hall expresses it, man can "put himself in his own zoo" (1976:5).

What we have said about the negative aspects of enculturation as habit-formation should make the minister of the Gospel, although always firm and uncompromising in regard to sin, truly empathetic, understanding, and patient, as was he who did not hesitate to defend the prostitute (Jn 8:7), who was known as "a friend of tax collectors and sinners" (Lk 7:34), and who said of himself, "Learn from me for I am gentle and humble of heart" (Mt 11:29). The frequent references in the Old and New Testament to "pagan" ways are really references to such culturally acquired habits (e.g., Dt 29:17; Est 4C:26; Is 17:10; Mt 5:47; 6:7; 1 Cor 5:1; l2:2; Eph 4:17; 1Pt 4:3). St. Paul had this undesirable habit formation in mind when he strongly urged the Ephesians:

> lay aside your former way of life and the old self which deteriorates through illusion and desire, and acquire a fresh, spiritual way of thinking. You must put on that new man created in God's image, whose justice and holiness are born of truth. [4:22–24]

A Positive Attitude Toward Enculturation. More important than all the negative observations we have made regarding the learning of a culture as habit-formation is the need to acquire a *positive* attitude toward enculturation. Despite the grip that systemic evil, whose roots are located in culture learning, may have on a society or on a segment of it, the learning of a way of life should be regarded rather as being primarily neutral or good in itself and, from the point of view of evangelization, as being a positive aid to a desired change. Rather than being the trap and cage that it sometimes is, it can give the Gospel message a true naturalness and permanency. Enculturation should be looked upon *positively*—as a network of habits in which the God of History in his providence and mercy has had an important hand. We are saying that despite the presence of evil in cultures there is a *basic goodness* in them. Father Edward J. Flanagan, the founder of Boys' Town, used to say that there was no such thing as a bad boy—only such that never had a chance. It is of this type of basic goodness that we speak. Such goodness is definitely there. It must, however, be looked for, discovered, and built upon. In the type of missiological anthropology that we are advocating, cultures are by no means to be looked upon exclusively, or even primarily, as a kind of ball and chain to which societies are shackled. They must be viewed, rather, as systems of habits containing at least in some limited sense a "hidden Christ," the result of God's own action and grace. The "hidden Christ" is a force that the Church must look for, discover, and build upon. Evangelization should, in fact, be built on no other foundation than on the one that God himself in his universal love, providence, and mercy (cf. 1 Tm 2:4) has already laid. That foundation is most clearly visible in a people's culture—in their "soul," which happens to be transmitted from generation to generation through the process of enculturation.

5.2.3.2.4 Enculturation and the Cross-Cultural Scope of Mission

Cultures, we have seen, are often subdivided into subcultures; and both cultures and subcultures consist of patterns that occur either as universals or as specialties or alternatives (*supra*, 5.2.2.2.2, 5.2.2.5). In proclaiming the Gospel and witnessing one's faith, the basic laws of communication must be observed. Among the most basic of such laws is the necessity of keeping the particular enculturation of the recipient of the Gospel message in mind, and therefore also of recognizing the variations at the specialties and alternative levels.

It is quite true that *Evangelii nuntiandi* speaks of five categories of beneficiaries of evangelization: (1) non-Christians (no.53); (2) active Catholics (no.54); (3) fellow-Christians not in full communion with Catholics (no.54,57); (4) inactive Catholics (no.56); and (5) the unchurched (no.57). This categorization, however, represents only a part of the cultural differences. Each category must be further divided and subdivided according to the particular cultures, subcultures, specialties, and alternatives involved. As communication theory clearly bears out and experience confirms, the starting point in any form of mission (be it social action, religious education, liturgy, or any other ministry) is a socio-cultural analysis of the situation here and now. There are, in fact, *many* variations of the five categories of beneficiaries, which must still be taken into account. The recipients of the message may be, for example, children, teenagers, young adults, older adults, or senior citizens; poor or well-to-do; mentally retarded, lame, blind, deaf, or terminally ill; alcoholics, drug addicts, juvenile delinquents, inmates of a penitentiary or mental hospital; married couples, divorced people or widows and widowers; highly educated professional people or illiterates; people from a big city or small town, from the suburbs or from the inner city; factory workers, farmers, peasants, fisher folk, migrant workers, college students, or the military. In a country like the United States, there are countless major cultural and subcultural differences that go well beyond specialties and alternatives. There are important ethnic and religious differences that make the United States a kind of cross-section of the world itself. The Good News must be preached to the "poor" (cf. Mt 11:4)—and the "poverty" of which the Bible speaks comes in a great variety of forms (*infra*, 8.4.2). The Good News must be preached to all the "poor," but always in *their* particular "language," in terms of *their* specific ways, needs, and values. The important principle to be remembered here is that all forms of mission will be at least to some extent "cross-cultural"; every evangelizer and every witness will at some level (cultural, subcultural, or at the level of specialties or alternatives) have to cross the boundaries of his or her own enculturation (Luzbetak 1987).

5.2.3.2.5 Enculturation and Primary Relationships

Enculturation theory suggests that *values are most effectively transmitted within the framework of the community* (*supra*, 5.2.2.6.2). The family dimension is particularly important; it is deserving of far more consideration than we might be able to give the topic. A few thoughts on enculturation and the home must, however, be mentioned here to substantiate our central point.

The Family and Enculturation. We have emphasized that an individual to a large extent reflects the values that he or she has *learned* (either through intended education, conscious imitation, or unconscious absorption) from those with whom he or she is in contact. In fact, the closer and the earlier the contact, especially if it is continuous, the greater is the impact. As Vatican II put it:

> parents must be acknowledged as the first and foremost educators of their children . . . the family is the first school of those social virtues which every society needs. [*Gravissimum educationis*, no.3]

The family is indeed the moral backbone of society, the best indicator of how deeply (or how superficially) the Gospel has been incarnated in a culture (cf. John Paul II, *Catechesi tradendae*, no. 68 and his *Familiaris consortio*).

Enculturation, as we have seen, is a process that begins with birth and, at least intermittently, continues until death. Parents, while in the process of parenting, have much to learn "on the job," as it were. Much of their learning takes place not in the abstract but in the actual cultural and social situations in which they must carry out their roles as Christian parents. One cannot, therefore, but applaud the practice of parishes and dioceses that have Christian formation programs geared to the given time and place specifically for parents. Perhaps the most meaningful, and admittedly the most difficult religious educational programs, are those that are planned and coordinated in such a way as to involve the whole family simultaneously, taking into account, of course, differences in age and responsibilities.[6] The best evangelizers are the members of the family, especially the parents, because they are also the best enculturators. The evangelization we are talking about is not so concerned about imparting theoretical knowledge about Christianity as it is concerned about an *effective and continuous Christian presence* in the family.[7] Spouse influences spouse, the parent influences the child, the child influences the parent, siblings influence siblings, and relatives, especially in an extended family system, influence relatives.

No one can deny that today we are witnessing the actual disintegration of family life in most countries and sectors of society. The forms of this disintegration are many. The causes are likewise many and closely interwebbed. In the total population of the United States, some 12 million children are brought up in a home with only one parent, usually the mother, who must serve not only as parent but also as homemaker, educator, role model, and breadwinner. The very nature of the nuclear family, especially in modern technically advanced societies, normally presupposes the presence of both father and mother for the proper functioning of the family and rearing of children.

The breakdown of the family has become for the inner-city blacks the greatest of all their tragedies (Moynihan 1965, 1986; Aschenbrenner 1975). As senator and sociologist Patrick Moynihan has been pointing out for the last twenty years, it is the breakdown of family life, more than anything else, that is perpetuating the plight of the American blacks. Unbelievable as it may seem, only 43 percent of American inner-city black children live in families with both parents, while the majority (57 percent) do *not*. By the year 2000, 70 percent of inner-city black families will be headed by single women. The causes are many and interdependent—not only racism and the inadequacies of the American welfare system, which are unquestionably major considerations—but, as many black leaders themselves decry, the inner-city culture and the associated enculturation. Such leaders are saying what anthropologists have long been saying: no change can be directed in any culture whatever, unless the society in question feels the need for the change. Unless the inner-city families feel the need for Christian family values, and do something about it, such values will never become a part of the inner-city culture. What must be of primary concern is to find a way out of a vicious circle. While striving to put an end to inner cities themselves, we must strive also somehow to restore family values in the black inner-city culture.

The community must itself (although not by itself) work from within to put an end to a deadly illness, namely certain inner-city culture patterns that promote and perpetuate family disintegration. To continue Moynihan's argument: Attitudes must change if the inner-city family is to revive and flourish. Meant are attitudes, for instance, toward promiscuity; toward teenage pregnancies; toward marriage as if it were an irrelevant white man's institution, with the father in the family as unnecessary ballast rather than a necessary role model; toward education (the high school drop-out rate for blacks is 40 percent, whereas 80 percent of available jobs in the United States presuppose a high school education). The key to full equality, according to sound sociological principles, is culture change initiated from within the family—through educational and other community programs, together with social justice. One cannot but applaud the efforts in this direction made by such organizations as PUSH and NAACP, Pre-Cana and Marriage Encounter programs, and the Catholic school system (cf. Coleman, Hoffer 1987). What we are emphasizing is that the attack from within the black community as well as from without be focused on *family values.* An extraordinarily insightful strategy is the set of Resolutions of the National Black Catholic Congress held in Washington, D.C., May 17–24, 1987 (*Origins,* December 10, 1987). As Moynihan has maintained over the years, the gains[8] made through the civil rights movement are being undone, and actually are being made impossible, through the disappearance of the very basis of human society (Moynihan 1965, 1986). The restoration of family values, we are saying, must go *hand in hand* with the struggle against discrimination, in fact, given the highest priority.

In contrast, it is estimated that about 10 percent of the white children in the United States and 20 percent of the Hispanics live in one-parent homes—one out of ten and one out of five respectively—a proportion which, however disheartening, is nonetheless incomparably more tolerable than that of the inner-city blacks. However, as is only too well known, the white family is also rapidly disintegrating. The sexual revolution, self-centeredness, tensions brought on by modern economic change, the divorce rate, and many other contributing factors are tearing out the very heart of family life. The "new poor" in the United States are, in fact, the *white* divorced and widowed mothers and their children.

Vatican II was both on solid moral ground and at the same time actually applying sound anthropological and sociological theory when it pointed out that

> with parents leading the way by example and family prayer, their children—indeed, all within the family circle—will find it easier to make progress in natural virtues, in salvation and in holiness. Husband and wife, raised to the dignity and the responsibility of parenthood, will be zealous in fulfilling their task as educators, especially in the sphere of religious education, a task that is primarily their own. [*Gaudium et spes*, no.48]

Enculturation and Modern Communications Media. In dealing with the influence of the home, we must point out at least briefly the role that modern communications media play in enculturation. Billions of dollars are spent on television advertising in the United States every year. At times, as much as a million dollars a minute are paid for a single advertisement (and this does not include the expense involved in research and production of the commercial). The cost-effectiveness of this is perhaps the best proof that television does indeed influence our ways and values. Many people, however, still refuse to recognize the impact that television has on present-day behavior for good or evil. Watching violence and pornography, they insist, does not turn one into a murderer or sexual deviate—and they produce statistics to "prove" this assumption. Overlooked is the fact that violence and pornography in the printed and electronic media can and do create the impression of social acceptability, especially in the minds of the young. If "everybody is doing it," the behavior can hardly be reproachable. Today the media are, knowingly or unknowingly, bent on making drugs and extramarital sex acceptable because "everyone is doing it," especially role models and popular heroes of the screen and sports field. As Mary Kenny describes the situation, television is actually destroying our "sense of appropriateness": the language of the barroom and the language of the home become one, and our children become a part of the adult world long before they reach it physically (Kenny 1987: 1235–1236). For better or for worse, the step from social acceptability to culture change, from actual behavior to culture change, is always small indeed.

Television must be regarded as a truly major enculturative influence, at least as important as the school and church, especially because it is so closely tied in with the family. The average American child will have watched 10,000 to 15,000 hours of television, with all its vice and violence, by the time he or she is sixteen. By eighteen, the teenager will have spent more hours before the television set than he or she will spend studying in college (Biernatzki 1978:9).

We can also not afford to overlook the fact that the child not only watches television; the child also watches the reaction of the family to the television program. All scandal, but especially within the family, owing to its deep and pervasive impact, is particularly serious (cf. Mt 18:6). The child cannot but observe the family's choice of programs, its laughter and other reactions, and, its approval or disapproval of what is being watched. Television has thus become not only an integral part of the home but also a major enculturative medium that has an extraordinary capacity for good or evil. How to deal with television is a challenge for the entire modern family. Parents must learn to appreciate its extremely important enculturative role in Christian formation today. It would be well for the reader to study William F. Fore's *Television and Religion: The Shaping of Faith, Values and Culture* (1987).

The Role of Peer Groups and Other Social Structures in Enculturation. The most important evangelizers next to the family are peer groups and other social structures, especially those that involve close interaction, dependence, and prestige in the particular community. No true Christian can afford to overlook that we *are* indeed our "brother's keeper" (Gn 4:9). Beyond the family, each member of the community is obligated, especially through an active, positive Christian presence in his or her given role, to evangelize the other; each must feel responsible for the enculturative process of conversion of the other. Peer pressure, to offer but one simple example, can do more to encourage or discourage drunk driving, alcohol and drug abuse, and illicit sex than any legislation or police enforcement, lectures at school, or sermons in church.

By no means do we wish to imply that a "cultural" or "socialized" Christian will ever be an adequate substitute for a truly converted one (cf. Loewen 1969a:1–17). To achieve so-called nominal Christianity can never be the goal of mission, a point we hope we have made clear by our repeated emphasis on "the mind of Christ," a "mind" that leaves no doubt whatsoever about the necessity of personal conversion (Mt 7:21; 15:11; Mk 7:6,20) and the need to rend hearts, not garments (Jl 2:13; Jer 9:25).

5.2.3.2.6 Christian Enculturation in a Pluralistic Society

Religious education in a pluralistic environment faces a special challenge: *Christians must learn to live as Christians even if the world around them does not.* An essential part of religious education (be it from the pulpit, in the classroom, or in the home) is the challenge of making decisions for oneself despite social pressures. How, for instance, is one to be a discriminating reader, movie-goer, television-viewer; in a word, how does one dare to be different? A religious educational program in a pluralistic society that fails to teach Christians how to be independent critics of the world in which they live leaves its task at best only half-accomplished. Christians, especially in pluralistic societies, must learn to be constantly aware of their vocation as prophets in their often unsympathetic world, not so much perhaps by proclaiming as by witnessing their faith. Anthropology, as we have seen, assures us that we are by no means shackled to culture. Christians can and should be at times countercultural. Is this not what Jesus meant when he said, "Whoever acknowledges me before men I will acknowledge before my Father in heaven" (Mt 10:32)? Especially in de-Christianized countries of the West, true Christians, as a subsociety, must be so enculturated as to be able to reject the rampant materialism, indifferentism, hedonism, scientism, and countless other *isms* that surround them. Among those other *isms* is, for instance, secular humanism, a very inadequate, compromised, watered-down "gentleman's-agreement-type" religion that in many points regards Christ and his Gospel as unimportant, if not irrelevant. This religion is referred to as "civil religion," identified, for instance, with American history, democracy, and ideals, and therefore in many ways is good in itself but unfortunately is a kind of "folk" or, as sociologist Peter Berger (1961) called it, a kind of "state" religion that leaves much to be desired as far as Christianity is concerned. Day in and day out, the Christian in a pluralistic society is exposed to a basically un-Christian ideology preached by the various media, modern commercialism, and a broadly accepted value system that judges right and wrong on the basis of economic advantage and disadvantage alone. There is also the widely accepted laissez-faire morality that, for instance, may decry extramarital pregnancies but condones, if not encourages, extramarital sex as long as it is "between consenting adults" and is done "safely."

We are saying that in a pluralistic society, Christian living will call for a very special kind of enculturation. Christians must be, so to speak, "bicultural"— citizens of *two* cities, citizens of this world without compromising their primary citizenship that is not of this world. In cold anthropological terms, Christians form a distinct, uncompromising subsociety within a larger society—a "little flock" (Lk 12:32) and a tiny "mustard seed" (Mt 13:31ff), a bit of yeast (Mt 13:33) called to help transform the world rather than to be transformed by it.

5.2.3.2.7 Culture Shock

Nature of Culture Shock. Excessive mental strain or physical exertion may lead to what is commonly called "burnout," "breakdown," "exhaustion," "collapse," or "shock." Thus, soldiers succumb to combat "fatigue." Victims of an accident may sometimes die not so much of the accident itself as of the accompanying "shock." Animals moved from their natural environment to that of a cage cease to eat and breed and often die when, theoretically speaking, they are placed into a veritable "paradise." Even flowers and trees that are transplanted invariably undergo "shock" and, in fact, frequently die. The respective syndromes are not unlike those of *culture shock*, which might be defined as the inability of an individual enculturated for a given physical, social, and ideational environment to adjust comfortably and more or less spontaneously to another environment. Culture shock is a common problem in all forms of cross-cultural activity. Asians and Africans are as susceptible to cultural shock as are Europeans and Americans. Migrant workers, overseas students, refugees, defectors, prisoners of war, hostages, people in hospitals or institutions, industrial managers abroad, government employees (e.g., those of the diplomatic corps, the Peace Corps, the Agency for International Development, the military), overseas employees of multinational corporations, foreign journalists, tourists, anthropologists doing fieldwork, and, not least of all, church workers, can all fall victim to culture shock. For church workers, it is not at all necessary to leave one's shores to be faced with the problem. A middle-class pastor or teacher assigned to an inner-city or ethnic parish may be exposed to culture shock no less than his or her counterpart overseas.

Symptoms of Culture Shock. The inability to adjust to strange cultural demands will inevitably lead to some degree of culture shock, the symptoms of which include (1) a growing negative and suspicious view of the "strange" people and their ways and values; (2) homesickness, loneliness, boredom, lethargy, and a tendency to withdraw; (3) rising stress, an overall feeling of dissatisfaction, disgust, irritability, and depression; (4) physical illness, especially chronic headaches and hypertension; (5) an overconcern about one's health; (6) excessive drinking or some other questionable compensation. Some twenty-five years ago, when talk about culture shock was still relatively new, Kalervo Oberg, a mission anthropologist, isolated the following concrete signs of culture shock found among mission personnel:

> excessive washing of the hands; excessive concern over drinking water, food, dishes, and bedding; fear of physical contact with attendants or servants; the absent-minded, far-away stare (sometimes called "the tropical stare"); a feeling of helplessness and a desire for dependence on long-term residents of one's own nationality; fits of anger over delays and other minor frustrations; delay and outright refusal to learn the language of the host country; excessive fear of being cheated, robbed, or injured; great concern over minor pains and irruptions of the skin; and finally, that terrible longing to be back home to be able to have a good cup of coffee and a piece of apple pie, to walk into that corner drugstore, to visit one's relatives and, in general to talk to people who really make sense. [1960:178]

Causes of Culture Shock. Culture shock results from the constant jolting and the consequent stress and fatigue associated with living in a society that has different ways and values from those that have become second nature to the outsider. Although human beings are perhaps more similar to one another than dissimilar, human similarities do not make us immune to cultural jolts. Here the word *cultural* refers also to subcultural differences and sometimes to differences on the microcultural level of specialties and alternatives within our own culture or subculture (*supra* 5.2.2.3, 5.2.2.5). If we fail to become at least to some extent bi- or multicultural in a "strange" cultural situation, we shall be constantly perplexed, disappointed, irritated, frustrated, fearful, apprehensive, and psychologically exhausted by our inability to respond "naturally" to the unfamiliar cultural demands made upon us.

As we shall see, there is a healthy as well as an unhealthy way of adjusting to a situation. But first, we shall offer some examples illustrating the frequency and variety of cultural stress. The examples we explore indicate some of the major *danger zones* that must be watched in any cross-cultural activity.

It should be noted that such danger zones are more than danger zones: they are important areas of opportunity and of needed sensitivity. We are taking a negative view of such areas only because our present consideration, culture shock, is itself a negative concept. Our negativeness at the moment should not suggest that we have forgotten the central goal of missiological anthropology, the incarnation of the Gospel into the very heart and soul of the local community—into the depths of the community's culture. "What else did the presence of the Holy Spirit indicate at Pentecost," asks a sixth century African author, "except that God's Church was to speak in the language of every people?" (Sermo 8, 1–3; PL 65, 743–744).

The illustrations are therefore intended to be more than isolated examples; they are *areas* that require needed self-examination, relearning, and constant adjustment. One should also not overlook one's own temperament as an important factor that must be taken into consideration when dealing with cultural stress. There can be a kind of "personality clash" between the *modal personality* of a society (that is, the statistically most frequent pattern of personality attributes of a given social group [cf. *supra*, 5.1.6.4]) and the type of person who has not been enculturated accordingly. A shy, reserved missionary, for instance, would find it far more difficult to adjust to a particular society's generally boisterous ways than would an outgoing and uninhibited individual; a routine-bound missionary would find it much more difficult to adjust to a society that seems to thrive on variety and a leisurely lifestyle (cf. Dye 1974:75–76).

Although climate and food come first to mind as areas of concern, the fact is that the most difficult adjustments are generally not physical but social and psychological. One can somehow bear unappetizing food (hunger somehow takes care of that), and one can somehow adjust to cold and heat (here, necessity somehow comes to one's aid). According to a study of Peace Corps volunteers, for example, only 1 percent found physical hardships a *serious* problem, and only 13 percent regarded such hardships as posing a *minor* problem; housing, food, health, and isolation were regarded by only 6 percent as a serious problem, and 20 percent considered these problems as minor (Pearson 1964:55). Thus the Peace Corps study bears out what perhaps most missionaries claim, namely that of all cultural jolts the most painful and most difficult to adjust to are the *psychological* frustrations. One should also note that it is not so much the *form* of the cultural pattern that causes stress as the clash of *meanings* that the forms express. We offer eight such categories of problems:

(1) Although we have de-emphasized the problem of *physical adjustment* compared to other areas of stress, we do not wish to deny that at times physical tensions can indeed pose difficult challenges.

The author (cf. Luzbetak 1970:85) well remembers the jolts he used to receive in New Guinea almost every time he entered his kitchen. He still fails to understand why he does not now suffer from a kind of mental disorder that might be called *cuisinophobia novaguenensis*. For example, one day he was surprised to discover how his potatoes were being peeled. He had been under the impression that there was only one way to peel potatoes—the way potatoes "should" be peeled, with a potato peeler or knife. But he was wrong. The cook felt that peeling potatoes was more efficiently done with one's fingernails, with his God-given "potato peeler," the way his culture taught him to peel potatoes in the first place. For a long time the author had been wondering why his potatoes were corrugated. The mystery was now finally solved. His cook, of course, had to master what appeared to him to be "just another useless and inefficient Western way of doing things." Or again, while setting the table one bright morning, the cook noticed that some of the eggs of a previous breakfast still clung stubbornly to the plate. He also noticed that he was being watched to see what he would do. The approach to cleaning the plate was simple, very natural, and culturally meaningful. A lick of the finger and, once again, the all-purpose fingernail, and the plate was "clean."

(2) Among the most painful jolts that one experiences in an unfamiliar cultural surrounding are those that come from new, unfamiliar *interpersonal relationships*. Statuses and roles will always be necessary for the simple reason that mutually understandable and acceptable relationships and support of fellow-humans are basic for human life itself. We have learned from our society, in the process of enculturation, how we are to relate to friends and relatives, to classmates and co-workers, to officials of all kinds, to individuals we immediately recognize as deserving special respect, to acquaintances, and to total strangers. In the new, unfamiliar cultural surroundings, the old cues for relating to others seem to vanish, leaving us in the dark as to proper behavior. New relationships must once again be built up and learned, through the same methods we used when we were infants and little children. There are many very subtle nuances to be learned. Our previous enculturation to a large measure becomes useless, and we begin to feel as helpless as children: we do not know, for instance, how a buyer should relate to a seller at the marketplace (one may, for instance, have to haggle as a matter of course); we do not know whom we are to greet, with what greeting, and how warmly; we also do not know how we are to relate to the different employees of a hotel or inn. In fact, we may not even know how to clothe ourselves, a most fundamental expectation in any code of human relations; for example, the ordinary conservative dress worn by American and European women may be regarded as immodest by Islamic or Hindu societies and in societies where sex play begins with the ankles or calves.

When missionary-anthropologist William D. Reyburn and his wife were in Cameroun (Reyburn 1960:6-8), they identified so much with the people that the community bestowed a native name on them to replace the old. In fact, they were even adopted ritually into the Bulu society. As psychologically satisfying as the new native name and adoption may have been, they soon learned that the privilege implied perhaps more than they had bargained for. Thus, according to Bulu thinking, the Reyburn possessions no longer were private property, and whatever they owned was now available for the collective use of the whole subclan. For instance, their gun had to be made available for an elephant hunt to a nephew visiting his maternal uncle. Reyburn himself was not allowed to join the hunting party and use the gun, because he, like all members of the subclan, had to observe the local pregnancy taboos (the Reyburns were expecting a child at the time).

(3) Interpersonal stress is also associated with *politeness and etiquette*. A newcomer must learn what is, or is not, "proper" and "dignified."

In Ethiopia, we are told (Fargher 1967:186-189), one never says "No" to a request; it is rather "Of course, I'd like to but. . . ." One never misses a chance to greet another person; if it is a friend, one dismounts from one's horse or mule and exchanges at least a few words, and if one passes the home of a friend, one must stop by at least for a few minutes. One must take an *active* part in a conversation; taciturnity is regarded as an insult. When passing by and seeing someone at work, one should never be too busy to lend a hand at least for a short time. "I'm in a hurry! I gotta run!"—so often heard in America—is entirely out of place. A direct business talk is quite normal perhaps in most cultures, but not in Ethiopia: you must rather use an *intermediary*, whether you want to purchase something, borrow some money, ask for permission, or beg for forgiveness. Politeness also demands that you never cut people short when they are talking, a sign of rudeness much more serious than in our culture—even when we feel justified in saying to someone, "I've heard all that before; come to the point."

An American touring some parts of Europe will be struck by the frequency of handshaking—a matter of politeness. The reasons for a handshake are not as momentous as in the United States, say a trip overseas or joining the army. Although the Latin American *abrazo* is catching on in North America, it still jolts some men, although not to the extent that the Russian "bear hug" does or the old-fashioned French accolade.

In America, there is no legitimate excuse for belching in public, no, not even if one has just emptied a large bottle of pop, tonic, soda water, or whatever your subculture has told you is the proper word for a carbonated soft drink. The one exception is the infant draped over its mother's or father's shoulder after having emptied a bottle of milk and gone through a few hundred taps and rubs on the back specifically in the hope of producing "a healthy burp." On the other hand, in China, things are quite different. A husband's manly burp in an exclusive restaurant would not embarrass his wife but please both her and the proprietor—since both would regard any emphatic belch in public as a way of saying "Thank you! Enjoyed it very much!"

Closely associated with etiquette and politeness are the *rules of friendship*. Not mastering the cues of friendship could be quite embarrassing, if not tragic.

Smiles, gestures, winks, greetings, pleasantries, and jokes appropriate for friends differ greatly depending on the culture. Although so-called bone-crushers are seldom called for, in America a firm handshake is always appropriate and to be preferred to a handshake that makes you wonder if a dead fish is being handed to you. In Latin America, however, a firm handshake between a man and a woman could very easily be misunderstood and suggestive. In Vietnam, to place one's hands on one's hips while facing another person (not an unusual nonchalant posture in America) is to challenge the other person to a fight. In Brazil, our "A-OK" gesture (the right hand raised with the tips of the thumb and forefinger touching and thus forming the "O" of OK) is obscene (cf. Luzbetak 1970:87).

(4) The issue of *territoriality* (the use of space) will vary according to the norms set down by the particular culture. Squirrels have their trees, and dogs know the property lines of their masters. Human beings recognize one another's territoriality, not however by instinct, the way animals do, but by learning the particular set of cultural norms. Disagreement regarding territoriality may lead to quarrels, if not to feuds and wars, over land ownership, national borders, parking spaces, or no-smoking areas.

What, for instance, is the proper use of space in conversations? In the New Guinea highlands, speakers may be several hundred yards apart exchanging their views "long distance." On the other hand, in Latin America one gets the impression that the people are crawling over you and breathing down your neck when they speak to you. They keep poking you and pulling your sleeve, as if you were not interested, or as if you were falling asleep, or perhaps trying to run away; and the more you draw back, the closer they get to you and the more persistent their tugging becomes. The comfortable conversational distance in South America is anything but comfortable to someone from North America and vice versa (cf. E. T. Hall 1959:204–209; *infra*, Figure 7).

E. T. Hall (1959:204–209) observes that in North America we stand four-five feet away from the person with whom we are discussing general matters such as sports, politics, or the weather. By contrast, we stand less than a yard away from the person with whom we are discussing such personal matters as where the nearest toilet is located. In Latin America, Hall points out, general matters are discussed at North American "personal distance," while personal matters involve what we have described as "tugging" and "breathing down one's neck." Hiebert illustrates the phenomenon in Figure 7.

Figure 7
Conversational Space in North and South America

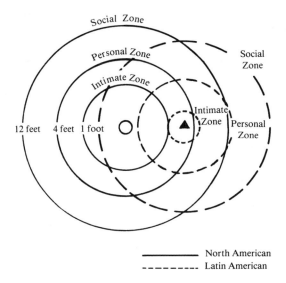

Use of space differs with cultures.

© P. G. Hiebert, *Cultural Anthropology,* Grand Rapids: Baker Book House, 1983. Figure 2.4.

Different attitudes toward territoriality can become particularly annoying or embarrassing when different sexes are involved. In some cultures, it is quite out of place, for instance, to have co-educational schools or to have men and women sit on the same side of the church. The territoriality of "his" and "hers" may go far beyond public lavatories. (Cf. E. T. Hall 1959:52, 60, 67–69, 187–209, 214.)

Closely associated with the concept of territoriality is that of *privacy*. The disregard of another's right to privacy is not only rude but painful. However, what is private in one cultural setting is not necessarily private in another (cf. Luzbetak 1970:89–90).

"Peeping Toms" in the United States can be "Ordinary Joes" in some missionary situations. The passengers in an Italian bus sometimes shock, or at least amuse, tourists by their understanding of privacy. An uninhibited jab in the ribs followed by a not-too-sweet "permesso" or "scusi," and you wedge your way with the aid of your elbow from one end of the bus to the other, ramming through twenty and more passengers with little regard for age, sex, social status, or broken ribs.

Generally, what enters my mouth becomes "mine" whether it be a toothbrush or a stick of gum; it is a matter of privacy. The author, for example, was jolted to see how chewing gum thrown away by Europeans would be picked up by New Guinea school children and then passed around like an Indian smoke pipe. (Speaking of smoke pipes, since they have been in someone's mouth, in our culture they are normally not to be used by anyone else.) We normally claim exclusive rights to whatever we put into our mouths, with such exceptions as forks and spoons.

(5) The manner in which societies deal with *time* is also culturally conditioned and can present a major area of possible jolts (cf. Luzbetak 1970:89).

In some cultures it may take you two or three times as long to do your shopping, cooking, or laundry. Worse still, it may take you months to get a simple replacement for a tractor, radio, or sewing machine part.

"Church services will begin promptly at 9:00 A.M." means one thing in North America and another thing in Latin America. "Long-range" planning in the United States is "short-range" planning in China. A "leisurely pace" in New York may be "top speed" in Trinidad or Haiti. The "*mañana* spirit" makes good sense in Latin America but is frowned upon in the United States, where one is taught in the earliest years of elementary school that what you can do today you should not leave until tomorrow and that "a stitch in time saves nine." Time may be money in the United States but it certainly does not seem to be such south of the border, where there is an entirely different sense of time.

In Ecclesiastes 3:1–8 we read that "there is a time for everything . . . a time to kill and a time to heal . . . a time to weep, and a time to laugh; a time to mourn, and a time to dance . . . a time to embrace, and a time to be far from embraces . . . a time to be silent, and a time to speak, a time to love and a time to hate." Many of such times are culturally determined and therefore an occasion for culture jolts. Christmas trees and poinsettias, like plum pudding and fruit cake, are out of place except around Christmas time. Having beer in the morning is regarded in the United States as being out of place, except for alcoholics. In Poland, on the other hand, as an old Polish saying has it, "drinking beer in the morning is like drinking cream."

(6) Another major set of jolts comes from what we might call *cultural incongruities* or *incompatibilities*—like wearing tennis shoes with a tuxedo (Luzbetak 1970:90–93).

A new missionary described in the following terms the jolts he had received from the incompatibilities between his own cultural expectations on the one hand and what he had observed upon his arrival in New Guinea: "I watched Father Mike hear confessions sitting on a five gallon can and then celebrate the Eucharist on a shaky-legged table that was full of holes. Sitting off to the side, I was amazed with his ability to concentrate on the Mass with pigs, dogs and chickens walking close to his legs and mixing freely with the people" (*Word/USA*, December 1979, p. 5).

The author found the custom of blessing fishing boats quite reasonable—after all, a fisherman's life is a dangerous and uncertain life, and he and his crew needed all the protection they could get. On the other hand, the author was at first surprised when New Guinea highlanders brought their pigs (their most prized possessions) to him for a blessing, or when Catholics in Rome asked prayers and a blessing not only on home and family but on the cat as well. On second thought, one can and should ask, "Are God, cats, and pigs really so incompatible as our culture seems to think?" Taking a siesta in North America is generally regarded as incompatible with good health and diligence; only little children, elderly people, the sick, and those working on a night shift are exempt. "Not so," say the Spaniards, "to take a midday nap makes excellent sense."

To Tanzanians, shaking water off one's hands over a fire is as incompatible as confusing sex roles (Singleton 1979:840).

Such incongruities and sources of cultural jolts reflect the presence or absence of what anthropologists call *functional linkages* (*infra*, chapter 6). These linkages provide logical or purposeful relationships between the various constituents of a culture (cf. Luzbetak 1970:90-92).

It is said that unless a person is pregnant, certain foods "just don't go together"—ice cream and beer for instance, or ice cream and pickles. Our teenagers sometimes make "impossible" sandwiches for themselves. In college cafeterias, one sometimes can see Latin American and Filipino students put heaps of sugar into their milk, while our sense tells us that one does not put sugar into one's milk except for baby formula perhaps or with cereal. Mint jelly with lamb and sweet cranberry sauce with turkey appear very compatible on the American table but almost unthinkable in most European countries, since "meat and sweets just don't mix." In Germany, milk and coffee go together but not milk and tea; in England, tea without milk is almost unthinkable.

Similarly, certain eating habits and civilization are supposed to be mutually exclusive. Thus, it is commonly believed that only animals and "savages" do not cook their meat. The fact is that the Japanese, a highly cultured people, eat raw fish, Americans eat raw oysters, and Germans are fond of "raw" (i.e., smoked but not fried or broiled) bacon—in fact, as we have seen, bacon tastes best to the Germans "before all the flavor is fried out." Germans actually eat totally raw, albeit spiced, ground beef as a delicacy, while Americans sometimes like their steaks "nice and rare," if not "still kicking."

Some behavior patterns are regarded as incompatible with masculinity or maturity. "Act your age!" and "Don't be a sissy, wimp or softy!" are powerful admonitions and jeers in most societies. Teenage girls may keep a favorite doll in their bedrooms but are too old to play house with them. Some societies regard dark beer as suitable for women and children but not for men. Sweet wine may be all right for women; men must have their dry wine or hard liquor. "*Macho*" societies (as well as others) are sometimes offended by women who come as tourists wearing "men's" trousers. Most important to remember is the fact that male and female roles vary from culture to culture, a major source of culture jolts.

Certain cultural patterns may be considered incompatible with a given place.

For men to wear a hat and to be barefoot in church is regarded in Western countries as disrespect for a holy place. Moslems, on the other hand, regard a head covering and bare feet as a sign of reverence. Moses had to take off his sandals before he approached the burning bush (Ex 3:5), for the place on which he stood was holy ground.

(7) *Communication*, verbal and nonverbal, produces one of the most serious areas of culture shock. Learning to communicate according to strange patterns is a difficult, tedious, frustrating, and often humiliating experience. It reduces an educated adult to the level of a child (cf. Luzbetak 1970:93–94). The difficulties to which we refer are not only those connected with pronunciation and grammar. We refer, also, especially to those problems connected with broader cultural subtleties and connotations. Sociolinguistics has contributed much to our understanding of what type of language is appropriate for what social occasion for what social group (Trudgill 1974).

Touches and bodily movements carry different meanings in different cultures: some are compatible with modesty, being in fact a form of kindness (e.g., an embrace or a warm clasp of the hand); in another culture, the same gesture may indicate an obscene intent. In most cultures as in Christianity, touch plays an important ritual role. In most cultures, too, touch is the ultimate proof of truth (Bronner 1982:352–355), reminding us of the Risen Lord's words to doubting Thomas, "Put your hand into my side. Do not persist in your unbelief, but believe (Jn 20:27)!"

Like a touch, silence can be an important form of communication. As we have seen, in Ethiopia to be silent when in a group can be very insulting. In liturgy, moments of silence can be particularly effective. In Buddhist philosophy, silence is the Symbol of the Ineffable. Silence is often used as a symbol of political protest and grief. Silence, as is only too well known, is used by angry spouses as "a cold treatment." Silence is indeed a part of the "silent language" that must be learned in any unfamiliar cultural setting to prevent misunderstanding and offense.

Women, as is quite generally the case, are not to communicate the way an angry truck driver or army sergeant does. In Japan, one must not only respect the hierarchical structure of society in one's vocabulary and grammar but also in what one does, for instance, how deeply one bows and who bows first and how many bows one makes. In World War II, American prisoners of war often suffered unnecessarily through their failure to appreciate the Japanese meaning of bowing. To an American, bowing was demeaning—

one bowed only to God, not to a fellow human; to the Japanese guards, a bow was nothing more than a simple recognition, the least one human being can expect of another (Hall 1959: 103–4).

A good example of nonverbal communication is the story told of an American lecturer on a lecture tour in Japan shortly after World War II. His task was to teach Japanese college students the meaning of democracy. Back in the United States he was regarded as a very capable lecturer, who knew how to present his message well. Creating a favorable atmosphere among his hearers, and not only preaching his message but demonstrating it as well, was one of his main techniques. When he entered a lecture room, he made sure that his face beamed with the friendliness and happiness of a true democracy—he was all smiles. Before beginning a lecture, he would first encourage all to feel at home, as in a true democracy, and to take off their coats as one would do in one's own home. He would even pass cigarettes around the room and take one himself. With a generous sweeping gesture, he would then very democratically begin to light the cigarettes. It was his practice not to sit behind the desk, as if he were an emperor sitting on his throne; instead, he paced up and down, leisurely smoking his cigarette, demonstrating true democracy while preaching it. One day, however, something went wrong. His young Japanese listeners had responded quite favorably at first; but then, suddenly, they began to rise from their seats, noisily discussing something among themselves in Japanese which the lecturer could not understand. Why the riot? What did the lecturer say that he should not have said? He inquired apologetically, but in vain. In desperation he hurried to the administrator's office. After questioning the students, the administrator approached the lecturer politely but very disappointedly, explaining in poor but unmistakable English, "Sir, in Japan table sacred; man's democratic bottom not!" The lecturer, in his enthusiasm for demonstrating true democracy, sat on the edge of the teacher's desk, communicating a totally unintended insult to his audience. "In Japan, table sacred; man's democratic bottom not!"

(8) The most difficult adjustment is associated with what we have called "third level" of culture, *the starting points of reasoning, reacting, and motivating*. This area involves the "mentality" of the people. We shall have much to say about these matters in chapter 6. The Hindu caste system, the deeply-felt Oriental need of face-saving, the inequality of sexes in Islam, and the overriding weight given to a society's needs over those of an individual will always be at the root of many painful misunderstandings. This area will cause much frustration, and many surprises, for a Westerner.

Cultural Adjustment. The seriousness of culture shock may vary in its symptoms from total psychological disability to less serious disorders. Culture shock may not necessarily result in a complete breakdown ("death" as it were), but it could cause something that is nevertheless serious, a kind of "lameness," "deafness," or "blindness." In any case, it could lead to a handicapped, ineffective, and unhappy ministry. Missionary anthropologist T. Wayne Dye (1974) provides us with six helpful ways to adjust to culture stress. (1) Do not deny, but recognize the culture stress. You may accordingly avoid much of the cultural fatigue that jolting normally causes. Bottle up or act as if you were not under stress, and the fatigue will be only that much greater. (2) Seek a reasonable amount of escape through light reading, music, or some other hobby, and allow yourself time for longer weekly and annual recreation. (3) Set goals for yourself that are realistic, and your frustrations will be proportionately reduced. (4) Build up acceptance for yourself by studying cultures in general and the culture of the local people in particular. (5) Improve communication with the people by studying the local language and observing nonverbal forms of communication. (6) Strengthen your emotional security through your own self-acceptance; that is to say, take yourself for what you are in the sense of T. Harris' *I'm O.K.—You're O.K.* (1967) and C. Osborne's *The Art of Understanding Yourself* (1967).

Normally, *some* form of adjustment is achieved by most humans forced to live in an unfamiliar cultural milieu. However, "some" adjustment will never be "enough" for Christian ministry and true witness. Business men and women, journalists, and government officials working in cultures different from their own might be satisfied with their adjustment if the society in question regards them as close and understanding friends. Being a good friend is, of course, a quality required of church workers as well (cf. W. H. Scott 1973). However, church workers, owing to the nature of mission, must set their sights much higher; their goals must be nothing less than *identification* with the local community—or at least nothing less than a relationship as close to identification as possible.

Identification means casting one's lot fully with the local community by becoming with it *one in communion* and *one in communication* (Reyburn 1960:15). To do so, we must, first of all, have genuine *empathy*, the capacity for participation in the local community's feelings. Empathy means understanding and appreciating as much as possible why the local community behaves as it does, no matter what it does. In mission, there are no reasons ever not to be empathetic, even if one cannot agree with or approve of the behavior in question. Jesus never turned away a sinner—no, not even when dealing with tax collectors, prostitutes, a guilty thief being justly punished for his crimes, or even a Judas.

Secondly, identification presupposes the *actual adoption* of as many ways and values of the community in question as possible. The goal must be nothing less than to be "all things to all men" (1 Cor 9:22) in imitation of Christ who "emptied himself" and took on human form in *all* things except sin (Phil 2:6f).

As a basic principle, the Christian engaged in mission should, like Christ and Paul, adopt *as much of the culture of the people served as possible*. To be avoided are only patterns that militate against sound reason and one's faith and conscience; only "sin" must be avoided.

This is, of course, an oversimplification of a complex problem. In an actual situation it may be quite difficult to say what is and what is not "sin" and what is and what is not a genuinely desirable adoption of local ways and values. We offer here three basic guidelines. (1) We have already indicated some of the more important principles for determining the limits to adoption; see our discussion of anthropological and missiological *professional ethics* (*supra*, 2.2.3.3; 2.3.2). (2) Further limits to actual adoption flow from the fact that there are patterns that are *beyond our reach*: even someone trained in cultural anthropology and in the latest, but still very imperfect, techniques for an emic understanding of culture will never really become perfectly bicultural. Therefore, even with the best of intentions, not one person will be able to achieve the ideal of which we speak.

Missionary-anthropologist William D. Reyburn (1960:1–4) describes how he thought that he had to adopt every possible trait of the Ecuadorean Andes Indians but soon discovered that he had not. He dressed like an Indian, ate what they ate, traveled by donkey the way they did, stopped off over night at cheap local inns where any Indian would, sleeping near his faithful donkey. He was convinced that he was like the Indians in all things. Nevertheless, even strangers would call him "mister" rather than "señor," a title by which Europeans were normally addressed. One day, when he could no longer control his curiosity, he asked an innkeeper why she called him "mister" even before he had opened his mouth. She could not quite pinpoint the reason, until she made him enter the inn exactly the way he had entered the day before for the very first time. "Now I know what it is," she said laughingly. "It's the way you walk. You Europeans swing your arms like you never carried a load on your back." Reyburn immediately stepped out into the street to see how the Indians really walked. "Sure enough," Reyburn tells us, "their steps were short and choppy, the trunk leaning forward slightly from the hips and the arms scarcely moving under their huge ponchos"—in a word, the way one would normally walk carrying a heavy load, as the Ecuadorean Indian only too often must and the European seldom does.

(3) Finally, *the community itself* will determine what any outsider, who may otherwise be considered to be a good, friendly, respectable, and sensible foreigner, should or should not adopt. The principle holds even for the foreigner who may have achieved an identification with the community to the extent that he or she is regarded as "one of us."

The author recalls how the indigenous population of the New Guinea highlands ridiculed a certain Australian gold prospector, referring to him as a "bush-kanaka" ("wild man") for walking barefooted and restricting his diet to native foods, although they themselves never wore shoes and lived mainly on sweet potatoes.

A Central American bishop once received a surprise gift from his friends in the United States—a beautiful air conditioner. However, the appliance was never placed in a window of his office or living room but left in the original packing hidden away somewhere in the attic and never used. To live or work in air conditioned comfort would have been regarded as a luxury by his people, no matter what air conditioning may have meant as far as the bishop's health and efficiency in his work were concerned. The bishop's good missionary sense told him that identification with his people was far more important.

Unless a particular culture expressly requires it and/or the local community would be pleased, an outsider should think twice before wearing the native garb—a fez, turban, sari, or G-string for that matter. Nor are missionaries in Alaska expected to live in igloos and to restrict their diet to that of the Eskimo.

Americans, as a rule, do not easily learn a foreign language. On the other hand, they expect foreigners coming to America to speak good English the moment their plane lands. Whether this expectation is justified or not, it is nonetheless an expectation that should be taken perhaps more seriously by foreigners coming to America than is sometimes done.

The author's new house in New Guinea, although made of native materials (bamboo) with a thatched roof commonly used by the local people, had quite a bit of sophistication about it, including a few wire-reinforced plastic windows (used generally for hen houses and cow barns in Australia), an interior furnished with curtains, a table cloth, an army cot serving as bed, a few folding chairs, a few crates varnished and converted into a desk, Chinese straw mats on the floor, the outside door and the frame of the house painted in the gaudiest red—all features as non-native as their missionary himself. The people welcomed this "palace," since, as they put it, "Father's new house now makes our tribe look important."

We shall, of course, become more and more specific about the limitations to actual adoption of local ways by outsiders as we progress. One important fact to keep in mind at all times, as suggested by someone well experienced in cross-cultural ministry, is that the local community will never forget that the missionary's mother was not a Zulu, a Navajo, or a Maori like theirs.

As the diagrammatic sketch in Figure 8 indicates, when we are subjected to culture jolts, we shall have to make an important decision: we may turn right and choose to go the way of identification, or we may turn to the left, the wrong way, and run the risk of culture shock. In the latter case, depending largely on our personality, we shall tend either to "go native" or to reject altogether the unfamiliar ways of the community served. By returning to the false security of our own culture, we become more and more "antinative."

Figure 8
Terminal Stages of Adjustment
to a New Cultural Environment

A diagrammatic sketch of possible form of adjustment
to a new cultural environment.

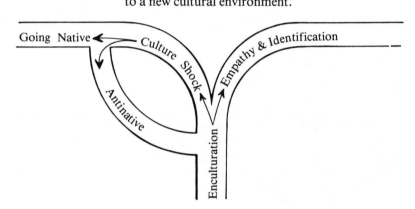

—*Going Native.* Going native is a neurotic form of identification, a compulsion for belonging to the society whose culture is responsible for the cultural stress being experienced. One is driven uncritically to giving up even one's most cherished values, in order to be accepted by the community and thereby once and for all to be free of the discomfort of cultural stress. The fact, however, is that by going native one is jumping from the frying pan into the fire.

Going native is an indiscriminate and, in fact, blind abandonment of one's own traditional norms for the hoped-for (but by no means guaranteed) satisfaction of being accepted. It begins as a reaction to stress, the reasoning being, "If you can't beat 'em, join 'em." In an attempt to adjust to cultural jolts, the person under cultural stress begins to romanticize the very culture that is causing the discomfort. Instead of objectively examining the culture patterns in question to see if they are opposed to sound reason and/or faith and therefore allowing for no compromise, or if on the other hand they are purely relative in value, the prospective candidate of culture shock increasingly exaggerates the "meaninglessness" of his or her own ways and values, romanticizes the very source of his or her pain and discomfort, and, at least in practice, declares the new ways and values automatically superior. The hunger for belonging sometimes drives such a person to form inordinate friendships with certain individuals from the society that is causing the culture shock. Going native may at times lead the unfortunate individual to alcohol abuse or to some other forms of compensation.

There is an essential difference between this pseudo-identification and the true type of identification that mission presupposes. In true identification, we *seek* oneness with the local community; in pseudo-identification we are *driven* into something that is really a neurotic or quasi-neurotic state. In true identification, we seek oneness with the community mainly for *altruistic* reasons, namely for the good of the community and for the spread of the Gospel message; in pseudo-identification we are driven to an imaginary hoped-for oneness out of strictly *personal and ultimately selfish reasons*.

—*Going Antinative*. Like going native, becoming antinative is a frantic, or at least unreasoned, attempt to escape the discomfort experienced from culture stress. The situation is very much like an itch: the more you scratch the itch, the more annoying it becomes. The budding antinativist becomes more and more uncomfortable in the strange cultural environment and at the same time becomes more and more inclined to put the blame not on his or her inability to adjust but on the strange culture causing the itch. Such a person begins to pull back into his or her shell of traditional norms, becoming more and more convinced that the problem lies in the ways and values of the local community. The person begins to limit his or her association to nonlocals, and if possible to compatriots alone. The person grows ever more and more suspicious of the local community's values, ever more and more defensive of his or her traditional ways, ever more and more negative, aggressive, and irritable. Name-calling becomes more and more intemperate: the people are "a bunch of kids" or "outright morons." The only country where everything is "right" is such a person's own home-country. If the person is forced to remain in this unpleasant environment, each culture jolt merely serves to widen the wound and to increase the nostalgia and antinativism.

Stages of Cultural Adjustment. What we have just described are the *terminal* stages of culture shock. As we mentioned earlier, most church personnel as a rule adjust more or less satisfactorily before they reach one of the terminal stages, or they are removed from the mission scene.

Mission anthropologists Oberg (1960:177–182) and Hiebert (1985:74–78; 1976:50–51) describe the stages of culture shock. No one seems to be spared from at least a touch of shock. (1) There is, first of all, the *Tourist Stage*, a honeymoon period that might last from a few weeks to several months, when culture differences of the unfamiliar society are not only novel but interesting, amusing, exciting, and challenging. Almost invariably one views cultural differences from the perspective of an onlooker, a tourist, as it were—from the perspective of what *others* do. There is the excitement of travel preparations, the purchase of suitable clothing and other needs, farewell parties and the admiring faces of friends; then there is the trip, and the photographs for friends back home. There are the first meals, the smiling faces, and helpful hands in the new cultural environment. There is the first experience of learning a few practical expressions in the local language and the encouraging reaction of the people. In about two weeks to several months the roller coaster is at its high point. The reaction is almost invariably the phrase: "I like the place. I'm staying!" (2) But soon the roller coaster starts its way down—at first slowly, then picking up speed. The meals become less and less interesting. The local people go back to their daily routines and begin to take the newcomer for granted. Culture jolts become more and more common and are more upsetting. The individual begins to realize that he or she is not a tourist, not someone on a honeymoon, not someone merely observing what *others* do but what *I* have to do. The roller coaster heads downward faster and faster, and now, after about a year in the new environment, the appearance of various symptoms of culture shock described in the previous section clearly indicate that the person has more than just a touch of cultural exhaustion. This is the *Stage of Disenchantment*, the "I-want-to-go-home!" stage. (3) Fortunately, this second stage is generally followed by a *Stage of Resolution*. Depending on the individual, this period may be short or long, but the sooner one begins to face the symptoms the better. (4) The final stage is that of *Adjustment*: one now feels relatively comfortable in the new culture; the culture jolts are now no longer as common or as painful as before. The person soon begins to feel not only more comfortable but also very much at home. An "I'm-staying!" feeling takes over. The individual is now able to think, act, and react very much the way the local community does. In all sincerity, the people keep telling the person verbally and nonverbally, "You are now really and truly one of us!"

Reentry: Reverse Culture Shock. In recent years, much attention has been given to the problem of reverse culture shock, the problem of cultural adjustment felt by church personnel returning to their home country after spending a longer time outside their native cultural environment. Strange as it may seem, often persons who have most easily adapted to the new culture are the ones who find the greatest difficulty in readapting when they finally return.

The explanation for reverse culture shock is simple enough: cultures change and vary not only geographically but also in time. Reverse culture shock is similar to what is known as the "generation gap." One's native culture is no longer what it used to be, and after one has been away, the cues formerly automatically present have somehow vanished. The culture has changed, in fact drastically. Homes and home appliances seem to have become excessively complicated; the traffic has become frightening and extremely dangerous. Worse still, old values seem to have vanished: family life is not what it used to be; pornography has entered the home through the media; interest in religion seems to have largely disappeared. Everyone seems to be impersonal and selfish, not like the people one learned to love and appreciate in the missions. Everyone dresses so differently; in fact, it is hard to say how one should dress.

Shopping centers have become enormous, complicated, overwhelming, and even threatening. Group conversations and the daily newspaper generally turn out to be very boring: one asks, What do I know, or care about, the latest Academy Awards, local sports, or national politics? Even the language used is at times unintelligible. In a word, the very same uneasiness and frustrations felt when the individual arrived at his or her overseas assignment now affects the returnee in his or her own native land. The symptoms of culture shock spoken of earlier in regard to the foreign culture once again appear, but in reverse, that is, in one's own native land. An adjustment must be made once again to a strange culture—or, to be more exact, to a culture that has *become* strange. Myron Loss has written a book on cultural adjustment called *Culture Shock* (1983) specifically designed for cross-cultural ministry. His book might provide additional useful reading on the subject. (*See* also Nida 1966:53–71; Hiebert 1985:78–80, 244–46, 282; Austin 1986.)

College Students from Third World Countries. Overseas students, especially from the Third World, often become disenchanted with the Western host country and Christianity, not because the foreign students have been mistreated in any way but because the overseas students fell prey to the type of culture shock we have just described. Campus ministries should, therefore, give particular attention to overseas students and their problem of cultural adjustment. Campus ministers and fellow students should go out of their way to be of assistance to such students and not wait to be called upon. Inaction cannot be justified merely by the claim that the foreign students are "clannish" and "unwilling" to mix.[9]

Perfectionism and Fear in Cultural Adjustment. It is vital for successful cross-cultural mission that one not be frightened into inactivity by the threatening cultural environment and by the difficulties one encounters in adjusting to it. Rather, the strangeness should be welcomed and looked upon as a challenge and adventure as exciting as the exploration of unknown lands at the time of Columbus or as the exploration of space today. Culture jolts should be taken as much as possible in stride. By studying the ways and values of the local community, of humankind around the world, and of one's own society, one should anticipate jolts. One may cushion or neutralize the blows by preparing oneself for advance internal acceptance. One should also not try immediately to master the whole culture, nor wait until one feels fully at home in the new way of life. Learning a strange culture is like learning a strange language. One does not remain silent until the entire dictionary has been learned and until every phonological and grammatical pattern has been thoroughly mastered. Rather, from the very first day, one should use as much of the language as one happens to know. One does not worry and fret about what one still does *not* know or what one handles only clumsily. *Perfectionism and fear of a strange culture are, in fact, as detrimental to apostolic work as the disregard for cultural differences itself.* Fear that leads to inactivity is like the fear of making a mistake in speaking a foreign language. If the fear keeps one from speaking, the foreign language will never be learned. A foreign language is learned by using as much of it as is known, and by dealing with the unknown as best as one can. Similarly, to master a strange culture one must not only study it but *use* it—use what one knows, learn from one's mistakes, and rely on the sympathetic understanding of the community, who more likely than not will be flattered by the efforts made. The magic word is *use*—use what you know and keep on learning! (Cf. Rosengrant 1960:51–65.)

Much more could be said about one's own enculturation as a source of cross-cultural problems, about culture shock, about proper adjustment to a strange culture, and about re-entry problems. Instead, we recommend a number of sources for supplementary readings. There is, first of all, the very useful and readable small book by John Rosengrant and others entitled *Adjustment to Overseas: How to Be a Welcome Resident and Worthy Christian Abroad* (1960). Then there is a rather long list of highly practical works available, including Judith N. Martin's edited "Theories and Methods in Cross-Cultural Orientation" (1986); Philip R. Harris and Robert T. Moran's *Managing Cultural Differences* (1986); Elise C. Smith and Louise Fiber Luce, eds., *Toward Internationalism: Readings in Cross-Cultural Communication* (1986); Lennie Copeland and Lewis Griggs' *Going International: How to Make Friends and Deal Effectively in the Global Marketplace* (1985); and Clyde N. Austin's *Cross-Cultural Reentry: A Book of Readings* (1986). Then there are the books dealing specifically with the American culture as a source of problems for Americans and for those coming to America, including Edward C. Stewart's *American Cultural Patterns: A Cross-Cultural Perspective* (1981); Alison R. Lanier's *Living in the U.S.A.* (1981); Zongren Liu's *Two Years in the Melting Pot* (1984); Conrad Kottak's *Researching American Culture: A Guide for Student Anthropologists* (1982); and Joseph G. Jorgensen and Marcello Truzzi's *Anthropology and American Life* (1974). Finally, there is Ted Ward's *Living Overseas: A Book of Preparations* (1984), in which emphasis is placed on attitude, rather than on culturological theory, and on down-to-earth practical tips on living overseas.

Chapter Six

INTEGRATION OF CULTURE

> *I find as impossible to know the parts without knowing the whole, as to know the whole without specifically knowing the parts.*
>
> Blaise Pascal

> *You can never do merely one thing.*
>
> Garrett Harden

Cultures are not a heap of odds and ends; they are *systems*. In this chapter we shall see how societies organize their cultures on three levels. (1) At the surface level are the individual building-blocks of culture, the meaningless *forms*, the "shapes," the signs or symbols minus their meaning, the *who, what, when, where, how,* and *what kind.* (2) The society relates such forms to one another through *function* to create a system of meanings (the immediate *why*s). (3) On the third and deepest level is the *basic psychology* (the underlying *why*s of a society; the starting points of thinking, reacting, and motivating; the fundamental premises, attitudes, and drives—the "mentality"). This inner logic on the third level of culture tends to give the middle-level relationships a general consistency and the whole culture a distinct character.

Although there is a difference of opinion among anthropologists today regarding the manner and degree of integration, the fact that cultural parts are integrated into some form of more or less integrated whole is now beyond question. Cultures are not like the countless random items on sale at an auto-parts shop. They are, rather, like assembled automobiles speeding along the highway. They are, in fact, more than *lifeless* machines; they are more like *living organisms*. Parts act and react—that is to say, they interact and "communicate" with one another. Cultures tend to be consistent and harmonious, and, generally speaking, one aspect of the design for living does not contradict or make impossible other aspects but tends to be supportive of the whole. Thus, integration—the manner in which the different aspects of culture affect each

223

other and how they work together—has become an important question in cultural anthropology.

Among the earliest theories were those of Emile Durkheim (1858–1917), who recognized the similarity between culture as a system and a biological organism. He insisted that, sooner or later, that which did not contribute to the survival of the whole would be eliminated. Durkheim explained this organic unity by assuming that members of a society had not only their own individual minds but shared also in a "group mind." "Collective representations" of that mind were expressed in religious and ritual activities.

Malinowski and Radcliffe-Brown independently took up Durkheim's organic analogy and were responsible for the development of a whole school of thought based on the notion of function. However, anthropologists were not satisfied: if the purpose of cultural integration was to maintain the whole and to assure its survival, why should cultures change? The earliest answers came from anthropologists like Boas and Robert Redfield (1897–1958) and their followers. Boas looked for the answer to the fact of change in acculturation; Redfield sought the answer in theories of modernization (evolution from folk to urban societies). Marxists, of course, had their standard ready answers involving class conflict (*supra*, 5.1.6.1.2).

Then came the psychological theories regarding cultural integration. Behind them was the wide influence of Freud. Ruth Benedict, Ralph Linton, Abram Kardiner, and others tried to explain integration by attributing "basic personality" types to particular cultures and by identifying "national characters." Morris E. Opler preferred to view cultures as having logical sets of underlying "themes" balanced off by "counterthemes." Lévi-Strauss argued that thought and behavior processes took place in basic opposing pairs (for example, death versus life, male versus female) that constituted the best answer for the harmony and mutual support of cultural components. Cognitive anthropology, a more recent perspective, presents culture as a system of meanings resembling the structure of language. Semiotic anthropology likewise speaks of meaningful interrelationships of component parts, utilizing the metaphor of a complex communications network, a system consisting of countless interwebbed pathways along which messengers carry their messages, with some circuits being tied more closely to one another but all pathways (relationships) together forming a single, unique communication system.

Whatever theory we may prefer, we arrive at more or less the same conclusion: a society tries to program itself, with varied amount of success, through its culture to survive and succeed in life by organizing its knowledge and creating for itself a more or less integrated system of symbolic communication designed to cope with the society's physical, social, and ideational environment. Despite the gear-grinding and dysfunctional aspects of a culture, anthropologists generally regard lifeways not as random conglomerations of unrelated parts but as more or less unified dynamic structures. Cultures are super-systems composed of interconnected systems; these, in turn, are themselves made up of subsystems. Underlying such interrelationships of parts at the second level of culture and giving them a certain—albeit far from perfect—harmony and consistency is the somewhat intangible but real "soul" of a people, at the third or "deep" level.

6.1 SURFACE LEVEL OF CULTURE: CULTURAL FORMS

Our focus in this chapter is not on the surface level of culture, not on the *forms* or "shapes" of behavior, the *who, what, where, when, how,* and *what kind.* These are the symbols *minus* their meanings.

We need not say more about *forms* than we have already said (*supra,* 3.1.3.3.1). The forms are the building blocks or "phonetics" of culture; they are "sounds" that can be described apart from the structure and meaning of the "language." Forms provide only a superficial (etic) understanding of the culture. By contrast, our concern in anthropology, and in this chapter, is with an *emic* or an "insider's" understanding of symbols—the form as it is structured in the particular symbolic system and as such carries meaning.

6.2 INTERMEDIATE LEVEL OF CULTURE: STRUCTURAL INTEGRATION

6.2.1 THE NOTION OF STRUCTURAL INTEGRATION

6.2.1.1 Minimal Contrasting and Meaningful Units

Some decades ago (*supra,* 5.1.6.3), functionalists were particularly fond of such terms as *institutions, complexes, traits,* and *items.* Such expressions seemed, at the time, best to describe the structure of cultures. Anthropologists defined *trait* as a culture's minimal constituent having an independent existence (e.g., an arrow). A trait was composed of *items* (e.g., the shaft or polish of an arrow shaft) that lacked an existence apart from the thought, action, or artefact of which they were parts. Traits were then united into complexes. A *complex* was considered to be a group of interrelated traits having a common immediate function. For instance, the bow, arrow, quiver, and way of shooting could be combined to produce an act. Complexes were then united to achieve a common response to a basic human need and formed *institutions,* small behavioral systems in themselves that together constituted the culture.

Whatever one wishes to call the different units and subunits just mentioned, structured units do exist and, in one way or another, enter into much of today's anthropological thought. Ecologists, while stressing the human environment, recognize the interplay between the physical, social, and ideational realms of culture (*supra,* 5.1.6.1.4). Configurationalists (*supra,* 5.1.6.4.1) exaggerated the organic unity on the third level. Cognitive anthropology (*supra,* 5.1.6.5.1) extended the structure of languages (Pike 1954–55) to include culture across the board. Symbolic anthropology (*supra,* 5.1.6.5.3) described the structure of culture in terms of modern communication theory.

The emphasis today is on describing cultures as the members of the society view and construe their world and as *they* deal with it in light of *their* understanding of reality (*supra*, 5.1.6.5). Often, complex terminologies based on the particular anthropological viewpoint are involved. Cognitive anthropology, which follows a linguistic model, is particularly interested in the study of how different cultures *form contrasting and meaningful basic units*. This school of thought uses such terms as *segregates*, *contrast sets*, *domains*, and *componential analysis* (terms that we shall not try to explain here). What is important to remember is that each culture has its own contrasting and basic units or domains. There is much to the assumption of cognitive anthropology that as people speak, so they view their world (Frake 1962:74). Every culture divides its world in its special way.

A classic example is that of the Manobos of Mindanao, Philippines, who consider it a sin to treat even in the slightest way a nonhuman as one treats a human, for instance, to speak to one's dog. At most one might give the dog a one-word order such as "Go!" or "Sit!" but it would be wrong to speak to an animal in a full sentence or phrase, or even to say, "*You* go!" Nor is it permissible to use a pronoun in reference to a dog. In the Manobo mind, the units "human" and "nonhuman" are as distinct as "human" and "divine" are to the Western mind; to mix the two becomes a kind of "blasphemy."

Metzger and Williams (1966) discovered that the Tzeltal of Mexico included under "things of mother earth" three major categories, "humans," "animals," and "trees-and-plants." The last category included as subcategory "trees-or-wood," while "trees-and-wood" included such sub-subcategories as "wood for house construction," "charcoal," "wood for bridge building," and "firewood." "Firewood," in turn, was differentiated into two still further subunits, whether one was speaking of "good" or "bad" firewood, with the latter two categories divided into such culturally vital and mutually exclusive units as "hard" or "soft" firewood, firewood that "dries quickly" or "dries slowly," and firewood that "creates a hot fire" vs. one that "creates a less-hot fire."

Our understanding of color differs considerably from that of the Hanunóo, who do not distinguish colors the way Westerners do but as "wet and lush" and "dry" (Conklin 1955). We also distinguish between a circle and an ellipse, while the Kpelle people of Africa use the same term to describe both the circle and the ellipse (Cole, Gay, Glick 1974:159–196). We speak of "four corners of the earth" and of "north, south, east, and west," orientating ourselves according to the rising and setting of the sun. The people along the Wahgi River in New Guinea orientate themselves by the direction of the current of the Wahgi River and whether one means the right or the left side of the river looking downstream.

Some technologically simpler societies view all motor vehicles as forming only one category of objects, while our feeling tells us that passenger cars, station wagons, buses, and trucks are "essentially" different and that, in fact, further distinctions and subdistinctions ought to be made. For example, our concept of "truck" calls for such further differentiations as "van," "pick-up truck," "dump truck," and "semi." Each of these would be broken into still further subcategories based for instance on differences in load capacity, number of wheels, usage (e.g., cement mixer, fire truck, tank truck, cattle truck), manufacturer, and model. "Passenger cars" have an even more complex hierarchical taxonomy. Our culture tells us not only the hierarchical arrangement of motor vehicles but "essential" contrasting features involved as well. If a Pacific Islander were to do ethnographical fieldwork in the United States, he would have to do a "componential analysis" to arrive at basic American categories of motor vehicles and the criteria we use to differentiate them.

Hiebert (1983:399) provides us with excellent examples of contrasting units taken from the classic dances of north India: "there are seven positions of the eyes, seven of the eyebrows, six of the nose, six of the cheeks, six of the lower lip, and sixty-seven of the hand, each of which conveys its own specific feeling and meaning"—"essential" distinctions as far as the Indians are concerned but hardly essential to other societies who dance no less than do the Indians.

Such component units of culture (symbols) are integrated at two distinct levels, at the functional or middle level and at the psychological or deeper level. We shall now proceed to examine these levels.

6.2.1.2 The Meaning of Meaning

Any relationship of a constituent part on the immediate level is called *function*. Bring all the functions of a cultural component together and you have its full meaning or value. Such interconnections may be causal or purposeful, or purely logical or ideational. Functions are frequently latent. Just as native speakers of a language may indeed feel and use the grammar of their language but at the same time may not be aware of the grammatical rules— much less be able to articulate them—so a society may not be aware of many interrelationships while unquestionably feeling and applying them. In fact, as we have seen when speaking of enculturation, such feelings and applications become a kind of second nature to the members of the society concerned. Some relationships may be irrational, nonrational, illogical, and even dysfunctional; they are often purely conventional, with no rhyme or reason behind them. Why, for instance, should racing always take place counterclockwise? Culture, as we have emphasized earlier (*supra*, 5.2.1.3), only *tends* to be harmonious, consistent, and successful.

In simpler and more tangible terms, we are saying that functions refer to the fact that constituent cultural domains (e.g., clothing, division of labor, kinship classifications, wedding customs) have a particular set of *meanings* and *values*. Viewed as a symbol, they have a very particular referent or set of referents. They are viewed by the society in question as being something more than what they are in themselves.[1] The more immediate meanings and values of symbols constitute the second level of culture. Thanks to functional interrelationships, cultural forms may be regarded by the society in question, for example: as "the purpose for" or the "cause of" or "result of" something; as "responsible for" or "the occasion for" something; as having "certain repercussions"; as "used for" something; as being "a prerequisite for" something else; as "playing a role in" something; as "filling the need for" something; as "performing the task of" or being "conducive to," as "promoting," "fostering," or "supporting" something; as "triggering" or "ensuring" something; as being "connected" or "associated" with something; as "reflecting," "suggesting," "expressing," or "presupposing" something; as "the reason" for something; as "giving value to" or "receiving value from" something else; as "evoking certain emotional responses" or as being "the motive" for something. And we might continue listing still other ways in which symbols might "mean" or "function" in a particular culture. (Cf. Firth 1955:237-258.)

We have used clothing as an example of such integrating interrelationships when first speaking about structure (*supra*, 3.1.3.3.2). We pointed out how clothing indicates the particular roles played, for instance, in religion, the military, police, and nursing. "The nurse's garb in its spotless whiteness gives encouragement to the patient. It enables the patients and hospital staff and administration to recognize the role of the wearer, facilitates interrelationships, promotes efficiency, very much as in the military. It projects an image of the professionalism of the institution, particularly its cleanliness, the traditional friendly image of a nurse, her dignity, self-control, patience, dedication, efficiency, peacefulness. It makes the wearer live up to the image of a nurse, e.g., nonpolitical, nonproselytising, nonflirting" (Argyris 1956, cited by Leininger 1970:79). Similar are the arguments for some kind of identifiable religious garb for Catholic priests and religious. Or again, the U.S. military opposed the wearing of the Jewish skullcap known as the *yarmulka* with the military uniform, not because the *yarmulka* expresses the otherwise beautiful thought of total submission to the God of Israel but because there would be endless repercussions affecting discipline and the intended functions of the military uniform.

Another apt example of meaning, value, and functional linkages concerns literacy. In technologically advanced societies, literacy means, for example, that I have gone through an elementary school and that I am not illiterate. Literacy *ensures* personal growth in culture and further education. It is a *prerequisite* for a good job, a political position, or to be a clergyman. Literacy is the *reason for* books, newspapers, road signs, advertisements, libraries. It is *associated* with school systems and Bible reading. It *fills the need* for communication as in letter writing and record keeping. The *repercussions* of illiteracy may very well be a low salary, unemployment, and poverty. In a word, literacy as a cultural form or symbol carries meaning and value well beyond what it is in itself, well beyond the *who, what, when, where, how*, and *what kind*.

In the West, the heart symbolizes love, as Valentine cards and carvings on tree trunks and park benches testify. The English word *heart*, in fact, has numerous connotations (functional linkages) involving emotions, intellectual and moral traits, affections such as compassion, generosity, courage, and especially one's innermost personality, reflecting the symbolical linkages between the heart and the rest of American culture. It is interesting to note how in much the same manner the written Japanese language builds on the radical symbol for "heart" (*shin* and *kokoro*) to construct the characters for terms like "courageous," "secure," "fidelity," "kindness," "consolation," "solicitude," "admiration," "devotion," "sorry," "feelings," "pure of heart," "thoughtful," "loyal," "fearless," "at peace," "mentality," "personality," and "innermost self." In many other cultures, the heart is simply a part of the human anatomy, while the liver or the bowels are used to express deep human values.

In New Guinea, where the valued and sacred animal is the pig, it would hardly be appropriate to offer to the ancestors or deceased relatives anything less valued (i.e., less functionally interrelated) than a pig, such as a goat or a sheep. Owing to the lack of appropriate linkages, the beautiful symbol of the Paschal Lamb loses much of its meaning in New Guinea without a certain amount of paraphrasing and commentary. "Sacrificial Pig," as abhorrent as the expression may sound to us, would be far less jarring to the New Guinea highlander than to call Christ a lesser-valued sacrificial animal, such as would be a lamb. Similarly, shepherds in India are often village drunkards; in Nigeria they are regarded as imbeciles. The touching parable of the Good Shepherd would accordingly not have the impact that it might have in a culture where shepherds are respected and where sheep are highly valued. Since the dove was regarded as a "dirty" animal in China and since it failed to express the true Christian connotation of the Third Person of the Blessed Trinity, some missionaries at one time thought that the bird-figure should be replaced by something more personal, and certainly something more inspiring than an ordinary pigeon or "meaningless" fiery tongues. This was not exactly a new idea, since in the fifteenth and eighteenth centuries promoters of the devotion to the Holy Spirit had faced the same problem in Europe and had consequently proposed, as was later done in China, that the Holy Spirit be depicted as a young man (cf. Rivinius 1982). The attempt not only met with strong resistance on the part of Church authorities but also by other Christian missionaries who argued that such representations would merely serve to make the Chinese conclude that Christians were polytheists and that their "gods" were homosexual.

Figure 9
A "Photographic" vs. a "Functional" Description of Culture

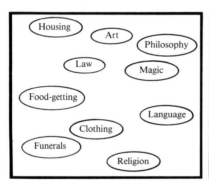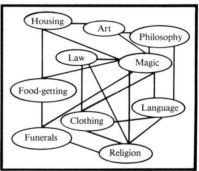

"photographic"   "functional"

An expatriate church worker who studies native dwellings, agricultural techniques, weddings, and funeral customs "photographically" (*supra*, Figure 9) would certainly not be following an anthropological approach to the understanding of the local community. Houses, gardens, weddings, and funerals (and all first-level components) must be viewed in all their details as they are interlocked by the local community in the particular community's organic-like design for living. Such relationships tend to fan out rather logically and consistently throughout the whole culture, as we shall see more clearly in the sections to follow dealing with configuration and the dynamics of culture.

To understand and appreciate polygamy, an extremely common problem in so-called mission countries, the local church will have to view the practice not as one would view a photo of a polygamous trio but rather as plural marriages are related to prestige, tribal friendships, interfamily obligations, wealth, family work, comfort, animal husbandry, feuding, tribal loyalty, ancestor worship, and with whatever else the society in question associates polygamy. Lust may very well be the last and least important of functions.

To understand the meaning of *radio* and *television*, one would have to analyze the countless relationships that the radio and television have in the mind of the particular society. In the United States, the radio and television are associated with news reporting; telephoning; sending telegrams; family recreation; teenage parties; family picnics; educational programs; sports casting; political campaigns and conventions; evangelization and religious services; as background music at work, in restaurants, airports, and bus stations, and sometimes while waiting for an answer on the telephone when the lines are busy; with law enforcement; spying and counterspying; terrorism; detonation of dynamite in construction work; with contact between bank robbers and their getaway car; navigation; traffic control on city streets, at airports and in harbors; with the task of dispatching taxis, buses, and service and delivery vehicles; with countless purposes of walkie-talkies; trucking; with hobbies; forest fire control; rocketry and outer space exploration; advertising goods, services, and events; weather forecasting; the paging of doctors in hospitals and other personnel in similar situations; civil defense; narcotics and border patrol; countless military applications; emergency communication (e.g., fire departments and paramedics); security police; and such practical devices as car telephones, car radios, and alarm clocks—and we might go on and on. The radio and television as items of the *American* culture cannot be understood by a non-American if viewed purely "photographically," that is, simply by themselves as electronic devices; they must be viewed as they are structured to function in the American way of life, as they are tied in with other parts of the American design for living. The words *radio* and *television* in the United States do not have the same meaning as *radio* and *television* have in Siberia.

One of the finest examples of functional linkages is the role that the pig plays in the culture of New Guinea highlanders (Rappaport

1968; Vayda, Leeds, Smith 1961; Luzbetak 1954, 1956). To a Westerner, a pig is hardly more than a potential ham and a source of income for certain individuals. In advanced Western countries, pigs have a very limited use and value: they are associated with farms, slaughter houses, butcher shops, and certain truck drivers—but that is more or less where the story ends. To the New Guinea highlanders, pigs mean much more because pigs are intermeshed in all aspects of life. The pig plays such a central role in the total lifeway that without the pig life itself would be well-nigh impossible. The pig provides the greatest security to the individual, family, and social group economically, socially, and religiously. The pig must be sacrificed to placate pork-hungry ancestors and more recently deceased relatives, on whom the well-being of the living members depends; no child is born into the world and no tribal battle is won without pig-sacrifices; often the only cure for a serious illness is a pig-sacrifice. Pigs are exchanged for the precious pearl shell (the equivalent of money and prestige); in fact, the pearl shell constitutes one of the main forms of wealth. Although eaten on a feast-or-famine basis, pork is the chief source of animal protein in the native diet. When a pig is sacrificed, the living eat most of the pork, leaving only special morsels and the souls of the pigs for the ancestors and for whomever the animal was slaughtered. Pork seals a great variety of social activities: it seals the friendship between individuals and tribes (a friend is called "a fellow-porkeater"), and a pork feast climaxes birth ceremonies, engagements, weddings, food-exchanges between friendly tribes and confirms truces with traditional enemies. Since there is no way of preserving meat, it is shared with family friends and groups with the understanding that those sharing in the feast will have to reciprocate when the occasion arises. Without pigs, a boy could not be initiated into the tribe and become a full-fledged member of the tribe. The number and quality of pigs owned give the owner prestige and power, while a pigless adult would be the equivalent of a penniless tramp. A woman's value is determined largely by her skill in caring for pigs, and it is this skill, perhaps more than anything else, that forms the major part of the training received from the future mother-in-law during the trial marriage and is the subject of the main test that a future bride must pass. It is, in fact, impossible for a young man to marry unless his family and friends provide the required number of pigs as a form of bridewealth. The prestige that a tribe enjoys among other groups depends largely on the number of pigs it has, and many a tribal battle is basically a quarrel over pigs. Since the pig is intertwined with all aspects of native life, the economic, social, and ideational, "pig" in New Guinea does not mean the same as "pig" in most of the world.

Both its meaning and value are determined by the way the concept functions in the New Guinea design for living—very much the way the meaning and value attached to the concept of "literacy," "radio," and "television" in the United States depend on their unique functional relationships within the American plan for coping with life, a plan we call "culture."

In India, the sacred cow reflects the Hindu belief *ahimsa*, which upholds the sanctity of life. Since the cow is a sacred animal, it may not be slaughtered. The fact that its sacred character allows it to roam around freely, eating much of the food that starving humans might otherwise eat, does not mean that the sacred cow is regarded by the Hindu mind as economically dysfunctional. On the contrary, allowed to roam about and to forage means that the farmer, who needs cattle for ploughing, does not have to stall-feed them for use the following season. Moreover, the sacred cow provides milk and a cheap source of fuel (dry dung). Thus the animal serves a double function, religious and economic.

Africa is said to "dance" its religion. In fact, in Africa, dancing is one of the main forms of communication, and therefore, like communication, dancing is tied in with many aspects of culture in a way unfamiliar to the Western mind. As William Smalley points out: "Africans dance to gain power and to appease the dead, to celebrate, and to mourn. They seem to us to dance for any excuse whatsoever, and if there is no excuse they dance for the fun of it. . . . The dance is a major instrument by which Africans transmit values, ideals, emotions, and even history. But more than once the African has been rebuffed by the missionary when he has attempted to worship God in dance—or for that matter, even to tell the Good News in this most natural form of communication" (Mayers 1974:193–194).

Art, whether it be music, sculpture, painting, dance, drama, poetry, or whatever, is essentially a form of human communication that pervades the total fabric of culture. Each art form includes styles, which are subsystems of communication in themselves, like dialects of a common language. A dance may be a form of worship, a form of recreation, a social event, an occasion for courtship, a means of educating a social group in its religion or tribal history and therefore to encourage group solidarity, a statement of a prophet, an important aspect of a shaman's cure. Carvings on an arrow may be magical to ensure success in hunting or in war. The fine needlework and glittering spangles on a Mexican sombrero may be purely decorative or a way of attracting visiting North

Americans to buy a product more readily. The artistic character of a ritual can instill tribal pride and identity, can be a form of education, a statement of a people's deepest aspirations and philosophy of life. A song may be a kindergarten ditty, a lullaby, a protest song at a rock concert, a church song, an elitist aria of an opera; each type of song thus serves a different function for a different class of people.

It is important to remember that the *full* meaning of a cultural component can never really be translated and still retain all the connotations that are derived from functional linkages. This fact, however, does not mean that concepts cannot be communicated cross-culturally with sufficient precision and impact, especially with the aid of supplemental information, further clarification, correction, and refinement. If adequate cross-cultural communication were impossible, we would have to say that education would be impossible. In fact, the very purpose of missiological anthropology (whether we call the purpose contextualization, inculturation, the incarnation of the Gospel, the evangelization of culture, local theology, or any other term) implies that verbal and nonverbal communication is indeed cross-culturally possible.

6.2.2 METHOD OF INQUIRY

Functions, it must be emphasized, may be *latent* or *manifest* to the members of a society. It could therefore be quite confusing to informants if we were to ask them such questions as "*Why* do you bury your dead in a crouching position?" or "*Why* does the hero in this myth marry a woman and a bird?" The fact is that many functions are latent and their meanings must be "dug out." The ideational models of culture (*supra*, 5.1.6.5) have methods for arriving at meaning, value, structure, and integration that are more sophisticated than those we shall propose, but for nonexpert "anthropologists," as are most church workers for whom this book is written, the following hints seem to be more in accord with our criteria for a good *missiological* model (*supra*, 5.1.4). In any case, to discover the network of linkages will call for an awareness of one's own ethnocentrism, keen observation, painstaking investigation, clever questioning and discussion, considerable reflection, and careful analysis.

1) *Never assume that cultural forms that happen to be similar to your own necessarily have similar or identical meanings and values* (*supra*, 5.2.1.6.4). Meanings, values, and all other relationships must be established, not assumed. Depending on the culture, the same symbol may have different referents.

Catherine Johns' *Sex or Symbol: Erotic Images of Greece and Rome* (1983) exemplifies how classical art, considered more often than not as being "erotic," may turn out to be not erotic at all but expressive of primitive fertility notions and sincere religious concerns when viewed within its social and religious context.

The Stars and Bars is the official ensign of the University of Mississippi. There were no problems or misunderstandings at the university until a few years ago when black cheer leaders at a sports event refused to wave the flag. To them, understandably, the Confederate flag symbolized slavery and all that the Ku Klux Klan stood for, hardly anything to cheer about.

Skirts worn by women are still regarded as immodest in China, where baggy pants seem more proper. On the other hand, Pope Nicholas I had to assure concerned missionaries sent to Bulgaria that women who insisted on wearing trousers were nonetheless worthy of Baptism. In some Muslim areas women are regarded as immodest unless they wear their veils and cover their faces. Meanings, we are saying, are always emic and therefore must not be assumed but established.

Dr. Fred Schwarz, a tea-loving lecturer from Australia, once tried a bit of his humor on his supposedly coffee-loving American audience. Coffee, he said, was made from castor oil beans soaked in shellac, the castor oil providing the taste and the shellac the color. Schwarz was totally dumbfounded when his American audience broke out in a loud applause. He had not realized that the audience was composed of a group of coffee-haters who regarded coffee drinking as something sinful (Schwarz 1960:137–138). The lesson to be drawn is that the same symbol can have a quite different meaning depending on the particular cultural or, as in this case, the subcultural linkages.

2) *Never lose sight of the fact that many meanings and values can be latent.* Culture is often not what people *say* but what they imply or even do not realize. Thus, people may say that a witchdoctor's incantations "cure" diseases, when actually the incantations instill confidence, provide needed security, and may have a psychosomatic effect on the patient, and therefore remain important elements in the society's plan for coping with life. Both latent and manifest relationships are a part of the people's design for living.

3) *Useful are POSITIVE observations of and inquiries into relationships.* For example, one might ask: What *purpose* does the local community attach to this cultural form? What do people say it can *cause*? What do they think it is the *result* of? What do the people believe the *repercussions* or *consequences* would be if the particular behavior were to be ignored?

More concretely, we might ask what, for instance, is an American high school? What does it really mean, that is to say, to *Americans*? Why do

Americans place so much value on this particular item? To be able to understand the true and full meaning of *high school* in the United States, one would have to analyze the functional implications of high school attendance *as this pattern is viewed by Americans*. Let us analyze some of the functional linkages involved.

1. To Americans, a high school education *means*:
   a. that the student has had more than eight grades of schooling;
   b. that he/she will most likely be eligible for college if four years of high school are successfully completed.
2. A high school education *ensures* one:
   a. a reasonably satisfactory and fulfilling employment, which, in turn, ensures him/her
      1) a middle-class home and neighborhood,
      2) a better education for a future family;
   b. a possibility for further growth in culture, education, and social advancement;
   c. an opportunity for a better understanding and appreciation of one's religious values.
3. A high school education *presupposes*:
   a. a high school system, which in turn presupposes
      1) teachers and administrators, which in turn presuppose
         a) teachers' training program,
         b) a teachers' union,
         c) continuing education for teachers;
      2) a school building;
      3) an educational program (especially a curriculum) and
   student and faculty discipline;
      4) school books and accessories;
      5) financial support for the above;
   b. students, who have completed grade school and meet other standards.
4. A high school education *performs the task*:
   a. of preparing youth for higher studies;
   b. of preparing them for marriage;
   c. of preparing them for skilled jobs;
   d. of forming their character;
   e. of training them in good citizenship.
5. A high school education *fills the need of*:
   a. keeping young people occupied and off the streets;
   b. keeping the unemployment rate down.
6. A high school education *is associated with*:
   a. extracurricular programs, which are in turn associated with

      1) sports, which in turn is associated with
        a) a gymnasium and other sports facilities,
        b) a sports director;
      2) drama, student newspaper;
      3) clubs and social activities;
    b. a parents-teachers association;
    c. a faculty lounge.
  7. High school education *is the reason for:*
    a. a library;
    b. bookstore;
    c. cafeteria;
    d. a fast-food restaurant and/or a malt shop or ice cream stand;
    e. traffic precautions, such as warning signs and a traffic patrol;
    f. a fleet of school buses.
  8. High school education *confers:*
    a. status (i.e., a new identity, inasmuch as the student is no longer a grade-school "kid");
    b. certain rights, such as the use of the high school facilities and the right to play on the school football team if qualified.
  9. High school education *is the result of:*
    a. the sophisticated economic system of the United States;
    b. state laws and city government;
    c. social consciousness on the part of taxpayers.
 10. To fail to attend high school or to drop out of the program will have the following *repercussions:*
    a. a lowering of status from that of "student" to that of "drop-out" or "failure";
    b. a reduction of opportunities to find employment other than a low-paying job of an unskilled laborer at best;
    c. a restriction of one's association and marriage to the uneducated, welfare-dependent class; and
    d. a stop to further intellectual development.

4) *Sometimes an INDIRECT and NEGATIVE approach may prove more productive than one that is direct and positive.* Often it is easier to observe and to pose questions about concrete tensions, disorganization, and disaster than to inquire positively into the functions of actual customs.

Recidivism and excuses for not living up to Christian principles may indicate that needs formerly filled by traditional un-Christian ways are not being met by the convert's new religion. Voodooism persists in Brazil and the Caribbean to no small measure because the Christian communities do not seem to be as interested and as effective as voodooism in an important function of religion—the preservation and restoration of health. The drunkenness and the apparent wastefulness of some Latin American fiestas are associated with such often legitimate but latent functions as prestige, local politics, friendship, and rivalry. Excuses for participation in dances considered to be immoral are sometimes more than just excuses. Such dances may indeed be "the only way I can find a decent wife for myself." Domestic and tribal disputes can be excellent clues for discovering functional linkages. The complaints of a wife may suggest genuine roles of a husband that are not being fulfilled. Fears and worries of adults, whether founded or unfounded, can likewise cast important light on functions from the insider's point of view. Dissatisfaction with Christian ways may also sometimes reveal that certain traditional uses, values, meanings, repercussions, connotations, and other functions like prestige and family obligations are being overlooked or underappreciated.

5) *Although actual case studies may be far more productive than mere THEORETICAL discussions, the latter can also prove useful for arriving at functions emicly.* A classroom discussion or assignment on a purely imaginary situation may reveal countless structural relationships that might otherwise go unnoticed—for instance, a discussion or composition on the consequences of a defeat in a tribal battle or of a contagious disease that would wipe out all the pigs in a New Guinea highland community will bring out the function or meaning of warfare and pig raising.

6.2.3 SUMMARY AND MISSIOLOGICAL APPLICATION

Among the more missiologically relevant points of the present section are the facts (1) that cultures are *systems*; they not only consist of parts but also have a unique *arrangement* of parts; (2) that the constituent parts of culture (*forms* or the "shapes" of *symbols*) occur on what we might call "the first level" of culture, the *who*, *what*, *when*, *where*, *how*, and *what kind*; (3) that forms have relationships (*linkages*) with one another, the *immediate whys*, called *functions*; (4) that meanings are *any and all* such relationships that exist among component parts occurring on the second or intermediate level of culture; (5) that the relationships may be causal, purposeful, logical, or purely ideational; (6) that such relationships or linkages may be *manifest* to the members of the society in question or they may be *latent* (i.e., they are unperceived but usually felt by them); (7) that meanings and values of symbols must be "dug out," not assumed, especially if one is an outsider; that is, functions must be understood *emicly* (rather than *eticly*), as the members of the society understand their culture; (8) that the second level of culture is known as *structural* integration; (9) that the third-level "psychological integration" (i.e., the underlying premises, attitudes, and goals) is responsible for the structural integration, as shall be explained in the subsequent section (*infra*, 6.3).

6.2.3.1 The Concept of Structural Integration and Mission

Why be so concerned about integration? There are three reasons we might offer for regarding integration (that is, considering culture as a *system*) as one of the most important concepts in all of mission anthropology. (1) *Empathy*. No matter how strange a culture may seem, it will cease to be strange as soon as it is viewed in its wholeness. (2) *Values*. Every component of culture has a value attached to it, namely the sum-total of relationships or meanings that the particular form or symbol has in the given culture. Polygamy, for instance, has a value that is unique to the particular culture, owing to the way it is integrated in that culture. The value of polygamy is the sum-total of its relationships or meanings. According to *the principle of functional substitution*, polygamy will remain a missiological problem until the sum-total of linkages is emically understood and until adequate, if not superior, substitutes or adjustments are found for the various functions. (3) *Contextualization*. From the anthropological point of view, *contextualization* is almost synonymous with *integration*. What concept could be of more importance to mission than the concept of contextualization? Christianity must become a twenty-four-hours-a-day affair. For Christ to be born into a culture, it is necessary that he become a living part of it; in fact, as we shall see in the section on psychological integration (*infra*, 6.3), Christ and his Gospel must become the very heart and soul of the way of life, the very raison d'être of human existence. Any cultural constituent (e.g., a religious rite, a burial, an American high school) has a genuine and full meaning only with reference to the whole.

6.2.3.2 A Theology of Cultural Forms and Functions

6.2.3.2.1 Priority of Function over Form

As is clear from the Old Testament, God's primary concern has always been *meaning*, not form. "For it is love [meaning] that I desire, not sacrifice [form], and knowledge of God [meaning] rather than holocausts [form]" (Hos 6:6). In similar vein, the prophet Joel cries out: "Rend your hearts [meaningfully], not your garments [symbolically only]" (Jl 2:13). The Psalmist expresses the very same sentiments in Ps 51:18f: "For you are not pleased with sacrifices; should I offer a holocaust, you will not accept it [the outward form]. My sacrifice, O God, is a contrite spirit [the inner meaning]." Speaking of a new covenant and contrasting it with the old, the Lord says through Jeremiah: "I will place my law *within* them, and write it upon their *hearts*" (Jer 31:33), not only in form but in meaning. In choosing David and having him anointed, God assures Samuel that "not as man sees does God see, because man sees the appearance [the form] but the Lord looks into the heart [the meaning]" (1 Sam 16:7). There are, of course, many other references in the Old Testament that leave no doubt whatsoever that God searches the *heart* and is primarily interested in what we *mean* and *intend*. In the New Testament, Jesus takes up the idea of meaning and intent repeatedly and stresses its priority over form. He has no room for pharisaical formalism (e.g., Mt 23:13–39) and insists that "the Sabbath [a form] was made for man, not man for the Sabbath" (Mk 2:27), a principle he confirmed again and again by word and example (e.g., Mt 12:1–8). As St. John Chrysostom in a homily on St. Matthew put it, "God does not want golden vessels but golden hearts" (Hom 50:3–4:PG 508–509).

6.2.3.2.2 Priority of Local Over Nonlocal Forms

The new People of God have indeed become "like the stars of the sky and the sands of the seashore" (cf. Gn 15:5, 22:17)—as wide as the world and as culturally diversified as humankind itself, each nation and tribe with its own ways (the first level of culture), its own meanings and values (the second level), and its own "soul" (the third level). As we have emphasized, forms in themselves, divested of God's intended meaning, are of little value in the eyes of God. By the same token, it matters little to God, as a rule, in what cultural form we express that meaning, as long as *his* meaning is safeguarded. We can please God by using any society's verbal or nonverbal forms. God understands every spoken and unspoken language under the sun and is equally pleased to hear his creatures praise and thank him in the Russian, English, or Cherokee language or in terms of the corresponding "silent language." God, especially as revealed in the New Covenant, in fact delights in this human pluriformity, but no language, verbal or nonverbal, seems so pleasing to him as the native *cultural* language, the language that both the Creator and creature understand best of all.

In other words, as a missiological principle we can say that the precedence of local symbols over nonlocal is to be regarded as the general norm, not as an exception. Local symbols have precedence over foreign symbols if for no other reason than the fact that they can better express both meaning and whatever is in the human heart. These are God's primary concerns. Moreover, as human beings we have a *right* to relate to our Heavenly Father in terms of our own providentially determined symbols. This is a right that *all* local churches enjoy; it is not a concession on the part of Church authorities. Because *local* symbols best express the true longings of the human heart and reflect God's own preference, they provide the *normal* way to relate to God and neighbor. In the words of Pius XII,

> the right to existence, the right to the respect from others, the right to one's own good name, the right to one's own culture and national character . . . are exigencies of the law of nations dictated by nature itself. [Allocution, December 6, 1953]

6.2.3.2.3 The Relative Nature of the Right to One's Cultural Forms

There are, however, exceptions to our general rule. Situations exist in which nonlocal symbols have precedence over local. We offer four arguments for the relative nature of the right to one's own cultural forms (Luzbetak 1981:44-47):

1) *God's Own Example.* As much as God respects a society's symbolic system, he nevertheless as Father of All has the right to insist that certain forms be adopted by his whole family, by all humankind irrespective of culture. He has, for instance, chosen to speak to most peoples through a *foreign culture and a foreign history*, that of his Chosen People. Jesus insisted that all nations, regardless of culture, adopt a washing ceremony we call "Baptism" (Mt 28:19; Mk 16:16) and a ritual meal we call "Eucharist" (Mk 14:22-24; Jn 6:51-56; 1 Cor 11:17-34). God himself has thus imposed nonlocal symbols on local churches. The most basic symbols, with their many ramifications, are the Bible itself, the Sacraments, and a specific form of fellowship we call the "Church." The local church may not, for instance, substitute the Koran or the sacred writings of the other great religions for the Bible. It was to help overcome some of the foreign aspects in the presentation of the Good News that John the Evangelist, without abandoning his Jewish tradition, wrote his Gospel with the Greek mentality in mind (*supra*, 3.2.1.1). Nor can a local church substitute a tatoo for Baptism even if a tatoo might, theoretically speaking, be far more meaningful. Neither can the Eucharistic meal be replaced by another form, no matter how truly local and timely such a form may be and how beautiful and inspiring such a local replacement might appear. Nor is the local church free to alter for itself an essential aspect of what we call "Church" (cf. *supra,* chapter 4) simply because the aspect does not coincide with the local church's particular way of thinking. As the African theologian Mbiti (1973) stated, mission does not consist in culturizing Christianity but in Christianizing culture. Or as John Paul II in his encyclical of October 16, 1979, On Catechesis in Our Time, expressed it:

> the Gospel message cannot be purely and simply isolated from the culture in which it was first inserted (the Biblical world or, more concretely, the cultural milieu in which Jesus of Nazareth lived), nor, without serious loss, from the cultures in which it has already been expressed down the centuries; it does not spring spontaneously from any cultural soil; it has always been transmitted by means of an apostolic dialogue which inevitably becomes part of a certain dialogue of cultures.

> On the other hand, the power of the Gospel everywhere transforms and regenerates. When that power enters into a culture, it is no surprise that it rectifies many of its elements. There would be no catechesis if it were the Gospel that had to change when it came into contact with the cultures. [*Catechesi tradendae*, no.53]

In the words of the U.S. Bishops' pastoral statement on world mission *To the Ends of the Earth*,

> the church must never allow herself to be absorbed by any culture, since not all cultural expressions are in conformity with the gospel. The church

retains the indispensable duty of testing and evaluating cultural expressions in the light of her understanding of revealed truth. Cultures, like individual human beings and societies, need to be purified by the blood of Christ. [National Conference of Catholic Bishops 1986a:no.44]

The precedence of local forms over nonlocal is indeed a *relative* norm.

2) *The Universal Character of the Church.* Moreover, the local churches are more than local; together they form a communion of churches, which is something more than the sum-total of its parts; it is more than just a federation (*supra*, 4.4.3.3). As the one Body of Christ and the one People of God, local churches share common needs, values, and goals with the rest of the Church. These needs go well beyond any local community's culture, tradition, and sociopolitical considerations. Although, generally speaking, local symbols have precedence over nonlocal, and although the local church must be as fully of the time and place as possible, Christian communities must not overlook their *universal* needs, values, and goals that call for symbols transcending the local community. The local community will need, besides its own local tradition and local symbols to assure its local identity, not a few broader symbols to establish and maintain its universal identity.

As basic as the symbols "one Lord, one faith, one baptism" (Eph 4:5) and "one bread" and "one body" (1 Cor 10:17) unquestionably are, there are lesser but nonetheless important worldwide (and therefore nontraditional) symbols that should not be overlooked. They too enter into mission. We refer to such symbols as Christian holy days, including Christmas, Easter, Ascension, and such sacred seasons as Advent, Lent, and Pentecost; and such ancient Christian symbols as the cross and baptismal names. Although these were perhaps unknown to the first-century churches, and certainly are not necessary for salvation, such nonlocal symbols and universal traditions of older churches should not be rejected by the local church just because such symbols happen to be foreign and Western. They are *good* ideas and as such should be made available to the whole Body of Christ. Such symbols may, in fact, be sociologically, psychologically, and practically speaking indispensable for a true sense of catholicity. Christians who view the veneration of Saints, especially of the Virgin Mary, exclusively from the point of view of undeniable excesses, generally fail to appreciate how a theologically sound veneration of martyrs and other exemplars of Christian living, especially the Virgin Mary, can contribute to the Christian sense of oneness and universality.

There is no denying that after two thousand years of history the Church is burdened with many weaknesses and sin, and is laden with countless cultural trappings. However, we should not overlook the fact that these same two thousand years indicate the presence and action of the Holy Spirit and much holiness. The Church has also participated, and in fact has led, in the tremendous human advancement of this period, both in social matters and in knowledge, including in advancement in theology. This is a rich legacy indeed. Over and above a hermeneutic of the *written* word, the Church needs a hermeneutic of the common Christian heritage that should be made available to the whole Body of Christ. Much of such tradition may be nonessential, but nonessential does not mean unimportant.[2]

3) *The Prophetic or Countercultural Character of the Church.* However important local symbols may be, they are nevertheless not to be romanticized or held inviolable. The fact is that Christian communities are not seldom called upon to be prophets among peers and contemporaries, and are actually called on at times to be countercultural. The civil rights and peace movements often, if not generally, represent a true Christian prophetic spirit. Today the prophetic challenge is almost limitless. It works against materialism, hedonism, rationalism, drugs, and the sexual revolution. The most powerful form of prophecy will, of course, always be Christian witness.

4) *The Fact of Cultural Borrowing as Evidence.* A final consideration that might be offered to show that sometimes nonlocal forms may actually be preferable to local ones. It is the undeniable anthropological fact that foreign symbols can be at times more effective than local forms in conveying a desirable meaning. For example, Western-type weddings seem to bring out the Japanese meaning of marriage to many Japanese more than their own traditional marriage ceremonies. Or again, many loan words enter faster than ever into the languages spoken in the "global village" today; they seem to be more expressive than the native term. For example, in English we use many musical terms that are taken from Italian, such as *largo, moderato, pianissimo*, and *ritardando*; many terms are taken from French, as in international politics the terms *detente, rapprochement*, and *coup d'état*; many are derived from Latin and Greek, as are the names for diseases and physiological processes such as *pneumonia, cancer*, and *metabolism*; and finally, some are derived from Russian, as are vodka and borscht. We shall see in the following chapter that when dealing with factors encouraging culture change, what is true of foreign verbal symbols is true also of foreign nonverbal behavior: much culture change occurs through borrowing deemed beneficial to the borrower.

6.2.3.3 Functional Linkages and Mission Strategy

6.2.3.3.1 Diagnosis of Problems

Mission anthropologist Jacob Loewen (1967) observed how South American Indians criticized missionaries for "scratching where it didn't itch." Functions of a culture tell the local church, whether in a missionary situation or not, where the itch is located. A good diagnosis is always half the cure.

To help bring about a desired economic, social, or religious change, a local church must deal with its whole culture and with culture as a whole. All linkages must be of interest and concern to the Christian, even from the purely anthropological point of view. As Cardinal Suhard declared, "the mission of the Christian is not only an apostolate: it is the convergence of three simultaneous actions, religious, civic, and social" (1953:104); or as the introductory quotation to this chapter says, "You can never do merely one thing." Diagnosis of any problem must be made in light of the whole, not as if culture were a heap of unrelated items, but in light of what it *is*—an integrated whole, a system. The disintegration of family life, the spread of drug abuse, the growing disregard for the Scriptures (for the Decalogue in particular), the lack of respect for Church authority, or any other problem facing local churches today cannot be diagnosed except in light of the given interrelationship of parts of the culture in question. People abuse drugs not only for pleasure and "kicks," but also for the camaraderie, because of peer pressure, for the forbidden-fruit attraction, for the mystique and the prestige connected with drugs, and sometimes, as in the case of LSD, for religious purposes. As Frederica de Laguna pointed out twenty-five years ago in her presidential address to the American Anthropological Association, "If we have learned anything, it is that all parts of a culture must be understood together, that the context and interrelationships are more essential than the specific parts, no matter how well the latter are known."

> Cultures are like a ball of tangled strings, one strand representing the economic life, another social institutions, another aesthetics and religious patterns. At different points the various strings are tied in knots, at some points more tightly than others. In order to untie one knot of any particular string, one must study the *whole* tangle; and just as no two tangles are alike, no two cultures are exactly alike. One must study the *particular* tangled whole and see which string must be tackled first, which knot must be untied now and which later, which string must be pulled and which relaxed, and which, in order to achieve the desired end, must be completely severed. [Luzbetak 1961:171]

Missionary work closely resembles this situation: to a large extent it consists in untangling cultural knots.

6.2.3.3.2 Functional Linkages and Predictions

Casey Stengel, the famous baseball manager, was known for his practical wisdom, good management skills, and planning ability. When he was once asked how he thought his team would end the baseball season, he said, "I don't believe in prophecies, especially about the future." Foresight yes, prophecy no! Anthropology is not a crystal ball; it is, however, an important aid to foresight and planning. Such "predictions," despite the uncertainty and associated risks, make as good sense in practical mission work as they do in sports and business. A carefully worked-out plan, even if it is fallible, is preferable to a blind stab in the dark. Many dioceses and religious institutes have wisely set up special planning offices, and not a few mission areas have research and development centers. Anthropology is no infallible crystal ball, but insights such as that which points to the organic structure of culture (1) can be a most propitious warning to decision makers of a possible undesirable *chain reaction* that might be triggered by their decision, (2) can suggest the most promising *starting point* in a mission program, and (3) can provide clues to solutions to many a pressing problem. The time has long passed when one might imagine that it is possible to solve, for instance, economic problems by economic means alone. The UNESCO has thus wisely declared a "World Decade of *Cultural* Development," i.e., a *holistic,* rather than merely an *economic,* development. The expression *evangelization of cultures* similarly implies an *integral* approach.

A classical case of *an undesirable chain reaction* frequently cited in applied anthropological literature is that of the introduction of the steel axe among the Yir Yoront aborigines of southwest Australia (Sharp 1952). The missionaries and white settlers had, of course, hoped for quite different results than the disaster that ensued:

> The steel axe, vastly superior to the traditional stone implement, was to give the aborigines more time for aesthetic activities and improve the standard of living. Instead, the standard of living remained the same, while the steel axe, the new time-saving device, merely made the men lazy and served to make them neglect and forget the arts they once had mastered. The art of making stone axes had formerly given the menfolk prestige and had instilled in them a sense of self-reliance. The making of stone axes had fostered friendship through trade and brought the older men respect from the rest of the people. In fact, the stone axe was *the* symbol of masculinity.

> The missionaries and white settlers, not realizing the important relationships that existed between the axe and the rest of the culture, would distribute the much superior steel axe to women and children as wages, prizes, and rewards in complete ignorance of and disregard for the role of the traditional stone axe. The old men, the onetime most highly-respected segment of society, were regarded by the whites as "no-hopers" and were consequently ignored. Formerly, women might be permitted at most to borrow an axe from their husbands, that is, if they were "ideal wives" and as such "worthy" to borrow this prestigious tool. Now, however, women could not only use a borrowed axe but actually possessed axes of their own which were far superior to the ones owned by their husbands. Similarly, while children could now easily acquire a steel axe, their fathers, the "no-hopers," could not. It was as if in Europe or America the father of a family could own only a bicycle while his wife and children could own Cadillacs and Rolls Royces. As wife and children grew more and more independent, insubordination gradually set in, and the former family head grew more and

more insecure. A confusion of age, sex, and kinship roles, and other serious disorganization followed. The concept of ownership became confused, which in turn encouraged theft and other forms of dishonesty and injustice totally unknown before. As the stone axe, once a source of prestige and masculine pride, became a mark of shame, the old festivals in which trading of stone axe heads and the initiation of the youth took place lost their excitement and significance; in fact, life itself seemed to have lost its zest, and the idea of suicide, formerly unknown, became a not-too-rare way of ending a confused, insecure, disorganized, and totally unsatisfying life.

Formerly the Yir Yoront had a closely-knit totemistic philosophy of life that permeated their whole way of life. Changes in their culture were orderly, occurring in accord with their totemic understanding of the world and the teaching of the ancestors. Explanations in myths for the rapid changes that were taking place as a result of the introduction of the steel axe could no longer keep pace with what was being experienced. A serious psychological and moral void was thus created which threatened the very existence of the Yir Yoront culture and the Yir Yoront themselves.

Although hindsight is always easier than foresight, the fact remains that much of this tragic story could have been prevented if only the all-important role of the stone axe had been understood and appreciated by the missionaries and settlers and if the superior steel implement had only been more selectively distributed in accord with the functions of the traditional implement.

The introduction of the steel axe among the Yir Yoront of Australia initiated a chain reaction in an undesirable direction. Yet, by struggling through the complexities of functional interwebbing, one might hope to discover the most promising *starting point in a desired direction*. The two processes, that is, avoiding mistakes and choosing the best and safest starting points, are actually the same. A good example of how through function we might get to the key to a desired chain reaction is the one suggested earlier for the black inner-city problems in the United States. The real key to racial equality is the restoration of the black family (*supra*, 5.2.3.2.5).

Functional linkages are important considerations in all problem solving. The following examples illustrate the principle.

Problems of Health and Illness. Such otherwise self-evident health practices as the boiling of water to prevent cholera and other diseases are self-evident only in technically advanced cultural settings as found in Europe and North America. The simple rule of drinking only boiled water may lose its simplicity in a most unexpected way through economic, social, and religious ties. Water may be associated with magic, kinship obligations, ritual purification, etiquette, friendship, daily routine, status, and many other aspects of the people's belief and behavior. As theoretically easy as it may be to boil water, the task can become difficult when it is a breach of etiquette not to drink the water that is offered by the host. Or perhaps a spirit may be annoyed if someone were to boil the cool water that came from the well or stream of which the particular spirit happened to be lord and master. Routine may make the boiling of water as awkward a procedure as is brushing our teeth after every meal (the best means of avoiding cavities). The medical missionary must be able to see health factors not as they are found in the home country, in a test tube of a modern laboratory, or in a medical manual but as they occur in the given sociocultural context (cf. Leininger 1970:111–144).

Problems in Agricultural and Technological Assistance. Anyone involved in technological assistance programs will soon find out that simple problems in one cultural situation may turn into very complex problems in another. Keeping a "simple" hand pump in good working order at the village well or increasing a crop through drainage, shading, mulching, fertilizing, and erosion control may be simple, but only when taken out of cultural context.

Edward T. Hall (1959:102–103) describes an interesting incident involving the Taos Indians and a U.S. government agronomist:

For some reason or other, the Indians were never able to have a satisfactory corn harvest. It did not take long for the expert to come up with a diagnosis and what he felt was the answer to the age-old problem: the Indians were planting their corn too late in the season. What could be simpler than to do the ploughing and sowing earlier, in early spring instead of early summer as they had customarily been doing?

The sad fact, however, was that the agronomist had little appreciation for anything but agronomy. Why bother, he thought, about such "irrelevant" matters as the religious beliefs and practices of the Indians? After all, was he not sent to Taos to *teach*, not to learn, to teach the people sound *agricultural* practices, not to meddle in other aspects of their lives?

Little did the expert care what the Taos Indians believed about Mother Earth and about such details as to when she was or was not pregnant. In any case, the agronomist was not there to study Indian "superstitions"—why, for instance, the Indians never drove their wagons to town in early spring, why their horses never wore horseshoes during this period, and why the Indians themselves very scrupulously avoided wearing shoes with hard soles during this time. If the expert had noticed such practices, he too would have realized that Mother Earth was pregnant in spring so that one could not be careful enough when walking over her. Needless to say, the agronomist and his ideas about the early ploughing were rejected outright. After all, was the agronomist not suggesting the "unthinkable" and the "most insane" idea imaginable? Who would want to dig into Mother Earth with a deep, sharp plough just when she was pregnant?

Problems Associated with Counseling and Other Pastoral Work. It is diffi-cult indeed to give any worthwhile advice to someone except in full cultural context, with all the functional linkages involved in view. Moral and other pastoral problems can never really be understood, much less solved, in isola-tion. Sermons and religious instructions will fall far short of their goal unless they are presented in terms of the total cultural context.

As we have seen, advice regarding polygamy makes little sense to the person seeking counsel unless the many possible intercon-nections between polygamy and the rest of the way of life are taken into consideration. In Malabar, child marriages can hardly be understood and appreciated by the outsider unless such mar-riages are viewed as a way to ensure the highly-valued premarital chastity of the pair. Besides, child marriages bind the two families and clans together even long before the couple begins to live as man and wife, an important value in the Malabar culture.

As a general rule, valid native monogamous marriages are recog-nized by Christian churches as valid. Problems arise, however, when one asks, "When is such a native marriage a valid native marriage?" Often a trial marriage precedes the finalization of the marriage. The question is: When does such a trial marriage end and when does the real marriage begin? Does the bride give her consent to the marriage when she is openly protesting against it? To determine whether a traditional (non-Christian) marriage is valid in the first place, the inquirer would have to study the network of relationships that marriage has with the rest of the culture. Where, for example, would any unmistakably married woman be buried, at her husband's burial grounds or in the cemetery of her original family? The follow-up question would be: Where would *this* still doubtfully married individual be buried? What property rights does a definitely married woman enjoy? The follow-up question would similarly be: What property rights does this still doubtfully married woman enjoy? What are the consequences of adultery in which a certainly married individual is involved? If this doubtfully married woman were to commit adultery, what would the consequences be? Whose ancestors and dead relatives do the two worship respectively? We are not saying that any particular question sug-gested above will be sufficient to determine whether a natural marriage bond exists or not but rather that by studying functional linkages as we suggest we might arrive at some strong clues and discover sufficient evidence to determine the case one way or the other.

Similarly, in keeping baptismal and other parish records, the data recorded should make sense in the culture in question. Sometimes it is relatively simple to arrive at meaningful vital information, as when a man is named after his child (teknonymy), but sometimes, especially for an outsider, it is anything but an easy task to identify what vital information is vital. The burial place (determined the moment a male is born), for instance, may sometimes tell one more about the identity of the individual than even the place of birth.

6.3 THIRD LEVEL OF CULTURE: PSYCHOLOGICAL INTEGRATION

6.3.1 THE "MENTALITY" OF A PEOPLE

6.3.1.1 The Meaning of Mentality

We have seen in the preceding section how functional linkages (the various meanings, functions, and values of cultural components) are the more immediate *why*s of a culture. There are deeper, implicit, and ultimate *why*s too, the so-called mentality of a people, which we shall now consider.

Of all the human potentialities in adjusting to life, why does a society choose certain more or less coherent ways of thought, attitude, and action and reject others? What is it that *makes* cultures into systems? What, in the last analysis, is *responsible* for such integration? The answer is the *mentality* of a society.

Philosophers of history, social psychologists, sociologists, anthropologists, and other researchers have long suspected that the overall consistency of which we speak is mainly due to a kind of "soul" that gives the culture its oneness and uniqueness or personality. This unifying psychological tendency has been called by various names, albeit with slightly different connotations. Among the names are *genius*, *philosophy of life*, *mentality*, *psychology*, *inner logic*, and *Geist*. Sumner spoke of *ethos*, while Sapir preferred the terms *style* and *patterning*. Benedict spoke of *mainspring* and *patterns* of culture. However, the problem does not lie in naming the "soul" but in explaining it.

Various attempts have been made to explain the fact of such psychological integration of culture. These explanations have claimed that (1) the very nature of the particular cultural form/symbol links the form/symbol to other forms/symbols; (2) life itself (the human life-cycle in particular) presupposes logical and purposeful linkages between the various constituents of a culture; (3) the human mind tends to operate in terms of logical relationships and categories. The American concept of an American high school (*supra*, 6.2.2) is an example of the first explanation; certain traits are constituents of the broader context, and therefore they demand such linkages. For the second instance, the explanation is founded on the fact that culture deals with life issues as a continuum, life being a single cycle of events beginning with conception and continuing into afterlife. Life is a continuous flow of the same river into which smaller tributaries flow and become one—it consists of birth, sibling relations, parental responsibility, filial respect, kinship, courtship, marriage, illness, and death. These two explanations, and others like them, however, are not the full answer. It is the third explanation that has the most to offer—it deals with the nature of the human mind and its tendency toward consistency. The human mind is programmed to be consistent (although not with guaranteed success). What is held to be "true," "valuable," and "useful" in one aspect of life will more likely than not be held to be "true," "valuable," and "useful" in other aspects as well. We have offered a number of examples of inner logic, for instance, the pig in the culture of the New Guinea highlanders (*supra*, 6.2.1) and the stone axe in the culture of the Australian aborigines (*supra*, 6.2.3.3.2). In both instances, there is something responsible for the close interlocking of constituent parts, something intangible but real. Meant are the *underlying* notions, values, and motives; meant are the *starting points* of reasoning, reacting, and acting; and meant are the *basic* premises, emotionally charged attitudes, and goals. Such an underlying and basic set of starting points in reasoning, reacting, and acting tends to be consistent in itself and is so basic that it permeates the whole culture and gives it a certain oneness. This is what is commonly referred to as a people's "mentality," "psychology," or "soul." It is what we call the *third* or *deep level* of culture.

It should be noted that when anthropologists speak of the mentality or the personality of a people, they may mean: (1) the *theoretical* character most in accord with the society's *configuration*, that is to say, the *ideal* character most in harmony with the society's norms and values; or (2) the personality that is *actually* shared most commonly in the society, the so-called *modal*, *basic*, or *communal* character.

We suggest that a number of distinctions be made so as to avoid the confusion that sometimes results from the jargon we are up against in anthropological literature when we discuss cultural integration (cf. F. Keesing 1958:159): (1) When referring primarily to the resulting *oneness* of a society's design for living, we might best speak of *the configuration, the dominant tendency, the orientation, the total-culture pattern, the focus, the plot, the set, the climax* of culture, and so on. (2) When speaking of the *starting points in the thought process*, one might best speak of *underlying premises, assumptions, hypotheses, master ideas, themes*, or *inner logic*. (3) When the focus is on *basic attitudes*, one might speak of *underlying values and interests*. (4) When the focus is on the *fundamental motivating forces*, one might speak of *underlying drives, goals, purposes, sanctions*, or *ideals*. (5) And when we speak of all these considerations, we are speaking of the *mentality* of a people.

6.3.1.2 Approach to the Identification of a Society's Mentality

We would be going well beyond the purpose of the present book if we were to attempt a description of the complex methods employed in present-day group personality studies. This we leave to professional researchers of personality and culture and to studies more specialized than the present work. In summary, the approach in question is three-pronged: it is (1) statistical, (2) involving rigorous psychological testing, and (3) relying on a careful emic analysis, especially of aspects of culture (such as world view, folk religion, cultural themes and counterthemes, art, myth, and ritual) that reflect more than do other aspects the society's understanding of its world, its life, its most deeply felt needs, its most serious conflicts, its most perplexing questions, and its most fundamental goals and drives. It is the third prong that will prove most useful for mission application and that at the same time is most easily understood by nonstatisticians, nonpsychologists, and nonanthropologists.

Whatever our specific preferred theory and corresponding method may be, valuable clues to the psychology of a people will be found in such areas of culture as the following:

(1) the world view, ideology, religion, philosophy, myths, ritual, art, folk tales, and proverbs—terms that will be explained later;

(2) all emotionally charged beliefs, attitudes, and motivations that at the same time have contradictory or limiting restraints (*themes* and *counter themes*);

(3) emotionally charged beliefs, attitudes, and motivations that occur very frequently and in a great variety of contexts—M. J. Herskovits' *cultural focus* (1950:542-560), the "high-density circuits" of semiotic anthropology;

(4) the image that the society has of itself;

(5) the violent resistance that the community has toward certain innovations;

(6) the violent resistance to legislation imposed on the community especially from the outside;

(7) the instructional emphases especially during initiation of the youth and at other points in the life-cycle (rites de passage);

(8) the constant admonition to small children and the curriculum in native educational programs;

(9) quarrels and disagreements among members of the same family or clan;

(10) more serious scoldings, reprimands, and penalties;

(11) the factors that seem to lead to the restoration of peace and security after a serious crisis;

(12) the nature of a preferred status and what must be done to acquire it;

(13) the motivations most frequently used by demagogues and native agitators;

(14) the reasons behind serious dissatisfaction and complaints;

(15) any violent hate or condemnation;

(16) the line of reasoning during tribal meetings or court sessions;

(17) the behavior that the more serious sanctions seek to control;

(18) the type of sanctions that are most feared;

(19) the more serious worries and the chief reasons for jubilation;

(20) the most severe ridicule, insults, curses, and threats;

(21) the most esteemed blessings and highest praise;

(22) the chief aspirations of families and individuals;

(23) the motives, true or false, highlighted in advertisements and commercials;

(24) occasions for war and legal conflicts;

(25) the motives for suicide and other "irrational" behavior, e.g., mutilation of one's own or another's body, or the willful destruction of one's property;

(26) the struggles, aspirations, beliefs, values, and goals of heroes and saints— why they are regarded as heroes or saints;

(27) the behavior of villains, witches, evil spirits—why they are feared and despised;

(28) the motives behind perjury and the reason for taking an oath or undergoing an ordeal. These are all examples of where one might look for clues to a society's psychology.

Such fundamental underlying premises, values, and drives are not only responsible for the *overall* consistency of a culture but are as a rule consistent among themselves and supportive of one another.

By constant inquiry and observation, careful analysis of field data, and an awareness of the danger of projecting one's own biases and values on the informant, we might, following any of the recognized emicly-oriented research approaches, draw up a tentative list of such starting points of reasoning, reacting, and acting. We might regard these as our beginning description of the so-called "mentality," "psychology," or "personality" of the people. Such a list should be constantly checked, discussed with informants and others, continually worked on, and appropriately revised. These tentative starting points in reasoning, reacting, and acting should then be carefully compared among themselves so as to identify ever broader and broader common denominators.

6.3.2 WORLD VIEW

We shall now look at some of the cultural domains that most clearly reveal a people's mentality. The domains include world view, religion, and mythology. The broadest of these concepts is the *world view*.

6.3.2.1 General Notion

A world view represents the deepest questions one might ask about the world and life, and about the corresponding orientation that one should take toward them. More concretely, the world view provides answers to such basic questions as: Who or what am I? Why am I in the world? What is reality? How do humans differ from nonhumans (animals, objects, the invisible beings)? Who belongs to the invisible world and what are the invisible forces in the world? What is the proper orientation to time and space? What about life after death? What in life or the world is desirable or undesirable, and to what degree?

The dozens of items that occur in most world views can be reduced to three or four categories, namely Supernature, Nature, Human Beings, and Time.

Various attempts have been made to classify world views. Robert Brow (1966) places world views in one of three groups: (1) those that regard existence as *meaningless*, e.g., atheistic world views; (2) those that regard existence as *meaningful*, namely theistic world views such as the Christian, Jewish, and Islamic; (3) the *irreligious* world views, such as those of humanists and communists. C. S. Lewis (1962) placed world views into somewhat similar groups: (1) the *materialistic* world views, which find the world meaningless, and which attribute its origin to pure accident; (2) the *religious* world views, which see a Mind behind the universe and regard Nature as reflecting Supernature; (3) the *partly materialistic and partly religious* world views, e.g., creative evolutionism.

6.3.2.2 The Threefold Nature of a World View

A world view, as we shall now explain and illustrate, is (1) cognitive, (2) emotional, and (3) motivational in nature.

6.3.2.2.1 The Cognitive Dimension of a World View

The world view tells the society what and how it is to think about life and the world. In fact, it shapes the cognitive process as such.

An assumption not questioned by Westerners is that the world is real, made up not only of human beings but also of other animals, plants, and lifeless reality. In vast areas of Asia, however, the world is looked upon as an illusion. In the West, not only what one can see, hear, smell, taste, or touch is real but what science tells us exists, like the countless invisible celestial bodies and the invisible atoms and components of atoms, the microscopic bacteria and viruses, and the mysterious electromagnetic waves. In New Guinea, ghosts are as real and as active as the living; in fact, they are constantly intervening and interfering, for better or for worse, in the lives of the survivors.

As Hiebert (1985:45) observes, Westerners view time as a unidirectional continuum which is broken into segments called years, days, minutes, and seconds and, we might add, even into light-years and nanoseconds. Others view time as a kind of pendulum going back and forth, not however as the pendulum of a clock in good running condition but a pendulum that moves back and forth at varied speeds and with pauses in between, i.e., sometimes time flies, sometimes it walks, and sometimes it stops. Still other societies view time as an endless circle, going round and round, repeating the cycle of seasons, of birth, life, death, and rebirth.

Looking at the cognitive process itself, one is struck by the emphasis placed by the Western mind on reasoning, rather than, say, on analogy, association, emotion, intuition, and mysticism to arrive at knowledge as does the Eastern mind. Actually, all minds use these various ways of thinking; however, depending on the world view, there is a fundamental difference in emphasis.

> To the Western mind, to know means above all else that one observes the sensible (i.e., the empirical), forms a hypothesis, and tests it; if it survives the test, it is upheld, otherwise it is rejected and another hypothesis is proposed. The Western mind proceeds from the particular to the general, emphasizing logical procedures. The Western mind, more than other minds, seeks concepts representing reality, categories, principles, and theories. More than other minds, it seeks statements, dogmas, and laws—in short, it seeks certitude and control.

> The Oriental mind, on the other hand, is fundamentally mythological, analogical rather than logical, relying heavily on feeling and intuition. The Hindu is basically a mystic: while the Western mind insists on "evidence," the Hindu arrives at truth intuitively, through a sense of identification with the whole universe, through a mystical union with a monistic god. While the Hindu is satisfied with something illusory and transitional rather than demanding proof and evidence, the Buddhist finds truth in analogues and associations—in beauty, simplicity, and peace.

6.3.2.2.2 The Emotional Dimension of a World View

A world view also tells the society how it is to feel about, evaluate, and react to the world and all reality. In other words certain values, interests and attitudes are so basic to the culture that they trigger deep emotional reactions throughout most, if not all, of culture.

> Face-saving, for instance, permeates all domains of the Japanese lifeway, even more so than do self-respect and the right to one's good name in the West.

> In the cultures of the Bible, there is a certain equality between the first-born son and the father. Although Christ admitted that as far as his human nature was concerned, the Father was greater than he (Jn 14:28), his Hebrew value system left no doubt behind that he and the Father were one and equal (Jn 10:30).

> Mafia behavior seems to be largely family loyalty, a deeply emotional value that permeates the whole Mafia way of life. Loyalty, for example, underlies Mafia discipline, family traditions, social relationships, and such Mafia values as bravery and revenge.

It is the emotional element in the Islamic world view that makes birth control a difficult commodity to sell. According to a report, a certain planned parenthood organization in an Islamic country had initiated a birth control program with heavy emphasis on "education." Large billboards with two contrasting pictures whose message was supposed to be "self-evident" were used. The one picture showed a large family, sad, undernourished, dressed in rags, with no less than ten children; the other picture was that of a small family of four, all well-fed, well-dressed, with only a boy and a girl, all smiling and happy, no doubt, because papa and mama practiced birth control. The impact on the Islamic viewers, however, was the very opposite of what had been desired: "Look at that poor, unfortunate family! They have only two children!"

Such basic emotionally charged attitudes shape a people's idea of art, literature, music, dancing, bodily decorations, dress, and architecture; they set the tone for ritual and ceremony; they identify the saint and the villain; and they spell out the flattering self-image that a society often has of itself, how it would like to be regarded by others, and how down deep in its innermost self it would like to be. Father Matthew Fox, O.P., speaking from a spiritual writer's point of view about his own culture, puts it well when he says as follows:

It is because we worship upness inside that we build skyscrapers outside. It is because we prefer aggression to gentleness inside that we invest so mightily in armaments and so punily in artists on the outside. [1979:268]

6.3.2.2.3 The Motivational Dimension of a World View

Motivational aspects of a world view are a society's basic priorities, purposes, concerns, ideals, desires, hopes, longings, goals, and drives corresponding to its understanding of the universe. This dimension shall be adequately illustrated in the following section on the U.S.A. world view.

6.3.2.3 The American World View

Some of the best illustrations of anthropological concepts are those taken from one's own culture. This is certainly true when speaking of world views. We are, of course, running the risk of stereotyping whenever we speak of a social personality of a fast-changing and heterogeneous population such as is found in the United States. Nor do we expect all readers to agree with all that will be suggested, especially because we are not providing sufficient statistical data or a description of the testing and analytical procedures involved. Our purpose is not to defend any particular thesis about American or Western ways of life but only to illustrate what *in concreto* a world view might look like.

Americans, as Jules Henry in his classic work *Culture Against Man* (1963:13–99) sees them, are individuals guided primarily by inner *drives*, such as ambition and expansion, with basic *premises* and *values* taking a back seat. In other words, not the cognitive or emotional but the motivational dimension of the American world view is of primary importance. We wish to emphasize, however, that although Americans may not be *primarily* cerebral or emotional, one will find in the American character these two dimensions as well.

Some recent and trustworthy comparative statistics are now available, thanks to a monumental international values study conducted in the early 1980s by the Gallup Organization, Inc. and other highly reputable research organizations of Europe and America.[3] The study involved some 25,000 in-depth interviews and an interview schedule of no less than 381 distinct items, covering such countries as Belgium, Canada, Denmark, France, Great Britain, Holland, Ireland, Italy, Japan, Northern Ireland, Spain, the United States, and West Germany.

Despite the image others may have of the American way of life as being essentially secularistic and amoral; despite the clearly secularistic interpretation of the Constitution of the United States by the Supreme Court since 1940; despite the drop in church attendance in some Christian groups; and despite the high divorce rate, the sexual revolution, and the ideological upheavals and confusion in recent decades, the Gallup Values Study confirmed what most Americans have always held of themselves—that they were a religious and highly moral people. The study showed that *religion and morality were in fact a very essential part of the core of assumptions, values, and drives that form the American mentality*. In fact, the survey showed that Americans were generally in the first or second place among the nations studied as far as spiritual values were concerned. Inquiries were made into such questions as belief in God, attitudes toward the Ten Commandments, life after death, and the attitude toward organized religion and family life. We offer only a few highlights of the survey.[4] The statistics given here are typical of the other items in the Gallup Values Study, which clearly show that the "melting pot," or more properly the "stew pot" we call "America," is basically religious and moral in its beliefs and values.

—A total of 95 percent of the U.S.A. sample expressed their *belief in God*, sharing the highest score with Ireland (also 95 percent). France had the highest percentage of professed atheists (29 percent).
—Italy had the highest percentage (83 percent) of those *who considered themselves religious*. Americans came in second with 81 percent.
—It was Catholic Ireland that had the highest percentage (76 percent) of those who believed in *life after death*, with Americans coming in second (71 percent).

—Northern Ireland responded with the highest percentage of people who believe that *clear norms for right and wrong* existed (34 percent). The United States was second, with 31 percent.

—In regard to belief in the First Commandment, that there is only *one God to whom worship is due*, the Irish Republic was the first (80 percent) among countries surveyed and the United States second (79 percent).

—In regard to belief in the Second Commandment, that one should have *respect for the Name of God*, the highest percentage was given by the United States (68 percent), with Canada second (52 percent).

—That the *Sabbath* should be kept holy as prescribed by the Third Commandment was held by 68 percent of those interviewed in Ireland, with the United States (57 percent) ranking second.

—Despite the sexual revolution, 87 percent of the Americans and 76 percent of the Canadians (the two highest) said *adultery* is wrong. Similar results were found for the Ninth and Tenth Commandments (United States 89 percent, Canada 79 percent; and United States 88 percent, Canada 82 percent, respectively). In a related question inquiring whether *moral rules should guide sexual behavior*, the highest percentage agreeing were the Americans (51 percent), with Canadians in the second place (45 percent). The lowest percentage of interviewees agreeing were the Dutch (28 percent).

—Some 88 percent of the Americans interviewed said they believed in the *existence of the soul*; Canadians provided the second highest number, with 80 percent. Only 33 percent of those interviewed in Denmark recognized the existence of the human soul, the lowest percentage of the countries studied.

—Americans again had the highest percentage (84 percent) of those believing in *heaven*, with Canadians second (69 percent). The highest belief in *hell* (67 percent) was among American respondents; the lowest was again Denmark, with only 8 percent.

—Belief in the reality of *sin* was similar: Americans produced the highest with 88 percent, Canadians second with 72 percent. The lowest Denmark and France, both with 51 percent.

—*Confidence in organized religion* was the highest for Americans (43 percent very high, 32 percent quite a lot, with only 20 percent saying "not very much" and 4 percent "not at all"). The Irish Republic alone was higher, with 52 percent regarding organized religion very meaningful.

What follows are further examples of the American world view not included in the Gallup Values Study.

1) *Basic Premises*. One of the most basic beliefs of Americans is the assumption that *human rights are innate, inalienable, and, in fact, supreme*. Respect for the individual is sacred. An individual has, for instance, the right to follow his or her conscience, to embrace any or no religion; humans as humans enjoy freedom of speech, assembly, and association; they are entitled to a fair trial (they are innocent until proven guilty). All humans are born equal, regardless of race, creed, ethnic group, or gender. Such human rights are God-given, i.e., they are rights that are not granted to the citizen by the state but come with one's humanity and which even the state must recognize. (Cf. Verba, Owen 1985; Berger 1986:72–114.)

2) *Underlying Values*. Americans are often criticized by friend and foe alike for allowing their fear of the Soviets to dominate their day-to-day and political lives. The fact, however, is that Americans are not afraid of the Soviet political or military might, as is supposed, as much as all that Soviet Marxism symbolizes. Soviet Marxism is in the American symbolic system a negation of values most appreciated by Americans: the freedom of religion, the freedom of conscience, the freedom of speech, the freedom of assembly, the freedom to travel and emigrate, the right to choose one's political leaders rather than merely be expected to rubberstamp decisions of a single party, and certain other basic American values. The American feels convinced that it is impossible to reconcile the Marxist ideology with the personal and other rights that are basic to Americans. "Rather dead than Red!" is in the last analysis not so much a political slogan as it is a seriously meant statement and summary of some of the most important American values. Americans, in other words, seem to love life's meaning more than life itself.

The American spirit of independence is reflected in such less than earth-shaking practices as car ownership, which gives the owner of the car the power to determine the travel schedule, speed, and route. Car ownership is a very special symbol to teenagers—a sign that as owners of a car they have passed from childhood to the independence of more responsible members of society. An important symbol of American independence is home ownership; in fact, 68 percent of American families own their own homes, the dream of every newly-married couple. The spirit of independence is also reflected in the popularity (but not necessarily wisdom) of credit cards. The growing reluctance to lifetime commitments, including a marriage "until death do us part" and the demand of some Catholics for an Ordination that would bind the priest only for a limited time, are but other indications of the high value placed (or misplaced) on personal independence. The frequent change of employment and careers in America is, among other things, an exercise of one's independence. The hippy lifestyle of the 1960s, which rejected the then-current American mores by dressing unconventionally, living communally, and advocating nonviolence and drugs, may have had other reasons for its sudden rise and rapid spread, but it certainly found very fertile ground in American cities where personal independence flourished and where counterthemes that otherwise limited independence were cast to the wind. The strong opposition to the military draft in peacetime is not so much an opposition to military draft as such as it is an expression of opposition to an encroachment on personal independence by the government.

Figure 10
American vs. Soviet Semantics

Time Magazine	*Pravda*
Western powers	imperialistic circles
imprisonment, arrest, banishment	re-education, rehabilitation, protective custody
invasion, intervention, subversion	invitation, brotherly assistance
religious oppression	religious freedom
dissident	subverter, enemy of the people
terrorist	freedom fighter
freedom fighter	terrorist
human rights	internal affairs

There are, of course, other values that might be regarded as starting points in the psychological process, for instance, honesty and truthfulness, and certain family values.

3) *Underlying Goals and Drives.* As pointed out, Jules Henry maintains that Americans are not moved so strongly by an inner logic or set of emotionally charged attitudes as they are by a set of drives. Americans are a *driven* people.

—Americans are driven *to achieve*, driven to ever higher goals, especially to a higher standard of living. Children are taught quite early in life such maxims as these: effort pays off; if you fail, try, try again; never say "die"; an ounce of pluck is worth a ton of luck. Or as William Ward put it, "What you can imagine, you can do; what you can dream, you can be." Achievement and success are powerful motivating forces. In a word, Americans are success-oriented.

—*Expansiveness*, especially in some American subgroups, is the fiercest of all drives. Americans are worshippers of progress. Not to advance is to lose ground. Americans set their sights high. Research and development are regarded as absolutely necessary in the business world. Professors must publish or perish. In a word, Americans must not only achieve but excel. If the American owns a business, the business must expand; if the individual is a member of the corporate hierarchy, he or she cannot remain satisfied for long with his or her present rank. An ordinary worker in a factory may express the drive of expansiveness if not through promotion then symbolically through the purchase of a new appliance, car, or home.

—Americans fear obsolescence. They are driven by *newness*, a theme expressed, for instance, in their countless programs of continuing education and training, and in their emphasis on research and development. Cars and home appliances are being unnecessarily replaced for questionably better *new* models. Perhaps no words are used more frequently in television commercials and on cartons and labels of products than *new*, *improved*, and *extra*, that is, something over and above the old. New Crest toothpaste is better than the old, and new Tide is a better detergent than the old because they are *new*. The same might be said of "New Theology": it is necessarily "better" because it is "new."

—Americans are driven *to compete.* Theirs is a highly competitive way of life, whether it be in sports, at schools (evident in spelling bees, science fairs, tuition grants), at places of employment, in politics, or in the marketplace or business world. The production and sales of trophies has become a major industry. Keeping up with the Joneses is a kind of national pastime, whether it be a matter of buying a new car, moving to a "better" neighborhood, acquiring additional farm land, or selecting for a son or daughter a college or an orthodontist to equip the boy or girl with the prestige symbol known as "braces." The element of competition is always there.

—Whether or not we agree with the thesis expressed in Christopher Lasch's *The Culture of Narcissism: American Life in an Age of Diminishing Expectations* (1979:xv), the American way of life does betray *a strong narcissistic tendency* euphemistically called "pursuit of happiness." The question, What do *I* get out of this? is a most natural starting-point for Americans in the psychological process. If the *I* should benefit from a piece of legislation, the *I* becomes highly motivated; otherwise, especially if a sacrifice is involved, there is a strong resistance to the idea. "Why should *I* be interested in a complete tax overhaul or in a five-cents increase in the gasoline tax? Why should *I* be concerned about a crop or dairy subsidy? I'm not a farmer." That individualism is a strong American value has been borne out by such major works as Robert N. Bellah et al., *Habits of the Heart: Individualism and Commitment in American Life* (1985).

—Closely related to the *now* and *me* of narcissism is *hedonism*. Pleasure-seeking, although not the full explanation, is certainly an important factor in the current sexual revolution and in the increase in drug addiction. Hedonism expresses itself even in not a few suicides. "I've tried everything. Why live if there is no fun in living?"

—*Economic* motivation underlies much of what Americans do— or better, it explains *why* they do it. The choices of education and career are determined largely on the basis of pecuniary benefits. Sports have ceased to be sports and have become business enterprises. One is respected largely by how much one owns or earns. Holidays like Christmas, Thanksgiving, and Mother's Day have become thoroughly commercialized. Americans are being bombarded with advertisements in the newspapers, on the radio and television, and in the constant flow of "junk mail." There are no social evils that the "almighty dollar" could not cure. Those medicines are being developed by the pharmaceutical industry which are most profitable, not those most needed; the latter must be taken care of through philanthropic research and government grants. Not justice but the open market (whatever is good for the economy) decides prices, salaries, interest rates, employment, locations of factories, and international trade. Economic benefits frequently determine the college courses pursued. While recognizing the imperfections of their style of capitalism, Americans firmly believe that theirs is nevertheless the most successful economic mechanism ever devised for advancing economic standards for a large number of people.

—That *science and technology* constitute a basic theme in American life is obvious, and little more need be said. Billions of dollars are spent by the government, foundations, and industry on scientific and technological research and development. The central role that science and technology play in the American educational system, in all aspects of employment (in offices, factories, and farms; in transportation, communication, production, management, and delivery), and in the most ordinary things of daily life, leaves no doubt about the position science and technology occupy in the American value system. Science and technology are an extremely important drive.

—As Bloom (1987) points out, a large segment of the U.S. university population worships *tolerance* to such an extent that tolerance ends up an absolute or in nihilistic relativism. Pluriformity seems to lead to tolerance, extreme tolerance to outright nihilism, which becomes the very goal of education.

In a more complex society there are, of course, important differences also at the subcultural level.

The Jewish and the Vietnamese communities in the United States are both known for their unsurpassed drive to excel whether it be at school, at work, or in a profession. Similarly, one is struck by the basic differences between Hispanic ethnics and the white American population. The Hispanic is, for instance, strongly person-oriented. Before "coming down to business," as does the so-called Anglo who believes that "time is money" (so let's not waste it), the Hispanic (who loves money no less than does his fellow-American) will insist on discussing strictly personal matters first, even if the two have met expressly to discuss business and not each other's wife and children. The white North American feels compelled "to get down to brass tacks" immediately (and therefore "not to waste one another's precious time"), while the Hispanic, who has a warm spot in his heart for the American dollar no less than does the Anglo, nevertheless feels that the human obligation of Hispanic courtesy must be taken care of first. The Hispanic *celebrates* time. A Hispanic theme insists that one should "keep pace with time and not rush it." Although countervalues keep reminding white Americans about "keeping their shirts on" and "holding their horses," they nevertheless often rush and regard the Hispanic attitude toward time as outright laziness and irresponsibility. To the Hispanic, however, to rush unnecessarily is to be impatient. While the Anglo is driven "not to leave off until tomorrow what can be done today," the Hispanic view of the world constantly reminds the Latin U.S. citizen that there will be a *mañana*, and therefore what you might be able to do tomorrow, you need not, or perhaps even shouldn't, do today. For the Hispanic, time walks, not flies: "time has been given to us by God so that we could be human." A final example of subcultural world-view differences is seen in the attitude of older Italian immigrants to the United States toward human laws: they are only "ideals," not "musts." As Benito Musso-lini, after having learned the hard way, used to say, "You can govern Italians, all right, but its not worth the effort."

Although North American ethnic groups share many assumptions, attitudes, and motivations with the American general population, they do have, as we have just seen, their important differences based on *their* particular world views.

6.3.3 RELIGION, IDEOLOGY, PHILOSOPHY

Religion, ideology, and philosophy are concepts closely related to world view, as we shall now explain.

6.3.3.1 Religion

There is no single definition of religion universally accepted by anthropolo-gists. We might offer an *essential* or *substantive* working definition, after Tillich and Eliade, by saying that *religion is a society's code for seeking and responding to the sacred and eternal*. Most anthropologists, however, prefer to describe religion "the easy way"—*functionally*—by indicating how religion fills human needs, what it *does* rather than what it *is*. Thus, (1) religion is said to provide socially acceptable answers to mysteries that the human mind longs to solve but that are beyond human experience. These questions concern the origin and destiny of humankind and the reasons for suffering, death, and evil. The Mystery of the Cross, which is the Christian explanation of suffering, is "a stumbling block to Jews, and an absurdity to Gentiles"; but to believers, suffering proclaims "the power of God and the wisdom of God, for God's folly is wiser than men, and his weakness more powerful than men" (1 Cor 1:23ff).

Suffering is the ultimate test of one's faith. Whereas atheists and skeptics argue that suffering merely proves either the Christian God's lack of love for human-kind or his powerlessness, "those who are called, Jews and Greeks alike" (1 Cor 1:24), find in the mystery of suffering God's infinite power, wisdom, and love, and an occasion (as it was for Jesus on the Cross) to make a supreme profession of faith and trust in him who is Creator—an opportunity to make an ultimate act of love for him who is Father. As Rahner stated,

> in our present concrete state, the acceptance of the suffering without an answer other than the incomprehensibility of God and his freedom is the concrete form in which we accept God himself and allow him to be God. If there is not directly or indirectly their absolute acceptance of the incomprehensibility of suffering, all that can really happen is the affir-mation of our own idea of God and not the affirmation of God himself. [*Theological Investigations*, XIX, 207].

(2) Religion legitimizes the social (and sometimes the moral) order of the particular society. We say "sometimes the moral" because, while Christianity regards God as ultimate norm of right and wrong and teaches that "None of those who cry out, 'Lord, Lord' will enter the Kingdom of God but only the one who does the will of my Father in heaven" (Mt 7:21), some religions do not consider morality as an aspect of religion. On the other hand, a religion like Hinduism, which believes in the law of Karma and observes the caste system, and therefore penetrates the whole lifestyle, or a religion like Islam, which covers not only spiritual and liturgical aspects of life but the social, economic, political, and personal as well (including dress, nomenclature, and sanitary habits), is highly moral in character. (3) Religion provides psychological sup-port to the society in times of frustration, failure, disaster, perplexity, crisis, and despair by instilling hope and courage and providing a sense of security in the believer. Religion intensifies solidarity and the sense of identity especially in times of crisis when solidarity and identity are most needed. Because religion is superempirical, it enables humans to transcend themselves.

Christianity *does* all this, and more; and so do other religions. *Religion* can, in summary, be functionally defined as *a system of beliefs and practices by means of which a group of people, in a culturally approved relationship with supernatural beings or powers, struggles with ultimate problems of human life* (cf. Yinger 1957:9). The difference between Christianity and other religions lies not so much in functions as in unique contents—Christianity in its unique *Christian* content.

Before concluding our brief description of religion, we would like to make a few final observations. (1) The main difference between *religion* and *world view* is that whereas religion always deals with the sacred and eternal, world view sometimes does not (note, for example, the Marxist outright rejection of the sacred and eternal). (2) It should also be noted that to categorize religions according to content is a very frustrating task owing to the combinations and mixtures involved. Thus, "animistic" religions (those that believe that objects of the natural world, such as trees, rocks, rivers, and mountains, are inhabited by spirits) may contain aspects of "totemic" religions (religions that claim a mystical relationship between a clan or subclan and an animal, plant, or natural phenomenon), whereas what we might call "ancestor worship" may contain elements of both animism and totemism. (3) Also of importance is the fact that religions consist of three essential components: beliefs, worship, and social relationships. It is the last (the social dimension of religion) that one is most frequently inclined to overlook. Private behavior may have aspects of religion, but religion as such, as Yinger emphasized,

> is a social phenomenon; it is shared; it takes on many of its most significant aspects only in the interaction of the group. Both the feelings from which it springs and the "solutions" it offers are social, they arise from the fact that man is a group-living animal. The "ultimate questions" which we have identified as the center of the religious quest are ultimate primarily because of their impact on human association. Even death is not fundamentally an individual crisis, but a group crisis, threatening to tear the fabric of family and community. [1957:12]

(4) Finally, most closely reflecting religion are myth and ritual (Firth 1967:284–292), terms we shall explain fully below (*infra*, 6.3.3.3). But first we must explain how ideology and philosophy differ from religion.

6.3.3.2 Ideology and Philosophy

The term *ideology* is sometimes used interchangeably with *world view*. As Honigmann understood the term,

> Ideology . . . includes socially standardized beliefs about the universe and man's place in it; conceptions about the sources of illness and other sorts of danger, attitudes of belonging, allegiance, and identification; sentiments about persons, objects, places, and times; and, finally, values concerning what to do and what not to do. [1959:589-590]

Sometimes the term *ideology* refers "to a cultural belief system, particularly one that entails systematic distortion or masking of the true nature of social, political, and economic relations" (R. Keesing 1976:558). We can thus speak, for instance, of a "Nazi ideology." (Cf. Geertz 1973:193-233). Sometimes, too, in a somewhat less pejorative or even non-judgmental way, *sets of closely related ideas, beliefs, and attitudes of a practical political, economic or social nature* (such as capitalism, socialism, Marxism, Confucianism, hedonism, positivism, materialism, scientism, and feminism) are referred to as *ideologies* or *philosophies*.

6.3.3.3 Myth and Ritual

The study of myth and ritual is as difficult as it is important. We shall, however, have to limit ourselves to a simple overview: we shall describe the meaning of myth, its significance for understanding the mind of a people, its structure, its function and dynamics, and its theoretical and practical missiological significance.

Perhaps the simplest and clearest introductory presentation of the subject of myth and mission will be found in the two issues of *Practical Anthropology* (1969, no. 4, 5) dedicated entirely to the topic. No less basic and readable are Roger Schmidt's sections on myth and ritual in his *Exploring Religion* (1980:126–140, 149–172). Most of what follows will be found in expanded and more fully illustrated form in these two superb introductory resources. For an anthropological overview of literature on myth, we recommend John Saliba, "Myth and Religious Man in Contemporary Anthropology" (1973). For an overview of Mircea Eliade's understanding of myth[5] we refer the reader to Eliade's very informative article, "Myth," in the *Encyclopedia Britannica* (1968:1132–1140; cf. Cunningham, 1973). To acquaint oneself more fully with the various approaches to mythology, it will, of course, be necessary to study more difficult and sometimes less readable works such as those of anthropologists Edward Evans-Pritchard, Mary Douglas, Victor Turner, Raymond Firth, Clifford Geertz, and Lévi-Strauss, of psychologists like Carl Jung, and of philosophers like Paul Ricoeur—and, of course, one should not overlook such classics on mythology as those by Joseph Campbell, Emile Durkheim, Bronislaw Malinowski, and A. R. Radcliffe-Brown.

6.3.3.3.1 Why Mythology?

Why should mission anthropologists be concerned about mythology? Before we even begin to suggest an answer, we must emphasize that the term *myth* as used here is quite different from what is generally understood by *myth* in popular usage. It does not mean something that is devoid of truth. It is not a synonym for error or fallacy. In the technical sense in which we use the term, *myth* means a story accepted as true by the people who narrate it. Thus the Incarnation and the Resurrection can be called mythical because, among other reasons, the Christian believer believes the story of the Incarnation and the Resurrection.

In many ways, a myth in the technical sense is like a parable, play, novel, or poem; even when not historical, scientific, or within the realm of human experience, it can nevertheless be a veritable treasurehouse of truth. Roger Schmidt (1980:126), in his excellent presentation of myth as a sacred narrative form, introduces the topic with a very beautiful and powerful statement from Milo C. Connick's *The Message and Meaning of the Bible*. The response answers our question, Why mythology?

> In terms of naked fact the poet's lines are false, but in terms of insight they are so profoundly true that they shout inspiration. So it is with

myths. A myth is not a fairy tale at odds with reality; it is designed to communicate truth. [Connick 1968:85]

Jesus' beautiful parable of the Prodigal Son lacks historical content but overflows with truth like a fountain of refreshing water that can never be exhausted. When we wish to transcend the superficiality of facts and data, we must resort to analogy and metaphor—to figurative language, such as is myth. Myth reveals the mind and heart of a people the way a poet reveals his inner feelings in poetry. What greater reason would anyone engaged in mission want for the study of culture than to be able better to understand and appreciate the heart and soul of the people being evangelized? At this juncture, we need not say more: concrete mission-related reasons for the study of myth and ritual will be taken up below (*infra*, 6.3.5.2.3).

6.3.3.3.2 What Is a Myth?

Originally *myth* (Gr. *mŷthos*) meant the same as "word," "message," "news," or "story." As the term is understood today by students of religion, and as understood in anthropology, a myth is a story of primeval or cosmic times, that is to say, times preceding the present order; it speaks of deities and other sacred beings; and it treats of ultimate questions—of a people's view of reality, of the meaning of life, of the origins of the universe and human-kind, of ancestors, of ancestral heroes and models, of the unknowable future. The Bible, inasmuch as it has certain characteristics of myth, can be said to be "mythical," whether we speak of the creation of the world, of Adam and Eve in the Garden of Eden, of the origin of languages at the Tower of Babel, of the Exodus, or of the epiphany of the Son of God and his final triumph. Humans deal mythically with the supernatural, their destiny, and the ultimate questions. A myth speaks of the unknowable (the unworldly) in terms of the world; and that is how God reveals himself to creatures—mythically. In referring to the Christian faith as "mythical" we do not mean that Revelation is derived from myth; we mean, for example, that Jesus is a "mythical figure" in the sense of John 14:9, "Whoever has seen me [in my humanity] has seen the Father." As Christians, we know God and all that he has revealed only mythically, that is, "indistinctly, as in a mirror" (1 Cor 13:12).

Christianity respects the mythologies of all peoples, as we respect all reli-gions. But even though we look upon non-Christian myth positively, we are not saying that Revelation and the Christian faith do not reject such non-Christian mythological contents as deal with the existence of gods, how the world came to be, and what the nature of human destiny is. Non-Christian mythology deserves respect because mythology is a society's best understanding and appreciation of the sacred (cf. Fries 1975:1011–1016).

Another characteristic of myth is that the story is viewed not as the creative work of some individual but rather as an account that has been *received* through revelation, a vision, or a dream. The myth is believed to be in some way derived from supernatural powers. As a result, myths enjoy extraordinary authority and respect.

Myths differ from such narrative forms as folktales, legends, sagas, and parables, all of which can be vehicles of truth and can reveal much about a people's mentality and spirit despite their fictitious content. *Folktales*, in contrast to myths, deal with the present rather than with the cosmic order of things; folktales are also focused on personal, rather than group behavior. *Sagas* are basically historical accounts, but are at the same time intertwined with legends. Exodus is regarded by many scholars today as a saga seen in the light of faith. *Parables*, unlike myths, are not fantastic stories but rather are stories about ordinary life familiar to everyone, with an underlying truth as their basic message.

Most closely related to the concept of myth is *ritual*.

> If myth is the "why" of religious life, then *ritual* is the "how" by which those concepts are put into practice. [Friedl 1981:255]

Ritual can be defined as sacred stylized behavior. There are, of course, secular rituals, such as showing reverence for the American flag, singing the *Star Spangled Banner*, and standing respectfully with hand placed on one's heart and reciting the Pledge of Allegiance. Our interest, however, is focused on *sacred* rites. The importance of such ritual for the understanding of a people's mentality derives from a number of facts. First of all, just as sacred rites powerfully reinforce beliefs (myths), so do beliefs reinforce rituals; thus, ritual and myth share their power and significance. Secondly, rituals are often dramatizations of myth. In a ritual, myths are not only narrated as a part of the ritual but are also performed through prescribed, repetitive social acts. In myth, the holy is *spoken* of; in ritual, one gets in *contact* with the holy. In a ritual, one not only *hears* or *reads* the story but participates in the communication process with *all senses*; in a word, one *lives* the myth: by employing sounds of drums, bells, bull roarers, flutes, melody; by touching, as one does with a handshake or embrace at the Kiss of Peace at Mass; by tasting, as in ritual feasting or Communion; by seeing symbolic objects and gestures such as dancing, sprinkling with water or blood, and slaughtering sacrificial animals; and by smelling incense and the burning of sacrificial animals. Further importance of ritual is derived from the association of sacred rites with the most central aspects of life. Thus, ritual is intimately associated with sustenance (e.g., the agricultural and hunting seasons), with the life cycle itself (consisting of the most important steps in life—birth, initiation, marriage, death), and with deities, ancestors, and supernatural powers on whom the individual's and community's well-being depends. In a word, myth and ritual are twin terms, the one adding its strength to that of the other. The old-time anthropological dispute about whether myth reflects ritual or whether ritual reflects myth has become a fruitless debate; both are extremely important human phenomena.

The most significant theoretical work done in recent years in the area of ritual is perhaps that of symbolist Victor Turner, represented especially in his *Dramas, Fields, and Metaphors* (1974) and *The Ritual Process: Structure and Anti-Structure* (1969). Although it is difficult to summarize his thinking in a few paragraphs, the substance of Turner's theory is encapsuled in what he calls *social drama*, the drama about how ritual, myth, and culture itself, evolve through a back-and-forth tension between two poles. It is not so much that a particular culture *functions*, as much as that it evolves.

Anthropologists, like Arnold van Gennep, and depth psychologists, like Carl Jung and Joseph Campbell, who have given much thought and study to ritual structures, are in general agreement with Turner. They view ritual as consisting of three stages, beginning with a rite of separation, then going into a rite of transition, and finally ending with an act of incorporation.

Turner uses a number of basic terms to express his understanding of myth, ritual, and culture dynamics, namely *social drama, root metaphor, structure* and *anti-structure, liminality,* and *communitas.*

(1) *Root metaphors* are basic value-laden analogies used to describe the world view. They pervade the whole culture and are expressed in social institutions, myths and, above all, in rituals that deeply influence the beliefs, emotions, and actions of a society. As an example we might suggest with Worgul (1979:9) that in a truly Christian culture, Christ's Resurrection is such a root metaphor (1 Cor 15:12-15). Christ's Resurrection is expressed, for instance, in the rite of Baptism, in the Eucharist, in funeral rites, in the Easter liturgy and season, in the crosses in cemeteries, and in such symbolic acts as Christian acceptance of death and martyrdom.

(2) Root metaphors of the normal culture (the *social structures* of the dominant cultural community) are in constant dialectic tension with *anti-structures.* Anti-structure should not be understood in a purely negative sense (Turner 1974:50-51) but rather as a kind of alternative way of expressing the society's core metaphors. The deviants involved regard their opposing ways (anti-structures) as an improvement on the ways of the cultural community. (Thus, as Jesus, a "deviant" himself, put it, he did not come to abolish the law and the prophets but to fulfill them [Mt 5:11].) Jesus' teaching was not so much *anti* as *counter*. Both poles, the Jewish structure and Christ's anti-structure, therefore, expressed the same Jewish root metaphors. The anti-structures come into play when structure seems to be losing its significance or becomes inadequate in expressing root metaphors. It should be remembered that deviants actually live partly by structure and partly by anti-structure. Again, to illustrate the point, some of Jesus' teaching represented anti-structure or marginal behavior to the then-existing mainline Judaism. Christ was anti-structural, inasmuch as he associated with tax collectors and sinners, "did not observe" the Sabbath, and insisted that his Kingdom was not of this world. He taught his disciples to be marginal and "not of this world." As a consequence, the "world" would hate them, bring them to court, and throw them into prison, while their persecutors would consider themselves as having done God a service (cf. Lk 21:12-13). However, anti-structure exists not to destroy but to

generate and perfect. It proposes alternate schemes for expressing root metaphors (cf. Worgul 1979:9-10).

(3) *Liminality* (V. Turner 1974:231-270) is an in-between condition. It means "on the threshold" or "on the boundaries" (derived from the Latin plural *limina*), "of law, custom, convention, and ceremonial" (V. Turner 1969:95), neither really in nor really out of the normal culture. Christ's apostles entered into a liminal, in-between state by "leaving all"—as one does when one goes on a pilgrimage or retreat or enters a novitiate (cf. Arbuckle 1987:186-201). In initiation rites, the initiates have left, or have been separated from, their old state but are not yet in the new. Christians are a pilgrim people: they have left home and are now "on their way" to their final goal. Initiates are invariably removed from the rest of the tribe, because they have outgrown childhood; they are now in a liminal situation, hidden deep in the forest, where by undergoing various ordeals they can prove their readiness for full-fledged membership in their tribes. In this liminal situation they listen to tribal myths, some of which women and children never hear, and in which tribal secrets are revealed. Then the initiates are ready to be incorporated into the community. Through myth and ritual, the initiates undergo an unforgettable, deeply spiritual experience that influences their behavior for the rest of their lives (Luzbetak 1954:115-128).

(4) *Communitas*, as Turner understands the term (1974:274), refers to the type of social relationships that one experiences outside the culture of normal community life. These relationships are found in liminality. They are basic, direct, one-to-one, informal relationships. Communitas describes the experience of initiates in Africa, Latin America, and Oceania, as well as the experience of monks and nuns, who are in many ways unhampered by cultural restraints.

Liminality and communitas are clearly present in ritual—in tribal initiation ceremonies; in Good Friday ceremonies when separation occurs in the ritualization of Christ's Death, followed by an in-between stage, and finally by the Resurrection on Easter Day; in the holy season of Lent, which begins with Ash Wednesday, is followed by a forty-day liminal period of penance, and finally ends in the normal Christian state of Easter. It occurs in the sequence of engagement, marriage, and, finally, of normal married life.

The transient, personal relationships in the in-between stage are indeed a unique communitas, basic direct one-to-one, informal relationships, ones of equality and statuslessness and homogeneity. They are expressed, for instance, in the nakedness in some initiation rites and rituals of submission (V. Turner 1974:274). Inasmuch as Christians belong to a Pilgrim Church, they too experience not only their normal day-to-day cultural or structural ties but, because they are in a liminal state, they feel the freedom associated with antistructure. A congregation attending a church service (a ritual) is similarly in a temporary liminal state in which the relationship is basically egalitarian. Although the liturgical process is by its very nature repetitive and formalized, liturgy is performed as by a community of equals, by brothers and sisters, free from the restraints of structure, around the same Lord's table, eating the same Loaf and drinking the same Cup. Whereas cultural structure tends to encourage formality and inequality, anti-structure encourages egalitarian relationships. Communitas is the bond uniting people over and above the formal bonds of culture, a bond that is distinctly undifferentiated and direct. Christ's disciples were scolded when ambition and unacceptable structural ways entered their thinking (Mt 20:20–27). They were to be so egalitarian, in fact, that they were to seek the lowest places at a banquet (Lk 14:9); they were to serve the "least" of Christ's brothers (Mt 25:40,45); in fact, they were to wash one another's feet as he, their Master, had washed theirs (Jn 13:12–17).

According to Turner, true cultural dynamism and creativity arises not so much from structure as from anti-structure. Historical developments and the development of culture, therefore, are a social drama. Turner sees the social drama taking place in four stages (1974:38–42). In the first stage, there is a breach in normal social interaction through contrary behavior or omissions. In the second stage, the disregard for interaction increases, until, in the third stage, a crisis is reached, when the normal culture community feels it can no longer tolerate such deviant behavior and begins to take repressive action against the deviants. In the fourth stage, the drama ends in reintegration: either the normal culture community succeeds in bringing anti-structure into line or it caves in by recognizing anti-structure as a new legitimate alternative. Ultimately, anti-structure itself becomes "normal," that is to say, culturally structured and reincorporated. The one time deviant ways now concretize the normal community's root metaphors.

It is ritual, according to Turner, that plays the central role in a social drama, that is, it is especially ritual that carries the core metaphors (the most basic values). Whether we speak of the rite of installation of a new tribal chieftain; of the ordination of a priest; of the investiture of a novice in a religious order; of the various life-cycle rites associated with birth, with Confirmation or the Bar Mitzvah, with a marriage, or with a burial; whether we speak of the liturgical year, we are observing the unfolding of a social drama involving separation, liminality, and incorporation.

To sum up—culture is by its very nature but a continuous dialectic between the two poles, between structure (i.e., the established way of life) on the one hand and anti-structure (liminality and communitas) on the other. Culture change is a veritable social drama, very much like myth and ritual. In this drama, anti-structure (that is, the opposing or alternate way of life) will eventually itself become structure through some form of reintegration. In this drama, it is ritual that plays the major role. (Cf. Worgul 1979:3–10).

6.3.3.3.3 The Structure of Myth

Motif. By *motif* we understand the smallest element of a myth. Such motifs generally fall into one of three categories: they refer either to the actors of a myth (e.g., a deity, an animal), to an unusual custom described, or to a magical object.

Themes. Certain mythological themes are worldwide; in fact they are at times almost universal. Any beginner in the study of mythology will be surprised by the worldwide distribution, for example, of creation-of-the-world myths, the loss-of-paradise myths, myths about women (or sex) as the origin of evil, about the end of historical time, about the Deluge, about the Babel-like origin of languages, and about afterlife. When comparing a particular theme in different cultures in different parts of the world, one is again and again struck by such similarities. Mythologists, of course, have always had a variety of explanations for such parallels—from traces of a primitive Revelation (Wilhelm Schmidt), to traces of history (E. B. Tylor), to cultural diffusion (diffusionists), to the fact of a common human psyche and that humans are by nature theory-builders and myth-dreamers (Durkheim, Mauss, Lévi-Strauss). Myths are particularly concerned with the origin of things: the origin of the universe, the origin of humankind in general and of particular tribes, and the origin of languages, fire, animal husbandry and agriculture, evil, illness, death, and such catastrophes as floods and earthquakes. The same myth, even of the same culture, may allow variants, depending on the particular situation or narrator. Myths, of course, cannot be taken at face value; exegetical interpretations must get at the deeper meaning. Roles played by animals, for instance, must be interpreted according to their symbolic meanings in the particular culture.

6.3.3.3.4 The Function of Myths and Rituals

Various functions have been attributed to myths by experts. Myths have been described as "a unifying device of society," as "a way of discharging emotions in socially accepted ways," as an "explanation of nature," as "a charter for belief and authority," as "a way of expressing basic human feelings toward the world," and as "a system of education into the total scheme of a society" (Saliba 1973:282–283). A very useful, missiologically significant coverage of such functions is that of Loewen (1969d:159–170).

The Cognitive Function of Myths and Rituals. Myths speak of reality as a people sees the world. A myth may claim that an animal, for example, will "allow" itself to be caught because it "knows" that the hunter is hungry. Myths depict the world view of a people, often in religious terms, and offer corresponding solutions to life's problems. Although, as we have just pointed out, myths have a strong tendency to speak of origins and are therefore greatly concerned with cosmology, they preserve and transmit more than knowledge about origins of the universe (cosmology). They preserve and transmit ontological knowledge as well, describing the purpose and destiny of the universe and its inhabitants, the problems of life and death, of good and bad fortune, and of natural catastrophes. The unexplainable is explained through mythical logic. Myths may describe the physical features that are "normal," the family life that is "ideal"; they speak of the "proper" orientation, of the norms, and of the self-image of a society (Saliba 1973:282–283).

Myths do not speak only of the past but attempt also to explain what is currently happening. Thus, contrary to official government policy, some extremist Israeli teachers are instilling into their pupils hatred for Arabs through the claim that Arabs are Amalek of Exodus 17:8–16, destined to be destroyed by God's chosen people. In myths, as Saliba points out (1973:266), "the past is not recalled for its own sake"; it is rather remembered because it "has significance for the present" and has a practical meaning for life.

The Integrating Function of Myths and Rituals. As Loewen (1969d:159–170) points out, myths not only preserve and transmit a society's knowledge but also integrate it in the form of a more or less unified "philosophy."

Myths also contribute greatly to the social integration of a people (i.e., to its identity and solidarity). (1) Myths are as a rule deeply ethnocentric. They present the society in question as *the* people. The tribes of the Middle Wahgi area of the New Guinea highlands call themselves *ye wei*—"real people," in contradistinction to Caucasians, who are *ye bang*—"[not real but] red people." (2) Myth and ritual integrate the present, past, and future generations; they are a unifying device. The Middle Wahgi tribes of New Guinea, for example, perform this function especially through their elaborate pig-killing festivals and initiation rites (Luzbetak 1954:59–80, 102–128).

The Validating Function of Myths and Rituals. Myths legitimize social behavior justifying the society's laws, expectations, mores, and taboos on the grounds that the ancestors have done so.

The Sanctioning Function of Myths and Rituals. Myths function as a very forceful social control. A society will submit to difficult conditions and will carry out burdensome customs because mythic truth makes such behavior reasonable: the customs, as we indicated earlier, were, after all, received from supernatural beings, through prophecies, revelations, or dreams. Thus, myths regarding transmigration of souls underlie the orderly but very demanding caste system of India. As a form of social control, myths help to maintain the social order. They also have an important part to play in the socialization process, especially at birth, initiation, marriage, and death. These so-called *rites de passage* are composed of rituals that dramatize the transition from one social state to another. At such times, myths form an integral part of the traditional instructions of the members of a society and are "cited" very much the way we cite the Sacred Scriptures in our own rites of passage, say at baptisms, confirmations, weddings, and funerals.

The Revitalizing Function of Myths and Rituals. Myths revitalize the rhythms of life and rejuvenate the spirit of the society. Individuals may pass away, but the society must live on and prosper even as one generation follows another. Crises and catastrophes come and go, but the social group must go on. By emphasizing origins, the narration and dramatization of myths revive the pristine power, recalling the time when the power was at its highest. Myths and rituals thus become particularly important when revitalization is most needed, that is, during the rites of passage and at times of personal or group crisis. Creation myths may be dramatized as a part of the initiation rites. Myths may be narrated on the occasion of a birth or during the planting season. The

Roman Catholic *Ritual* offers us countless examples of the revitalizing function of myth and ritual in present-day Christianity. It is interesting to note that Australian aborigines repaint rock drawings supposedly painted by the ancestors at the time of creation so as to revive the original creative power, and the New Guinea highlanders paint their fertility shields (*geru*) at festivals. After the great fertility rite, the *Gol Kerma* (Luzbetak 1954:59-80, 102–128), that is celebrated in honor of the ancestors by each clan only about once every generation, ritual gardens are planted around the central shrine of the ancestors by individual families to recoup some of the original fertility of the soil. Health is restored by the Bhils of India by recreating a miniature universe around the patient.

The Transcendentalizing Function of Myth and Ritual. Through myths and ritual, humans can transcend their humanness. Hostility and aggressiveness can be channeled in culturally more acceptable directions. The New Guinea fertility rite referred to above includes a mock battle to placate the ancestors for having made peace with their traditional enemy. At least symbolically—once an enemy, always an enemy. Through ritual, humans can transcend their limitations and mythically participate in divine nature. Mask-wearers in a rite not only represent a deity but through the ritual mask participate in the very life of the deity (Bühler 1960). In the Eucharistic ritual, we not only eat at the same table *with* the Lord but become *one* with him.

6.3.3.3.5 Dynamics of Myth and Ritual

Myths resist change, but they, like any other component of culture, are nevertheless subject to change. Basically the same factors come into play as with any other culture change (cf. *infra*, chapter 7). Changes may enter into a myth intentionally by innovators, or they may enter unnoticed through a kind of "cultural drift." Certain details, owing to other changes taking place, may become less interesting and less relevant, and therefore are de-emphasized and eventually forgotten. On the other hand, to bring a myth or ritual more in harmony with the rest of the changing culture, the priest, prophet, shaman, or some other narrator or performer may introduce a new slant to the myth, combine a new element with an old, fuse the two, or deliberately substitute the new for the old. These changes may be occasioned by a new dream, inspiration, or revelation. Myths, although possessing strong tendencies to resist change, are not immune to the various processes involved in *acculturation*, the change arising from contact with other societies. The latter is particularly true when a tribal community accepts Christianity or Western scientific ways.

6.3.3.3.6 The Interpretation of Myths

It might be well to preface this section by pointing out the fact of *polysemy*, a characteristic of symbol emphasized in Victor Turner's research. The polysemous quality is the ability of a symbol (and therefore of myth and ritual) to have more than one meaning, in fact even to have contradictory meanings. The interplay of meanings gives additional dynamism to the symbol. The original

Jewish symbol of wine and cup meant family oneness, conviviality, hope, and joy—all distinct meanings that have been carried over to the Mass through the one symbol, the Last Supper.

Various anthropological theories have been proposed to explain myth.[6] Roger Schmidt (1980:136–140) reduces the various approaches to the analysis of myth to four distinct ways of viewing myths.

1) *Myth Viewed as an Ultimate Explanation*. Myths, as we have seen, are basically a religious phenomenon, a response to the sacred, a statement about ultimate reality and purpose. Myths are not too concerned about succession of events, and they often blend the past with the present. Their concern is to provide a kind of religious commentary and a statement of social values. Eliade sees myth as a reflection of a people's view of authentic existence—how to recreate life by doing what was done by the gods or the ancestors. The paradox between the human and the divine is resolved through a mythological explanation: the sacred reconciles the polarity.

2) *Myth Viewed as a Projection of the Unconscious*. Carl Jung and other psychologists consider myths to be a public form of dreams. Because the human psyche is the same regardless of culture, not entirely unexpected is the rather broad distribution of such mythical symbols as paradise, water, mother-earth, and twins—to mention only a few examples—in both myths and dreams. Myths are but public dreams reflecting the common psychic life of humans as humans.

The Freudian psychological term *Oedipus complex* was derived from Hellenic myths to explain the origin of incest taboos and certain psychoneurotic conditions. According to a Greek myth, King Oedipus had an unintended sexual relation with his mother and, also unintentionally, murdered his father. The taboo against incest has its psychological origin in the guilt feeling arising from a common incestual hostility and jealousy. The Electra complex is likewise based on Greek mythology as the female counterpart of the Oedipus complex. A similar hostility and jealousy is expressed in the myth about Uranus, the sky deity, who was castrated by his own son Cronus. Eventually, Cronus married his sister Rhea and cannibalized all of his offspring except Zeus, whom Rhea had successfully managed to hide from him.

3) *Myth Viewed as a Validation of the Social Order*. According to Bronislaw Malinowski, the true function of myth is not to be sought in the details of mythical accounts but in its social contexts—that is, in the situation in which the myth is told or ritualized. The purpose of myth is to reinforce tradition, social interaction, and tribal morality. Thus, for instance, according to a myth of the Trobriand Islanders, the ancestors originally lived in the underworld. The various clans emerged through a hole in the earth that then became the center of the ancestral territory. The theme thus confirms the land rights of the people and, at the same time, depending on the sequence of the emergence from the underworld, the rank of the particular clan.

4) *Myth Viewed as a Mediation of Conflicts and Contradiction*. The main proponents of the conflict-contradiction interpretation of myths are the struc-

turalists with Lévi-Strauss as their leader. Just as humans are language-speaking animals with inborn linguistic competency, so too humans are myth-making animals with a special inborn myth-making ability. The human mind is constantly faced with contradictions demanding resolution. There are, for instance, the contradictions of life and death, the opposition between male and female, the conflict between the younger and older generations, the differences between good and evil, darkness and light, and the tension between reason and emotion, natural inclinations and cultural restraints. Myths are a reflection of this constant opposition; at the same time, however, myths present ways of solving such contradictions. R. Schmidt uses the biblical story of Cain and Abel to illustrate the binary nature of myth: the story of Cain and Abel is not so much an account of the first murder as it is a case of opposition between the values of two cultures, that of herders and that of agriculturalists. God resolves the tension by accepting Abel's animal sacrifice and cursing Cain: "Therefore you shall be banned from the soil that opened its mouth to receive your brother's blood from your hand. If you till the soil, it shall no longer give you its produce. You shall become a restless wanderer on the earth" (Gn 4:11–12).

6.3.4 THEMES AND COUNTERTHEMES

In studying approaches to world views and social personalities, an investigation particularly appropriate for missiological application is Morris Opler's Theme and Countertheme Theory.

Early attempts at describing world views and group characters produced such stereotypic portrayals of peoples as found in the *Histories* by Herodotus (fifth century B.C.) and *Germania* by Tacitus (c. 56-117 A.D.). As we have seen in our overview of models of culture (*supra*, 5.1.6.4.1,5.1.6,.4.2), personality and culture studies have made considerable changes in the last fifty years, thanks especially to a more rigorous application of scientific methods. Today, anthropologists do not look for a single, unique, all-pervading "pattern" or "mainspring" as Ruth Benedict once did for at least a number of cultures. Cultures are not that simple, clearcut, and unified. Margaret Mead suggested that a distinction be made between primary and secondary trends in a culture. The Maori, for instance, were supposed to have an economic system that was primarily cooperative and secondarily self-centered. Real progress, however, was not made until Morris Opler (1945; 1946) suggested a theory of *themes and counterthemes*, providing us with important insights that remain useful to this day. It would indeed be difficult for us to deny the existence of themes—*a basic set* of generally consistent postulates and core attitudes and motivating forces that run more or less through the whole culture and that give the culture its character and dominant emotional tone. Balancing such dominant themes, according to Opler, are certain opposing, limiting, and circumscribing *counterthemes*.

Opler defined *theme* as "a postulate or position, declared or implied, and usually controlling behavior or stimulating activity, which is tacitly approved or openly promoted in a society." He proposed as example a basic Apache premise according to which men are supposed to be not only physically but also intellectually and morally superior to women. Themes, Opler observed, are made manifest through *formalized* or *unformalized* and *primary* or *symbolic* expressions. A *formalized* expression (e.g., a ritual practice) is always specific; it is insisted on; and it is rarely disobeyed. An *unformalized* expression is one that is less strict and that allows occasional modification. Apache women, for instance, are expected to be reserved and deferential toward men; however, sometimes age or a special relationship between the man and the woman concerned may justify a modification of the rule. The fact that Apache men are to precede women in walking and eating is a *primary* expression; excessive movement in the mother's womb, on the other hand, is a *symbolic* expression believed to indicate that the baby will be a boy, because the excessive movement symbolizes male strength and superiority.

Themes, according to Opler, can often be recognized by the presence of counterthemes. Because themes are central and pervading in the given way of life, other basic assumptions, attitudes, and goals are called for to restrain and balance the themes. For example, men may be all-important, *but* women are important too. Women may be excluded from certain rituals, *but* they have their special parts to play in certain ceremonies. Men may be dominant, *but* women have their special rights and privileges too. Counterthemes are definitely weaker, serving mainly as "brakes" on themes. Though, on the whole, themes are antagonistic toward counterthemes, a society is unable to function without the latter. In fact, some counterthemes may be used "as veils" to conceal underlying motivations (cf. Henry 1963:14).

The presence of counterthemes does not make cultures unchangeable; it does, however, help to explain the balancing process that enters into the imbalance that accompanies any culture change (*infra*, chapter 7). Most important to remember is that, as themes and counterthemes are indeed starting points in the psychological process, they are taken for granted by the society and, as a rule, are never, or very seldom, questioned. They are indeed the *starting points* in reasoning, evaluating, and motivating.

A few concrete examples of what we mean by *counterthemes* may help us better to understand the theory just enunciated.

When describing American values and drives, we pointed out, for instance, how much individual freedom and personal rights meant to Americans. However, to balance off this extremely important value, the American is reminded of the existence of a countertheme, the existence of "a common good" which at times may have precedence over private rights, for instance, at times of war or pestilence. Also there is the countertheme that human rights, such as the freedom of speech, are not absolute but must be exercised responsibly. Civil libertarianism absolutizes such themes by removing counterthemes altogether and allowing total freedom to the individual. For example, women have a right over their bodies to the extent that they may have an abortion for any or no reason; cohabitation and homosexuality are "options," legitimate "sexual preferences" or "alternatives"; pornography is but an exercise of the "freedom of speech." On the other hand, sometimes so-called state rights and occasionally the Bible itself are resorted to as a kind of countertheme to circumvent the constitutionally sanctioned human rights.

Another readily recognizable American theme (shared with other Western cultures) is the assumption that judgments are to be made in dualistic or polarizing terms; that is, something will be either/or, right/wrong, clean/dirty, good/bad, wise/stupid, work/play, with no middle or gray area. History and current events are generally interpreted in terms of "good guys" and "bad guys," although a countertheme reminds the American that the truth most likely lies in the middle.

The countertheme to American competitiveness is the not-too-comforting thought that "it is not whether you win or lose, but how you play the game that counts" and that one should find satisfaction in being "a good loser" and a "good sport."

We also pointed out the narcissistic tendencies in the American society. Fortunately, strong counterthemes appear on the scene to remind the American that responsibility goes far beyond oneself. The counterthemes referred to are Christian charity and the Golden Rule, "American generosity," the spirit of sharing, community involvement, team spirit, and, for the wealthy, philanthropy. Such counterthemes put the brakes on otherwise strong narcissistic tendencies.

A countertheme to the American demand for newness and the fear of obsolescence is a certain form of conservatism. In not a few respects Americans are ultraconservative, for example in constitutional matters and sports.

(For a further example of a missiological application of Opler's theme theory, *see* William Conley's *The Kalimantan Kenyah: A Study of Tribal Conversion in Terms of Dynamic Cultural Themes* [1976].)

Themes, as intimated earlier, can vary also on the subcultural level, or even on the level of specialties and alternatives. "Single-issue" voting is often criticized in the United States as being narrowminded. The Moral Majority, the backers of a disarmament or freeze on nuclear testing, the feminists and their Equal Rights Amendment, the opponents of abortion, the environmentalists, the advocates of the black or Hispanic cause, the dairy or wheat farmers, and similar interest groups are really not voting on the basis of only one issue; they are voting according to a central *theme* (not unlike Turner's "core metaphor") that in their case penetrates and underlies all, or mostly all, of their other values. Affirmative Action, dairy prices, nuclear plants, and the Equal Rights Amendment are something more than what they are in themselves: they are like the American flag, representing not so much American politics as American ideals. That is to say, they symbolize not just one issue but everything else associated with it as well.

In concluding this section on themes and counterthemes, we might note that every society regards itself and other societies as great—or not so great—on the basis of its themes. Unfortunately, the not-so-flattering stereotyping of other cultures is only too often based on one's own themes rather than on those of the society being judged. Discussions about national differences, such as the following, are frequently heard in European circles.

The *question*: What is the real difference between heaven and hell? (One little *hint*: It's not the temperature.) It's *heaven* if the British govern, the French cook, the Germans take care of the technological problems, and the Italians do the loving. It's *hell* if the English do the cooking, the French take care of the technological matters, the Germans do the loving, and the Italians do the governing.

6.3.5 SUMMARY AND MISSIOLOGICAL APPLICATION

6.3.5.1 Summary

1) What ultimately makes culture into a system is the so-called *mentality of a people* (including the set of underlying premises, root values, and basic goals and drives; the starting points of a people's reasoning, reacting, and motivating). A mentality will be more or less consistent and organized and is therefore referred to as *psychological integration*.

2) As important as, and more difficult than, an analysis of functions (the immediate *whys*, and the more immediate meanings and values) is an analysis of the basic or ultimate *whys* of a culture. Numerous clues, however, are evident, the most important of which are the people's *world view*. A world view has a cognitive, emotional, and motivational dimension. The cognitive dimension refers to the way a people reasons and perceives reality. The emotional dimension refers to root values and attitudes. The motivational dimension refers to the people's basic drives and goals. A world view is most clearly revealed in a people's religion, mythology, and ritual.

3) *Functionally*, religion can be defined as a system of beliefs and practices

by means of which a group of people in a relationship with supernatural beings or powers struggles with the ultimate problems of life. Religion consists of beliefs, worship, and corresponding social relationships. Among the chief functions of religion are to provide answers to problems beyond human experience; to legitimize the social order; to instill and support group solidarity and identity; and to provide support to the individual and the community especially in times of perplexity, crisis, and tragedy. *Substantively*, religion is the underlying code of a society regarding the proper way of responding to the sacred and eternal.

4) *Myth* underlies religion and reveals its spirit. Myth is a story about ultimate questions; it provides an answer to the *why* of religious life. *Ritual* is the sacred stylized behavior of a society. Myths and rituals have a cognitive, integrating, validating, sanctioning, revitalizing, and transcendentalizing function.

5) Various *interpretations* are given to myths, depending on the mythologist's particular perspective. Accordingly, myths are viewed as an ultimate explanation; as a projection of the unconscious (Jung and Freud); as a validation of the social order (Malinowski and the functionalists); as a mediation of conflicts and contradictions (Lévi-Strauss and the structuralists).

6) A useful approach to the study of a people's mentality and the psychological integration of a society is M. Opler's *theme and countertheme* theory. By *themes* we mean the basic set of generally consistent postulates, core attitudes, and motivating forces running more or less through the whole culture. These give a special character and a dominant emotional tone—the so-called soul or spirit of a people. Balancing such dominant themes are certain opposing, limiting, and circumscribing counterthemes.

6.3.5.2 Missiological Application

6.3.5.2.1 Mission and the Degree of Integration

The missiological terms *contextualization*, *inculturation*, and *incarnation* of the Gospel are the equivalents of functional and psychological *integration*. The term *integration* is therefore of no little significance to missiological anthropology.

We have stressed that no culture is perfectly integrated. The "oneness" of an organism is never really attained. As there are degrees of integration, so there are degrees of contextualization. On the one hand, there is the so-called nominal Christianity in countries like France and Denmark, and there are the poorly instructed syncretistic countries of Middle and South America and the Caribbean. On the other hand, there is the fervent Christianity of the New Testament churches and of many truly Christian communities today; these survive and thrive despite, or perhaps on account of, difficulties and persecution. Hinduism and Islam are totally integrated with the rest of culture, more than Christianity generally is. The Inca culture was so thoroughly integrated that the removal of its central component, the Inca leadership, caused the entire culture to disintegrate.

We propose three criteria for judging how thoroughly a culture is integrated. These criteria enable us to measure the extent to which the Gospel has become functionally and psychologically one with the rest of the lifeway. The criteria are: (1) the number and intensity of linkages; (2) the degree of consistency; (3) the extent of reciprocity.

The Number and Intensity of Linkages. The more numerous and intense the ties are between cultural forms and the message of the Gospel (*supra*, 6.2) and the more intense the bond between the Gospel and the mentality of a people (*supra*, 6.3), the deeper is the integration or incarnation of the Gospel. Not only must the functional interwebbing between a Christian community's ways and the Gospel be as intense as possible ("*Whatever* you do, whether in speech or in action, do it in the name of the Lord Jesus" [Col 3:17]), but the Gospel also must become the very heart and nerve center of the community. For a community to be truly Christian, it must be of "the mind of Christ" (1 Cor 2:13–16); in fact, the word *life* must become synonymous with *Christ* (Phil 1:21). True Christian living is a twenty-four-hours-a-day affair, touching all aspects of life—the physical, social, and ideational. Mission has no lesser goal than "Thy Kingdom come!"

The Degree of Consistency. Integration calls for consistency and harmony within the culture-whole. Contextualization implies harmony between the teaching of the Gospel and the three levels of culture (the forms, functions, and psychology; the symbols, their meanings, and the core metaphors). The more consistency there is between the traditional expectations and those of the Gospel, the higher the degree of integration.

The local community must do more than tenderly plant, gently water, faithfully weed, and carefully cultivate the Lord's vineyard (cf. 1 Cor 3:4–6). The acceptance of the Gospel consists in true repentence (Mk 6:12; Acts 30:21; Col 3:9–10; 1 Pt 3:9), in taking up a cross (Mt 10:38; 16:24; Mk 8:34; Lk 9:23; 14:27; Gal 6:14), in "engrafting" Christ (Rom 11:19, 24)—in fact, in "gouging out" eyes and "cutting off" limbs (Mt 5:29f). Contextualization does not mean romanticizing local ways. A compromise of the Gospel is impossible where there is a true conflict between cultural structure and Gospel anti-structure.

> If your right eye is your trouble, gouge it out and throw it away! Better to lose part of your body than to have it all cast into Gehenna. Again, if your right hand is your trouble, cut it off and throw it away! Better to lose part of your body than to have it all cast into Gehenna. [Mt 5:29f]

Applied to a society, these startling analogies certainly call for nothing less than "cultural surgery." If a cultural form or symbol, a meaning or value, or an underlying premise, basic attitude, or core goal is the society's trouble and serves only as a stumbling block, the society has no choice but to "cut it off" or "gouge it out." A Christian community must not compromise the Gospel or try to escape its own prophetic call to be countercultural. No society is forced to follow Christ, but if it opts for Christ, it has no choice but to take up its cross and follow him (Lk 14:27). Although Christ called the peacemakers blest (Mt 5:9), and although he was the Prince of Peace (Is 9:5) and after his Resurrection could not wish his faithful followers anything more precious than peace (Mt 28:9), it was he who asked:

> Do you think I have come to establish peace on the earth? I assure you, the contrary is true; I have come for division. From now on, a household of five will be divided three against two and two against three; father will be split against son and son against father, mother against daughter and daughter against mother, mother-in-law against daughter-in-law, daughter-in-law against mother-in-law. [Lk 12:51ff]

Evangelization, whether it be to non-Christians or to fellow Christians, will, according to Jesus' own warning, involve a certain amount of interference with the smooth operation of a society. In Turner's terminology, by choosing Christianity, a community breaks from all that is un-Christian, becomes a "deviant," and a threat to non-Christian tradition; tensions rise; an impasse is reached; and then either the non-Christian mass accepts Christianity itself, or at least tolerates Christianity as a legitimate alternative, or the Christian community surrenders through compromise and unfaithfulness (*supra*, 6.3.3.3.2). The Gospel may be a source of untold peace, but it nevertheless brings unavoidable tension and pain. It is a cross that demands the greatest "absurdity" (1 Cor 1:23)—the giving up of one's treasured ways and values.

In other words, at times the Christian community must play the disagreeable role of "culture surgeon." The type of "culture surgeon" we are talking about, of course, is a prophet who is full of compassion, who, like Christ, can weep over a sinful city (Mt 23:37), one who is constantly aware of the complexity and consequences of functional linkages and the power of a people's mentality. Mission will therefore at times call for the removal of an existing custom or value. As in surgery, so in evangelization: the removal as well as the engrafting ("functional substitution") call for a genuine, far-seeing appreciation of the interwebbing of the various parts of the cultural organism at all levels. Like a conscientious and sympathetic surgeon, the responsible decision makers must make the operation as painless as possible. Every move must be well planned and well-timed; and just as now careful preparation for the operation is made necessary, so, later on, a careful convalescence, a period of patient waiting for complete health and recovery, is called for. "Surgery" will be resorted to only because, after careful consultation with others, "surgery" was deemed unavoidable. A local community, especially through its decision makers, should make good use of experts and specialists to the extent that they are available—including theologians, missiologists, psychologists, sociologists, economists, linguists, anthropologists, and others. Above all, consultation with the local community itself is indispensable. The best answers to pastoral problems are to be found in the well-instructed, faithful Christian community and in their yearnings as expressed in the deeper meanings of their myths, rituals, and folk religion. Unless such procedures are followed, the removal of a "diseased" portion of the body may prove to be more destructive than the disease itself. A good surgeon will be deeply concerned about every linkage, whether on the second or third level of culture; and, as far as it is humanly possible, compensation will be made through compatible Christian substitutes.

The true Christian is indeed paying a great price for "the pearl of great price" and is willing to sell "all that he or she has" to buy it (Mt 13:44ff). Two questions should be a part of the examination of conscience of every decision maker and everyone engaged in a ministry—in fact, by the entire Christian community: (1) Are we courageously fulfilling our prophetic role? (Or perhaps is it true, as someone has warned, that we were given a Gospel that was a wild tiger but that we unfortunately tamed and domesticated it into a pussy cat?) (2) Do we appreciate the weight of the cross that the individual Christian is carrying? Only an understanding of the theory of cultural integration will enable one to answer such questions.

Extent of Reciprocity. *Reciprocity* refers to the manner in which the different elements of a culture reinforce each other. The greater the reciprocity, the more integrated the culture. By encouraging reciprocity, we are not advocating compromise, distortion, or betrayal of the Gospel. Not even the least "jot" or "tittle," the least "iota" or "stroke of a letter" (Lk 16:17) essential to the Good News is negotiable. Pope Benedict XIV, writing to the Bishop of Peking in 1744, expressed the official policy of the Catholic Church, still valid today, in the following words:

> Let it be known to everyone that in matters pertaining to religious truth, when it is a question of superstition or idolatry, sympathy or tolerance is utterly impossible, as Tertullian put it: "Any such tolerance is itself a form of idolatry." [*Collectanea*, I:349]

This is not to say that serious mistakes have not been made both on the side of unwarranted compromise as well as on the side of unjustifiable rigor, as our survey of mission models (*supra*, chapter 4) has revealed. The secular purposes of ambitious rulers were served in the name of Christ not only during the Reformation but also throughout history: under Charlemagne, the Teutonic Knights, the Crusades, the Spanish Inquisition, the tandem Cross-and-Crown policy of Rome, and the arrangement between Protestant missions and the British and Dutch trading companies. Today, there is a serious struggle going on, within and without the Church, between cultural structures and Christian antistructures, between a commitment to local tradition and Christian orthodoxy, between those who stress that the Christian is *in* the world (even if not of it) and those who stress that the Christian is not *of* the world (even if in it). Ultimately, it will be the local Christian community that will have to resolve such tensions through a tripolar dialectic between the Gospel, the universal tradition, and the local tradition. The more a culture supports a people's faith, the more integrated is the faith with the culture. A Christian community's goal should be at least to achieve recognition as a legitimate alternative in the larger society so that it might through its presence serve as the yeast in the whole mass of dough (Mt 13:33).

6.3.5.2.2 World View and Mission

The world view of a people is really the only medium through which a society is able to understand anything, including the Gospel message and anything else that the Church may wish to communicate. It is the main measuring-rod of a people used for evaluating the Gospel message, and, humanly speaking, it ultimately determines what will or will not move a society to accept and live the Gospel. Owing to the expatriate missionary's world view, it will seem quite natural and not out of the ordinary to demand from converts that they assume personal blame for their actions. The fact is, however, that individuals brought up in a neo-Confucian world view will tend to think in terms of *group* (not personal) responsibility. Similarly, some societies hold that one should hide one's emotions, or at best express them only indirectly, a fact that may, for example, make it difficult for them to adopt the evangelical emphasis on a public affirmation.

6.3.5.2.3 Myth and Mission

Mission anthropologist Loewen determined seven benefits that the church worker might expect from a knowledge of local mythology (1969d:185–192): (1) myths can provide contact points for the transmission of the Christian message; (2) myths can help preprogram the Church's message to a society; (3) myths can help locate points of conflict between the Gospel and traditional ways of thinking and behaving; (4) myths can help identify the people's values and felt-needs; (5) myths provide invaluable information for problem solving; (6) myths provide useful information for translation; (7) myths help reduce the danger of syncretistic interpretations of the Christian message. We shall now explain and comment on each of these points.

Myths as Contact Points. A right start is always half the task in effective communication. To discover the right start may, in fact, be the most important challenge facing an evangelizer. Achieving proper entry and acceptability is therefore always vital.

A very common and effective general field technique in anthropology is the swapping of information between the fieldworker and the informant. This technique has proven particularly useful for collecting myths. Exchanging stories about the creation of the world, the origin of humankind, or about how a people has come to appreciate certain values generates mutual trust and respect and creates interest and an atmosphere of openness. The similarities and differences between biblical accounts and the local myths provide important contact points for religious and other instruction.

Myths and Message Preprogramming. The necessity of preprogramming one's message is a principle in communication theory going back to the ancient

Greek and Latin authors and orators. Preprogramming is particularly important in cross-cultural communication. Mythology suggests metaphors that are solemn, sacred, and sometimes deeply moving. Mythology also provides a key to the effective structuring of a message; it reveals how what is said best fits together. Mythology provides symbols that are both understandable and have impact, that is, symbols that not only do not distort the desired message but move the listener emotionally in the desired direction of joy, admiration, determination, or outrage.

The Role of Myth in a Conflict Between Christianity and the People's World View. Christianity, as we emphasized, must be uncompromising in its rejection of mythological content incompatible with Revelation and the Christian faith. In this regard, a knowledge of local mythology can contribute much to the necessary dialectic that must go on between local tradition, universal tradition, and the Gospel (*supra*, 3.1.3.6.2) if true contextualization is to be realized. A knowledge of local mythology makes one aware of points of conflict. Theologically inadmissible content must be uncompromisingly but empathetically confronted with the Christian version. Sometimes local churches in the Third World try to justify their failure to correct theological error by claiming for themselves a "broadmindedness" and an appreciation of the people's "simple faith" when they should really be prophetic and countercultural. This is not to say that nativistic movements and prophetism do not often reflect in their mythologies inner longings that merit a hearing. In fact, such longings, coming as they do from the depths of the soul of a people, can be opportunities for preaching a truly relevant Christianity. Some Latin American myths, for example, are interpreted in terms of current social injustice, an injustice that began with the arrival of the Spanish and Portuguese colonialists. Thus traditional mythology makes Jesus a most welcome Liberator from all forms of sin and captivity. Here liberation theologies are clearly on the right track.

Myth and Local Values and Felt-Needs. If the Gospel is to be communicated with the desired impact, it will have to be preached as much as possible in terms of the particular people's value system, not in terms of the value system of the outsider. What guidance can be offered if the people's value system is not taken fully into account? Communication, such as is involved in mission, must as much as possible be in terms of the values of the receptor society; it must proceed from the known to the unknown, from the wanted to the still unwanted, from the felt to the still unfelt (*supra*, 5.2.1.6.2). Myths, we are suggesting, reveal much that is already known, intensely wanted, and deeply felt. They are therefore of great value to the evangelizer.

Myth and Problem Solving. Mission problems are often encrusted in tribal beliefs. These beliefs are in turn often reflected in myths. Parishioners may refuse to part with a small piece of land for a parish school or church, not because they do not value the project under discussion but, as is the case in parts of Africa, because "only what you make can be given away or sold, and no one except God has made the land." It may take a myth to reveal such "self-evident" reasons and sources of problems.

Myth and Translation. Mission calls for a considerable amount of translation work. First and foremost, there is the need for the translation of Scripture into the vernacular. There are, however, many other translation needs, such as for the translation of Christian concepts for catechisms, homilies, theological studies, liturgical books, and hymns—not to mention the needs of socio-economic programs. Anyone who has done linguistic field research will appreciate what a great resource myths are not only for lexicographical and grammatical purposes but also for the study of literary styles used in various genres—for instance, in rituals, storytelling, proverbs, songs, prayers, and oratory.

Myth and Syncretism. Christian communities are frequently shocked by the thought of utilizing something as "pagan" as mythology. Many argue that myths merely perpetuate "paganism" through a "hodgepodge of Christianity and paganism." We shall have more to say about this issue (*infra,* 7.3.4.2.3). The fact is that, on the contrary, an appreciation of mythology and a proper application of it to evangelization may, for instance, enable the religious educator to contrast the message of the Gospel with that of myths and thereby clarify the Good News. Myths make it possible for a local church to build on the already known, appreciated, and felt. Mythology thus suggests to the alert educator or preacher where to begin, what to emphasize, and where to suggest warnings. (Cf. Loewen 1969d:191–192.) Mythology may also provide some enlightening and interesting illustrations, including metaphors with deep emotional and motivational ramifications. Myth, therefore, does not necessarily increase the danger of syncretism but, if properly used, may serve as a salutary antidote against whatever negative aspects that the particular syncretistic beliefs and practices may have. The insights of anthropologists like Lévi-Strauss, Geertz, and V. Turner should be made use of as much as possible.

6.3.5.2.4 Application of Opler's Theme Theory to Mission

The "mentality of the people" is a very common topic of discussion in missionary gatherings. Much that is said is impressionistic and anecdotal. Surprise is expressed about the general uniformity of thought habits, emotions, and predictability of behavior. Much that is said may be nothing more than an affirmation of ready-made stereotypes. Nevertheless, such discussions represent a considerable amount of experience and evidence—not scientific evidence, but evidence nonetheless. To put such invaluable experience into good use in a somewhat more systematic, albeit tentative manner and in accord with some of the anthropological theory presented in this chapter, we suggest an approach based especially on Morris Opler's thinking (*supra,* 6.3.4). The approach is applicable not only for overseas missions but also for countries like the United States where the cultural communities are almost as diversified as in the world itself.

In our presentation of Opler's theory of themes and counterthemes, we suggested the possibility of isolating assumptions, attitudes, and goals that might be regarded as common denominators; such common denominators, we said, might be further reduced to a lowest common denominator called *themes. Common* denominators, as opposed to *lowest* common denominators, are really extensions of themes and might be called *corollaries*. The evidence for such generalizations one might call *practices*. The New Guinea mentality of thirty years ago, prevalent in the Middle Wahgi area, illustrates what we mean.

Theme I: The ultimate norm for "good" or "evil," "right" or "wrong" is the clan.
Corollary A: Behavior is "good," "evil," or "indifferent," depending on how it affects the clan.
>*Practice 1*: One may steal, rape, or do bodily harm to another person provided that the victim is not a member of one's own clan or someone friendly to it and provided that the act does not have repercussions detrimental to the clan (e.g., by occasioning an unwanted war or feud).
>*Practice 2, 3, 4, etc.*
Corollary B: To disagree with one's clan is shameful, if not a betrayal.
>*Practice 1*: My "brother" (fellow-clansman) must be preferred to others.
>*Practice 2*: In quarrels, my "brother" is always "right." Not to side with him would be a betrayal of the clan.
Corollary C: Personal rights and advantages are subservient to those of the clan.
>*Practice 1*: No personal advantage is to be sought at the expense of the clan.
>*Practice 2*: Women should be satisfied with their relatively inferior status, since thereby they serve the clan.
>*Practice 3*: Forced marriages occur for the good of the group, e.g., to strengthen intratribal friendships.
>*Practice 4*: Individuals may be expected to confess crimes of which they are not guilty so that the real culprit who happens to be more important to the clan might avoid imprisonment.
Corollary D, E, F, etc.

Theme II: Security is found primarily in the clan.
Corollary A: Group prosperity and group prestige have precedence over personal or family goals.
>*Practice 1*: Brotherly cooperation is expected of all clan members in all crises and important phases of life, e.g., by contributing to the bridewealth, helping another in constructing a house, participating in the various ceremonies associated with birth, marriage, funerals.
>*Practice 2*: Selfishness is frowned upon. Sharing of one's for-

tune or success is proper behavior; however, the favor obligates the recipients to reciprocate.

Practice 3: Intratribal competition is improper. On the other hand, competition is expected between clans, e.g., at festivals, in sports. Most games, except those recently introduced, are noncompetitive.

Practice 4: One must be ready to die for one's clan. Bravery in battle is never forgotten. Cowardice in battle constitutes an impediment to marriage.

Corollary B: Every member of the clan is vitally important to the clan.

Practice 1: An injury done to one member is an injury done to all.

Practice 2: The clan assumes the guilt and consequences of the actions of the individual member—actions, for example, that result in feuding and hostage taking.

Practice 3: Disregard of tradition by one or a few members may bring down the wrath of the ancestors on all.

Practice 4: The education of the young is the responsibility of the whole clan, not only of parents or immediate kin.

Theme III: Successful living consists in close cooperation among ALL members of the clan, the living as well as the departed and even with the future generations.

Corollary A: The Living: Cooperation within the clan is a primary obligation.

Practice 1: Instructions given to initiates stress cooperation.

Practice 2, 3, etc.: see Theme II.

Corollary B: The Departed and Ancestors: The living members of the clan are totally dependent on the departed and the ancestors, e.g., for their health, harvest, pigs, victory in battle. (Luzbetak 1956:81-96.)

Practice 1: Traditional ceremonial dances, mockbattles, feasts, and pig sacrifices are not only socioeconomic in character but are also basically religious; the primary beneficiaries of the ritual are the ancestors and more recently departed kin.

Practice 2: Elaborate funeral and memorial rites, chopping off of fingers to prove one's sympathy for the departed, and consultation of spirit-mediums are an expression of the dependence of the living on the kin and clan members in the other world.

Corollary C: The departed clan members are dependent on their descendants for their happiness in the otherworld.

Practice 1: The departed are constantly threatening the living with misfortune, haunting them, and interfering in their lives, so that the living will be mindful of the needs of the dead. The religion is largely a religion of fear.

Practice 2: The happiness of the living depends on the number and quality of pigs that the living can sacrifice (i.e., send the soul of the pig to the otherworld, leaving only some morsels of the pork for the deceased).

Corollary D: The most important possession is one's herd of pigs. (We refer the reader to our discussion on the functional linkages of pigs in New Guinea, *supra*, 6.2.1.)

Although additional themes, corollaries, and practices might be suggested, there is a definite focus on *clan* concepts and *clan* values that might be outlined in terms of themes, corollaries, and practices as we have just done. One should note how closely interwebbed this clan complex is. Group-oriented assumptions, attitudes, and interests permeate all aspects of the people's culture—economic, social, and religious.

It would make good missiological sense for expatriate missionaries, sending churches, outside agencies, and other outsiders, whenever possible, to do what the Christian community following its own cultural "instinct" would do naturally and most spontaneously, namely, to build its religious and socioeconomic programs on *group* concepts and *group* values. We offer some concrete, although quite incomplete, examples of what we mean.

Religious Education. In order to emphasize the centrality of Christ in Christianity, the word for *Church* might be "Christ's Clan" rather than some meaningless loan word. This indeed would make Christ the Head of the Body and us its members (1 Cor 12:12–30), all sharing one and the same Spirit (Eph 4:4); the name "Christ's Clan" would clearly state that he is the First-Born of many brothers (Rom 8:29) and declare his Lordship over all that is (Phil 2:11; Col 1:16); it would proclaim him as *the* clan hero, who is "the way, the truth, and the life" (Jn 14:6) and the Clan's Exemplar par excellence, for when the Clan looks at him, they see the perfect image of the Father (Jn 14:8). Without him, in fact, the Clan could do nothing (Jn 15:5).

We become members of Christ's Clan through faith and a washing ceremony of adoption called "Baptism" through which we are born again and made to share the common Life of the Clan. We thus become God's own adopted children (Rom 8:15). Membership in Christ's Clan brings many rights and privileges, the greatest of which is this sharing of common "Clan Life" (Sanctifying Grace, the Holy Spirit who takes his abode within us) much the way we share the life of our parents and ancestors. We become Christ's brothers and sisters. In return for the privilege of being a member of the Clan we must adopt the ways and values of the Clan.

The desirable qualities that one would wish for one's own natural clan are found to an eminent degree in Christ's Clan, but in an entirely different sense, for Christ's Clan is not of this world (Jn 18:36). We all want our natural clans to be numerous, rich, admired by others, powerful. Christ's Clan has all these characteristics beyond compare. Christ's Clan is numerous, with brothers and sisters over the whole world and over all ages, not confined to a small portion of a valley, mountain side, or river bank. Many of the Clan's brothers and sisters were outstanding heroes (called Saints, Martyrs, Confessors), witnessing to the world and showing us what it means to be true and loyal members of Christ's Clan. The greatest of these Clan heroes was Christ's own mother, the Virgin Mary. She was purely human, although her son was divine, but since he, our Clan Head, came to us through her, she is also the Clan's Mother, loving us and concerned about us as a mother. Of all human beings, she was most like Jesus her son, and therefore is our Model showing us how we should be devoted to the Head of our Clan. Like human ancestors of a natural clan, the ancestors of Christ's Clan are honored especially by our imitation of them. Like the members of a natural clan, they are deeply interested in our welfare. Christ's Clan is "rich" and "powerful" in the sense that God the Almighty Father is rich and powerful. Christ's Clan is "rich" and "powerful" because its Head is Christ, who is God with the Father and the Spirit.

Although we cannot understand *how* the Father, Son, and the Holy Spirit are only *one* God, our clan tradition, originally revealed to us through our Clan Head and the Word of God we call "the Bible," tells us so and we believe.

Our true Clan Home, called "Heaven," is not in this world but in a place prepared for us by Jesus, the Head of our Clan (Jn 14:2).

Much more, of course, would have to be said to cover the basic teachings of Christianity: for instance, we would have to explain the origin of the world; the origin of human beings; the origin of evil; the death and resurrection of Jesus and what they mean for the individual and the whole Clan of Christ; and the Christian virtues, especially love for one another as *the* distinctive mark of Christ's Clan. In all cases, the doctrine could be presented from the easily understood and naturally sympathetic perspective of a clan-oriented people. *Sin*, for instance, might be translated as "a betrayal of Christ's Clan" or as "an insult" to the Heavenly Father. Other doctrines can be similarly presented in terms of group concepts and group values. Such doctrines include the Sacraments, the Ten Commandments, the Sacred Scriptures, and the Liturgy.

Christian counterthemes would also have to be added to balance such narrowly defined explanations of the Good News, especially of *universal* values of Christians. For example, the fact must be stressed that one must love *all* humankind, whether Christian or not.

Other Mission Activities. A focus on group structure and group values as just described makes sense in whatever the Christian community does or is asked to do. Church vocations and the recruitment of lay catechists and other lay ministers may be more appealing if made from the point of view of "clan needs" and "clan growth." In fact, group consciousness should be considered in any community project. Thus, the building of schools, hospitals, and roads might rely less on volunteers and more on the existing social structure and natural esprit de corps. Not least of all, care must be taken to present the Church and its mission in the broad comprehensive terms that will be explained in chapter 8.

Chapter Seven

CULTURAL DYNAMICS

Attentiveness to the signs of the times is part of our vocation.
                    Society of the Divine Word,
                    Constitution no. 507

You must change with the times unless you are big enough to change the times.
                                        Anonymous

7.1 GENERAL NOTIONS

7.1.1 THE NATURE OF CULTURAL DYNAMICS

By its very nature, an organism is dynamic: it changes and it adjusts, sometimes successfully, sometimes less so. At the same time, organisms have a tendency to persist, to remain what they are. Culture is such an organism, a living system, in structure as well as in its dynamic character. New elements are constantly being added while other elements are lost, substituted or fused. Generally speaking, the changes that take place are not haphazard but are in harmony with the culture-whole and are in response to the whims and demands of the time and place.

Cultures are constantly changing because the individuals of the society—the architects of culture—are constantly modifying their "plan for successful living," constantly seeking to improve their underlying code of behavior in accord with the growth of their experience and their ever-changing physical, social, and ideational environment.

As any architect will maintain, sometimes changes creep into blueprints unnoticed. Moreover, one change will trigger other changes in the attempt to restore balance and harmony.

Sometimes change in an organism gets out of control, and disorganization sets in. Some cultures, like some organisms, change more rapidly and more

292

thoroughly than others. Organisms grow, develop, multiply from generation to generation; and sometimes they deteriorate and disappear. In any case, the nature of both organisms and societies is to grow and develop, to react and adjust, and to continue their lives. Even though individual members of society eventually leave the scene, the society lives on, perpetuating itself from generation to generation.

7.1.2 ANTHROPOLOGY AND CULTURE CHANGE

There is much that we do not know about culture change. Questions about how, at what rate, and why culture elements are added, lost, substituted, and blended have kept anthropologists busy researching and debating ever since anthropology was born. Nevertheless, much *is* known, as the present chapter will show. Anthropological explanations will, of course, vary according to the particular perspective (*supra*, 5.1.6; for example, V. Turner's theory, *supra*, 6.3.3.3.2).

No single book could possibly provide all such available information. Consequently, we refer the reader, first of all, to a number of anthropological classics on the subject. The studies we name may prove particularly useful for missiological anthropology. Foremost is Homer G. Barnett's *Innovation: The Basis of Culture Change* (1953). Also useful is the collection of classic articles edited by Paul Bohannan and Fred Plog, *Beyond the Frontier: Social Process and Cultural Change* (1967). Useful, too, are works that, while they focus on *directing* culture change, take the theory of culture dynamics into consideration. There are a number of such older, but by no means outdated, works that go back to the 1960s and earlier. The excellence of these works is evident in the concreteness of their presentation; they not only *apply* anthropology but *base* their applications on still valid anthropological theory regarding culture change. See, for example, Arensberg, Niehoff (1964), Niehoff (1966), Erasmus (1961), G. Foster (1969, 1973), Goodenough (1963), Niehoff (1966), Paul (1955), and Spicer (1952). More recent applied anthropological publications that might be recommended for a better understanding on a practical level are Angrosino (1976), Eddy, Partridge (1978), Chambers (1985), and van Willigen (1986).

7.1.3 THE LOCUS OF CULTURE CHANGE

The issue of where culture is located is not a purely academic problem. In applied anthropology, it makes a great difference where our target is—inside the mind or outside it. We have dealt with the question earlier when speaking of the nature of culture. Now we wish to look at the problem once more, this time from the point of view of culture change.

7.1.3.1 Culture Change and Psychology

We emphasized that culture is a *design* for a society's behavior. Culture does not consist of the actual historical events and things themselves but is the *underlying code* of things and events (*supra*, 5.2.1.2, 5.2.2.2.4). Culture is not history; history reflects culture. Many things and events may, of course, be used as symbols by the society in its underlying code for and of behavior. When culture changes, it is not so much that clothing, agricultural techniques, wedding customs, and funeral rites have experienced alterations but that *ideas* about clothing, agriculture, weddings, and funerals have changed. Culture change is essentially a change of knowledge and attitude, and therefore of design—of *ideas about* behavior. Culture change is the process by which new ideas regarding social behavior are generated and interpreted. To direct cultural change, therefore, means to propagate new *ideas* according to *psychological* laws. We are really speaking of laws of thinking, feeling, and evaluating: how thoughts, attitudes, and goals change; how they are substituted by other thoughts, attitudes, and goals; how they fuse with other thoughts, attitudes, and goals, and how they may even disappear. The basic tool in applied anthropology, we are saying, is something essentially psychological—symbolic.

7.1.3.2 Cultural Change and Sociology

But culture is more than a thing of the mind. There is a close interaction between culture and society, between the code for behavior and actual behavior. In fact, culture is the central force that affects behavior; and yet behavior more than anything else affects the code. As Geertz (1957:34) pointed out, we are dealing with abstractions of the same phenomenon—reality. As anthropologists, and especially as *applied* anthropologists, we are therefore intensely interested in both, actual behavior and the code.

7.1.4 KINDS OF CULTURE CHANGE

There are various kinds of culture change and persistence. They may be categorized according to (1) the extent of change, (2) the rate of change, (3) the object of change, and (4) the manner of change.

7.1.4.1 Type of Change Based on Extent of Change

By *general persistence*, anthropologists mean the tendency of a society to resist change in a wide area of life.

The Amish are a classic example: *anything* "worldly" is frowned upon. Since the Amish are "not of this world," they avoid all "worldly" frills including automobiles, television sets, and radios. Their dress style, beards, hairdos and haircuts allow little choice for the individual. In fact, even lapels and buttons smack of "worldliness" and must be avoided. Most dangerous of all forms of such "worldliness" is secondary education, which threatens to undermine the Amish lifeway at its roots. A true child of God does not place his trust in modern technology or schooling but sees his or her goal in life to be that of a simple, hardworking, honest, devout, cooperative, God-fearing tiller of the land.

Sectional persistence, on the other hand, affects only certain aspects of culture, the so-called "hard" parts of a way of life that are especially resistant to change. Americans, for example, show clear sectional persistence in regard to sports, political organization, the Constitution of the United States, and certain aspects of religion and personal freedom. However, as we have seen (*supra*, 6.3.2.3), Americans also have a passion for achievement, for expanding and competing, for economic growth, and for advancing science and technology.

Partial persistence refers to a custom that is carried out with reduced frequency or only in restricted situations. For example, nowadays in many, if not in most, American cities and towns a wake is held in a funeral home, rather than in the family parlor as was the general custom some decades ago. The use of horses at funerals is generally restricted to special ceremonies for outstanding military leaders or for funerals at Arlington National Cemetery.

Survivals are culture components that have with the passing of time changed their function and have become mere conventions and formalities.

The Easter rabbit and the custom of coloring eggs on Easter are survivals of old fertility magic. The fake slit on the lapels of men's suits and the useless buttons on the sleeves are survivals of one-time functioning parts of men's clothing. The fake woodpaneling on some station wagons is a survival of actual wood panels common at one time on similar vehicles called "beach wagons." The word for "train" in present-day baby-talk is "choo-choo train," although steam engines that used to go "choo-choo" have long disappeared.

7.1.4.2 Type of Change Based on Rate of Change

Revolution. As Kroeber (1948:408) defined the term, revolution is a "change suddenly precipitated with more or less violence, affecting a considerable total portion of a culture, and due to an accumulation of arrears, or lag, in progressive change." Classic examples include the Industrial and Bolshevik Revolutions and the spread of Christianity throughout Europe.

Style. A style is the very opposite of a revolution. It is a short-lived, more or less insignificant modification in a single element of culture, as, for instance, the modifications made annually in new car models.

Long-term Trends. Very much like a style, a long-term trend is a rather insignificant modification in a single element of culture, but it continues over a long period of time. Men's suits undergo at most very insignificant changes over a long period of time, while women's dresses must be different every season.

Cultural Drift and *Historic Accident.* Cultural drift is the process whereby "minor alterations slowly change the character and form of a way of life, but where the continuity of the event is apparent" (Herskovits 1950:581). Examples might be found in the pronunciation of English words or in the passage of the grammatical "it's I" to the ungrammatical but now correct "it's me." An historic accident (for instance, the many changes brought to the islanders of Manus by World War II [Mead 1956]) contrasts with a cultural drift and might be defined as "the more abrupt innovations, whether arising from within a culture or coming from outside a given society" (Herskovits 1950:581).

7.1.4.3 Type of Change Based on the Object of Change

Change may occur at any of the three levels of culture: in the form, in the function, or in the basic assumptions, values, and drives. It may affect a trait, complex, institution, or even a wider range of behavior. (Each of the various anthropological perspectives described in chapter 5 have, of course, their own designations for the "parts" of culture.)

7.1.4.4 Type of Change Based on Manner of Change

Changes can occur through (1) substitution, (2) loss with no replacement, (3) incrementation with no displacement, and (4) fusion.

Substitution. Substitution takes place when a traditional element is dislodged by a new element.

In Roman Catholic liturgy, Latin has been dislodged by the vernacular. The automobile has almost completely dislodged the horse. The ballpoint pen has dislodged the fountain pen. In grade schools, paper has dislodged the slate. Corporal punishment has disappeared from many American schools and homes not because children no longer need to be punished but because other disciplinary measures have dislodged the proverbial rod or because parents and teachers have adopted new theories regarding the rearing of children that place the rod in the same era as the horse and buggy.

Substitution may be *complete* or it may be *partial.* As a rule, it is partial. Such is the case because innovations are generally unable to fill some or most of the functions that the original form has filled. In other words, new symbols, perhaps more often than not, do not perfectly coincide in meaning and value with the old. Some down-to-earth examples of substitution follow.

Except for ethnic baking, homemade cakes have been completely displaced in the United States by a whole new industry of substitute ready-mixes and frozen pastries, while homemade bread has practically disappeared by giving way to bakery bread. Such is also the sad history of homemade ice cream and homemade sausage.

Complete replacement of old armament and ammunition with ever-more sophisticated instruments of war is perhaps the rule rather than the exception with the military, for such is the nature of the beast. Cannons have been replaced by planes, helicopters, rocketry, jet-propulsion, computerized "seeing" weapons, and nuclear arms; horses have been replaced by airplanes, helicopters, tanks, armored troop carriers, trucks, and jeeps. Although, with the military, complete substitution is, as we have just pointed out, perhaps the general rule (or at least the goal), cadets in military academies must, nevertheless, learn to manipulate swords, ride horses, and shoot old-fashioned cannons for ceremonial purposes, a function that no modern equipment has succeeded in replacing. Thus even in the most modern and most efficient army, navy, or air force there will also be some *partial* substitutions.

The safety razor, especially the more recent versions like the double-track type, has completely displaced the straight razor—except, of course, in the case of professional barbers and professional cut-throats, who still insist that the old-time straight razor is easier to handle and indeed more effective for their particular purpose. Electricity, to offer another example, has not been able completely to dislodge the old-fashioned kerosene lantern or pressure lamp on some camping trips and wherever electrification is still impractical or impossible. Similarly, even in civilian life, the horse has been only partially displaced: even in our supersonic age, horses are needed for parades and they are found indispensable in modern cities like New York for crowd control. Large ranches are, in fact, maintained in Wyoming for raising horses for such present-day needs as rodeos, parades, and circuses, while ranches for breeding race horses are found especially in Kentucky.

In New Guinea the otherwise highly appreciated steel knife is sometimes regarded less suitable for butchering pigs than the simple traditional bamboo knife because the latter can be easily sharpened by pulling off a fine strand of fiber at the implement's cutting-edge. The New Guinea highlanders also may prefer their traditional wooden digging-stick to obtain their day's supply of sweet-potatoes from the garden because the clumsy heavy steel spade may damage the roots, vines, and the still-immature potatoes.

Our examples show that although complete substitutions occur, partial replacements are the more common. In fact, complete substitution is generally reached in stages by way of partial change. Generally, a new pattern will completely dislodge the old only if the innovation seems to fill a need more satisfactorily than the traditional pattern and, at the same time, perform *all* the functions of the old. This fact should be remembered by all engaged in socioeconomic and religious educational programs. If a Christian community is to be relevant and its message acceptable, it must offer clearly better "products" than its "competitors." Otherwise, the acceptance will be at best only partial, selective, and syncretistic.

Loss with No Replacement. Loss consists in the dislodgement of a traditional pattern without at the same time providing a substitute. This type of culture change often takes place as a kind of chain reaction: one element in a culture disappears and many things associated with it disappear as well.

Loss through a chain reaction occurs, for instance, when a myth is shattered and everything tied to the myth disappears with it. Or, with the disappearance of earrings, the custom of piercing the earlobes disappears. Men's trousers used to have a little "watch pocket" on the right side just below the belt line; with the arrival of the wrist watch and its advantages over the traditional pocket watch, the special little pockets also disappeared. One also wonders if men's vests have not largely disappeared because they were no longer needed for a place to keep the pocket watch.

Incrementation. Incrementation is the introduction of additional elements into the culture without a corresponding displacement. A good, easily understandable example is the impact that television has had on American ways.

When television became a part of the American way of life, such increments appeared on the American scene as television antennas on rooftops, factories that manufactured television sets, stores and salesmen that sold them, advertisements in newspapers that promoted television set sales. Architects began to design special rooms and nooks specifically for television sets. Furniture manufacturers designed special easy chairs for television watching. Television newscasters and television performers had to be found and developed. A new section of the newspaper was needed to comment on programs. A weekly, *TV Guide,* soon appeared. Television called for an army of specialized photographers and reporters around the world; engineers, writers, choreographers, and directors at various levels, called the "television industry," had to be organized. Federal laws and special commissions had to be created to regulate the industry and the sponsors of programs and their commercials.

Fusion. Fusion is the amalgamation of an innovation with a traditional pattern. One of the finest examples of fusion is Neo-Melanesian, commonly known as "Pidgin English." Neo-Melanesian is a true language that was spontaneously formed when European sailors and settlers arriving in New Guinea tried to communicate with the native population. The resulting language was "English" only in the sense that most words showed some semblance in sound and were remotely close in meaning to those in "Pidgin"— "business"—English. The phonological, morphological, and syntactic structure and the underlying thought patterns of Neo-Melanesian are definitely more Melanesian than English. (Some of the vocabulary is of German, Oceanic, and other origin.) To offer an example, the word *han* evidently derives from English *hand*. A fusion of English and Melanesian linguistic structures and thought patterns is illustrated in the following interesting phrases:

brukim han (literally, "break the hand") = to make a fist; also to fracture one's hand or arm.

han bilong pam (lit., "a hand belonging to a pump") = a pump handle.

han bilong em nogut (lit., "his/her hand is no good") = she is menstruating. This is a euphemism. During such periods a woman is not allowed to cook or touch certain things; hence her hand is "sick, useless, and not at all good."

han bilong diwai (lit., "the hand of a tree") = a branch.

han bilong singlis (lit., "the hand of a singlet [British for 'under-shirt']) = a sleeve.

han pensil (lit., "a hand serving as a pencil") = a fingerprint of illiterates used in contracts instead of a signature.

han wara (lit., "a water's hand") = a tributary of a river.

paitim han (lit., "fight," i.e., "strike the hand") = to clap one's hands.

plentihan (lit., "plenty/many hands") = centipede.

sekan long haus lotu (lit., "shake hands in a house of worship) = to get married.

han bilong pik, dok, pusi (lit., "a hand of a pig, dog, pussy cat") = the foreleg of a pig, dog, or cat. The Melanesian pictures quadrupeds as having two arms and two legs like humans. (Cf. Mihalic 1957:41–42; 1971.)

7.1.5 SUMMARY AND MISSIOLOGICAL APPLICATION: GENERAL NOTIONS REGARDING CULTURAL CHANGE

7.1.5.1 Summary

1) Some cultures tend to change more rapidly than others, but all cultures change; they all have a double tendency: a tendency to persist and a tendency to change.

2) Because culture is the underlying code of behavior (a set of ideas or norms), it is a thing of the mind. The locus of culture change is therefore in the mind of the individual member of society, and culture change takes place in accord with psychological laws. These laws, however, become externalized outside the mind: culture is, in fact, the central force influencing behavior, whereas behavior deeply affects culture.

3) There are various types of cultural change. Depending on the extent, rate, object, and manner of change, culture change may be described in the following ways: as general, sectional, or partial persistence; as a revolution, culture lag, or historic accident; as change affecting the first, second, or third level of culture; as a substitution, a loss with no replacement, an incrementation with no displacement, or a fusion.

7.1.5.2 Missiological Application

7.1.5.2.1 Theory of Culture Dynamics and Mission Action

If the Church *is* mission, it is by its very nature an agent of culture change. In anthropological and therefore purely human terms, the work of the establishment of the Kingdom of God is culture change.

Despite the limited nature of our present knowledge about culture dynamics, what *is* known can cast considerable light on the most promising approach to mission. Any worldly enterprise, such as that of government or business, will do its best to predict future trends and to plan its course; diagnosis and foresight are a part of worldly undertakings. There is always an element of gamble present, but the choice before the wise of the world is not between knowing infallibly what the future has in store but rather to come up with a wise and reasonable calculation. In the words of the Gospel, it is unfortunate that like the wily manager "the worldly take more initiative than the otherworldly when it comes to dealing with their own kind" (Lk 16:8), or as the King

James version has it, "the children of this world are in their generation wiser than the children of light." Too often, Church policy and strategy are based on tradition and guesswork rather than on analysis and on the light obtained from scientific research and study. Every industry has its team of researchers whose sole task is to discover more effective and more efficient ways of manufacturing and marketing the product in question. The Church needs besides "salesmen" also capable researchers who are deeply interested in applying human light to mission action; not the least important area of needed research and study is that of culture dynamics.

Change can be slow and superficial; that is, there can be a change merely in *style* that gives the Church time to adjust. But change can be deep and sudden—*revolutionary*. Only a century ago, speed was judged by the clap of hoofs; today, speed is calculated to one-billionth of a second. Pebbles, fingers, the abacus, and mechanical calculators have given way to unbelievably fast computers. Satellite communication has indeed turned the globe into a "village." Jets have given way to supersonic planes, orbiters, and the space shuttle. Contact between cultures in even the most remote parts of the world, for better or for worse, is a fact that must be dealt with. Western national economies have suddenly been transformed into international economies that have worldwide problems. New giant cities with equally gigantic social, economic, political, and moral problems have mushroomed around the world. Ideologies of every ilk are now in fierce competition with the Gospel, and no society is spared.

Today as Christians we cannot afford to take a leisurely pace. Radical changes are taking place all around us, overnight. Christians must somehow keep up with this breakneck speed. Unfortunately, little is known about revolutionary change and how to deal with it. Today, scholars and experts in every field, especially at Christian universities and research centers, must look beyond their purely secular responsibilities and help those engaged in mission better understand the meaning of revolution and what mission in a revolutionary age really entails. *Revolutionary* approaches are needed in *revolutionary* times. Willy-nilly, revolutionary apostolic methods are no longer a matter of choice for the Church. In the mad race forced upon the Christian today, there is no choice for the Church, unless, of course, the Church does not mind being left behind in the dust.

7.1.5.2.2 The Locus of Culture Change and Mission

The locus of culture change is the individual *mind*. When culture changes, it is the set of ideas that individuals share with one another that changes. Because the commission given the Church is to "make disciples" of all nations, the Church's task is that of an educator: its task is to bring about a change in the mind and heart of "disciples." It is "the mind of Christ" (1 Cor 2:16) that must be adopted. To be effective, the approach employed by church workers in bringing about any change, religious or socioeconomic, must be aimed at the *mind and heart* of people. Human efforts in mission are therefore essentially *psychological*—in other words, educational and communicational.

The awareness that mission consists in altering the socially defined *mental* content should set the whole tone to ministry, whatever its nature may be. In ministry, we are ultimately dealing with the acceptance of ideas. It is not the number of tractors or the size and sophistication of hospitals, schools, and churches that determine how much progress has been made in agriculture, medicine, education, or religion and morality. One must look into the minds and hearts of people. What ideas and values do the individuals have about agriculture, health, education, religion, and morality?

The church worker is, in a word, primarily an *educator*, and the primary tool of the Church is *communication*. The church worker's primary task is not so much to deliver things as it is to communicate ideas. The church worker, whatever the ministry, is not a delivery man who drops off hybrid corn seed for poor farmers or medicines and bandages at various points called "mission dispensaries" or "hospitals." The task is not so much to deliver things, however desperately needed such deliveries sometimes are, but to communicate. As the Chinese saying goes, "If you give a man a fish, you feed him once; if you show him how to fish, you feed him forever." The words of the Great Commission to "make disciples" are well chosen indeed, and the Great Commission's emphasis and focus on communication and culture as a symbolic system are as anthropologically as they are missiologically sound. It goes without saying, of course, that communication and education do not make action unnecessary. The Gospel cannot be communicated unless it is also practiced (*supra*, 1.2).

7.1.5.2.3 Loss and Functional Substitutes in Mission Action

Karl Rahner has rightly complained that today theological truths are only too often "being silenced to death" and, we might add, that with the demise of such truths, many other truths disappear from the lives of Christians as well. For instance, not only has the concept of sin vanished from many minds, but truths that are associated with sin are gone as well. We refer, for example, to the obligation of avoiding occasions of sin, to the gravity of scandal, to the fact that thoughts, desires, and omissions could be evil too, to the teaching regarding final judgment, to the fear of God, and to no small measure to the Ten Commandments themselves. In a word, the theory enunciated in this section on culture dynamics tells us that any cultural loss may involve more than the loss itself; there may be a *string* of associated losses.

Sometimes important values are unavoidably, and in fact unintentionally, cast off. When abandoning the undesirable, we should not overlook the fact that even treasured values may be linked to the undesirable. Without wishing to justify Catholics of the extreme right in any way, there is no denying that when the vernacular liturgy replaced the old Latin form of worship, unavoidably lost were such associated positive benefits as the Gregorian chant. One might, of course, rightly argue that this was but a part of the price paid for something of greater value. It nevertheless does illustrate the principle of loss through association.

As a basic principle in applied anthropology, every effort should be made to foresee undesirable losses and, if these losses are foreseen, every effort should be made to provide appropriate substitutes. This principle has always been part of the thinking underlying traditional missionary accommodation, a principle that makes good sense in modern missiological anthropology as well.

For instance, with the great emphasis on liturgical worship and the de-emphasis of nonliturgical devotional practices after Vatican II, overlooked were the benefits associated with certain aspects of traditional Catholic devotional life. Instead of regarding nonliturgical devotions as competing with and obstructing liturgical goals, the liturgical movement should have tied private devotional life more closely to present-day theological thinking, to Scripture reading, and to liturgy itself. Instead, a void was created. Spiritually wholesome popular practices, such as the devout and meditative recitation of the Rosary and the Sacred Heart Devotion, should have been updated, and the updated forms of such devotions should have been encouraged (cf. Luzbetak, Mehok, Smith 1975:v–xxx).

Similarly, with the virtual abolition of the traditional meatless Fridays and the Lenten fast, an important symbol was officially removed without providing an adequate substitute. Until recent times, Fridays and Lent in many American Catholic homes and parishes had a deep symbolic meaning, evidenced, for instance, by the number of people that would go to weekly confession and daily Mass during Lent and abstain voluntarily from alcohol, luxuries, and parties. For various reasons (e.g., legalism on the part of Church authorities and religious educators regarding the rules of fast and abstinence, the awkwardness and difficulties involved in observing Friday and Lenten rules in modern times, and the many dispensations that had to be made) the age-old fast and abstinence rules were abolished with little thought given to the need for meaningful updated functional substitutes. Except for a few days of the year on which fast and/or abstinence was still regarded as "obligatory," Catholics were encouraged "to do something on their own." Penance, however, to be *communal* can never be vague. To be a symbol, expectations must be far more concrete than "something" and "on your own." Consultations should have been held throughout the U.S. dioceses to find ways to symbolize in a meaningful, updated, and *social* fashion sincere repentance—ways to humble one's self, ways to plead for forgiveness of God and community, ways to express one's total surrender to God. Instead, Fridays and Lent seem simply to have been stripped of the last few vestiges of meaning, with no adequate substitute provided. Moreover, by participating in communal penance, such as Fridays and the season of Lent, one was formerly able to profess his or her belonging to the group doing the penance, and thus Fridays and Lent contributed to religious identification and solidarity. Fridays and Lent also provided a further opportunity to confess one's faith openly, the way one does on Sundays when one goes to church. Friday was another small but salutary reminder (besides Sunday) of belonging to the Body of Christ, a very salutary reminder especially today in a world that does not recognize sin or Redemption.

The fact is that communal penance is thoroughly human, found throughout the world and throughout the history of religion, found in the Koran, in Judaism, in the life and teaching of Christ, in the early Church, and throughout Church history. Although the only prescribed cultic fast day in the Old Testament was the Day of Atonement (Lv 16:29ff; Nm 19:7), fasting is frequently mentioned by the Sacred Writers (McKenzie 1965:274). Fasting was practiced, for example, as a sign of repentance (Neh 9:1ff), as a sign of mourning (2 Sm 1:12), and as a form of prayer of petition (Ezr 8:21ff; Ps 35:13). Fasting was practiced by the infant Church as a common form of prayer of petition, repentance, and longing for Christ's Second Coming (e.g., Acts 13:2ff; 14:23).

Instead of watering down and, for all practical purposes, abandoning the practice of communal penance which is so deeply rooted in the Judaeo-Christian tradition and in human nature itself, Fridays and Lent as symbolic sacred times should have been updated, emphasized rather than de-emphasized, and the legalistic concern about the obligatory nature "under pain of sin" should have been appropriately changed. Unfortunately, with the virtual abandonment of the social character of the symbol, an important educational and ascetical value was sacrificed, with little or no meaningful replacement.

In much the same manner, by attacking magical practices as mission churches must so often do, newer Christian communities may sometimes actually undermine important community and family values. Fear of black magic may sometimes be the only effective way a wife can force her husband to be faithful and to responsibly care for his family. Or sometimes by eliminating magic, tribal discipline may be threatened.

This does not mean, of course, that Christian communities in which superstition plays a major role have an unresoluble dilemma. The missiological principle of functional substitution must enter into the picture: substitutes compatible with the Gospel must be a part of the community's strategy. Much better use must be made of existing liturgical, paraliturgical, and scriptural possibilities, including the annointing of the sick and the general concern for the ill, disabled, and elderly; and the ritual blessing of children, homes, land, stock, farming implements, plants and seeds, fishing boats and equipment. Religious processions through the gardens of an agricultural community in the spirit of the old Rogation Days may indeed be very much in place today. Exorcism itself may, in fact, be a special need among certain peoples. All this should, of course, be accompanied by fervent prayer, fasting, almsgiving. Appropriate instructions on God's providence, love, and concern for his children must also be provided.

What we are trying to emphasize with these illustrations is the fact that in devising a mission strategy we should be aware of the various types of culture change. A change might be brought about intentionally or unintentionally through loss, substitution, incrementation, or fusion; it may be slow or it may be rapid. In any case, functional replacements must as much as possible not be overlooked or regarded as unimportant. Even if one is unable to accept the examples given, one cannot deny that we are speaking of anthropological concepts that have extremely important missiological bearing.

7.2 THE PROCESSES BY WHICH CULTURES CHANGE

Three distinct processes are involved in culture change: (1) the primary or innovative processes that give rise to change; (2) the secondary or integrative processes that attempt to fit the innovation into the existing culture-whole; and (3) terminal processes that bring about the more or less final result of change, e.g., equilibrium or disequilibrium.

7.2.1 THE PRIMARY OR INNOVATIVE PROCESSES OF CULTURE CHANGE

How is culture change triggered? It may be triggered from within or from without the society. If it is triggered from within the society, we speak of *origination*; if from without, we speak of *diffusion*. Diffusion may be *unconscious*, *voluntary*, or *forced*.

7.2.1.1 Origination

Origination occurs through (1) invention or (2) discovery. *Invention*, which includes not only objects but abstractions as well, results from the application of previous knowledge, whereas *discovery* does not use previous knowledge as much as it adds to it. Discovery is totally unintended, whereas inventions are sometimes the result of a positive quest for new ideas. Even the simplest societies do a certain amount of deliberate experimentation, whereas throughout the world many of the greatest innovations have been accidental (among these discoveries were vulcanization and penicillin). Inventions generally have important antecedents, often resulting from the unconscious pooling of many hardly noticeable previous innovations by members of the society. If Jules Verne had been an Australian aborigine, he probably would never have been dreaming about trips to the moon; Jules Verne's culture had prepared him for such fantastic, but now realized, dreams.

An invention or discovery need not be a unique event in history. Parallel inventions and discoveries have constantly taken place. Some interesting examples of simultaneous originations suggested by Kroeber (1948:342) are the telescope, by Jansen, Lippershey, and Metius in 1608; sunspots, by Fabricius, Galileo, Harriott, and Scheiner in 1611; logarithms, by Napier in 1614 and Bürgi in 1620; calculus, by Newton in 1671 and Leibniz in 1676; nitrogen, by Rutherford in 1772 and Scheele in 1773; oxygen, by Priestley and Scheele in 1774; the steamboat, by Jouffroy in 1783, Rumsey in 1787, and Fitch and Symington in 1788; the telegraph, by Henry, Morse, Steinheil, Wheatstone, and Cooke about 1837; the phonograph, by Cros and Edison in 1877; the North Pole, by Cook and Peary in 1909.

There are a number of reasons for such more or less simultaneous inventions and discoveries. (1) Often the very nature of the invention or discovery demands a multiple origin. For example, practically all humans, and monkeys, peel their bananas the same way. In all cultures, we wash with water; Cleopatra was a remarkable exception when she washed in milk. (2) Some parallels are pure coincidences. For example, the word for *river* in a language spoken in the Caucasus Mountains is the same as *river* in one of the Micronesian languages; and, for all we know, the word for "big toe" may be the same in the Greek *koiné* as in one of the Polynesian dialects. (3) Human needs and human psychology are often the same; that similar solutions should be stumbled on is therefore to be expected. (4) When societies have similar or identical knowledge and beliefs and share similar purposes, there is a great possibility of similar inventions and discoveries. The feverish military competition between the Soviet and the Western blocs has brought about many very similar inventions that may not all be attributed to spying. The Nobel prizes are sometimes shared by several individuals, as their scientific contributions are similar and interdependent.

We speak of *basic*, *developmental*, or *revolutionary* origination when we refer to inventions or discoveries that give rise to a large number of other innovations. This is the case with steam power, electricity, the gasoline engine, the radio, television, and computers. A *secondary* or *modificational* origination is a further elaboration of a previous invention or discovery, as, for instance, in the application of computer science and technology to domestic appliances and automobiles.

7.2.1.2 Diffusion

Far more common than origination is change from without—known as *diffusion*. The fact is that the cultures that are situated at crossroads of contact today, as throughout the history of humankind, are the ones most likely to grow and develop most rapidly.

Diffusion can take place without direct contact between the borrowing culture and the culture of origin. Symbols, with or without the objects they signify, are able to migrate. In fact, the object itself may migrate. Thus, potatoes came to Europe from South America by way of Spain in 1560; from Spain the potato migrated to England in 1586 and was adopted as a wholesome and basic food; from England it diffused to Ireland in 1590, to Germany in 1651, Scotland in 1683, Sweden in 1725, and Russia in 1744 (Honigmann 1959:210).

Anthropologists speak of different types of diffusion (after Honigmann 1959:212–215). (1) *Stimulus diffusion* occurs when an idea, the "stimulus," is borrowed and is then independently elaborated upon by the borrowing society. Today, Japan is accused of borrowing the original idea for most of its successful products from the West instead of being involved in costly and risky original research. Japan is said to develop such ideas further; in fact, its products surpass the prototype in quality and Japan is able to outmarket the originator. In New Guinea, a steel axe head without a handle is preferred to one with a handle, because the owner likes to add his own handle to fit his personal grip. When English is adopted by a Third World country as a trade language—as, for instance, in many African countries, India, and the Philippines—it is adopted not without changes in pronunciation in accord with the borrowing country's own phonological patterns. When diffusion takes place without alterations, it is referred to as *pure diffusion*. Thus franchises such as Coca Cola, McDonald's hamburgers, and Colonel Sanders' Southern fried chicken are meticulously controlled against any type of unauthorized alterations. (2) Diffusion is described by anthropologists also as *gradual* and as *rapid,* depending on how fast or how slowly the process takes place. The adoption of birth control is rapid in some countries, gradual in others. (3) Diffusion is spoken of as *objective* or *technical,* depending on whether the object itself or the technique was adopted. The Yir Yoront of Australia adopted the steel axe itself, not, however, the technology associated with the manufacturing of the implement (*supra,* 6.2.3.3.2). (4) The diffusion may be *strategic* or *nonstrategic,* depending on whether or not the diffusion calls for extensive preparation for its adoption. Industrialization, for example, demands extensive modification in trade, transportation, housing, education, food production, and, in fact, in the whole lifestyle. Computerization, too, calls for extensive preparation, even in technologically advanced countries. (5) Diffusion is described also as *active* and *passive.* Watching a Russian ballet does not require participation and is therefore passive diffusion as far as American culture is concerned, whereas eating Russian caviar and drinking vodka is quite active. (6) Diffusion is described also in terms of the *object* of change—as diffusion of a form, function, or the underlying mentality (of a symbol, meaning, or core metaphor) or of a simple trait, complex, institution, or larger complex of institutions. (7) Finally, diffusion may be *by direct contact*. That is, elements of a culture may be first borrowed by a neighboring people and then spread by direct contact to other societies; on the other hand, diffusion may be brought about through *indirect contact*, through intermediaries such as traders.

In concluding our brief discussion on diffusion, we must mention two important situations that are closely related to direct diffusion: *acculturation* and *force*.

Some decades ago, acculturation was the primary concern of not a few anthropologists. It was soon felt that a distinction had to be made between diffusion and acculturation. In accord with the recommendation of Redfield, Linton, and Herskovits, who served on a special committee for the Social Science Research Council, the term was defined as "those phenomena which result when groups of individuals having different cultures come into continuous firsthand contact, with subsequent change in the original culture patterns of either or both groups." Although acculturation is closely related to diffusion, the concept includes a whole gamut of dynamic processes. It is not any single process but rather a special contact *situation*, one that is direct, continuous, involving extensive borrowing, and extending over a longer period of time. Moreover, today the term generally refers to a contact between a weaker and a more powerful people, with the subordinate society adapting itself to the stronger, usually Western, society.[1]

Sometimes the quickest and most radical change comes about through a second form of direct diffusion, namely *force*, *violence*, and *rebellion*. Here, too, we are not talking about a single process but about a whole spectrum of dynamic processes, about a *situation* in which direct diffusion plays a major role. Meant is, for example, the violent suppression of peoples by an elite, a ruling group, or a tyrant, by a conqueror, by colonial powers, revolutionists, or terrorists. Understandably, under pressure the weaker social group may at least partially adopt the behavior of the more powerful. In a matter of decades, the Bolshevik Revolution has radically transformed Eastern Europe and most of Asia. Within a relatively short period of human history, colonization had similarly changed the world for better or for worse. Mission history (*supra*, chapter 3) can also, unfortunately, provide us with many examples of forced diffusion.[2] It should be noted, however, that even pressure cannot bring about culture change without the inner acceptance and collaboration of and by those being pressured (*infra*, 7.3.1.1).

7.2.2 SECONDARY OR INTEGRATIVE PROCESSES

The primary or innovative processes just described trigger a whole series of secondary processes which we shall call *integrative*. Although even philosophers of repute are not always perfectly logical, the human mind, however simple or sophisticated, strives for harmony and consistency. In response to this universally valid tendency, there is a certain amount of imbalance and uneasiness created whenever a new idea enters a people's underlying code of behavior. Conflicting symbols begin to compete and interfere with one another. The secondary processes aim to restore balance and to integrate the innovation with the traditional design for living. However, as we shall see in our section on the terminal processes of change (*infra*, 7.2.3), sometimes changes fail to keep pace with the innovations, and disorganization sets in. The members of the society, the architects of the society's design for living, are, as a result, constantly adjusting and modifying the design, sometimes more successfully, sometimes less so, with one change in the blueprint requiring many others. To bring about the desired consistency, either the novelty undergoes change or the traditional ways and values are modified. The balancing and integrating modifications of which we speak may affect all three levels of culture—form, function, and mentality (the symbol, its meaning, and the core metaphors).

The innovation itself may be modified through *reinterpretation*, or additional changes may enter into the culture-whole through *ramification*, or both processes may be involved. Important in this connection are the concepts already described regarding the various types of culture change, especially loss, accretion, substitution, and fusion.

7.2.2.1 Reinterpretation

Reinterpretation is sometimes called reformulation, contextualization, redesigning, reorientation, reworking, reconstellation, readaptation, recasting, and reintegration.

But before we enter more deeply into our discussion of the process of reinterpretation, we must point out a very important principle, important in a particular way to missiological anthropology. Our concern is the *principle of selectivity*, a point to which we shall have to return again. Suffice it here to point out that, as a general rule, a society will hesitate or refuse to adopt any new idea that it senses to be inconsistent with its cultural system or for which it feels no need. If, on the other hand, the new idea appears at least in some respect desirable, the society will, as we shall see, begin to reinterpret it so that it does fit into the symbolic system. It is, of course, possible for the unwary architects of the cultural blueprint, the individual members of the society, to allow a novelty to enter into their plans without realizing it. Reinterpretation would then also most likely take place unconsciously.

7.2.2.1.1 Reinterpretation of a Borrowed Form

Of the three levels of culture, the first level (form) is usually the least likely to undergo modification. When borrowed by a tribe just recently out of the Stone Age, a steel spade would most likely remain a steel spade, an ordinary tin can would remain a can, and a sweater would remain a sweater—that is to say, as far as the *form* is concerned. We underscore the word *form*. The Ten Commandments and the Sacraments likewise tend to remain as borrowed in their *form*.

A change in form would occur, for example, if for the Palm Sunday procession local flora were to be used instead of palms. The Decalogue would be changed in form if an additional commandment or an omission of one were involved. The Eucharist would be changed in form if, instead of bread and wine, rice and tea were to be used, or if, instead of the traditional words of consecration, some other passage of Scripture (for instance, the account of the Annunciation, Birth, or Ascension) were to be used. In such cases, we would say that the forms themselves were reinterpreted, recast, and reformulated.

7.2.2.1.2 Reinterpretation of Meaning/Function

As we have just seen, the form of the cultural element borrowed tends to remain the same; it is the meaning that changes (Luzbetak 1970:215–220).

Napoleon's soldiers were known for their eagerness to ingratiate themselves with the Russian peasantry whenever and wherever possible. Not being able to speak Russian, the soldier would refer to himself in French simply as *bon ami*, i.e., "Call me 'Good Friend'!" That is exactly what the Russian peasants did; they called the French soldiers *bonamicheski*, retaining the French form (*bon ami*) but reinterpreting the word to mean "scoundrel." (Herskovits 1950:555.)

A devout artist, quietly painting in his studio in an old Spanish monastery, will portray the Blessed Virgin in harmony with the aesthetic and moral values of Spain and will depict his sacred subject as the ideal of moral integrity, spiritual purity, and womanly dignity, while his Protestant Scandinavian counterpart would try to express slightly different aesthetic as well as spiritual values corresponding to the Scandinavian and Protestant ethos. The same holds true of the African artist painting his Black Madonna.

In America a spade is (i.e., *means*) an ordinary practical tool of an unskilled laborer and is usually kept in the garage by most people for occasional use around the house. The function, meaning, and usage of a spade, and the corresponding symbolic impact may be quite different in another culture. In the highlands of New Guinea the author has observed how men would carry their heavy long-handled spades with them even on long journeys, not because spades were practical tools to have around like a pocket knife but because they were a way of "keeping up with the New Guinea Joneses"; the spade was reinterpreted as a status symbol.

To a North American, a Mexican poncho is a poncho; to a Mexican, some ponchos are for men and some for women. Not to appreciate the difference would be like a North American male wearing a woman's dress—not quite kosher, to say the least. The author recalls the shock he received in the Wabag area of New Guinea when two of his altarboys entered the sacristy each sharing a part of a lady's dress that they had obtained from a European settler, the one lad wearing the blouse and the other the skirt—and nothing else. Here was a total recasting of the meaning of clothing in general and women's clothing in particular.

The Hawaiian *hula* was originally a semi-sacred dance. However, when performed on a New York stage it is completely stripped of its religious significance. Americans have reinterpreted the dance as pure secular entertainment. (Linton 1936:409.)

The author can recall countless examples of such reinterpretations of *meanings* of borrowed forms that he has personally witnessed in the New Guinea highlands during his four-year sojourn there.

Newspapers, for example, were greatly appreciated by the illiterate highlanders, not for the news contained but for rolling cigarettes. The newspaper remained what it was, newsprint, but its use, hence meaning, changed.

Plastic saucers could not be successfully introduced by storekeepers; that is, not *as* saucers. But as soon as an imaginative New Guinean thought of drilling holes on the edge of the dish so that the saucer might be tied and worn like a *maiduma*-shell on the forehead, the stocks of saucers were soon sold out.

The author had often wondered why the schoolchildren were always so eager to empty his waste basket. The mystery was solved one day when he had to stop a fight between two small children battling over a few sheets of crumpled up carbon paper that had been thrown away and which the children now reinterpreted as a beauty aid for making their hair jet-black.

Or again, despite the fact that the people wore only loin cloths or cotton *laplaps*, men and boys were eager to acquire a belt as a decorative belly band, while some pregnant women sought them, as was learned later, for the purpose of abortion. Similarly, thick woolen sweaters, although out of place in the hot tropical sun, were sometimes worn nevertheless not to keep the body warm but "beautiful."

And there is the story told of the pioneer New Guinea missionary and explorer Father Willy Ross. When he arrived in Mt. Hagen he soon found out that despite the cool, even cold, rainy days, long underwear were a bit too warm. Since he realized that he would never use his long johns, he discarded them one day with his rubbish. The following Sunday he was to receive the shock of his life. Proudly strutting down the middle aisle with chin held high, deliberately late for Mass, came the ghostlike figure of the headman of the tribe dressed in his pastor's discarded snow-white underwear—or, should we say, "outfitted in his brand-new reinterpreted tuxedo"?

Reinterpretation, it must be remembered, does not proceed in some haphazard way but, as a rule, it occurs in accord with the lifeway of the borrowing society. Thus the wheel, the so-called greatest invention of all times, first appeared in the Old World, and from there diffused to Assyria, Iran, India, and then on to Egypt. In Egypt, domestication of animals was unknown when the wheel was introduced; however, pottery was an important element. Consequently, the wheel was not utilized (reinterpreted) in terms of a vehicle drawn by an animal but as the potter's wheel. In Europe, the wheel arrived after the domestication of animals; there the wheel was utilized in terms of a vehicle. (Benedict, R. 1956:191.)

7.2.2.1.3 Reinterpretation of Basic Assumptions

Innovations that experience the strongest resistance are those that are on the third level of culture. These types of innovations directly contradict the society's world view or religion, as we shall see when we deal expressly with the factors involved in change (*infra*, 7.3).

7.2.2.2 Ramification

By *ramification* we mean the fanning out of secondary processes within a culture. Owing to the interrelatedness of cultural patterns (a theme stressed in the preceding chapter), when a change occurs in one aspect of culture, other changes take place as well. Such changes take place especially through additional loss, increment, substitution, and fusion, and are usually reinterpreted according to the existing cultural structure. We have seen how the indiscriminate introduction of the steel axe among the Yir Yoront of Australia had deleterious consequences throughout the culture (*supra*, 6.2.3.3.3). We have seen also how the introduction of the radio and television had ramifications for perhaps most people living today. Urbanization and industrialization invariably initiate profound ramifications. We now offer some additional examples to show the importance of the concept for a proper understanding of culture dynamics.

Blankets, bush knives, steel axes and spades, cotton loincloths, and other Western goods not only served the general Western purposes of such items when taken over by the New Guinea highland peoples but immediately were ramified in reinterpreted form as symbols of prestige and as objects appropriate for gift exchange and the bridewealth.

The word for "pick-axe" in the Middle Wahgi language is *kongmam*, literally meaning "mother-pig." Since the language has no voiced G-sound at the end of a word, the local people interpreted the Pidgin English *pik* to mean "pig" rather than "pick." Asked why they called the tool "pig" and, in fact, a "mother-pig," the reply given was, "The pick is very much like a pig; in fact, very much like a mother-pig. You see, when we build roads for the government, one man (the one with the 'mother-pig') roots up the ground the way a real mother-pig does, while her 'piglets' (the men with the spades) break up the clumps." The original confusion of "pick" with "pig" and the further ramification of the word as "mother-pig" are very much in harmony with the important role pigs play in the New Guinea way of life.

Formerly the Winnebago Indians were supposed to have had rather lax attitudes toward toilet training for children. Their philosophy was quite sound: No diaper, no bother! But as soon as the Indians introduced wooden floors, no diaper meant plenty of bother. Tired of trying to keep the floor clean, the Winnebago Indians introduced two additional novelties, diapers and early toilet training, two unexpected ramifications of the new-fangled flooring. (Honigmann 1959:14.)

Ramification affects not only the material and social life of a people but the ideational as well. The Western world view reaches the remote areas of the world through the various news media and educational lessons. One new idea ramifies into a dozen others, and these into still others. Art, music, dance, philosophy, and ritual may all be similarly affected.

A concept closely related to ramification is *culture lag*. Innovations do not ramify evenly throughout a culture or society. Some aspects of culture are clung to with far more resistance than others. Owing to the process of *selectivity*, for example, the integration of the Gospel in the culture of mission lands as well as in the West is generally uneven. We shall have more to say on the subject when we discuss syncretism (*infra*, 7.3.4.2.3). Such *lag* occurs not only in the culture itself but also in the actual behavior of the community. Some individuals of the community may accept the novelty; others will hesitate or oppose it. Invariably, tensions will arise among individuals and groups. The educated classes, professionals, and the elite may accept a novelty, whereas the others may resist it. There seems to be such tensions arising among Roman Catholics in the United States today: the college-educated more likely than not lean toward the acceptance of liberal ideas, while the others tend to be opposed, indifferent, or confused. A very common form of social conflict is the type that occurs between immigrant parents and their American-born children. It takes place among other reasons because the parents are reinterpreting the novelties in terms of their old-country cultural experiences.

7.2.3 THE TERMINAL PROCESSES OF CULTURE CHANGE

When we speak of terminal processes of culture change, we mean the overall results or direction of the constant shifting from balance to imbalance in the society's struggle for integration and equilibrium.

The terminal processes of special interest to missiological anthropology are (1) development as opposed to decline, (2) elaboration as opposed to simplification, (3) growth and reduction-segregation, and (4) equilibrium as opposed to disequilibrium. Just which processes will win out will depend on the interplay of the many factors (cf. Luzbetak 1970:220–228). The issue of interplay will be discussed fully in a later section (*infra*, 7.3).

7.2.3.1 Development

We have seen how culture is a design for living, a blueprint for life. The adaptive system of a society "develops" as the society's experience with the world and life grows and its contact with other cultures increases. Although *development* takes place in all aspects of life, the term most frequently refers to a development in regard to the physical environment. Humans can control their climate through improved housing, heating, air conditioning, awnings, bathtubs and showers, swimming pools, clothing, umbrellas and raincoats; they control distance through improved means of travel—from the invention of sandals to horseback riding, from automobiles and trains to airplanes and luxury liners; distance is controlled also through such means of communication as telephone and telegraph systems, radio and television, satellite communication, the printed word, film, and video-cassette recorders. Humans are able to control energy by training animals and using steam, electrical, petroleum, and nuclear power. Humans control their food supply through various agricultural techniques and animal husbandry, and through various methods of preserving food. At least to some extent, humans are also in control of bacteria and viruses, as well as of their broken limbs and deteriorating organs.

Such technical development by no means implies that a technologically advanced society is necessarily able to deal more successfully with its social problems or that it has a greater capacity to cope with its ideational environment more satisfactorily than a less technologically developed society. As advanced as the United States and similar nations may be technologically, their social and spiritual problems become proportionately that much more complex and overwhelming. We refer, of course, to such only-too-well-known problems as delinquency, drug addiction, alcoholism, social and racial strife, crimes, terrorism, wars, and the general loss of a moral sense and spiritual values.

7.2.3.2 Elaboration

By *elaboration* is meant the growing diversification and complexity of the cultural content. The concept as such prescinds from desirability or undesirability. It does, however, imply the presence of a greater number of alternatives and specialties. Thus, tools become more specialized; clothing becomes more differentiated according to status, social roles, and usage; the varieties of food increase; buildings become more diversified and more specialized; social roles become more complex; philosophies increase and compete with one another; the arts, science, and religion become more sophisticated.

Factors related to elaboration include, especially, the presence of a potential for elaboration (elaboration begets elaboration); the presence of a large population; and the presence of cultural elements that are cumulative in nature, that is, elements that persist and allow for cultural additions. (Honigmann 1959:279-280.)

7.2.3.3 Equilibrium

Despite the constant shifting from balance to imbalance through growth and development and elaboration, somehow cultures generally seem to maintain a more or less satisfactory overall balance or *equilibrium*. This general state of balance is known as *eunomia* or *euphoria* (after Radcliffe-Brown), a "feeling of well-being" characterized by an overall steadiness in culture, a high morale, self-confidence, and a sense of security. Such steadiness, of course, should not be exaggerated; we are speaking of only a more or less satisfactorily established, smoothly operating state of culture and society, not of a utopia.

An important gyroscope for maintaining balance despite the constant shifting between balance and imbalance is the process known as *reduction-segregation*. To cope with the growing complexity of culture, the individuals of the society (the architects of life's blueprint) begin to divide the rapidly expanding cultural inventory through the process called *reduction-segregation*. The inventory is arranged into specialties based on age, sex, occupation, and other social norms so that less and less of the culture-whole need be mastered by any individual. The ideas, norms, and knowledge are systematized and reduced to more generalized concepts, principles, laws, theories, disciplines, and schools of thought. Today in more technologically advanced countries, reduction-segregation is having a hard time keeping up with development and elaboration, so that some speak of an "information glut or revolution" and of a "future shock."[3]

As in the case of cultural elaboration, here, too, when speaking of equilibrium we are not making any value judgments as to the desirability or undesirability of the balance. Equilibrium merely implies balance, efficiency, and smoothness of operation. Equilibrium does not connote correctness, justice, or truth. A godless materialistic culture may sometimes be better balanced than a struggling but God-fearing one. A harmful weed may be a healthier and stronger specimen of plant life than a highly valued flower.

In an acculturative situation (the close, firsthand, and more or less continuous contact between a weaker and more powerful neighbor), a society may achieve equilibrium in one of three ways. (1) In a *symbiotic* situation, each of the cultures specializes in certain activities, the one becoming dependent on the roles and service of the other. Thus, a fisherfolk may supply the fish for an island agricultural society, while the latter provides for the vegetable needs of the fisherfolk. (2) In a situation of *stabilized pluralism*, each of the cultures in contact remains basically independent, as in the case of the indigenous Indian populations and the so-called ladinos in Central America. (3) Equilibrium may also be achieved through *assimilation*, the complete blending of the two cultures (Honigmann 1959:270–271).

7.2.3.4 Disequilibrium

Sometimes the integrating processes fail to keep up with the changes taking place. Disintegration then begins to set in. Disintegration is a form of cultural pathology. It renders one's enculturation useless. The traditional symbols, their meanings, and the underlying premises, values, and goals no longer serve as a map for living. The mastery of the design for living gives the individual and the society a sense of confidence, an assurance of being able to cope with the particular physical, social, and ideational environment. Disintegration brings uncertainty, confusion, frustration, and low morale; behavior loses its meaning and becomes unpredictable; the values become doubtful and hazy.

Such *dyspattern*, *dysfunction*, and *dysconfiguration* (and consequent decay) can come from within as well as from without the society. History is full of tragic disappearances of cultures, notable examples being Ancient Egypt, Greece, and Rome. We shall briefly examine four situations particularly significant in today's world.

7.2.3.4.1 Culture Decay and Death through Violence
The division of Europe after World War II has destroyed such national identities as Latvia, Estonia, Lithuania, and Eastern Germany—and possibly all of Eastern Europe—not only politically but in other ways as well. Today, wars are being waged around the globe that will certainly change the cultural face of tomorrow's world. The greatest of all threats, of course, is the ever-present danger of a nuclear holocaust.[4] As Albert Einstein so succinctly put it: "I don't know what kind of weapons we'll be using in World War III, but I do know for sure what weapons will be used in World War IV—bows and arrows." Yes, if there should ever be another world war, and if humans should survive, fire may again have to be rediscovered and the wheel reinvented.

7.2.3.4.2 Culture Decay and Death through Contact

As history tells us, many cultures have disappeared as a result of war, conquest, and the injustices of colonialism. The mighty empire of the Incas came to a tragic end when its highly integrated society collapsed under the pressure of the Spaniards. No less than two-thirds of the total population died as a result of forced labor and diseases introduced by their colonizing European overlords. The remaining third was subjected to intolerable serfdom and a life of frustration, with only alcoholism and debauchery able to satisfy the once-proud and culturally rich Inca heart.

Discussing the unfortunate effects of European contacts and colonialism in Melanesia, William Halse Rivers summed up the situation as "a loss of the will to live." The expression may sound somewhat exaggerated; however, the contact did indeed bring about so much disorientation, disorganization, and uncontrollable change into the lives of some tribes that they had only boredom, frustration, disgust, and despair to look forward to. It is known that the Tasmanians and some American Indian tribes completely disappeared with their cultures through Western contact.

The Swiss anthropologist Alfred Bühler (1957:1–35) provides us with a case from the Sepik River area of New Guinea. Despite the fact that the ruling white population has always been relatively small, since World War I the native people have nevertheless been subjected to intensive acculturative pressures. The result was not one of symbiotic cooperation and independence or balanced reintegration but cultural disorganization. Formerly the tambaran-houses served very important functions in the community: they were the main symbol of tribal solidarity; they were the art studios and museums of the people; they were the temples, the sources of supernatural power and security; they were, in fact, the very heart of native life. Christianity did not succeed in becoming a satisfactory alternative for the old ideology, while the material benefits derived from Western contact left the native heart cold and lifeless. Patterns that formerly gave the individual prestige, such as the possession of shells, ceased to stir up pride and admiration in the native heart, while no real substitute was found to fill this void. With the coming of the government, plantations, and mission stations, many individuals began to dream of the day when they would be able to achieve the same material advantages as the Europeans. Full of expectations they flocked to plantations, government posts, and mission stations for work and education, the two roads that promised success. However, serious frustration set in and the hope of ever participating in the white man's world of wonder seemed to have been shattered. Associated with this disillusionment was the deep feeling of inferiority; subconsciously the New Guinean was convinced that he was far below the white man in intelligence, ability, and value, a point impressed on him in various ways by the white population. Countless changes thus entered into the native way of life and made the culture meaningless—indeed a classic situation for the rise of Cargo Cults and a total cultural disorganization.

7.2.3.4.3 Disintegration and Death of Cultures through Modernization

Today the greatest danger of serious disintegration of cultures comes from the understandable but often misguided craving of societies around the world for rapid and even instantaneous technological change. Multinational corporations are speeding up the process by moving to the Third World, where the wages are incomparably lower than in the West and where there are no fringe benefits and unions to worry about.

In Africa, Latin America, India, and elsewhere, an ever-increasing proportion of the population is moving into urban and industrialized localities. Thousands of Latin Americans are daily leaving their sheltered, although usually not ideal, traditional environment in favor of poverty-stricken, filthy shanty towns that usually skirt the larger cities. Cities like Caracas are a beautiful picture to behold, except for the frame containing the numberless shacks that encircle the city.

It is not the physical inconveniences and health conditions alone that are deplorable. Perhaps the most painful consequences of urbanization are the depersonalization and cultural disorganization that accompany migrants to the shanty towns. As uninviting as the conditions of the home-village may have been, there was always the comforting sense of belonging, a sense of solidarity; there was law and order and cooperation in the community and among kin; there was a sense of responsibility for the common welfare and a satisfying feeling that "someone is interested in my well-being." With the abandonment of social ties, however, the migrant frequently loses his or her sense of responsibility toward others and one feels totally isolated. In the traditional environment, the individual had a definite status and a corresponding role to play. In the new surroundings, the person is alone. Self-centeredness is a typical trait of dwellers of shanty towns, where you have to "stand on your own feet" and "shift for yourself": nobody helps you; why should you help anyone else? The enculturation process did not teach the individual much about what one had to do to stand on one's own feet. Even in traditional conditions, a death in the family is an indescribably painful and tragic experience, especially if a father or mother dies, but at least the shock is somewhat softened by the warmth of kinship, tribal, and community patterns. In a shanty town, one is largely alone, especially at times when others are needed most.

The problem of eking out a living in the poverty-stricken home-village was bad enough, but in the shantytown one soon learns that moving was hardly the solution. The migrant family leaves behind much of its old value system and traditional controls of behavior. The father becomes an alcoholic or a drug addict and the mother becomes the breadwinner, leaving the children on their own. Mental disorders become a major problem. Respect for elders disappears and delinquency grows. Overcrowding seriously affects the moral life of all. Family quarrels become almost as common as the shacks in which the squatters live.

The picture just described may not be true of every family, nor perhaps of every shanty town; however, the picture is unfortunately common enough to be painted in the terms that we have employed (cf. Puebla Conference, Final Document, in Eagleson, Scharper 1979: no.71, 418f).

In almost any rapidly industrialized area, one finds mining camps, laborers' quarters, and so-called company towns. South Africa is a typical example. Sometimes, as in New Guinea, young men are recruited for temporary service on a coastal plantation. The experience is not entirely negative, but it does call for special pastoral care to counteract what might be considered as *partial* cultural disorganization. Describing the situation of a few decades ago, the author observed that

> employment on the coast has definitely widened the young man's horizon. His interests now seem to extend well beyond the tribal territory. He is now able to speak Pidgin English fluently. He has become sure of himself and has now a better chance of succeeding on a mountain plantation near home. He feels superior to his less-traveled brother. However, not everything that he has learned on the coast is necessarily a boon to him: he now knows how to gamble and has perhaps grown fond of gambling; types of sexual perversion unheard of in the mountains may have been ordinary plantation gossip; his respect for the white man has definitely diminished and perhaps the dangerous seed of the Cargo Cult has been planted among the mountain people while a few of the young men were laborers on the coast. Although the anopheles mosquito is present in the mountains . . . the recruits return with much more malaria than they had when they went to the coast and much more than their natural resistance permits. One wonders if the romance was really worth the price. [1958a:73]

The mining camps and company towns of South Africa, India, and elsewhere have their own, but similar, stories of woe to tell. A whole new field exists today, called urban anthropology (*infra*, 8.4.4).

7.2.3.4.4 Disintegration through External Migration

One of the earliest and most important studies on the subject of migrations is the classic pioneering work in empirical sociology by W. I. Thomas and F. Znaniecki (1918–20). This five-volume study, titled *The Polish Peasant in Europe and America,* documented for the first time the disorganization that can result from the decrease in the influence of traditional social patterns on migrants. The researchers contrasted Polish family life as found in the home-country with that of Poles in America.

In Poland, "the large-family group" (including relatives to the fourth degree) rather than the nuclear family owned the land on which the peasants worked. The large family was closely linked to other such groups through marriage. Authority was in the hands of the older members and was duly respected by all. Interests centered around the farm and the closely interacting socioeconomic group into which the individual was born. When the Polish peasants migrated to America, the New World was indeed a *new* world to them, a world for which they had not been prepared by their particular enculturation. As a result, the immigrant had to be satisfied with a job that required no special skill and had to become a city-dweller rather than a farmer as in the old country.

In America, the immigrant not only lacked economic security but also greatly missed the solidarity and support of the old large-family group. Formerly, everything had been predetermined by custom; in the new environment, the immigrants had to plan every step for themselves.

The Polish immigrants, despite the prejudice against them and despite language barriers and associated clannishness, somehow managed to adjust to their new environment. They nevertheless felt greatly threatened by their new surroundings. To protect themselves against the danger of losing their "Polishness," they settled in Polish neighborhoods where Polish for a generation or so remained the primary language. They erected large parish churches and schools of which they could be proud and through which they hoped to preserve their Polish heritage. The immigrants formed a variety of social organizations with others who spoke the same language and understood each other's problems.

Despite the low salaries that they received in coal mines and steel mills where they usually worked, they managed to build for themselves relatively comfortable homes in the security of Polish neighborhoods. They also discovered new sources of security in the American way of life, such as insurance policies and bank accounts.

However, life was basically difficult and the transition was not smooth or successful in all cases. Because wives were no longer involved in farm chores and farm work, and their activities were limited to housekeeping and their responsibilities to those of homemakers, the fathers were the sole breadwinners. Strict paternal authority, traditional to the Poles, rapidly declined as the children and wives became more and more Americanized. Not seldom did it happen that the low salary of the unskilled Polish laborer forced him to become involved both in heavy debts and sometimes also in heavy drinking. Their American-born children could not help but be confused by the conflict they felt between the values of their American environment and those of their foreign-born parents. At times, moral values taught by their parents appeared unreal and questionable. Delinquency, in fact, became a serious problem in not a few of the Polish immigrant families. Despite the ups and downs, the Poles turned out to be among the most successful of immigrants in business, finance, education, politics, in church leadership, and in general adjustment (cf. Greeley 1977). The key to their success was the ever-present hope that their *children*, not so much they themselves, would enjoy the fruits of their labor and many sorrows.

Problems like those just described are being experienced today by countless refugees and immigrants around the world. America, of course, continues to be *the* land of immigrants. In fact, as late as 1960, no less than half of the adult Roman Catholics in the United States were themselves foreign-born or had foreign-born parents (Greeley 1977:184). No less than 17 million European immigrants passed through Ellis Island alone between 1892 and 1954. In recent times, America has seen the influx of thousands of Vietnamese, Filipinos, and others from Asia, and millions of others from Latin America and the Caribbean and elsewhere. Certainly one of the major challenges of the Church in the United States is the challenge of meeting the cultural needs of immigrants during the process of Americanization (Fitzpatrick 1987:95–165). Without overlooking the uniqueness of present-day immigration problems, much might be learned from the Polish and other earlier ethnic experiences.

7.2.4 SUMMARY AND SELECTED MISSIOLOGICAL APPLICATIONS: PROCESSES BY WHICH CULTURES CHANGE

7.2.4.1 Summary

1) Three distinct processes are involved in culture change: (1) the primary or innovative processes that give rise to change; (2) the secondary or integrative processes that attempt to fit the innovation into the existing cultural whole; and (3) the terminal processes that are the final result of change.

2) The primary or innovative processes are origination and diffusion. Origination occurs from within the society, diffusion from without. The latter may be unconscious, voluntary, or forced.

3) Origination may be an invention or discovery. Invention is generally understood as an innovation based on previous knowledge, whereas discovery is not. Discovery may, in fact, be unintended.

4) Diffusion is change from without; that is, through borrowing. There are various types of diffusion: (1) stimulus diffusion, wherein the "stimulus" for borrowing is borrowed and then the novelty borrowed is independently elaborated; (2) gradual or rapid diffusion; (3) objective or technical diffusion, depending on whether the idea of the object or the idea of the technique is adopted; (4) strategic or nonstrategic diffusion, depending on whether a long preparation for the adoption is necessary or not; (5) active or passive diffusion, depending on whether participation is required in what is borrowed or not; (6) diffusion affecting the form, function, or underlying philosophy; (7) diffusion affecting a trait, complex, institution, or a complex of institutions; (8) diffusion achieved through direct or indirect contact.

5) Closely related to diffusion are acculturation and force. *Acculturation* is the direct and continuous contact and borrowing extending over a long period of time, generally between a weaker and a more powerful society. The former

adapts itself to the latter. By *force,* we understand the involuntary adoption of behavior that eventually leads to culture change.

6) Secondary or integrative processes are triggered by the primary or innovative processes. Such secondary processes aim to restore the consistency that has been disturbed by the novelty. On the one hand, there is the drive to reject the foreign element as foreign and "out of place"; on the other hand, there is the urge to accept it and make it into an integral part of the system. To solve the tension, the society must either reject or modify the novelty, or it must change its own traditional ways through reinterpretation and/or ramification.

7) According to the principle of selectivity, a society tends to reject or adopt novelties in accord with its felt-needs.

8) Borrowed forms are least likely to undergo reinterpretation. Generally speaking, it is the meaning of the novelty that undergoes modification. Most resistant to adoption are novelties that contradict deeply felt needs, especially those on the third level (e.g., those affecting the existing world view or religion). However, such felt-needs can be in regard to economic and social aspects of life as well.

9) Culture lag refers to the fact that innovations do not ramify evenly throughout a culture or society.

10) Terminal processes are those associated with the end result of change. They include development, elaboration, reduction-segregation, equilibrium, or their opposites. Development is growth and generally refers to technological advancement; elaboration is a gain in complexity; reduction-segregation is the process by which the complexity of culture is simplified especially through categories, principles, theories, laws, and specializations; equilibrium is the general feeling of balance and well-being, of satisfaction and trust in the culture, a feeling that life's plan (culture) is indeed working. The opposite of equilibrium is disequilibrium or imbalance brought about especially by violence, suppression, cultural contact and conflict, urbanization, or migration.

11) By ramification we mean the fanning out of secondary processes within a culture.

7.2.4.2 Missiological Application: The Processes of Change

7.2.4.2.1 Mission and Interpersonal Relations with Innovators

Although culture is a *societal* possession and mission is the discipling of *nations* (Mt 28:19), the only way a church worker can achieve a religious or socioeconomic change is not through an abstract society but through concrete *individuals.* There is no other way of introducing or incarnating the Gospel or bringing about a desired socioeconomic change than by involving *individuals* who deviate from the traditional ways. There is also no other way of directing reinterpretation, controlling selection and ramification, or restoring equilibrium than through the individual bearers of culture. They are the "yeast" of the Gospel (Mt 13:33), whose new ideas and values eventually penetrate the whole "mass of dough" (the whole society). These individuals are the all-important *innovators* of anthropology who must be reached to initiate change.

Correct interpersonal relations with the "yeast" will stimulate it to rise and penetrate the whole mass of dough. Sometimes it seems that the business world is more conscious of the need for human sensitivity than those engaged in mission. We refer to the down-to-earth treatment of interpersonal relationships as found, for instance, in the Dale Carnegie classic *How to Win Friends and Influence People*, the excellent training manuals of the Peace Corps, and the many recent handbooks and guides now available for people preparing themselves for overseas business or government assignments.[5]

We call this practical interpersonal sensitivity *rapport*. Rapport presupposes three basic principles: (1) respect the individual person as an *individual*; (2) in fact, respect the person as an *important* individual; and (3) respect and treat this important individual as a *friend* (cf. Luzbetak 1970:229–239).

To respect an individual as an individual is difficult enough in one's own social and cultural environment, but to do so becomes doubly difficult when subconsciously there is a feeling of superiority, such as often exists in a Christian toward a "pagan," in a "knower and lover of God" toward an "idolator," an educated Westerner toward a simple, illiterate non-Westerner. To recognize and treat individuals as individuals—that is, taking into account their own temperaments, talents, handicaps, preferences, and name, and not lumping them all under one stereotype—will be particularly difficult to the newcomer to a strange cultural milieu where all people seem to look alike, have names that sound alike, and seem to act in the same peculiar and seemingly inferior manner.

To treat an individual as an individual means, first of all, that we recognize that the person has *feelings*. These feelings are often culturally defined.

At times one cannot very well argue with one's stomach, but heroes do exist. We refer to the gentleman who is supposed to have nonchalantly wrapped up in a lettuce leaf a caterpillar he found crawling about in his salad and quickly and heroically swallowed it so as not to embarrass his hostess.

Without going that far, he might have done something suggested in a Peace Corps manual (cf. Spector and Preston 1961:46). The story goes something like this: a government overseas worker was once invited to a dinner at which he was offered a fish head to eat, a way of singling him out as the guest of honor. To refuse the fish head would have been a grave insult, but to gulp it down would have been to tempt the Lord. The fish head looked even larger than it was, and the longer he looked at it the larger it became. Very cleverly he suggested: "Back in America, where I come from, we have the custom of saving the delicacies for the ladies; so, if Madame Hostess wouldn't mind, it would make her humble and unworthy guest extremely happy to see *her* eat this most delicious-looking fish head." The man was not exactly honest but he certainly was sensitive to the feelings of others, including his own.

To respect culturally defined feelings is difficult, especially when one does not share the same culture as the person whose feelings one wishes to respect.

What might be regarded as maintaining discipline in a classroom through firmness and consistency in the United States may very well be harshness and inconsiderateness toward children in another country.

What Americans regard as snobbishness Japanese teachers may regard as ordinary respect due to them as teachers, just as American parents expect a certain amount of deference from their children. When going on a school outing with their students, for instance, Japanese teachers would consider it degrading if they were to be "piled into the bus" indiscriminately with the students, whereas American teachers would most likely find camaraderie on this rare occasion as being very much in place.

Not only must we treat individuals as individual beings; we must also treat them as *important* individuals. Once again, in so doing we must use the native yardstick to determine what the word *important* means.

Depending on the culture, victory in an objectively insignificant local election or an appointment to an objectively insignificant government post may be anything but insignificant in the eyes of the individual and his community. Missionaries visiting their bush-schools or mission doctors checking their medical outposts should encourage and publicly praise and award the native teacher or nurse whenever praise is due, using, of course, not the sophisticated educational and medical standards of the expatriate's home-country but the realistic standards here and now.

The least that one can do to make a person feel important is to recognize that he or she has a personal *name*, as any good politician can tell you. In fact, politicians believe that they can never shake enough hands or kiss enough babies.

Al Smith, the first Roman Catholic to run for the presidency of the United States, had the reputation of remembering names. Once a person had been introduced, Al never forgot the name. As was later learned, however, his trick was a very simple one. Whenever he could not remember the name of someone he was supposed to have met at some time, he would apologetically ask in a very friendly tone of voice, "So sorry! What was the name again?" As soon as the name of the unfamiliar potential vote-getter was uttered, "I'm Martinelli, Hasenschwanz, Majewski, or whatever," Al Smith would interrupt the person and say laughingly, "O no, no! I mean your *first* name." The stranger was, of course, flattered, and Al Smith got himself an additional vote-getter.

However, the proper use of personal names and titles is closely tied to local customs and to the statuses of persons concerned. In cross-cultural relations, it is the customs of the local people that should be observed, not the preferences of the outsiders.

In most American offices and factories it is not unusual to call one's boss by his or her first name, a practice that is unthinkable in most European countries. To address supervisors by their first names may be quite offensive and demeaning. Many American blacks seem to prefer to be called by their title and family name rather than by their informal first name, e.g., Mr. or Mrs. Jones rather than Jack or Bess.

It is the culturally preferred name that should be learned and used in dealing with people.

Rapport demands that the individual be treated not only as being important but as a friend. Without going into a long treatise on the meaning of friendship, it may be sufficient to point out that friendship anywhere in the world presupposes the following: (1) mutual understanding, (2) common taste, (3) common interests, (4) mutual support, (5) mutual admiration, and (6) mutual accessibility. Such traits will lead to mutual trust, affection, and identification. Other traits might be mentioned, but these will suffice to make our point, namely that to a large extent *such traits are culturally defined*.

—*Mutual Understanding*. A friend is never a stranger, nor can a stranger ever be a friend. Anyone engaged in mission should know his or her people, understand their ways, and appreciate their values. It may not be out of place to stress here the need for pastors, teachers, or any other church workers not to remain a closed book. The community must know them to love them as friends. To speak of oneself every now and then, especially if the pastor, teacher, or any other church worker is of another culture, is very much in place. We should not, of course, extol our native land in a triumphal and haughty way but speak about our ways to let the community understand the "strange" person that we happen to be. Once the community appreciates that their pastor is culturally different, it will be more inclined to overlook the (culturally) "naive" remarks, the "foolish" decisions, the "impolite" behavior, and the occasional "rudeness." Just how often one should speak of one's cultural background, family, or home-country will depend on the expectations of the local community.

In Japan, for instance, a spiritual person ought to be detached
from things of this world, including one's own family. Elsewhere,
on account of the emphasis placed on family loyalty, such detach-
ment may scandalize the people, since it would give them the
impression that the spiritual person is disloyal to the family and
ungrateful to the parents, the two worst sins imaginable, certainly
incompatible with the role of a spiritual person.

—Common Taste. Conflicting tastes, no less than strangeness, will discourage friendship and identification. Tastes are largely determined by one's culture, especially in more homogeneous societies that have not experienced the
impact of the terminal process that anthropologists call "elaboration" (*supra,*
7.2.3.2). Hence, the adoption of local ways and values should be of great
concern to all engaged in mission. It is a question of sacrificing one's own
cultural tastes rather than of sacrificing friends.

—Common Interests. A pastor, director of a school or hospital, and in fact
anyone called to a ministry must learn as soon as possible not only to work for
the community but also to share responsibilities with it. Nothing generates
common interest as much as common involvement. A "none-of-your-
business" attitude discourages the growth of such interest. It is easy for the
community to sense an "I'll-call-you-when-I-need-your-advice" spirit. Such
pastors, directors of schools or hospitals, and other church workers make
cooperation and corresponding interests impossible by their constant attitude
of "*I* am the boss around here." Church workers should be as much as possible
partners with the community they serve by sharing their burdens and successes
with them.

In turn, those called to a ministry, whatever it be, should be deeply involved
in the interests of the community they serve—in their crops, their fiestas, and in
the expected additions to their families. Again, the pastor should be aware of
the native understanding of "interest." Especially in a society or subsociety in
which family solidarity is stressed, the preacher and the teacher in particular
would do well to emphasize family values, to uphold family authority, and to
share the community's respect for family ties.

—Mutual Support. Interest and good wishes, however, are never enough to
cement true friendship. Needed is actual assistance. "A friend in need is a
friend indeed" is not only a saying; it is true anthropological and missiological
wisdom. But here once again we must point out that the meanings of "assistance" and "need" are going to depend on the community's culture.

Paternalism is generally not what the people are looking for. Paternalism
humiliates. Although outright charity is necessary and indeed in place, the
emphasis should always be on providing opportunities for self-help.

True charity will be tailored to the local felt-needs. In a highly elaborate
culture (*infra,* 7.3.3.2), the most needy are perhaps the mentally handicapped,
as such an elaborate culture calls for a design for living that presupposes a

healthy mind. However, in simple societies of Africa or the South Seas, it is often the *physically* handicapped that seem to be most needy. In many such societies, the economic system is so simple that even mentally handicapped individuals can "make a living"—that is, they can take part in the economic system, perhaps work in a garden, or even climb a coconut tree and feed themselves. It is the physically handicapped who need the greatest assistance. In highly elaborate economies, physically handicapped individuals are not only able to survive but also to compete and even outdo their physically sound colleagues in medicine, law, literary work, business, and politics. Franklin Delano Roosevelt was handicapped but served longer in the White House than any other individual and that during the most difficult years in American history—during the great Depression and World War II. *Disabled* does not mean *unable*. Gallaudet University in Washington, D.C. is a university exclusively for students who have hearing and speaking disabilities. In other words, when we speak of assistance, we mean filling the *real* needs of a community, especially those determined by the culture and the actual situation.

We hasten to add that the type of assistance that encourages friendship must be *mutual* rather than one-sided. As early as possible, the Christian community must learn to support the local and universal Church. Friendship is a give-and-take relationship.

—Mutual Admiration. Friends are people we admire. If missionaries expect to be admired by the community they serve and thereby become friends, they must master the "silent language" of the community, the meanings behind their behavior. Even the way a person walks and closes doors communicates an idea—not seldom the wrong idea, one of timidity, suspicion, haughtiness, and disregard for others. If missionaries fail to learn the people's silent language they may, in fact, be communicating a message of harshness, timidity, stupidity, impoliteness—qualities that one would normally not find in one's best friend.

Of special importance is to learn and appreciate the self-image of a people. Every society has its own picture of a good person. The self-image represents the ideals of the society, ideals which, even if perhaps never reached, deserve to be admired. Respecting the self-image of the people is one of the surest ways of achieving entry into a community and winning the confidence, friendship, and cooperation of its members.

—Mutual Accessibility. Friends are mutually accessible. Habitually to brush people off and to have little time to listen to their worries, problems, and needs does not encourage friendship. A regular leisurely stroll through the village or market place, with an appropriate greeting for all and a short chat here and there, is one of the ways of making oneself accessible and of promoting friendly relations. Availability during "office hours," in the church, classroom, or clinic, generally is not sufficient to form the friendly ties between the community and those engaged in ministry. Time must be set aside for contacts *outside* of such official hours—once again in accord with the expectations and

the "silent language" of the community. A pioneer missionary in New Guinea gave as reason for walking rather than traveling by horse, bicycle, or jeep from station to station, at times over long distances, the fact that in this way he was able to exchange a few words with everyone he would meet along the road.

Nothing could be more detrimental to friendly relations than not being accessible even during "office hours." Just what reasonableness means in regard to office hours should be determined not only by the culture of the pastor but by the culture of the parishioners as well. Especially in missionary situations, the pastor is regarded as "a public servant," someone to be on call twenty-four hours a day. Worse still is the fact that the importance of the business to be discussed is determined by local norms that may very well appear unreasonable to outsiders.

Nonetheless, accessibility does not mean excessive familiarity. Here, too, local norms must be respected. The fact is that most cultures impose a certain distance on roles of respect. This distance governs relationships with teachers, leaders, and persons dedicated to religion. The culturally imposed distance sometimes makes those in authority and highly respected positions the loneliest persons on earth. Most painful is such loneliness if a difference exists in attitudes in this matter, with the culture of the religious person having one set of expectations and the culture of the Christian community another.

All that we have just said about rapport, however, fades into nothingness compared to the importance of learning the language of the people and to the importance of what was said in our opening chapter, our "Theological Preamble," where we tried to paint a portrait of a truly ideal instrument of God—ideal theologically as well as anthropologically.

7.2.4.2.2 Mission and the Integrative Processes of Change

As we have seen, after a change has been initiated it must be integrated with the rest of culture through secondary processes of change. A sufficient number of individuals must accept the new idea and live by it. To accelerate the process, as already suggested, the mission approach should be focused on societal goals (*supra*, 5.2.2.6.2). Mission success should, therefore, not be judged by numbers alone but rather by how many individuals are influenced, who in turn will influence others. Innovators should include individuals who are able to reach beyond themselves and to touch others. In other words, we are saying that a good mission strategy will not lose sight of those individuals who are most suited for mission on the secondary or integrative level of change.

Unfortunately, too many pastors, religious educators, and other church workers, whether their direct involvement is in the religious or in the socioeconomic field, only too often seem to think that they alone are the laborers in the vineyard of the Lord, the sole contextualizers of the Gospel. It would be far more in accord with the Gospel parable of the yeast and mass of dough for these church workers to regard themselves as mere catalysts and to ascribe the transformation of the community to grassroots witnesses and leadership, the primary integrators of innovations.

Baptism is not a purely personal matter, a kind of certificate entitling one to membership in the Church and a kind of pass to enter heaven. The pastor, and all religious educators, should emphasize again and again, in season and out of season, that Baptism is rather a commitment to share one's faith with others. Mission is inseparable from one's own acceptance of Christ.

Cardinal Suenens is supposed to have expressed the thought in the following terms: "There is something wrong with the answer given in our old catechisms to the question 'Why did God make us?' " the Cardinal complained. "We should not say 'God made us so that we might know God, love God and serve God and thereby gain heaven' but 'God made us so that we might know God and lead others to know him, to love God and lead others to love him, to serve God and lead others to serve him, so that we might together gain heaven.' "

A missionary in India had the same understanding of what it meant to be a Christian, when he insisted that his converts say immediately after the words of their Baptism ("I baptize you in the name of the Father and the Son and the Holy Spirit") the admonition of Paul, "Woe to me if I do not preach Christ and him crucified" (cf. 1 Cor 9:15–17).

If the candidates for Baptism are not convinced of the missionary nature of Christianity, they are not really prepared for Baptism. The same holds for religious instruction in so-called de-Christianized countries of the West: conversion begins with oneself but does not end there. As St. John Chrysostom put it in his homily on the Acts of the Apostles, "There is nothing colder than a Christian who does not seek to save others. . . . It is easier for the sun not to give warmth and shine than for a Christian not to shed his light" (Homily 20,4:PG: 162–164).

7.3 CONDITIONS FAVORING CHANGE/PERSISTENCE

When cultures change, usually no single factor by itself brings about the change; rather, there is an interplay of factors, with one factor outweighing the other. It is the cumulative effect that ultimately decides the actual direction in which the scale tilts—toward change or against it.

We shall enumerate the more important factors involved in change known from anthropology, sociology, psychology, and history: first those affecting change in general, that is to say, factors affecting change or persistence either from within the culture through origination or from without the culture through diffusion; then we shall consider factors associated primarily, if not exclusively, with origination; and finally those that are responsible for diffusion. The study of culture change was at its height perhaps in the 1950s and 1960s. To this day, some of the best studies of change factors go to this period.

We shall make abundant use especially of H. Barnett's classic *Innovation* (1953) and J. Honigmann's *World of Man* (1959:204-272).

7.3.1 CONDITIONS FAVORING CHANGE IN GENERAL

7.3.1.1 Presence of Suitable Innovators

To innovate, there must be an innovator. Some individual or individuals must begin in their own minds to visualize a revision of their society's ways and values; they must (1) analyze and (2) mentally reorganize the change.

They must, first of all, analyze one or more cultural units that we have been calling *domains*. Some anthropologists prefer to use the term *mental configurations*, a concept used in a sense different from our earlier usage of *configuration*. A mental configuration here is a unit or cluster of closely related ideas viewed as distinct from any other unit in the given culture.

> For example, the essential elements of a birthday party form a unit quite distinct from a Christmas party or a wedding anniversary. We could not very well use Christmas decorations, including the Christmas tree and Santa Claus, in the middle of July at a birthday party. Such an analysis and revision would indeed be a remarkable innovation.

> Similarly, our mental configurations of the respective roles of a husband and wife are quite distinct. However, today, because of the women's liberation movement, the differences are being re-examined and revised. Today the majority (51 percent) of the labor force in the United States is composed of women; 60 percent of the children between the ages of seven and fourteen have mothers who are employed away from home. Changing diapers, bathing children, and doing the family laundry used to be the exclusive role of women, but not anymore. Elements of the husband-wife mental configuration have undergone considerable reshuffling—that is, considerable analysis and reformulation of a possible new arrangement in parental roles have taken place.

Secondly, innovators must not only analyze such mental configurations; they must (mentally) reorganize them as well.

> The guitar not so long ago used to belong to a purely secular context, although, judging by some classical art, angels seem to have been playing guitars for a long time. The guitar was regarded as an element of mental configurations called "romance," "cowboys," and "campfires." Polkas were likewise regarded as something purely social and secular, suitable especially for Polish weddings and taverns. It was unthinkable at one time that such

secular items as guitars and polkas would ever be used in a sacred context. Today, however, thanks to successful innovators, "Guitar Masses" are an ordinary event in parish liturgies, and "Polka Masses," although still causing a considerable amount of eyebrow-raising, are on their way to acceptance in some U.S. Polish parishes. To many, however, polkas are still as much out of place in church as a German "oom-pa-pa" band.

But before an actual revision in the culture is made, a sufficient number of individuals besides the innovator must accept it in real life, at least as an alternative or specialty. They are the integrators—in missiological terms, the actual inculturators. Such practical adoption of new knowledge anthropologists call *performance* (cf. Spradley, McCurdy 1980:302–325).

Let us look more closely at what is meant by *suitable* innovators. No value judgment is implied other than that which is contained in the phrase "suitable to effect a change for better or for worse." Regardless of what theory we may favor regarding culture change, the fact remains that unless there are suitable innovators, there will be no innovation. *Someone*, we said, must invent or discover the novelty from within the society, or *someone* must borrow it from without and rework it. Eventually, a sufficient number of *individuals* will have to accept and live accordingly so as to integrate the innovation into the existing culture. Whereas one society may have a relatively large number of dreamers, eccentrics, radicals, Utopians, "idea-persons," prophets and prophetesses, and charismatic individuals—in other words, a large number of "suitable" innovators—other societies may have a relatively large number of conservative ideologists, *immobilistas*, and diehards.

Good innovators have a penchant for change or at least are open to certain types of innovations. They often have a flair for going beyond the socially permissible range of variability; they are fond of experimentation. They also often have courage; to be different sometimes calls for considerable daring. For example, it must have taken no little courage for the first man to venture out into the streets in downtown Chicago or New York in a pair of Bermuda shorts, as it must have taken considerable courage or eccentricity for the first woman to wear the almost frightening tarantula-like attachments called "false eyelashes."

In a word, societies that are "blessed" with an abundance of suitable innovators and integrators at any given time will, for better or for worse, tend to change their ways more rapidly than societies that lack individuals with innovative talents and personalities. *Other things being equal, the greater the number and the more suitable the innovators, the greater the change.*

7.3.1.2 Social Attitude Favorable to Change

Just as individuals can be favorably or unfavorably inclined toward culture change, so can entire societies and cultures. *A favorable attitude of a society toward culture change stimulates change*. This atmosphere produces the ideal climate for origination and diffusion. We have pointed out how the Amish culture shows a *general overall* resistance to change (*supra*, 7.1.4.1). On the other hand, we have seen how Americans as a whole resist change in certain areas of life involving sports, political structure, and religious and other personal freedoms. However, Americans also have deep internal drives as far as scientific and technological change is concerned (*supra*, 6.3.2.3). We can expect relatively little change in the Amish way of life and much change in certain areas of American behavior. The principle we are stating here is: *A society that expects and favors change will change more readily than one that considers change undesirable, impossible, unthinkable, or evil.*

The intensity of the desire for change or the abhorrence of it may vary greatly. Margaret Mead, in her *New Lives for Old* (1956), describes how the people of Manus were not only favorably disposed toward change but also had an extraordinary craving for it, so that within a matter of twenty-five years the entire culture had been transformed.

7.3.1.3 Freedom of Inquiry and Action

Cultures differ as to the amount of freedom of inquiry and independence of action allowed. Islam, with its literal interpretation of the Koran, leaves little room for inquiry and innovation. Soviet authors, journalists, artists, and scientists must toe the party line, as perhaps nowhere else in the world, whereas freedom is the boast of journalists, artists, and scientists of the West. No society, of course, allows its members total freedom. Such freedom would be tantamount to anarchy and to not having a culture at all. It is interesting to note how epithets like "eccentric" and "crackpot" are labels used even in strictly scientific circles, where freedom of inquiry is almost a fetish. Even in the West, one must stay within the sometimes arbitrary bounds set by professional associations and "authorities" and "keep pace" with one's field (cf. Barnett 1953:68). Even in social work, in the religious life, and in mission work itself, there are "bandwagons" and fads.

The greatest freedom of inquiry and action exists during periods of cultural and social disorganization (*supra*, 7.2.3.4), as is the case during wars and revolutions, economic depressions, migrations, and during rapid urbanization and industrialization. This fact is appreciated, for instance, by Marxists and other revolutionists. They usually time their strategy to coincide with such periods of freedom of inquiry and action, when cultures are most vulnerable. Once the revolutionists have taken over and established themselves, they immediately deprive the society of its freedom of speech, assembly, and information lest such freedom undermine the newly won gains through counterrevolutionary innovations. Here the principle is: *The greater the freedom of inquiry and action, the greater are the chances for innovation.*

It should be noted, however, that political dictatorships, tyrannical regimes, and authoritarianism do not make all innovation impossible. Such obstacles to inquiry and action generally merely channelize cultural dynamics rather than put an end to innovation.

7.3.1.4 The Force and Effectiveness of Social Control

Individuals tend not only to conform to the norms set down by their culture but personally insist that other members of the society observe those norms as well. To see how deeply ingrained this tendency is, one need but observe children at play: they keep reminding each other about fairness and about accepted norms, and do not hesitate to ridicule and temporarily ostracize each other and occasionally blacken an eye or two so as to force an uncooperative playmate to comply. The growing child not only observes certain rules of etiquette at table but voices annoyance when a younger brother or sister fails to do the same.

For a similar reason New Guinea schoolchildren returning from boarding schools to their homes for vacation are sometimes pressed to discard their "sophisticated" cotton loincloths and dress "properly," that is, not to put on airs but to live like ordinary and genuine members of the tribe.

But over and above this personal urge to make others conform is the society's set of social controls. By *social control* we mean the set of beliefs, precepts, and institutions that serve to pressure the society as a whole to conform to accepted ways. According to a belief among the Indians of Guatemala, for instance, one of the most serious sins that might be committed is "to show off" and act like a *ladino*.

The members of society are thus both slaves and tyrants—slaves when they must wear tuxedos on a hot summer day, tyrants themselves when they invite others to a formal dinner and make the guests wear long-sleeved starched shirts, tight bow ties, and unbearably warm black woolen tuxedos instead of light trousers, sport shirts with open neck, and sandals.

Social control will vary from society to society, not only as to form but also as to severity, extent, and actual application of pressures. *Other things being equal, the more forceful and effective the social controls, the more persistent the culture. Aspects of culture to which little or no pressure is applied will tend to change more readily than those to which are attached severe and effective sanctions.*

7.3.1.5 Change as a Factor in Innovation

As we have seen earlier (*supra*, 7.1.5.2.3; 7.2.2.2), *change begets change* and therefore change itself is a factor in innovation. The introduction of literacy, for example, may effect a whole chain of increments, losses, and other changes: a school system, teachers, teacher-training programs, textbooks, libraries, newspapers, printers, publishers, higher standards of living, higher employment requirements, higher salaries, a different division of labor, adjustments in domestic chores and routines, and so on. One innovation gives birth to a chain of others.

7.3.1.6 Compatibility as a Factor in Culture Change

Among the most important factors in culture change and persistence is the cultural compatibility between the novelty and the existing culture, especially the novelty's compatibility with the basic assumptions, attitudes, and goals—in a word, with the deep, third level of culture that we have been calling "mentality," "psychology," "themes," and "core metaphors" of a people (*supra*, 6.3). According to the imperative of selection (*supra*, 7.2.2.1), a society tends to choose those novelties from among the many possibilities that are in harmony with its basic structure, its "soul." The third level of culture has, therefore, rightly been dubbed the "watchdog" of culture: nothing dare enter a culture that this watchdog does not allow. As a rule, a novelty will be accepted by the society only if the novelty and the starting points of reasoning, reacting, and motivating, which form the particular third level of culture, are compatible or if the otherwise incompatible novelty can somehow be fitted into the total cultural system through reinterpretation and reformulation (*supra*, 7.2.2). The following examples will illustrate what we mean.

A universal phenomenon is the tendency of languages to adopt words and expressions from other languages. Foreign loan words enter, for instance, into English and German without much difficulty since such loan words do not affect the rest of the culture. In fact, some seem to be more to the point and, for some reason or other, more appropriate, e.g., *liverwurst*, *wiener*, and *schnapps*. The form, i.e., the pronunciation of the loan word, may be somewhat reinterpreted, e.g., when an American pronounces the name of the city of Bonn, or when a German speaks of New York, both pronunciations follow the phonological patterns of the respective borrowing language. On the other hand, the meanings of *Bonn* and *New York* remain the same. The meanings of many loan words, however, are reformulated. The German word *Kontrolle* and the English word *control* are both derived from the medieval French, but the meanings have been reformulated. Similarly, the English word *character* does not coincide in meaning with the German *der Character* which can mean "willpower." Foreign words and expressions generally do not involve inconsistency with the borrowing culture, except that overuse of foreign words gives the impression of bombast and affectation, which collides with the American sense of equality. As a rule, loan words, if properly used, do not face much resistance. French, however, seems to be an exception; it is very resistant to foreign words, since the French regard linguistic purity as a matter of national pride, an important cultural value.

English has always been open to borrowing. Thus according to the estimates of lexicographers, as high as 90 percent of the English vocabulary may be of Latin origin, although English is a Germanic language. The borrowing from Latin entered into English especially as a result of the Norman Conquest in 1066 A.D., the spirit of the Renaissance, and the demands of modern times for a suitable, easily coined, and historically consistent scientific and technological nomenclature.

Birth control devices often face serious resistance in Moslem countries because the idea of birth control is inconsistent with the premise that children are a gift from Allah.

The apartheid in South Africa persists, among other reasons, because the white population finds the idea of equality with the black and the so-called colored population a threat to the very existence of the white culture and society. It is feared that if the nonwhite people were to be given their rights, the whites would not remain equal with the nonwhites for very long. The tables would be turned, and the political and economic power would pass over to the nonwhites who would then become the oppressors and the Europeans the oppressed. Whether such reasoning is valid or not, the inconsistency between the "one-person one-vote" novelty and traditional apartheid values gives rise to fierce resistance to change.

Until recent times, competitive civil service was unthinkable in Japan. According to an old Japanese never-questioned underlying assumption, *hereditary* rank alone made sense (Honigmann 1959:230). The idea of competitive civil service was incompatible with the established inner-logic of the people. The Japanese, to offer another example, had accepted many Chinese ways but rejected such customs as footbinding, since this novelty was incompatible with the Japanese abhorrence of mutilation.

The underlying set of assumptions, values, and drives, we said, serves as a kind of watchdog for a people's culture. Nothing enters the home that the watchdog does not allow. However, this is perhaps saying too much. The fact is that watchdogs are not all equally good watchdogs. Not seldom, incompatible elements are linked to desirable elements, so that they enter the home hidden behind desirable novelties. Many of our family values have been affected in this manner; for example, attitudes toward sex and violence have been adversely affected through otherwise extremely useful technological advancements called television (*supra*, 5.2.3.2.5), the automobile, and sports. At times, the cultural watchdog dozes off, as all watchdogs are wont to do, and an incompatible element enters the culture through *cultural drift* (*supra*, 7.1.4.2). At times, too, the watchdog's master (the society in question) may wish to quiet down the watchdog by reformulating an underlying theme to accommodate the visitor (the desired novelty).

7.3.1.7 Factionalism

Within societies, we find distinct interest groups, each with its own biases, grievances, concerns, and goals. If a novelty should appear advantageous to a particular group, that group will be inclined to accept and develop it; if, on the other hand, it appears to threaten the group, the novelty will generally face resistance. Among the important variables in culture change, therefore, are group interests and loyalties—in a word, factionalism. One of the chief obstacles to social and economic change in Latin America is factionalism: the wealthy classes insist on the status quo and label everything else Marxism. In the United States, issues concerning federal aid to parochial schools, tax reform, racial justice, immigration laws, and similar legislation brought before the Congress meet with opposition chiefly on account of "constituencies," interest-groups who see the world only from their own point of view. In a word, *the relative force of opposing factions and interest-groups constitutes an important factor in culture change and persistence.*

Although the individuals of a society generally support the traditional ideology, more complex societies often include individuals who are discontented, disillusioned, and ready for radical change. Although such "revolutionaries" and "utopians" may not be a factor as important as Karl Mannheim claimed in his *Ideology and Utopia* (1936), the role of interest-groups, factions, utopians, and revolutionaries in culture change must not be underestimated.

7.3.1.8 Catastrophe as Factor in Culture Change

Almost any type of major catastrophe will create social instability and a climate favoring change. Such disasters include wars, typhoons, hurricanes, earthquakes, floods, epidemics, volcanic eruptions, starvation, major crop failures, or any other so-called act of God. In times of disaster, the society is open to almost *any* "solution." In desperation, a society may reach out like a drowning man for a floating straw; the feeling is that there is no harm in trying. As in every major destabilization, the climate is "ideal" for experimentation— open to any, even revolutionary, idea that at least remotely looks promising. Revolutionaries in fact thrive on destabilization.

Catastrophes sometimes bring to isolated populations totally unexpected contacts and ideas from the outside. Contacts arrive from the churches around the world, from the Red Cross, and from the United Nations. Starvation recently brought assistance from those groups to the tragically struck areas of Africa, and World War II to the Pacific islanders of Manus (Mead 1956).

Catastrophe can also unite a people as nothing else can. It is quite true that in such times a people's faith in their traditional values is tested and often strengthened rather than weakened or destroyed. People adjust to the severest calamities by having recourse to their basic traditional values and religious beliefs. (Cf. Lessa 1964:1–47; R. Keesing 1976:429–477.) Nothing has, for example, united the Jewish community world wide more than the tragedy of the Holocaust.

7.3.2 CONDITIONS FAVORING ORIGINATION

Homer G. Barnett in his classic *Innovation* (1953:39–181) provides us with a vast amount of useful information on the subject under discussion. Our question is: What conditions are conducive to invention and discovery?

7.3.2.1 Proper Motivation

Inventors and discoverers are highly motivated individuals. Almost invariably, inventions and discoveries can be traced to deep and powerful motivations. The motivations may be as varied as the innovations themselves. We shall, however, try to reduce them to a manageable number of major categories.

Conscious Wants. Inventors usually have a definite goal or need in mind, a reward that stirs them on to find an answer to a problem. The reward may be mainly financial, as was the case in the quest for a substitute for fossil fuel during the oil shortage in the 1970s or as is the case today in regard to the many inventions and discoveries of pharmaceutical companies and the so-called high-tech industry.

Subliminal Wants. As Barnett rightly points out, involved are not only conscious wants but also a complicated interplay of wants, many of which are unconscious peripheral goals. The inventor is sometimes said to have stumbled on a solution to a particular problem accidentally when actually the inventor has been pondering over the problem for many days, months, and years. Although he or she may claim that "the answer came from nowhere" and others may attribute the invention or discovery to "intuition," the fact is that the subconscious was constantly at work. Such was, for instance, the case when Edison discovered that carbon could be employed as an incandescent lamp filament. Such was also the case with the "accidental" discovery of the back-folding wings for military planes when an engineer was absentmindedly toying with two paper clips. Many discoveries have been made by compulsive explorers; many, by individuals totally taken up with some subliminal dream, unconscious drive, or ego-need; many, again, by persons obsessed by power, a guilt complex, or a deep-seated all-absorbing jealousy. Such inventions and discoveries are not to be attributed to accident but to subliminal wants and motivations.

Creativity. More than half a century ago, Joseph Rossman in his study *The Psychology of the Inventor* (1931, cited by Barnett 1953:42) pointed out how, among the 710 inventors questioned, the most frequently mentioned motivations for their new ideas were love of inventing and the desire to improve. An artist often works for no other reward than "for art's sake." Similarly, scholars spend countless hours in deep thought and study out of pure love for truth and knowledge. The best musicians play their instruments for hours, day after day, not so much because they will receive a stipend for an upcoming concert but out of true love for music. It is such creativity that is responsible more than anything else for new art techniques and styles and the most important scientific insights. Inventors sometimes work under great financial handicaps, and often without recognition, purely out of their commitment to their art or science. Thus many years elapsed before the so-called Mendel's law was recognized, a fact that did not stop the botanist in relentless research into the laws of heredity. The best evidence for what we are saying is exhibited by the perhaps millions of subsidized publications for which authors themselves receive no recompense other than a few copies of their book or article and the satisfaction of having made a contribution to science.

The Reconciliation of Conflicting Ideas. Conflicting ideas are a kind of psychological itch; itches must somehow be gotten ridden of. Solutions to psychological conflict *must* be found. An example of the type of psychological conflict we have in mind is that of the whites of South Africa. They are told by their constitutions that racial discrimination is just and reasonable, while Christians around the world keep reminding them that such attitudes are diametrically opposed to the Gospel. Being members of their society and at the same time devout and believing Christians, they must reconcile the two views in their minds and hearts. This is done through novel interpretations of the Gospel. In much the same way, the equal-but-separate opportunities for all citizens regardless of race or creed used to be a not uncommon interpretation of the United States Constitution by many Americans, who attempted to justify and reconcile their psychologically conflicting prosegregationist views about equal rights and democracy.

Obstacles and Handicaps. There is a deep conviction in human beings that obstacles and handicaps are there to be conquered. This rather common view of life is responsible for many innovations, such as the great variety of today's medicines and therapies, plastic surgery, artificial limbs and organs, transplants, and such less dramatic inventions as eyeglasses, hearing aids, false teeth, crutches, toupees, and the various so-called beauty aids.

Quest for Relief. Not a few inventions and discoveries result from attempts to cope with boredom. Sports and games serve this purpose. Hobbies, which should be placed in this category of quests for relief, have likewise been responsible for countless originations, as for instance in carpentry and in crocheting. Not a few liturgical innovations seem to reflect this quest for relief.

Desire for Efficiency and Effectiveness. Giving rise to countless inventions and discoveries is the desire for efficiency and effectiveness, evidenced by constant innovations in the business world and in the military and medical fields.

7.3.2.2 The Size and Complexity of the Culture

Innovations do not fall from the sky but grow out of the given culture. Inventions and discoveries are always in some way built upon the past. Innovations, although at times revolutionary, as in the case of the discovery of electric power or the invention of the printing press, depend on previous knowledge, techniques, and the existing cultural inventory. If Beethoven had been a contemporary of Palestrina, he would certainly have been a great composer but he would not have been a Beethoven; a Beethoven symphony with its complex and greatly refined instrumental techniques, orchestration, and rich variation of sound and rhythm was unthinkable in Palestrina's time. Originators are individuals who somehow manage to climb over the wall of traditional behavior; but to do so they must use a ladder provided them largely by tradition. The richer the cultural inventory, the greater are the possibilities of new combinations.

7.3.2.3 Channeling of a Cultural Inventory into the Same Individual

A highly elaborate culture with its complexity and differentiation (*supra*, 7.2.3.2) is no guarantee that much origination will take place. What is still needed is the assurance that the rich cultural inventory is funneled into the same individuals. Because culture change is a thing of the mind, any loss, incrementation, substitution, or blending and any reinterpretation or reformulation must take place in the mind and therefore in the individual. If there is any reworking of ideas as is presupposed by origination, the reworking must be done in the same minds. Origination thrives in cultures that encourage collaboration and where there is unrestricted sharing of knowledge through, for instance, public libraries, publications, professional associations, research centers, and universities. Origination is held back when opportunities for mutual stimulation and enlightenment are lacking.

Such channelization of ideas presupposes also a meeting of *divergent* ideas. A clash of ideas provokes critical discussion and frees the individual from one-track thinking. This is unquestionably one of the great strengths of academic freedom. Some political ideologies and religious systems tolerate a greater divergence of opinion than others; the greater the political or religious freedom of inquiry, the greater is the origination. (We need not, of course, remind the reader that the term *origination* does not necessarily connote *improvement*). A church that fears all origination tends to stagnate.

7.3.2.4 Competition

Competition is one of the most important factors involved in culture change. It may be motivated through the offers of prizes, bonuses, and scholarships; it may occur in struggles that take place between such groups as political parties, religious denominations, and sects. It is found, also, in international commerce. Competition that stimulates origination can become rather fierce among rival products, companies, and entire industries.

The United States largely owes its rapid industrial growth to its competitive spirit. Despite the presence of giant corporations in all major industries, Americans frown upon monopolies and cartels, and the government forbids, breaks up and penalizes amalgamations and business practices that threaten "fair competition." While nationalization of industries is common in most countries, Americans are strongly opposed to any form of government takeover that removes competition, whether it be of banks, railroads, natural resources, or any other form of business.

During World War II, when competition was a matter of survival, inventions and discoveries were made at an unprecedented rate. Today Russia and the United States are in a fierce economic, political, social, and ideological struggle, a fact that explains many of the radical changes taking place around the globe today.

Competition not only encourages change but also clears the way for and triggers *other* factors conducive to origination. Thus, for instance, competition creates a general atmosphere for origination by stimulating a craving for innovations; it funnels ideas into the same individuals through friendly or inimical challenges; it initiates organized and subsidized experimentation; it frequently creates symbols, slogans, and rituals that intensify existing rivalries.

However, competition has a built-in handicap. Because competition is a form of stress, it tends to stimulate invention and discovery in its own limited direction.

7.3.2.5 Deprivation

Necessity is indeed the mother of invention. According to a very natural human inclination, whenever we are deprived of some necessity, we try to improvise. During World War II, Germany became a country of so-called *ersatz* products, from fuel for vehicles to food for humans. Marxism finds much of its appeal in have-not nations and during periods of depression. In democracies, people will change party allegiance and vote accordingly when they feel that the party they supported in the previous election "let them down" and "deprived" them of some expected benefit.

Deprivation thus opens the mind to innovation; it encourages change. It should be noted, however, that as in the case of competition, so in deprivation: the resulting origination is highly focused and therefore limited in the direction of the deprivation.

7.3.2.6 Leisure and Peace of Mind

As just pointed out, stress tends to limit the scope of innovations. When there is sufficient leisure and quiet, and the mind is free and relaxed, the interests are varied rather than forced into a single direction. *Simulated leisure* refers to the structures in a culture that provide the needed peace and quiet by removing financial and other worries so that the inventor can invent and the discoverer can discover. These structures provide for subsidies and grants, collaboration in research, tenure and promotions, and public recognition such as the Nobel Prize.

7.3.3 CONDITIONS FAVORING DIFFUSION

We have just considered the conditions that favor change from within a culture. Our present concern is, What favors change from without? What favors borrowing? We shall try to place the different factors under four heads: (l) the type of community that is borrowing or lending; (2) the type of contact between the two societies; (3) the type of motive for borrowing; (4) the type of idea borrowed (cf. Honigmann 1959:209–72). In other words, borrowing by its very nature presupposes a lender, a borrower, contact between the two, a reason for borrowing or lending, and something borrowable.

7.3.3.1 Community Factors: The Type of Borrowers and Lenders

The donor and the recipient may be a large or small social group; homogeneous or heterogeneous; aggressive, indifferent, or passive; constituting a dominant or minority group; possessing a simple or complex way of life. How do these variables affect diffusion? Or do they?

Community Size. There is too much evidence against the supposition that a numerically larger society necessarily becomes the donor while the smaller becomes the recipient. The fact is that the size of communities in a potential borrowing-lending situation is easily outweighed by other factors. The pygmies of the Ituri forest are a classic example of how a numerically weaker people can remain uninfluenced by a numerically stronger neighbor. There are also many examples of numerically smaller groups influencing larger ones. As colonial history shows, the European planters, traders, government and business people, and missionaries throughout Africa, the Pacific, Latin America, and elsewhere have been outnumbered by far by the indigenous people; nevertheless, it was more often the numerically smaller European group that influenced the larger native populations. Active Marxists generally are at first only a small minority in a country, but in a matter of sixty or so years Marxism has been able to influence the cultures of more than a third of the world.

The fact is that the size of a community can work either way, for borrowing or against it. In a smaller community, the members generally interact with one another much more closely than in a large community, and close interaction favors change. However, a small community is usually more homogeneous than a larger one, and homogeneity favors persistence rather than change.

The Subcommunity Directly Involved in Diffusion. Five factors are important here. First, in a borrowing-lending situation, *the recipient may be either the whole community or only a segment of it.* Although at first sight it may appear that contact with an entire society would be more favorable to diffusion than contact with only a segment, there are many counterbalancing factors.

Second, *the character of the borrowing and lending groups* must be considered. The segment of society directly involved in borrowing may consist of *active, indifferent,* or *passive* individuals. The UNESCO, the World Health Organization, the Food and Agricultural Organization, the Peace Corps, the Agency for International Development, Communist cadres, and missionaries are examples of *aggressive* agents of diffusion. What matters is not so much how many individuals are working but how zealous and efficient they are in spreading their cause. As Douglas Hyde, once a leading protagonist and propagandist for Communism and later a convert to Roman Catholicism, pointed out some twenty-five years ago in a seminar on Marxist methods attended by the present author,

> Communists in any country are usually at first a relatively small segment of the population but they make up for their small numbers by their organizational skill, dedication, and action. The small Communist group consists mainly of teenagers and young adults between the ages of fifteen and twenty-five. This age group is precisely the one that is most idealistic, just beginning adult life with its responsibilities and overflowing with energy and hope for a better world, ready to make any sacrifice demanded of them. In Douglas Hyde's view, more Communists have died in our times for the cause than Christians have for Christianity in all its history. Group enthusiasm, a sense of leadership and mission, and belief in their cause have more than made up for the smallness of their original numbers. "Every Communist a leader! Every factory a fortress!" was never meant to be a mere slogan.

Third, a consideration that must be kept in mind in analyzing the character of the segment of society as a factor in diffusion is *the position of the segment in the overall structure of the borrowing society.* Some individuals and subsocieties may constitute the main centers of power and influence and the chief currents of communication. As our survey of mission history (chapter 4) has shown, it has happened that once an influential individual or segment of society has accepted Christianity, the rest of the society often did the same. During the Reformation, it was often *Cujus regio ejus religio* ("As the ruler, so the religion").

Fourth, there is the consideration whether the borrowers belong to *the dominant or to the minority group*. Although a dominant group is, more often than not, too proud to borrow minority ways, it does not follow that the minority is eager to adopt the majority values; both sides are usually selective. By itself, the relative position of the groups is as a rule not a deciding factor; rather, the diffusion will depend on the cumulative effect of the various factors that come into play.

Fifth, there is the consideration of *migrant groups* as opposed to members of a society that choose to remain in the homeland or home village. Are migrant groups more prone to borrow novelties than the society at large remaining in the homeland, and are those moving to the cities more prone to borrow than those remaining in the village? As we have seen when discussing disequilibrium (*supra*, 7.2.3.4), the social and cultural disorganization connected with internal or external migration does indeed predispose the migrant for culture change. Moreover, physical separation from the old country or home village, the totally absent or greatly reduced force of traditional social pressures abroad or in the big city, and the urge to adjust to the new cultural milieu make the migrant particularly open, if not vulnerable, to change.

More Irish have given up their faith in England and America than in Ireland. It is said that there are more Roman Catholic Japanese in Brazil than in Japan. Migrant laborers leaving their tribal areas and settling in the company towns and slum districts of Africa quickly give up their traditional moral standards and other patterns of behavior.

7.3.3.2 Contact Factors in Diffusion

No borrowing can take place unless the potential borrower and lender come in contact with each other. This contact may be continuous, direct, and long-lasting as in acculturation (*supra*, 7.2.1.2), or it may be remote and indirect as often happens when individual elements of a culture diffuse. The contact may be friendly or unfriendly. What bearing do such variables have on culture borrowing?

The Intensity of Contact as a Factor. It is quite true that *other things being equal, the more intense the contact, the more open is the contact to diffusion*. On the one extreme is *tarriance*, the total isolation with no communication with the outside world; on the other extreme is *acculturation*, the direct, first-hand, long-lasting contact with a more powerful neighboring society; a third possibility is *symbiosis*, the mutually beneficial and cooperative relationship between neighboring societies with each respecting the ways of the other but each going its own way; a fourth possibility is *positive avoidance* or disregard of each other by neighboring peoples.

Today, total isolation is more hypothetical than real, for even the most remote peoples are at least in some indirect contact with other cultures. Particularly today, even the most isolated island peoples of the Pacific are in contact with the industries of Hong Kong. The contact is indirect, but it is contact nonetheless. Contacts may be made through a single gold-prospector, hunter, government official, or scientist collecting entomological or botanical specimens. In such relatively rare contact situations, artifacts rather than beliefs and values are usually diffused. Beliefs and values, however, can and do "migrate" over long distances (through such media as art forms or myths). Nonetheless, even if it is true that geographic isolation does not make diffusion impossible, it does make the culture relatively stagnant. Archaeological and other anthropological evidence suggests that the richest cultures tend to be those that are fortuitously situated on the crossroads of cultural contact. Thus, God's Chosen People providentially originated and developed as a nation in the culturally rich, ancient Near East, from which they were able to borrow and further develop many of their literary and artistic models, religious, social, political, and legal forms, and much of their wisdom tradition (*infra*, 7.3.4.2.3). Providentially, too, because of the propitious cultural, social, and political situation, the one-time tiny Jewish sect, Christianity, located in the heart of the Roman Empire, could by the year 400 A.D. become the dominant religion of the Mediterranean basin (*supra*, 3.2.1) and become the heart of the rich European cultural history.

Anthropologists speak of isolation caused by *blocked communication*. Meant is the relative isolation resulting from illiteracy and linguistic barriers, xenophobic attitudes as have existed in places such as China until rather recent times, as well as political and religious barriers. Yet despite blocked communication and actual geographic isolation, the growing literacy among peoples of the world, the growing knowledge of foreign languages (especially English), the availability of books, newspapers, radios, and other media are all contributing to the eventual development of what McLuhan termed "the global village."

Friendly Versus Hostile Contact. Inasmuch as friendship encourages close interaction, it is conducive to diffusion. In fact, friends are known for exchanging gifts, borrowing things, and sharing ideas. Friendship encourages admiration and even intermarriage. Intermarriage in particular links one community to another and may become a particularly powerful channel of diffusion.

Hostility, on the other hand, encourages suspicion, prejudice, and avoidance. Hostility, however, does not make contact ineffective and borrowing impossible, as once again the cumulative effect of all variables determines how the scale will tilt. The Japanese have perhaps never imitated the Americans more than during World War II when the superior engineering techniques of the Americans were considered desirable.

The Duration of the Contact. Duration is no doubt a factor but it is once again dependent on the cumulative effect of other variables. It took Manus Island only twenty-five years to be totally transformed (Mead 1956).

7.3.3.3 Motivational Factors in Diffusion

7.3.3.3.1 Felt-Needs

A cultural pattern will diffuse most easily if the potential borrower is aware of its rewarding nature and conscious of the fact that the pattern might bring a possible answer to a pressing problem (*supra*, 5.2.1.6.2).

Sometimes the reward is self-evident, in which case the innovation tends to be accepted without questioning. The advantage of adopting certain material objects like the rifle and the steel axe has always been obvious. Such basic discoveries as agriculture and animal husbandry have spread rapidly over the world, not because they involved skills that are easily mastered but because they promised rewards that are easily comprehended. The success that Christian and Moslem missionaries experienced in Africa was due in no small measure to the "climate" of the times: the Africans were feeling a dissatisfaction with their traditional ways.

A society will remain sceptical about ideas that are at best doubtfully rewarding, especially if their adoption involves great expense and sacrifice. From the standpoint of the unbeliever, "the price of Christianity is far above its worth." Christianity is indeed a very difficult "product" to sell because its value is not immediately apparent. Generally, innovations that cannot be fully understood and appreciated, such as Christianity and many aspects of medicine and hygiene, are *selectively* accepted and are adopted in *addition* to what has been traditionally held; we are thus up against the whole problem of syncretism (*infra*, 7.3.4.2.3), of having doctors and witchdoctors at the same time treating the same patient. When consulting the university-trained physician, the people will also consult the shaman; while believing in the God of the Bible they will also trust voodooism. In some value systems, there is the additional problem that delayed rewards seem to be no rewards at all. Offer someone five dollars today or five hundred tomorrow, and the person will take your first offer as the preferable. "A bird in the hand is worth two in the bush" may be a truism, but the fact is that Christianity, although ultimately otherworldly, has many and great immediate rewards that are neither delayed nor postponed. "The reign of God is already in your midst!" (Lk 17:21). This truer image of the Kingdom is the one that must be proclaimed. To quote a Saint of our own times, "I do not know what I possibly could have in heaven that I do not now already possess."

7.3.3.3.2 Prestige

One value all cultures seem to share is prestige, a value very frequently associated with diffusion. A foreign idea is easily diffused if it brings prestige to the adopter. Thus, the steel axe diffused rapidly in Australia—in fact too rapidly—because it was regarded as a prestige-object.

The German immigrant of the low artisan class in Brazil took to horseback riding, according to Honigmann (1959:219), because in Germany horseback riding was regarded as a privilege of the nobility while in Brazil, his new home, it was a gaucho status symbol.

American public-relations consultants, advertisers, and politicians capitalize on prestige because "Prestige sells!" Prestige, we hasten to add, also diffuses.

Leading American magazines advertise whiskeys of distinction in full-page colored pictures of elegantly dressed people at a party served by a dignified-looking butler-like figure who pours out the particular potion, the choice of people who know and who can afford good whiskey. Similarly, automobiles are advertised in pictures showing the arrival of a chauffeur-driven luxury vehicle in front of a fancy hotel or nightclub to bring home a smiling formally dressed couple (the man in tuxedo and the lady in gown and mink stole) after a pleasant but unquestionably expensive evening.

In political campaigns, lesser candidates love to be photographed with such well-known figures as the President of the United States, outstanding football players, and popular movie stars. Products are advertised by associating them with prestigious people, whether it's a product like Polident to make your false teeth sparkle or Wheaties, "the breakfast of champions," to make you into a future Olympic star.

Father Matteo Ricci tried this approach in China in the sixteenth century by dressing like a native bonze, accepting visitors only in accordance with high-class Chinese etiquette, assuming the dignity of a mandarin, and associating himself with the upper elite and the Emperor himself.

Unconscious as well as subconscious rewards play an important role in culture change, as the many studies in ecological anthropology suggest (*supra*, 5.1.6.1.4).

7.3.3.3.3 Interest

Felt-needs that do not include a *practical* appreciation of the novelty will have little influence on diffusion. The Chukchee, for example, never adopted the Eskimo igloo, and the Eskimo never adopted the Chukchee reindeer-breeding, not because the Chukchee did not appreciate the need for igloos or because the Eskimo did not theoretically appreciate reindeer, but because *interest* or *practical appreciation* in igloos and reindeer breeding was lacking (Benedict, R. 1956:185–186).

> Health programs in underdeveloped areas of the world often find little practical interest as far as preventive medicine is concerned. While aspirin, sulfa drugs, penicillin, and other wonder-drugs are appreciated, sanitation, improved diet, vaccinations, and mosquito control often arouse relatively little excitement. Even in better educated regions of the world, loss of weight, regular exercise, sufficient rest and recreation, avoidance of fatty and salty foods, abstention from tobacco, alcohol, and drug abuse, and especially regular checkups find far less practical acceptance than calling a doctor or going to a hospital when one has actually fallen ill.

A further reason for the lack of practical interest in a novelty is the fact that sometimes *the advantages that might be derived are neutralized or even outweighed by the disadvantages*, or, at least, so thinks the potential borrower.

> The British are still not convinced that they drive their cars on the "wrong" side of the street. Americans appreciate the metric system and learn it in school, but in their daily lives insist on yards, feet, and inches, on pounds and ounces, and on gallons, quarts, and pints.

> English orthography certainly calls for a thorough reform, but as in the case of the "proper" side to drive on and the metric system, a worthwhile change in spelling is regarded as not worth the cost. Entire libraries would have to be reprinted, or one would have to learn both the old and the new spelling. ("And we have enough problems with spelling as it is.") It might be argued that the change need not be so drastic; but then the advantages of the spelling reform would also be greatly reduced and not worth the trouble. A perfectly phonemic spelling (i.e., with one symbol for each speech sound that differentiates the meaning of words) would be impossible: whose dialect would be used as standard? the BBC, Manchester, Boston, Southern USA, Indian, Ghanaian, Filipino, Australian? Most likely, each dialect would insist on its own pronunciation, in which case English orthography would be in a worse situation than it is now. At least so goes the argument.

Sometimes a felt-need is regarded by the members of a society as *impossible*. An impossible dream will most likely not be pursued; it will never reach the stage of being a practical interest that is needed for diffusion. A sense of helplessness immobilizes a culture.

The hopelessness felt by some blacks in the United States is unfortunately a self-fulfilling prophecy. Similarly, the fatalism that is found in much of Latin America makes the direction of desired change extremely difficult. Hence the emphasis in the Latin American church on *conscientization*.

Despite the unreasonableness of expensive weddings and funerals and our theoretical opposition to them, we still insist on our traditional ways when the time comes and have unnecessarily expensive weddings and funerals. Despite the complaints about the expense involved in sending Christmas cards to friends, most people continue their tradition and the U.S. Post Office Department thrives on the increasing volume of cards year after year. "There is nothing I can do about it" is a rather general feeling— and nothing is done.

Finally, there are *negative* rewards that must be mentioned as influencing diffusion. We accept a change not because a novelty is rewarding but simply to obtain relief from the pressure of an aggressive innovator or an enthusiastic house-to-house peddler who has somehow managed to get a foot in our door together with his or her set of brushes, assortment of beauty aids, vacuum cleaner, or the newest and handiest can-opener ever.

A small pressure group often succeeds in imposing its views and preferences in a community simply by "sticking to its guns"; sooner or later the majority will tire and cave in.

Sometimes a nation may submit to a foreign government or an unfair military dictatorship, accept heavy burdens, and obey unjust and tyrannical laws, not because the nation accepts such injustice but because it simply prefers the lesser of two evils, the relief from pressure.

7.3.3.3.4 Emotions

A final dimension of motivation that must be considered in connection with factors involved in diffusion is *emotion*. Like felt-needs, prestige, and interest, emotions play an important part in borrowing. Among the chief emotions involved are bias/prejudice, fear, and discontent. These emotions, of course, are important factors in the acceptance and rejection of the Gospel and the Church's socioeconomic efforts.

Prejudice. Often associated with hate and fear, prejudice renders individuals blind to potential rewards that might otherwise have served as strong incentives for borrowing. Christian denominations have much to learn from one another but, owing to prejudice, pass up many opportunities for such mutual enrichment; there is also much that might be learned from non-Christian faiths, especially from our Jewish brothers and sisters.

> Prejudice against Roman Catholics until President Kennedy arrived on the scene kept much talent and dedication from important government posts and leadership roles in the United States—and with the loss of potential talent and leadership many useful ideas. The same is still true in regard to women and minorities; not only is the source of talent and leadership diminished but the country's growth and development is limited as well.

Prejudice and fear are frequently the result of a past experience. The hatred, suspicion, and fear with roots going back to the Reformation lingers on in both Protestant and Catholic groups. A classic example of how an historical experience can be perpetuated and can block diffusion is the following.

> A Navaho chanter once tried to introduce a new fertility dance that was to guarantee a rich harvest of potatoes. The innovator painted potatoes on the backs of the dancers, who had been instructed to cough and vomit as if from overeating. It just so happened that soon after the performance many of the Navaho Indians died. The deaths were blamed on the dance, in which coughing had resembled the wheezing and choking associated with the whooping cough. Other Navahos died of diarrhea which in turn was blamed on the vomiting in the dance. Still others died of measles, sores, and small pox which looked very much like the potato buds painted on the backs of the dancers. As Herskovits (1950:486) observed, there is little chance of a dance with the elements of coughing, vomiting, and potatoes ever being introduced among the Navaho; the one-time experience lives on together with the prejudice against such a dance.

Bias. Bias inclines one to exaggerate the rewarding nature of a novelty and therefore unduly inclines the potential borrower toward its acceptance. Americans generally prefer French wines, German beer, Italian salami, Swiss cheese, and Polish ham to domestic counterparts, although there is little evidence that some American wines, beer, salami, cheese, and ham are not as good as, if not better than, some or most imports.

7.3.3.4 Diffusability

Diffusion presupposes not only a lender and a borrower, contact between the two, and a reason for borrowing and lending. It also demands a *diffusable idea.* What ideas are diffusable? Which ones are more readily diffused than others?

Simple Versus Complex Ideas. Simple ideas are definitely more easily borrowed than complex ones. It is easier for simple tribal peoples to borrow such Western utilitarian objects as steel axes, beads, matches, and cotton textiles than it is for them to adopt the complex technology associated with their production.

Usefulness and Attractiveness. A naturally useful and attractive element tends to diffuse more rapidly than one that is indifferent, useless, or unattractive. Foreign words and expressions often seem to be more appropriate than similar words and expressions in the vernacular. For example, we tend to use Latin in law (e.g., *habeas corpus, in absentia*), Greek and Latin in designating parts of the human body and in naming diseases and medicines (e.g., *epiglottis, vitamin*), French in diplomatic matters (e.g., *coup d'état, détente*), and Italian in music (e.g., *pianissimo, fortissimo*). The Japanese are among the world's greatest admirers of European classical music, so much so that Beethoven, Mozart, and Schubert have become household names as in the West.

Form, Function, Underlying Mentality/Symbol, Meaning, Core Metaphor. Most easily diffused is form. It is easier to accept a creed or ritual as such rather than the doctrine or meaning behind the creed or ritual. Most difficult to diffuse is the third or deep level of culture (as are, for instance, the basic premises, attitudes, and motivations underlying Christianity).

Early Learning. What one learns in early life tends to persist more than what is learned in later life. Certain sexual tendencies, speech habits, gestures and facial expressions, fear of black magic and wicked spirits, and fondness for certain foods—all of which are associated with early learning—are among the most difficult of habits to change. Voodoo persists for a variety of reasons, not least of all because it is associated with early life experiences. Health programs meet stiff opposition when new dietary habits are suggested because they go counter to the pleasant and satisfying childhood experiences associated with eating.

Basic Survival. Any custom regarded as basic for survival will be the most difficult to alter. Owing to the close ties of ancestor worship with survival and prosperity, this feature of society will not be easily given up in Melanesia, even when traditional practices have been outwardly rejected in Baptism. The Catholics of Poland regard their faith as a matter of life and death. Their faith is in fact so much for them a part of their culture and a matter of survival that every effort made so far to counteract the influence of Catholicism in their public and private lives has ended in failure.

Alternatives. Patterns that allow a large range of alternatives and leave much to personal taste, self-expression, and open competition are usually among the most mobile.

Cultural Focus. An idea taken up more recently by symbolical anthropology (*supra*, 5.1.6.5.3) is what Herskovits (1950:411–412) had called *cultural focus*. The most mobile of all culture elements are the ones that fall within the *center of interest*, where the circuitry becomes particularly close and intertwined and where the back-and-forth flow of communication is most intense. Thought and discussion are centered around premises, values, and goals located here, and it is thought and discussion that give birth to new experiments, new risks, and new interpretations. It is here that openness to and interest in change (i.e., in growth and development) is the greatest. It is here that the greatest elaboration (*supra*, 7.2.3.2) occurs. It is here that the climate for origination and diffusion is indeed most favorable and actually takes place. On the other hand, if an innovation threatens the center of interest, the cultural focus becomes the area of greatest resistance.

7.3.4 SUMMARY AND MISSIOLOGICAL APPLICATION: CONDITIONS FAVORING CHANGE

7.3.4.1 Summary

1) *Conditions Favoring All Change.* There are certain conditions that favor *all* culture change, whether the change is initiated from within the culture (through invention or through discovery) or from without (through borrowing).

The basic requirement is the presence of *suitable innovators*, that is to say, individuals who can analyze and reorganize mental configurations in their own minds. Innovators must then be able either by themselves or through others to lead a sufficient number of members of the society to accept the innovation so that it is practiced universally by the society or so that it becomes an alternative or specialty and is integrated with the rest of culture.

The factors encouraging change are a favorable attitude of the society toward change; freedom of inquiry and action; social control; change itself; compatibility of the novelty with traditional ways and values; factionalism; and catastrophe.

2) *Conditions Favoring Origination.* Specifically favoring origination are the presence of wants, both conscious and subliminal; creativity; the presence of conflicting ideas demanding reconciliation; obstacles and handicaps; quests for relief; desires for efficiency and effectiveness; the size and complexity of the particular society; the possibility of channeling the same ideas through the same minds; competition; deprivation; and leisure and peace of mind.

3) *Conditions Favoring Diffusion.* Into question come the following: the type of community that is borrowing or lending the novelty; the type of contact between the borrower and lender; the type of motivation involved; and the type of idea borrowed.

As far as the *community* is concerned, the relative size of the borrowing or lending society as such does not of itself favor or inhibit diffusion; on the other hand, the character and position of the segment of society actually adopting the new ways do.

Other things being equal, the more intense the *contact*, the greater are the chances for diffusion.

Motivation is an important consideration in diffusion. Especially important are felt-needs, prestige, interest, and such emotions as prejudice and bias.

Diffusability of the idea itself is a factor. More diffusable are simple, rather than complex, ideas; useful and attractive ideas; forms, rather than their meanings and underlying philosophy; patterns that allow for many alternatives; and ideas that fall within the cultural focus. Most resistant are ideas opposed to early learning, basic survival, and the society's center of interest.

7.3.4.2 Selected Missiological Applications

The basic reasons for studying factors involved in culture change are to understand more clearly the difficulties associated with mission action, to reduce the chances of making serious mistakes, and to direct desired change more effectively. We shall now examine such factors more closely. Some factors we shall treat very briefly because their practical significance is easily grasped, for example, a lack of freedom of inquiry, incompatibility with the rest of culture, or threats to survival. By contrast, other factors will call for lengthier explanations.

7.3.4.2.1 Innovators

If the Church *is* mission, every Christian must be a witness, but one that is truly an "innovator" for Christ and his Kingdom. In whatever circumstances or situations Christians find themselves, they must be constantly "innovating," constantly making the Gospel relevant here and now. Christians are "deviants" and form what V. Turner called the "anti-structure." Their faith must be generative, ever adapting, ever finding new ways of loving God and their brothers and sisters in accord with the particular time and place. As the epigram introducing the present chapter reminds us, "Attentiveness to the signs of the times is part of our vocation." Let us take a close look at a Christian "innovator."

There are different types of innovators, some of whom are more suitable for change and mission than others. To be a Christian innovator—the yeast that penetrates the mass of dough (Lk 13:21) and the salt and the light of the world (Mt 5:13–14)—to be a truly effective Christian witness and leader in a community will call for vision, courage, and steadfastness as well as other characteristics found in any good innovator, whatever the nature of the innovation.

Some innovators are unstable and inconsistent: they at first reach out for the Way, the Truth, and Life, accept Christ for a while and then abandon him as soon as they experience some difficulty or pressure. Some, on the other hand, have the vision, wisdom, boldness, and faith that true witness and Christian leadership demand. Some Christian communities are indeed blessed with the type of seed that produces a hundred-, sixty-, and thirtyfold (Mt 13:4–8). These are the ones best suited for effective witness and leadership. The importance of selecting and training Christian leaders (lay as well as ordained) cannot be stressed strongly enough. Unfortunately, too many religious educators fail to judge their success by their best criterion, the number of Christian "innovators" that they discover and help form.

A good case study of the mission scene in which the local people, to use Barnett's terminology, are the "innovators" and the missionaries are the "advocates" is Darrell Whiteman's *Melanesians and Missionaries* (1983).

7.3.4.2.2 The Christian and Sectional Resistance

We have also discussed the different types of resistance to change, among which were *general* and *sectional* forms of resistance (*supra*, 7.1.4.1). Christians are citizens of *two* cities; theirs, therefore, must not be a general resistance to the world but a sectional one.

Christians must at all times be *in* the world but not *of* it (Lk 9:25; 12:30; Jn 8:23; 15:19; 17:11-18; 18:36; Jas 1:27; 1 Jn 2:15ff). We are reminded of the beautiful *Letter to Diognetus* that describes the true modern Christian as much as it did the Christian of the second century when the letter was written:

> Christians cannot be distinguished from other people whether it be in nationality, language, or custom . . . with regard to dress, food, or ways; they behave according to the customs of whatever city they happen to live in, be it Greek or foreign.

> Nevertheless, there is something rather strange about them. They live in their own country as if they were only passing through it. . . . Any country can be their homeland, but they regard their country, whatever it be, as a foreign land. As anyone else, they take wives and have children but they do not expose them. They share their meals with others but not their wives. They live in the flesh, but they are not ruled by the desires of the flesh. They live their lives in the world but they are citizens of heaven. Obedient to the laws, their lives transcend the laws. . . . As the soul is present in every segment of the body while remaining distinct from it, so Christians are to be found in all cities of the world but cannot be identified with the world. [No. 5-6, Funk, 397-401]

7.3.4.2.3 Cultural Consistency and Desired Change

Anthropologists stress the fact that *new ideas that are at least partially consistent with traditional ways have a better chance of being accepted and integrated than those that are not* (*supra*, 7.3.1.6). This principle is, of course, of no surprise to missiologists, because it is a mere restatement of the principle of *missionary accommodation*, a principle as old as the Church itself (*supra*, 3.1.2).

7.3.4.2.4 Motivation and Desired Change

Only too often, religious educators are overconcerned about instructing their hearers *about* the Christian faith and give relatively little attention to their other, equally important task, Christian motivation. It can be quite enlightening to go through the Gospels with focus on the effort Jesus placed on motivation in his instructions.

7.3.4.2.5 Channeling of Ideas into the Same Minds and Church Action

Channeling of ideas into the same minds was another factor stressed in our theoretical section on culture change (*supra*, 7.3.2.3). This simple principle confirms the wisdom of such approaches to mission as are the various forms of the university apostolates, continuing educational programs, conferences, and grassroots study groups. They are all different ways of channeling ideas in the direction of the desired change.

7.3.4.2.6 Openness to a Difference of Opinion and Mission

Conflicting opinions, as we have seen, tend to stimulate change (*supra*, 7.3.1.3, 7.3.2.4). A fearful attitude toward change in the Church in the hope of preserving orthodoxy and a distrust of local churches has sometimes served merely to generate at best a short-term security while obstructing long-term growth and development. The Slavonic and Chinese Rites Controversies are good examples of what is meant here (Fitzpatrick 1987:53–93). Or as Andrew Greeley (1977:34–35) observes, the heresy of *Americanism* condemned by Leo XIII in his *Testem benevolentiae* was vindicated by Vatican II some eighty years later. To the extent that it existed at all, the heresy was to be found in the writings of French authors, not in the United States:

> Many of the [liberal] themes and practices of American Catholic life at the turn of the century . . . were profoundly threatening to Rome. Ironically, most of these emphases—openness to non-Catholics, strong social concern, consultation with clergy and the laity in decision making, optimism about the modern world, willingness to conduct a dialogue with anyone, endorsement of scientific and technical progress—became Church policy after the Second Vatican Council. Phantom heresy or not, Americanism has now become official policy. [Greeley 1977:34]

This is, of course, not to say that the Church is a democracy and that the Gospel can be voted on. Nor, as John Paul II in his 1984 Christmas message "One Church, Many Cultures" (no.7) pointed out, can the Church, when dealing with the difficult question of local culture versus the Gospel or the universal doctrine and tradition of the Church, abdicate her authority and responsibility as teacher and guardian of truth. Change without restraint is anarchy; it is change run wild. Conflict may always encourage change, but not all change is desirable.

7.3.4.2.7 The Character of the Local Christian Community as a Factor in Change

As we have emphasized earlier (*supra*, 3.1.3.1) and implied throughout, the chief agents of contextualization are the Holy Spirit and the *local community*. What anthropology has to tell us about community factors in culture change (*supra*, 7.3.3.1), therefore, should be of great interest to missiologists and those engaged in mission, and in fact to every Christian community. We refer to the relative size of the community, the zeal or apathy characteristic of the community, the respect enjoyed by the Christian community as a segment of the general population, all of which has a direct bearing on mission and the effectiveness of Christian witness. For example, Christianity began as a tiny, insignificant sect (*supra*, 3.2.1.1). In fact, Christ compared his Kingdom to the "least of all seeds" (Mt 13:31–32). Not the size of the infant Church but the hidden potential mattered. The zeal, the dedication, the sense of mission, the willingness to sacrifice, and the enthusiasm for witness and readiness for leadership compensated for the infant Church's smallness. Even when the infant Church seemed most powerless, her enemies had to admit that the blood of Christians was but "the seed of Christians."

7.3.4.2.8 Felt-Needs

We have been stressing throughout how *felt-needs were a most basic factor in directing culture change* (see, for instance, *supra*, 5.2.1.6.2). We therefore need not say more here except to re-emphasize that it is impossible for the Church to "sell" its "foreign wares" except in terms of felt-needs.

We have also pointed out (*supra* 7.3.3.3.3) that another important ingredient must be added to felt-needs. This ingredient consists of *practical interest*. In addition, *emotions*, especially fear, prejudice, and bias, have much to say in the process of change and conversion. Liturgists might profit by studying opposition to liturgical reform with this in mind.

7.3.4.2.9 Social Control and Mission

Every society has, and indeed needs, social controls to ensure compliance with the rules of culture. For the same reason, organizations, large or small, including the local and the universal institutional Church, must have their sets of laws and by-laws with their penalties and rewards to encourage order and cooperation.

Fortunately, Christians no longer look to Caesar to spread the Kingdom of God. We have seen how insistent Vatican II was that the Gospel be accepted freely and how professional ethics connected with the direction of culture change reject all forms of force and manipulation (*supra*, 2.3.2.3).

We have also seen (*supra*, 7.3.1.4) that, for better or for worse (i.e., for or against the Gospel), the more forceful and effective the social controls of a society are, the more persistent will be its traditional ways. Aspects of culture to which the society applies little or no pressure will tend to change more readily than those which the society insists on and to which it attaches severe and inevitable sanctions. Here again one might review what was said earlier about V. Turner's *structure* and *antistructure* (*supra*, 6.3.3.3.2). Church workers, whether concerned about socioeconomic betterment or spiritual needs, will do well to study the social control system of the society in question: they must determine which aspects of culture are insisted on, how severe the pressures are, how inevitable the sanctions, and which sanctions are attached by the society to which behavior. To understand the apparent lack of cooperation, the recidivism, apathy, resistance, or opposition on the part of the members of a Christian community, the society's social control system should be carefully analyzed. Social pressures, whatever their form, do play an important part in human behavior, including the behavior of Christians.

Although insisting on a free acceptance of the Good News, the Gospel leaves no doubt about the need for social controls. They must, however, be fair, just, and charitable. While Jesus forgave repentant sinners (Lk 7:37ff; Jn 8:7), he suggested

> if your brother should commit some wrong against you, go and point out his fault, but keep it between the two of you. If he listens to you, you have won your brother over. If he does not listen summon another, so that every case may stand on the word of two or three witnesses. If he ignores them, refer it to the church. If he ignores even the church, then treat him as you would a Gentile or a tax collector. I assure you, whatever you declare bound on earth shall be held bound in heaven, and whatever you declare loosed on earth shall be held loosed in heaven. [Mt 18:15–18]

Before proceeding to enumerate some of the main types of social controls, it should be noted that when studying a society's social control system we must view the system from the *insider's* perspective. Public humiliation, for instance, is a far more painful form of social pressure in Japan than in America, where face-saving does not play the role that it does in the Orient.

There are two categories of controls, the positive and the negative. Among the main *negative* controls that must be studied are especially the following: (1) *Physical punishment.* These include such pressures as beating, imprisonment, exile, mutilation, execution, duels, and ordeals. (2) *Fines.* (3) *Gossip.* All peoples are sensitive to group comment, a fact that makes gossip an important form of social control. Individuals have been known to drop out of catechumenates simply because it was being whispered that they were taking instructions merely to escape work at home. (4) *Commands* are a common but forceful way to make people comply with traditional behavior and to avoid novelties. The effectiveness of the command will depend on the particular culture; thus, for instance, the orders of a father may be disregarded with little repercussion but not the orders of a maternal uncle. Authority figures like priests, witchdoctors, shamans, teachers, policemen, and parents generally are able to give more forceful commands than others in the community. (5) *Ridicule* is usually a very effective control. Children learn the "correct" way to speak the vernacular to a large extent for fear of ridicule by their peers. (6) *Threats* and *fear* of physical punishment, sorcery, or the anger of a secret society or any other pending evil will make a person think twice before he or she parts from the structured path. To illustrate—a Christian girl may agree to marry a polygamist because she fears that a hex will be placed on her to make her barren. (7) *Taboos* are traditional prohibitions to which such sanctions as the vengeance of the ancestors, a spirit, or a god are annexed. Even after Baptism, a new convert may feel compelled to continue traditional ways incompatible with Christianity for fear of illness or death. The impression made on the Melanesian mind from earliest childhood by the oft-repeated ghost stories about vengeful deceased relatives is deep and lasting, subconsciously compelling the new convert to return to former ways and placate the dead with pig-sacrifices. (8) *Scolding* as a kind of humiliation—and always as an irritant—may force the individual to do "what is right" and observe the "proper" ways. Sometimes the person submits for the sake of peace and to escape painful nagging.

A society makes use of a great variety of *positive* pressures as well. (1) *Education* in the broadest sense of the term is one of the most basic of controls. (2) The danger of losing traditional *rewards* may keep certain individuals from accepting new untraditional but desirable socioeconomic, moral, or religious ways. On the other hand, sometimes questionable rewards attract individuals to Christianity (as in the case of so-called "rice Christians" in former China, and in the case of some sects that are said to be enticing Latin American shanty-town squatters by taking advantage of their destitution). An individual may not wish to be baptized because once baptized the man will not be able to exercise his traditional right to marry a second wife. (3) *Praise, prestige*, and *admiration*, appreciated by all peoples, are special types of rewards that support a structure. A child who is not accepted by good companions may seek the affirmation of a gang of delinquents instead. In response to this psychological need, the Christian community and the Church at large should try to provide sufficient outlets for affirmation; otherwise it will be sought elsewhere. Even if as a person of faith the Christian ought perhaps to be satisfied with otherworldly rewards—the Gospel warns us against the behavior of hypocrites who have already received their reward (Mt 6:16ff)—the fact is that Christians have the human need for affirmation itself. Besides, outstanding achievement awards are given not so much to flatter the ego of the recipient as to encourage and support his or her efforts and to urge others to do likewise. Parochial, diocesan, regional, and international awards do indeed have a place in mission. (4) *Security* is an extremely powerful social control. Culture, the underlying code of behavior, may be observed because one's food, bridewealth, general welfare, protection against one's enemies, and survival itself sometimes depend on such observance. Not to observe the code may be looked upon as a betrayal of one's family or tribe, a crime that will inevitably bring punishment from the ancestors not only on the offender but on the whole tribe or clan as well. (5) *Symbols* in art and ritual have a far wider impact on the observance of cultural norms than most people realize. If all church bells and steeples were to be removed from Western cities, towns, and villages, Christians of the West would certainly lose much of their sense of God's presence in the world and their awareness that their destiny is "upwards." Thanks to art, Buddhism was able to spread throughout the East as rapidly as it did. One of the chief functions of the highly symbolical liturgy of Christians is to encourage Christian living. The Cross has from earliest centuries been a powerful symbol for Christians. Marxist governments are particularly fond of elaborate parades and demonstrations, flaming-red banners, giant images of Marx and Lenin, and especially of the symbol of all Marxist symbols, the hammer and sickle. (6) Sociologists include among positive social controls also *slogans, propaganda, disinformation,* and *advertising*.

To sum up, a local Christian community should be aware of the social controls of the broader society. There are positive as well as negative controls, overt controls, and the subtly hidden controls. An understanding of traditional social controls will help the Christian community understand the recidivism and the persistence of less desirable patterns. Among the inventory of controls there will also be some controls that might be well-suited for use by Christian organizations, parishes, and movements—and here we mean especially the positive controls.

7.3.4.2.10 Diffusability of Ideas and Change

We have seen that diffusability of ideas is a major factor in diffusion (*supra*, 7.3.3.4). Anthropology tells us that most easily diffused is the form, the symbol minus its meaning; less diffusable is the second level of culture, the function or meaning; most difficult is the third level of culture, the underlying premises, values, and drives. It is easy to teach children to recite the Lord's Prayer, but it will take more than a lifetime to grasp its full meaning and to put the various petitions into practice. It is also easy for converts to memorize the Ten Commandments—to learn the form—but it is an entirely different matter to teach the meaning of the Ten Commandments in terms of one's real life twenty-four hours of the day. It will take a considerable amount of formation before a Christian can truly appreciate the fact that the Ten Commandments are God's way of making divine wisdom available to his creatures and that the Commandments are God's way of expressing his love and concern.

7.3.4.2.11 Social Structure and Mission

When we discussed the nature of culture, we said that culture is a *society's* design for living; accordingly, we stressed the importance of following a societal rather than an individual approach to mission (*supra*, 5.2.2.6.2). Mission goals extend beyond the individual. Mission is to "nations" and to "the world" (Mt 28:19; Mk 16:15), to societies and, by analogy, to cultures. This premise is in harmony with Paul VI's *Evangelii nuntiandi* (no.18-20), and the final Puebla Document (no. 385-393), and John Paul II's constant references to "the evangelization of cultures" (Carrier 1987:118-139; Gremillion 1985:187-234). A number of consequences flow from our premise.

In developing a mission strategy, the Christian community should never lose sight of status and roles. In fact, as the Christian community develops its mission strategy, the whole social structure should lie open like a map (*supra*, 5.2.2.6.2, 5.2.3.2.5; cf. Reed 1985:33-58; Filbeck 1985; Holland, Henriot 1983). We offer a few simple illustrations. To rely on children as innovators and to neglect the adults, especially the menfolk, is sociologically naive, to say the least. To deal directly only with the ordinary, more or less cooperative villagers and to bypass the uninterested elders of the village shows a total lack of understanding of how societies operate. Certain individuals, such as emperors, popes, dictators, kings, presidents, governors, and mayors, have with a single stroke of the pen or a simple nod of the head changed the whole course of history and the character of cultures. The educated, even when outnumbered, usually wield far more power than the illiterate. What we are saying is that

Christian innovators must be strategically placed. The presence of Christian witnesses and leaders is needed most where the power for good or evil is the greatest.

Although it is not the task of the Church to determine for others the political structures and activities, it is the task of the Church through its teaching and through Christian witness and leadership to *conscientize not only the willing individual as individual but the "powerhouses" of the particular societies*, powerhouses that are as varied as the societies themselves.

Such "powerhouses" of change in more complex societies constitute the very foundation of social structure, and include (1) the government, central as well as local; (2) the military and police force with their power to legislate and enforce; (3) the churches with their organizations; (4) the education system, ranging from daycare centers to graduate schools and related associations; (5) the various cultural, health-related, and recreational associations; (6) such economic forces as corporations (large multinational as well as smaller local ones), bank systems, important and less-important business people, and employers of every kind; (7) political parties and their leaders with their ability to control the lives of others; (8) the communications industry, including transportation, television, radio, newspapers, cinema, publishers, and booksellers; (9) civic organizations; (10) interest groups of every kind with their particular concerns, esprit de corps, ambitions, grievances, and techniques—including civil rights organizations, women's liberation groups, labor unions, professions, student organizations, farmers, factory workers, merchants, landowners, renters and tenants, landlords and owners of tenement houses. This listing, of course, is meant to be illustrative rather than enumerative.

Such powerhouses are the various circuits of communication for good as well as for evil; they can be integral parts of systemic injustice or channels for counteracting systemic sin—indeed, they are powerhouses of communication that must carefully and fully enter into mission strategy. After a social analysis has been made, the local Christian community, especially its leaders, should be able to identify the centers of power and the direction and relative force of the various currents of communication.

Although, as Pope John XXIII stressed in his *Princeps pastorum* (no.17), it is quite true that generally speaking the uneducated follow the lead of the educated and the ordinary citizens follow the more respected persons and personalities (one need but observe the use of persons of prestige for advertising and political purposes), *it does not follow that the influences of change are always from up to down and from the elite to the less educated*. The fact is that *leadership is present among peers* whether rich or poor, educated or uneducated. We must not overlook the leadership of the poor. The wealthy and elite often form the immobile segment of society, the one that most staunchly defends the status quo whether it is right or wrong. Thus in Latin America, for several decades now, the greater potential for change, hidden in many cases but still there, has been not the conservative aristocrat but the poor shanty town dweller.

The spirit of the Gospel, we are saying, must penetrate *all* channels of communication. Some powerhouses are more powerful than others. These powerhouses can also be powerhouses for mission as well. It is, of course, not the business of the Church to tell governments what economic or political system they should have; nor should the Christian impose his or her faith values on others; it is nevertheless the role of the Church to preach in season and out of season the moral principles underlying the choices before the particular society *as it is structured*, while the Christian in his or her discussions, public statements, political stand and participation, and ordinary living must boldly "proclaim" the Gospel to all possible power-houses of change.

7.3.4.2.12 "Christopaganism": Syncretism and Dual Religious Systems

General Notion of Syncretism. Syncretism as understood in anthropology is any synthesis of two or more culturally diverse beliefs or practices, especially if of a religious character. Inasmuch as it is a synthesis, syncretism is a terminal process (*supra*, 7.2.3). Anthropologists qua anthropologists are, of course, interested in religion, not in theology: to them, *any* synthesis of religious beliefs and practices is syncretistic. Thus, in anthropological terms, Christianity itself can be said to be a syncretistic religion, an amalgam composed of Judaism, new ideas taught by Jesus and his followers, and the many later cultural accretions and theological developments and recombinations of beliefs and practices that have occurred over the centuries. In this sense, Judaism is itself a deeply syncretistic religion. The Chosen People originated in the very heart of the great civilizations. The cultural debt that they owe to their surrounding world is great indeed. To the cultures of the ancient Near East the Jews owe such basic aspects of their culture as circumcision; the creation stories; the spring sacrifice of nomads (later, the Paschal sacrifice); the Sabbath; certain patriarchal customs; such agricultural feasts as those of Unleavened Bread and Pentecost. Judaism, of course, purified (reinterpreted) the meanings and added new ones to the elements they borrowed from the surrounding countries. Much of its art, sacred literature, and wisdom tradition were likewise borrowed. The temple with its Phoenician craftsmanship and its liturgy came from outside. Much of the Jewish political and legal system came from the non-Jewish world. In a word, the Old Testament uses "pagan" forms to express its faith in Yahweh. In this sense, Israel was indeed syncretistic.

In missiology, however, the term *syncretism* involves Christian theology and may accordingly be more narrowly defined as any theologically untenable amalgam. Moreover, to the missiologist, syncretism is not necessarily terminal and may be an intermediate stage or process, as we shall explain. The differ-ence in usage of the anthropological and missiological term must be clearly kept in mind. When we use the term in missiological anthropology, we speak of a combination of beliefs and practices that are *theologically* untenable.

There are three basic problems associated with theologically untenable amalgams: (1) as far as their content is concerned, they are *untenable,* for they are forms of Christopaganism; (2) as a process, they are *largely unavoidable* and *subliminal* inasmuch as they reflect psychological "laws" associated with all culture change; (3) they often reflect important, and sometimes central, values of a society that demand respect. Their existence produces an enormous missiological dilemma. The problem is discussed in Tetsunao Yamamori and Charles Taber (eds.), *Christopaganism or Indigenous Christianity?* (1975).

Figure 11
Correspondence between African Gods and Catholic Saints in Brazil, Cuba, and Haiti ☆

African deities as found in:	Brazil	Cuba	Haiti
Obatala		(O) ☆ ☆ Virgen de las Mercédes; the Most Sacred Sacrament; Christ on the Cross	
Obatala; Orisala; Orixala (Oxala)	(I) (N) (R) "Nosso Senhor de Bomfim" at Bahía; (N) Saint Anne; (R) "Senhor do Bomfim" at Rio (because of the influence of Bahía)		
Grande Mambo Batala		(O) Santa Barbara	(M) Saint Anne
Shango	(I) (N) (R) Santa Barbara at Bahía; (R) St. Michael the Archangel at Río; (R) St. Jerome (the husband of Santa Barbara) at Bahía (see Yansan below)		
Elegbara, Elegua, Alegua		(O) "Animas benditas del Purgatorio''; "Anima Sola"	
Legba			(M) (H) St. Anthony; (W) (H?) St. Peter
Esu	(I) (N) (R) the Devil	(O) St. Peter	
Ogun	(I) (R) St. George, at Río; (N) St. Jerome; (I) (N) (R) St. Anthony, at Bahía		
Ogun Balandjo Ogun Ferraille			(M) St. James the Elder; (H) St. Joseph; (H) St. James

Osun	(N) Virgin Mary; N.D. de Candeias	(O) Virgin de la Caridad del Cobre	
Yemanjá	(N) Virgin Mary; (R) N.S. de Rosario (at Bahía); N.D. de Conceição (at Rio)	(O) Virgin de Regla	
Maitresse Erzulie; Erzilie; Erzilie Freda Dahomey			(M) (S) the Holy Virgin; especially the Holy Virgin of the Nativity; (P) Santa Barbara (?); (H) Mater Dolorosa
Saponam	(I) the Sacred Sacrament		
Osa-Osé (Oxóssi)	(I) (N) (R) St. George, at Bahía; (R) St. Sebastian, at Río	(O) St. Alberto; (occasionally) St. Hubert	
Ololu; Omolú	(R) St. Bento	(O) St. John the Baptist	
Agomme Tonnere			(M) St. John the Baptist
Ibeji (Brazil and Cuba); Marassa (Haiti)	(R) Sts. Cosmas and Damien		(H) Sts. Cosmas and Damien
Father of the Marassa			(H) St. Nicholas
Orumbila (Odumbila?)		(O) St. Francisco	
Loco	(R) St. Francisco		
Babayú Ayí		(O) St. Lazarus	
Iía	(R) The Most Sacred Sacrament		
Yansan (wife of Shango)	(R) Santa Barbara (wife of St. Jerome)		
Damballa			(W) (H) St. Patrick
Father of Damballa			(H) Moses
Pierre d'Ambala			(M) St. Peter
loa St. Pierre			(H) St. Peter
Agwe			(H) Expeditius
Roi d'Agouescau			(M) St. Louis (King of France)
Daguy Bologuay			(M) St. Joseph
la Sirène			(M) the Assumption (H) N.D. de Grâce

loa Christalline	(H) Ste. Philomena
Adamisil Wedo	(H) Ste. Anne
loa Kpanyol	(H) N.D. de Ab Gracia
Aizan	(H) Christ (?)
Simbi	(H) St. Andrew
Simbi en Deux Eaux	(H) St. Anthony the Hermit
Azaka Mede	(H) St. Andrew (?)
'Ti Jean Petro	(H) St. Anthony the Hermit (?)

☆ Reprinted with permission from M. J. Herskovits, "African Gods and Catholic Saints in New World Religious Belief," *American Anthropologist,* XXXIX (1937), 635-643.

☆ ☆ In this table, the initials before the names of the saints indicate the sources from which the correspondences have been derived:

(H) Herskovits, field data (see also *Life in a Haitian Valley,* Ch. 14).	(W) Wirkus and Taney.
	(N) Nina-Rodrigues.
(I) Ignace.	(O) Ortiz.
(M) Price-Mars.	(P) Parsons.
(S) Seabrook.	(R) Ramos.

Examples of Syncretism in Simpler Societies. Every case of syncretism is unique. Nor is syncretism to be looked upon as a phenomenon that occurs exclusively in newer churches and in technologically simpler societies.

The Caribbean and Brazil. As Herskovits (1950:554; *supra,* Figure 11) pointed out, Caribbean and Brazilian black Catholics have identified many of their African deities with Catholic Saints and with statues and pictures of Catholic origin. For example, in Haiti St. Anthony has become one with the West African Dahomean and Yoruban trickster Legba, an identification based on the fact that both St. Anthony and Legba were known as lovers of the poor. St. Patrick becomes identified with Damballa, a West African rainbow-serpent. The Blessed Virgin, frequently represented in regal garments, has been identified with Erzulie, a goddess of water, who is in control of all riches. The River Jordan becomes identified with certain African rivers. In Trinidad, the head of the Shouter Baptists corresponds to the African cult-head, and much of the baptism ritual is traceable to African initiatory rites.

American Indians. Some traces of Christianity can be found in the Peyote Cult (also known as Peyote Religion, Peyote Way, and the Native American Church). The Peyote Cult is perhaps the most widespread religion among the present-day North American Indians. It seems to have originated in the state of Oklahoma among the Kiowa and Comanche Indians in the late nineteenth century.

Peyote, after which the religion is named, refers to a spineless cactus that grows in the northern part of Mexico and in some southern parts of Texas. When eaten it produces an alkaloid-drug effect. It seems to have some minor curative properties; it also reduces fatigue and is said to help concentration. As Slotkin (1955-56:64-70) tells us, the plant is the focal point of Peyote religion. The fresh peyote or its dried tops are eaten or a tea is brewed and taken sacramentally. It is taken both in time of minor illnesses as well as when serious sickness strikes—in the latter case a special ritual is prescribed. It is also taken to ward off harm and to provide protection to warriors. It is regarded as a source of knowledge superior to that of the Christian Bible: "it is an experience with God rather than a mere reading about him." In fact, under ritual conditions it enables the communicant to have visions of God or of "some intermediary spirit like Jesus" and to experience Revelation. To profit from such "communion" one must be disposed, that is, externally disposed through bodily cleanliness, internally through humility, recollection, and an ardent desire to receive the benefits of peyote. The plant may, in fact, have telepathic effects and bring the communicant a kind of gift of tongues.

Mexico. A syncretistic belief and practice reported by E. Pike and F. Cowan (1959:145-150) is very similar to the Peyote Cult. It is found among some southern Mexican Indians where a species of mushroom instead of the peyote cactus is used sacramentally. The mushroom has hallucinatory powers and, as the Mazateco Indians believe, Christ speaks to people through the mushroom. Jesus is supposed to have spat on the ground, thus miraculously creating the mushroom, has been perpetuated to our own times.

The Chols of Mexico have reinterpreted a Roman Catholic ceremony, making it into a corn-planting ritual. According to a Catholic tradition, the crucifix is covered with a black or purple cloth immediately before Easter as a symbol of Jesus' death. The Chols reinterpreted this ritual by saying that Jesus is covered over with a cloth so he would believe that it was dark and cloudy and be reminded to send sunshine so as to dry out the recently felled trees and underbrush resulting from the preparations made for corn-planting. When on Easter day the cloth is removed from the crucifix, God will see the sun and send the needed rain for the newly planted corn. (Cf. Beekman 1959:241-250.)

The Mayas were known for their human sacrifices, a practice they insisted on even after accepting Christianity, for it was believed that human sacrifice was absolutely necessary for maintaining order in the cosmos. The practice merely went underground in syncretistic form: the underground Mayan Christians *crucified* their victim and called him "Jesus Christ."

Guatemala. Guatemala (after Nida 1961:1–14) offers perhaps the best example of syncretism, with its sorcerers (*brujos*), medicine men (*curanderos*), sacrifices, shrines (*ermitas*), and polytheism. It is believed that there are two gods, the Christian God and the traditional Dios Mondo, the owner of the world. The Blessed Virgin is identified with the moon deity, the symbol of benefits and fertility. In pre-Columbian (and therefore pre-Christian) times the "God of the Dead" was the son of the moon and the sun. It was, therefore, no difficult matter to identify the Crucified Christ with the traditional "God of the Dead." It was also easy to identify the Virgin Mary with the moon deity. Because the Spanish missionaries referred to God as "the God of Heaven," it was also easy to conclude that he was their Sun-God. Dios Mundo, who was regarded as basically wicked, was identified with the Christian Satan who was referred to by missionaries as the "Prince of the World." The custom of naming people, towns, villages, shrines, and churches after Catholic Saints was readily accepted by the Guatemalans since in pre-Columbian times they used to do the same in regard to the *dueños*, their traditional wicked spirits. The idea of prayer was also readily accepted, because the Spanish custom of bargaining with the Saints corresponded rather closely with their own traditional idea of supplication. The missionaries' idea of vows and penance also harmonized with theirs. Christianity was, in fact, so interpreted as to function very much like the traditional religion, a way of assuring or restoring temporal well-being. As the Indians were fond of ceremony, especially of the use of fire and *copal*, they welcomed the Spanish ritual usages which were similar to their own: the abundant use of candles, joyful processions, and fiestas. The sorcery, not uncommon in present-day and recent Guatemala, is really a blend of pre-Columbian black magic and the beliefs of Spanish settlers and missionaries. Among the most serious sins that one might commit is to offend Nature as, for instance, by pulling up a corn plant or by disturbing the social order as one does when someone puts on airs and acts like a *ladino*. The *pecadillos* or small sins include such "trivial" matters as fornication, while drunkenness, polygamy, and prostitution are not sins at all; in fact, prostitutes have a patroness, Santa Maria Magdalena. Sin is not evil in itself because by blindfolding statues one may sin with impunity, and once a year, while Jesus lies in the tomb and God is dead, all sins are allowed.

Africa. Not a few African religions regard God as totally transcendent. Just as intermediaries are necessary if one wishes to speak to a tribal potentate, so the Supreme Being is viewed as beyond the immediate reach of humans. As true to the particular culture as this attitude may be, it is a case of syncretism when transferred to Christianity. The Gospel leaves no doubt whatsoever that God is as near to us as a father (or maternal uncle in Africa, for that matter) and that we should address him accordingly, "Abba!" (Gal 4:6). We read in Matthew 1:23 that "they shall call him Emmanuel, a name which means 'God is with us.' " In fact, we are temples of the Holy Spirit (1 Cor 3:16), and the Blessed Trinity lives *within* us. There is no choice in the matter: somehow any such African pure-transcendence must be replaced with the Christian blend of transcendence-and-immanence. Regardless of what any African culture may suggest, Africans must feel that they are more than subjects of the King of Heaven; they are his children and heirs and must learn to relate to the King of Heaven as a royal African family would relate to their King and Father.

Western Syncretism. Lest we think that untheological amalgams occur only in non-Western cultures, we offer the following list of European and American instances. Yes, older churches are syncretistic too, no less than the Zulu, Fijian, or Eskimo. The fact is that Western Christians absolve themselves too easily of syncretism. In fact, we can speak of a de-Christianization of Europe, which is but a syncretization of Christianity or an example of structure prevailing over antistructure. It should be noted that syncretism is not a matter of an occasional nonobservance of a Christian norm that continues to exist but rather a matter of actually altering the code of behavior itself.

Religious educators in the West have too easily put the *First Commandment* aside as nonapplicable. The fact is that Western Christians have their own Golden Calves and Baals: hedonism, scientism, positivism, individualism, commercialism, and materialism.

Sin, hell, and *other truths of faith* are being denied or forgotten. Karl Menninger has aptly entitled his book *Whatever Became of Sin?* (1973). The British novelist David Lodge makes the interesting observation that "sometime between 1950 and 1975 hell was abolished." Karl Rahner (*supra*, 7.1.5.2.3) expressed more or less the same thought when he said, "Some truths are being silenced to death." Among such truths certainly are, for example, the communion of saints, sinfulness of some thoughts, the sacrificial nature of the Eucharist, much of eschatology, the sinfulness of extramarital sex, alcohol abuse, and keeping holy the Sabbath Day. Somehow the ideas of sin, hell, and other truths have ceased to exist—notwithstanding the Sacred Scriptures, Church tradition, and the teaching of the Church.

The evils of *capitalism* are now taken for granted as slavery was over the centuries—capitalism with its selfishness, its little concern for the needs of the employee and the effect on Third World economies. Profit justifies almost any business decision. (*See* the National Conference of Catholic Bishops' Pastoral Letter of 1986 on the subject.)

The *sexual revolution* is as unchristian as can be and is still wholly acceptable to many Christians: (1) Homosexuality is regarded as a healthy, good, and natural way of being in the world, a legitimate option on a par with heterosexuality. (2) Cohabitation is regarded by not a few as an alternative to marriage. The practice tripled in a decade (1970–1980)—1,500,000 households (out of 67 million) in the United States alone. (3) Pornography in print and in popular music is rampant throughout Christian Europe and America. (4) The majority of Western youth regard premarital sex as permissible. (5) Sex education has become totally amoral, consisting in how to avoid pregnancy and venereal disease. According to a survey, in the United States there are 2.6 sex acts on television on an average afternoon watched and supported by Christians. (6) In some U.S. cities the majority of black children are born out of wedlock. (7) Prostitution in various forms is growing and is receiving more and more public approval. Child pornography, abuse, and prostitution are on the rise.

Alcohol abuse has become so much a part of Western cultures that in "the most Christian country" of Europe, Poland, it is an integral part of hospitality and joviality. Some five million Poles (of 35 million) are alcoholics. Poland consumes more alcohol than any other country in the world. One out of every ten Polish workers does not appear for work at least once a week because of drunkenness. Among many Catholics in the United States and elsewhere, Mardi Gras and St. Patrick's Day, two supposedly Christian feasts, are as much a time for sin as they are for fun.

"*Thou shalt not kill!*" (1) The Decalogue does not say anything about responsible *driving*, but it certainly includes that responsibility. However, every year in the United States alone some 25,000 deaths (about half of all automobile-related casualties) result from car accidents involving drunken drivers. (2) A million and a half *abortions* are performed every year in the United States alone. It is said that Catholic Poland and Italy lead all European countries in the number of abortions. (3) *Tobacco-related deaths* are likewise staggering, resulting in no less than 350,000 deaths in the United States each year—more than the number killed in both world wars. Innocent spouses, and especially infants of smoking mothers, become the victims of culturally approved and often sinful habits of others. The wife of a smoker has double the chance of dying of lung cancer than the wife of a nonsmoker. (4) *Professional boxing* is immoral but is supported by thousands of Christians. The intent is to "knock out" and "hurt" the opponent. The fact is that 87 percent of boxers have boxing-related brain damage. North Americans condemn the cruelty of bullfighting in the neighboring countries south of the border but condone the cruelty of boxing. (5) Drug abuse has become a worldwide epidemic and is growing. (6) The highest rate of suicides in the world is in Christian Hungary. In the United States, suicide is the second most common cause of teenage deaths.

Biblical Syncretism and Dual Loyalty. In biblical times, Baal was the unquestionable lord of the earth in the fertile Golden Crescent: he was the god of rain, fertility, and harvest. In Bernard W. Anderson's words, "To have ignored the Baal rites in those days would have seemed as impractical as for a modern farmer to ignore science in the cultivation of the land" (1957:106).

It is not surprising, then, that the Israelites, unaccustomed to the ways of agriculture, turned to the gods of the land. They did not mean to turn away from Yahweh, the God of the Exodus and the Sinai covenant. To Yahweh they would look in times of military crisis; and to Baal they would turn for success in agriculture. Thus they would serve Yahweh and Baal side by side. [Anderson, B. 1957:106]

Belief in Baal and in Yahweh in fact, as Anderson goes on to tell us, began to coalesce almost the day the Israelites set foot on Canaanite soil: figurines of Ashtart, the goddess of fertility, were kept; elements of Israelite and Canaanite ritual and mythology were fused; children were named after Baal, and, in fact, Yahweh himself was sometimes addressed as "Baal" (Hos 2).

Yahweh, however, was anything but indifferent. He presented himself ever more as a "jealous" God who tolerated no other gods. The distinction between a God of History (Yahweh) and a God of Fertility (Baal) was intolerable to him. The bold proclamations and actions of the prophets throughout the Old Testament left no doubt that Yahweh was indeed absolute, the Lord of *all* aspects of life. (Anderson, B. 1957:106–107.)

Despite Israel's paganisms, Yahweh did not abandon his People. Yahweh is a patient God. He takes men and women as and where they are, in accord with the anthropological "laws" of culture change in mind. He seems to be viewing syncretism as a process rather than as content. God accepts Israel as Israel is, but challenges her to ever greater perfection. Jonah seems to have had a syncretistic view of Yahweh, as he believed in other gods as well. However one may wish to interpret the story of Jonah, Yahweh is presented as a patient God. God does not disown Jonah because the man's faith contains elements of paganism. God accepts him where and as he is and works with him from there. As anthropology tells us, syncretistic combinations are a very normal process in religious change and growth (cf. Salamone 1975:33–43). God does not reject those in the process of purification just because they are not yet pure—he rejects only those who refuse purification, as the parable of the barren fig tree tells us (Lk 13:6–9).

While rejecting any compromise of Christian truth as such, we are proposing that, nevertheless, a positive, rather than a negative, attitude be taken toward the process of syncretism, as the God of the Bible does. It is best to view the process as a way of removing the slag from the precious gold ore. Conversion is a continuing purification. A syncretism-free Church is an eschatological hope, not a reality. A positive attitude is called for also because syncretism often indicates human needs and demands responses to true human values, such as a tribe's appreciation of its traditions and ancestors. Finally, syncretism can also provide important clues to a mission strategy. Syncretism may thus be a bridge and an accelerator in the acculturative process from unchristian to Christian ways and beliefs (cf. H. Burger 1966:103–115). In God's time and with God's help, the Pilgrim Church will reach her destination as did the Israelites, and will "be made perfect as your Heavenly Father is perfect" (Mt 5:48).

Typology of "Christopaganism". A distinction is frequently made between *syncretistic* and *dual religious systems.* R. Schreiter (1985:146–148) sees three foci around which syncretistic phenomena might be grouped: (1) where Christianity and another tradition come together to form a new reality, with the other tradition providing the basic framework; (2) where we have a similar combination but where Christianity provides the basic framework; and (3) where only selected elements of Christianity are borrowed. Here one should note that the basic anthropological concepts in all three forms of syncretism are *acculturation* (*supra*, 7.3.3.2) and *integration* (chapter 6): aspects of one religious system are integrated with those of another religious system either totally or partially.

Dual religious systems do not integrate outside elements; rather, the systems operate alongside one another. The author has studied the phenomenon in the highlands of New Guinea (1958a:52–87). The New Guineans lived by two distinct sets of norms, the one for dealing with whites, the other for dealing among themselves. The one system was used in all relations with the government, the missions, and settlers; the other system was for all "internal" affairs. In many parts of the world, in cases of serious illness, the pastor is called to anoint and to pray over the dying person, but as soon as the priest leaves the scene, the local witchdoctor or shaman is called, as still another, equally valid way of dealing with illness and death. Such dual systems occur in three forms: (1) one system becomes dominant, but elements of the other are also maintained; (2) both systems are followed more or less equally; (3) sometimes culture and traditional religion become so identified with the rest of life that a "double belonging" appears inevitable, making one wonder, for instance, whether a Christian in Japan has to cease being Japanese to be a true Christian or whether one can be both. In other words, the question that is sometimes raised is whether a Japanese can be a Shinto by culture and a Christian by his or her Christian faith. (Schreiter 1985:147–149.)

Such categorization of syncretism and dual systems, however, does not seem to be very useful. Each case of syncretism is unique. More meaningful would be to look upon syncretism and dual systems as *any other culture change*, using the general notions regarding culture dynamics that we have described, the general kinds of change, the general processes of change, and the factors applicable to culture change in general especially what anthropologists have to say about acculturation and integration.

In dealing with syncretism and dual religious systems, therefore, we cannot but insist on making the important distinctions suggested between content and process. As far as the *content* of syncretism is concerned, such amalgamations or combinations are by their very definition theologically untenable, impermissible, and therefore undesirable. Our attitude as Christian anthropologists toward the *content* cannot be but negative: the Gospel may not be compromised and the principle of cultural consistency suggested earlier (*supra*, 6.3.5.2.1), according to which the Gospel has priority over culture, must be upheld. When essentials of faith are in question, the Christian community must, as far as is humanly possible, strive to Christianize its cultural content rather than culturize (i.e., alter) the Gospel.

Syncretism can also be viewed as *process*—in fact, as just emphasized, it may be seen as involving all the processes discussed in our theoretical section on culture dynamics (chapter 7). In dealing with syncretism, we must further distinguish between intermediary or integrative processes (*supra*, 7.2.2) and those that are terminal (*supra*, 7.3.3). A theologically untenable amalgam as a *terminal* process or a symbiotic dual religion as *terminal* are both diametrically opposed to mission. Our attitude here, as in the case of content, can be but negative. If, however, we are speaking of secondary or integrative processes (*supra*, 6.2), such syncretistic or dual processes allow for, and in fact demand, a certain amount of patience. One need not, of course, approve or encourage unchristian beliefs and practices.

Viewed as an integrative process rather than a terminal one, syncretism is in an "in-between" stage; that is to say, the culture under consideration is in a state of imbalance. The theologically untenable amalgam is still, so to speak, en route to the Good News. It is in a process of purification and everything possible must be done not to allow it to become terminal. Through sound religious education and sound pastoral strategy, the local Christian community must challenge its members to work toward the total elimination of the incompatible unchristian content, with as little tarrying as possible. This is done, as we have emphasized on a number of occasions, especially through a tripolar dialectic between the community's local tradition, the universal Church tradition, and the Gospel. We are speaking of a dialectic, not an edict, so that the needs and ideals of the people, often veiled in syncretism, are listened to, built upon, and used as much as possible as steppingstones to the Gospel.

Also to be noted is the fact that there is much we do not know about the human dimension of conversion, especially at the unavoidable, subconscious level. Even after conversion has taken place, a certain amount of syncretism and double loyalty will remain; a craving for the fleshpots of Egypt will still be experienced; and entirely new allurements will arise as the Pilgrim Church wends its way up the rocky and treacherous road toward its destination. The problems of syncretism present a constant struggle. As Paul describes the situation,

> you must no longer live as the pagans do. . . . They are estranged from a life in God because of their ignorance and their resistance. . . . That is not what you learned when you learned Christ! I am supposing, of course, that he has been preached and taught to you in accord with the truth that is in Jesus: namely, that you must lay aside your former way of life and the old self which deteriorates through illusion and desire, and acquire a fresh spiritual way of thinking. You must put on that new man created in God's image, whose justice and holiness are born of truth. [Eph 4:17-24]

Syncretism, when and where it exists, should be in reality, and not merely as an excuse, a part of the struggle against sin and human imperfection, a part of the conversion process. The struggling Christian must remain confident "that he who has begun the good work . . . will carry it through to completion, right up to the day of Christ Jesus" (Phil 1:6). In missiological anthropology, the attitude toward syncretism should be one of optimism, that of a group of Pilgrims, joyfully and hopefully singing "Thy Kingdom come!" In the words of St. Augustine,

> You should sing as wayfarers do—sing but continue your journey. Do not be lazy, but sing to make your journey more enjoyable. Sing, but keep going. . . . Keep on making progress. [*Sermo* 256: PL 38, 1193]

Some Specific Controls for Directing Syncretism. We have suggested two *general* principles regarding syncretism: first of all, that the attitude of the Church toward syncretism should be *positive* despite an uncompromising spirit toward any essential unchristian content; secondly, that the *general* concepts, principles, and theories of social change should be applied to syncretism and double loyalty, because religious hybridization follows quite faithfully the patterns or "laws" of social change. We feel, therefore, that there is little indeed that might be said specifically about religious combinations that has not already been said. Here, however, we wish only to make a few observations and to emphasize the usefulness of some of the general theory of culture change.

Religious hybridization is worldwide and affects almost *any* two religions or world views that meet. It is one of the chief challenges facing the Church, not only in mission countries but in the West as well. The seriousness and complexity of the problem are often downplayed as ignorance on the part of Christians and are attributed to a lack of proper instruction, as if preaching and teaching and waiting were the full answer. Culture change is far more complex than is the process of making someone understand. Sometimes the advice given to newcomers by veteran pastors can be expressed in one word, "Patience!" The fact is that theologically untenable syncretistic beliefs and practices will not vanish by patience alone and by wishing syncretism away. Unless something more positive is done to direct the course of the syncretistic process than merely being patient, the result will indeed be a *terminal* condition.

A general principle in applied anthropology that we suggested earlier was *to study the history* of culture change (*supra*, 5.1.6.2.3). In our case, the first step is to study syncretism with a historian's fine sense of detail, proportion, and habit of interrelating events, occasions, and causes.

Christopagan mixtures and blends are to a large extent the result of untended *selectivity* (*supra*, 7.3.1.6). As we have seen in our study of cultural integration and dynamics, there is a tendency for a society to select from the many possibilities those innovations that are most compatible with the rest of its culture, especially with the underlying premises, basic attitudes, and fundamental goals. The Church as Herald and Teacher must, therefore, not only proclaim its message but must at the same time direct the process of selection that necessarily goes on in the minds and hearts of the recipients of the message. Relatively minor elements of the Good News are sometimes selected and emphasized by the recipients of the message, whereas the truly important aspects of the message are passed over and not "heard." The essentials will thus remain on the periphery of the lives of the ones receiving the message, while the theologically minor aspects, which have the greater appeal and consistency with traditional ways and values, will be accepted, emphasized, and overemphasized. More time and effort, therefore, will have to be given to those aspects of the Church's message that are more important but culturally less attractive. Otherwise, candles and incense may become more important than the Eucharist or the Scriptures; vows and promises, more important than the Ten Commandments; the crucifix or a "miraculous" statue, more important than Christ's death and resurrection; or a patron Saint or the Virgin Mary, more important than God himself. Not seldom, too, Christians select the first "Great Commandment" but pass over the second (Mk 12:30f) as irrelevant.

Similarly, untended *reinterpretation* (*supra*, 7.2.2.1) will inevitably lead to syncretism. No matter how clearly the religious educator may present Christian doctrine, the message will necessarily be filtered through the traditional cultural inventory, structure, and underlying mindset. Even if the catechism, the creed, and the Ten Commandments are recited correctly word for word, the meaning will be reinterpreted, at times incorrectly, unless the educator guides the reinterpretation. Less lecturing and more listening, less ready-answers and more observation and discussion will go a long way toward the control of undesirable reinterpretation.

One of the more common reasons for syncretism and dual loyalty is the fact that innovations often do not provide for some of the functions of the traditional ways and values displaced by the Gospel message. Unless satisfactory Christian functional substitutes are found for undesirable unchristian ways, one should not expect polygamy, black magic, superstitious charms, voodooism, or any other unchristian deeply felt need to be replaced by Christian beliefs and practices. A partial explanation for the rise and growth of the African Independent Church Movement is the fact that Christians have failed to give adequate attention to such people's needs as exorcism and faith healing. Folk piety gets out of hand and becomes syncretistic not because not enough rules have been imposed on the worshipping public but because there is a felt-need for a more spontaneous outlet for religious feeling than is generally allowed in strict liturgical functions.

Syncretism arises largely from the fact that Christianity as actually preached and officially practiced is often not where people really hurt—or in Jacob Loewen's terms, where it itches. To cater to the needs and preferences of the society in question may sound like a contradiction to what we have just said about the local church's obligation to guide the process of selectivity, reinterpretation, and ramification. The fact is, however, that the Church must not only guide selectivity, reinterpretation, and ramification but must *also* respond to the deeply felt needs of the people. It is not a question of either/or but both/and. All that we have thus far said about felt-needs and about the importance of social analysis comes into play. An elitist or culturally irrelevant religion, rather than one deeply aware of the felt-needs of the people, will merely encourage untheological forms of popular piety, a return to pre-Christian ways, unchristian beliefs and practices borrowed from neighboring societies, or neopaganism. Christian formation must, therefore, not overlook such basic concerns as the community's need for recreation, concerns about crops and livestock, diseases, earthquakes, storms, menacing neighbors, and ever-present evil spirits. Besides formalized liturgy, opportunities for meaningful personal religious expression are also needed, for instance, for theologically sound devotions and popular religiosity.[6]

Nativistic leaders, *prophets*, and *messiahs* often give rise to revolutionary forms of syncretism. Here we refer to such movements as the Black Muslims in the United States, who have completely repudiated Christianity. For some four hundred years, Indian tribes of Brazil and Paraguay, led by prophets and messiahs, moved back and forth across the country in quest of a promised land. In Africa there was, for example, the great prophet and messiah Simon Kimbangu with his highly syncretistic religion. In India there was the "Back to the Vedas" movement of over a hundred years ago under Dayanand Sataswati. Oceania has seen the sporadic rise of Cargo Cults and other syncretistic religious movements.

In concluding this section on change factors and mission, we wish to emphasize again that culture change is a *very* complex phenomenon and that there is much—very much, in fact—that we still do not know. Nonetheless, it is a wise person that will use whatever knowledge he or she has and whatever the state of his or her art may be.

Chapter Eight

EPILOGUE: ANTHROPOLOGY AT THE SERVICE OF FAITH

Never overlook the obvious.
Leo Burnett

An Indian Jesuit expressed it well when he complained to a group of missionaries about the mission methods employed in his native India: "You say that you bring Jesus and new humanity to us. But what is this 'new humanity' you are proclaiming? We would like to *see* it, *touch* it, *taste* it, *feel* it. Jesus must not be just a name, but a *reality*. Jesus must be illustrated *humanly*." And how right on the target he was! All human beings are *cultural* beings. Jesus must be *culturally* relevant if he is really to be understood and appreciated. This is *a most obvious fact unfortunately only too often overlooked.*

Until recent times, anthropological concepts and principles were regarded as relevant only to newer churches. Little thought was given to the need for a culturologically orientated mission for the *universal* Church or for *all* local churches including those of the West.

The universal Church needs anthropology, first of all, to understand the Scriptures—sacred writings that represent many cultures over many centuries. The Church needs anthropology if it is to be able to evaluate and be in a position to offer to nations around the globe a two-thousand-year-old tradition, much of which is both spiritually and culturally precious, while much might best be described as mere trappings of history. The Church needs anthropology because it must be able to speak today as it did on that first Pentecost (Acts 2:1–12), in a way that all peoples of the world might understand. The Church ought to be able to speak in respective native tongues about the marvels God has accomplished—whether the people be Parthians, Medes, or Elamites; whether they be from Mesopotamia, Judea, Cappadocia, Pontus, or the province of Asia; from Phrygia, Pamphylia, Egypt, or Libya; whether they be Romans, Cretans, or Arabs. The Church must understand *all* peoples and be understood *by all*, despite deep cultural differences. It would be unfortunate indeed if the Church were to overlook the fact that it has today at its disposal, as never before, a vast treasury of human knowledge in the social sciences, not the least important of which is the Science of Human Beings called *Anthropology*.

But even local churches *qua local* addressing their own people, with whom they share the same culture, need a *culturally oriented* approach to mission and therefore should avail themselves of the Science of Culture. As we have emphasized over and over again, there is no more effective or more genuine way of being Christian—that is to say, of being "of the mind of Christ" (1 Cor 2:16)—than in terms of culture. The local church is not fully and effectively proclaiming the Kingdom unless the Gospel is preached in the cultural "language" of the community concerned: in other words, unless the proclamation of the Word, the participation in worship and manifestation of God's presence, and the specific forms of communication, fellowship, service and organization are all as closely as possible tailored to the culture and social situation of the time and place. What every local church needs is a truly local theology, local in understanding and local in practice.

Such goals can never be achieved except through truly local symbols. Because cultural anthropology is the study of symbolic systems, a basic but systematic grasp of culture in general and especially of one's own culture should be an essential part of *all* training for mission.

Such a training should include the study of culture from three points of view: one should be acquainted with the culture of humans in general, with one's own culture, and with the culture of the community ministered to. The present book has sought to provide especially a grasp of culture in general. It has also sought to provide some insight into the culture of the chief readers of the book, the cultures of the West (mainly the English-speaking world, and the United States in particular). At least by now the reader should be disabused of the old notion that anthropology was only for those dealing with "exotic" or "primitive" ways of life.[1]

In this epilogue to *The Church and Cultures*, we shall once more emphasize "the obvious" by reviewing in broad terms the culturological theory we have discussed in these many pages. We shall do this from the point of view of the nature and mission of the Church.

Whatever the philosophical distinction between the nature of the Church and the nature of its mission may be, the two terms are closely related: what the Church *does* should flow from what the Church *is*. The Church, as we have seen (*supra*, 4.4.3.3), is being described today in terms of models or perspectives, as partial views of a reality too difficult to describe in a single, simple definition. We shall briefly review the role of cultural anthropology in mission action accordingly from the point of view of the Church (1) as a community—that is, as the Body of Christ and as People of God, (2) as a Sacrament or sign of Christ's Grace and God's active presence, (3) as a Herald of God's Kingdom,

(4) as a Servant, and (5) as an institution or organization. There are, of course, dozens of other images of the Church in the Scriptures (Minear 1960). They are all, however, more or less reducible to the five major models as subimages. What we are saying is that the Church, whether viewed as universal or local, cannot afford to neglect modern culturological concepts, principles, theories, and methods such as those that we have tried to present, explain, and illustrate.

When applying anthropology to mission, we might best select for our pivotal ecclesiological perspective that particular model of the Church that seems to be most consistent with the given problem, task, client's preference, or the society's underlying set of basic assumptions, attitudes, and goals (*supra*, 6.3; cf. Dulles 1978:200). Thus, the community model of the Church might be used especially when dealing with problems of communication, ecumenism, cooperation, community development, identity, solidarity, reconciliation, and communal worship. The sacramental model is appropriate for symbolizing the Christian faith in word, creed, and ritual. The kerygmatic or "herald" model might be used for dealing with Christian witness, religious educational programs, seminary education, role of the laity, schools, and church growth. The diaconal model is suited for dealing with poverty, socioeconomic reform, civil rights, alcoholism, health and illness, abortion, crime, child abuse, care of the aged, care of the mentally handicapped and homeless, racism, women's rights, or nuclear war. And finally the institutional model can be applied to structural and administrative questions and new ministries.

In selecting a dominant image or perspective of the Church, one should keep the clustering of strengths and weaknesses associated with a particular model clearly in mind. The strengths should be capitalized on; the weaknesses should be compensated for through insights from other, compatible models so as to bring in the needed balance and correction. The institutional model will, of course, need the most correction, and, as Dulles maintains (1978:205), this pattern can hardly serve as one's dominant perspective of the Church. Most importantly, missiological anthropology must not lose sight of the fact that Christians, whether they are witnessing their faith or are active in a ministry, are builders of a Temple of which *Christ* must always remain the cornerstone and the *apostles* the foundation (Eph 2:20–22). In applying anthropology to mission, a sound christology and ecclesiology are therefore indispensable.

8.1 THE CHURCH AS COMMUNITY

The communal model views the Church as the Body of Christ, as God's People, as a fellowship in Christ deeply committed to the well-being of its members. Theologically, the strength of this model lies in its deep Scriptural roots; anthropologically, its strength lies in a deeply ingrained human trait, the human need and subconscious craving for fellowship in almost everything we do as humans. The favorite model of Vatican II, as the Extraordinary Synod of Bishops of 1985 emphasized, was precisely this communal model, the Church as a People of God. The Church exists because human beings *need* each other; they need community.

The basic danger that lurks in this otherwise sound and indeed beautiful understanding of the Church is the fact that the image may lead people to become too introspective and not concerned enough about the world outside the Church-community. To get lost in the joy and blessing of Christian fellowship means to forget the Kingdom for which the Church exists; it is also to forget that the Church *is* mission. There is also the danger that when we speak of the Church as the People of God and as the Body of Christ we become too mystical and possibly get lost in clichés and platitudes. Finally, there is the danger that the communal character can become so dominant that the institutional dimensions of the Church can be made to appear unimportant. These and similar dangers, strongly emphasized by such theologians as Dulles (1978:187–188,202) and McBrien (1980:713), must not be lost sight of.

8.1.1 THE COMMUNAL MODEL: ITS MEANING, STRENGTHS, AND WEAKNESSES

A genuinely Christian community was meant to be as perfect a community as possible. It was meant to be profoundly unique—unique in concept, unique in its oneness and solidarity, unique in its source of life and strength, and unique in its purpose. When applying anthropology to Christian community building, this uniqueness must remain in focus. For an idea of what such a unique community might look like, we might best go to the New Testament churches and to Christ and the Apostles who inspired them.

At the Last Supper Jesus prayed "that all may be one as you, Father, are in me, and I in you" (Jn 17:21), the very ultimate in unity! The love that members of a Christian community should have for one another is the type of love the Father had for humankind when he gave up his only Son (Jn 3:16), the type of love that Jesus had when he laid down his life so that his friends might live (Jn 15:13). The New Testament churches argued: "If God has loved us so, we must have the same love for one another" (1 Jn 4:11).

The Acts of the Apostles tells us that as a result of this striving for nothing less than perfect unity, "the whole group of believers was united, heart and soul" (cf. Acts 4:32). This is, of course, not to say that the early Christian communities did not have their share of jealousies, selfishness, misunderstandings, grudges, anger, lies, quarrels, acts of revenge, divisions, and scandals (*see*, for instance, 1 Cor 1:10–11; 6:7ff; 8:9,12; Gal 5:15; 6:1; Eph 4:31f; Phil 2:3,4,14; Jas 3:16). Despite such imperfections, the New Testament churches strove relentlessly for nothing less than the ideal. It is this *perfect* New Testament model that missiological anthropology must keep in mind when called upon to help build a Christian community, be it a diocese, parish, or a smaller religious organization or institution. Accepting anything less than this perfect New Testament model would entail failing to recognize the meaning of "*Christian* community" and not understanding a primary and essential task and challenge facing missiological anthropology. A closer look at this uniqueness and perfection will, therefore, be necessary. Truly Christian communities strive to maintain the following features:

1) Other communities might be built on self-interest and on a variety of worthy, or conceivably even less worthy, goals. Christian communities rest primarily on *faith-values*.

2) Other communities are formed because the members are in search of freedom from fear, from want, from boredom, from oppression, and the like—that is, freedom from *without*; Christian communities, by contrast, seek freedom from *within*—that is, freedom *to* love God and neighbor *unshackled to selfishness*.

3) Other communities may be built on a less perfect unity; Christian communities can be satisfied with nothing less than *organic* oneness and wholeness.

> I am the vine, you are the branches. He who lives in me and I in him, will produce abundantly, for apart from me you can do nothing. A man who does not live in me is like a withered, rejected branch, picked up to be thrown in the fire and burnt. [Jn 15:5f]

Paul takes up this organic model and elaborates on it in a number of his Letters (e.g., Rom 12; 1 Corinthians 12; Eph 4; Col 1:18), notably in 1 Corinthians 12, the substance of which we quote:

> The body is one and has many members, but all the members, many though they are, are one body; and so it is with Christ. It was in one Spirit that all of us, whether Jew or Greek, slave or free, were baptized into one body . . . If the foot should say, "Because I am not a hand I do not belong to the body," would it then no longer belong to the body? . . . If the body were all eye, what would happen to our hearing? If it were all ear, what would happen to our smelling? As it is, God has set each member of the body in the place he wanted it to be. . . . The eye cannot say to the hand, "I do not need you," any more than the head can say to the feet, "I do not need you." Even those members of the body which seem less important are in fact indispensable. . . . God has so constructed the body as to give greater honor to the lowly members, that there may be no dissension in the body, but that all the members may be concerned for one another. If one member suffers, all the members suffer with it; if one member is honored, all the members share its joy. You, then, are the body of Christ. [1 Cor 12:12–27]

Like any living body, the Christian community has but one soul, the Holy Spirit (1 Cor 12:4,11,13). The members of this Body partake of the one and the same Food, Christ: they partake of the One Christ in prayer, for "where two or three are gathered in my name, there am I in their midst" (Mt 18:20; cf. Mt 5:23–24; 18:19–20); they partake in the One Christ as presented in the Sacred

Scriptures, because the Scriptures are an extension of the apostolic oral preaching (Jn 20:30–31; 1 Jn 5:13) and a way of seeing the Father himself (Jn 14:8–9); they partake in the One Christ above all in the Eucharist, the One Loaf and the One Cup (1 Cor 10:16–17; 11:26).

4) Other communities are built on laws and by-laws. Christian communities are, of course, institutions (Moberg 1984) that similarly need laws and by-laws; however, Christian communities are founded primarily on something far more effective, more durable, and more reliable—on actual mutual trust, respect, forebearance, caring, sharing, and on the promise to serve one another.[2]

Consider *mutual respect*, for instance. The early Christian communities respected each other because each was created according to the image and likeness of God (Gn 1:26). Each member had a unique charism worthy of the highest respect (1 Cor 12:14–24, 28–31). The charism of even the weakest and lowliest was appreciated, for it was regarded as a part of God's plan that allowed for no substitutes (cf. *supra*, 1.2.3). Each member was respected because each had been redeemed at the same Price, the Blood of the Son of God himself (Jn 3:16). Each was respected because whatever was done to the least member of the community was regarded as having been done to God himself (Mt 25:40). Those in positions of responsibility were respected because true authority came from God, and those in authority were accountable not only to the community but to God himself (cf. Rom 12:8; 13:1; Eph 6:1,5; Col 3:20,22; 1 Tm 2:2; 1 Pt 2:18–21).

Or consider the very distinctive characteristic of *bearing one another's burden* (Gal 6:1–10). Meant here is not only a tolerance for each other's weaknesses but also sincere forgiveness and the implication that people must genuinely listen to each other with true human warmth, meaningful encouragement, affirmation, and brotherly and sisterly compassion.

Not to be overlooked, however, is the fact that community life of the New Testament churches went well beyond respect and bearing with one another: the members of the community were actually involved in one another. Of the church of Jerusalem we read that

> the community of believers were of one heart and one mind. None of them ever claimed anything as his own; rather, everything was held in common. [Acts 4:32]

In other words, the early Christians *shared* their blessings—not only their material goods (Gal 2:10; Rom 15:26; 2 Cor 8:9–14) but their spiritual blessings as well. They did this through sharing their personal testimonies (2 Cor 12:2–10; Gal 1:11–20), by confessing their sins to one another (Acts 19:18; Jas 5:16), and by constant prayer for one another (Acts 2:42; 8:24; 2 Cor 1:11; Eph 1:16; Phil 1:19; Col 1:3,9; 1 Thes 1:2; 2 Tm 1:3). Actual sharing of one's time and talent in service of one another was routine; in any case, good wishes were never enough.

If a brother or sister has nothing to wear and no food for the day, and you say to them, "Good-bye and good luck! Keep warm and well fed," but do not meet their bodily needs, what good is that? [Jas 2:15-16]

The early Christians could not forget that their Heavenly Father actually had "shared" his Son with them (cf. Jn 3:16) and that Jesus actually had given them all he had, and had actually "emptied himself" (Phil 2:7). As he had done, so they would have to do for one another.

The way we came to understand love was that he laid down his life for us; we too must lay down our lives for our brothers. [1 Jn 3:16]

Although much more could be said about the first Christian communities, there is only one more observation that space will allow us to make. As the Acts of the Apostles and the various epistles in the New Testament bear out, this deep concern for one another did not make people forget the needs of other communities (Rom 15:25; 1 Cor 16:1-12; 2 Cor 8, 9; Gal 2:10); other communities were, after all, integral parts of the same Body. Nor did the infant Church, despite persecution, forget the Great Commission to make disciples of all nations (e.g., Gal 2:9, Acts *passim*). Without becoming introspective the community was always deeply concerned about its own members. The danger of introspection, however, always lurks in this otherwise excellent view of the Church.

8.1.2 ANTHROPOLOGICAL APPLICATION

What we have said about the ideal Christian community may sound a bit too mystical for any practical application. Nevertheless, we have produced a clear and important statement of a very basic mission goal, and have given a true description of an actual challenge facing Christians in our day. This challenge is faced by all church leaders, all who are responsible for the development of local theologies, all who must preach or teach, all who must prepare liturgical services, all who are engaged in social apostolates, and not least of all by those anthropologists who would wish to apply their field to mission. Building community is a very basic and essential part of the Church's mission. The specific challenge to every Christian community is none other than to "demystify" the New Testament community model by translating it into the concrete sociocultural situation and real life here and now. As we have seen in chapters 5-7, each society has *its* way of respecting an individual, *its* way of bearing another's burden, *its* way of listening, forgiving, caring, sharing, serving, spending oneself for others—in a word, *its* way of becoming a true New Testament Christian community, *here* in Fiji, Angola, Guatemala, or the United States, and *now*, two thousand years after that first Pentecost. *The building of New Testament Christian communities in our own times is, in fact, one of the most central objectives of mission, if not the very heart of mission, the very key to mission success, and therefore a major and fundamental goal of mission anthropology as well.*

8.2 THE CHURCH AS UNIVERSAL SACRAMENT

8.2.1 THE SACRAMENTAL MODEL: ITS MEANING, STRENGTHS, AND WEAKNESSES

By a *sacramental model*, we mean that the Church is viewed as a sign of Christ's continued action in the world through the Holy Spirit toward the fulfillment of God's promises. The sign becomes visible especially in the liturgy of the Church. Originally the word *sacrament* or *mystery* referred to God's love manifested in Wisdom Incarnate working to restore fallen humanity to glory through his death and resurrection. When we speak of the Church as being the "universal sacrament," we mean that Christ *the* Sacrament now works through his Body the Church. "Where two or more are gathered in my name, there am I in their midst also" (Mt 18:20), and where Christ is, there is also his Church. The Church's structure and action (especially its action through the word and sacraments) make the Church into a sign and instrument of God's loving presence and grace. (*Lumen gentium*, no.48; *Gaudium et spes*, no.45; *Ad gentes*, no.2–5; *Sacrosanctum concilium*).

As we pointed out when discussing the concept of model in general (*supra*, 5.1.4), a good model will always be useful, open, fitting, and stimulating. To a large extent, such is the sacramental model. Its strength lies especially in its theological possibilities. Not only is the sacramental view of the Church rooted in basic faith values and well-founded in the Scriptures, but it also opens up a whole new vista for modern theology, suggesting new areas of useful investigation and casting new light on hitherto unsuspected theological relationships. But it goes well beyond theory. When anthropology is applied to mission, the sacramental model provides many useful insights and deeply spiritualizes the whole pastoral approach. The sacramental model, however, shares the introspective weakness of the communal model, with a concentration on the individual's own growth rather than on mission that goes beyond oneself. There is a danger—some say a tendency—for someone who views the Church in this light to become complacent and forgetful of such Christian roles as that of prophet, herald, and servant. In Dulles' words, the sacramental model

> could lead to a sterile aestheticism and to an almost narcissistic self-contemplation. As a remedy, attention must be called to the values of structures, community, and mission brought out in the other models. [1978:202]

8.2.2 ANTHROPOLOGICAL APPLICATION

An important dimension of the Church as Universal Sacrament is *ritual*. As cultural anthropology bears out, religion is never divorced from ritual. This is, of course, particularly true of the Christian faith. Ritual fortifies belief as belief fortifies ritual. It would, therefore, be well to review what was said earlier about the importance of sacred rites (*supra*, 6.3.3.3.2): how, for instance, sacred rites are *dramatizations* of beliefs; how in ritual the holy is reached not only by the spoken word, the read word, or the listened-to word, but also in a communication process *involving all senses*. Thus in ritual, beliefs are not only read and heard but are also *experienced*: experienced through sounds and melodies, using drums, bells, musical instruments, or the clapping of hands; experienced by touching, as in the imposition of hands at an Ordination, or the Anointing of the Sick, or the handshake or embrace at the Kiss of Peace; experienced by tasting, as in Communion; experienced by watching and smelling the fragrant smoke of incense as it rises heavenward toward the throne of God together with the assembly's prayers and sacrifices; experienced by feeling the sprinkling or pouring of water symbolizing the washing away of sin and a dying to the world; experienced by "listening" to colors, such as the flaming red of Pentecost, or to objects like the glowing candles of Easter Vigil that cry out joyful praise to the Light of the World whose light we share and must pass on to others; experienced in bodily gestures and postures (Krosnicki 1987), such as the sign of the cross, the reverent removal of shoes or hat, the devout folding of hands and bowing of the head, the raising of one's arms toward Heaven—the source of unfailing help— through respectful standing, humble kneeling, joyful dancing, and even prostration on the ground as an act of complete abandonment and pouring out of oneself before God and people in absolute trust in God's goodness and mercy. Sacred rites are associated with the most important events in a person's life, such as one's birth, initiation, marriage, and death; and with such fundamental human needs as health, protection against bodily harm, and sustenance itself. What is important to remember is that, just as in the case of community building each culture has *its* own way of respecting an individual, bearing one another's burdens, listening, forgiving, caring, sharing, serving, and spending oneself for another, so it is in the case of ritual: *each culture has its own set of ritual symbols and meanings that should be used as much as possible to make the local church even more recognizable as God's Universal Sacrament.*

But before we conclude our general observations on ritual, there are a number of important culturological precautions that must be kept in mind when contextualizing Christian rites. (1) Sacred ritual is associated with *mystery*, with beliefs that are so rich in content that they can neither be exhausted nor fully comprehended. Contextualization must never become so explicit that it removes the element of mystery and stifles the endless flow of thought, emotion, and motivation associated with the mysterious, the beyond-comprehension. This is especially true in societies such as those we find throughout Africa and Asia. (2) Christian ritual is highly *aesthetic*, and here inculturation has a major role to play (cf. Maldonado, Power 1980). Ritual should represent the best of a community's aesthetic culture—the very best of its literary and poetic ability, the best of its musical and dramatic skills, the best of its sculpture and architecture. The sanctuary and the ark (Ex 35:30-35; 37:1-9), and later the Temple in Jerusalem, represented the acme of Jewish artistic genius. St. Peter's in Rome is the product of the best of European art of its time. While Baroque architecture cries out, *"Only the richest and best* is good enough for the Lord!"*, true modern artistic simplicity states an alternate and no-less-beautiful truth, namely that *nothing* is really good enough for God. We hasten to add, however, that liturgy must not become elitist. Liturgy is for the *people*, not only for priests and monks. We are, therefore, not necessarily speaking of sophisticated art forms; a simple people's folk art—even children's drawings or dance—the *best* they are capable of and coming from their innermost selves, can be art truly worthy of worship. Africans are said to *dance* their religion, as they dance so many other aspects of their lives. (3) Contextualization of Christian ritual must be imaginative but must at all times be primarily concerned about *worshipping*, rather than about *worship*. Contextualization should be concerned more about creating a genuinely prayerful "God-is-with-us" and "He-is-risen" atmosphere than about rules governing art, however important such rules may be for homilies, singing, organ playing, or arrangement of candles and flowers. There is something not quite right when the preacher, choir, or others are more concerned about performing well than they are about worshipping well. (4) Contextualization must never overlook the fact that ritual, although imaginative and constantly aware of the need to keep pace with culture, is nevertheless by its very nature *repetitive* and *traditional*. Ritual is, after all, the memory of a faith community. Many dangers lurk in the craving of our times for newness and originality at the expense of essential repetition and tradition. As anthropology tells us, unless ritual is repetitive and remains traditional, it is not ritual at all. (Cf. Mead 1965.)

Much more could, of course, be said about anthropology and the contextualization of the Church as a universal sacrament. However, as this concluding chapter is intended as a brief epilogue, we shall limit ourselves (1) to reminding the reader of the very pertinent concepts, principles, and illustrations discussed especially in chapters 6-7, and (2) to recommending further study of works that directly relate to the Church as sacrament and that treat the topic more fully than we have been able to do. Much has been written in recent years about cultural adaptation in regard to Christian ritual life, especially since Vatican II. The *Sacrosanctum concilium* (no.3: 37-40) expressly points out that such contextualization is not only proper for mission lands but for all cultures as well, with adjustments to be made to the temperament and traditions of peoples and the times. Speaking expressly but not exclusively of newer churches, the Decree on the Church's Missionary Activity encourages Catholics to

borrow from the customs, traditions, wisdom, teaching, arts and sciences of their people everything which could be used to praise the glory of the Creator, manifest the grace of the Saviour, or contribute to the right ordering of Christian life. [*Ad gentes*, no.22; *see* also *Lumen gentium*, no.13]

Recommended for further study of the Church as sacrament are the following publications. (1) There are the *general* works on myth, religion, and ritual, such as Roger Schmidt's *Exploring Religion* (1980), a *must* for any beginning student of missiological anthropology. There are also such *strictly anthropological* works as Victor Turner's *The Ritual Process* (1969) and *Dramas, Fields, and Metaphors* (1974), Michael Banton's *Anthropological Approaches to the Study of Religion* (1966), Raymond Firth's *Symbols: Public and Private* (1973), Mary Douglas' *Natural Symbols* (1973), and Clifford Geertz's "Religion as a Cultural System" and his "Ethos, World View, and the Analysis of Sacred Symbols" (1973:87–141). For an overview of what anthropologists are saying about ritual symbolism one might consult Nancy D. Munn's "Symbolism in a Ritual Context: Aspects of Symbolic Action" (1973). (2) There are works that provide *historical, theological, cultural, and liturgical backgrounds*. The reader might, for instance, consult Anscar J. Chupungco's *Cultural Adaptation of Liturgy* (1982) and Frank Senn's *Christian Worship and Its Cultural Setting* (1983), to see how one might apply cultural principles to liturgy. (3) For specific regional examples of contextualization there are such still useful pre-Vatican II collections of articles as Johannes Hofinger's *Liturgy and the Missions: The Nijmegen Papers* (1960) and the more recent Concilium publications, *Liturgy and Cultural Religious Traditions* (edited by Herman Schmidt and David Power, 1977). Such liturgical journals as *Worship* and *Ephemerides Liturgicae* similarly contain localized illustrations. Consult, for example, Chupungco (1977), Diekmann (1971), Escamilla (1977), Gusmer (1977), Puthanangady (1977), Ramirez (1977), and Smits (1976). (4) There are the culturologically oriented studies of *specific sacraments and of such aspects of liturgy* as time and place. These works include studies about the Africanization of the rites of Baptism, Confirmation, and the Eucharist by Sanon (1985); indigenous penitential rites by Loewen (1969b, 1969c, 1970a, 1970b); cross-cultural studies about food as symbol by Douglas (1984), S. R. Johnson (1982), Chang (1977), and Firth (1973:243–261); and Thiel's cross-cultural studies of marriage (1970) and ritual times and places (1981). A remarkable example of detailed inquiry into gestures and movements is the work being done by mission anthropologist Herman Hochegger and his Centre d'Etudes Ethnologiques Bandundu in Zaire. A general study of nonverbal communication that might be of particular interest to the liturgist is Mark L. Knapp (1978). (5) The Church as herald and servant, as we shall see, must be there where the people hurt most of all. Much more, therefore, could be said about the relationship of the sacramental role of the Church and the Church as herald and servant. Much more could be said, for instance, about such matters as sacramentals, faith healing, exorcism, and popular piety, all of which represent important forms of both ritual and human needs. These are culturoreligious issues calling for further study to supplement what we have been able to offer in the present text.

8.3 THE CHURCH AS HERALD

8.3.1 *THE KERYGMATIC MODEL: ITS MEANING, STRENGTHS, AND WEAKNESSES*

The kerygmatic model of the Church focuses on *communication as the Church's main human tool*. As Paul stated,

> But how shall they call on him in whom they have not believed? And how can they believe unless they have heard of him? And how can they hear unless there is someone to preach? And how can men preach unless they are sent? [Rom 10:14-15]

The Church is both teacher and prophet—teacher in matters of faith and morals, and prophet when humans part from the message of the Gospel. The Incarnate Word continues to have meaning in the world today through the Church. The Church may not be an expert in economics, politics, or military affairs, but it is the authoritative teacher in what, in God's mind, it really means to be truly human. In a word, the mission of the Church is to be the *vox Dei* in matters of faith and morals, in matters of love and justice, in matters of peace, reconciliation, and salvation.

To speak of teaching and prophesying (i.e., in calling cultures to task) is to speak of communicating. No matter how we look at the mission of the Church—no matter what model we choose—we see the Church communicating. Thus the communal character of the Church is maintained largely through communication; the Church as a sign of God's active presence produces in itself a form of communication; the Church as servant must serve in word and action, communicating the Church's human and divine knowledge and proving the validity of its message by living in accord with what the Church believes and teaches. It is also through communication that the Church progresses along its arduous pilgrim path toward the fulfillment of the Kingdom and through which the Church organizes itself into a visible body.

Both *verbal* and *nonverbal* communication is required by the kerygmatic nature and mission of the Church. Scripture and the teaching authority of the Church are, of course, basically dependent on verbal skills. The Church's communication, however, does not stop there. Christian witness is, in fact, mainly nonverbal; actions *do* indeed speak louder than words, and it is action that makes the Church's words understandable and credible.

Like all models, the kerygmatic model has its advantages and disadvantages (cf. Dulles 1978:202). It has, for instance, the distinct advantage of giving the Church members a deep sense of mission and identity. It generates a deep love for and commitment to the Scriptures, and it produces zeal for the Kingdom. On the other hand, a kerygmatic image of the Church may make Christians so absorbed in the word that they may neglect other dimensions of the Church, including the institutional, the sacramental, and the social. In Dulles' words, this perception of the Church

> tends to oversimplify the process of salvation, to advertise "cheap grace," to be satisfied with words and professions rather than to insist on deeds, especially in the social and public arena. [1978:202]

8.3.2 ANTHROPOLOGICAL APPLICATION

What we are saying is that to be true to its nature and mission, the Church has no choice but to follow *the human laws of communication*. Culture, we have seen, is the underlying code for social behavior; it is the symbolic system of a society. The more clearly we understand the underlying cultural codes for behavior and the symbolic systems of peoples, the more concretely we understand the mission of the Church itself.

But what are those "human laws of communication" of which we speak? We have identified and explained the main "laws," especially in chapters 5–7. Available today are a large number of introductory works on cross-cultural communication: among these are John C. Condon and Fathi S. Yousef's *An Introduction to Intercultural Communication* (1975); K. S. Sitaram and R. T. Cogdell's *Foundations of Intercultural Communication* (1976); Mark L. Knapp's *Nonverbal Communication in Human Interaction* (1978); and Larry A. Samovar and Richard E. Porter's *Intercultural Communication: A Reader* (1982). There are also a number of excellent works that we mentioned earlier (*supra*, 2.3.3.2) that are focused on the communication of the Gospel as such, from which a selection should be made and carefully studied to supplement the present text. The author's own choice of the clearest, most concise, most concrete, and missiologically perhaps most useful works are the following: David J. Hesselgrave, *Communicating Christ Cross-Culturally* (1978), Eugene A. Nida and William D. Reyburn, *Meaning Across Cultures* (1981), and Charles H. Kraft, *Communication Theory for Christian Witness* (1983). For a Roman Catholic perspective, one might best consult Eilers (1987:110–122).

8.4 THE CHURCH AS SERVANT

8.4.1 THE DIACONAL MODEL: ITS MEANING, STRENGTHS, AND WEAKNESSES

By viewing the Church as a servant, we emphasize a very basic characteristic of the mission of Jesus himself. His mission was a total self-giving and an unreserved commitment to the Kingdom of God, a Kingdom of love, justice, peace, and freedom in a world of oppression and sin. The Church continues this self-giving and commitment in Jesus' name. Peace, justice, reconciliation, and love are not secondary to the mission of the Church; they are, instead, *constitutive.* To be the Church of *Christ*, the Church must be the servant of humanity. Or as the great China missionary Blessed Joseph Freinademetz would say, "I am happy to be where there is the cross and suffering, for God is there." In a word, the diaconal model of the Church rests on solid theological ground. Perhaps the chief weakness of the model is in its tendency to downplay other dimensions of the Church and to identify the Church and the Kingdom of God. One might wonder with McBrien (1980:714) why anyone would even want to become a member of a church that would be primarily or exclusively diaconal in nature when one could be even more effective in bringing about social change outside such a church. Also among the weaknesses of this perspective of the Church are the many dangers and temptations associated with the more radical liberation theologies (Ratzinger 1984, 1986; Kloppenburg 1974a).

8.4.2 THE DIACONAL TASKS OF THE CHURCH: WHO ARE THE POOR?

One frequently hears today that the Church, in imitation of Christ, has cast its lot with the poor. Logically enough, missiological anthropology is there to serve "the Church of the Poor." It is, therefore, important for the mission anthropologist to know who the "poor" are.

No single passage of Scriptures is by itself able to tell us what the word *poor* means. The Old Testament in particular is ambiguous (Léon-Dufour 1973:436–438; McKenzie 1965:681-684.) Israel regarded poverty as a despicable state, a punishment from God, whereas riches were a reward for faithfulness to God (Ps 1:1-6), a theme that was picked up later by the Calvinists. Poverty is sometimes attributed to laziness, intemperance, and frivolity (e.g., Pr 28:19). At other times, we are told that it is best to be neither rich nor poor (Pr 30:8-9). Much of this ambiguity comes from the fact that the wisdom tradition in particular comes from a wide range of cultures, over many years. Even though the Qumran indicates that a kind of ascetical poverty was practiced, rabbinical sources before 70 A.D. regard poverty simply as a curse (McKenzie 1965:683). Nevertheless, many passages of the Old Testament urge compassion for the oppressed, the powerless, the hungry, the widow and the orphan, and the exiled (all regarded as "poor"). Such passages declare Yahweh as the avenger and deliverer of the poor (e.g., Ex 3:7-12; 22:21-24; 35:10; 37:11). The Psalmist (e.g., Ps 22:27) and the prophets in particular (cf. Is 1:16f; Jer 22:13-17; Am 5:10-14) hark back again and again to the concern that Yahweh has for his poor, who are regarded as his special friends and servants. Those who are like the poor, that is, those who are humble, meek, God-fearing, and trusting—in a word, those who are "lowly" (e.g., Ps 149:4)—are likewise "Yahweh's poor."

What is beyond the least shadow of doubt is the fact that the Messiah is the Messiah of the Poor. In the sermon on the mount Jesus assures us that the poor are not cursed but blessed indeed (Mt 5:3); they are the privileged heirs of his Kingdom. It is to them that the Messiah brings the Good News (Is 61:1; Lk

4:18), and it is of them that Mary the Handmaid of the Lord sang her Magnificat (Lk 1:46–55). The Messiah of the Poor is himself poor, born in a stable (Lk 2:7), with no place to lay his head (Mt 8:20), and only a cross to die on. The Acts of the Apostles tells us that Jesus did not limit his ministry to preaching but that "he went about doing good works and healing all" (Acts 10:38). The Gospels describe numerous instances that show his deep concern for all types of poverty: he instructed the ignorant, consoled the bereaved, gave sight to the blind, speech to the mute, hearing to the deaf. He cleansed the lepers and made the lame walk. He condemned the wealthy for injustices done to the poor and powerless, fed the hungry multitudes in the desert, and forgave and defended prostitutes. His command to the Apostles was, interestingly enough, twofold: "He sent them forth to proclaim the reign of God and heal the afflicted" (Lk 9:2). The "poor" are, therefore, first and foremost, the hungry, homeless, naked, and all who have been deprived of their basic human rights and voice in society—in a word, they are those who need healing.

There is the type of poverty that strikes certain individuals as individuals; there is also the type of poverty that strikes entire groups. A fundamental task of Christians is to speak for the voiceless, whoever they are: the illiterate, the unemployed, the aged poor, the mentally disturbed, the undocumented aliens, the migrant farmers, the juvenile delinquents, the mentally disturbed street-people digging through the garbage, the bag-ladies dragging themselves and their "precious" belongings to the nearest run-down hostel, the winos and dope addicts, the countless slum and shanty town dwellers—and we might, of course, go on and on in this vein for several more pages describing the world of the poor.

But besides such examples of individual poverty, there are the systemic forms of impoverishment that affect whole nations and large groups qua groups within a society (B. Ward 1966). We refer to such general deprivation of human rights as the helplessness that affects the unborn and their right to life (with 1,500,000 abortions annually in the United States alone); racism in its many subtle forms and disguises; sexism, with women "holding up half the sky" (as Chairman Mao liked to put it) but not quite enjoying half the basic human rights; the deprivation of political, social, economic, and religious rights as is shown by the situation in South Africa, in most Marxist countries and in those governed by military dictatorships (with some 600 million Christians forbidden to exercise their faith freely, with countless others deprived of their property rights or forbidden to form independent labor unions or political parties or to enjoy equal access to education with those who are "fortunate" enough to belong to the "right" party, class, or race). There are also many other injustices, too many to enumerate here, such as the deprivation associated with the policies that are set by international bankers, multinational corporations, and rapid industrialization or those resulting from a fossilized feudal system that for centuries has deprived the masses of their most basic human needs. There are, finally, millions of refugees, victims of war or politics, and millions of poverty-stricken migrant workers who have no voice and an uncertain future. These too are the voiceless for whom the Christian must speak and who must be healed, and whom applied anthropology must serve.

However, some of our examples of poverty may be misleading. Poverty must be looked upon *holistically* (John Paul II 1987b: no. 15). Since "not on bread alone is man to live" (Mt 4:4), there are other essential needs that deprive a person of human dignity besides basic bodily requirements. Walter Burghardt, for instance, speaks of "Seven Hungers of the Human Family" (1976); these include spiritual needs such as forgiveness of sin and knowledge of God. In an address in the United States, Mother Theresa, the world's greatest authority on poverty, called the attention of her stunned audience to the fact that the United States, as rich as it was, had more poverty than India. "Poverty of loneliness!" she explained. People can be "poor," regardless of how large their bank accounts may be and no matter in what sort of luxurious homes they may live.

> Poor is poor,
> Rich is rich,
> Who can tell me
> Which is which?

This is true not only of death but also of all human "poverty." In other words, with all the different types of human needs and misery connected with the human condition, there is no doubt that "the poor you will always have with you" (Mt 26:11). Whether you are rich or poor, you are poor indeed if, for example, you are terminally ill from cancer or AIDS (in some cultures, if you are a leper or an epileptic); if you lose your sight, become paralyzed, or become otherwise seriously handicapped; if you become a victim of extreme depression or are otherwise mentally disturbed; if someone in your family commits suicide; if your family breaks up; if a child runs away from home (and there are today a million such children in the United States alone); if you are an abused child; if you yourself or a member of your family, rich or poor, is an alcoholic or drug addict; if you, whether rich or poor, are a hostage in Lebanon or perhaps have been taken prisoner and have been tortured by your own government. This is, of course, only a partial and very imperfect picture of the poverty of today.

From the earliest times, Christians carried out the twofold command given to the Apostles "to proclaim the reign of God and heal the afflicted" (Lk 9:2). This command binds every follower of Christ. In the words of John XXIII,

> We have today an undeniable duty toward men, in justice and charity, to do everything possible to ensure the subsistence of undernourished peoples, to develop everywhere a more reasonable exploitation of the riches of the soil and underground for the benefit of a rapidly-growing world population and to safeguard at the same time the social equilibrium of the regions affected by this economic development. [Semaine Sociale, Angers, July 1959]

These words are seriously meant, for, according to John XXIII, this "duty" is nothing less than a matter of "justice and charity." Or as his predecessor Pius XII in his missionary encyclical *Evangelii praecones* (no.73) put it, "To disregard this plea [for assistance], to pass it over in silence would not be without guilt in the sight of the Eternal God." We are speaking of nothing less than of a basic *constitution* of the Kingdom of God. Other more notable encyclicals and directives include, for instance, John XXIII's *Mater et magistra* (1961) and his *Pacem in terris* (1963); Vatican II's Pastoral Constitution on the Church in the Modern World (*Gaudium et spes*, 1965); Paul VI's *Populorum progressio* (1967), the Medellín Documents (Eagleson, Scharper, 1979), the *Octogesima adveniens* (issued on the occasion of the eightieth anniversary of the social encyclical *Rerum novarum*, 1971); the document of the Second Synod of Bishops *Justice in the World* (1971); John Paul II's *Redemptor hominis* (1979), *Laborem exercens* (1981a), and *Sollicitudo rei socialis* (1987b); the National Conference of Bishops' pastoral letter on war and peace (1983) and their *Catholic Social Teachings and the U.S. Economy* (1986); and, finally, the *Instruction on Christian Freedom and Liberation* of the Congregation for Doctrine of Faith (Ratzinger 1986:no.44–70). The basic message of all these documents is the same, all echoing Dom Helder Camara's well-known theme, which in turn echoes the inaugural message of the mount (Mt 5:3): "The Church must be the voice of those who cannot speak! The Church is the Church of the Poor or it is not the Church of Christ!"[3] Similar guidance, concern, and commitment to peace and justice have come from the World Council of Churches and other religious communities, from the United Nations, and from countless private organizations throughout the world. Some of the more significant evangelical sources on social justice issues are, for instance, Miriam Adeney, *God's Foreign Policy: Practical Ways to Help the World's Poor* (1984); Ronald J. Sider, ed., *Evangelicals and Development: Toward a Theology of Social Change* (1981); Tom Sine, *The Mustard Seed Conspiracy* (1981); Andrew Kirk, *The Good News of the Kingdom Coming: The Marriage of Evangelism and Social Responsibility* (1983).

8.4.3 ANTHROPOLOGICAL APPLICATION

As St. James reminded the early Christians, it is not sufficient to wish the poor well and simply tell them "Good-bye and good luck! Keep warm and well fed!" (Jas 2:16); the Christian must *do* something about it. The subfield of anthropology known as applied anthropology seeks to do just that (*supra*, 2.2.3). It applies anthropological concepts and principles, such as we discussed in Chapters V–VII, to human needs, for the betterment and advancement of peoples, for the defense of human dignity, and for human self-realization (*supra*, 2.2.3.3). This is but another way of saying that applied anthropology exists, like the Church itself, to serve humanity.

There is much that the Church can learn from applied anthropology, particularly regarding (1) the objectives of and (2) the approach to social betterment.

8.4.3.1 The Objectives of Social Action

Self-Help. Post-World War II reconstruction programs were known for their emphasis on self-help. *To help people help themselves* became the basic aim of such agencies as the United Nations Educational, Scientific, and Cultural Organization (UNESCO), the Food and Agricultural Organization (FAO), and of such national assistance programs as those of the Peace Corps Volunteers. The best food and medicines come packaged in the form of education and corresponding culture change—a change that enables the needy people to produce their own food and to take care of their own illnesses. Whether applied anthropology is focused on food, agriculture, health, technology, or on urban problems, its primary concern is placed where it should be—*on helping people help themselves*. Paternalism is definitely out.

The Root Causes. Moreover, as important as charity may be—and in emergencies it must be given top priority—normally, applied anthropology emphasizes justice rather than charity. The fact is that charity, as important as it is, often fails to ask the *hard* question: What is *the root cause* of the particular problem? Or, perhaps, should we not say that the *greatest* act of charity would be to ask hard questions? As Dom Helder Camara complained, "When we help the poor we are called saints; when we ask why they are poor, we are called communists." In terms of practical anthropology, it is the "communist" question that is more important. Applied anthropology is not against soup-kitchens or works of charity; rather, it seeks to make soup-kitchens obsolete and unnecessary by finding the root cause of hunger and other social evils and by working toward nothing less than *structural* reform. To ask the hard question, to get to the root cause, to aim at structural reform—these must always be the ultimate aim of a Servant Church. As mission history shows (*supra*, chapter 3), such goals have always been present, but unfortunately not without a strong admixture of paternalism.

8.4.3.2 The Approach to Social Action

Good applied anthropology believes in a *holistic* approach to identifying as well as to solving human problems (*supra*, 2.2.1.1). (1) Both *macro* (nonindigenous and worldwide) and *micro* (indigenous and local) factors are taken into account and, as much as possible, dealt with. (2) As basic as injustice is in regard to the problems of poverty, hunger, and other human disorders, it would be simplistic to place all the blame on injustice, as religious workers are sometimes wont to do. Causes can be as complex as humans themselves. (3) Although natural factors such as ecology and the interplay among ecology, technology, and social and religious patterns may be exaggerated by ecological anthropologists (*supra*, 5.1.6.1.4), the fact of ecological influences in human problems cannot be denied. Similarly, a good anthropological analysis will not put all the blame on others but will take the local history and ethnohistory into consideration (*supra*, 5.1.6.2.3) when studying human suffering. (4) Applied anthropology also makes good use of sociological and psychological theory (*supra*, 2.2.4.1; 5.1.6.4) in diagnosing and solving problems. (5) A holistic approach recognizes that sometimes the oppressed may at least partly be responsible for their sad plight. They, too, can sometimes be quite materialistic, pleasure-seeking, living beyond their means, not availing themselves of opportunities, wasteful in the use of their limited resources, and undisciplined; their own priorities, government policies, and culture can, in fact, be their worst enemy (*supra*, 5.2.3.2.5). Not being infallible or impeccable, the oppressed can even become oppressors themselves.

A number of applied anthropological models come into question (cf. van Willigen 1976:83–85). Because they are models that a Servant Church can use, we shall examine them a bit more closely.

The Applied Ethnological Model. This is the model used by George Foster (1969, 1973). The client selects a strictly anthropological problem and passes it on to a professional ethnologist who researches the relevant ethnology. It is the client, not the ethnologist, who is directly involved in the social action as such.

The Social Advocacy Models: The Vicos and Fox Models. Applied anthropologists do not merely wait to be asked for advice. A major task of applied anthropology and a major aspect of the mission of the Servant Church is to *promote* desirable change. Although ultimately it is the oppressed who must decide what is desirable and what is not, the needy may sometimes be so utterly helpless that they cannot extricate themselves from their oppression without outside advocacy and priming. Very often nothing less than a *structural* change in society is required, and there is little, short of violence, that the voiceless and disenfranchised might be able to do to bring about such a change. Someone else, therefore—someone like the Church (or social scientists, for that matter)—must begin the process of liberation. Some applied anthropologists are professional advocacy strategists. Their knowledge and experience should be adopted by the Church, especially when the basic problem seems to be cultural. Sometimes the oppressed must first be made aware of their own true needs, of their potential, and of their hidden power. The oppressors themselves must be made aware and convinced of the rights of the oppressed. Advocacy calls for organization that may be totally unfamiliar to the oppressed.

There are two well-known models employed in advocacy work by applied anthropologists that might be adapted for church-related social action: the Cornell-sponsored Vicos *project model* mentioned earlier (*supra*, 2.2.3.1) and Sol Tax's *action model*.

Vicos was a Cornell University demonstration project in Peru directed by anthropologist Holmberg and some colleagues. A large, landed estate was rented in the hope of putting an end to the exploitation of Indian tenant farmers. At first the anthropologists assumed the role of *patrons* with a view to guiding the Indians away from the dependency that is generally associated with Latin American large-scale farms called *haciendas*. After ten years of

research, careful planning, and corresponding community education, the unthinkable was achieved: agricultural, social, and structural changes were successfully introduced; the Indians chose
their own representatives; they purchased the land, and, in a word,
the one-time serfs became self-sufficient farmers.

The other model, known as "action anthropology," or sometimes "the Fox
model," (in reference to the Fox Indians) is more common. Action anthropology does not believe in *directing* a project as did the Vicos project. It prefers to
take the local people where they are, expand their range of alternatives, help
them to define their socioeconomic goals, and provide them with corresponding skills necessary to achieve such goals. It tries to provide the legal and other
expertise to document tribal land ownership or the medical expertise for setting
up neighborhood health centers. It takes into consideration the lack of time for
research. It stresses the need to maintain and strengthen the community's
identity, and it emphasizes locally controlled strategies rather than external
services and bureaucracies (van Willigen 1976:83).

The Community Development Model believes in community betterment
from within the community itself. It therefore relies on the theory of "cooperation in change." Ward Goodenough's classic *Cooperation in Change* (1963)
should be read by every church worker, as it contains idea after idea directly
applicable to the type of church-related advocacy proposed in the present
book. In this model, the anthropologist does not direct change but stimulates
the community, serves as consultant and facilitator, and works closely from
within the communal framework of the people. The model relies primarily on
education and cooperation.

The Clinical Model is a recently developed approach in which the anthropologist, in the capacity of researcher and consultant, serves as a cultural specialist
in solving such clinical problems as drug addiction and alcoholism (Rosenstiel,
Freeland 1973). Here, too, there is much that the Servant Church can learn
from anthropology.

8.4.4 SUPPLEMENTARY READINGS

A considerable amount of experience has been gained by anthropologists,
especially in the last fifty years. These anthropologists worked not only as
analysts and advocates but also as planners and policy formulators, consultants, and decision makers. Their invaluable experience is now available for
church-related social action.

We have explained and illustrated much anthropological theory in the
foregoing chapters. Much more, of course, could have been said. We therefore
once again urge the reader to supplement the present book, first of all, with
studies in *general* applied anthropology, especially Chambers (1985), Eddy,
Partridge (1978), Bodley (1976), G. M. Foster (1973), Arensberg, Niehoff
(1964), Goodenough (1963), and Spicer (1952). At the same time, we must call

the reader's attention to the vast literature now available to church workers in such *specializations* as community development, education, rural and urban development, health and illness, and social pathology.

For comprehensive bibliographies in the various applied anthropological specializations, we recommend especially Chambers (1985:96–99, 132–136), Partridge (1984:95–117), and van Willigen, Dewalt (1985:93–117).

Medical anthropology is perhaps the best-developed specialization (Wirsing, McElroy 1981). Available are bibliographical resources such as Todd and Ruffini's *Teaching Medical Anthropology* (1979) and specialized journals like *Social Science and Medicine, Medical Anthropology*, and the *Medical Anthropology Quarterly*. There are also a number of medical anthropological textbooks and readers that prove useful especially for beginners in the field; among them are G. M. Foster and B. Anderson's *Medical Anthropology* (1978), A. McElroy and P. K. Townsend's *Medical Anthropology in Ecological Perspective* (1979), and L. Tancredi's *The Anthropology of Medicine* (1983). Nutritional problems, of special interest to the Church, are well represented in medical anthropological literature. For a survey of the field, one might consult, for instance, E. Montgomery and J. W. Bennet's "Anthropological Studies of Food and Nutrition: The 1940s and the 1970s" (1979). This specialization of medical anthropology has several professional journals, among them, *Ecology of Food and Nutrition*. Books specifically on nursing and culture are also available, e.g., Leininger (1970); likewise available are applied anthropological resources on culture and aging, e.g., Fry (1981), Gelfand and Kutzik (1979). There is also considerable literature on culture and drug abuse, e.g., Michael Agar's *Ripping and Running* (1973). Studies on the relationship of culture and alcoholism have been published in such edited works as Mac Marshall, *Beliefs, Behaviors, and Alcoholic Beverages* (1979), Michael W. Everett et al., *Cross-Cultural Approaches to the Study of Alcohol* (1976), and Edith Lisensky Gomberg, Helene Raskin White, and John A. Carpenter, eds., *Alcohol, Science and Society Revisited* (1986).

Of quite general interest to church workers should be the rapid development of the field of educational anthropology, which has produced a literature almost as vast as that of medical anthropology. General works in educational anthropology include J. Friedman Hansen's *Sociocultural Perspectives on Human Learning* (1979). Of special interest to churches in highly heterogeneous societies like that of the United States are the many studies related to the education of ethnic groups, e.g., J. U. Ogbu, *Minority Education and Caste* (1978). The journal that focuses on the subject of educational anthropology is the *Anthropology and Education Quarterly*. Regarded as classics in the field are Spindler (1955, 1963) and Kimball (1974). Missiological work in educational anthropology has been done by Marvin K. Mayers (1974, 1985).

The dominant demographic trend of the last several decades, second only to the growth of population itself, has been urbanization (Brown, Jacobson 1987). Since 1950 the urban population increased from 600 million to no less than 2 billion. Around the year 2000, the majority of humanity will live in cities. As a result urban anthropology has grown by leaps and bounds. Useful are, for example, the reference works of A. Southall, *Urban Anthropology* (1973); the reader edited by T. Weaver and D. White, *The Anthropology of Urban Environments* (1972); Ulf Hannerz, *Exploring the City: Inquiries Toward an Urban Anthropology* (1980); and E. Eames and J. G. Goode, *Anthropology of the City: An Introduction to Urban Anthropology* (1977). For a survey of urban anthropology and a review of the state of the art one might consult Wulff (1976), Gulick (1973), R. Keesing (1976:503–516), and P. Gutkind in Southall's book referred to above (1973). Unfortunately, despite the deep interest of the churches in urban ministries, there seems to be relatively little awareness or appreciation of the developments made in the field of urban anthropology.[4]

In community and regional development, available are such resources as: Charles Erasmus' *Man Takes Control: Cultural Development and American Aid* (1961), G. Dalton's *Economic Anthropology and Development* (1971), and D. C. Pitt's *Development from Below: Anthropologists and Development Situations* (1976).

In agricultural and rural development there are such useful works as Dobyns, Doughty, and Lasswell's *Peasants, Power, and Applied Social Change* (1971) and J. B. Brown's *Rural Revitalization: A Challenge for Public-Interest Anthropology* (1977).

It should finally be noted that a number of the specializations referred to above have formed professional associations that should be of interest to mission anthropologists. Among these are the Society for Urban Anthropology, the Society for Psychological Anthropology, the Society of Medical Anthropology, the Council on Anthropology and Education, and the Council on Nutritional Anthropology. All have headquarters in Washington, D.C.

8.5 THE CHURCH AS INSTITUTION

8.5.1 THE INSTITUTIONAL MODEL OF THE CHURCH: MEANING, STRENGTHS, AND WEAKNESSES

The institutional model views the Church as being primarily an identifiable society, an organization with offices, structure, order, discipline, and obedience. The Church is intended by God as his visible instrument of salvation.

But as Dulles warns us, a clear distinction must be made between *institution* and *institutionalism*. "A Christian," he says, "may energetically oppose institutionalism and still be very much committed to the Church as institution" (1978:40). *Lumen gentium*, the Dogmatic Constitution on the Church of Vatican II, which we regard as a basic guide for missiological anthropology, clearly does not endorse institutionalism even while it supports the institutional character of the Church. The Council strongly emphasizes the fact that the Church is far more than a visible society—that it is a mystery, the Body of Christ, a Sacrament, and Herald. In other words, Vatican II views the juridical organizational aspect of the Church in a much broader and deeper context than did the institutionalists of the late Middle Ages and especially the defenders of the papacy during the Counter-Reformation and particularly in the last few centuries up to 1950. Dulles goes on to point out that institutionalism tends to be clericalist, juridicist on the pattern of the secular state, and triumphalistic. He states that

> in spite of the overemphasis on the institutional in official Roman Catholic theology, especially since the Reformation, the institutional model of the Church has rarely been advocated in its purity. . . . They tempered the institutional with more spiritual and organic conceptions, such as those of the communion of grace or the Body of Christ. For a fuller understanding of moderate institutionalism, therefore, one must draw upon the communitarian and mystical views of the Church. [Dulles 1978:50]

The main advantages of viewing the Church as institution are due to (1) its strong endorsement in official Catholic teaching in the past few centuries; (2) its insistence on continuity with Christian origins; and (3) its ability to instill a strong sense of corporate identity and loyalty. However, the model has some very serious disadvantages: (1) the theory lacks the strong basis in Scripture and in early Church tradition that the other models discussed have; (2) its clericalism makes the laity passive and exaggerates the role of human authority in the Church; (3) it stifles theological growth; and (4) it militates against the spirit of the times, especially against interfaith dialogue and ecumenism. (Dulles 1978:47–50.)

8.5.2 ANTHROPOLOGICAL APPLICATION

What is of special importance to Christians is the fact that the Church as institution (Moberg 1984) is far more than an institution; it is a *mystery*, a unique institution that transcends human understanding. Although it is true that the Church as institution is not the primary image that Christians must keep in mind, it is nevertheless the dimension of the Church that applied anthropology as a purely human tool serves most directly. Applied anthropology has much to offer the local as well as the universal Church regarding human organization. It assists in policy analysis, program evaluation, needs-assessment, cost-benefit issues, intrainstitutional communication, corporate identity and loyalty, social forecasting, and other aspects of management and development of institutions.

We have illustrated the relevancy of anthropological theory to human organization when we spoke, for instance, of group contact and conflict within Christian communities, institutions, and agencies (*supra*, 5.2.2.6.4). We have also illustrated the importance of cultural integration and how useful such theory can be for forecasting the impact or chain reaction resulting from a decision and how the knowledge of cultural linkages might identify the most promising starting points and the least disorganizing approaches to goals. We have also seen how important the underlying psychology of a society is for any organization (chapter 6). We have seen also how, in making decisions, individual Christians and their institutions must keep culture dynamics constantly in mind (chapter 7). In fact, without making the institutional model our dominant image of the Church, we could have nevertheless included the applications regarding the communal, sacramental, kerygmatic, and diaconal roles of the Church under the head of "Church As Institution."[5] Many of the supplementary readings suggested there could also have been suggested here. The Church is indeed a genuinely *human* institution, but it is an institution that is called to be a perfect New Testament community, a true reflection of God's presence, God's mouthpiece as herald and prophet, and God's servant. We might add that it is a human institution called to live up to almost a hundred other subimages scattered throughout the Bible.

Good introductions to organizational anthropology are, for instance, S. Nagel and M. Neef's *Policy Analysis in Social Science Research* (1979), Erve Chambers' *Applied Anthropology: A Practical Guide* (1985:138–211), and van Willigen and Dewalt's *Training Manual in Policy Ethnography* (1985).

CONCLUSION

What better way is there to conclude the present work than to hark back to our "preamble" (chapter 1)—to the theological foundations of missiological anthropology? Why should the Church be concerned about cultures? By "Church" we mean, of course, every Christian, but especially those called to a ministry and those in leadership roles. We pose the same question now. Why, we ask, should the Church be concerned about cultures? Our answer was and is: *We are concerned about cultures so that the Church may be as perfect a channel of Grace as possible, as worthy an instrument in the hands of God as possible, as good, wise, and faithful a servant as is humanly possible*—this, and this alone, is our aim and our theological justification for a Church-related applied science of culture that we have called "Missiological Anthropology."

NOTES

1. The Theological Foundations of Missiological Anthropology

1. Other considerations that must enter into any full discussion of mission spirituality include (1) the scriptural and theological basis of the spirituality in question; (2) the specific psychological and situational context—that is, the education, health, talent, the socioeconomic situation, and the spiritual level of the person concerned; (3) the culture of the society; and (4) the type of ministry or witness in which one is engaged.

2. Christian spirituality has been treated, for example, by such authors as Pourrat (1953-55), Bouyer (1963-69), Goldbrunner (1964); Besnard (1965); Boyd (1965); Aumann, Hopko, Bloesch (1968); Sudrack (1968); Goodall (1968); Gannon and Traub (1968); Carter (1971); Fox (1972, 1976,1979); Metz (1978), Miles (1983). For specifically mission spirituality, *see* Reilly (1978), Godwin (1977), Bosch (1978), Nemer (1983), Raguin (1973), and the National Conference of Catholic Bishops' *To the Ends of the Earth: A Pastoral Statement on World Mission* (1986, no. 55-60). For a scripturally based spirituality praised highly by Christians of all traditions, *see* Richard J. Foster's *Celebration of Discipline: The Path to Spiritual Growth* (1978), *Freedom of Simplicity* (1981), and *Study Guide for Celebration of Discipline* (1983a). For a general overview of Protestant spiritual tradition, *see* Senn (1986).

2. Missiological Anthropology

1. Kluckhohn's actual wording is: "Anthropology holds up a great mirror to man and lets him look at himself in his infinite variety" (1949:11).

2. *See*, for instance, McGavran's classic *The Bridges of God* (1955, rev. ed. 1981), *How Churches Grow* (1966), and *Understanding Church Growth* (1970).

3. For more about Schmidlin, Streit, and their associates, *see* K. Müller 1980, 1984; Henkel 1982; Glazik 1961.

4. At this juncture it would be advisable to scan available bibliographies on missiological literature and to page through publication notices and bibliographies in such journals as the *International Review of Mission*, *Missiology*, and the *International Bulletin of Missionary Research*. (*See* below, note 9.)

5. *Infra*, 4.4.2.1 and 4.4.2.3.

6. For bibliographies and evaluation of Bavinck, Kraemer, and Hoekendijk, *see* van den Berg 1983,7:171-175; Hoedemaker 1980,4:60-64; 1977,2:71-11.

7. For more about this revolutionary thinker, *see* Allen 1962, 1964; Paton 1960, 1968; Beyerhaus, Lefever 1964:33-39; Branner 1977.

8. More comprehensive coverage of the history of U.S. Protestant missiology will be found in Chaney 1976 and Forman 1974.

9. The outstanding *Catholic* mission libraries are those of the Gregorian University and the Sacred Congregation for the Evangelization of Peoples, the Pontificia Biblliotheca delle Missioni (Henkel 1982:19), the latter library containing no less than

100,000 volumes. Excellent collections of missionary study resources will be found also at various centers and institutes of mission orders and congregations, such as that of the Divine Word Missionaries located at St. Augustin, near Bonn. This center has besides strictly missiological and theological holdings, an outstanding general anthropological collection of 80,000 volumes and a specialized sinological library of 75,000 volumes. Other very useful missiological resources in Europe are those at Louvain, Münster, Madrid, and Lisbon. In the United States, good resources will be found especially at such Catholic missionary training centers as the Catholic Theological Union in Chicago and the Maryknoll School of Theology in Maryknoll, N.Y.

In the United States, the richest *Protestant* holdings were at one time those located at the Mission Research Library (now a part of the Union Theological Library of New York), with 100,000 items catalogued by author, title, and subject, followed by such collections as those of the Day Missions Library at Yale and the holdings at Princeton, the University of Chicago and neighboring theological schools, Duke University, Harvard, Hartford Seminary Foundation, Southern Methodist University, Southern Baptist Theological Seminary in Louisville, School of World Mission at Fuller Theological Seminary, and Wheaton College in Wheaton, Illinois. In Britain, the better-known missiological resources are the libraries of the Church Missionary Society, the United Society for the Propagation of the Gospel, Selly Oak Colleges at Birmingham, and the New College at the University of Edinburgh. In Scandinavia, good missiological resources are located at Vahls Missions Library (Aarhus), the Egede Institutet (Oslo), and Uppsala University. In Germany, they are found at the Universities of Hamburg and Tübingen as well as at the Hackmannsche Bibliothek at Marburg, and at the library of the Rhenish Missionary Society in Wuppertal Barmen and the Norddeutsche Mission in Bremen. (Cf. Neill, Anderson, Goodwin 1971:407.)

One should, of course, not overlook the vast amount of information that is to be found especially in the larger general libraries and the many specialized resources at various research centers and schools around the world. Within the relatively small area of Washington, D.C. alone, for instance, one has at one's disposal unbelievably large library resources. The Library of Congress alone has about 14,000,000 volumes and well over 44,000,000 other catalogued material, much of which would be of interest to missiologists. There are also in Washington many specialized libraries that are at least indirectly related to missiology, such as those of the National Geographic Society, the School of Advanced International Studies of the Johns Hopkins University, the Smithsonian Institution, and countless other libraries of various research centers, theological schools, and universities of the area. Many are focused on specific geographical areas (Africa, Latin America, Far East and Asia, etc.), art, linguistics, health, and other aspects of missiology (Tra, Rashke, Luzbetak 1969:40–56). In England, such large general resources, often with invaluable missiological significance, are, for example, at the so-called "copyright" libraries containing all copyrighted publications of Britain, namely the British Museum (especially its vast collection of periodical literature), the Bodleian Library at Oxford, and the Cambridge Library (Neill, Anderson, Goodwin 1971:407f)—not to mention the splendid specialized collections of materials on former colonies available in England and elsewhere.

Important *archival resources* are those of the Sacred Congregation for the Evangelization of Peoples (Vatican), covering Catholic missionary action ever since the founding of the Congregation in 1622, with selections of the archives made available since 1893 as *Collectanea* and since 1938 as *Sylloge*. Other important missiological depositories are found at various headquarters of Catholic and Protestant mission societies and boards, in general national archives (e.g., at London, Madrid), and in such holdings as the former Missionary Research Library (Neill, Anderson, Goodwin 1971:31f).

For *the current status of Catholic missions*, one might consult such general resources as the *Origins* (Washington, D.C.), SEDOS (*see* Motte,Lang 1982:245f, 281, 459f, 633–49, 655–673), *Fides* (Rome), *Agenzia Informazioni: Missionarie* (Rome), *Pro Mundi Vita* (Brussels), *Acta Apostolicae Sedis* (Vatican). Information-gathering on current Protestant missions is being conducted today by the Mission Advanced Research and Communication Center (MARC) of Pasadena, California in collaboration with the School of World Mission at the Fuller Theological Seminary and the World Council of Churches (Geneva) and various national councils. Also useful are such ecumenical resources as the *International Documentation on the Contemporary Church* (IDOC).

Bibliographical resources, despite the relative newness of the field of missiology, are considerable, thanks especially to the monumental *Bibliotheca Missionum* (1911–1974, 31 volumes) and since 1935 the annual supplementary volumes *Bibliografia Missionaria* (beginning 1935, 49 volumes as of 1985). In fact, bibliographical interests have been largely responsible for the very birth of modern Catholic missiology (Henkel 1982:16–19). To this day bibliographical work is given high priority by missiologists, especially by the International Association for Mission Studies, which has established an active documentation, archives, and bibliographical network.

General missiological reference works, such as dictionaries and encyclopedias, were among the missiologist's felt needs as early as 1891, when Edwin M. Bliss published his work. It was, however, not until eighty years later that missiologists had anything resembling an "encyclopedia," actually an informative one-volume *Concise Dictionary of the Christian World Mission*, edited by Stephen Neill, Gerald H. Anderson, and John Goodwin (1971). This work is presented mostly from the Protestant perspective. *The Encyclopedia of Modern Christian Mission* (Goddard, ed., 1967) is focused on information about Protestant mission organizations. *The New Catholic Encyclopedia* (vol. 1–16, 1964; supplement, 1979) is a general coverage of Catholicism, including the missiological dimensions. A recent, ecumenical, epoch-making encyclopedia of direct concern to missiologists is the *World Christian Encyclopedia: A Comparative Survey of Churches and Religions in the Modern World, A.D. 1900–2000* edited by D. Barrett in 1981 (*see* the special issue evaluating this monumental work in *Missiology*, 1984,1:5–78) and Paul Cardinal Poupard's edited *Dictionaire des Religions* (1984). Most recently to appear is the German ecumenical *Lexicon Missionstheologischer Grundbegriffe* (1987) edited by K. Müller and T. Sundermeier. Most welcome, of course, is the new monumental *Encyclopedia of Religion*, (1987) edited by Mircea Eliade and his associates.

Missiological literature is largely *periodical*. The Missionary Research Library of New York in its halcyon days could boast of no less than 750 current mission-related periodicals; today, the Pontifical Missionary Library has in its collection some 3,416 periodicals that have ceased publication (Henkel 1982:19) and 630 current journals (Metzler 1981:125). The leading professional English-language missiological journals are the *International Bulletin of Missionary Research*, the largest missiological periodical today, with a subscription of 9,000 (in existence since 1950 under slightly different names and now published by the Overseas Ministries Study Center of Ventnor, N.J., now located in New Haven, Connecticut); the *International Review of Mission* (in existence since 1912, originally called the *International Review of Missions*, published by the World Council of Churches, Geneva); and *Missiology* (with the subtitle of *An*

International Review, published since 1973 by the American Society of Missiology). Perhaps the oldest Catholic missiological journal in the United States is the *Worldmission* (New York). Somewhat less known to English-speaking readers are such excellent Catholic journals as the *Neue Zeitschrift für Missionswissenschaft* (Beckenried, Switzerland), *Zeitschrift für Missionswissenschaft und Religionswissenschaft* (Münster), *Anzeiger für Seelsorge,* and *Missio-Pastoral* (Aachen), *KM* (Bonn), *Eglise Vivante* (Louvain), *Missi* (Lyon), *Parole et Mission* (Paris), *Spiritus* (Paris), *Misiones Extranjeras* (Burgos), *Mensaje* (Madrid), *Het Missiewerk* (Nijmegen), *Euntes Docete* (Rome), among others. Among the more outstanding European Protestant journals, perhaps somewhat less known to English-speaking readers, are *Evangelisches Missions-Magazin* (Basel), *Evangelische Missions-Zeitschrift, Svensk Missionstidskrift* (Uppsala), and *De Heerbaan,* (Amsterdam). Also less known are such recent publications as the new Catholic periodical *Kosmos* (Washington, D.C.), *Inculturation: Working Papers on Living Faith and Cultures* (Rome), the *FABC Papers* (Federation of Asian Bishops' Conference, Hong Kong), and the many valuable newsletters like the Protestant *Scan* (Abington, Pennsylvania), *Pulse* (Wheaton, Illinois). Also noteworthy are the *Church and Cultures* of the Pontifical Council for Culture and the many newsletters of missionary orders and societies and research centers, for example, the *SEDOS BULLETIN* (Rome), the *Westfriars* (Franciscan Province of St. Barbara, California), and *Inter-Religio* (Nagoya, Japan). Still other journals directly relevant to mission problems are specialized according to discipline or geography. There are also the journals of particular religious orders; for instance, the professional periodicals of the Divine Word Missionaries *Anthropos, Verbum,* and *Monumenta Serica* (all three published at St. Augustin, West Germany), *Folklore Studies* (Nagoya, Japan), *Philippine Studies* (Cebu, Philippines), *DiWA, Studies in Philosophy and Theology* (Tagaytay, Philippines); or the many Jesuit journals, such as the *Japan Missionary Bulletin* (Tokyo), *Inculturation,* sponsored by the Columban Fathers (Seoul, Korea); and the Franciscan contributions, such as the *The Americas* (Washington, D.C.). There are, of course, many periodicals of varying quality that are basically promotional and popular.

The leading Catholic *publishers* of mission studies in the English-speaking world today are, no doubt, the Maryknollers and their Orbis Books. The leading Protestant counterparts are such publishing houses as the Friendship Press, an interdenominational agency of the National Council of Churches, and Eerdmans of Grand Rapids. Not to be overlooked, however, are such basically denominational publishers as the Abingdon Press of Nashville and the British Lutterworth Press. Appreciated especially by a large number of active missionaries is the steady flow of missiological publications coming from the William Carey Library of Pasadena, California. For additional information on missiological resources, *see* Neill, Anderson, Goodwin (1971), s.v. *Archives, Bibliographies, Periodicals for Missionary Study,* and *Mission Libraries;* Müller, K. and T. Sundermeier (1987:206-225).

10. An art or science can hardly prosper unless opportunities are available to the particular group of specialists for cross-fertilization, challenge, mutual support, and transference of knowledge from the older to the younger specialist. Such services are provided by professional missiological associations, research centers, conferences, symposia, and the like. The American Society of Missiology (ASM), for instance, is the type of professional association we have in mind. Founded in 1973, today, the society can boast of about five hundred members (W. Shenk 1987:20). Its articles of incorporation describe its goals as:

to promote the scholarly study of theological, historical, social and practical questions relating to the missionary dimension of the Christian church; to relate studies in missiology to the other scholarly disciplines; to promote fellowship and cooperation among individuals and institutions engaged in activities and studies related to missiology; to facilitate mutual assistance and exchange of information among those thus engaged; to encourage research and publication in the study of Christian mission. [W. Shenk 1987:36]

The American Society of Missiology holds an annual meeting and publishes the journal *Missiology*, a quarterly continuing the original journal *Practical Anthropology*. It has a worldwide circulation of about two thousand. The organization is interconfessional and multidisciplinary and is a member of the Council on the Study of Religion (Luzbetak 1976b:11f). It also publishes a monograph series. Such national and regional associations bring their members into contact with one another. Such is also the case with the International Association for Mission Studies (IAMS), whose official aims are

to promote the scholarly study of theological, historical, and practical questions relating to mission; to disseminate information concerning mission among all those engaged in such studies and among the general public and to publish the results of research; to relate studies in mission to studies in theological and other disciplines; to promote fellowship, cooperation and mutual assistance in mission studies; to organize international conferences of missiologists; to encourage the creation of centers of research; and to stimulate publications in missiology.

IAMS publishes *Mission Studies* (formerly *IAMS NEWSLETTER*), from which are quoted the aims of the organization. IAMS sponsors workshops and consultations on bibliography, documentation, and archives. In post-World War II years, professional missiological associations have multiplied around the world. For listings of such associations, *see* Verkuyl 1978:72f, 87; IAMS publishes a register of its member-institutions in its *Directory of Centers for Religious Research*. For a history of the Association of Professors of Mission in North America, *see* Horner 1987: 120-124.

Despite the slow and uncertain start that graduate training in missiology had in the United States, considerable progress has nevertheless been made (Beaver 1976:75-87). The *International Bulletin of Missionary Research* (1983:104-134) lists no less than 145 degree-granting institutions and 934 doctoral dissertations from 1945-1981 in North America alone, while the 1982 *Directory of Study Centers* of MARC/World Vision International (Monrovia, California) provides 82 pages listing Protestant study centers. Note also the general report, "Doctor of Missiology Degree in North American Theological Schools," *International Bulletin of Missionary Research* (1986:177).

11. In chapter 5 we shall discuss the author's technical usage of the terms *social* and *cultural*. The practitioner, especially the experienced administrator, may be more knowledgeable about certain *social* patterns (i.e., actual behavior); the anthropologist, on the other hand, may know much more about the code underlying actual behavior, (i.e., culture in the strict sense of the term). We shall emphasize this distinction and show the necessity of studying and dealing with both dimensions when applying anthropology to mission.

12. For the Catholic biblical basis for missionary action, *see* Senior, Stuhlmueller

1983. For Protestant theology of missions, *see* Glasser, McGavran 1983; Bassham 1979; Verkuyl 1978:89–117; G. Peters 1972.

13. Important collaborators of *Practical Anthropology* were such professional mission anthropologists/linguists as James O. Buswell, Joseph Grimes, Donald R. Jacobs, Charles Kraft, Jacob A. Loewen, Eugene A. Nida, Lowell L. Noble, William D. Reyburn, William Smalley, Claude E. Stipe, Charles R. Taber, Robert B. Taylor, Alan R. Tippett, and William L. Wonderly.

14. That there was a felt need for systematic manuals was evidenced especially by the reception of Nida's pioneer works, especially his excellent *Customs and Cultures* and *Message and Mission*, and the handbooks by various authors that soon followed. For example, Mayers' *Christianity Confronts Culture* deals with the educational dimension, and Hesselgrave's *Communicating Christ Cross-Culturally* focuses on communications theory. See also the present author's own *Church and Cultures*.

15. Held at Willowbank, Bermuda, in January 1978, with thirty-three theologians, anthropologists, linguists, missionaries, and pastors in attendance.

16. When on May 20, 1982 John Paul II founded the Pontifical Council for Culture, he declared:

> I have decided to found and institute a Council for Culture, capable of giving the whole Church a common impulse in the continuously renewed encounter between the salvific message of the Gospel and the multiplicity of cultures, in the diversity of cultures to which she must carry her fruits of grace.
>
> The Council will pursue its ends in an ecumenical and brotherly spirit, promoting also dialogue with non-Christian religions, and with individuals or groups who do not profess any religion, in a joint search for cultural communication with all men of good will. [*Church and Cultures: Bulletin of the Pontifical Council for Culture*, 1984,1:3]

The aims of the Council are spelled out as follows in its newsletter *Church and Cultures*.

—To witness to the Holy See's deep interest in the progress of culture and in the dialogue between cultures and the Gospel.
—To participate in the Roman Departments and the cultural institutions of the Holy See so as to facilitate co-ordination.
—To enter into dialogue with the Episcopal Conferences with the aim of encouraging a fruitful exchange about the research, initiatives and cultural accomplishments carried out by local Churches and of enabling the whole Church to benefit from them.
—To collaborate with international Catholic organizations of a university, of a historical, philosophical, theological, scientific, artistic and intellectual nature, and to promote their reciprocal cooperation.
—To ensure the effective participation of the Holy See in international congresses concerned with science, culture and education.
—To facilitate Church-culture dialogue at the level of universities and research centres, organizations of artists and specialists, researchers and scholars, and to promote worthwhile meetings between these cultural groups.
—To welcome to Rome representatives of culture interested in a better under-

standing of the Church's activities in this field, and in benefiting the Holy See with their rich experience. (Aims as stated in *Church and Culture: Bulletin of the Pontifical Council for Culture*)

17. This is largely a summary of the author's article "Prospects for a Better Understanding and Closer Cooperation Between Anthropologists and Missionaries," in *Studies in Third World Societies*, no.25 (1985), pp. 1–53.

18. For further reading on the subject, *see* Claude E. Stipe's excellent bibliography (1980) and No.25 and 26 (1985) of *Studies in Third World Societies* (Williamsburg, Virginia: College of William and Mary).

19. For examples of some of the worst type of antimissionary negativism, *see* Chagnon 1974 and Tonkinson 1974; for a well-intentioned but nonetheless biased example of negativism, *see* "The Declaration of Barbados for the Liberation of Indians," 1972. For examples of outright diatribe, *see* Loth 1963 and H. Mohr 1965.

20. *See* U.S. Catholic Mission Association, *Mission Institutes: Programs in North America for Missionaries—1987*, Washington, D.C., 1986.

21. *Supra*, chapter 2, note 10.

22. *Supra*, chapter 2, note 9.

23. For more about missionary contribution to linguistics, *see* Burgmann 1967; for more on the Summer Institute of Linguistics, *see* the articles by Stipe and by Taylor in *Studies in Third World Societies*, 1985, no.25 and no.26.

24. For a bibliography and fuller account of Wilhelm Schmidt's accomplishments, *see* Luzbetak, "The Wilhelm Schmidt Legacy" in the *Occasional International Bulletin of Missionary Research*, 1980,4:14-19; *see also* note 26.

25. December 30, 1950. Article by Dr. Heine-Geldern, reprinted from *Furche* (Vienna).

26. Some four hundred publications are credited to Schmidt, two hundred of which are full-length books and articles. His monumental work *Der Ursprung der Gottesidee* ("The Origin of the Idea of God") consists of twelve large volumes. A considerable amount has been written about Father Wilhelm Schmidt, including full-length books. For bibliographies of works about Schmidt, *see*, for instance, Henninger (1956), Luzbetak (1980), and Brandewie (1983, 1985).

3. Mission Models

1. The term *paganism* is placed in quotation marks to indicate our awareness of the pejorative connotation of the term.

2. *See*, for instance, *Studies in the International Apostolate of Jesuits* (1978). Carrier (1987:146) claims that the term was used already in the 1930s.

3. For some Catholic reservations regarding the application of the otherwise excellent principle, *see* Luzbetak 1981:43–47.

4. For more about the Slavonic Rite controversy, *see* F. Dvornik's *Byzantine Missions Among the Slavs* (1970); Fitzpatrick 1987: 54–61; *see* also John Paul II's encyclical *Slavorum apostoli* of June 7, 1985 in which he regards the mission approach of the two apostles to the Slavs as nothing less than "incarnational."

5. Although it is quite true that the pope condemned the enslavement of Indians in 1537, slave trade as such was not condemned by a pope until the 1830s by Gregory XVI, while slavery itself was not condemned until years later.

6. The three "selves" refer to the local community's self-support, self-governance, and self-propagation. For a concise history and exposition of the "three-self" formula, *see* Beyerhaus 1979:15–30.

7. The first specifically missionary training center for Catholics in the United States had opened at Techny, Illinois near Chicago in 1908 by the German missionary society, the Society of the Divine Word. Three years later an American mission society was founded at Maryknoll, N.Y.—no small achievement for American Catholicism considering that the United States was officially a "mission land" until June 29, 1908.

4. Signs of the Times

1. A whole issue of the *International Review of Mission* was devoted to the moratorium in 1975. *See* also Bosch 1978:287–291; Luzbetak 1977:69; Wagner 1975:165–176; G. Anderson 1974:133–141; IDOC 1974,9:49–86; Tippett 1973b:275–278.

2. Cf. Barrett 1971, 1968; H. W. Turner 1965. *Missiology* devotes an entire issue to "New Primal Religious Movements" (1985,1).

3. *See* the rapidly growing literature on the subject of basic communities, e.g., Cook 1980, 1985; Barreiro 1982; Eagleson, Torres 1981; Healey 1983.

4. E.g., the Vatican II documents; encyclicals like *Mater et magistra, Pacem in terris. See* especially *The Gospel of Peace and Justice: Catholic Social Teaching since Pope John*, presented by Joseph Gremillion (Maryknoll, N.Y.: Orbis Books, 1976. 623pp.). *See also* Permanent Observer to the UN, 1987.

5. Excellent English translations of Vatican II documents are available. *See*, for instance, Abbott 1966 and Flannery 1975. For Catholic commentaries, *see* Kloppenburg 1974b, Vorgrimler 1967–1969, J. H. Miller 1966. For Protestant commentaries, *see* Lindbeck 1970, Outler 1967, and Pawley 1967.

6. *See* the special issue of the *International Bulletin of Missionary Research*, vol. 9, no. 4, October 1985 on "Mission since Vatican Council II." *See also* the special issue of *Missiology* entitled "Papers of Annual Meetings: Vatican II Missiology," vol. 13, no. 4, October 1985; the proceedings of the symposium of the National Catholic Evangelization Association commemorating the 20th anniversary of the *Evangelii nuntiandi*, Boyack, ed. 1987; and such useful contributions as those of Ryan 1977:210–231 and Bohr 1977:66–82.

7. For reports and documents of the Extraordinary Synod of Bishops (Rome, November 24–December 8, 1985), whose chief task was to evaluate the impact of Vatican II after twenty years and to review challenges that still lie ahead, *see* the special issues on the Synod in *Origins*, December 12, 1985 (Washington, D.C.: United States Catholic Conference) and *Priest*, April, 1986, vol. 42, no.4 (Huntington, Indiana: Our Sunday Visitor, Inc.). *See* also Lobkowicz (1986) and Stackpoole (1986).

8. "Finding Christ" in non-Christian religions is a metaphor used by missiologists in a variety of senses: one may be looking for "other Christs" as does Panikkar, or for traces of revelation, i.e., for the working of the God of History and the signs of salvific benefits ultimately derived from and through Jesus Christ, the Savior of *all* humankind.

9. For examples of what we mean by "extremes" in liberation theology, *see* Ratzinger 1984, 1986; Kloppenburg 1974a; Petulla 1972, 1973; Eagleson 1975.

10. For an excellent discussion of the relation of the Church to the world, *see* Rahner 1975:237–250.

11. Much has been written about Anonymous Christianity. One of the best presenta-

tions of Rahner's theory is Anita Roper's *The Anonymous Christian* (translated by J. Donceel, New York: Sheed and Ward, 1966). Excellent insights can be found in R. Schreiter's "The Anonymous Christian and Christology," *Missiology*, 1978,1:29–52. For concise readable presentations, *see* Verkuyl 1978:340–372, Richard 1981:31–35, and P. Knitter 1985:126–130.

5. The Nature of Culture

1. So-called operating models, models depicting action, are generally referred to as *simulations*. Today they are frequently computerized.

2. Although today reports of cannibalism or *anthropophagy* are more or less limited to the remotest parts of New Guinea and South America, some anthropologists claim that according to historical and archaeological evidence at one time the custom had been widespread and practiced around the world. The fact is that very little undeniable evidence based on actual *participant observation* is available. It would, of course, be going too far to claim as does William Arens in his *The Man-Eating Myth: Anthropology and Anthropophagy* (1979) that cannibalism as an approved institution has never existed. For an evaluation of our current state of knowledge about cannibalism, *see*, Paula Brown and Thomas Gregor (eds.), *The Ethnography of Cannibalism* (1983).

3. The universal catechism proposed at the special 1985 Synod of Catholic Bishops will hardly make local catechisms unnecessary; local catechisms will, in fact, be as necessary as local theologies and local catechetical programs. A universal catechism may well fill the needs stemming from the universality of the Church, but there are still the special requirements flowing from the unique sociocultural situation of the local church. Although a universal catechism provides for the needed unity, there is still the no-less-important diversity that must not be overlooked. The papal catechetical commission, it should be noted, has been wisely composed of Cardinals representing not only Roman Congregations directly involved in religious education but also representing a cross-section of the Catholic world: two members are from the United States, two from India, and one each from Germany, Poland, Czechoslovakia, Benin, Italy, Syria, Belgium, and Paraguay.

4. For a brief but excellent coverage of the so-called culture areas of the world, *see* Hunter, Whitten (1976:104–111).

5. For the problem of terminology, *see* Leach (1976:9–16).

6. Such attempts have been made before, and therefore the idea is not new (for example, in the Catholic Archdiocese of Chicago and the Diocese of Cleveland). At a workshop conducted in Moshi, Tanzania, in March 1986, the idea was taken up by the Eastern African Catholic Bishops, and guidelines were issued for "a catechesis of the family in which each family member, starting at an early age" would participate (*Mission Intercom*, June 1986).

7. For the important role of the family as enculturator in society, *see* John Paul II, *Familiaris consortio* (The Christian Family in the Modern World, November 22, 1981), an apostolic exhortation following the Sixth Synod of Bishops, Rome, September 26–October 25, 1980 (*see* especially Flannery 1982:845, 857–860).

8. It is estimated that 55 percent of U.S. blacks are now of the middle class, earning $15,000 to $50,000.

9. Recent books on the subject include, for instance, Lawson Lau, *The World at Your Doorstep: A Handbook for International Student Ministry* (1984) and Gary Althen, *The Handbook of Foreign Student Advising* (1984).

6. Integration of Culture

1. Taking *culture* as "a system of symbols," *function* becomes synonymous with meaning. Function is not what a cultural form actually does but what it is perceived or intended to do.

2. Because the local church is both local and universal in character, the right to one's own symbolic system will involve tensions and responsibilities on the part of the particular churches and the universal Church. On the one hand, the particular churches, whether in the Third World or in the West, have a right to their ways and values, and this must be respected by the rest of the churches; on the other hand, particular churches must respect the *magisterium* and the need for liturgical and other discipline, Canon Law in particular (cf. Martinez y Alire 1986). Sometimes they will be called upon to make painful sacrifices of their ways and values for the common good. Purely human laws, however, must not make unreasonable demands on local churches, especially such that would call for daily and prolonged heroism. The solution to such tensions is what we have been calling with R. Schreiter a tripolar dialectic between the cultural tradition, the universal tradition, and the Gospel.

3. The Gallup Values Study was initially devised for six European countries. By the early 1980s, it became one of the largest social science projects ever, with eventually as many as twenty-five–thirty countries projected, including those of the Eastern Bloc as well as the Far East, the Middle East, and North and South America (*Gallup Values Study: Progress Report No. 2: September 1982*).

4. The U. S. and Canadian sections of the study were under the direction of the Center for Applied Research in the Apostolate (*CARA*) of Washington, D.C. The official report was to appear sometime in 1987. Our data are from various *CARA* press releases and commentaries such as von Feldt's editorial in *Columbia*, January 1982.

5. For a critique of Eliade's approach, *see* Ivan Strenski, "Mircea Eliade: Some Theoretical Problems," in *The Theory of Myth*, Adrian Cunningham (ed.), 1973.

6. For an evaluation of such theories, *see* Percy S. Cohen, "Theories of Myth," *Man*, 1969,4:337–353.

7. Cultural Dynamics

1. For further reading on acculturation, recommended is R. H. C. Teske, Jr. and B. H. Nelson, "Acculturation and Assimilation," *American Ethnologist*, 1974:351–368 and Honigmann (1959: 255–272).

2. Recommended for further reading on the subject of violence are Martin Hengel's *Victory Over Violence: Jesus and the Revolutionists* (1973) (a political theology showing that Jesus was opposed to violence) and the Documents of the Puebla Conference. The latter regard violence as nothing more than a way of engendering new forms of bondage and as being by its very nature unchristian (Eagleson, Scharper 1979; *see* especially Final Document no. 508, 509, 521, 532, 534, 1259).

3. Alvin Toffler, *Future Shock* (1970); William L. Wonderly, "Insights from Alvin Toffler's 'Future Shock'," *Missiology*, 1973:31–46.

4. The pastoral letter of the National Conference of Catholic Bishops on War and Peace, *The Challenge of Peace: God's Promise and Our Response* (1983), was a splendid show of ecclesiastical leadership in a most difficult area.

5. E.g., Rosengrant (1960); Martin (1986); Smith, Luce (1986); Austin (1986); Copeland, Griggs (1985).

6. Such would be an updated devotion to the Heart of Jesus (*see* Luzbetak, Mehok, Smith 1975; cf. Pius XII, *Haurietis aquas* 1956) or a theologically sound devotion to the Virgin Mary as proposed by Vatican II (*Lumen gentium* no.62–69; *see* also the National Conference of Catholic Bishops' pastoral letter *Behold Your Mother* of November 21, 1973, Paul VI's apostolic exhortation *Marialis cultus* of February 2, 1974, and John Paul II's encyclical *Redemptoris Mater* of March 25, 1987).

8. Epilogue: Anthropology at the Service of Faith

1. For a systematic study of general introductory anthropological concepts and principles, we recommend as supplementary reading one or the other of the many excellent handbooks used in undergraduate programs. Among these are James P. Spradley and David W. McCurdy's *Anthropology: The Cultural Perspective* (1980) and Paul G. Hiebert's *Cultural Anthropology* (1983). Or better still perhaps, one might prefer a general introduction to anthropology that has a distinctly Christian perspective, such as Stephen A. Grunlan and Marvin K. Mayers' *Cultural Anthropology: A Christian Perspective* (1979). For more advanced supplementary general reading in anthropology, one might study Roger M. Keesing's very readable and balanced *Cultural Anthropology: A Contemporary Perspective* (1976) and John J. Honigmann's edited work, *Handbook of Social and Cultural Anthropology* (1973). For supplementary reading on one's own (specifically American) culture, we recommend Conrad P. Kottak's *Researching American Culture: A Guide for Student Anthropologists* (1982) and Joseph G. Jorgensen and Marcello Truzzi's collection of articles and bibliography dealing with the theory of analysis of American cultures, organization of U.S. kinship, socialization, language, religion, education, work, leisure, subcultures, and social change. This work is entitled *Anthropology and American Life* (1974).

2. The author has personally received much inspiration from group discussions regarding community building based on the New Testament according to a plan developed by the Oblate Community of Hurtsville, N.S.W., Australia, called "New Testament Way to Community." Not a few of the author's thoughts on the spirit of the New Testament churches are traceable to this group experience. The Oblate program in detailed outline form is strongly recommended and is available from Oblate Missionaries, New Testament Community, Lewis Lane, Godfrey, IL 62035 U.S.A.

3. For papal documents on world issues, *see*, for instance, Joseph Gremillion's *The Gospel of Peace and Justice: Catholic Social Teaching since Pope John* (1976) and *Paths to Peace* (1987) compiled by the Permanent Observer Mission of the Holy See to the United Nations.

4. One of the earlier attempts was the present author's edited interdisciplinary volume, *The Church in the Changing City* (1966), which includes a bibliography covering the literature prior to 1966.

5. This seems to be the thinking also of Richard J. Todd when he sets up as criteria for true maturity of a local institutional church the following characteristics:

(1) A significant group of believers.
(2) A church that is evangelized and catechized in what is fundamental to the faith.
(3) A church which offers ecclesiastical services sufficiently established and inculturated: preaching, liturgy, sacraments and a church life that has some established order.
(4) A church where ecclesiastical services are realized with native pastoral

agents: bishop, priests, deacons, lay ministers and those living the evangelical life.

(5) A church with organized works or personal initiatives ready to serve the community with prepared people, and economical resources that come from that same church, all sharing a prophetic social commitment according to gospel principles.

(6) A church with mission awareness and with some significant contribution to developing churches according to its means.

(7) A church which is ecumenical and thus partakes in dialogue with other Christians and/or with non-Christians.

(8) A church with the ability of analysis and criticism of the world around it which can assume a prophetic role; it has the capacity for self-analysis and self-criticism for its own reform and renewal; it is able to say what it should be. (Todd, R. 1984:184-185)

REFERENCES

Abbott, Walter M., ed.
    1966   *The Documents of Vatican II*. New York: America Press.

Adeney, Miriam
    1984   *God's Foreign Policy: Practical Ways to Help the World's Poor*. Grand Rapids: Eerdmans.

Agar, Michael
    1973   *Ripping and Running: A Formal Ethnography of Urban Heroin Addicts*. New York: Seminar Press.

Allen, Roland
    (1912)   *Missionary Methods: St. Paul's or Ours?* Grand Rapids: Eerdmans.
    1962
    (1927)   *The Ministry of the Spirit*. Grand Rapids: Eerdmans.
    1964

Althen, Gary
    (1983)   *The Handbook of Foreign Student Advising*. Yarmouth, Maine: International Press.
    1984

American Anthropological Association
    1973   *Social Ethics*. Washington, D.C.: American Anthropological Association.

Anderson, Bernard W.
    1957   *Understanding the Old Testament*. Englewood Cliffs, N.J.: Prentice Hall, Inc.

Anderson, Gerald H.
    1967   "A Moratorium on Missionaries?" In G. H. Anderson and T. F. Stransky, eds., *Mission Trends*, pp. 133-141. New York/ Paramus/ Toronto: Paulist Press.

Anderson, Gerald H., ed.
    1976   *Asian Voices in Christian Theology*. Maryknoll, N.Y.: Orbis Books.

Anderson, Gerald H., and Thomas F. Stransky, eds.
    1974-81   *Mission Trends*. 5 vols. New York/ Paramus/ Toronto: Paulist Press. Grand Rapids: Eerdmans.

Angrosino, Michael V., ed.
    1976   *Do Applied Anthropologists Apply Anthropology?* Southern Anthropological Society Proceedings, no. 10.

Arbuckle, Gerald A.
    1987   *Strategies for Growth in Religious Life*. New York: Alba House.

Arens, William
    1979   *The Man-Eating Myth: Anthropology and Anthropophagy*. London: Oxford University Press.

411

Arensberg, Conrad M., and Arthur H. Niehoff
  1964   *Introducing Social Change*. Chicago: Aldine.
Argyris, C.
  1956   *Discovering Human Relations in Organizations: A Case Study of a Hospital*. New Haven: Labor and Management Center, Yale University.
Aschenbrenner, Joyce
  1975   *Lifelines: Black Families in Chicago*. New York: Holt, Rinehart and Winston.
Aumann, Jordan, Thomas Hopko, and Donald G. Bloesch
  1968   *Christian Spirituality East and West*. Chicago: Priory Press.
Austin, Clyde N.
  1986   *Cross-Cultural Reentry*. Abilene, Texas: Abilene Christian University Press.
Banton, Michael, ed.
  1966   *Anthropological Approaches to the Study of Religion*. London: Tavistock Publishers.
Barbour, Ian G.
  1974   *Myths, Models and Paradigms: A Comparative Study in Science and Religion*. New York: Harper and Row.
Barclay, William
  (1956)   *The Daily Study Bible*. Rev. ed. Translated with an Introduction and
  1975   Interpretation. Philadelphia: Westminster Press. (First published by Saint Andrew Press, 1956.)
Barnett, Homer G.
  1953   *Innovation: The Basis of Cultural Change*. New York: McGraw-Hill Book Co., Inc.
Barnouw, Victor
  1973   *Culture and Personality*. 2nd ed. Homewood, Ill.: Dorsey.
Barreiro, Alvaro
  (1977)   *Basic Ecclesial Communities: The Evangelization of the Poor*. Mary-
  1982   knoll, N.Y.: Orbis Books.
Barrett, David B.
  1968   *Schism and Renewal in Africa: An Analysis of Six Thousand Contemporary Religious Movements*. Nairobi, Kenya: Oxford University Press.
  1971   "African Independent Church Movement." In Neill, Stephen, Gerald H. Anderson, and John Goodwin, eds., *Concise Dictionary of the Christian World Mission*, pp. 9–10. Nashville/ New York: Abingdon Press.
  1982   *World Christian Encyclopedia*. New York: Oxford University Press.
Bassham, Rodger C.
  1979   *Mission Theology: 1948-1975. Years of Worldwide Creative Tension Ecumenical, Evangelical, and Roman Catholic*. S. Pasadena, Calif.: William Carey Library.
Baum, Gregory, and Charles W. Forman
  1974   "Is There a Missionary Message?" In Gerald H. Anderson and Thomas F. Stransky, eds., *Mission Trends, No. 1: Crucial Issues in Mission Today*, pp. 75-86. New York/ Paramus/ Toronto: Paulist Press. Grand Rapids: Eerdmans.

Bausch, William J.
  (1973)   *Pilgrim Church: A Popular History of Catholic Christianity.* Rev. ed.
             Notre Dame, Ind.: Fides
Beaver, R. Pierce
  (1967)   *To Advance the Gospel: Selections from Writings of Rufus Anderson.*
  1981   Grand Rapids: Eerdmans.
  1970   "The History of Mission Strategy." In Winter, Ralph D. and Steven C.
             Hawthorne, eds., *Perspectives on the World Christian Movement: A
             Reader*, pp. 191-205. Pasadena, Calif.: William Carey Library. (Origi-
             nally appeared in *Southwestern Journal of Theology*, 1970.)
  1979   "The Legacy of Rufus Anderson." *Occasional Bulletin of Missionary
             Research* 3:94-97.
Beaver, R. Pierce, ed.
  1973   *The Gospel and Frontier Peoples: A Report of a Consultation Decem-
             ber 1972.* S. Pasadena, Calif.: William Carey Library.
Beekman, John
  1959   "Missionizing Religious Syncretism among the Chols." *Practical An-
             thropology* 6:241-250.
Beidelman, T. O.
  1982   *Colonial Evangelism: A Socio-Historical Study of an East African
             Mission at the Grassroots.* Bloomington: Indiana University Press.
Bellah, Robert N., Richard Madsen, William M. Sullivan, Ann Swidler, and Steven M.
Tipton
  1985   *Habits of the Heart: Individualism and Commitment in American Life.*
             Berkeley: University of California Press.
Benedict XV
  1919   *Maximum illud.* An Apostolic Letter on Spreading the Catholic Faith
             Throughout the World. Translated by William Connolly, S.J. Issued
             November 30, 1919. In J. M. Burke, S.J., ed., *Four Great Encyclicals:
             Incidental Papers of the Institute of Mission Studies*, No. 1, pp. 9-23.
             New York: Fordham University Press. (Also in Gerald C. Treacy, S.J.,
             ed., *Two Encyclicals on the Foreign Missions by Pius XI and Benedict
             XV.* New York: The America Press, 1944.)
Benedict, Ruth
  1942   *The Chrysanthemum and the Sword: Patterns of Japanese Culture.*
             New York: Houghton Mifflin Co.
  (1934)   *Patterns of Culture.* New York: New American Library of World
  1950   Literature (Mentor Books, 1950). (Originally published, New York:
             Houghton Mifflin Co., 1934.)
  1956   "The Growth of Culture." In L. Sapiro, ed., *Man, Culture, Society*, pp.
             182–195.
Bennet, John W. et al.
  1956   *Some Uses of Anthropology: Theoretical and Applied.* Washington,
             D.C.: The Anthropological Society of Washington.
van den Berg, J.
  1983   "The Legacy of Johan Herman Bavinck." *International Bulle-
             tin of Missionary Research* 7:171–175.
Berger, Peter L.
  1961   *The Noise of Solemn Assemblies: Christian Commitment and the*

Religious Establishment in America. Garden City, N.Y.: Doubleday.

1986   *The Capitalist Revolution: Fifty Propositions about Prosperity, Equality, and Liberty.* New York: Basic Books, Inc.

Besnard, Albert Marie

1965   "Tendencies of Contemporary Spirituality." *Spirituality in Church and World.* Concilium Series, no. 9. Christian Duquoc, O.P., ed. New York: Paulist Press.

Beyerhaus, Peter

1979   "The Three Selves Formula: Is It Built on Biblical Foundations?" In Charles Kraft and Tom N. Wisley, eds., *Readings in Dynamic Indigeneity,* pp. 15–30. Pasadena, Calif.: William Carey Library

Beyerhaus, Peter, and Henry Lefever

1964   *The Responsible Church and the Foreign Mission.* (Based on the German work by Beyerhaus *Die Selbstständigkeit der jungen Kirchen als missionarisches Problem.*) Grand Rapids: Eerdmans. (Reprinted by William Carey Library of S. Pasadena, California, in *Crossroads in Missions.*)

Bibliografia Missionaria

1935–   Rome: Macioci and Pisani (Vol. 46, 1982).

Bibliotheca Missionum

1916-70   Freiburg: Herder Verlag (30 vols.).

Biernatzki, W. E.

1978   *Catholic Communication Research: Topics and a Rationale.* London: The Research Facilitator Unit for Social Communication.

Bloom, Allan

1987   *The Closing of the American Mind: How Higher Education Has Failed and Impoverished the Souls of Today's Students.* New York: Simon and Schuster.

Böckle, Franz, ed.

1970   *The Future of Marriage As Institution.* Concilium Series, no. 50. New York: The Seabury Press.

Bodley, John H.

1976   *Anthropology and Contemporary Human Problems.* Menlo Park, Calif./Reading, Mass./London/Amsterdam/Ontario/ Sydney: Cummings Publishing Co.

Boff, Leonardo

1986   *Ecclesiogenesis: The Base Communities Reinvent the Church.* Maryknoll, N.Y.: Orbis Books.

Boff, Leonardo, and Clodovis Boff

1987   *Introducing Liberation Theology.* London: Burns Oates/Maryknoll, N.Y.: Orbis Books.

Bohannan, Paul, and Fred Plog, eds.

1967   *Beyond the Frontier: Social Process and Cultural Change.* Garden City, N.Y.: Natural History Press.

Bohr, David

1977   *Evangelization in America: Proclamation, Way of Life and the Catholic Church in the United States.* New York/ Ramsey, N.J./ Toronto: Paulist Press.

Bornemann, Fritz
    1975   *Arnold Janssen: Founder of Three Missionary Congregations, 1837-1909. A Bibliography.* Translated by John Vogelgesang. Rome: Esse-Gi-Esse.
    1982   *P. Wilhelm Schmidt, S.V.D. 1868-1954.* Analecta Societatis Verbi Divini, no. 59. Rome: Generalizia del Verbo Divino.

Bosch, David J., ed.
    1971   *Church and Culture Change in Africa.* Pretoria: N. G. Kirk-Boekhandel.
    1978   "Toward True Mutuality: Exchanging the Same Commodities or Supplementing Each Others' Needs?" *Missiology* 6:283-296.
    1979   *A Spirituality of the Road.* Scottsdale, Pa.: Herald Press.
    1980   *Witness to the World: The Christian Mission in Theological Perspectives.* London: Marshall, Morgan and Scott/Atlanta: John Knox Press.

Bourguignon, Erika
    1973   "Psychological Anthropology." In John J. Honigmann, ed., *Handbook of Social and Cultural Anthropology*, pp. 1073-1118.

Boutilier, James A., Daniel T. Hughes, and Sharon W. Tiffany, eds.
    1978   *Mission, Church, and Sect in Oceania.* Association for Social Anthropology in Oceania. Monograph Series. Mac Marshall, series editor. Ann Arbor: University of Michigan Press.

Bouyer, Louis et al.
    1963-69   *A History of Christian Spirituality.* Vol. I: Louis Bouyer, *The Spirituality of the New Testament and the Fathers* (translated by Mary Perkins Ryan). Vol. II: Jean Leclerq, Francois Vandenbroecke, and Louis Bouyer, *The Spirituality of the Middle Ages* (translated by the Benedictines of Holmes Eden Abbey). Vol. III: Louis Bouyer, *Orthodox Spirituality and Protestant and Anglican Spirituality* (translated by Barbara Wall). New York: Desclée.

Boyack, Kenneth, ed.
    1987   *Catholic Evangelization Today: A New Pentecost for the United States.* New York/Mahwah: Paulist Press.

Boyd, Malcolm
    1965   *Are You Running with Me, Jesus?* New York: Holt, Rinehart and Winston.

Braaten, Carl E.
    1980   "Who Do We Say He Is? On the Uniqueness and Universality of Jesus Christ." *Occasional Bulletin of Missionary Research* 4:2-8.

Brandewie, Ernest
    1983   *Wilhelm Schmidt and the Origin of the Idea of God.* Lanham, Md.: University Press of America, Inc.
    1985   "Wilhelm Schmidt and the Roots of Culture-History." In Darrell Whiteman, ed., *Studies in Third World Societies*, no. 35, pp. 369-386.

Branner, John E.
    1977   "Roland Allen: Pioneer in a Spirit-Centered Theology of Mission." *Missiology* 5:175-184.

Bria, Ion, ed.
1986   *Go Forth in Peace: Orthodox Perspectives on Mission*. Geneva: World Council of Churches.

Bronner, Simon J.
1982   "The Haptic Experience of Culture." *Anthropos* 77:351–362.

Brow, Robert
1966   *Religion: Origin and Ideas*. Chicago: InterVarsity.

Brown, Jerry B.
1977   *Rural Revitalization: A Challenge for Public-Interest Anthropology*. Washington, D.C.: Anthropology Resource Center.

Brown, Lester R. and Jodi Jacobson
1987   "Assessing the Future of Urbanization." In *State of the World 1987*. Washington, D.C.: Worldwatch Institute. Brown, Paula, and Donald Tuzin, eds.

Brown, Paula, and Thomas Gregor, eds.
1983   *The Ethnography of Cannibalism*. Washington, D.C.: Society for Psychological Anthropology.

Brown, Raymond E., Joseph A. Fitzmyer, and Roland E. Murphy
1968   *The Jerome Biblical Commentary*. 2 vols. in one. Englewood Cliffs, N.J.: Prentice-Hall, Inc.

Bühler, Alfred
1957   "Kulturkontakt und Kulturzerfall: Eindrücke von einer Neuguineareise." *Acta Tropica* 14:1-35.
1960   *Die Maske: Gestalt und Sinn*. Führer durch das Museum für Völkerkunde und Schweizerische Museum für Volkskunde Basel. Ausstellung vom 17. Januar bis 24. April 1960.

Bühlmann, Walbert
1977   *Courage Church!* Maryknoll, N.Y.: Orbis Books.
1978   *The Coming of the Third Church: An Analysis of the Third Church*. Maryknoll, N.Y.: Orbis Books.
1979   *The Missions on Trial*. Maryknoll, N.Y.: Orbis Books.
1980   *The Search for God: An Encounter with the Peoples and Religions of Asia*. Maryknoll, N.Y.: Orbis Books.
1982   *God's Chosen Peoples*. Maryknoll, N.Y.: Orbis Books.
1986   *The Church of the Future: A Model for the Year 2001*. Maryknoll, N.Y.: Orbis Books.

Burger, Henry G.
1966   "Syncretism, An Acculturative Accelerator." *Human Organization* 25:103–115.

Burghardt, Walter J.
1976   "Seven Hungers of the Human Family." Washington, D.C.: United States Catholic Conference.

Burgmann, Arnold
1967   "Linguistics, Missionary Contribution to." In *New Catholic Encyclopedia*, pp. 776-781. New York/ St. Louis/ San Francisco/ Toronto/ London/ Sydney: McGraw- Hill Book Co.

Burke, Carl F.
1966   *God is for Real, Man: An Interpretation of Bible Passages and Stories*

As Told by Some of God's Bad-tempered Angels with Busted Halos to Carl F. Burke. New York: Association Press.

Burke, Thomas J. M.
1957 *Catholic Missions: Four Great Encyclicals*. Edited by Rev. Thomas J. Burke, S.J., with Introduction, Study Plans and Topical Index. Incidental Papers of the Institute of Mission Studies No.l. New York: Fordham University Press.

Burridge, Kenelm O. L.
1978 "Missionary Occasions." In Boutilier, Hughes, Tiffany, eds., pp. 1–30.

Burrows, William R.
1980 *New Ministries: The Global Context*. Maryknoll, N.Y.: Orbis Books.
1985 "Tension in the Catholic Magisterium about Mission and Other Religions." *International Bulletin of Missionary Research* 9:2–4.

Cardenal, Ernesto
1976-82 *The Gospel in Solentiname*. 4 vols. Maryknoll, N.Y.: Orbis Books.

Carrier, Hervé
1985 "Understanding Culture: The Ultimate Challenge of the World–Church?" In Gremillion, ed., 1985, pp. 13–30.
1987 *Evangile et cultures de Léon XIII á Jean-Paul II*. Vatican: Libreria Editrice Vaticana. Paris: Mediaspaul.

Carter, Edward
1971 *Spirituality for Modern Man*. Notre Dame, Ind.: Fides.

Cassell, Joan, and Sue-Ellen Jacobs
1987 *Handbook on Ethical Issues in Anthropology*. Special Publication 23. Washington, D.C.: American Anthropological Association.
   Catholic International: A Documentary Publication. Brookline, Mass.: Bayard Press.

Chagnon, Napoleon A.
1974 *Studying the Yannomanö*. New York: Holt, Rinehart and Winston.

Chambers, Erve
1985 *Applied Anthropology: A Practical Guide*. Englewood Cliffs, N.J.: Prentice-Hall.

Chaney, Charles L.
1976 *The Birth of Missions in America*. Pasadena, Calif.: William Carey Library.

Chang, K. C.
1977 *Food in Chinese Culture*. New Haven: Yale University Press.

Chapple, Eliot D.
1970 *Culture and Biological Man: Explorations in Behavioral Anthropology*. New York: Holt, Rinehart and Winston.

Chupungco, Anscar J.
1977 "A Filipino Attempt at Liturgical Indigenization." *Ephemerides Liturgicae* 91:370–376.
1982 *Cultural Adaptation of Liturgy*. New York/ Ramsay, N.J./ Toronto: Paulist Press.

Cobb, John
1975 *Christ in a Pluralistic Age*. Philadelphia: Westminster Press.

Codrington, Robert Henry
(1891) *The Melanesians: Studies in Their Anthropology and Folklore.* (Origi-
1957 nally published by Oxford: Clarendon Press). New Haven: Human
Relations Area Files.

Cohen, Percy S.
1969 "Theories of Myth." *Man* 1969:337–353.

Cole, M., J. Gay, and J. Glick
1974 "Some Experimental Studies of Kpella Quantitative Behavior." In J. W.
Berry and P. R. Dassen, eds., *Culture and Cognition*, pp. 159–196.
London: Methuen.

Coleman, James and Thomas Hoffer
1987 *Public and Private High Schools: The Impact of Communities.* New
York: Basic Books.

Collins, Gary
1975 "Stress!! and the Missionary." *Trinity World Forum* (newsletter, vol. 1,
no. 1).

Comblin, José
1977 *The Meaning of Mission: Jesus, Christians and Wayfaring Church.*
Maryknoll, N.Y.: Orbis Books.

Commission on World Mission and Evangelism
1980 *Your Kingdom Come: Mission Perspectives.* Report on the World
Conference on Mission and Evangelism. Melbourne, Australia, 12–25
May 1980. Geneva: World Council of Churches.

Condon, John C., and Fathi S. Yousef
1975 *An Introduction to Intercultural Communication.* Indianapolis:
Bobbs-Merrill Educational Publishing.

Conklin, Harold C.
1955 "Hanunoo Color Categories." *Southwestern Journal of Anthropology*
11:339–344.

Conley, William
1976 *The Kalimantan Kenyah: A Study of Tribal Conversion in Terms of
Dynamic Cultural Themes.* Nutley, N.J.: Presbyterian and Reformed
Publishing Co.

Conn, Harvey M.
1984 *Eternal Word and Changing Worlds: Theology, Anthropology, and
Mission in Trialogue.* Grand Rapids: Zondervan.

Connick, Milo C.
1968 *The Message and Meaning of the Bible.* Belmont, Calif.: Dickenson.

The Constitutions of the Society of the Divine Word.
1983 Rome: Generalizia del Verbo Divino.

Consultation on World Evangelization (1980: Pattaya, Thailand)
1980 *How Shall They Hear?* Consultation on World Evangelization. Official
Reference Volume. Thailand Reports. Wheaton, Illinois/London:
Lausanne Committee for World Evangelization.

Cook, Jr., A. William (Guillermo)
1980 "Base Ecclesial Communities: A Study of Reevangelization and
Growth in the Brazilian Catholic Church." *Occasional Bulletin of
Missionary Research* 4:113-117.

| 1985 | *The Expectation of the Poor*. American Society of Missiology Series, No. 9. Maryknoll, N.Y.: Orbis Books. |

1987 "Base Communities: A Suggesed Bibliography." *Latin American Pastoral Issues* 14:72-75.

Copeland, Lennie, and Lewis Griggs

1985 *Going International: How to Make Friends and Deal Effectively in the Global Marketplace*. New York: Random House.

Costas, Orlando E.

1977 "Missiology in Contemporary Latin America: A Survey." *Missiology* 5:90–114.

1982 *Christ Outside the Gate: Mission Beyond Christiandom*. Maryknoll, N.Y.: Orbis Books.

Crollius, Ary A. Roest

1980 "Inculturation and the Meaning of Culture." *Gregorianum* 61:253–275.

1984 "What Is So New about Inculturation?" In *Inculturation: Working Papers on Living Faith and Cultures*, (Rome: Gregorian University), 5:1–18.

Cunningham, Adrian, ed.

1973 *The Theory of Myth*. London: Sheed and Ward.

Dale, John T.

1966 "The Home as an Evangelizing Agent." *Practical Anthropology* 13:122–128.

Dalton, George

1971 *Economic Anthropology and Development*. New York: Basic Books.

Damboriena, Prudencio

1971 "Aspects of the Missionary Crisis in Roman Catholicism." In William J. Danker and Wi Jo Kang, eds., *The Future of the Christian World Mission*, pp. 73-87. Grand Rapids: Eerdmans.

Danker, William J., and Wi Jo Kang, eds.

1971 *The Future of the Christian World Mission*. Grand Rapids: Eerdmans.

"The Declaration of Barbados for the Liberation of Indians."

1972 *International Review of Mission* 61:243. (Reprinted in R. Pierce Beaver, ed., *The Gospel and Frontier Peoples*, pp. 369-380.)

Devos, George

1980 "Psychological Anthropology: Humans As Learners of Culture." In Ino Rossi, ed., *People in Culture*, pp. 170-204.

Dickson, Kwesi, and Paul Ellingworth

1969 *Biblical Revelation and African Beliefs*. Maryknoll, N.Y.: Orbis Books.

Diekmann, Godfrey L.

1971 "Is There a Distinct American Contribution to the Liturgical Renewal?" *Worship* 45:578-587.

Diognetus, Letter to

c.250 A.D. 5–6, Funk, 397–401. Quasten, 248–253.

Dirven, Peter J.

1971 "Missions, Roman Catholic." In Neill, Anderson, Godwin, *Concise Dictionary of the Christian World Mission*, pp. 412-414.

Dobyns, H. E., P. L. Doughty, and H. D. Lasswell
1971   *Peasants, Power, and Applied Social Change: Vicos as a Model.* Beverly Hills: Sage Publications.
Donovan, Vincent J.
1978   *Christianity Rediscovered: An Epistle from the Masai.* Notre Dame, Ind.: Fides/Claretian Press. Maryknoll, N.Y.: Orbis Books.
Douglas, Mary
1973   *Natural Symbols: Explorations in Cosmology.* New York: Vintage Books (Random House).
1984   *Food in the Social Order: Studies of Food and Festivities in Three American Communities.* New York: Russel Sage Foundation.
Drewery, Mary
1979   *William Carey: A Biography.* Grand Rapids: Zondervan.
Dulles, Avery
1976   "Contemporary Approaches to Christology: Analysis and Reflections." *Living Light* 13:119–144.
(1974)   *Models of the Church.* Garden City, N.Y.: Doubleday, Image Books.
1978
1985   *Models of Revelation.* Garden City, N.Y.: Doubleday, Image Books.
Dumoulin, Heinrich
1963   *A History of Zen Buddhism.* New York: Random House.
1974   *Christianity Meets Buddhism.* LaSalle, Ill.: Open Court Publishing Co.
Dvornik, Francis
1970   *Byzantine Missions among the Slavs.* New Brunswick, N.J.: Rutgers University Press.
Dye, T. Wayne
1974   "Stress-Producing Factors in Cultural Adjustment." *Missiology* 2:61-78.
Eagleson, John, ed.
1975   *Christians and Socialism: Documentation of the Christians for Socialism Movement in Latin America.* Translated by John Drury. Maryknoll, N.Y.: Orbis Books.
Eagleson, John, and Philip Scharper, eds.
1979   *Puebla and Beyond: Documentation and Commentary.* Translated by John Drury. Maryknoll, N.Y.: Orbis Books.
Eagleson, John, and Sergio Torres, eds.
1981   *The Challenge of Basic Christian Communities.* Maryknoll, N.Y.: Orbis Books.
Eames, E., and J. G. Goode
1977   *Anthropology of the City: An Introduction to Urban Anthropology.* Englewood Cliffs, N.J.: Prentice-Hall.
Eddy, Elizabeth M., and William L. Partridge, eds.
1978   *Applied Anthropology in America.* New York: Columbia University Press.
Eggan, Fred
1977   "The History of Social/Cultural Anthropology." In F. C. Wallace et al., *Perspectives on Anthropology—1976*, pp. 1–13. Washington, D.C.: American Anthropological Association.

Eilers, Franz-Josef
1987 *Communicating Between Cultures: An Introduction to Intercultural Communication*. Roma: Editrice Pontificia Università Gregoriana.

Eliade, Mircea
1968 "Myth." In *Encyclopedia Britannica*, vol. 15, 1968 edition, pp. 1132–1140.

Eliade, Mircea, editor in chief
1987 *The Encyclopedia of Religion*. 15 vols. New York: Macmillan/ London: Collier Macmillan.

Elkin, A. P.
1953 *Social Anthropology in Melanesia*. Issued under the auspices of the South Pacific Commission. London/ Melbourne/ New York: Oxford University Press.

Ellen, R. F.
1984 *Ethnographic Research: A Guide to General Conduct*. ASA Research Methods in Social Anthropology Series. Orlando, Florida: Academic Press.

Engel, Heinrich
1980 *Silberschatz und goldener Schlüssel: Volksmärchen—theologisch erzählt*. St. Augustin, (W. Germany): Verlag Wort und Werk.

Engel, James F.
1979 *Contemporary Christian Communications: Its Theory and Practice*. Nashville/ New York: Thomas Nelson.

England, John C.
1982 *Living Theology in Asia*. Maryknoll, N.Y.: Orbis Books.

Erasmus, Charles J.
1961 *Man Takes Control: Cultural Development and American Aid*. Minneapolis: University of Minnesota Press.

Erdozain, Placido
(1980) *Archbishop Romero: Martyr of Salvador*. Foreword by Jorge Lara-
1984 Braud. Maryknoll, N.Y.: Orbis Books.

Escamilla, R.
1977 "Worship in the Context of Hispanic Culture." *Worship* 77:290–293.

Everett, Michael W. et al.
1976 *Cross-Cultural Approaches to the Study of Alcohol*. The Hague: Mouton.

Fargher, Brian L.
1967 "The Pith Helmet Attitude." *Practical Anthropology* 14:186–189.

Ferguson, James
1982 *Salvation and the Mission of the Church: A Comparative Study of the Writings of A. Seumois and W. Bühlmann*. Dissertation, Catholic University of America.
1984 "A Paradigm Shift in the Theology of Mission: Two Roman Catholic Perspectives." *International Bulletin of Missionary Research* 8:117-119.

Ferm, Dean William, ed.
1986 *Third World Liberation Theologies: An Introductory Survey*. Maryknoll, N.Y.: Orbis Books. (Vol. 1.)

Third World Liberation Theologies: A Reader. Maryknoll, N.Y.: Orbis Books. (Vol.2.)

Filbeck, David
    1985   *Social Context and Proclamation: A Socio-Cognitive Study in Proclaiming the Gospel Cross-Culturally*. Pasadena, Calif.: William Carey Library.

Firth, Raymond
    1955   "Function." In W. L. Thomas, Jr., ed. *Current Anthropology*, pp. 237-258.
    1967   *Tikopia: Ritual and Belief*. Boston: Beacon Press/ London: Allen and Unwin, Ltd.
    1973   *Symbols: Public and Private*. In the Symbol, Myth and Ritual Series edited by Victor Turner. Ithaca: Cornell University Press.

Fitzpatrick, Joseph
    1987   *One Church Many Cultures*. New York: Sheed and Ward.

Flannery, Austin, gen. ed.
    1975   *Vatican Council II: The Conciliar and Post Conciliar Documents*. Collegeville, Minn.: Liturgical Press.
    1982   *Vatican Council II: More Post Conciliar Documents*. Boston: St. Paul Editions.

Fonseca, Claudia
    1982   "Some Considerations on the Limits of Anthropological Theory as Applied to Community Development." *Anthropos* 77:362–384.

Fore, William T.
    1987   *Television and Religion: The Shaping of Faith, Values and Culture*. Minneapolis: Augsburg Publishing House.

Forman, Charles W.
    1974   "The South Pacific Style in Christian Ministry." *Missiology* 2:421–436.
    1978   "Foreign Missionaries in the Pacific Islands during the Twentieth Century." In Boutilier, Hughes, Tiffany, eds., pp. 35–64.

Foster, George M.
    1969   *Applied Anthropology*. Boston: Little, Brown and Co.
    (1962)   *Traditional Societies and Technological Change*. 2nd ed.
    1973   New York/Evanston/San Francisco/London: Harper and Row.

Foster, George M., and Barbara Anderson
    1978   *Medical Anthropology*. New York: John Wiley.

Foster, Richard J.
    1978   *Celebration of Discipline: The Path to Spiritual Growth*. New York/ Hagerstown/ San Francisco/ London: Harper and Row.
    1981   *Freedom of Simplicity*. New York/ Hagerstown/ San Francisco/ London: Harper and Row.
    1983a   *Study Guide for Celebration of Discipline*. Cambridge/ Hagerstown/ New York/ Philadelphia/ London /Mexico City/ São Paulo/ Sydney/ San Francisco: Harper and Row.
    1983b   "The Ministry of the Towel: Practicing Love through Service." *Christianity, Today*, January 7, 1983.

Fox, Matthew
    1972   *On Becoming a Musical Mystical Bear: Spirituality American Style*. New York: Paulist Press.

| 1976 | *Whee! We, wee All the Way Home: A Guide to the New Sensual Spirituality.* Wilmington, N.C.: Consortium Books. |

| 1979 | *A Spirituality Named Compassion and the Healing of the Global Village, Humpty Dumpty and Us.* Minneapolis: Winston Press. |

Frake, Charles O.

1962 "The Ethnographic Study of Cognitive Systems." In T. Gladwin and W. G. Sturtevant, eds., *Anthropology and Human Behavior*, pp. 72-85. Washington, D.C.: Anthropological Society of Washington.

1964 "Notes on Queries in Anthropology." *American Anthropologist* 66:132-145.

Frazer, Sir James George

1922 *The Golden Bough: A Study in Magic and Religion.* One volume abridged edition. New York: Macmillan.

Friedl, John

(1976) *The Human Portrait: Introduction to Cultural Anthropology.* Engle-
1981 wood Cliffs, N.J.: Prentice-Hall, Inc.

Fries, Heinrich

1975 "Myth." In Karl Rahner, ed., *Encyclopedia of Theology: The Concise Sacramentum Mundi*, pp. 1011-1016. New York: Seabury Press.

Fry, Christina

1981 *Dimensions: Aging, Culture, Health.* New York: Praeger.

Fuchs, Stephen

1963 "Messianic and Chiliastic Movements among Indian Aboriginals." *Studia Missionalia* 13:85-103.

1976 "The Religio-Ethical Concepts of the Chamars in Northern India." *Missiology* 4:43-52.

Gallup Organization, Inc.

1982 *Gallup Values Study: Progress Report No. 2, September 1982.* Princeton, N.J.: Gallup Organization, Inc.

Gannon, Thomas M., and George W. Traub

1968 *The Desert and the City: An Interpretation of the History of Christian Spirituality.* London: Macmillan.

Geertz, Clifford

1957 "Ritual and Social Change: A Javanese Example." *American Anthropologist* 59:32-54. (Reprinted in Geertz 1973:142-169.)

1966 "The Impact of the Concept of Culture on the Concept of Man." In J. R. Platt, ed., *New Views on the Nature of Man*, pp. 93-118. Chicago: University of Chicago Press. (Reprinted in Geertz 1973:33-54.)

1973 *The Interpretation of Culture: Selected Essays.* New York: Basic Books, Inc.

1984 "Distinguished Lecture: Anti Anti-Relativism." *American Anthropologist* 86:263-278.

Gelfand, Donald E., and Alfred J. Kutzik

1979 *Ethnicity and Aging: Theory, Research, and Policy.* New York: Springer.

Gensichen, Hans-Werner

1984 "Were the Reformers Indifferent to Missions?" *Verbum SVD* 25:3-10.

Gibellini, Rosino, ed.

1979 *Frontiers of Theology in Latin America.* Translated by John Drury. Maryknoll, N.Y.: Orbis Books.

1988 *The Liberation Theology Debate*. London: SCM Press. Maryknoll, N.Y. Orbis Books.

Gilliland, Dean S.
1986 "How 'Christian' Are African Independent Churches?" *Missiology* 14:259–272.

Glasser, Arthur F., Paul G. Hiebert, C. Peter Wagner, and Ralph D. Winter, eds.
1976 *Crucial Dimensions in World Evangelization*. S. Pasadena, Calif.: William Carey Library.

Glasser, Arthur F., and Donald A. McGavran
1983 *Contemporary Theologies of Mission*. Grand Rapids: Baker Book House.

Glazik, Josef
1961 *50 Jahre katholische Missionswissenschaft in Münster 1911–1961: Festschrift von Josef Glazik MSC*. Münster: Verlag Aschendorf.

Godwin, Clement
1977 *Spend and Be Spent: A Reflection on Missionary Vocation, Spirituality and Formation, with Particular Reference to India*. Bangalore, India: Asian Trading Corporation.

Goldbrunner, Josef
(1955) *Holiness Is Wholeness and Other Essays*. Notre Dame, Ind.: University
1964 of Notre Dame Press.

Goldschmidt, Walter, ed.
1960 *Exploring the Ways of Mankind*. New York: Holt, Rinehart and Winston.
1979 *The Uses of Anthropology*. A special publication of the American Anthropological Association, no. 11. Washington, D.C.: American Anthropological Association.

Gomberg, Edith Lisensky, Helene Raskin White, and John A. Carpenter, eds.
1986 *Alcohol, Science and Society Revisited*. Ann Arbor: University of Michigan Press.

Goodall, Norman, ed.
1968 *The Uppsala Report: Official Report of the Fourth Assembly of the World Council of Churches, Uppsala, July 4–20, 1968*. Geneva: World Council of Churches.

Goodenough, Ward Hunt
1956 "Componential Analysis and the Study of Meaning." *Language* 32:195–216.
1957 "Cultural Anthropology and Linguistics." In P. Garvin, ed., *Report of the Seventh Annual Round Table Meeting on Linguistics and Language Study*. Monograph Series on Language and Linguistics, No. 9. Washington, D.C.: Georgetown University.
1961 "Comment on Cultural Evolution." *Daedalus* 90:521–528.
1963 *Cooperation in Change: An Anthropological Approach to Community Development*. New York: Russell Sage Foundation.
1970 *Description and Comparison in Cultural Anthropology*. Chicago: Aldine.
1971 *Culture, Language and Society*. McCaleb Module in Cultural Anthropology, 1–24. Reading, Mass.: Addison–Wesley.

Gorer, Geoffrey

1943 "Flowers in Japanese Culture." *Transactions of the New York Academy of Sciences* (2nd series) 5:106–124.

1948 *The American People*. New York: W. W. Norton and Co.

Gorer, Geoffrey, and J. Rickman

1949 *The People of Great Russia*. London: Cresset Press.

Gorski, John F.

1983 "The Future of Missiology in Latin America." *Verbum SVD* 24:63–76.

Greeley, Andrew M.

1977 *The American Catholic: A Social Portrait*. New York: Basic Books, Inc.

1984 "The Ways of Knowing." *Commonweal*, August 10, 1984: 431–433.

Gremillion, Joseph, ed.

1976 *The Gospel of Peace and Justice: Catholic Social Teaching since Pope John*. Maryknoll, N.Y.: Orbis Books.

1985 *The Church and Culture since Vatican II: The Experience of North and Latin America*. Notre Dame, Ind.: University of Notre Dame.

Gritti, J.

1975 *L'expression de la foi dans les culture humaines*. Paris: Centurion.

Grunlan, Stephen A., and Marvin K. Mayers

1979 *Cultural Anthropology: A Christian Perspective*. Grand Rapids: Zondervan.

Grutka, Andrew G.

1977 *Grateful Reflections of a Bishop*. Gary, Ind.: Bishop A. G. Grutka.

Gulick, John

1973 "Urban Anthropology." In John J. Honigmann, ed., *Handbook of Social and Cultural Anthropology*, pp. 979–1029.

Gusinde, Martin

1958 *Die völkerkundliche Ausrüstung des Missionars*. Nr. 1 Steyler Missionsschriftenreihe, herausgegeben von P. Dr. Anton Freitag. Kaldenkirchen: Steyler Verlagsbuchhandlung.

Gusmer, C.

1977 "A Bill of Rites: Liturgical Adaptation in America." *Worship* 51:283–289.

Gutiérrez, Gustavo

1973 *A Theology of Liberation: History, Politics and Salvation*. Translated and edited by Sister Caridad Inda and John Eagleson. Maryknoll, N.Y.: Orbis Books.

Haas, Mary R.

1977 "Anthropological Linguistics: History." In Anthony Wallace et al., eds., *Perspectives on Anthropology*, pp. 33–47. Washington, D.C.: American Anthropological Association.

Haekel, Josef

1959 "Zur gegenwärtigen Forschungensituation der Wiener Schule der Ethnologie." In *Beiträge, Symposium 1958*. New York: Wenner–Gren Foundation.

1970 "Source Criticism in Anthropology." In Raoul Naroll and Ronald Cohen, eds., *A Handbook of Method in Cultural Anthropology*, pp. 147–179. New York/ London: Columbia University Press.

Hall, Edward T.
  1959   *The Silent Language.* Garden City, N.Y.: Doubleday.
  1976   *Beyond Culture.* Garden City, N.Y.: Doubleday.
Hall, Edward T., and William Foote Whyte
  1960   "Intercultural Communication: A Guide to Men of Action." *Human Organization* 19:5-12.
Hallencreutz, Carl F.
  1970   *New Approaches to Men of Other Faiths 1938-1968: A Theological Discussion.* Research pamphlet no. 18, World Council of Churches. Geneva: World Council of Churches.
Hannerz, Ulf
  1980   *Exploring the City: Inquiries Toward an Urban Anthropology.* New York: Columbia University Press.
Hansen, Judith Friedman
  1979   *Sociocultural Perspectives on Human Learning.* New York: Prentice-Hall.
Harris, Marvin
  1968   *The Rise of Anthropological Theory.* New York: Thomas Y. Crowell.
  1971   *Culture, Man and Nature: An Introduction to General Anthropology.* New York: Thomas Y. Crowell.
  1979   *Cultural Materialism: The Struggle for a Science of Culture.* New York: Random House.
Harris, Philip R., and Robert T. Moran
  1986   *Managing Cultural Differences.* Houston: Gulf Publishing Co.
Harris, T. A.
  1967   *I'm O.K.—You're O.K.* New York: Harper and Row.
Harrold, Charles Frederick, ed.
  1945   *A Newman Treasury: Selections from the Prose Works of John Henry Newman.* London/ New York/ Toronto: Longmans, Green and Co.
Healey, Joseph G.
  1983   "Let the Basic Christian Communities Speak: Some Pastoral Theological Reflections on Portezuelo and Beyond." *Missiology* 11:15-30.
Hengel, Martin
  1973   *Victory Over Violence: Jesus and the Revolutionists.* Translated by David E. Green. Philadelphia: Fortress Press.
Henkel, Willi
  1982   "The Legacy of Robert Streit, Johannes Didinger, and Johannes Rommerskirchen." *International Bulletin of Missionary Research* 6:16-21.
Henninger, Joseph
  1956   "P. Wilhelm Schmidt SVD (1868-1954): Eine biographische Skizze." *Anthropos* 51:19-60.
Henry, Jules
  1963   *Culture Against Man.* New York: Random House.
Herskovits, Melville J.
  1950   *Man and His Works: The Science of Cultural Anthropology.* New York: Alfred A. Knopf.
Hesselgrave, David J.
  1978   *Communicating Christ Cross-Culturally: An Introduction to Missionary Communication.* Contemporary Evangelical Perspectives. Grand Rapids: Zondervan.

Hick, John
1973   *God and the Universe of Faiths*. New York: St. Martin's Press.
Hiebert, Paul G.
1976   "An Introduction to Mission Anthropology." In Glasser, Hiebert, Wagner, Winter, eds., pp. 41–88.
1978   "Missions and Anthropology: A Love/Hatred Relationship." *Missiology* 6:165–180.
1983   *Cultural Anthropology*. 2nd ed. Grand Rapids: Baker Book House.
1985   *Anthropological Insights for Missionaries*. Grand Rapids: Baker Book House.
Hoebel, E. Adamson
1958   *Man in the Primitive World: An Introduction to Anthropology*. 2nd ed. New York/ London/ Toronto: McGraw–Hill.
Hoedemaker, Libertus A.
1977   "Hoekendijk's American Years." *International Bulletin of Missionary Research* 1:7–11.
1980   "The Legacy of Henrik Kraemer." *International Bulletin of Missionary Research* 4:60–64.
Hoffman, Ronan
1967   "Missiology." In *New Catholic Encyclopedia*, vol. 9, pp. 900–904. New York: McGraw–Hill.
Hofinger, Johannes, ed.
1960   *Liturgy and the Missions: The Nijmegen Papers*. New York: P. J. Kenedy and Sons.
1961   *Teaching All Nations*. New York: Herder and Herder.
Hogg, William Richie
1978   "The Legacy of Kenneth Scott Latourette." *Occasional Bulletin of Missionary Research* 2:74–80.
Holland, Joe, and Peter Henriot, S.J.
(1980)   *Social Analysis: Linking Faith and Justice*. 2nd rev. and enlarged ed.
1983   Maryknoll, N.Y.: Orbis Books.
Holmberg, A. R.
1965   "The Changing Values and Institutions of Vicos in the Context of National Development." *American Behavioral Scientist* 8:3–8.
Honigmann, John J.
1959   *The World of Man*. New York: Harper and Row.
Honigmann, John J., ed.
1973   *Handbook of Social and Cultural Anthropology*. Chicago: Rand McNally College Publishing Co.
Horner, Norman A.
1987   "The Association of Professors of Mission in North America: The First Thirty-Five Years, 1952-87," *International Bulletin of Missionary Research* 11:120–124.
Horowitz, Irving Louis
(1965)   "The Life and Death of Project Camelot," *Trans–Action*, December,
1973   1965. (Reprinted in M. T. Weaver, ed., *To See Ourselves*. Glenview, Ill.: Scott, Foresman and Co.)
Howard, Leslie G.
1981   *The Expansion of God*. Maryknoll, N.Y.: Orbis Books.

Hunter, David E., and Phillip Whitten, eds.
1976   *Encyclopedia of Anthropology*. New York/ Hagerstown/ San Francisco/ London: Harper and Row.

Hymes, Dell
1974   *Foundations in Sociolinguistics*. Philadelphia: University of Pennsylvania Press.

Hymes, Dell, ed.
1964   *Language in Culture and Society: A Reader in Linguistics and Anthropology*. New York: Harper.

IDOC, International Documentation on the Contemporary Church
1962–   Headquarters Rome, Italy; USA office, New York.
1974   "Moratorium: Retreat, Revolt or Reconciliation?" no. 9, pp. 49–86.

Idowu, E. Bolaji
(1973)   *African Traditional Religion: A Definition*. Maryknoll, N.Y.: Orbis
1975   Books.

Jarvie, I. C.
1965   "Limits of Functionalism and Alternatives to It in Anthropology." In D. Martindale, ed., *Functionalism in the Social Sciences*, pp. 18–34. Monograph no. 5 of the American Academy of Political and Social Sciences. Philadelphia. (Reprinted in Robert A. Manners and David Kaplan, eds., *Theory in Anthropology: A Sourcebook*, pp. 196–203. New York: Aldine, 1968.)
1984   *Rationality and Relativism: In Search of a Philosophy and History of Anthropology*. Boston: Routledge and Kegan Paul.

John XXIII
1959a   *Princeps pastorum*. The Prince of Shepherds. Encyclical issued November 28, 1959. English translation by International Fides Service, Rome.
1959b   Allocution. Semaine Sociale, Angers, July 1959.
1961   *Mater et magistra*. Mother and Teacher. Encyclical Letter on Christianity and Social Progress, May 15, 1961. Translation by Rev. H. E. Winstone. Washington, D.C.: The Pope Speaks.
1963   *Pacem in terris*. Peace on Earth. Encyclical issued April 11, 1963. English translation. New York: Paulist Press.

John Paul II
1979a   *Redemptor hominis*. The Redeemer of Humankind. Dated March 4, 1979, released March 5. English translation in *Origins* 8:625–644.
1979b   *Catechesi tradendae*. On Catechesis in Our Time. Encyclical issued October 16, 1979. English translation in Flannery 1982:762–814.
1981a   *Laborem exercens*. On Human Work. English translation in *Origins* 11:225–244.
1981b   *Familiaris consortio*. The Christian Family in the Modern World. An apostolic exhortation dated November 22, 1981. A follow-up on the Sixth Synod of Bishops, Rome, September 26–October 25, 1980. English translation in Flannery 1982:815–898.
1984   "One Church Many Cultures." Christmas message to the College of Cardinals, December 21, 1984.
1985   *Slavorum apostoli*. Apostles of the Slavs. Encyclical issued June 7, 1985. English translation in *Origins* 15: 113–125.

1986   Address to the Bishops of Brazil. *Origins*, April 3, 1986, 15:681-685.

1987a   *Redemptoris Mater*. Mother of the Redeemer. Encyclical issued March 25, 1987. English translation in *Origins* 16:746-766.

1987b   *Sollicitudo rei socialis*. The Social Concern. Issued December 30, 1987. Released February 20, 1988 for the twentieth anniversary of *Populorum progressio*. Vatican City: Libreria Editrice Vaticana.

Johns, Catherine
1983   *Sex or Symbol: Erotic Images of Greece and Rome*. Austin, Texas: University of Texas Press.

Johnson, S. Ragnar
1982   "Food, Other Valuables, Payment, and the Relative Scale of Ommura Ceremonies." *Anthropos* 77:509-523.

Jorgensen, Joseph G., and Marcello Truzzi
1974   *Anthropology and American Life*. Englewood Cliffs, N.J.: Prentice-Hall.

Jorgensen, Joseph and Eric Wolf
1970   "Anthropology on the Warpath in Thailand." In *New York Review of Books,* pp. 26-35.

Juste, Ramon et al.
1981   *La religiosidad popular paraguaya: Aproximación a los valores del pueblo*. Asunción del Paraguay: Ediciones Loyola.

Kane, J. Herbert
1984   "The Legacy of J. Hudson Taylor." *International Bulletin of Missionary Research* 8:74-78.

Kasdorf, Hans
1980   "The Legacy of Gustav Warneck." *International Bulletin of Missionary Research* 4:102-107.

Keesing, Felix M.
1958   *Cultural Anthropology: The Science of Custom*. New York: Rinehart.

Keesing, Roger M.
1974   "Theories of Culture." In Siegel, Biels, Tyler, eds., *Annual Review of Anthropology*, pp. 73-97. Palo Alto, Calif.: Annual Reviews Inc.

1976   *Cultural Anthropology: A Contemporary Perspective*. New York/ Chicago/ San Francisco/ Atlanta/ Dallas/ Montreal/London/ Sydney: Holt, Rinehart and Winston.

Kellogg, W. N., and L. A. Kellogg
1933   *The Ape and the Child*. New York: McGraw-Hill.

Kenny, Mary
1987   "TV's Hidden Programme." *Tablet* 14 November 1987, pp. 1235-1236.

Keyes, Lawrence
1982   *The Last Age of Missions: A Survey of Third World Mission Societies*. Pasadena, Calif.: William Carey Library.

Kimball, Solon
1974   *Culture and the Educative Process*. New York: Teachers College Press.

Kirk, Andrew
1983   *The Good News of the Kingdom Coming: The Marriage of Evangelism and Social Responsibility*. Downers Grove, Ill.: Inter-Varsity Press.

Kirschbaum, P., and F. Fürer-Haimendorf
1934   *Anleitung zu ethnographischen und linguistischen Forschungen mit*

          besonderer Berücksichtigung der Verhältnisse auf Neuguinea und den umliegenden Inseln. Mödling bei Wien: Anthropos-Verlag.

Kloppenburg, Bonaventure
1974a   *Temptation for the Theology of Liberation*. Chicago: Franciscan Herald Press.
1974b   *The Ecclesiology of Vatican II*. Chicago: Franciscan Herald Press.

Kluckhohn, Clyde
1939   Preface to the English translation of *The Culture Historical Method of Ethnology: A Scientific Approach to the Racial Question* by Sylvester A. Sieber. New York: Fortuny's.
1949   *Mirror for Man: The Relation of Anthropology to Modern Life*. New York/ Toronto: McGraw-Hill.

Kluckhohn, Clyde, and William H. Kelly
1945   "The Concept of Culture." In Ralph Linton, ed., *The Science of Man in the World Crisis*, pp. 78–106. New York: Columbia University Press.

Knapp, Mark L.
1978   *Nonverbal Communication in Human Interaction*. New York: Holt, Rinehart and Winston.

Knitter, Paul F.
1978   "A Critique of Hans Küng's *On Being a Christian*." *Horizons* 5:151–164.
1985   *No Other Name? A Critical Survey of Christian Attitudes Toward the World Religions*. American Society of Missiology Series, No. 7. Maryknoll, N.Y.: Orbis Books.

Köhler, W.
1925   *The Mentality of Apes*. New York: Harcourt, Brace.

Kokot, Waltraud, Hartmut Lang, and Eike Hinz
1982   "Current Trends in Cognitive Anthropology." *Anthropos* 77:329–350.

Komonchak, Joseph
1986   *Toward a Theology of Local Church*. The First Colloquium of the FABC Theological Advisory Committee, 1986. *FABC Papers*, no. 42. Hong Kong: Federation of Asian Bishops Conferences.

Kottak, Conrad Philip, ed.
1982   *Researching American Culture: A Guide for Student Anthropologists*. Ann Arbor: The University of Michigan Press.

Koyama, Kosuke
1974   *Waterbuffalo Theology*. Maryknoll, N.Y.: Orbis Books.

Kraft, Charles H.
1979   *Christianity in Culture: A Study in Dynamic Biblical Theologizing in Cross-Cultural Perspective*. Maryknoll, N.Y.: Orbis Books.
1983   *Communication Theory for Christian Witness*. Nashville: Abingdon Press.

Kraft, Marguerite G.
1978   *Worldview and the Communication of the Gospel: A Nigerian Case Study*. S. Pasadena, Calif.: William Carey Library.

Kroeber, Alfred L.
1948   *Anthropology: Race, Language, Culture, Psychology, Prehistory*. New York: Harcourt, Brace and Co.
1950   "Anthropology." *Scientific American* 183:87–94.

Kroeber, Alfred L., and Clyde Kluckhohn
  1952   *Culture: A Critical Review of Concepts and Definitions.* With the assistance of Wayne University and appendices by Alfred G. Meyer. Papers of the Peabody Museum of American Archaeology and Ethnology.

Krosnicki, Thomas
  1987   "Dance within the Liturgical Act." *Worship* 61:349–357.

Küng, Hans
  (1967)
  1976a   *The Church.* Garden City, N.Y.: Doubleday and Co.
  1976b   *On Being a Christian.* (Translated by Edward Quinn from the German *Christ Sein.*) New York: Doubleday.
  1986   *Christianity and World Religions.* New York: Doubleday.

Lane, Dermot A.
  1975   *The Reality of Jesus: An Essay in Christology.* New York: Paulist Press.

Lanier, Alison R.
  1981   *Living in the U.S.A.* Chicago: Intercultural Press.

Lasch, Christopher
  1979   *The Culture of Narcissism: American Life in an Age of Diminishing Expectations.* New York: W. W. Norton.

Latourette, Kenneth Scott
  1933   "Mission." In *Encyclopedia of Social Sciences*, vol. 9. Edwin R. A. Seligman, editor in chief; Alvin Johnson, associate editor. New York: Macmillan.
  (1937–45)   *A History of the Expansion of Christianity.* 7 vols. New York: Harper
  1970   and Row. Grand Rapids: Zondervan, 1970.

Lau, Lawson
  1984   *The World at Your Doorstep: A Handbook for International Student Ministry.* Downers Grove, Ill.: InterVarsity Press.

LCWR and CMSM (Leadership Conference of Women Religious and The Conference of Major Superiors of Men)
  1976   *Hopes and Concerns for Mission.* Prepared by LCWR Global Ministry Committee and the CMSM Mission Committee for the Eighth Annual Assembly U.S. Catholic Mission Council, May 6–7, 1976. Washington, D.C.: LCWR, CMSM.

Leach, Edmund
  (1970)   *Claude Lévi-Strauss.* Middlesex/ New York/ Victoria/ Ontario/ Auck-
  1974   land: Penguin Books. Rev. ed. 1974.
  1976   *Culture and Communication: The Logic by Which Symbols Are Connected.* An Introduction to the Use of Structuralist Analysis in Social Anthropology. Cambridge/ London/ New York/ Melbourne: Cambridge University Press.

Leininger, Madeleine M.
  1970   *Nursing and Anthropology: Two Worlds to Blend.* New York/ London/ Sydney/ Toronto: John Wiley and Sons, Inc.

Léon-Dufour, Xavier, ed.
  (1962)   *Dictionary of Biblical Theology.* 2nd ed., revised and enlarged. New
  1973   York: The Seabury Press. (Original French edition, 1962; revised, 1968. First English printing, 1973; second printing, 1977.)

Lessa, William
1964   "The Social Effects of Typhoon Ophelia (1960) on Ulithi." *Micronesia* 1:1–49.

LeVine, Robert A.
1973   *Culture, Behavior, and Personality: An Introduction to the Comparative Study of Psychosocial Adaptation.* Chicago: Aldine–Atherton, Inc.

LeVine, Robert A., and Donald T. Campbell
1972   *Ethnocentrism: Theories of Conflict, Ethnic Attitudes and Group Behavior.* New York/ London: John Wiley.

Lévi–Strauss, Claude
(1958)   *Structural Anthropology.* Translated from the French by Claire Jacob-
1963   son and Brooke Grundfest Schoepf. New York: Basic Books, Inc.
1966   *The Savage Mind.* Chicago: University of Chicago Press.

Lewis, C. S.
1962   *The Case for Christianity.* New York: Macmillan.

Lewis, Oscar
1959   *Five Families: Mexican Case Studies in the Culture of Poverty.* New York: Basic Books.

Lindbeck, George
1970   *The Future of Roman Catholic Theology: Vatican II Catalyst for Change.* Philadelphia: Fortress Press.

Linden, Eugene
1986   *Silent Partners: The Legacy of the Ape Language Experiments.* New York: Time Books.

Lingenfelter, Sherwood G., and Marvin K. Mayers
1986   *Ministering Cross–Culturally: An Incarnational Model for Personal Relationships.* Grand Rapids: Baker Book House.

Linton, Ralph
1936   *The Study of Man: An Introduction.* The Century Social Science Series. Student's ed. New York: Appleton–Century–Crofts, Inc.
1945   *The Science of Man in the World Crisis.* New York: Columbia University Press.

Liu, Zongren
1984   *Two Years in the Melting Pot.* San Francisco: China Books and Periodicals.

Lobkowicz, Nikolaus
1986   *"Was brauchte uns das Konzil?"* Würzburg: Näuman.

Loewen, Jacob A.
1967   "Religion, Drives, and the Place Where It Itches." *Practical Anthropology* 14:49–72.
1969a   "Socialization and Conversion in the Ongoing Church." *Practical Anthropology* 16:1–17.
1969b   "Confession, Catharsis, and Healing." *Practical Anthropology* 16:63–74.
1969c   "Confession in the Indigenous Church." *Practical Anthropology* 16:114–127.
1969d   "I. Myth and Mission: Should a Missionary Study Tribal Myths?" *Practical Anthropology* 16:150–159.

"II. The Structure and Content of Myths." *Practical Anthropology* 16:150–159.

"III. The Function of Myth in Society." *Practical Anthropology* 16:159–170.

"IV. The Dynamics of Myth: Changing and Mythmaking." *Practical Anthropology* 16:170–178.

"V. Myth Analysis." *Practical Anthropology* 16:178–184.

"VI. Myth As an Aid to Missions." *Practical Anthropology* 16:185–192.

1970a   "The Social Context of Guilt and Forgiveness." *Practical Anthropology* 17:80–96.

1970b   "Four Kinds of Forgiveness." *Practical Anthropology* 17:153–168.

1970c   "A Message for Missionaries from Mopass." *Practical Anthropology* 17:16–27.

Lonergan, Bernard
1972   *Method in Theology*. New York: Herder and Herder.

Loss, Myron
1983   *Culture Shock*. Middleburg, Pa.: Encouragement Ministries.

Loth, H.
1963   *Die christliche Mission in Südwestafrika*. East Berlin: Akademie Verlag.

Lowie, Robert H.
1937   *The History of Ethnological Theory*. New York: Rinehart and Co., Inc.

Luzbetak, Louis J.
1954   "The Socio–Religious Significance of a New Guinea Pig Festival." *Anthropological Quarterly* 27:59–80, 102–128.

1956   "Worship of the Dead in the Middle Wahgi (New Guinea)." *Anthropos* 51:81–96.

1958a   "The Middle Wahgi Culture: A Study of First Contacts and Initial Selectivity." *Anthropos* 53:52–87.

1958b   "Treatment of Disease in the New Guinea Highlands." *Anthropological Quarterly* 31:42–45.

1961   "Toward an Applied Missionary Anthropology." *Anthropological Quarterly* 34:165–176. (Reprinted in *Practical Anthropology* 10 [1963]:199–208.)

(1963)   *The Church and Cultures: An Applied Anthropology for the Religious*
1970   *Worker*. Pasadena, Calif.: William Carey Library.

1966–67   "Anthropological Factors in Adolescent Catechesis." *The Living Light* 3:27–39.

1969   "Man Today." In Edna McDonagh et al., *The Church Is Mission*, pp. 117–130. London/Dublin/Melbourne: Geoffrey Chapman.

1975   "Understanding 'Cross–Cultural Sensitivity': An Aid to the Identification of Objectives and Tasks of Missionary Training." *Verbum SVD* 16:3–25.

1976   "Missiology Comes of Age." *Missiology* 4:11–12.

1977   "Two Centuries of Cultural Adaptation in American Church Action: Praise, Censure or Challenge?" *Missiology* 5:51–72.

1979a   "The Mission of the Church." In the *New Catholic Encyclopedia*, vol. 17. New York: McGraw-Hill.

1979b   "Missiology." In the *New Catholic Encyclopedia*, vol. 17. New York: McGraw-Hill.

1980   "The Wilhelm Schmidt Legacy." *Occasional Bulletin of Missionary Research* 4:14–19.

1981   "Signs of Progress in Contextual Methodology." *Verbum SVD* 22:39–57.

1985a   "If Junipero Serra Were Alive: Missiological Anthropological Theory Today." *The Americas* 41:512–519. (Reprinted in *Junipero Serra and the Northwestern Mexican Frontier, 1750–1825*, pp. 85–92. Washington, D.C.: Academy of American Franciscan History, 1985.)

1985b   "Prospects for a Better Understanding and Closer Cooperation Between Anthropologists and Missionaries." In Darrell Whiteman, ed., *Studies in Third World Societies*, pp. 1–53. Williamsburg, Va.: College of William and Mary.

1985c   "Cross–Cultural Missionary Preparation." In *Trends and Issues: No. 1, Missionary Formation*, pp. 61–79. Epworth, Ia.: Divine Word College.

1987   "The Beneficiaries of Evangelization." In Kenneth Boyack, ed., *Catholic Evangelization Today: A New Pentecost for the United States*, pp. 69–83. New York/ Mahwah: Paulist Press.

Luzbetak, Louis J., ed.
1966   *The Church in the Changing City*. Techny, Ill.: Divine Word Publications.

Luzbetak, Louis J., William Mehok, and Frances A. Smith
1975   *The Sacred Heart Devotion: A Christocentric Spirituality for Our Times*. Vol. l, A Study Sponsored by the De Rance Foundation. With Critical Commentaries. Milwaukee/ Rome: International Institute of the Heart of Jesus, Inc.

Lynd, Robert S., and Helen M. Lynd
1929   *Middletown: A Study in Contemporary American Culture*. New York: Harcourt, Brace.

Maldonado, Luis, and David Power, eds.
1980   *Symbol and Art in Worship*. Edinburgh: T. and T. Clark/ New York: Seabury Press.

Malinowski, Bronislaw
(1922)   *Argonauts of the Western Pacific*. London: Routledge and Kegan Paul
1932   Ltd., 1922/ New York: Dutton, 1932.

Manners, R.A. and D. Kaplan, eds.
1968   *Theory in Anthropology: A Sourcebook,* Chicago: Aldine.

Mannheim, Karl
1936   *Ideology and Utopia*. New York: Harcourt, Brace.

Marshall, Mac, ed.
1979   *Beliefs, Behaviors, and Alcoholic Beverages*. Ann Arbor: University of Michigan Press.

Martin, Judith N., ed.
1986   "Theories and Methods in Cross–Cultural Orientation." *International Journal of Intercultural Relations*, vol. 10, no. 2.

Martindale, Don, ed.
1965   *Functionalism in the Social Sciences: The Strengths and Limits of Functionalism in Anthropology, Political Science, and Sociology.*

Monograph no. 5 of the American Academy of Political and Social Sciences. Philadelphia, February 1965.

Martinez y Alire, Jerome J.
1986   *Cultural Adaptation of the Liturgy: Legal Notion and Competent Authority*. Dissertation, Catholic University of America, Washington, D.C.

Mayers, Marvin K.
1974   *Christianity Confronts Culture: A Strategy for Cross-Cultural Evangelism*. Grand Rapids: Zondervan.
1985   "The Missionary as Crosscultural Educator." In Darrell L. Whiteman, ed., *Missionaries, Anthropologists, and Cultural Change*, pp. 387–395. *Studies in Third World Societies*, no. 25. Williamsburg, Va.: College of William and Mary.

Mbiti, John S.
1973   "African Indigenous Culture in Relation to Evangelism and Church Development." In R. Pierce Beaver, ed., *The Gospel and Frontier Peoples: A Report of a Consultation December 1972*. Pasadena, Calif.: William Carey Library.
1977   *Confessing Christ in Different Cultures: Report of a Colloquium Held at the Ecumenical Institute, Bossey, 2-8 July 1977*. Geneva: Ecumenical Institute, Chateau de Bossey.

McBrien, Richard P.
1980   *Catholicism*. 2 vols. Minneapolis: Winston Press.

McCulloch, Robert
1978   "Gregorian Adaptation in the Augustinian Mission to England." *Missiology* 6:323–334.

McElroy, Ann, and Patricia K. Townsend
1979   *Medical Anthropology in Ecological Perspective*. Duxbury Press.

McGavran, Donald Anderson
(1955)   *Bridges of God*. London: World Dominion Press. Revised and enlarged
1981   edition, New York: Friendship Press.
1966   *How Churches Grow*. New York: Friendship Press.
1970   *Understanding Church Growth*. Grand Rapids: Eerdmans.

McKenzie, John L.
1965   *Dictionary of the Bible*. New York: Collier Books, Macmillan Publishing Co./ London: Collier Macmillan.

McNaspy, C. J.
1982   *Lost Cities of Paraguay: Art and Architecture of the Jesuit Relations*. Photographs by J. M. Blanch. Chicago: Loyola University Press.

Mead, Margaret
1928   *Coming of Age in Samoa*. New York: William Morrow and Co., Inc.
1942   *And Keep Your Powder Dry*. New York: William Morrow. (British title, *The American Character*. London, 1944.)
1956   *New Lives for Old: Cultural Transformation—Manus, 1928-1953*. New York: William Morrow.
1965   "Ritual Expression of the Cosmic Sense." *Worship* 40:66–72.
1977   "Applied Anthropology: The State of the Art." In A. F. C. Wallace et al., eds., *Perspectives on Anthropology*, pp. 142–161. Washington, D.C.: American Anthropological Association.

1978 "The Evolving Ethics of Applied Anthropology." In Elizabeth M. Eddy and William L. Partridge, eds., *Applied Anthropology in America*, pp. 425–437. New York: Columbia University Press.

Mead, Margaret, Elliot Dismore Chapple, and G. G. Brown
1949 "Report of the Committee on Ethics." *Human Organization* 8:20–21.

Meggers, Betty J.
1971 *Amazonia: Man and Culture in a Counterfeit Paradise*. Chicago: Aldine–Atherton, Inc.

Menen, Aubrey
1953 *Dead Man in the Silver Market*. New York: Charles Scribner's Sons.

Menninger, Karl
1973 *Whatever Became of Sin?* New York: Hawthorn Books.

Metz, Johannes
1978 *Followers of Christ: Perspectives on the Religious Life*. New York: Paulist Press.

Metzger, Duane, and G. Williams
1963 "A Formal Ethnographic Analysis of Tenejápa Ladino Wedding." *American Anthropologist* 65:1076–1101.

1966 "Some Procedures and Results in the Study of Native Categories: Tzeltal 'Firewood'." *American Anthropologist* 68:389–407.

Metzler, Josef
1981 "The Sacred Congregation for the Evangelization of Peoples or the Propagation of the Faith: The Mission Center of the Catholic Church in Rome." *International Bulletin of Missionary Research*. 5:127–128.

Meyendorff, John
1974 "The Orthodox Church and Mission: Past and Present Perspectives." In G. H. Anderson and T. Stransky, eds., *Mission Trends No. 1*, pp. 59–71. New York: Paulist Press/ Grand Rapids: Eerdmans.

1978 "Eastern Orthodoxy" and "Eastern Orthodoxy, History of." In *Encyclopedia Britannica*, vol. 6, pp. 142–161.

Mihalic, Francis
1957 *Grammar and Dictionary of Neo–Melanesian*. Techny, Ill.: The Mission Press.

1971 *The Jacaranda Dictionary and Grammar of Melanesian Pidgin*. Milton, QLD: The Jacaranda Press.

Miles, Margaret R.
1983 "The Recovery of Asceticism." *Commonweal*, January 28, 1983, pp. 40–43.

Miller, John H., ed.
1966 *Vatican II: An Interfaith Appraisal*. Notre Dame, Ind.: University of Notre Dame Press.

Minamiki, George
1985 *The Chinese Rites Controversy*. Chicago: Loyola University Press.

Minear, Paul
1960 *Images of the Church in the New Testament*. Philadelphia: Westminster.

Mission Intercom. Newsletter of the U.S. Mission Association, Washington, D.C.

Missionary Oblates of Mary Immaculate
s.d. *New Testament Way to Community*. Godfrey, Ill.: Oblate Missionaries.

Moberg, David O.
1984   *The Church As a Social Institution*. Grand Rapids: Baker Books.
Mohr, H.
1965   *Katholische Orden und deutscher Imperialismus*. East Berlin: Akademie Verlag.
Mohr, Richard
1959   *Richtlinien für eine Missionsmoral*. Nr. 2 Steyler Missionsschriftenreihe herausgegeben von P. Dr. Anton Freitag. Kaldenkirche: Steyler Verlagsbuchhandlung.
Molnar, Thomas
1987   "The New Vatican Document." *The Human Life Review* 13:114–116.
Montgomery, Edward, and John W. Bennett
1979   "Anthropological Studies of Food and Nutrition: The 1940s and the 1970s." In Walter Goldschmidt, ed., *The Uses of Anthropology*, pp. 124–144. Washington, D.C.: American Anthropological Association.
Moore, Robert L., and Frank E. Reynolds, eds.
1984   "Anthropology and the Study of Religion." Chicago: Center for the Scientific Study of Religion.
Motte, Mary, and Joseph R. Lang, eds.
1982   *Mission in Dialogue: The SEDOS Research Seminar on the Future of Mission*. Maryknoll, N.Y.: Orbis Books.
Moynihan, Daniel Patrick
1965   "Report on the Negro Family." (A government report from D. P. Moynihan, Assistant Secretary of Labor.)
1986   *Family and Nation*. New York: Harcourt, Brace, Jovanovich.
Mulders, Alphons
1961   *Missionsgeschichte: Die Aüsbreitung des katholischen Glaubens*. Aus dem Niederländischen von Johannes Madey. Regensburg: Verlag Friedrich Pustet.
Müller, Karl
1980   "Legacy of Joseph Schmidlin." *International Bulletin of Missionary Research* 4:109–113.
1984   *Friedrich Schwager: Pionier katholischer Missionswissenschaft*. Studia Instituti Missiologici Societatis Verbi Divini, no. 34. Nettetal (W. Germany): Steyler Verlag.
Müller, Karl, and Theo Sundermeier
1987   *Lexikon missionstheologischer Grundbegriffe*. Berlin Dietrich Reimer Verlag.
1987   *Mission Theology: An Introduction*. Studia Instituti Missiologici Societatis Verbi Divini, no. 39. St. Augustin (W. Germany): Steyler Verlag/ Berlin: Riemer Verlag.
Munn, Nancy D.
1973   "Symbolism in a Ritual Context: Aspects of Symbolic Action." In John J. Honigmann, ed., *Handbook of Social and Cultural Anthropology*, pp. 579–612.
Murdock, George P. et al.
(1937)   *Outline of Cultural Materials*. New Haven: Yale University Press.
1982

438   REFERENCES

Myklebust, Olav Guttorm
    1955,   *The Study of Missions in Theological Education.* 2 vols. Oslo: Forlaget
    1957   Land of Kirke/Egede Institute.
Myrdal, Gunnar
    1944   *An American Dilemma.* 2 vols. New York: Harper.
Nader, Laura, and Tomas W. Maretzki, eds.
    1973   *Cultural Illness and Health.* (Anthropological Studies, David H.
                 Maybury–Lewis, ed., no. 9.) Washington, D.C.: American Anthropo-
                 logical Society.
Nagel, Stuart, and Marion Neef
    1979   "What's New about Policy Analysis Research?" *Society* 16:24–51.
Naroll, Raoul, and Ronald Cohen, eds.
    1970   *A Handbook of Method in Cultural Anthropology.* New York/ Lon-
                 don: Columbia University Press.
National Conference of Catholic Bishops
    1983   *The Challenge of Peace: God's Promise and Our Response.* Pastoral
                 Letter on War and Peace. Washington, D.C.: United States Catholic
                 Conference.
    1986a   *To the Ends of the Earth: A Pastoral Statement on World Mission.*
                 Washington, D.C.: United States Catholic Conference. Reprinted in
                 International Bulletin of Missionary Research (1987:50–57). Study
                 guide available from the Society of the Propagation of the Faith, New
                 York, N.Y.
    1986b   *Pastoral Message and Letter On Economic Justice for All: Catholic
                 Social Teachings and the U.S. Economy.* Washington, D.C.: United
                 States Catholic Conference.
Neill, Stephen
    1964   *A History of the Christian Missions.* Pelican History of the Church,
                 vol. 6. Baltimore: Penguin Books.
    1966   *Colonialism and Christian Missions.* New York: McGraw–Hill.
Neill, Stephen, Gerald H. Anderson, and John Goodwin, eds.
    1971   *Concise Dictionary of the Christian World Mission.* London:
                 Lutterworth/ Nashville: Abingdon.
Nemer, Lawrence
    1979   "Models of Missionary Activity in the Church's History: Encounters
                 with Pluralism." MS. Paper read at the Symposium of Chicago Consor-
                 tium of Theological Schools, April 1979.
    1981   *Anglican and Roman Catholic Attitudes on Missions: An Historical
                 Study of Two English Missionary Societies in the Late Nineteenth
                 Century.* St. Augustin (W. Germany): Steyler Verlag.
    1983   "Spirituality and the Missionary Vocation." *Missiology*: 11:419–434.
Newbigin, Lesslie
    1986   *Foolishness to the Greeks: The Gospel and Western Culture.* World
                 Council of Churches Mission Series No. 6. London: SPCK/ Grand
                 Rapids: Eerdmans.
Newman, Cardinal John Henry
    (1875)   *Meditations and Devotions.* London: 1875. Reprinted in Charles Fre-
    1945   derick Harrold, *A Newman Treasury: Selections from the Prose Works
                 of John Henry Newman.* London/ New York/ Toronto: Longmans,
                 Green and Company.

Nida, Eugene A.

1954   *Customs and Cultures: Anthropology for Christian Missions*. New York: Harper and Brothers.

1960   *Message and Mission: The Communication of the Christian Faith*. New York: Harper and Row. (Reprinted 1972, Pasadena, Calif.: William Carey Library.)

1961   "Christo-Paganism." *Practical Anthropology* 8:1–14.

1966   "Cultural Variety." In Rosengrant et al., *Assignment Overseas*, pp. 53–71.

Nida, Eugene A., and William D. Reyburn

1981   *Meaning Across Cultures*. American Society of Missiology Series, No. 4. Maryknoll, N.Y.: Orbis Books.

Nida, Eugene A., and Charles R. Taber

1969   *The Theory and Practice of Translation*. Leiden: Brill.

Nida, Eugene A., and William L. Wonderly

1963   "Selection, Preparation, and Function of Leaders in Indian Fields." *Practical Anthropology* 10:6–10.

Niehoff, Arthur H.

1966   *A Casebook of Social Change*. Chicago: Aldine.

Oberg, Kalervo

1960   "Culture Shock: Adjustment to New Cultural Environment." *Practical Anthropology* 7:177–182.

O'Collins, Gerald

1977   *What Are They Saying About Jesus?* New York/ Ramsay/ Toronto: Paulist Press.

O'Connell, Hugh J.

1968   *Keeping Your Balance in the Modern Church*. Catholic Lay Series, No. 9. Liguori, Mo.: Liguorian Pamphlets.

Ogbu, John U.

1978   *Minority Education and Caste*. New York: Academic Press.

Ogden, Shubert M.

1961   *Christ Without Myth*. New York: Harper and Row.

"One Hundred Years of Ethnological Theory in the German–Speaking Countries: Some Milestones." *Current Anthropology* 5:407–418.

Opler, Morris Edward

1945   "Themes as Dynamic Forces in Culture." *American Journal of Sociology* 51: 198–206.

1946   "An Application of the Theory of Themes in Culture." *Journal of the Washington Academy of Sciences* 36: 137–165.

Origins: NC Documentary Service

     First issue, May 24, 1971. Published weekly by the National Catholic News Service, Washington, D.C.

Osborne, Cecil

1967   *The Art of Understanding Yourself*. Grand Rapids: Zondervan.

Outler, Albert

1967   *Methodist Observer at Vatican II*. Westminster, Md.: Newman Press.

Panikkar, Raimundo

1978   *The Intrareligious Dialogue*. Ramsey, N.J.: Paulist Press.

Pannenberg, Wolfhart

1967   "The Revelation of God in Jesus of Nazareth." In J. M. Robinson, ed., *Theology as History*. New York: Macmillan.

1968   *Jesus: God and Man*. Philadelphia: Westminster Press.
1985   *Anthropology in Theological Perspective*. Translated by Matthew J.
            O'Connell. Philadelphia: Westminster Press.

Parratt, John
1983   "Theological Methodologies in Africa." *Verbum SVD* 24:47–62.

Partnership
            News and notes from six continents to encourage the renewal of church
            and mission. 1564 Edge Hill Rd., Abington, Pa. 19001.

Partridge, William L.
1984   *Training Manual in Development Anthropology*. A special publication
            of the American Anthropological Association and the Society for
            Applied Anthropology. Washington, D.C.: American Anthropological
            Association.

Paton, D. M., ed.
1960   *The Ministry of the Spirit: The Selected Writings of Roland Allen*.
            Grand Rapids: Eerdmans.
1968   *Reform of the Ministry: A Study in the Work of Roland Allen*. Lon-
            don: Lutterworth Press.

Paul, Benjamin D., ed.
1955   *Health, Culture, and Community: Case Studies of Public Reactions to
            Health Programs*. New York: Russell Sage Foundation.

Paul VI
1967   *Populorum progressio*. On the Development of Peoples. Issued March
            26, 1967. English translation. Washington, D.C.: U.S. Catholic Con-
            ference.
1974   *Marialis cultus*. For the Right Ordering and Development of Devotion
            to the Blessed Virgin Mary. Issued February 2, 1974. In *Osservatore
            Romano*, English edition, April 4, 1974.
1975   *Evangelii nuntiandi*. Issued December 8, 1975. English translation.
            Washington, D.C.: U.S. Catholic Conference.

Pawley, Bernard C.
1967   *The Second Vatican Council: Studies by Eight Anglican Observers*.
            New York: Oxford University Press.

Paz, Octavio
1970   *Claude Lévi-Strauss: An Introduction*. Translated from the Spanish by
            J. S. Bernstein and Maxime Bernstein. New York: Dell Publishing Co.,
            Inc.

Pearson, David
1964   "The Peace Corps Volunteer Returns." *Saturday Review*, October 17,
            1964.

Pelto, Pertti, and Gretel H. Pelto
(1970)   *Anthropological Research: The Structure of Inquiry*. Cambridge/
1978   London/ New York/ Melbourne: Cambridge University Press.

Permanent Observer Mission of the Holy See to the United Nations
1987   *Path to Peace*. Brookfield, Wisc.: Liturgical Publications.

Peters, George W.
1972   *A Biblical Theology of Missions*. Chicago: Moody Press.

Petulla, Joseph
1972   *Christian Political Theology: A Marxian Guide*. Maryknoll, N.Y.:
            Orbis Books.

Pike, Eunice V., and Florence Cowan
  1959   "Mushroom Ritual Versus Christianity." *Practical Anthropology* 6:145–150.
Pike, Kenneth L.
  1954–55   *Language in Relation to a Unified Theory of the Structure of Human Behavior*. Glendale, Calif.: Summer Institute of Linguistics.
Pitt, David C.
  1976   *Development from Below: Anthropologists and Development Situations*. The Hague, Netherlands: Mouton.
Pius XI
  1931   *Quadragesimo anno*. Forty Years After. On Reconstructing the Social Order. Issued May 15, 1931. English translation. Washington, D.C.: U.S. Catholic Conference.
  1937   *Divini Redemptoris*. Issued March 19, 1937. English translation with discussion outline by Rev. Gerald C. Treacy, S.J. New York: Paulist Press.
Pius XII
  1945   Christmas Message.
  1951   *Evangelii praecones*. Messengers of the Gospel. On Promoting Catholic Missions. Issued June 2, 1951. English translation. Washington, D.C.: U.S. Catholic Conference.
  1953   Allocution, December 6, 1953.
  1956   *Haurietis aquas*. Encyclical Letter on Devotion to the Sacred Heart. Issued May 15, 1956. English translation. Washington, D.C.: U.S. Catholic Conference.
  1957   *Fidei donum*. The Gift of Faith. On the Present Conditions of the Catholic Missions, Especially in Africa. Dated April 21, 1957. English translation. New York: Society for the Propagation of the Faith.
Pobee, John S., ed.
  1986   *Theology by the People: Reflections on Doing Theology in Community*. Geneva: World Council of Churches.
Poupard, Paul Cardinal (directeur)
  1984   *Dictionaire des Religions*. Paris: Presses Universitaires de France.
Pourrat, Pierre
  1953–55   *Christian Spirituality*. Translated by W. H. Mitchell, S. P. Jacques, and Donald Attwater. 4 vols. Westminster, Md.: Newman.
Puthanangady, P.
  1977   "Liturgical Renewal in India." *Ephemerides Liturgicae* 91:293–298.
Radcliffe–Brown, A. R.
  1922   *Andaman Islanders*. Cambridge: Cambridge University Press.
Raguin, Yves
  1973   *I Am Sending You: Spirituality of the Missioner*. Manila: East Asian Pastoral Institute.
Rahner, Karl
  1961–   *Theological Investigations*. New York: Crossroads.
  1975   *Encyclopedia of Theology: The Concise Sacramentum Mundi*. New York: Seabury Press.
  1979   "Toward a Fundamental Theological Interpretation of Vatican II." *Theological Studies* 40. (Reprinted in the *Catholic Mind*, 1980, pp. 44–56.)

Ramirez, R.
1977   "Liturgy from the Mexican American Perspective." *Worship* 51:253–298.
Rappaport, Roy
(1968)   *Pigs for the Ancestors: Ritual in Ecology of a New Guinea People*. New
1984   Haven, Conn.: Yale University Press.
Ratzinger, Cardinal Joseph
1984   *Instructions on Certain Aspects of the Theology of Liberation*. Re-
            leased September 3, 1984. English translation in *National Catholic
            Reporter*, September 21, 1984, pp. 11–14.
1986   *The Congregation for Doctrine of the Faith: Instruction on Christian
            Freedom and Liberation*. Issued March 22, 1986. English translation in
            Origins 15:713–728.
1987   *Instruction on Respect for Human Life in Its Origin and the Dignity of
            Procreation: Replies to Certain Questions of the Congregation for the
            Doctrine of Faith*. *Origins* 16:697–707.
Redfield, Alden, ed.
1973   *Anthropology Beyond the University*. Proceedings, Southern Anthro-
            pological Society, No. 7. Athens, Ga.: University of Georgia Press.
Redfield, Robert
1947   "The Study of Culture in General Education." *Social Education*
            11:260–275.
Reed, Lyman E.
1985   *Preparing Missionaries for Intercultural Communication: A Bicultural
            Approach*. Pasadena, Calif.: William Carey Library.
Reilly, Michael Collins
1978   *Spirituality for Mission: Historical, Theological, and Cultural Factors
            for a Present-Day Missionary Spirituality*. Maryknoll, N.Y.: Orbis
            Books.
Reyburn, William D.
1960   "Identification in the Missionary Task." *Practical Anthropology* 7:1–15.
Richard, Lucien
1981   *What Are They Saying About Christ and World Religions*? New York/
            Ramsey, N.J.: Paulist Press.
Richardson, Don
(1976)   "Do Missionaries Destroy Cultures?" In Ralph D. Winter and Steven
1981   C. Hawthorne, eds., *Perspectives on the World Christian Movement: A
            Reader*, pp. 482–493.
Rivinius, Karl Josef
1982   "Zur Darstellung des Heiligen Geistes in menschlicher Gestalt. P. Jo-
            hannes Janssen im Konflikt mit der römischen Kurie." *Verbum SVD*
            23:43–64.
Robinson, John A. T.
1973   *The Human Face of God*. Philadelphia: Westminster Press.
Roper, Anita
1966   *The Anonymous Christian*. Translated by Joseph Donceel, S.J., with
            an afterword "The Anonymous Christian According to Karl Rahner"
            by Klaus Riesenhuber. New York: Sheed and Ward.

Rosengrant, John, et al.
 1960 *Assignment: Overseas. How to Be a Welcome Resident and a Worthy Christian Abroad.* New York: Thomas Y. Crowell.
Rosenstiel, C. Ronald, and Jeffrey B. Freeland
 1973 "The Rehabilitation of Institutionalized Narcotic Addicts." In Alden Redfield, ed., *Anthropology Beyond the University*, pp. 97–119. Athens, Ga.: University of Georgia Press.
Ross, Eric, ed.
 1980 *Beyond the Myths of Culture: Essays in Cultural Materialism.* New York: Academic Press.
Rossi, Ino
 1974 *The Unconscious in Culture: The Structuralism of Claude Lévi-Strauss in Perspective.* New York: E. P. Dutton and Co., Inc.
Rossi, Ino, ed.
 1980 *People in Culture: A Survey of Cultural Anthropology.* New York: Praeger (Holt, Rinehart and Winston/ CBS, Inc.).
Rossi, Ino, and Edward O'Higgins
 1980 "Theories of Culture and Anthropological Method." In Ino Rossi, ed., 1980, pp. 29–78.
Rossman, Joseph
 (1931) *The Psychology of the Inventor.* Washington, D.C.: Inventor's Pub-
 1964 lishing Co.
Ryan, Tim
 1977 "Contemporary Roman Catholic Understanding of Mission." In Beaver, ed., pp. 210–231.
Rynkiewich, Michael A., and James P. Spradley, eds.
 1976 *Ethics and Anthropology.* New York: John Wiley.
Sahlins, Marshall
 1958 *Social Stratification in Pilgrimage.* Seattle: University of Seattle Press.
 1976 *Culture and Practical Reason.* Chicago/London: The University of Chicago Press.
Salamone, Frank A.
 1975 "A Continuity of Igbo Values after Conversion: A Study in Purity and Prestige." *Missiology* 3:33–43.
 1980 Response to Claude E. Stipe's article "Anthropologists versus Missionaries: The Influence of Presuppositions." *Current Anthropology* 21:174.
Saliba, John A.
 1973 "Myth and Religious Man in Contemporary Anthropology: Survey of Literature." *Missiology* 1:281–283.
Samovar, Larry A., and Richard E. Porter, eds.
 1982 *Intercultural Communication: A Reader.* 3rd ed. Belmont, Calif.: Wadsworth Printing Co.
Sanday, Peggy Reeves, ed.
 1976 *Anthropology and the Public Interest: Fieldwork and Theory.* New York/ San Francisco/ London: Academic Press.
Sanon, Bishop Anselme Titsianma
 1985 *Das Evangelium verwurzeln: Glaubenserschliessung im Raum afrikanischer Stammessituationen.* Band 7: Theologie der dritten Welt. Freiburg: Verlag Herder.

SCAN   A six-continent reading service for the renewal of church and mission. Abington, Pa.: Partnership in Mission.

Schillebeekx, Edward, ed.

1967   "The Synod of Bishops: Crisis of Faith and Local Church." *IDOC, International Documentation on the Contemporary Church,* 23 July 1967, p. 7.

1970   *Dogma and Pluralism.* Concilium Series: Theology in the Age of Renewal. New York: Herder and Herder.

Schmidlin, Joseph

1931   *Catholic Mission Theory.* (*Katholische Missionslehre im Grundriss.*) Edited by Matthias Braun, S.V.D. Techny, Ill.: Mission Press.

1933   *Catholic Mission History.* A translation. Edited by Matthias Braun, S.V.D. Techny, Ill.: Mission Press.

Schmidt, Herman, and David Power

1977   *Liturgy and Cultural Religious Traditions.* New York: The Seabury Press.

Schmidt, Roger

1980   *Exploring Religion.* Belmont, Calif.: Wadsworth, Inc.

Schmidt, Wilhelm

1926-55   *Der Ursprung der Gottesidee. Eine historisch-kritische und positive Studie.* 12 Bände. Münster in W.: Aschendorfsche Velagsbuch-handlung.

1939   *The Culture Historical Method of Ethnology: A Scientific Approach to the Racial Question.* Translated by Dr. S. A. Sieber; preface by Dr. Clyde Kluckhohn; notes by Professor W. Koppers. New York: Fortuny's.

Schneider, Jane, and Shirley Lindenbaum, eds.

1987   *Frontiers of Christian Evangelism.* Special issue of the *American Ethnologist.* Washington, D.C.: American Anthropological Association.

Schreiter, Robert J.

1977   "Theologie in context. Naar een sociologie van de theologie." *Tijdschrift voor Theologie.* 17:3-23.

1978   "The Anonymous Christian and Christology." *Missiology* 6:29-52.

1980   "Issues Facing Contextual Theologies Today." *Verbum SVD* 21:267-278.

1981   "Local Theologies in the Local Church: Issues and Methods." In *Catholic Theological Society of America Proceedings*, pp. 96-112.

1985   *Constructing Local Theologies.* Maryknoll, N.Y.: Orbis Books.

Schwarz, Fred

1960   *You Can Trust the Communists (to be Communists).* Englewood Cliffs, N.J.: Prentice-Hall.

Scott, William Henry

1973   "The Missionary as a Good Foreigner." *Missiology* 1:383-387. *SEDOS Bulletin.* Roma: Servizio di Documentazione e Studi.

Senior, Donald, and Carroll Stuhlmueller

1983   *The Biblical Foundations for Mission.* Maryknoll, N.Y.: Orbis Books.

Senn, Frank C., ed.

1983   *Christian Worship and Its Cultural Setting.* Philadelphia: Fortress Press.

1986   *Protestant Spiritual Traditions.* New York/Mahwah: Paulist Press.

Seumois, André

1973–81 *Théologie missionnaire.* 5 vols. Rome: Editiones Urbanianae. Vol. I: *Délimitation de la fonction missionnaire de l'Eglise* (1973). Vol. II: *Théologie de l'implantation ecclésiale* (1974). Vol. III: *Salut et religions de la Gentilité* (1974). Vol IV: *Eglise missionnaire et facteurs socioculturels* (1978). Vol. V: *Dynamisme missionnaire du Peuple de Dieu* (1981).

Shank, David A.

1985   "Mission Relations with the Independent Churches in Africa." *Missiology* 13:23–4 ˙.

Sharp, P. Lauriston

1952   "Steel Axes for Stone Age Australians." In Edward Spicer, ed., *Human Problems in Technological Change: A Casebook.* New York: Russell Sage Foundation, pp. 69–90. (Also reprinted in *Practical Anthropology* 7:62–73. Originally appeared in *Human Organization*, 1952, vol. 11.)

Sheehan, Thomas

1984   "Revolution in the Church." (A review of Hans Küng's *Eternal Life? Life After Death as a Medical, Philosophical, and Theological Problem*.) *The New York Review of Books*, June 14, 1984, pp. 35–39.

Shenk, Wilbert R.

1977a "Henry Venn's Legacy." *Occasional Bulletin of Missionary Research* 1:16–18.

1977b "Henry Venn's Instructions to Missionaries." *Missiology* 5:477–485.

1981   "Rufus Anderson and Henry Venn: A Special Relationship?" *International Bulletin of Missionary Research* 5:172–176.

1983   *Henry Venn: Missionary Statesman.* Maryknoll, N.Y.: Orbis Books.

1984   "The 'Great Century' Reconsidered." *Missiology* 12:133–146.

1987   *The American Society of Missiology 1972–87.* Elhart, Ind.: The American Society of Missiology.

Shorter, Aylward

(1973) *African Culture and the Christian Church? An Introduction to Social*
1974   *and Pastoral Anthropology.* Maryknoll, N.Y.: Orbis Books.

(1975) *African Christian Theology: Adaptation or Incarnation?* London:
1977   Geoffrey Chapman Publishers/ Maryknoll, N.Y.: Orbis Books.

(1978) *African Christian Spirituality.* London: Geoffrey Chapman (1978)/
1980   Maryknoll, N.Y.: Orbis Books (1980).

1985   *Jesus and the Witchdoctor: An Approach to Healing and Wholeness.* Maryknoll, N.Y.: Orbis Books.

Sider, Ronald J., ed.

1981   *Evangelicals and Development: Toward a Theology of Social Change.* Philadelphia: The Westminster Press.

Sine, Tom

1981   *The Mustard Seed Conspiracy.* Waco: Word Books.

Sine, Tom, ed.

1983   *The Church in Response to Human Needs.* Monrovia, Calif.: Mission Advanced Research and Communication Center (MARC).

Singleton, M.

1979   "*Dawa*: Beyond Science and Superstition (Tanzania)." *Anthropos* 74:817–863.

Sitaram, K. S., and R. T. Cogdell
1976   *Foundations of Intercultural Communication*. Columbus: Merrill.
Slotkin, J. S.
1955-56   "The Peyote Way." *Tomorrow* 4:64–70.
Smith, Edwin W.
1934   "Anthropology and the Practical Man." *Journal of the Royal Anthropological Institute* 64:xiii–xxxvii.
Smith, Elise C., and Louise Fiber Luce, eds.
1986   *Toward Internationalism: Readings in Cross-Cultural Communication*. Cambridge, Mass.: Newbury House Publishers.
Smith, Gordon Hedderly
1945   *The Missionary and Anthropology: An Introduction to the Study of Primitive Man for Missionaries*. Chicago: Moody Press.
Smith, Simon E.
1977   "The American Role in World Wide Mission: The Roman Catholic Church." In R. Pierce Beaver, ed., *American Missions in Bicentennial Perspective*, pp. 403–432. Pasadena, Calif.: William Carey Library.
Smits, K.
1976   "Liturgical Reform in Cultural Perspective." *Worship* 50:98–110.
Sobrino, Jon, and Juan Hernandez Pico
1985   *Theology of Christian Solidarity*. Maryknoll, N.Y.: Orbis Books.
Song, Choan-Seng
1980   *Third-Eye Theology: Theology in Formation in Asian Settings*. Maryknoll, N.Y.: Orbis Books.
1984   *Tell Us Our Names: Story Theology from an Asian Perspective*. Maryknoll, N.Y.: Orbis Books.
1986   *Theology from the Womb of Asia*. Maryknoll, N.Y.: Orbis Books.
Southall, Aidan
1973   *Urban Anthropology*. New York/ London: Oxford University Press.
Spector, Paul, and Harley O. Preston
1961   *Working Effectively Overseas*. Prepared for the Peace Corps by the Institute for International Services of the American Institute of Research. Washington, D.C.: American Institute for Research.
Spicer, Edward H., ed.
1952   *Human Problems in Technological Change: A Case Book*. New York: Russell Sage Foundation.
Spindler, George, ed.
1955   *Education and Anthropology*. Stanford, Calif.: Stanford University Press.
1963   *Education and Culture: Anthropological Approaches*. New York: Holt, Rinehart and Winston.
Spradley, James P.
1979   *The Ethnographic Interview*. New York: Holt, Rinehart and Winston.
1980   *Participant Observation*. New York: Holt, Rinehart and Winston.
Spradley, James P., ed.
1972   *Culture and Cognition: Rules, Maps, and Plans*. San Francisco: Chandler.
Spradley, James P., and David W. McCurdy
1980   *Anthropology: The Cultural Perspective*. 2nd ed. New York/ Chichester/ Brisbane/ Toronto: John Wiley and Sons.

Stackpoole, Alberic, ed.
  1986   *Vatican II by Those Who Were There.* London: Geoffrey Chapman.
Stamoolis, James
  1984   "Eastern Orthodox Mission Theology." *International Bulletin of Missionary Research* 8:59–63.
  1986   *Eastern Orthodox Mission Theology Today.* Maryknoll, N.Y.: Orbis Books.
Steward, Julian H.
  1955   *Theory of Culture Change.* Urbana: University of Illinois Press.
Stewart, Edward C.
  (1972)   *American Cultural Patterns: A Cross-Cultural Perspective.* Chicago:
  1981   Intercultural Press.
Stipe, Claude E.
  1980   "Anthropologists versus Missionaries: The Influence of Presuppositions." *Current Anthropology* 21:165–179.
Stott, John, and Robert T. Coote, eds.
  1979   *Gospel and Culture.* The Papers of a Consultation on the Gospel and Culture Convened by the Lausanne Committee's Theology and Education Group. Pasadena, Calif.: William Carey Library.
Stransky, Thomas F.
  1985   "The Church and Other Religions." *International Bulletin of Missionary Research* 9:154–158.
Strenski, Ivan
  1973   "Mircea Eliade: Some Theoretical Problems." In Adrian Cunningham, ed., *The Theory of Myth,* pp. 40–78. London: Sheed and Ward.
Sturtevant, William G.
  1964   "Studies in Ethnoscience." *American Anthropologist* 66:99–131.
Sudbrack, Joseph
  1968   "Spirituality." In Karl Rahner, ed., *Sacramentum Mundi: An Encyclopedia of Theology,* vol. 6. New York: Herder and Herder. (In one-volume edition, *The Concise Sacramentum Mundi,* pp. 1623–1634.)
Suhard, Emmanuel Celestin
  1953   *The Church Today: Growth or Decline.* Notre Dame, Ind.: Fides Press.
Taber, Charles R.
  1969   "Why Mythology?" *Practical Anthropology* 16:145–146.
  1978   "The Limits of Indigenization in Theology." *Missiology* 6:53–79.
Takenaka, Masao
  1986   *God Is Rice: Asian Culture and Christian Truth.* Geneva: World Council of Churches.
Tancredi, Lawrence
  1983   *The Anthropology of Medicine.* New York: Praeger.
Tax, Sol
  1958   "The Fox Project." *Human Organization* 17:17–19.
  1977   "Anthropology for the World of the Future Thirteen Professions and Three Poposals." *Human Organization* 36:225–334.
Teske, Jr., R. H. C., and B. H. Nelson
  1974   "Acculturation and Assimilation." *American Ethnologist,* 1974: 351–368.

Thauren, Johannes
1927 *Die Akkommodation im katholischen Heidenapostolat.* Münster: Aschendorff.
1928 "Zur Frage der missionarischen Anpassung unter Berücksichtigung des Museo Missionario Etnologico in Rom." In *P. Wilhelm Schmidt Festschrift.* Wien.

Thiel, Josef Franz
1970 "The Institution of Marriage: An Anthropological Perspective." In Franz Böckle, ed., *The Future of Marriage: As an Institution*, pp. 13–24. New York: The Seabury Press.
1981 "Die Bedeutung von Raum und Zeit als religiöse Dimension." *Verbum SVD* 22:19–37.

Thomas, William I., and Florian Znaniecki
1918-20 *The Polish Peasant in Europe and America.* 5 vols. Chicago: University of Chicago Press/ Boston: Badge.

Tippett, Alan R.
1970 *Church Growth and the Word of God.* Grand Rapids: Eerdmans.
1973a *Aspects of Pacific Ethnohistory.* Pasadena, Calif.: William Carey Library.
1973b "The Suggested Moratorium on Missionary Funds and Personnel." *Missiology* 1:275–279.
1974a "Research Method and the Missiological Process at the School of World Mission." In Alvin Martin, ed., *The Means of World Evangelization: Missiological Education*, pp. 498–504. S. Pasadena, Calif.: William Carey Library.
1974b "Toward a Technique for Extracting Anthropological Data from Oceanic Missionary Records." Paper presented at the 1974 Annual Meeting of the American Society of Ethnohistory. Mimeographed.
1980 *Oral Tradition and Ethnohistory: The Transformation of Information and Social Values in Early Christian Fiji 1835–1905.* Canberra: St. Mark's Library.

Tippett, Alan R., ed.
1973 *God, Man and Church Growth.* Grand Rapids: Eerdmans.

Todd, Harry F., Jr., and Julio L. Ruffini, eds.
1979 *Teaching Medical Anthropology.* Washington, D.C.: Society for Medical Anthropology.

Todd, Richard J.
1984 "From the Concept of Missions to the Concept of Developing Churches: A Proposal." *Missiology* 12:179–194.

Toffler, Alvin
1970 *Future Shock.* New York: Random House.

Tonkinson, Robert
1974 *The Jigalong Mob: Aboriginal Victors of the Desert Crusade.* Menlo Park, Calif.: Cummings.

Torres, Sergio, and John Eagleson, eds.
1976 *Theology in the Americas.* Maryknoll, N.Y.: Orbis Books.
1981 *The Challenge of Basic Christian Communities.* Maryknoll, N.Y.: Orbis Books.

Torres, Sergio, and Virginia Fabella, eds.
1978   *The Emergent Gospel: Theology from the Underside of History*. Mary-
            knoll, N.Y.: Orbis Books.
Tra, John, Richard Rashke, and Louis J. Luzbetak
1969   *National Mission Institute: A Missionary Training Coalition*. Washing-
            ton, D.C.: Center for Applied Research in the Apostolate (CARA).
Tracy, David
1984   "Levels of Liberal Consensus." *Commonweal*, August 10, 1984, pp.
            426–429.
Truax, James
1979   *Student Mission Power: Student Volunteer Movement*. Pasadena,
            Calif.: William Carey Library.
Trudgill, Peter
1974   *Sociolinguistics: An Introduction*. Middlessex, England/ New York:
            Penguin Books.
Turner, Harold W.
1965   "Pagan Features in West African Independent Churches." *Practical
            Anthropology* 12:145–151.
Turner, Victor
1969   *The Ritual Process: Structure and Anti–Structure*. Chicago: Aldine.
1974   *Dramas, Fields, and Metaphors: Symbolic Action in Human Society*.
            Ithaca/ London: Cornell University Press.
Turner, Victor, and Edith Turner
1978   *Image and Pilgrimage in Christian Culture: Anthropological Perspec-
            tives*. New York: Columbia University Press.
Tybor, Sr. M. Martina
1984   "SS. Cyril and Methodius: Times, Places and Peoples in Christ." In
            Joseph C. Krajsa, ed., *Jednota Annual Furdek,* pp. 147–149.
Tyler, Stephen A., ed.
1969   *Cognitive Anthropology*. New York: Holt, Rinehart and Winston.
Umiker–Sebeok, Jean, and Thomas A. Sebeok
1981   "Clever Hans and Smart Simians: The Self–Fulfilling Prophecy and
            Kindred Methodological Pitfalls." *Anthropos* 76:89–165.
1982   "Rejoinder to the Rumbaughs." *Anthropos* 77:574–578.
Vatican II (N.B. Only documents referred to in the text are listed here in alphabetical
order.)
1962–65   *Ad gentes*. The Decree on the Church's Missionary Activity. December
            7, 1965.
            Apostolicam actuositatem. The Decree on the Apostolate of Lay Peo-
            ple. November 18, 1965.
            Dei Verbum. The Dogmatic Constitution on Divine Revelation. No-
            vember 18, 1965.
            Dignitatis humanae. The Declaration on Religious Liberty. November
            7, 1965.
            Gaudium et spes. The Pastoral Constitution on the Church in the
            Modern World. December 7, 1965.
            Inter mirifica. The Decree on Means of Social Communication.
            December 4, 1963.
            Lumen gentium, The Dogmatic Constitution on the Church, Novem-
            ber 31, 1964.

Nostra aetate. The Decree on Non–Christian Religions. October 28, 1965.

Sacrosanctum concilium. The Constitution on Sacred Liturgy. December 4, 1963.

Unitatis redintegratio. Decree on Ecumenism. November 21, 1964.

Vayda, Andrew P., ed.
    1968   *Peoples and Cultures of the Pacific: An Anthropological Reader.* Garden City, N.Y.: The Natural History Press for the American Museum Natural History.
    1969   *Environment and Cultural Behavior: Ecological Studies in Cultural Anthropology.* New York: Natural History Press.

Vayda, Andrew P., Anthony Leeds, and David B. Smith
    1961   "The Place of Pigs in Melanesian Subsistence." In V. E. Garfield, ed., *Proceedings of the 1961 Annual A.E.S. Meetings*, pp. 69–77.

Verba, Sidney and Gary R. Owen
    1985   *Equality in America: The View from the Top.* Cambridge, Mass.: Harvard University Press.

Verkuyl, Johannes
    1978   *Contemporary Missiology: An Introduction.* Translated and edited by Dale Cooper. Grand Rapids: Eerdmans.

Vessels, Jane
    1985   "Koko's Kitten." *National Geographic* 167:110–113.

Voget, Fred W.
    1973   "The History of Cultural Anthropology." In John J. Honigmann, ed., *Handbook of Social and Cultural Anthropology*, pp. 1–88. Chicago: Rand McNally.

Vorgrimler, H., ed.
    1967–69   *Commentary on the Documents of Vatican II.* New York: Herder and Herder.

Wagner, C. Peter
    1975   "Colour the Moratorium Grey." *International Review of Mission* 64:165–176.
    1979   *Our Kind of People.* Nashville: Knox Press.

Walliga, J. M., et al.
    1987   *Inculturation: Its Meaning and Urgency.* Kampala, Uganda: St. Paul Publications-Africa.

Ward, Barbara
    1966   *World Poverty: Can It Be Solved?* (In-depth analysis of the problem of world poverty with sensible suggestions toward a solution.) Chicago: Franciscan Herald Press.

Ward, Ted
    1984   *Living Overseas: A Book of Preparations.* New York: The Free Press, Macmillan Co./ London: Collier Macmillan Publishers.

Warner, W. Lloyd
    1941   "Social Anthropology and the Modern Community." *American Journal of Sociology* 46:785-796.
    1962   *The Corporation in the Emergent American Society.* New York: Harper.

Warner, W. Lloyd, and Josiah Low
1947 *The Social System of the Modern Factory*. New Haven: Yale University Press.

Warner, W. Lloyd, and Paul Lunt
1941 *The Social Life of a Modern Community*. New Haven: Yale University Press.

Warren, Max A. C.
1955 *Caesar—the Beloved Enemy: Three Studies in the Relation of Church and State*. London: SCM Press.
1971 *To Apply the Gospel: A Selection from the Writings of Henry Venn*. Grand Rapids: Eerdmans.

Wax, Murray L.
1978 "Once and Future Merlins: The Applied Anthropologists of Camelot." *Human Organization* 37:400–408.

Weaver, Thomas, and Douglas White, eds.
1972 *The Anthropology of Urban Environments*. Washington, D.C.: Society for Applied Anthropology.

Werner, Oswald, and G. Mark Schoepfle
1986 *Systematic Fieldwork*. 2 vols. Beverly Hills, Calif.: Sage Publications, Inc.

Whiteman, Darrell
1983 *Melanesians and Missionaries: An Ethnohistorical Study of Social and Religious Change in the Southwest Pacific*. Pasadena, Calif.: William Carey Library.
1985 "Missionary Documents and Anthropological Research." In Darrell Whiteman, ed., *Missionaries, Anthropologists and Cultural Change*, pp. 295–322.

Whiteman, Darrell, ed.
1984 *An Introduction to Melanesian Cultures*. Goroka, Papua New Guinea: The Melanesian Institute.
1985 *Missionaries, Anthropologists and Cultural Change*. (Studies in Third World Societies, no. 25.) Williamsburg, Va.: College of William and Mary, Dept. of Anthropology.

Williams, Thomas Rhys
1972 *Introduction to Socialization*. St. Louis, Mo.: C. V. Mosby Co.

van Willigen, John
1976 "Applied Anthropology and Community Development Administration: A Critical Assessment." In Michael V. Angrosino, ed., *Do Applied Anthropologists Apply Anthropology?* pp. 81–91. Athens, Ga.: University of Georgia Press.
1980 *Anthropology in Use: A Bibliographic Chronology of the Development of Applied Anthropology*. Applied Anthropology Documentation Project. Pleasantville, N.Y.: Redgrave Publishing Co.
1986 *Applied Anthropology: An Introduction*. South Hadley, Mass.: Bergin and Garvey Publishers, Inc.

van Willigen, John, and Billie R. Dewalt
1985 *Training Manual in Policy Ethnography*. A special publication of the American Anthropological Association, no. 19. Washington, D.C.: American Anthropological Association.

Wilmore, Gayraud S., and James H. Cone, eds.
1979   *Black Theology: A Documentary History, 1966–1979.* Maryknoll, N.Y.: Orbis Books.

Winter, Ralph D., and Steven C. Hawthorne, eds.
1981   *Perspectives on the World Christian Movement: A Reader.* Pasadena, Calif.: William Carey Library.

Wirsing, Rolf, and Ann P. McElroy
1981   "Medizinische Anthropologie in den USA." *Anthropos* 76:743–783.

Wonderly, William L.
1973   "Insights from Alvin Toffler's 'Future Shock'." *Missiology* 1:31–46.

Worgul, George S., Jr.
1979   "Anthropological Consciousness and Biblical Theology." *Biblical Theology Bulletin: A Journal of Bible and Theology* 9:3–12.

World Council of Churches
1961   "The Missionary Task of the Church: Theological Reflection." *Bulletin, Division of Studies.* Geneva: World Council of Churches.

Wulff, Robert M.
1976   "Anthropology in the Urban Planning Process: A Review and an Agenda." In Michael V. Angrosino, ed., *Do Applied Anthropologists Apply Anthropology?* Athens, Ga.: University of Georgia Press.

Yamamori, Tetsunao and Charles Taber, eds.
1975   *Christopaganism or Indigenous Christianity?.* S. Pasadena, Calif.: William Carey Library.

Yerkes, R. M., and A. W. Yerkes
1929   *The Great Apes.* New Haven: Yale University Press.

Yinger, J. Milton
1957   *Religion, Society and the Individual: An Introduction to the Sociology of Religion.* New York: The Macmillan Company.

Zabawa, Robert
1987   "Macro–Micro Linkages and Structural Transformation: The Move from Full–Time to Part–Time Farming in a North Florida Agricultural Community." *American Anthropologist* 89:366–382.

INDEX

Accommodation: approach to, 83; how differs from inculturation, 82-83; need for, in mission, 80-81. *See also* Mission models, accommodational

Acculturation: basic readings on, 330; not to be confused with inculturation, 69; notion of, 69, 308, 321-22

Action anthropology, 391

Adaptation. *See* Mission models, accommodational

Adjustment to a second culture: approach to, 215-22; basic readings on, 221. *See also* Relativity, cultural

African Independent Church Movement, 107-108

Agricultural development: basic readings on, 395; and functional linkages, 147-48

Alcohol abuse: basic readings on, 394; as a form of Western syncretism, 367

Allen, R., mission approach of, 21

Alternatives: as factor in culture change, 350; notion of, 159, 170

Americanism, as "heresy," 354

Anderson, B. W., 368

Anderson, G. H., 21-22

Anderson, R., 16, 98

Angrosino, M. V., 39, 293

Anonymous Christianity: basic readings on, 124, 132, 406 (ch. 4, n.11); description of, 124-26, 132

Anthropoids and culture, 189-92

Anthropologist-missionary relations, 53-61, 63

Anthropology: approaches to, 23-42, 139-56; basic readings in, 409 (ch. 8, n.1); comparative method in, 27; difference between psychology and, 43; holism in, 15, 24-26; nature and scope of, xix, 23-24; subdisciplines of, 27-36

Anthropos, 60, 61-63. *See also* Schmidt, W.

Applied anthropology: basic readings on, 39, 393-95; contemporary, 39; goal of, 168; history of, 36-39, and the institutional Church, 396-97; in mission, 374-97; nature and scope of, 34-36; and social action, 391-95; and value judgments, 40-42

Archaeology, 30

Archives, missiological, 400-401 (ch. 2, n.9)

Arensberg, C. M., 38, 293

Associations, professional: in missiological field, 402 (ch. 2, n.9); for social action, 395

Atheism, 165

Augustine, Saint, 15, 115, 163

Barclay, W., 87, 160

Barnett, H. G., 293, 338

Barrett, D. B., 104, 108

Barth, K., 21, 118

Basic ecclesial communities, as sign of the times, 108

Basic readings: on acculturation, 330; on agricultural anthropology, 395; in applied anthropology, 39; on communication, 386; on cultural adjustment, 222; on culture dynamics, 293, 330; on enculturation, 182; on ethnohistory, 146; on general anthropology, 409 (ch. 8, n.1); on the institutional Church, 396, 397; on the kerygmatic mission, 386; on liturgy and culture, 384; in missiological anthropology, 50-53; on models of culture, 139; on models of mission, 85; on myth and ritual, 266; on the sacramental model of the Church, 384; on semiotic anthropology, 156; on Slavonic Rite Controversy, 405 (ch. 3, n.4); on social action, 393-95; on social structure and mission, 174; on spirituality for mission, 399; on theological foundations for mission, 404 (ch. 2, n.12); on Vatican II, 406 (ch. 4, n.4 and n.5); on world issues, 409 (ch. 8, n.4)

Basic units of culture, 225-27

Bassham, R. C., 20, 107

Beaver, R. P., 21, 85, 93, 98, 99, 100

Bellah, R. N., 261

Benedict XV, 2

Benedict, R., 32, 36, 37, 148, 187, 224

Beneficiaries of evangelization, and enculturation, 197-98

Bernard, Saint, and religious liberty, 91

Bibliographical resources in missiology, 401

Biculturalism. *See* Adjustment to a second culture; Culture shock

Bishop, his ministry and authority, 128

Bloom, A., 262

Boas, F., 36, 144

Body of Christ. *See* Church as community

Boff, L., 22, 79, 122

Boniface, Saint, and his approach to mission, 90

Boundaries of culture: and communication, 175-76; and society, 171-72

Braaten, C. E., 120, 121

Brandewie, E., 145

Bühler, A., 274, 317

Bühlmann, W., 18, 23, 105, 107, 123

Burridge, K., 28, 59

California missions: accommodational approach of, 94; paternalism of, 94

Camara, H. P., 390, 391

Camelot, ethics of project, 35-36, 39

Campbell, J., 266

Campus ministries, and overseas students, 221

Capitalism, as a form of Western syncretism, 367

Carey, W., and his approach to mission, 98

Cargo cults, 373

Caribbean, Church expansion into the, 93

Carrier, H., 53, 59, 69, 113, 358

Charlemagne, and mission, 89

de las Casas, B., his mission approach, 93

Chambers, E., 39, 41, 293, 393, 394, 397

Chimpanzees, and culture, 189-92

Chinese Rites Controversy, 16, 92-93, 164, 354

Chomsky, N., 30

Chrysostom, Saint John, 15, 89, 240

Christian anthropology, nature and scope of, 41

Christianity, as a minority religion, 104-105

Christocentricity, in mission, 2-4

Christology: "from above," 115; "from below," 115; uniqueness of Christ, 124-26, 158, 164

Christopaganism. *See* Syncretism

Chupungco, A. J., 384

Church, mission of, 375-97

Church, models of, 375-97

Church, official teaching on the, 126-30

Church, universal, defined, 128. *See also* Models of Church; Mission of Church

Church as community: described, 376-80; strengths/weaknesses of model, 377

Church as herald: basic readings on, 386; notion of, 385; strengths/weaknesses of herald model, 385-86

Church as institution: basic readings on, 396, 397; maturity of, 408-10 (ch. 8, n.5); notion of, 395; strengths/weaknesses of model, 395-96

Church as local, 128

Church as mystery, 396

Church as a pilgrim people, 155

Church as sacrament: notion of, 381; strengths/weaknesses of model, 381

Church as servant: basic readings on, 390, 394-95; notion of, 386-87; anthropological models for, 392-93; strengths/weaknesses of model, 386-87. *See also* Mission of Church, social; Social action

Church as a *world* Church, 109-110

Church growth, history of, 85-132

Civil religion, described, 203

Client-anthropologist relations, 48-49

Clinical model, for social action, 393

Cognitive anthropology: approach and perspective, 150-52, 225; basic readings in, 151-52

Colonialism, and Church growth, 91-105, *passim*

Comblin, J., 72

Comity arrangements, 94

Commonalities, in culture, 158

Communication: among animals, 189-92; basic readings on, 386; cross-cultural, 213-14; and cultural boundaries, 175-76; and genres, 83-84; and mission, 8; nonverbal, 213-14, 386; and social structure, 359; verbal, in mission, 385. *See also* Church, as herald

Communications media, and enculturation, 201-202

Communitas, V. Turner's conception of, 270-71

Community development: basic readings on, 395; models for social action, 393

Comparative method of anthropology, 27, 38

Compromise of Gospel, inadmissible, 354. *See* Unity in diversity

Conditions favoring change. *See* Factors in change

Configuration, defined, 159

Configurationalism, described, 148-49

Conflict theory, in sociology, 166-67

Consistency, and the degree of inculturation and integration, 281-83. *See also* Selectivity; Relevancy, cultural

Contacts, cultural: and conflicts in Church institutions, 176-81; as source of disequilibrium, 317; type of, as factor in change, 343-45

Contextualization. *See* Inculturation

Conversions, types of, 64-105

Coote, R. T., 8, 52

Costas, O. E., 22, 107

Counseling, and functional linkages, 248-49

Countercultural nature of mission, 160. *See also* Compromise of Gospel, inadmissible; Consistency; Prophetic role, of Christians; Structure/Anti-Structure; Unity in diversity

Counterthemes, 277-79. *See also* Theme and Countertheme

Crollius, A. A., 41, 53

Crusades, as approach to mission, 91

Cultural anthropology, 29-34. *See also* Archaeology; Ethnography; Ethnology; Linguistics; Social Anthropology

Cultural dynamics: basic readings in, 293; and mission, 300-305, 322-29, 352-73; nature of, 292-93

Cultural ecology, 143-44

Cultural materialism, 143

Cultural vs. *Social,* 403 (ch. 2, n.11, 14)

Culture: an adaptive system, 156, 161, 163; as an anthropologist's construct, 167-68; as a code of and for behavior, 167, 168-69; cognitive anthropological model of, 150-52; as communication, 157; configurationist model of, 148-49; criteria for a good model of, 136-37; defined, 74, 133, 134-35, 156, 224; as a design for succeeding in life, 156; diffusionist models of, 144-45; ecological model of, 143-44; evolutionistic models of, 139-40, 142; functionalist model of, 147-48; holistic nature of, 158-59; ideational models of, 150-56; ideational and public, 168-69; as an individual's perception, 167; as learned, 181-222; Marxist model of, 140-42; materialistic models of, 139-44; missiological model of, 137-39, 156; neoevolutionist model of, 142; psychoanalytic approach to, 149; psychological models of, 149; relation of, to actual behavior, 168-69; semiotic model of, 154-56; as a set of ideas and norms, 156-57; as socially acquired, 166-81; structuralist model of, 152-54; and success in life, 157-58; symbolic anthropological model of, 154-56; and tradition, 170-71

Culture area, 171

Culture change: basic readings on, 330; ideational nature of, 293-94; types of, 294-300; innovative (primary) processes in, 305-308; integrative (secondary) processes in, 308-14; origination as form of, 305-306; role of individual in, 322-30; terminal processes of, 314-21. *See also* Cultural dynamics; Factors in change

Culture circle theory. *See Kulturkreislehre*

Culture disintegration. *See* Disequilibrium; Dysfunction

Culture dynamics: basic readings on, 293, 330; types and factors, 292-373

Culture focus: defined, 350; importance of, 351

Culture jolts, as cause of culture shock, 204-14. *See also* Relativity, cultural; Enculturation

Culture shock: basic readings on, 222; causes of, 204; nature of, 203; symptoms of, 204. *See also* Adjustment to a second culture

Cyril and Methodius, Saints, approach of, to mission, 90-91, 354, 405 (ch. 3, n.4)

Darwinism, 139-40

Decalogue, and Western syncretism, 366-68

De-Christianization, 161

Degrees of inculturation, criteria for determining, 281-83, 353

Development, notion of, 314-15

Dewalt, B. R., 39, 394, 397

Diaconal model of Church. *See* Church, as servant

Diagnosis of problems, role of functional analysis in, 243-44

Dialectical approach to mission, 78, 79, 81, 82-83, 160, 161, 164-65, 246, 283, 316

Dialectical materialism. *See* Marxism

Diffusion: contact factors in, 343-45; factors involved in, 341-51; notion of, 306-308; types of, 306-308

Diffusionism: American, 144; European, 144-45

Discovery, defined, 306

Disequilibrium, through migration, 318-21; through modernization, 318; notion of, 316-21

Divine Word Missionaries: and anthropological research, 60, 61-63; origins, 99; missiological resources of, 400 (ch. 2, n.9); pioneers in missiology, 17; and spirituality, 2-3, 7-8

Dobyns, H. E., 36, 395

Dominicans, mission models of, 91, 93

Donovan, V. J., 71, 72, 174

Doughty, P. L., 36, 395

Douglas, M., 52, 154, 266

Drug abuse, basic readings on, 394. *See* Syncretism: Western

Dual religious systems, 368, 369-70

Dulles, A., 118, 129, 130, 138, 376, 377, 381, 385, 395, 396

Durkheim, E., 33, 266, 272

Dye, T. W., 205, 215

Dynamic equivalence approach to inculturation, 79-81

Dysfunction, notion of, 316

Ecology, cultural, 143-44

Eddy, E. M., 36, 38, 293, 393

Educational anthropology, basic readings on, 394

Eilers, F. J., 52, 386

Eliade, M., 266

Emic, defined, 150, 225

Empathy: and crosscultural adjustment, 215-18; in mission, 160-61; and structural integration, 239

Enculturation: basic readings on, 182; and cultural relativity, 182-86; and early learning, 198-201; and ethnocentrism, 64-66; and family values, 198-201; as habit formation, 196-97; in mission, 196-98; nature and scope of, 182-92; and peer groups, 201-202; in a pluralistic society, 202-203; positive attitude toward, 197; and primary relationships and early learning, 198-201; as process, 167, 188-89; role of communications media in, 201-202. *See also* Culture jolts; Culture shock

Equilibrium, cultural, notion of, 315-16

Ethics: in applied anthropology, 40-42; in missiological anthropology, 44-49

Ethnocentrism: in mission, 64-66; in history, 84-105, *passim;* nature and types of, 64-66

Ethnography, 31-32

Ethnohistory: notion of, 145-46; basic readings in, 146

Ethnology, 31-32

Etic, defined, 150, 225

Ethnoscience. *See* Cognitive anthropology

Ethnosciences in missiology, 13-14

Ethnosemantics. *See* Cognitive anthropology

Evangelii nuntiandi: on beneficiaries of evangelization, 197-98; on charity in evangelization, 4; commentaries on, 406 (ch. 4, n.6); contents of, 112-13; on evangelization of culture, 69, 358; on holism, 82; on Holy Spirit in mission, 2; importance of, 112; on spirituality for mission, 2, 24

Evangelization of culture. *See* inculturation

Evolutionism, 139-40

Factors in change: affecting diffusion, 341-51; affecting origination, 337-41; affecting both origination and diffusion, 329-37

Faith, in mission spirituality, 3-4

Family values, importance of, 198-201. *See also* Primary relationships

Felt-needs: and cultural boundaries, 176; and the diaconal role of the Church, 162; as a diffusion factor, 345; in mission, 162-63; in myth, 285; notion of, 162-63; in syncretism, 373

Ferguson, J., 123

Ferm, D. W., 22, 79

Filbeck, D., 174, 358

"Finding" Christ in non-Christian faiths, 73-74. *See also* "Hidden" Christ; Religious liberty

Firth, R., 63, 148, 154, 156, 228, 265, 266

Fitzpatrick, J., 52, 69, 321, 354

Force: and conversion, 73-74, 91; and culture change, 308. *See also* "Hidden" Christ; Religious liberty

Form, cultural: in inculturation, 74-76, 225; notion of, 74-76, 159, 225; priority of function over, 239-40; relativity of right to, 240-43

Forman, C. W., 5, 21

Foster, G. M., 38, 293, 294

Foundations, theological, for missiological anthropology, 1-11, 397

Fox project, 392

Frake, C. O., 151, 226

Francis of Assisi, Saint: spirit of, for mission spirituality, 10; approach of, to conversions, 91

Franciscans, approach to mission, 93-94, 99

Free will, and culture, 188

Freedom of conscience. *See* Force; Religious liberty

Freudianism: and myth, 275, 280; in psychological anthropology, 149, 224

Friedl, J., 153, 268

Friendly relations: as factor in change, 344; in rapport, 325-28

Function: in inculturation, 76-77; and cultural relativity, 212-13; meaning of, 76-78, 159, 227-34; and values, 76-77

Functional linkages: and chain reaction, 245-46; and diagnosis of problems, 243-44; and health, 246-47; and mission, 243-44; and predictions, 244. *See also* Referents; Yir Yoront

Functional substitutes: and structural integration, 239; in mission, 302-305; in dealing with syncretism, 372-73

Functionalism: in anthropology, 147-48; defined, 134; in sociology, 166-67

Fusion, defined, 299

Geertz, C., 40, 52, 154, 156, 169, 266, 286, 294

Generation gap, a cultural view, 164, 220

Genres, in communication, 83-84; in inculturation, 83-84

Gibellini, R., 22, 79, 122

Glasser, A. F., 15, 20, 107

"Going native," 218-19. *See also* Adjustment to a second culture; Culture shock

Goldschmidt, W., 39, 41

Goodenough, W., 38, 39, 151, 293, 393

Greeley, A., 320, 321, 354

Gregory the Great, Saint, approach of, to mission, 89

Gremillion, J., 53, 59, 69, 113, 358

Group conflicts, 176-81

Gutiérrez, G., 22, 23
Habits, personal, and enculturation, 196-97
Hall, E. T., 191, 196, 209, 247
Harris, M., 36, 143
Health, and functional linkages, 246-47
Henriot, P., 162, 358
Henry, J., 260, 277
Herskovits, M. J., 32, 36, 251, 296, 308, 310, 349, 350, 361-63
Hesselgrave, D. J., 52, 386
"Hidden Christ," meaning of, 73-74, 197. *See* Religious Liberty
Hiebert, P. G., 15, 27, 41, 52, 135, 136, 209, 219, 221, 227, 253
Historical anthropology, 144-46
History: as basis for understanding syncretism, 372; of mission models, 84-132
Holism: in anthropology, 15, 24-27; in culture, 157, 159; in development, 245; in the meaning of poverty, 389; in a missiological model of culture, 138-39; in mission, 164
Holland, J., 162, 358
Holmberg, A. R., 36, 38, 41, 392
Holy Spirit: as primary agent in mission, 1-2; and spirituality for mission, 1-2
Honigmann, J. J., 141, 149, 313, 314, 316, 335, 346
Human effort, and spirituality for mission, 8-10
Human rights, and mission, basic readings on, 390
Humanities, principle difference between anthropology and, 43
Identification, crosscultural, 215-18
Ideology, meaning of, 265
Idiosyncrasy, defined, 169
Illness, and functional linkages, 246-47
Incarnation. *See* Inculturation
Incrementation, defined, 298-99
Inculturation: approaches to, 79-81, 83; beneficiaries of, xv, 374-76; cultural depth in, 73-78; cultural dynamics involved in, 78; and cultural translation of, 79-81; degrees of, 280-84; dialectical approach to, 79, 81-84; dominant

process in, 82; dynamic equivalence approach to, 79-81; emphasis in, 83; goal of, 72-73, 82; justification for, 83; liberational approach to, 79; not to be identified with accommodation, 68-81, 82-83; not to be identified with acculturation, 308; notion of, xvii, 69-84, 374; in older churches, xvii, 82, 375; primary agents in, 48, 70-72, 82; relation of, to culture, 133; translational approach to, 79-81
Independent Church Movements, as a sign of the times, 107
Indigenization. *See* Inculturation; Mission models: accommodational; "Three-self" formula
Individual, and culture change, 322-30
Individual variability, in culture, 168
Innovation, in mission, 322
Innovators: and culture change, 330-31; suitability of, for directing change, 330-31; suitability of, for mission, 352-53
Institution: defined, 225; identified with inculturation, 69
Institutional Church. *See* Church as institution
Institutionalism, not to be identified with Church as institution, 395
Integralism in development, 245. *See also* Holism
Integration: degrees of, 280-84; meaning of, 223-25; and diagnosing problems, 243-44. *See* Function; Mentality
Integrative processes, in change and mission, 328-29
Intensity of linkages with Gospel: and degree of inculturation, 281; and degree of integration, 281
Intermediate level of culture. *See* Function
Janssen, Arnold, Blessed, 7, 17
Jarvie, I. C., 58, 148
Jesuits, 92-96, 99. *See also* Chinese Rites Controversy; Reductions; Religious orders
Jews, conversions of, to Christianity, 91
John Paul II, 81, 199, 241, 254

John XXIII, 67, 359, 390

Keesing, F., 134, 159

Keesing, R., 40, 53, 54, 60, 144, 157, 167, 168, 169, 337, 395

Kelly, W. H., 187

Kerygmatic model of Church. *See* Church as herald

Kimball, S., 394

Kloppenburg, B., 79, 122, 142

Kluckhohn, C., 32, 38, 134, 187

Knowledge: nature of, 135; and skill, in mission, 8-10

Kraft, C. H., 52, 79, 386

Kroeber, A. L., 36, 133, 134, 295, 306

Kulturkreislehre, as diffusionism, 134, 144-45

Küng, H., 121

Lasch, C., 261

Lasswell, H. D., 36, 394, 395

Latourette, K. S., 13, 15, 21, 85, 89, 91, 97, 100, 104

Levels of culture, 224-25. *See also* Form, cultural; Function; Meaning; Mentality

Lévi-Strauss, C., 154, 275, 286

Liberation theology: basic readings in, 22-23, 79, 399-400

Liminality, 270

Linguistics: 30-31. *See also* Basic readings: on communication

Linton, R., 32, 37, 38, 224, 308

"Little flock," Church as: 132, 203. *See also* Minority religion; Anonymous Christianity

Liturgy, 355, 381-84. *See also* Ritual

Local church: its need of universal symbols, 242-43; primary agent in inculturation, xvii, 354-55; as subject to judgment of communion of churches, 72; as also universal, 48, 72, 83

Local theologies: and the concept of culture, 157; as a sign of the times, 108. *See also* Inculturation

Locus of culture, 157, 168

Locus of culture change, 168, 293, 302

Loewen, J. A., 84, 202, 243, 272, 273, 286

Lonergan, B., 71, 155

Love: of God, 3-4; of neighbor, 4

Lowie, R. H., 36, 63, 134, 159

Lull, Ramon, approach of, to mission, 15, 91

Luzbetak, L. J., 41, 44, 51, 56-57, 73, 79, 80, 84, 112, 138, 165, 186, 210, 211, 212, 213, 232, 244, 270, 273, 274, 310, 314, 323

Macrochange, in history, 146

Magisterium. *See* Church as herald; Prophetic role of Christians

Malinowski, B., 33, 37, 147, 148, 266

Mariology, and inculturation, 242

Marxism: as anthropology and ideology, 140-42; as conflict sociology, 166-67; and culture change, 224, 336, 342; and human rights, 388; in liberation theology, 122; types of, 141; world view in, 258

Mayers, M. K., 52, 394

McBrien, R. P., 41, 118, 377, 387

McGavran, D. A., 13, 20, 174, 176

McKenzie, J. L., 193, 387

Mead, M., 36, 37, 40, 149, 296

Meaning, notion of, 76-78, 227-34

Media, and enculturation, 201-202

Medical anthropology, basic readings in, 394

Mellitus, Letter to, 89

Mennen, A., 194-95

Menninger, K., 147, 366

Mentality: alternate terms for, 250; approach to study of, 250-52; and cultural relativism, 214; as deepest level of culture, 159; as factor in culture change, 334-36; and inculturation, 77-78; notion of, 249-50; terms for, 250

Merton, R., 148

Messianism, and syncretism, 373

Migration: and diffusion, 343; and disintegration, 318-21

Minority religion, Christianity as, 104-105. *See also* "Little flock"; Anonymous Christianity

Missiological anthropology: basic readings in, 50-53, 54-56; and the Church as institution, 395-97; and client relations, 48-49; and communal nature of

Church, 376-80; current, 51-53; goals of, 12, 374-75; history of, 49-53; nature and scope of, xix, 12-14; professional ethics, 44-49; in Church social action, 386-95; theological foundations of, 1-11; and theology, 12-15, 109-32, 374-97. *See also* Applied anthropology; Mission.

Missiology: defined, 13, 14; history of, 15-23; as history, 13-14; multidisciplinary character of, 14; name of, 12-13; nature and scope of, 12-14; resources in 22-23, 339-403; as theology, 13-14; Third World, 22

Mission: to cultures (*see* Inculturation); crosscultural scope of, 197-98, 281-82; and the Holy Spirit, 1-2; and religious liberty, 46-48; official Catholic teaching on, 130-32; prophecy and, 281-82; theological foundations of Christian, 44; worldwide character of, 109-10

Mission methods. *See* Mission models

Mission models: accomodational, 67-69, 94; contextual, 69-84 (*See also* Inculturation); defined, 64; ethnocentric, 64-66; history of, 84-132

Missionaries, and anthropologist, 53-61. *See also* Schmidt, Wilhelm

Missionary accomodation. *See* Mission models, accomodational

Missionary antrhopology. *See* Missiological anthropology

Moberg, D. O., 379, 396

Model: concept of, 135-36; criteria for a good, 136, 137-39; of culture, basic readings on, 139; of Church, 129-30, 375, 376-80, 381, 385-86, 386-89, 395-96; of culture, for missiology, 137-39. *See also* Culture; Mission models

Modernization, and disintegration, 317

Moratorium, on mission aid, as sign of the times, 107

Motivation: in culture change, 337-38, 345; in religious education, 353-54

Moynihan, D. P., 199, 200

Mystery, Church as, 396

Myth: basic readings on, 266; dynamics of, 274; functions of, 272-74; interpretation of, 274-76; and message

programing, 284-85; notion of, 267-68; structure of, 271-72; and structuralism, 153; and syncretism, 286; and translation, 386; use of, in mission, 266-67, 284-86

National character studies, 149

National churches, 94

National Council of Catholic Bishops (NCCB), 47, 73, 113, 367, 390

Nationalism, and missionaries, 102

Nativism, and syncretism, 373

Neill, S., 20, 85

Nemer, L., 101-103

Neopaganism, 161. *See also* Syncretism

New ethnography. *See* Cognitive anthropology

New ministries, as a sign of the times, 108

New Testament churches: and dynamic equivalence theory, 79-81; history of, 85-87

Newbigin, L., 1, 161

Newman, J. H., 6, 10

Nida, E. A., 51, 52, 80, 174, 184, 221, 311, 386

Niehoff, A. H., 38, 293

de Nobili, R., approach of, to mission, 92

Non-Christian religions. *See* Anonymous Christianity; Religious liberty

Nutrition, readings in applied anthropology on, 394

Oberg, K., 204, 219

Oblates of Mary Immaculate, 99

O'Higgins, E., 41, 141, 154

Opler, M. E., 224, 276, 277

Organizational anthropology, 176-81

Orthodox missiology, 22

Panikkar, R., 22, 121

Pannenberg, W., 41, 120

Parsons, T., 148, 166

Partridge. W. L., 36, 38, 39, 293, 393, 394

Pastoral work, and functional linkages, 248-49

Paternalism: as form ethnocentrism, 65-66; in California missions, 94

Patrick, Saint, approach of, to mission, 89

Patristic literature, on missiology, 15

Paul, B. D. 38, 293

Paul VI, 2, 4, 20, 24, 69, 73, 82, 106, 111, 112-13, 197-98, 358, 390, 406 (Chapter 4 n. 6)

Peer group, role in enculturation, 201-202

People of God. *See* Church as community

Performance, as condition for changes, 331

Periodicals, missiological, 401-402

Persistence, cultural, 294-95. *See* Culture change

Personality and culture studies, 149

Peyote cult, 363-64

"Philosophy" of a people. *See* Mentality

Philosophy vs. world view and ideology, 265

Physical anthropology, 28-29

Pidgin English, as an example of cultural fusion, 299

Pietism, a mission model, 91

Pike, K., 150, 151, 225

Pius XI, 93, 103, 240

Pius XII, 46, 67, 103

Pluralism, and religious education, 202-203

Poor: Christian commitment to, 108-109; meaning of, 387-90. *See also* Poverty

Pope, role of, in the Church, 128

Popular religiosity: and culture, 176; the Sacred Heart devotion and veneration of the Virgin Mary as, 409 (ch. 7, n.6): as a sign of the times, 108

Poverty: basic readings on, 390; causes of, 391-92; meaning of, 387-90; Protestant evangelical teaching on, 390. *See also* Poor

Prediction, and functional linkages, 244-45

Prejudice, and culture change, 348-49

Primary relationships, and enculturation, 198-201

Processes of culture change, 305-29

Professional associations, for mission anthropology: 402-403 (ch.2, n.10)

Project Camelot, ethics of, 35-36

Prophetic role, of Christians, 160, 243, 281-82. *See also* Church as herald

Prophetism, and syncretism, 373

Psychoanalytic aprroach to culture, 149

Psychology, difference between anthropology and, 43

Psychological anthropology, 148-49

Psychological integration. *See* Mentality

Publishers of mission studies, 402 (ch.2, n.9)

Racism, as a form of ethnocentrism, 66

Radcliffe-Brown, A. R., 33, 37, 147, 266, 315

Rahner, K., 41, 109, 123, 124, 125, 264, 366

Ramification, notion of, 312-14

Rappaport, R., 143, 231

Rapport, in directing cultural change, 323-38

Ratzinger, J., 22, 23, 40, 79, 122, 142, 390

Recidivism, and cultural needs, 160-63

Reciprocity: and degree of inculturation, 283-84; and degree of integration, 283-84

Redfield, R., 37, 193, 308

Reductions, 94-96

Reed, L. E., 52, 176, 358

Reentry, as reverse culture shock, 220-21

Re-evangelization, 161

Reference works in missiology, 401, (ch.2, n.9)

Referents, notion of, 227-34. *See also* Meaning

Regional development, basic readings in, 395

Reinterpretation: notion of, 309; and syncretism, 372; types of, 309-12

Relativity, cultural: in aesthetics, 185-86; in anti-missionary prejudice, 56-58; in communication, 210; in ethics, 185-86; and food, 182-84, in incongruities, 211-13; and mentality, 214; in mission, 161; in missionary-anthropologist relations, 56-58, 59; and muscular habits, 184; in nonverbal communication, 213-14; and the physical environment, 205-206; and politeness, 207-208; relative vs. absolute, 56-58; and the social environment, 206-210; in social action, 161-62; and space, 209-210; and territoriality, 208-210; and time, 210-

11. *See also* Enculturation; Ethnocentrism

Relevancy, cultural. *See* Accomodation; Inculturation; Felt-needs

Religion: civil, 203; functions of, 263-64: notion of, 263-65; and science, 8-10. *See also* World view

Religious education: motivation in, 353-54; and Opler's theme theory, 286-90; in a pluralistic society, 202-203; programming of, 163, 165, 166

Religious freedom. *See* Religious liberty

Religious liberty, 46-48, 101; and Vatican II, 161, 283. *See also* Force

Religious orders, and mission models, 89-105, *passim*

Respect: for cultures, 46-48; for individuals, 323-25; for non-Christian religions, 46-48. *See also* Religious liberty

Reverse culture shock, 220-21

Revolution: defined, 295; and mission, 301; in history, 146

Reyburn, W. D., 52, 80, 207, 216, 386

Ricci, M., 92-93, 346, 354. *See also* Chinese Rites Controversy

Ricoeur, P., 41, 266

Ritual: and art, 382-83; basic readings on, 266, 384; dynamics of, 274; functions of 272-74; and inculturation, 381-84; as mystery, 382; nature of, 381-84; notion of, 268; and myth, 268-70; as repetitive and traditional, 383; V. Turner on, 268-71; as worship, 383

Root causes, of social problems, 391

Root metaphor, 269

Rossi, I., 41, 141, 154

Rural development, basic readings on, 395

Sacramental model of Church. *See* Church as Sacrament

Sacrifice, and spirituality for mission, 4-6

Sahlins, M., 77, 142, 143

Saints, veneration of, in popular religiosity, 242

Salamone, F., 53, 55

Saliba, J., 266, 272, 273

Salvation, official Catholic teaching on, 123-24

Schleiermacher, F. E. D., 13, 16

Schmidlin, J., 13, 15, 16, 17, 89, 99, 100, 104

Schmidt, R., 266, 275, 276

Schmidt, W., 51, 144, 145, 272; achievements of, 61-63; bibliographies of works about, 405 (ch. 2, nn.24, 26)

Schoepfle, G. M., 41, 151

Schreiter, R. J., 53, 79, 81, 138, 148, 156, 369, 370

Science and mission, 8-10

Scientific standards, and mission anthropology, 45-46

Sebeok, T. A., 30, 192

Secularization, 161. *See also* Modernization

Selectivity: in culture change, 163, 334-36; in syncretism, 372

Self-determination: and missiological anthropology, 46-48; and the "three-self" formula, 100, 356-57

Self-help, in social action, 391

Semiotic anthropology. *See* Symbolic anthropology

Sense of personal mission, in mission spirituality, 6-8, 329

Seumois, A., 123

Sexual revolution, a form of Western syncretism, 367

Shanty towns, and disequilibrium, 318

Sharp, P. L., 245. *See also* Yir Yoront

Sheehan, T., 115, 116

Shenk, W., 99, 104

Shorter, Aylward, 22

Signs of the times, 98-111

Slavonic Rites Controversy: 354; basic readings on, 405 (ch.3, n.4). *See also* Cyril and Methodius, Saints

Smith, E. W., 60

Social action: approaches to, 391-93; basic readings in applied anthropology on, 393-95; models of, 392-93

Social anthropology, 33-34

Social controls: and culture change, 333; types of, 357-58

Social drama, according to V. Turner, 269, 271

Social structure: basic readings on, 174; and communication, 359; and mission, 173-75, 358-59: and the World Council of Churches, 175. *See also* Societal approach to mission

Social vs. *cultural*, 403 (ch.2, n.11)

Socialization, defined, 166

Societal approach to mission, basic readings on, 174-75

Society: defined, 166-67; and the individual, 167-69

Sociolinguistics, 213

Sociology vs. anthropology, 42

Specialty: defined, 159; notion of, 169-70

Spicer, E. H., 293

Spindler, G., 39, 394

Spirituality for mission: 2-8, 10, 328, 397; basic readings on, 399 (ch.1, n.2)

Spradley. J. P., 41, 15, 331

Stabilization, notion of, 316

Stamoolis, J., 22

Stipe, C. E., 41

Stott, J., 8, 52

Stransky, T., 22, 73

Streit, R., 17

Structural integration: methods of inquiry into, 234-38; in mission, 239; notion of, 225-38; theories regarding, 225

Structuralism: basic readings in, 153-54; critique of, 152-53; described, 152-54; types of, 152; usefulness for mission, 153

Structure/Antistructure: in change, 355-56; in mission, 352: according to V. Turner, 269-70

Subculture: Christianity as, 203; notion of, 171-72; and world view, 262-63

Substitution, described, 296-98

Surface level of culture. *See* Form, cultural

Symbiosis, notion of, 316

Symbol, notion of, 76, 223-38, 249-50. *See also* Cognitive anthropology; Function; Structuralism; Symbolic anthropology; Meaning

Symbolic anthropology, basic readings in, 156: critique of, 155-56; in mission, 155-56; the name, 154; types of, 154-56

Syncretism: in Africa, 366; biblical, 368; in Brazil, Cuba, and Haiti, 363; in the Caribbean, 363; as content, 368-71; and cultural boundaries, 176; defined, 360; in Guatemala, 365; in Mexico, 364-65; and mission, 371-73; and myth, 286; among North American Indians, 363-64; notion of, 360; as process, 368-71; proper attitude toward, 369; typology, 367; and unity of faith, 283; Western, 366-68

Synod of Bishops: of 1974, 111; of 1985, 108, 111, 376

Taber, C. R., 55, 80, 361

Taboo, as social control, 356-57. *See also* Social controls

Teaching authority, of Church. *See* Church as herald; Magisterium

Technological development, and functional linkages, 247-48

Television and enculturation, 201-202

Teutonic Knights, and religious liberty, 91

Theme and countertheme: in culture, 276-79, 286-91; in mission, 286-91

Theocentricity, in spirituality for mission, 2-4

Theological foundations, 1-11

Theology: crosscurrents in, 113-23; historico-critical method in, 116; of human rights, 387-90; and narrative, 83-84; paradigm shift in, 114-18; and tradtion, 79, 81-84, 117

"Three-self" formula, 98, 100, 406 (ch.3, n.4)

Third level of culture. *See* Mentality

Third World missiology, 22

Thomas Aquinas, Saint, 15, 41, 103

Thomas, W. I., 319

Tippett, A. P., 14-15, 146

Tobacco abuse, as form of Western syncretism, 368

Touch, meanings of, 213

Tracy, D., 116, 117

Tradition vs. culture, 170-71. *See also* Theology: and tradition; Tripolar dialectic

Training for missions, 59, 375

Trend, long-term, defined, 295-96

Tripolar dialectic, 77, 79-80, 160, 161, 164-65, 246, 316, 370-71

Triumphalism, as form of ethnocentrism, 66. *See also* Mission models

Trust in God, in spirituality for mission, 6-9

Turner, V., 52, 84, 148, 154, 156, 266, 269, 270, 271, 286, 293, 352, 355

Tylor, E. B., 36, 134, 151

Umiker-Sebeok, J., 30, 192

UNESCO: and holistic development, 245; and self-help, 391

Uniqueness of Christ, 124-26, 158, 164

Unity in diversity, 48, 72, 83. *See also* Prophetic role, of Christians; Countercultural nature of mission

Universal Church, role of, in inculturation, 72, 83

Universality of Christ, 124-26

Universals, notion of, 159, 170

Universities, and mission, 100-101

Urban anthropology, basic readings in, 394-95

Urbanization, 394. *See also* Modernization

Value judgments, in applied anthropology, 40-42

Values. *See* Functional linkages; Meaning; Mentality

Vatican II: and Americanism, 354; and atheism, 161; basic readings on, 406 (ch.4, nn.5,6); documents of, 110-11; on ecumenism, 110; on family values, 199, 201; fundamental feature of, 109-110; on Holy Spirit in mission, 2; importance of, 106, 109-110: on inculturation, 69, 73, 74; on the institutional nature of the Church, 395-96; on interfaith cooperation, 110; on justice as basis for inculturation, 110; on liturgy, 381, 383-84; on mission of Church, 109-111, 130-32; on nature of Church, 110, 126-30; on the nature of the local church, 110; on nonChristian religions, 125-26; on the People of God, 376-77; on religious liberty, 46-48, 73, 74, 126, 161; and ritual, 383; on sacramental nature of Church, 381; on salvation, 123-24; as a sign of the times, 109-110; on Christian social responsibility, 110, 143; on the theological basis of mission, 44; on the universality of Christ, 124-26; on the worldwide character of the Church, 110

Vayda, A. P., 143, 232

Venn, R., 16, 98

Verkuyl, J., 13, 85, 99

Vicos project, 36, 392-93

Viennese School. *See Kulturkreislehre*

Violence, 316

Vocation. *See* Sense of personal mission

Warneck, G., 12, 13, 16, 68

Warren, M., 20, 98, 99

Werner, O., 41, 151

Whiteman, D. L., 52, 53, 146, 353

van Willigen, J., 39, 293, 393, 394, 397

Women, in mission, 94

Worgul, G. S., 53, 270, 271

World view: American (USA), 255-63; cognitive dimension of, 253-54; emotive dimension of, 254-55; and mission, 284; of missionaries vs. anthropologists, 56-58; motivational dimension of 255, 260-63; notion of, 252-63; types of, 252-53

Yir Yoront: disorganization and functional linkages, 245-46, 307, 312, 345-46

Znaniecki, F., 319-20